SYMBOLIZATION AND DESYMBOLIZATION

SYMBOLIZATION AND DESYMBOLIZATION

ESSAYS IN HONOR OF NORBERT FREEDMAN

EDITED BY

RICHARD LASKY

KARNAC

New York

London

Production Editor: Robert D. Hack

This book was set in 11 pt. Berkeley by Alpha Graphics of Pittsfield, NH.

10 9 8 7 6 5 4 3 2 1

 Printed in the United States of America on acid-free paper. For information write to Other Press LLC, 307 Seventh Avenue, Suite 1807, New York, NY 10001. Or visit our website: www.otherpress.com.

Library of Congress Cataloging-in-Publication Data

Symbolization and desymbolization / editor, Richard Lasky.
p. cm.
Includes bibliographical references and index.
ISBN 1-892746-99-9
1. Symbolism (Psychology) 2. Psychoanalysis. 3. Freedman, Norbert.
4. Psychoanalysts—United States—Biography I. Freedman, Norbert.
II. Lasky, Richard.
BF175.5.S95 S96 2002
150.19'5'092—dc21

2002025782

Contents

Contributors

John S. Auerbach is Professor, James H. Quillan College of Medicine, East Tennessee State University; Coordinator, Posttraumatic Stress Disorder Program at James H. Quillan Veterans' Administration Hospital; Research Affiliate, Yale University Department of Psychiatry; and Member, Editorial Board, *Psychoanalytic Psychology*.

Sheldon Bach is Clinical Professor of Psychology, New York University Postdoctoral Program in Psychoanalysis; Fellow, Institute for Psychoanalytic Training and Research; Training and Supervising Analyst, New York Freudian Society; and Visiting Lecturer, New York Psychoanalytic Institute.

Alan Bass is Fellow and Faculty, Institute for Psychoanalytic Training and Research; Faculty and Training Analyst, New York Freudian Society; and Graduate Faculty, New York University.

Sidney J. Blatt is Professor, Departments of Psychiatry and Psychology, Yale University; Faculty, Western New England Psychoanalytic Institute; and Visiting Professor, University College London.

Wilma Bucci is Professor and Director of Research, Derner Institute, Adelphi University; Honorary Member, American Psychoanalytic

Association; Chair, Research Associates of the American Psychoanalytic Association; Honorary Member, Institute for Psychoanalytic Training and Research; Member and Faculty, International Psychoanalytical Association Research Training Program; Research Director, Pacella Parent Child Center at the New York Psychoanalytic Institute; and Coeditor, *Psychological Issues Monograph Series*.

Monica Carsky is Clinical Assistant Professor of Psychology and Psychiatry, Weill Medical College of Cornell University; Member, Personality Disorders Institute at New York Presbyterian Hospital; Member, Institute for Psychoanalytic Training and Research and International Psychoanalytical Association; and Supervising and Training Analyst, Institute for Psychoanalysis and Psychotherapy of New Jersey.

Andrew B. Druck is Past President, former Dean of Training, Fellow (Training and Supervising Analyst) and Faculty Member, Institute for Psychoanalytic Training and Research; Faculty and Supervisor, New York University Postdoctoral Program in Psychotherapy and Psychoanalysis; and a Diplomate in Psychoanalysis, American Psychological Association.

Steven J. Ellman is Professor Emeritus, CUNY Graduate Center; Training Analyst and Fellow, Institute for Psychoanalytic Training and Research; Supervisor and Visiting Professor, New York University Postdoctoral Program in Psychoanalysis and Psychotherapy; President, Independent Psychoanalytic Societies of the United States; and Member, Editorial Board, *Psychoanalytic Quarterly*.

Lawrence Friedman is Clinical Professor of Psychiatry, Weill Medical College of Cornell University; Associate Editor, *Journal of the American Psychoanalytic Association*; and Faculty, New York University Psychoanalytic Institute.

Alan Frosch is President, Fellow (Training and Supervising Analyst), and Faculty, former Dean of Training, and former Codirector of the Clinical Center, Institute for Psychoanalytic Training and Research.

Jesse D. Geller is Associate Clinical Professor of Psychology, Yale Department of Psychiatry; Adjunct Associate Professor, Teachers College, Columbia University; Honorary Member, Institute for Psychoanalytic Training and Research; and Member, Society for Psychotherapy Research.

Stanley Grand is Fellow, Institute for Psychoanalytic Training and Research; Training Analyst, New York Freudian Society; and Faculty and Supervisor, New York University Postdoctoral Program in Psychoanalysis and Psychotherapy.

Mark Grunes is Faculty, Institute for Psychoanalytic Training and Research; and Training and Supervisory Analyst, New York Freudian Society and New York University Postdoctoral Program in Psychotherapy and Psychoanalysis.

Marvin Hurvich is Training and Supervisory Analyst, Institute for Psychoanalytic Training and Research, New York Freudian Society, and New York University Postdoctoral Program in Psychoanalysis and Psychotherapy; Professor of Psychology, Long Island University; and Diplomate in Psychoanalysis, American Board of Professional Psychology.

Gil A. Katz is Dean of Training, Fellow (Training and Supervising Analyst), and Faculty, Institute for Psychoanalytic Training and Research; and Supervising Analyst and Clinical Associate Professor of Psychology, New York University Postdoctoral Program in Psychoanalysis.

Naama Kushnir-Barash is Faculty and Fellow (Training and Control Analyst), Institute for Psychoanalytic Training and Research; and Faculty (Training and Control Analyst), Israel Psychoanalytic Society.

Richard Lasky is Faculty and Fellow (Training and Control Analyst), Institute for Psychoanalytic Training and Research; Clinical Professor of Psychology and Supervising Analyst, New York University Postdoctoral Program in Psychotherapy and Psychoanalysis; Past President, Psychoanalytic Society of the New York University Postdoctoral Program; Diplomate in Psychoanalysis, American Board of Professional Psychology, American Psychological Association; Fellow, American Academy of Psychoanalysis; and Member, American Psychoanalytic Association and International Psychoanalytical Association.

John Rosegrant is Member, New York Freudian Society and Institute for Psychoanalytic Training and Research; and Adjunct Assistant Professor of Psychology, Teachers College, Columbia University.

Jean B. Sanville is Founder, currently Training Analyst, Los Angeles Institute and Society for Psychoanalytic Studies; Founder, first Dean, California Institute for Clinical Social Work; and former Editor, *Clinical Social Work Journal*.

Jean Schimek was Faculty and Fellow (Training and Control Analyst), Institute for Psychoanalytic Training and Research; former Faculty, Psychology Department, New York University; former Faculty, Departments of Psychiatry, Yale Medical School and Downstate Medical Center (Brooklyn, NY); and Member, International Psychoanalytical Association. He passed away just before publication of this book.

Elaine Schwager is Member, Institute for Psychoanalytic Training and Research; Faculty, Washington Square Institute Family Forensic Program; certified Imago Couples Therapist; and a published poet, screenwriter, and playwright.

Doris K. Silverman is Faculty and Fellow (Training and Control Analyst), Institute for Psychoanalytic Training and Research; Clinical Associate Professor and Supervising Analyst, New York University Postdoctoral Program in Psychotherapy and Psychoanalysis; and Editorial Board Member, *Psychoanalytic Psychology* and *The International Journal of Psychoanalysis*.

Riccardo Steiner is Member, British Psychoanalytical Society; Honorary Archivist of the British Psychoanalytical Society; and Coauthor, with Pearl King, of *The Freud-Klein Controversies 1941–1945*.

Irving Steingart is Faculty and Fellow (Training and Control Analyst), Institute for Psychoanalytic Training and Research; Clinical Professor of Psychology and Supervising Analyst, New York University Postdoctoral Program in Psychotherapy and Psychoanalysis; and Member, Association for Child Psychoanalysis and International Psychoanalytical Association.

Isaac Tylim is Faculty and Fellow (Training and Control Analyst), Institute for Psychoanalytic Training and Research; Clinical Associate Professor and Supervising Analyst, New York University Postdoctoral Program in Psychotherapy and Psychoanalysis; Member, International Psychoanalytical Association; and Coordinator, Inpatient Psychology, Maimonides Medical Center.

Robert S. Wallerstein is Past President, American Psychoanalytic Association; Past President, International Psychoanalytical Association; Professor Emeritus and former Chair, Department of Psychiatry, University of California School of Medicine; and Emeritus Training and Supervising Analyst, San Francisco Psychoanalytic Institute.

Introduction

RICHARD LASKY

Norbert Freedman was born in Hamburg, Germany. Bert and his immediate family fled Nazi persecution in 1933. Traveling by different routes they all made it safely to the United States where a 16-year-old Bert began his new life. Bert was one of the lucky ones, a German Jew saved from the Holocaust, traumatized but not beyond repair. Part of that repair involved developing a perspective on his experience, a perspective that began when he was still in Germany and that matured as he continued to grow up in America, a perspective that has served him to good advantage his whole life. The development of a perspective involved the process of symbolization, not in the sense of symbol making (which might be better called the process of symbol formation), but in the sense of being able to gain psychological distance from raw (internal or external) experience. The question of how people are able to symbolize experience and how, once symbolized, it can subsequently become desymbolized, has been a major focus of Bert's professional attention.

A brief anecdote will serve to show how this worked for Bert. One day, in Germany, on the local soccer field, Bert kicked a particularly good goal. Rather than being cheered he was stoned. How dare a Jew, less than human, better an Aryan, a member of the master race? Bert's friend Helmut (an "Aryan" but no Nazi) held a handkerchief to Bert's bloody head and said, "Let's get out of here!" That experience initiated what became for Bert a lifelong motto: "Let's keep moving." "Let's keep moving" did not mean running away, a passive bloodied victim, but continually moving on to higher ground, in moral terms, in educational accomplishments, in human relations, and as a human being. That triumph of the symbolizing process (but not of that process alone, of course) has carried Bert from the object of the Nazis' lowest category, subhuman, to an exemplar of the Jews' highest compliment: a "mensch."

Bert's psychological development did not begin on the soccer field, of course, but it was tempered by growing up with such experiences. He came from an assimilated family, Jews who thought of themselves as Germans who happened to be Jewish. Bert spent the seven years before the family escaped learning that in German eyes he was a Jew, not a German, and he learned it the hard way. In those years he and his brother Ralph reconnected with their Jewish roots. At the very same time—and especially after Kristallnacht—Bert became an expert on the immigration policies of many other countries; he knew the pathways to Cuba, to Guatemala, to Shanghai, and, of course, to the United States (the grand prize of all destinations for the Jews of Germany and Eastern Europe).

Like many others who managed to escape, Bert's family was able to see the writing on the wall, and his father made the best preparations for flight that he could. That required both risk and hope. He packed up all their furniture and belongings and had them sent to Hoboken, New Jersey, for storage, not knowing whether he would ever see them again. Ralph was successfully sent to England and eventually got to America on a Liberty ship. A young Danish woman, a family friend, smuggled the family jewelry in her brassiere to Denmark, where it was sold to book passage to New York for Bert's father. Another friend, an American, signed an affidavit guaranteeing that the Freedmans would not be left destitute and dependent on the state, and sent $2,000 to pay for Bert and his mother to come to America.

These were not easy, comfortable passages; they were long, dangerous trips filled with surprise, drama, and confrontation. Bert and his mother did not have a seven-hour transatlantic flight with dinner service and movies; they had a 26-day journey, the long way around. From Hamburg they traveled to Berlin, where they managed to get passage on a Lufthansa flight to Koenigsberg. From Koenigsberg they went to Minsk, from Minsk to Pinsk, from Pinsk to Moscow. After a four-day delay in Moscow they made the long passage across Siberia. From Irkutsk they went to Novisibirsk, to Chetta, and to Lake Baikal, facing arrest by the NKVD the entire way. Then they arrived in Manchuria, which was at that time occupied by the Japanese, an Axis ally of Germany. After interrogation by the Japanese police in Manchuria they made their way to Harbin, China, where they were warmly received by a community of emigrant Russian Jews who fed them challah, chicken soup, and strudel. From Harbin they passed through the Korean peninsula on the way to their penultimate destination, Yokohama, Japan. Throughout that exhausting journey they never really felt certain that they would reach America until, finally, they were in motion on a Japanese ship (with a swastika flag snapping in the breeze) bound for Seattle, Washington. And it was not until they were on that ship that they learned the fate of the other family members; crossing the Pacific they received a telegram from Bert's father, now safe in New York, telling them that Ralph, too, was saved and was on a Liberty ship bound for America.

Bert arrived in Seattle on August 29, 1940, and his first home in the United States was among the small immigrant group that had settled there. Within two weeks he got his first job, working in a pawnshop (how ironic that Bert's first job in America was in a business so closely tied to abandoned and retrieved memories). He wasn't thinking about psychoanalysis at that time; he was obsessed with the idea of being an American. That meant a period of hating everything German and getting rid of his German accent. It is not surprising that an adolescent, persecuted and displaced, might hate the place he was forced to flee, but would that necessarily lead to an obsession with being a total, dyed-in-the-wool American? Consider this: For the first time in his life Bert could sit at a soda counter and flirt with a girl without fear of being arrested! When he became old enough he tried to enlist in the Army but, even then, his eyes prevented him from doing so. It may not have interrupted Bert's love affair with America, but he did receive a disturbing culture shock when, after Pearl Harbor, he saw his Japanese-American friends and neighbors shipped off to internment camps.

Bert worked at various jobs, helped his parents run their boarding house, and went to night school. The boarding house was made possible only because it was furnished with the belongings Bert's father had shipped to Hoboken; some of them can still be seen today in Bert's New York apartment. His research career may be said to have started with his senior project at the University of Washington. The title of that project was "The Ecological Redistribution of European Immigrants from 1939 to 1944." One of the more interesting findings was that although 5 percent of all American college students were, at that time, elected to Phi Beta Kappa, among the European students the rate was 70 percent.

Between 1940 and 1946 Bert's problems with his eyes progressively worsened and he was sent to Chicago for a complex and unusual operation. He had no inkling at that time that he would eventually become blind, although he had a foreshadowing of what was to come when his eyes were bandaged shut for many weeks after the operation.

Although Bert's professional interest has closely focused on processes of symbolization and desymbolization, he has also had a deep, lifelong interest in nonverbal communication. With his eyes bandaged for weeks he became acutely aware of sound, smell, and touch. That experience, while he was vulnerable and dependent, simultaneous with being protected and taken care of, may have been central in the choice of his research interests in the years to follow. One can make a natural comparison here, juxtaposing Bert's early years in Nazi Germany and his visual difficulties against the general problem of childhood trauma, and one might ask the obvious question about why some traumatized children develop formal stress-related neuroses and others, like Bert, do not. The nature of the trauma can be decisive, but more often, the deciding factor is not so much the nature of the trauma but rather whether or not the child had immediately available, supportive parents who could help him process what, as a child, he could not process on his own. Apparently, Bert had that kind of help. From Bert's senior project to the accomplishments of the rest of his life we see the evidence of, and a testimony to, both his internal and his external resources. In terms of his external resources we see a testimony to the doctors and nurses (and to one nurse in particular) at the time of his eye surgery and, of crucial importance, a testament to his family and to the sheltering immigrant community that kept him from becoming a stunted human being as he moved from the persecution that characterized his childhood to adolescent freedom and safety in America. In terms of his internal resources we see a testimony to the strength of his own ego.

When Bert finally left the tight-knit German-Jewish immigrant community of Seattle it was to come to New York, his brother Ralph, and his graduate studies. His doctoral dissertation (in 1954) also gives us an indication of the thread of his life experience, and how Bert could neutralize and sublimate even the worst of it. Using the reaction of college-age girls to seeing subliminal sexual and aggressive words, he elaborated some of George Klein's ideas about perceptual defense. His dissertation title was, "Discrimination Without Awareness." Now let us ask some questions, similar to the one we posed about trauma: Was there an unconscious relation between Bert's seeing but not seeing and his work on material that was "subliminal"? Was there an unconscious relation between Bert's childhood experience of being stoned and his subjects being exposed to sexual and aggressive stimulation (another kind of bombardment, however subliminal)? Was there an unconscious relation between Bert's childhood persecution and the "Discrimination" in the title of his dissertation? To suggest those unconscious connections is only speculation, a form of armchair analysis. However, let us suppose those connections are there. What, then, would we see? We would see that, for Bert, they did not signal psychic disorder; they signaled the very opposite. If all that were true, his early work can only be viewed as an impressive structure of adaptation and mastery.

The 1950s were good years for Bert; in addition to getting his doctorate and entering into the world of psychoanalysis, he also met and married Njuty (but not until they had lived together for some years). Living together unwed, as they did, was a radical departure from the social norm and it gives a clear indication of their independence of thought and spirit (but not quite so independent that they let Bert's mother know about it). That degree of personal freedom and assurance was unusual, particularly during those years of McCarthy-inspired lock-step conformity. After living through what they did—having both been victims of, and then refugees from, Nazi hatred—how could even a McCarthy scare them? (Bert's mother was another matter.) A year after they married Jeff was born, and Carol was born four years later. Jeff had a special status as the firstborn son, but Carol had a special status, too; on Bert's father's side there had been a long string of only boys—thirteen boys in the last three generations—and Carol was the first girl.

It was during this time that Bert also developed his famous reputation as a workaholic. Among his friends Bert is well-known for his fifteen-hour days and his weekend and midnight telephone calls. Unlike many workaholics, however, who do not have a life outside their work, Bert has made psychoanalysis his life without giving up on the rest of life. He is deeply involved in culture, in the arts and in music and literature, and he also manages to shoe-horn a very rich and active social life into his crazy schedule. But the pattern began back in the 1950s. That was when he started what would become his training analysis, when he was getting plenty of "bootleg" supervision, and when he also began working three jobs. He worked as a research consultant in advertising (believe it or not), he worked at a mental health clinic in Queens, and he began his private practice.

Despite having written a doctoral dissertation, Bert really learned the basic methodology of the research trade, the bread-and-butter tools of research one might say, while at Downstate (Downstate Medical Center, State University of New York) doing psychopharmacological research. While his psychiatric colleagues at Kings County Hospital (just across the street) assured him that there was no longer any need for dynamic psychotherapy or for a dynamic model of the mind, Bert went his own way. And, rather than faltering, he intensified his study of psychoanalysis; his research at Downstate (about which more will be said later) went far beyond psychopharmacology and, paralleling his development as a psychoanalyst, he addressed questions like: What is the role of transference in psychopharmacological treatment? What is the role of the patient's subjective somatic experience in psychopharmacological treatment? What is the role of different personality structures in psychopharmacological treatment?

If the 1950s were good to Bert, the 1960s were not; they were tough, difficult years. In 1962 Bert had a recurrence of the retinal detachment that had been successfully operated on in Chicago fifteen years earlier. The operation was again successful, but Bert got hit with devastating news; he was informed that he was suffering from progressive macular degeneration and that he had to begin preparing himself for blindness.

Next, he applied to the psychoanalytic institute at Downstate (now the Psychoanalytic Association of New York) for acceptance as a research candidate. In those days, research candidacy was the category that psychologists, as non-physicians, were relegated to in the institutes of the American Psychoanalytic Association; they had to promise to use their psychoanalytic training only for research purposes, and to swear that they would never engage in the clinical practice of psychoanalysis. Some swore and meant it, others swore and disregarded it, others sought training at the very few other places (some of which were not even in the United States) where they were not treated like second-class citizens, and others arranged privately for training analysis and supervision with the very people they would have worked with if they had gone to those institutes. The latter is what was known as bootleg training. It was called bootleg not only because the student got psychoanalytic training outside the institute, but also because the training analysts and control analysts who taught them were forbidden to do so by the American Psychoanalytic Association, and so they had to keep their participation in training these people a secret. As if this were not sufficiently absurd, one of the senior analysts on the Downstate faculty took Bert aside one day and, reminding him of Freud's paper on "the exceptions" and of the case of Richard III, told him that because the prevailing wisdom was that a person suffering from a physical handicap also receives a narcissistic wound that can never be overcome (i.e., Bert was therefore considered by him to be unanalyzable), he could not recommend Bert's application and, therefore, the Training Committee would not be able to accept him.

After he had digested and then evacuated this, Bert turned to IPTAR (the Institute for Psychoanalytic Training and Research) instead. By the time he approached IPTAR he had already had lots of training analysis, bootleg supervision, and control experience. In recalling this, Bert said: "The IPTAR community welcomed me with open arms."[1]

---

1. It seems appropriate to quote his exact words about this because they have such a familiar ring in Bert's life. As analysts our antennae tend to go up when we hear something repeated again and again, even if it is a positive statement and even (or perhaps, especially) when the contexts are continually shifting. Over and over Bert found himself in hostile and dangerous environments from which he escaped into the welcoming arms of a good object (i.e., person, community, or country). In another rash episode of armchair analysis, would it be too procrustean a stretch to suggest that the attitude and the behavior of that senior analyst, and the policies of the Downstate program and the American Psychoanalytic Association, may have unconsciously been connected to memories of Nazi Germany? The unconscious parallels do not make them really equivalent, of course, but consider the following: On the one hand Bert was handicapped and, therefore, unanalyzable; on the other hand he was one of a group biologically ("racially") so different and inferior, so subhuman, that no amount of mixing with Aryan blood could wash them clean. On the one hand because Bert was a psychologist he was to be only a "research" candidate, a second-class citizen, marginalized during training and discriminated against both at admission and in the opportunity, even after graduating, to be considered a "real" psychoanalyst. On the other hand he was a member of a marginalized people, a "race" not really members of German society, a group Germany had to keep itself and the world as free of as possible, a member of a group where only a few rare individuals could be tolerated, and then only under special and deprived conditions. On the one hand that senior analyst's lack of tact and his willingness, in the name of both honesty and science, to subject Bert to a severe narcissistic injury (his application was no good because *he* was no good); on the other hand the vicious hatred and the regular propaganda about and against Jews as a group, and even against Jewish children in their schoolrooms where they learned "Nazi science." On the one hand "this analytic society has no place for defectives like you," "there is no analytic 'existence' available for people like you—here, or anywhere else if we had our way"; on the other hand ghettos, "Madagascar," and Auschwitz.

I will soon say more about the warmth he found at IPTAR and you will note that both the welcome and the warmth reminded him of "the safe havens of the 1930s" (his words, again). A conscious idea of that sort gives some credence to the

The next trauma was a worse one than his projected blindness, and it made his rejection by Downstate insignificant by comparison. This was the news, in 1967, that Njuty had cancer. By the time it was discovered it had already metastasized and they went through a terrible time of second-guessing themselves, wondering whether, if they had only been more vigilant, they could have caught it earlier and perhaps have saved her. All told, they had four long years of preparing for her death. Those years were not unrelievedly somber and in the first two they lived well, with one trip to Europe and another across the southwest and into California, but the last two years, 1970 and 1971, are best not remembered.

The decade of the 1970s was complex, with highs and lows all mixed up together. There was, of course, the low of losing Njuty, and Bert's struggle to simultaneously cope with mourning and the problems of single parenthood. There was the ambivalence and awkwardness of having to relearn dating. But finally, at the end of the tunnel, there was the high of meeting Joyce Beckett, his present wife.

During this period, there was a sudden miraculous regaining of his vision. As high as that high was, he also had the low of having to go through the experience of losing it once again. But for two or three years, he knew what his kids looked like.

Another high for Bert was the feeling that, after ten years of involvement at IPTAR, he had finally and fully found his professional home. IPTAR offered him a wonderful haven, in some important ways reminiscent to him of the days in the 1930s when, despised by his so-

---

kinds of unconscious, or possibly not even fully unconscious, connections I have hypothesized above. It guarantees no certainty about what may have been stimulated in Bert but it is very suggestive. On the possibility that my hypothesis is accurate, let us fast-forward into the present for one final comparison: On the one hand Bert is, indeed, a "real" psychoanalyst, considerably more respected than most, both here in the United States as well as internationally; on the other hand the Third Reich is dead, institutes of the American Psychoanalytic Association have lost lawsuits over the very premise that there is creditable evidence that physically handicapped people are unanalyzable (and many have gone on not only to graduate but to join their faculties), and psychologists are now *actively* recruited by American Psychoanalytic Association institutes for "full" training. One imagines that Bert derives considerable satisfaction, consciously and unconsciously, from both sides of that equation.

called Aryan friends, he was warmly taken in by the Jewish community and institutions of Hamburg. The study groups at IPTAR, its commitment to social consciousness, a caring attitude toward its students, the depth of the curriculum, the spirit of "the Eddies" (Ed Weil and Ed Frankel) and Stan Berger: these are what Bert remembers as having been influential in solidifying his commitment to, and identification with, this exciting new group that had been formed in an uncharted ocean of varying forms of analytic thinking and practice.[2] Bert was IPTAR's President three times (1974–1976, 1984–1986, and 1990–1992) and although he was not himself a founding member he has, from the 1960s on, done what he could to shape IPTAR, to protect it, and to ensure that it would have the place in the larger psychoanalytic community that he believed it deserved. Today, in no small part due to his efforts, it does.

In the late 1970s and early 1980s Bert and Doris Bernstein spearheaded the effort that made IPTAR the first American group *not associated with the American Psychoanalytic Association* to become a full component society of the International Psycho-Analytical Association (IPA).[3] In the late 1980s and the early 1990s Bert once again took the helm in spearheading the creation of the Confederation of Independent Psychoanalytic Societies of the United States (IPS). Both of those stories are part of the public record and need not be recounted here; however, leaving the arena of IPTAR's "foreign affairs" aside, there is still one thing more to say about Bert's contribution to IPTAR's "domestic affairs" during those years. Back in the 1970s Bert joined the Freudian Faculty of the New York University Postdoctoral Program

2. As a historical point: after the original, founding members (Reuben Fine, Edward Frankel, Lillian Gordon, Irwin Herbst, May Fine Lipson, Elizabeth McNeill, Edmund Weil, and Rose Palm) and the additional three charter members (Stanley Berger, Gertrude Blanck, and Daisy Franco) who then put the organization together from scratch, Bert was only the third person subsequently admitted to membership at IPTAR, preceded only by Abe Levine and Ruth Lax.

3. IPTAR was quickly followed by the New York Freudian Society and, the year after that, by the Los Angeles Institute for Psychoanalytic Studies and, finally, by the Psychoanalytic Center of California.

in Psychotherapy and Psychoanalysis.[4] He was not merely well-liked there (which he was, very much, and still is), he was so highly esteemed that he became a magnet, drawing many among the NYU faculty to IPTAR.[5]

Moving now to look more closely at Bert's professional development: his career as a psychologist and psychoanalyst deeply involved

4. The NYU Postdoctoral Program has four "tracks." The other three are Interpersonal-Humanistic, Relational, and Independent (not to be confused with the British middle school independents).

5. Bert (linked at NYU with Stanley Grand) was not just a little magnet, he was like one of those monster magnets in the wrecking yards that can pick up tons and tons of metal at once, and the flow to IPTAR was copious and continuous. Among those new "recruits" were Jean Schimek, Marvin Hurvich, Sheldon Bach, Lloyd Silverman, and Irving Steingart, followed shortly thereafter by Louis Lauro, Joyce Steingart, Andrew Druck, me and my wife, Judith Lasky, Isaac Tylim, Gil Katz, Mary Libbey, Ben Roth, David Webb, Carolyn Feigelson, and Anita Katz. You will recognize many of those names among the contributors to this book: among those names you will also find many past and present committee chairpersons at IPTAR, deans of the IPTAR Institute, and presidents of IPTAR. These NYU faculty were followed by other NYU faculty and graduates, from the 1970s through the 1980s (the first integration of NYU people into IPTAR); they were then followed in the 1990s by many NYU candidates (with a sprinkling from other institutes) who entered into candidacy at IPTAR prompted by the access to the IPA this gave them (the second integration of NYU people into IPTAR). This, too, in a funny sort of symbolical way, parallels Bert's life of migration and "keeping moving." As one of those "migrants" I believe this cross-fertilization has been extremely good for both the organization and the people in it (the people who "grew up" at IPTAR and the "immigrants" equally). IPTAR, an organization rich to begin with (if it were not, Bert's attraction alone could not have drawn us), was made richer by our participation and we, on the other hand, found new colleagues and friends and a professional home that was eminently satisfying. A detailed account of those "migrations," the benefits accrued and the growing pains endured, is interesting from both a personal and a historical perspective; unfortunately, to pursue it farther at this time would take us too far from Bert's story. The point of having mentioned it, however, must be obvious: it is to recognize publicly how much Bert was the catalyst for that migration. One of the things that makes it so impressive is that this was not a migration from a hated country but from a well-loved one. The way so many "outsiders" flocked to IPTAR and worked to become IPTAR "insiders," not prompted by being rejected or by the need to reject, illustrates two very important truths: the innate attractiveness of IPTAR as a place we wanted to make our professional home, and the power of Bert as a friend, a colleague, and an object in the ego-ideal of many of us.

in research can be divided into four relatively distinct areas. In the 1950s and 1960s Bert, as coprincipal investigator with David Engelhart at the Psychiatric Treatment Research Center and at the Psychopharmacology Research Unit (both in the Department of Psychiatry of the Downstate Medical Center), focused his research on studies of treatment evaluation. These were studies with a twist, however; in a highly medicalized psychiatric environment deeply affected by the development of psychotropic medications, Bert took it as his task to single out for study the so-called nonspecific treatment effects. Nonspecific treatment effects in that psychopharmacological setting were often the very factors associated with relational and stylistic aspects of the psychiatric treatment process. They included the quality of the doctor–patient relationship, the expectations the patient brings to the treatment, the willingness of the doctor to provide treatment, the patient's experience of pill ingestion, and the long-term consequences of treatment by psychoactive drugs. In addition to his many papers on the effects of medication itself, those other studies, about twenty all told, constituted a countercurrent and a new wave in the biochemical revolution of the 1950s and 1960s.

It is important to remember how dramatically the landscape of mental illness was changed by the development of psychoactive medications, medications that seemed to be able to help with conditions previously thought to be intractable. Although psychoanalysis was also at the height of its popularity in America at that time, it was clearly helpful only to the walking wounded, not the mortally wounded populating the back wards of state mental hospitals all across the country. Psychosurgery was discredited, ECT and insulin coma therapy also did not live up to the hopes they originally stimulated, and for the first time, with psychoactive medications, it really looked like something other than long-term storage might be possible for the severely mentally ill. The possibilities of medication-based treatment seemed almost limitless and the psychiatric community, as well as patients and their families, was enthusiastic and optimistic. The long-term failure rate of drug therapy was unknown and, therefore, not a matter of active concern; the deleterious side effects of long-term drug treatment had yet to be observed; the problem of noncompliance in unsupervised settings was still a matter for the future; and the failure of the community mental health movement—a policy venture directly stimulated by the success of drug therapy with long-term patients—had not yet occurred. The intense excitement among doctors and patients was based on imagining a vast population of deeply impaired patients who, as a result of biochemical intervention, would no longer be lost to themselves, their families, and society, but restored to happy and useful lives. No matter how we see some of its limitations today, it was undoubtedly an important advance in psychiatric treatment and, in some quarters, it was treated as nothing short of miraculous.

In the midst of all this, and anticipating developments that would not occur in psychoanalysis until about a half century later, Bert's research offered a perspective on the role of the treatment relationship in the modification of mental states that was otherwise being exclusively attributed to the effects of medication. Moreover, his research examined the effects of the relationship with a very special group: severely disturbed, borderline, and even actively psychotic individuals, a group of patients who were, at that time, generally thought to be refractory to just about everything except, occasionally, heavily administered drug therapy. It is fascinating to see how those studies, conducted half a century ago, presaged and have complete relevance to exactly what occupies the interest—in, fact, the cutting edge of interest—of contemporary psychoanalysts in America.

If we review some of the highlights of Bert's findings during that period of his life, we find them quite congruent with some of the findings we are getting today at the IPTAR Clinical Center. (Bert is IPTAR's Director of Research, quite naturally.) He was able to show, for example, that when paranoid patients improved in psychopharmacological treatment the improvement was regularly related to the experience of subjective body complaints, that is, diffuse body sensation was highly correlated with drug effectiveness. He identified two kinds of paranoid structures, those they called "modifiers" and those they called the "hard" paranoid patients; the "hard" patients did better on drug therapy (and they were the ones who showed subjective somatic complaints) whereas the "modifiers" got better on placebos and got worse on drugs. These were double-blind, double-crossed studies where the identity of the drug was concealed from both the patient and the prescribing psychiatrist; the point of that particular design was to test the element of suggestion in both the therapist and the patient. Finally, Bert developed the Hospital Proneness Scale. He found that psychiatric hospitalization was not linked to psychiatric diagnosis; it was linked, instead, to such factors as aggressivity, social isolation, and psychological differentiation on the TAT (Thematic Apperception Test).

The next period of Bert's research life focused on communication as expressed through linguistics and kinesics (i.e., body movement). Prompted by the findings of the first period, Bert also became interested in indicators of clinical "shape" (much of this work was done with Stanley Grand and Irving Steingart). Collaborating with Merton Gill, who was on the faculty and staff of the Psychiatric Treatment Research Center in the late 1960s, Bert hoped to explicate the "shape" of the transference during drug treatment. The cornerstone of his entire research program during the 1970s was an innovative scoring system applied to nonverbal behavior (here we see the "shape" that Bert's interest, mentioned earlier in this introduction, in nonverbal communication took). He developed a classification of object-focused and body-focused movements that were then brought to bear on video-recorded clinical interchanges and video-recorded psychotherapy sessions. In the classification system he devised, body activity was not approached as an attempt to communicate mentalized thoughts or feelings; bodily acts were seen, instead, as organizers, attempting to regulate self states and object states. His research now became more explicitly psychoanalytic in nature, its objectives to understand the psychic meaning of these acts. He studied the role of object-focused and body-focused movements during associative narratives, then during silences, then during listening, and also in relation to certain affective conditions (e.g., aggressive and depressive states). He then attempted to give this an epigenetic foundation by conducting a developmental study in which he explored these categories of bodily movement in children from 4 to 16 years of age.

There were important implications of this that were brought to bear on verbal communication as well—specifically, the relationship between these categories of kinesic actions and the structure of language itself. Studies conducted with Irving Steingart examined the connection of kinesic action to syntactic structure. Other studies connected kinesics to newly emerging ideas about the referential process. In 1977, Bert wrote the first study on referential activity with Wilma Bucci.

The psychoanalytic implications of Bert's work in this period were summarized in the book *Communicative Structures and Psychic Structures* (1977, Plenum Press: NY), a volume edited in collaboration with Stanley Grand.[6] During this period Bert was appointed Director of Psychology at the University Hospital (Downstate). He was also appointed Director, succeeding Herman Witkin, of the Program in Research Training for Psychiatrists (the D.M.S.—Doctor of Medical Science—degree) then offered by Downstate.[7]

---

6. A historical note of interest is connected with this book. It was there that Lester Luborsky's very first version of the Core Conflictual Relationship Theme was published. As Bert tells it, when Luborsky called to notify Bert of his intent to include that paper, he said: "Bert, you will be the first one to get it, and you'll hear a lot more about it afterwards."

7. An additional little piece of history: I too worked at Downstate, during the mid- to late 1960s. I first began working as a research assistant for Herman Witkin and Helen Block Lewis, conducting (among others) the rod-and-frame tests, tilted-room tests, and embedded figure tests (and doing the statistics—with a mechanical hand calculator no less, an absolute horror) for the work they did on field dependence and independence, which culminated in their book *Psychological Differentiation*. I then shifted my interest to the newly emerging field of sleep and dream research, and worked for Fred Baekeland and with David Koulack, both of whom were part of the D.M.S. program, as were many others whose names may be familiar to the reader. To mention only a few: Ismet Karachan, Fred Pine, Arthur Shapiro, Charles Fisher, Leo Srole, Karen Machover, Phil Oltman, Susan Deri, and Don Goodenough. However, Bert and I worked on different sides of the campus, so to speak, physically as well as hierarchically; Bert was a high-powered, accomplished researcher and I was a lowly research assistant. I left Downstate just before Bert took over as Director of the D.M.S. program, so despite working in the same program for a number of years, we never met. I had, of course, heard of him but I feel sure he had never heard of me.

Using observations from that period of his work, Bert's research in the 1980s focused in on issues that he believed are of critical importance in psychoanalysis, and two sets of observations became central: first, the shielding response, a continuous form of self-stimulation of the body surface (here Bert was using Freud's metaphor of creating a shield or sheath); and, second, the transformational unit, a brief instrumental form of self-touching embedded in a pause during the associative flow (this form of nonfluency Bert dubbed "the Coca-Cola phenomenon," the pause that refreshes). Bert drew the conclusion that these kinds of action functioned as organizers of thought. The shielding activity appeared to point to some kind of associative impasse and the transformational unit, with its momentary interruption and gestural action, seemed to assist in developing both new meanings and more complex syntactic functioning. These observations clarified for Bert some important aspects of the analytic listening process. First, it suggested something about the timing of interpretations following a period of listening; second, it suggested something about the nature of transformational processes in analysis; and, finally, it suggested something about enactment in analysis. Here again, we see how prescient Bert's research interests were, dovetailing with developments that are now critical in the minds of working theorists and clinicians, matters that were just about to emerge in the field, but had not yet appeared.

Along with this, Bert followed an additional set of research interests having to do with specific clinical constellations. He began to look at the construction and deconstruction of meaning in splitting and in depression. In addition he used direct observations (videotapes) of the bodily actions and movement of therapists as they listened to "difficult" and "not-so-difficult" patients. These were studies in which Bert distinguished some of the differences between symbolizing and nonsymbolizing countertransference reactions, differences that were subtly embedded in unconsciously determined bodily action rather than in language or gross enactment. This gave them a special meaning in addition to their fantasy and transference content; it gave them meaning as a regulatory principle, that is, one of the ways analytic process is regulated by patient and analyst.

It was also during that period that Bert rejuvenated the Research Committee at IPTAR. Together with a small group of colleague-investigators[8] Bert was able to muster significant support for research in terms of both talent and money from both the IPTAR Society and from the IPTAR Clinical Center, the upshot of which was a comprehensive research program at IPTAR evaluating both the outcome and the process of long-term treatment. A study of process, in psychoanalysis proper, has been undertaken by Bert, Marvin Hurvich, and me as its coordinator, and studies of effectiveness, retrospective recollection, and internalization of the therapist and the therapeutic experience in analytically oriented psychotherapy have been conducted at the IPTAR Clinical Center (variously coordinated by Joan Hoffenberg and Neal Vorus, and including the essential participation of Donna Bender, Allan Frosch, and Jesse Geller). A report of that work was published by Bert, Joan Hoffenberg, Neal Vorus, and Allan Frosch in the *Journal of the American Psychoanalytic Association* in 1999 ("The Effectiveness of Psychoanalytic Psychotherapy: The Role of Treatment Duration, Frequency of Sessions, and the Therapeutic Relationship," 47[3]:741–772).

---

8. I use the term *colleague-investigators* because of its special meaning at IPTAR. At most analytic institutes (including IPTAR) the divisions among candidates and members, faculty, and training and supervising analysts are usually quite discrete for reasons readily understood, and considered right or wrong depending on whom you read concerning the organizational psychology of analytic training. At IPTAR those divisions exist and are broken down simultaneously; candidates are integrated into selected committees of the various Boards, giving them some representation in how IPTAR is governed and how the curriculum develops. But nowhere at IPTAR is there a greater mutuality between candidates and even the most senior of members than in the Research Committee; a special quality of colleagueship has emerged there and it was intentionally planned that way by Bert (which tells us something, once again, about his character and not just his accomplishments). This is very important in both practical and philosophical terms as it is relatively rare for candidates at psychoanalytic institutes, subjected to an extremely hierarchical structure, however well-intentioned and necessary, forced into an artificial return to adolescence as students yet once again, and subjected to the superheated reactivation of the conflicts of their childhood in their training analyses, to be treated like the accomplished, professional adults that they are.

As one can see from the date of that paper, this has segued into the fourth period of Bert's research, a period in which all that he has worked on in the past has been brought together and then refocused into the work of the present: Bert's intense interest in symbolization. To explain why Bert has centered his interest so strongly in symbolization, I give you his own words:

> The psychoanalytic attitude is a symbolizing attitude. We listen to our patients' stories as signifiers of multiple meanings. And, we listen to ourselves from multiple perspectives. Our patients deal not only with drives, self, or objects, but they also try to deal with the symbolization of drives, self, and object relationships. What matters, consistently, is the process of translation and transmutation. Psychoanalysis may have been born in the theory of dreams and matured in the theory of transference and countertransference, but these are all unthinkable without a concept of mediation and transformation. It is a process of linking items in different spheres of the mind where one represents the other. It is a process where experience, stated as a fact through self reflection, becomes symbol. It is through such a network of mediation that psychoanalytic work accrues and when this is throttled impasse ensues. Hence, it is along lines of symbolization that we can account for psychoanalytic work and psychoanalytic change. It is this perspective that has given rise to my most recent interest in symbolization as a process specific to analytic treatment. And it is a process that belongs to common ground because every analyst, in every theoretical orientation, finds him- or herself embracing a symbolizing attitude. Such a recognition calls for a specific psychoanalytic theory of symbolization, rooted in but over-riding known cognitive or information processing approaches. [Freedman, in press]

Bert approached this work, as usual, through an empirically driven perspective; he developed the idea of "incremental symbolization," a concept that operates on four developmentally (dynamic, not chronological, development) sequential levels: desymbolization, incipient symbolization, discursive symbolization, and dynamic symbolization. Bert's ideas about symbolizing processes are quite distinct from two other approaches that are now current in the field and should not be condensed with or confused with them: a view of psychic life (mainly developed by French analysts) that is divided into either symbolic or imaginary spheres, and what might be termed the phenomenological approach, which fails to acknowledge that in psychoanalytic treatment what is symbolized in part had been unconscious. Bert's emphasis on dynamic symbolization sets his theory firmly apart.

Bert's four levels of symbolization are not just research constructs, they are concepts of clinical importance, so rather than discussing the research findings of the particular studies on which they were based I will present, instead, short clinical descriptions of each of them:

Desymbolization is concrete and repetitive, with an insistence not only on the sameness of things and situations but also on sameness of the self and of others. Defensively, this mode of mentalization is based on profound disavowal, implementing the wish not to know.[9] It also guards against psychological differentiation within the self and between the self and the other. Psychic space can be said to be frozen. One finds a serious inability to use experience, external, situational, and internal, to create complex and varied meanings. Only single, unwavering perceptions of experience are used and they are treated as concretized facts, rather than being understood as a construction, that is, as one of many possible interpretations. There is a reification of affective experience, somatic experience, object relational experience, and perceptual experience. Desymbolization may become apparent in a variety of different clinical syndromes: for example, in the delusional aspects of some kinds of psychosis, in the projective identification one so often sees in borderline states, in the absolute fixation on body weight and body weight only in the eating disorders, and in the frozen constellations of narcissistic

9. At the time of this writing Bert is hard at work distinguishing the differing roles of evacuative defenses versus the defense of disavowal in the various impediments to symbolization.

states. Desymbolization is the condition[10] in which a transformation cycle begins, as Bert understands it.[11]

Transformation cycles are meta-events that describe the movement of mentalization (not cognition and not meta-cognition) through the four hierarchical levels of symbolization; they "unfreeze" frozen constellations of any sort, not just narcissistic. Transformation cycles are, from Bert's point of view, the bread and butter of the working-through process; they are an operational description of analytic process itself.

Incipient symbolization involves the ability to name emotional states that are linked to the inner body self, states that exist in the affecto-sensory-motor language that Edith Jacobson described so well. Here one finds the possibility of articulating body-linked emotions by the use of metaphor and through the specification of emotional experiences as they are present in current and past contexts. This ability suggests a link between the spoken word and what are often thought of as prelinguistic codes. Thus, incipient symbolization is not descriptively dissimilar to Wilma Bucci's referential activity, which rests on the linking of two codes, the verbal and the nonverbal. It is true that from a linguistic perspective incipient symbolization is fully a form of symbolizing work, but it is important here to make a clinical distinction. From an analytic view it is important to note that it is only an incipient event; that is, it is dramatically different from desymbolization but it is still only a precursor to the symbolization of dynamic conflict in the transference.

In choosing the term **discursive symbolization** Bert took the word "discursive" from Susan Langer's emphasis on discourse as a

10. Although desymbolization is obvious and highly symptomatic in the more primitive disorders, it is not restricted to primitive pathology; it operates in everyone with an unconscious.

11. Although the impetus for the concept of transformation cycles grew out of the transformation(al) cycles that Bert described in his research on kinesics, this is by now a much more complex phenomenon that should not be confused with the earlier concept. The earlier concept referred to a consolidating moment in an analytic or a therapeutic hour, and the present concept is about analytic process (although it is not entirely irrelevant to analytic psychotherapy) and it can cover days, weeks, months, and years.

crucial aspect of symbolizing. Can one imagine discourse in therapy without the interplay between the self in interaction with an other? It would be unthinkable. Discursive symbolization in analysis involves the telling out loud of relationship episodes in which one can recognize not only the presence of one's self but also the presence of the other. The relationship episode will be told with affective interaction between the two, perhaps with mutual recognition. And the recounting of it takes place with a coherent narrative. So in discursive symbolization we see the patient moving from the earlier realm of only body-self space that is present in incipient symbolization to the realm of object-relational space,[12] in which self and other are articulated in a coherent narrative. Discursive symbolization not only alludes to the events depicted in the narrative, it alludes to something else as well. As these relationship episodes are expressed in treatment, we find the kernel of the transference making its appearance. One might say that everything in treatment is transference, but in discursive symbolization in particular, a special emphasis is placed on a narrativization of the transference. That implies a widening of inner psychic space. That widening allows for the give and take, the projection and introjection, all the intramural activity necessary for the development of internal as well as external object relations. This is Bert's model of the way an expansion of inner space occurs, and expansion of inner space sets the stage for the expansion of analytic space. Contracting down now to the operationalism of clinical events, discursive symbolization involves the beginning of the type of self-awareness we hope to see in analytic therapy, a nascent reflectiveness about the impact of relationships on the self. But however much this narrativization of the transference sketches the frame of prototypical relational episodes, as in Lester Luborsky's Core Conflictual Relationship Themes, it does not yet capture the signs of inner conflict that are a defining aspect of analytic work.

12. The concept of space (body-self space, psychic space, object-relational space, symbolizing space, analytic space) is very important for Bert; different kinds of space are a subfeature of every component of a transformation cycle and it is the basis for his concept of *spatialization*.

As an introduction to defining the attributes of **dynamic symbolization** it is important to first point out that, in Bert's view, the symbolic mode of thought, in all its variants, is governed by an invariant structure, a triangular one. What this means is that two discrete items from different spheres of the mind are joined through the action of an observing ego. This is true in all three forms of symbolization: it occurs in incipient symbolization, where we see the linking of spoken language with emotion structures; and it occurs in discursive symbolization, when we see the emergence of relationship sequences that allude to the transference. This generalization does not hold, however, for desymbolization, since there triangularity collapses. Getting now to the definition of dynamic symbolization, we are not just dealing with the linking of affects or relationship episodes, which can be quite conscious, but with experiences that are conflictual, irreverent, or chaotic. These experiences are reconciled with experiences that are rational, coherent, or bound. Said another way: both in psychoanalysis and in dynamic symbolization we are concerned with the symbolization of the dynamic unconscious. Thus, dynamic symbolization rests on notions of integration: the accomplishment of binding and linking. What marks dynamic symbolization is that something previously unknown or unconscious is being integrated, bound, linked. To see the representation of dynamic symbolization in the clinical setting, what do we look for? We look for the recognition of multiple, incompatible, contradictory perspectives on the self or on the other, often driven by pleasure or unpleasure. These contradictions, despite the process of linking or binding, will always vary in structure from chaotic and incoherent to cohesive and realistic. From his earlier work on kinesics and body rhythmicity Bert has recognized that in dynamic symbolization signs of symbolizing work also occur in the form of discontinuities, gaps, and breaks in the frame, not only from signs of the intrusion of the unconscious. At the very beginning of this introduction I made a distinction between the process of making symbols and the process of symbolization as a means of gaining distance from raw experience. Obviously symbols may be used regressively but the ability to make a symbol itself depends on a capacity for doing some kind of symbolic work. Bert stresses that only when the symbolic product has been preceded by that inner work can we speak of psychic attainment. That is why dynamic symbolization is, in his opinion, a good criterion for both treatment process and outcome.

These are ideas about clinical process at a relatively high level of abstraction; the ideas accrued slowly from the work of dozens of empirical studies and then, in true Norbert Freedman style, Bert applied them to further empirical studies of importantly related clinical ideas: the mechanisms of spatialization, and the transformation cycle. After working out these concepts, his work with them (rather than on them) continued. In one study Bert examined patterns of long-term clinical change through the identification of transformation cycles; he examined, in another study, specific patterns of symbolized and desymbolized transference; in another study, he examined these concepts to identify some of the phenomena operative in symbolized and desymbolized countertransference; and, in a fourth study, he examined transformation cycles in the termination phase. In his work Bert has focused not only on the transformation cycle within which one finds the sequence of incremental symbolization; he has also focused his attention on incremental spatialization, and that is because it is so closely linked to the allied concept of creating symbolizing space. Bert uses the idea of spatialization in both a metaphorical and a literal sense; thus he has studied this phenomenon cross-culturally (in comparisons with mobile and stationary groups); he has studied it in early infant–caregiver interactions; and he has studied it in the biorhythmicity of clinical interchange, thereby making it possible to identify some of the nonverbal signifiers of symbolizing space.

Earlier, when I quoted Bert, he finished his statement with a call for "a specific psychoanalytic theory of symbolization rooted in but overriding known cognitive or information processing approaches." I think it is clear that Bert has done just that. In our research on psychoanalytic process (using tape-recorded analyses) Bert's concept of symbolization, along with Marvin's ideas about annihilation anxiety, are pivotal. And this brings us fully to the present. Bert is now Professor Emeritus at Downstate, Clinical Professor at NYU, and the Director of Research at IPTAR. He has developed an ambitious research program at IPTAR that includes not only our work on analytic process but also a number of simultaneously running studies of analytically oriented treatment at the IPTAR Clinical Center. At present the research environment at IPTAR is so rich that we have been able to establish a number of research externships for doctoral candidates in psychology and social work, another one of Bert's ideas, transformed into a very gratifying accomplishment.

As I draw this introduction to a close it seems appropriate to bring Bert's life, apart from just his research, back into the picture. At IPTAR, but not only at IPTAR, Bert is held in the kind of esteem the Japanese reserve for their "national treasures." He is a personal, analytic, and organizational elder statesman so highly regarded that one is reminded of the commercial for a brokerage house that used to appear on television a few years ago: the screen is full of action and noise which, all of a sudden, is brought to a total halt with the screen characters frozen in raptly attentive postures; in the resonating silence a resounding voice intones, "When E. F. Hutton speaks, everyone listens."

Although this is a *festschrift* and not a monograph, this book is part of IPTAR's Monograph Series. It was specifically commissioned by IPTAR to honor Bert's career and his life. All of the contributors to this book were eager to be included simply because of the strength of their personal feelings for him; unfortunately, many others had to be turned away. On March 12, 2000, IPTAR held a magnificent (and expensive) dinner in his honor and, again, there was fierce competition over who could have the podium because one evening was not enough to accommodate the amount of praise his friends, family, and colleagues wanted to give him. IPTAR has also established a Norbert Freedman Fund for Psychoanalysis, which will be used to support psychoanalytic and psychotherapeutic research. The proceeds of the dinner, the contributions from many friends and colleagues who could not attend that event, and all of the royalties from this book are directed into that fund (which is still accepting contributions).

Now it is time to turn to the contributions made by the authors in this *festschrift*, all of whom have made some aspect of the symbol-making or symbolizing process a central part of their contribution. In fact, this was a condition of their participation. This is particularly impressive when one considers that they all have their own interests, which they spend considerable time pursuing, and which they endeavor to work on in schedules that are frequently hectic and overburdened. They have all agreed to stop their own work long enough to show how these symbolizing processes are relevant to it, and that is a very special statement about Bert and also about them.

A SELECTIVE (CHRONOLOGICAL) BIBLIOGRAPHY OF THE WRITINGS OF NORBERT FREEDMAN

Freedman, N. (1953). Early childhood recollection: an integrative technique for analysis of personality test data. *American Journal of Individual Psychology* 1:86–91.

Freedman, N., Engelhardt, D. M., Glick, B. S., Kaye, H., Buchwald, J., and Stark, P. (1958). Drop-out from outpatient psychiatric treatment. *A.M.A. Archives of Neurology & Psychiatry* 80:657–666.

Hankoff, L. D., Freedman, N., and Engelhardt, D. M. (1958). The prognostic value of placebo response. *American Journal of Psychiatry* 115(6):549–550.

Freedman, N., Warshaw, L., Engelhardt, D. M., Blumenthal, I. J., and Hankoff, L. D. (1959). The effect of various therapies upon fecal incontinence in chronic schizophrenic patients. *Journal of Mental and Nervous Disease* 128(6):562–565.

Engelhardt, D. M., Freedman, N., Glick, B. S., Hankoff, L. D., Mann, D., and Margolis, R. (1960). Prevention of psychiatric hospitalization with use of psychopharmacological agents. *Journal of the American Medical Association* 173:147–149.

Freedman, N., Engelhardt, D. M., Hankoff, L. D., Schwartz, S., and Zobel, N. (1961). Patterns of verbal group participation in the drug treatment of schizophrenics. *International Journal of Group Psychiatry* 11(1):60–73.

Engelhardt, D. M., and Freedman, N. (1961). An approach to the evaluation of long-term psychopharmacological therapy of schizophrenic patients. In *Mental Patients in Transition*, ed. M. Greenblatt, pp. 322–335. Springfield, IL: Charles C Thomas.

Engelhardt, D. M., Rosen, B., Freedman, N., Mann, D., and Margolis, R. (1963). Phenothiazines in prevention of psychiatric hospitalization II: Duration of treatment exposure. *Journal of the American Medical Association* 186:981–983.

Freedman, N., Engelhardt, D. M., Mann, D., Margolis, R., and London, S. (1965). Communication of body complaints and paranoid symptom change under conditions of phenothiazine treatment. *Journal of Personality and Social Psychology* 1(4):310–318.

Freedman, N., Cutler, R., Engelhardt, D. M., and Margolis, R. (1967). On the modification of paranoid symptomatology. *Journal of Nervous and Mental Disease* 144(1):29–36.

Freedman, N., and Hoffman, S. (1967). Kinetic behavior in altered clinical states: an approach to objective analysis of motor behavior during clinical interviews. *Perceptual and Motor Skills* 24:527–539.

Freedman, N., Rosen, B., Engelhardt, D. M., and Margolis, R. (1967). Prediction of psychiatric hospitalization I: The measurement of hospital proneness. *Journal of Abnormal Psychology* 72(6):468–477.

Rosen, B., Engelhardt, D. M., Freedman, N., and Margolis, R. (1968). The hospitalization proneness scale as a predictor of response to phenothiazine treatment. *Journal of Nervous and Mental Disease* 146(6):476–480.

Cohen, M., Freedman, N., Engelhardt, D. M., and Margolis, R. (1968). Family interaction patterns, drug treatment and change in social aggression. *A.M.A. Archives of General Psychiatry* 19:50–56.

Grand, S., Freedman, N., and Jortner, S. (1969). Variations in REM dreaming and the effectiveness of behavior in group therapy. *American Journal of Psychotherapy* 23(4):667–680.

Freedman, N., Cutler, R., Engelhardt, D. M., and Margolis, R. (1970). On the modification of paranoid symptomatology II: Stylistic considerations and the effectiveness of phenothiazines. *Journal of Nervous and Mental Disease* 150(1):68–76.

Freedman, N. (1972). The analysis of movement behavior during the clinical interview. In *Studies in Dyadic Communication*, ed. A. Seigman and B. Pope, pp. 58–72. New York: Pergamon.

Steingart, I., and Freedman, N. (1972). A language construction approach for the examination of self/object representations in varying clinical states. *Psychoanalysis and Contemporary Science* 1:132–178.

Freedman, N., O'Hanlon, J., Oltman, P., and Witkin, H. A. (1972). The imprint of psychological differentiation on kinetic behavior in varying communicative contexts. *Journal of Abnormal Psychology* 79(3):239–258.

Freedman, N., Blass, T., Rifkin, A., and Quitkin, F. (1973). Body movements and the verbal encoding of aggressive affect. *Journal of Personality and Social Psychology* 26(1):72–85.

Grand, S., Freedman, N., and Steingart, I. (1973). A study of the representation of objects in schizophrenia. *Journal of the American Psychoanalytic Association* 21(2):399–434.

Blass, T., Freedman, N., and Steingart, I. (1974). Body movements and verbal encoding in the congenitally blind. *Perceptual and Motor Skills* 39:279–293.

Freedman, N., and Steingart, I. (1975). Kinesic internalization and language construction. *Psychoanalysis and Contemporary Science* 4:355–403.

Steingart, I., and Freedman, N. (1975). The organization of body-focused kinesic behavior and language construction in schizophrenic and depressed states. *Psychoanalysis and Contemporary Science* 4:423–450.

Freedman, N. (1976). Hands, words, and mind: on the structuralization of body movements during discourse and the capacity for verbal representation. In *Communicative Structures and Psychic Structures*, ed. N. Freedman and S. Grand, pp. 109–132. New York: Plenum.

Freedman, N., and Grand, S. (1976). A gesture toward a psychoanalytic theory of communication. In *Communicative Structures and Psychic Structures*, ed. N. Freedman and S. Grand, pp. 293–306. New York: Plenum.

Grand, S., Marcos, L. R., Freedman, N., and Barroso, F. (1977). The relation of psychopathology and bilingualism to kinesic aspects of interview behavior in schizophrenia. *Journal of Abnormal Psychology* 86(5):492–500.

Barroso, F., Freedman, N., Grand, S., and van Meel, J. (1978). The evocation of two types of hand movements in information processing. *Journal of Experimental Psychology: Human Perception and Performance* 4(2):321–329.

Bucci, W., and Freedman, N. (1978). Language and hand: the dimension of referential competence. *Journal of Personality* 46:594–622.

Freedman, N., Barroso, F., Bucci, W., and Grand, S. (1978). The bodily manifestations of listening. *Psychoanalysis and Contemporary Thought* 1(1):153–194.

Freedman, N. (1980). On splitting and its resolution. *Psychoanalysis and Contemporary Thought* 3:237–266.

Barroso, F., Freedman, N., and Grand, S. (1980). Self-touching, performance, and attentional processes. *Perceptual and Motor Skills* 50:1083–1089.

Bucci, W., and Freedman, N. (1981). The language of depression. *Bulletin of the Menninger Clinic* 45:334–358.

Freedman, N. (1983). On psychoanalytic listening: the construction, paralysis, and reconstruction of meaning. *Psychoanalysis and Contemporary Thought* 6(3):405–434.

Freedman, N. (1985). The concept of transformation in psychoanalysis. *Psychoanalytic Psychology* 2(4):317–339.

Freedman, N., and Grand, S. (1985). Shielding: an associative organizer. In *From Research to Clinical Practice*, ed. G. Striker and R. Keisner, pp. 353–374. New York: Plenum.

Gilani, Z. H., Bucci, W., and Freedman, N. (1985). The structure and language of a silence. *Semiotica* 56:99–113.

Freedman, N. (1986). On depression: the paralysis, annihilation, and reconstruction of meaning. In *Empirical Studies of Psychoanalytic Theories, Vol. 2*, ed. J. Masling, pp. 109–129. Hillsdale, NJ: Analytic Press.

Freedman, N., van Meel, J. M., Barroso, F., and Bucci, W. (1986). On the development of communicative competence. *Semiotica* 62:77–105.

Freedman, N. (1988). The setting and the issues. *Psychoanalysis and Contemporary Thought (Special Issue: Psychoanalysis and Values: Reflections on the Hamburg Congress)* 2:197–212.

Freedman, N. (1989). Two principles of communicative functioning. In *The Individual, Communication, and Society: Essays in Memory of Gregory Bateson*, ed. R. W. Reiber, pp. 279–300. Cambridge, England: Cambridge University Press.

Freedman, N. (1991). Varieties of symbiotic manifestations. *Psychoanalytic Reflections on Current Issues* 10:58–77.

Barroso, F., and Freedman, N. (1992). The nonverbal manifestations of cognitive processes in clinical listening. *Journal of Psycholinguistic Research* 21(2):87–110.

Freedman, N. (1994). More on transformation: enactments in psychoanalytic space. In *The Spectrum of Psychoanalysis: Essays in Honor of Martin S. Bergmann*, ed. A. K. Richards and A. D. Richards, pp. 93–110. Madison, CT: International Universities Press.

Freedman, N., and Berzofsky, M. (1995). The shape of the communicated transference in difficult and not-so-difficult patients: the symbolized and desymbolized transference. *Psychoanalytic Psychology* 12(3):363–374.

Freedman, N., and Lavender, J. (1997). On receiving the patient's transference: the symbolizing and desymbolizing countertransference. *Journal of the American Psychoanalytic Association* 45(1):79–103.

Freedman, N. (1998). Psychoanalysis and symbolization: Legacy or heresy? In *The Modern Freudians*, ed. C. Ellman, S. Grand, M. Silvan, and S. J. Ellman, pp. 79–97. Northvale, NJ: Jason Aronson.

Freedman, N., Hoffenberg, J., Vorus, N., and Frosch, A. (1999). The effectiveness of psychoanalytic psychotherapy: the role of treatment duration, frequency of sessions, and the therapeutic relationship. *Journal of the American Psychoanalytic Association* 47(3):741–772.

Freedman, N. (in press). Ein bericht von mid-Manhattan. In *Research Conference on Long-Term Treatment Effects*, ed. German Psychoanalytic Association. Hamburg (German language edition).

1

Norbert Freedman: Psychoanalytic Therapy Researcher

ROBERT S. WALLERSTEIN

In his biographical chapter, Richard Lasky has painstakingly and lovingly surveyed the life and the career of Norbert Freedman as psychoanalytic scholar—as student, as clinician, as educator, as investigator, and above all, pervading every aspect of Bert's activities, as an innovator of novel psychoanalytic perspectives that have enduringly enriched our psychoanalytic landscape. In his most appreciative overview of Bert's career, Lasky has segmented Bert's research investigations, and the many publications to which they gave rise, by decades, according to the successive central research themes that Bert and his different research colleagues were addressing. These will only be summarily restated here, in order to indicate their incremental unfolding and their gradual shift into the increasingly incisive study of the central problems of psychoanalytic therapy research: what changes are (or can be) brought about in psychoanalytic therapy, that is, the outcome question; and how are those changes brought about, through the interaction of what factors or variables in the patient, in the therapy and the therapist, and in the patient's evolving life situation, or in Bert's favored language, via what mediating mechanisms, that is, the process question.

After receiving his doctorate in the early 1950s, with a thesis on subliminal perception along the experimental psychoanalytic lines laid out by George Klein and his colleagues, Bert worked into the '60s at the Downstate Medical Center of the State University of New York in Brooklyn, in the beginning and rapidly burgeoning field of psychopharmacology research, the impact of the new psychoactive drugs on the spectrum of severe psychopathological disorders, efficacy and outcome research into the treatment of psychiatric illness. But as Lasky has carefully delineated, Bert's interests from the start were in the psychological meanings of the drug-induced somatosensory changes, and the altered psychological self-states accompanying (or reflecting) these changes, what the more biologically oriented drug researchers subsumed in all too facile a manner as placebo effects or nonspecific treatment effects.

To Bert Freedman this research was an avenue into outcome studies of major psychiatric illnesses treated by the new psychopharmacological agents, but from the perspective of psychological meanings and of achieved altered and improved psychological states, a kind of combined process and outcome study of psychiatric treatments. Bert's work at the time was thus through a different prism—via the medication-induced physiological bodily changes—rather than the simultaneously developing psychotherapy research projects devoted to the study of the *psychological* treatments of those mental and emotional disorders felt to be amenable to purely psychological interventions, such as Carl Rogers' research program built on his client-centered therapeutic approach (Rogers 1951, Rogers and Dymond 1954), or the psychoanalytically framed Psychotherapy Research Project of The Menninger Foundation with which I was associated (Wallerstein 1986, Wallerstein et al. 1956). However, in his efforts to encompass both process and outcome aspects of drug-induced therapeutic changes, again, of course, via a psychological vantage point, Bert was certainly au courant with the similar thrust of our Menninger project, and well ahead of his time, if viewed from the perspective of the then prevailing state of the art of psychotherapy research.

Following further in Lasky's accounting, from the latter '60s and into the '70s, Bert's investigative interests shifted—and deepened—

into the study of therapeutic communication in its broadest and totalistic sense, as the fullest complex of verbal, nonverbal, and kinesic expression, the imbricated relationship of body movement within the therapeutic dyad, to semantic and syntactic expression. I would expand on Lasky's extensive discussion of this new era of Bert's research by adding my conception of the intent, to wit, to explore the role of all the nonverbal, somatosensory, and kinesic manifestations as markers and as expressions of the inner psychological change process, reflections perhaps of the mediating or linking mechanisms that are the motors of therapeutic change. This concern with psychic change I see as the organizing red thread of research preoccupations of Bert Freedman's professional lifetime. What I am asserting is that long before Bert set his current sights as an explicit process and outcome psychotherapy researcher, he was indeed, perhaps not quite consciously, a cryptopsychotherapy researcher all along, and it is in this context, including the gradual evolution of his linguistic and kinesic preoccupations into his major studies of what he calls symbolization and desymbolization—for which he is so justly recognized and which has been set as the overall theme of this *festschrift* in his honor—that I wish to set out my own take on Bert Freedman's place within the growing edifice of contemporary psychotherapy research.

But to return first to Lasky's chronology: in the mid-'70s, and into the '80s, Bert's investigative ardor, fueled by the newly available technology of videorecorded psychotherapy hours, turned to the fullest exploration, empirically and conceptually, of the realm framed by the side-by-side study of verbal expression alongside the whole array of nonverbal interactive parameters, centrally, of course, the kinetics of posture and body movement. From this came such creations as (1) a scoring system for nonverbal behaviors; (2) the collaboration with Wilma Bucci in the evolution of the conceptions of referential activity, the referential cycle, and the multiple code theory of mental functioning—a cognitive, science-based modification of psychoanalytic understandings of the thinking process (Bucci 1997)—all becoming an avenue for the study of the process of psychotherapeutic change; (3) the conceptions of the shielding response, the transformational process, and the transformational unit; (4) and finally, in the '90s, the full flowering of the conceptions of the symbolizing attitude, signifying, to quote from Lasky's citation from Bert, "the psychoanalytic attitude is a symbolizing attitude. We listen to our patients' stories as signifiers of multiple meanings. . . ." (p. 18).

In his chapter Lasky has developed at some length Bert's various, related conceptions having to do with the translation and transmutation of symbols, incremental symbolization comprising the succession of incipient symbolization, discursive symbolization, and dynamic symbolization, all defined and characterized, as well as the reverse, desymbolization, and then in the ever-oscillating therapeutic process, the capacity for reversal, in turn, of the desymbolization, by disembedding and thus restoring the psychic space within which the symbolizing function can be incrementally restored—all of this worked out in intensive study of videotaped psychotherapy sessions with "difficult" (borderline, narcissistic, character disordered, etc.) and "not-so-difficult" (normal-neurotic) patients, and described in these sessions both transferentially and countertransferentially. Of this symbolizing process, Bert rightly states that it is "a process that belongs to common ground because every analyst, in every theoretical orientation, finds him- or herself embracing a symbolizing attitude. Such a recognition calls for a specific psychoanalytic theory of symbolization" (p. 18), which Bert and his co-authors tried to build in his sequence of papers across the past decade.

My own intent in this chapter is to elaborate, building on the developmental outline provided by Lasky, my own assessment of Bert Freedman's achieved place—now at the zenith of his undiminished and astonishingly productive research career—within the contemporary universe of psychotherapy research, as an impressive investigator of both psychotherapy process and psychotherapy outcome. And I will do this by explicating Bert's observations and conceptions, and their relationship to the current state of the field, through study of his quite recent publications in these two realms, a 1997 article with Joan Lavender on process studies (together with reference to an unpublished recent manuscript with Stanley Grand), and a 1999 article with Joan Hoffenberg, Neal Vorus, and Allan Frosch on outcome studies.

I turn first to the process studies because they, in a direct line, represent the fullest development of Bert's impressive conceptualizations of the vicissitudes of the symbolizing process, his major theoretical activity over the past decade and a half. Bert's focus here has been on issues of countertransference as varyingly impeding or facilitating the interpretive analytic activity, and this is indeed fully congruent with the concerns that have burgeoned, both clinically and in research, during this same time period, with the significance of countertransference exploration as a guide to understanding and promoting the clinical treatment process (see in this connection, for example, Jacobs [1991] and many others), that is, the change process in psychoanalytic therapy.

In the 1997 paper (Freedman and Lavender), the thesis is stated early: "Here it is posited that the usefulness of the countertransference depends on the partial retention of the symbolizing functions within the analyst" (p. 81), and then, after reference to the analyst's capacity to achieve a state of disembedding, with the creation of an inner psychic space within which to face the transference onslaught, and to restore the symbolizing function, the authors go on to state, "These are the ideas that lead us to attempt an objective definition of the constructive elements within countertransference phenomena" (p. 81).

Here the focus becomes squarely Bert's particular vision, and his exemplification of these "constructive elements" within the countertransference: "There is, however, a sphere other than countertransference [in its impeding or deflecting sense] in which the patient's psychic life lives on in the analyst's consciousness. This sphere, defined by the essence of the analyst's work ego (Fliess 1942), involves tact, caring, transitory identification, and controlled regression. . . . This form of participation has generally been discussed within the vast literature on empathy. . . . Annie Reich (1966) noted some thirty years ago that it behooves us to draw the boundary between empathy and countertransference. Despite the apparent complexities, these boundaries are not so vague; indeed they are definable. What we would like to show here are the definable constituents of empathy, the *useful countertransference*, and the countertransference that is *destructive* of the treatment process" (pp. 81–82, italics added).

These constituents are to be discerned, "Through the Window of the Listening Process" (p. 82), but not only through the hearing of the recorded verbal interaction, but also—and this is Bert Freedman's very special focus on the countertransference—through the bodily manifestations of listening, granted that others, like Jacobs and McLaughlin, have also paid attention to the postural elements, on both sides of the couch, in the interplay within the transference–countertransference matrix. Most specifically, "We believe that rhythmicity of bodily actions during listening is associated with heightened attunement and the capacity to create symbolizing space. The failure of rhythmicity—continuous arrhythmicity, or shielding—indicates disrupted attunement and a breakdown in the analyst's capacity to create such space" (p. 84). And the authors state that this conviction is built on the correlation of the bodily movements as captured in the videorecorded therapy session with the retrospective accounts of the therapists of their experience of the interactions of the same session, the latter conveyed in illustrative detail.

They also define rhythmicity, and its obverse, arrhythmicity or shielding, empirically: "Rhythmicity during listening is manifest in head nods, lateral hand-to-body motions, foot kicks and posture shifts. . . . In general rhythmicity refers to kinesic acts phased in with the ebb and flow of speech" (p. 84). Contrarily, "Arrhythmicity involves ongoing, repetitive bilateral self-stimulation usually at the midline with one hand or finger acting upon the other . . . or a particular form of self-regulatory head nods. It involves a restricted range spatially. Shielding during listening is unresponsive to variations in the patient's phonemic rhythm and inevitably occurs under conditions of stress or interference" (p. 84).

And of course there are also intermediate forms: "We also considered an intermediary phenomenon, transitory discontinuities within the network of bodily rhythmicity. . . . One gets the impression that transitory arrhythmia is a reparative withdrawal, for while the transitory arrhythmia *is* arrhythmic, its very time-limited nature indicates that it is embedded within a general frame of rhythmic engagement, representing a moment of discontinuity within a framework of continuity" (pp. 84–85). Then using a quantitative assessment of the bodily movements recorded in the videotaped hours and what the authors call the "contextual analysis" of the same hours, meaning an interview focused on the experienced psychic states of the therapist as recalled after the therapy session, all tied together with pertinent inferences linking the observed kinesic activity to the recounted experiential narrative, Freedman and Lavender could evaluate "fluctuations in symbolizing activity against fluctuations in bodily listening rhythmicity by assessing the therapist's use of language to determine where she was able to sustain the symbolic function necessary for effective attunement and therapeutic work and where her symbolizing activity failed" (p. 87). They could conclude therefore that "Rhythmicity thus serves as a kinesic frame for empathy. Arrhythmicity, by contrast, signifies the disruption of symbolizing functions and may be regarded as a kinesic marker for the presence of a desymbolizing countertransference" (p. 89).

The ways in which these processes are conceived to work is spelled out in more specific detail in the unpublished manuscript written with Stanley Grand, built around the study of the videotaped therapy hours of the same three therapists, each with a "difficult" and a "not-so-difficult" patient, that are the basis of the findings presented in the paper with Lavender. The specified aim of the paper with Grand was to clearly depict "the vulnerability, the resiliency, and the efficacy of the analyst's mind at work" (p. 1), with special focus, of course, on what Bert has called constructive and destructive countertransferences. This is done, again, via the linking of the observed kinesic actions with the therapists' accounts of their experienced mental states. It is during the therapist's listening process, the receiving of communications and their intrapsychic restructuring, that the sensorimotor matrix of the early body gets reactivated and expressed. And it is when transference resistance appears that the question arises of the analyst's capacity to ward off its impact and sustain the listening process, or, failing that, to have derailment ensue.

This is illustrated by the detailed dissection of the encounters of the three therapists, each with their "difficult" and their "not-so-difficult" patient. With the not-so-difficult patients, there is a perceived rhythmic alternation from receiving through restructuring, which implies a symbolizing process, with transitory identifications and patterns of optimal empathic attunement. And concomitantly, the language of the therapists' interventions is described as articulate, affectively appropriate, and reflective. The transitory arrhythmias, which may appear within this "symbolizing" or productive countertransference, invariably involve only temporary disruptions of the orderly sequences of the listening process, and at these points, of course, the threshold is reached between empathic attunement and an impeding countertransference.

By contrast, with the difficult patients there are characteristically periods of continuous bilateral self-stimulation or shielding. The language during interventions is often staccato, nonattuned, inappropriate. This is a manifestation of the desymbolizing countertransference, where vicarious introspection has been replaced by immersion into the therapist's subjectivity, often experienced as drowsiness, restlessness, or being "zonked" in the patient's material. It reflects what the authors call a "state of embeddedness" in which the process of constructing meanings is interfered with, and it is this work of meaning construction that is at the heart of the symbolizing process.

The resolution of this embeddedness depends on an inner process in the mind of the therapist, triggered by some alerting signal, like the perceived discomforts just referred to. Disembedding, when successful, becomes then a transformation of mental functioning, the re-creation of a listening space, and the ability again to represent and convey meanings. Such gradual connecting is again clearly represented in the visually perceived sensorimotor sphere, with a shift from the arrhythmic to the recovery of rhythmicity, from a pattern of continuous, monotonous self-stimulation to intermittent and multiple sensorimotor stimulation, from a body focus to an object focus. This recovery of rhythmicity represents an entering again into the symbolic realm of the patient, a resymbolization through the designated steps of the symbolizing process. And it is a nonverbal working through.

This disembedding is thus an escape from the desymbolizing countertransference, and when it fails to occur, therapeutic stagnation ensues. It is marked by the described motor actions, and has directionality, movement in the direction of psychoanalytic agency. It is not just a pulling away from the desymbolized countertransference, but a positive movement toward the regaining of analytic work capacity. The listening space has been restored and the therapist is enabled once more to make appropriate, attuned, and effective interpretations. This is what leads to the concluding sentence in the manuscript: "It is in the dynamics of the listening process before interpretation that we can delineate the therapeutic action of psychoanalysis" (p. 18).

How does all of this, as finally encapsulated in the sentence just quoted, relate to the realm of psychotherapy research and to my conception of Bert Freedman as all along a cryptotherapeutic process researcher? The relationship is essentially in Bert's longtime struggle to conceptualize the nature of the therapeutic action of psychoanalytic therapies, to conceptualize the mechanisms of change, and to establish empirical markers of the change process that become amenable to systematic and replicable inquiry, observable as well by investigators independent of the original proponent. Bert's vital linkage of "the view from within," namely the therapist's retrospective recounting of the shifting mental states experienced within the therapy session, to "the view from without," the observed concomitant kinesic behaviors of the therapist as captured in the videotaped record of the same session, clearly adds a novel and important new dimension to the universe of therapy process research, a dimension that is almost entirely absent in the established array of functioning, recognized psychotherapy process researchers.

Let me explain. Research into psychotherapeutic processes has had a much shorter history than into therapy outcomes, because, unlike outcome research, it has depended on the development of appropriate technology, recorded therapy sessions (and subsequently the capacity for large-scale computer search and data retrieval), and the willingness of the psychoanalytic clinical community to accept the intrusion of recording devices within the consulting room. I have described elsewhere (Wallerstein 2001) the several-generation development of therapy research, starting as far back as 1917, within the first decade of the introduction of psychoanalysis in America, when

Isidor Coriat, in Boston, reported on the therapeutic results achieved in 93 cases, of whom 73 percent were declared either recovered or much improved, with these rates nearly equal across all his diagnostic categories. This was followed in the 1930s by several comparable but larger-scale reports from the collective experiences of the psychoanalytic treatment centers of some of the pioneering psychoanalytic training institutes; by Otto Fenichel from the Berlin Institute in 1930, by Ernest Jones from the London Psychoanalytic Clinic in 1936, and by Franz Alexander from the Chicago Psychoanalytic Clinic in 1937. In all these early statistical accountings, which I have called the "first generation studies," the judgments of improvement were made (only) by the treating clinician, according to (usually) unspecified criteria, and without individual clinical detail or supporting evidence. But they were the beginnings of formal outcome research in psychoanalysis, and in my paper (Wallerstein 2001) I trace what I then demarcate into four successive generations of psychotherapy research, each a development beyond the shortcomings and research pitfalls of the prior generation, and with methods and designs of increasing complexity and research sophistication.

Because of its inherently greater conceptual and methodological complexity, counterpart research into the nature of the *processes* by which change comes about, or is brought about, in psychoanalytic therapies has been more recent in origin, and has not yet undergone generational transformations. Also, since it necessarily (or at least usually) entails more detailed focus on moment-to-moment therapeutic interactions, process research, as already stated, has only been rendered feasible on a significant scale by the more recent—meaning basically since the 1970s—development and deployment of suitable technology, namely the possibilities for audio and then video recording, as well as of computerization and high-speed computer word or situation searches.

Audiorecording was actually introduced into psychoanalytic research as early as 1933, when Earl Zinn was known to have made dictaphone recordings of psychoanalytic sessions with a patient at Worcester State Hospital (Carmichael 1956). Since then, recordings have been advocated and used by a gradually widening array of analytic investigators. In a major overview in 1971 of "Issues in Research in the Psychoanalytic Process," a colleague and I (Wallerstein and Sampson 1971) reviewed the literature to that date on the use of audio recording in therapy sessions and discussed the various arguments for and against such use, as well as the arguments comparing the different advantages or disadvantages of recorded sessions vis-à-vis therapists' process notes of those sessions. I won't restate here any of those arguments except to say that it is only within the past two, or perhaps three, decades that an adequate consensus has emerged that analytic therapy *can* go on under these observed circumstances—that is, that a properly therapeutic process can nonetheless evolve, contra Freud's long accepted dictum that a therapeutic process can brook no third party involvement, and, concomitantly, that computer technology has advanced to where the enormous database generated can be feasibly managed.

This has led to the recent, almost explosive proliferation of psychoanalytic therapy process research, mainly in the United States and Germany, but also in Great Britain and elsewhere. The elaboration of modern-day empirical psychoanalytic process studies is exemplified by the contents of a 1988 book, *Psychoanalytic Process Research Strategies*, edited by Hartvig Dahl, Horst Kächele, and Helmut Thomä, a close American-German collaboration, the proceedings, actually, of a major workshop of American and German researchers on "Empirical Research in Psychoanalysis," held in Ulm, Germany, just prior to the 1985 International Psycho-Analytical Association Congress in Hamburg.

Among the therapy process research strategies presented at Ulm, in relation to an anonymous specimen hour, were such major additions to the process research armamentarium as (1) Wilma Bucci's Dual Code Model scoring Referential Activity (RA),[1] the referential connections between the verbal (linguistic) and nonverbal (emotional) systems; (2) Hartvig Dahl's Fundamental Repetitive and Maladaptive Emotion Structures (FRAMES); (3) Merton Gill and Irwin Hoffman's

1. A coding scheme developed originally with the collaboration of Bert Freedman (see Bucci and Freedman 1978).

Patient's Experience of the Relationship with the Therapist (PERT); (4) Lester Luborsky's Core Conflictual Relationship Themes (CCRT); and (5) several others, less widely used. What these various process research strategies have in common is what Bert Freedman has dubbed "the view from without," that is, the laying out of the verbatim verbal record of the properly transcribed—in accord with a set of rules worked out by Erhard Mergenthaler of Ulm, Germany, and Charles Stinson of San Francisco—audiorecorded hour, so as to discern and identify successive sequences of the verbatim material that reveal the patterns of mental and emotional dysfunction, patterns that would be expected to be modified into less maladaptive directions in the course of a successful therapeutic process.

The focus by Bert Freedman and his different collaborators on the kinesics and semantics of the therapist's listening process as markers of psychic states and of changes of psychic states, and therefore as an avenue of access to a theory of therapeutic action, is, on the one hand, on all fours with each of the other models just referred to, with its own equally appropriate place then, as a potential methodological and conceptual contributor to an ultimately empirically elaborated and validated full-bodied theory of therapeutic change, of the process of change. But Bert's perspective is more than each of the others in two salient respects. First, he combines his "view from without," the patterns of kinesic rhythmicity and arrhythmicity, with equal attention to the "view from within," the therapist's retrospective reconstruction of his or her psychic experience of the session, and to the pattern of relationship between the two views, from without and from within. Second, Bert's view from without encompasses a dimension not available to the others who work essentially from audiorecorded and transcribed sessions. Bert adds the dimension of kinesic patterns made accessible through videotaping of therapy sessions, and adds thus to the overall comprehensiveness of methods advanced to study therapeutic processes. It is in this sense that I see Bert Freedman as a major figure, as empiricist and conceptualizer, in psychotherapy process research.

To turn now to Bert Freedman as psychotherapy outcome researcher. Outcome research into psychiatric illness has come a long way since Bert was first involved in this area, as a collaborator, from the perspective of changes in mental states and mental functioning attendant upon psychoactive drug treatment of the array of more severe mental and emotional disorders. The field of psychoanalytic therapy research has been steadily growing in the number of workers (albeit still all too small a cadre), and in geographic spread into a worldwide fraternity (with its main centers still in North America and northern and western Europe). This research activity has been given enhanced impetus and increased urgency by the growing demand from governmental and private insurance carriers across the industrialized world for demonstrated efficacy and cost effectiveness of our psychological therapies, in order to warrant appropriate claim upon the reimbursement purse. Indeed, the accelerating internal growth dynamic of psychotherapy research, and the surge of external socioeconomic pressures for justification of efficacy, have combined to bring us to a present state in which, in the recently published *Open Door Review of Outcome Studies in Psychoanalysis* (1999), Peter Fonagy and his collaborators could categorize and discuss some 50 established and currently ongoing psychotherapy research projects around the world, and only 19 of them in the United States.

It was within this context of current, rapidly burgeoning psychoanalytic outcome studies, and with the impetus provided by the creation of the IPTAR Clinical Center (ICC), that Bert Freedman has rejuvenated the IPTAR Research Committee and, with the support of a large number of colleagues, has undertaken a comprehensive research program with the ICC patients for the evaluation of the process and outcome of long-term psychoanalytic therapies. A first report of that methodically created research program has recently been published (Freedman et al. 1999). This marks Bert's return as an explicit outcome researcher, but now in the realm of purely psychological (psychoanalytic) treatment methods.

The aims of this current program have been several: (1) to assess the role of treatment frequency (one, two, or three times per week) in treatment effectiveness; (2) to assess the role of treatment duration (from less than six months to more than two years) in treatment effectiveness; (3) to assess the role of an established positive therapeutic relationship in treatment effectiveness; (4) to discern differential treatment effectiveness with varying diagnostic clusters; and (5) to explore the usefulness of the patients' reports of their therapies, based on a modified version of the *Consumer Reports* study (Seligman, 1995, 1996) as the essential database for this outcome research enterprise. To pursue these aims, the modified *Consumer Reports* questionnaire was sent to all 240 patients (all, of course, outpatients), past and present, who had been or were still in treatment at the ICC; 99 completed questionnaires were returned (41 percent). Given that the therapists for these patients were not involved in the data collection and did nothing to encourage compliance with the questionnaire request, this was deemed a satisfactory enough rate of return. Demographically, the research sample seemed quite congruent with the entire ICC population, except diagnostically. The research sample was psychologically better integrated, with depressive reaction being the dominant diagnostic category, as compared with schizophrenic reactions and bipolar disorders being the more common in the overall clinic population, that is, a more normal-neurotic vis-à-vis a more borderline population.

Out of the questionnaire data, the research investigators constructed a number of measures, all described in detail: an Effectiveness Questionnaire (EQ), an Effectiveness Score (ES), a specific improvement score (a measure of Focal Symptomatic Gains), a satisfaction with one's therapist score, and a global improvement score (the latter three being transformed into 100-point scales), a Positive Relationship Index (PRI), and an Index of Adaptive Life Gains.

Using appropriate statistical techniques, predicted findings emerged along every line of research inquiry: an increased Effectiveness Score clearly correlated with incrementally increasing treatment duration from one month to over 32 months; the same increased effectiveness also correlated with increased treatment frequency when once weekly was compared with both twice and three times weekly, though there was not a significant difference in effectiveness between two and three sessions weekly. And beyond that, using linear multiple regression, a model was constructed using frequency and duration together as predictors of effectiveness. The combined predictive power of frequency and duration turned out to be quite significant, and interestingly, by partialing out the linear relation between duration and frequency, these variables turned out to account for separate portions of the variance in effectiveness. The authors therefore could conclude "that in the sample as a whole, frequency and duration contribute to outcome in qualitatively different ways" (Freedman et al. 1999, p. 758).

The authors also explored the quality of the treatment relationship, PRI (Positive Relationship Index) vis-à-vis NRI (Negative Relationship Index) as an independent source of variance, regardless of frequency or duration, therefore also as a determinant of treatment outcome, and again found a positive correlation between the PRI and the overall treatment effectiveness (which, of course, still leaves the unanswered question of whether the positive relationship operates as a vehicle of therapeutic change in its own right, or merely provides the frame within which veridical interpretations leading to appropriate insights are the central mutative factor, or of course, some interaction between the two, relationship and insight). In relation to the five major diagnostic clusters to which they assigned the research sample, the authors found that for four of the five clinical groupings, selective responses were indeed found to the two defined parameters of treatment conditions, that is, duration and frequency. For two of the four clusters (those representing more acute conditions), frequency of treatment was the more salient consideration, and for the other two (those representing more chronic conditions), treatment duration was more determinative. And last, not explicitly stated in the article but certainly implicit throughout, there was general satisfaction with their adaptation of the *Consumer Reports* questionnaire, that is, the patient's self-report via a detailed questionnaire concerning the treatment experience as an adequate enough database on which to construct reliable, and, it is hoped, valid, assessments of the effectiveness of the treatment (the treatment outcome) and of some of the determining variables of that outcome.

However, additionally, the authors were able to add another data source, audiorecorded interviews after the termination of the treatment, in order to secure narrative accounts of how the patients had experienced their treatment and its impact on the quality of their lives and on their current state of well-being. This they call the method of "recall validation," and, at the time of writing, this had taken place with eight patients. It was designed to give clinical validity to their concept of effectiveness, the idea that an alteration within the patient's quality of life experience, as assessed by the questionnaire response, had indeed taken place. Another objective, more exploratory, was to try to ascertain some of the mediating conditions accounting for the perceived treatment effects. The authors express the hope that this method of retrospective reconstruction of the therapeutic experience will provide a fruitful database for the identification of mediating mechanisms, which is, of course, music for the future, to be substantiated or not, as this research program progresses.

What does all this add up to within the context of the current wide panoply of psychoanalytic outcome research as portrayed in Fonagy and colleagues' (1999) *Open Door Review*? After their very brief overview of the prior historical development of psychoanalytic outcome research, Bert and his colleagues (Freedman et al. 1999) state: What is largely missing from these evaluations [the prior studies that they mentioned] is the study of the role of conditions of treatment exposure as an independent source of variance" (p. 744). This led them to focus on duration and session frequency as the first, most obvious dimensions to study in relation to analytic work and effectiveness. There have been very few psychoanalytic outcome studies that have focused on treatment duration as a major determinant of outcome. There have been two well-known studies focusing on frequency as a major variable affecting treatment process and outcome. These have both had to do with children (Fonagy and Target 1996, Heinicke and Ramsey-Klee 1986, Target and Fonagy 1994). Both these studies have focused on this as a comparative assessment of the efficacy of child psychotherapy vis-à-vis child analysis; in both these studies, as in the Freedman and colleagues (1999) study, patients were differentially assigned, not randomly, but rather in terms of presumptive differing clinical indications, and thus, of course, other determinants (other variables), beyond frequency, have been involved in the differing outcomes. In the Freedman and colleagues study, specific effort has been addressed toward partialing out the effects of variables other than frequency, and the proffered modality was in every case designated psychoanalytic psychotherapy (of differing frequency), but not psychoanalysis, with its other usual dimensions, such as recumbency on the couch, expectation of a free association process, and so on.

Given these considerations, the Freedman and colleagues study, with its specified parameters and a carefully constructed and sound method and design, does occupy a unique niche within the panoply of currently ongoing analytic therapy outcome studies, and has already borne substantial fruit, though still in its beginnings. What still awaits doing is the conceptual bringing together of this outcome study from the ICC, devoted to the question of *what* changes can be expected and achieved in psychoanalytic therapies, under what conditions of frequency, duration, and so on, and what I have called Bert Freedman's exploration of the process question: *how* those changes come about, through what mediating mechanisms, using, of course, the window of his own conceptions of the oscillating vicissitudes of the symbolizing and desymbolizing process.

Here the challenge is to bring about the conceptual congruence expressed in the principle enunciated by Strupp and colleagues in the first chapter of the book edited by Dahl, Kächele, and Thomä, "that the description and representation, theoretically *and* operationally, of a *patient's conflicts*, of the *patient's treatment*, and of the *assessment of the outcome*, must be congruent, which is to say, must be represented in comparable, if not identical, terms" (Dahl et al. 1988, p. ix). This fundamental integrative principle—proposed to subsume conceptually the entire array of process and outcome researches, however seemingly disparate their concepts and their instruments—is called the Principle of Problem-Treatment-Outcome Congruence, "PTO congruence" for short (Strupp et al. 1988, p. 7). The establishing of this congruence, the integrating of process studies and outcome studies within one conceptual framework, is what I have called the major direction that fourth generation psychotherapy research studies need take (Wallerstein 2001). I have just called this the challenge that the ever innovative and creative Bert Freedman, with his gathering of collaborators, is in as good a position as anyone I know to meet.

Which brings me to my conclusion on a personal note of great appreciation and admiration. I have known Bert a good many years now, as a psychoanalytic scholar and a psychoanalytic researcher, in a number of contexts, as a fellow participant in IPA Congresses, as a devoted member of the Collaborative Analytic Multi-Site Program (CAMP), a consortium of psychoanalytic process and outcome therapy researchers, meeting regularly under the auspices of the American Psychoanalytic Association, and as a friend with whom I have shared discourse in person and by phone and mail, on a considerable variety of clinical and research issues in our shared discipline. I have always been truly amazed that Bert, whose vision has been totally lost now for so many years, is able to participate in so many research meetings, where complicated and detailed data are presented, both verbally and projected upon a screen, and to participate, with a fine grasp of the overall structure of the presentation, combined with a keen memory for the presented detail, including the graphic detail he cannot see, and can then make such discerning comments and ask such probing questions, fully the equal of each of the other conference participants. And this is not to speak of a seemingly eidetic memory for a vast literature, clinical and research, that must have been laboriously read to him over a considerable time span. What prompts me to this personal note now is that it was not until I immersed myself, for the purposes of this article, in studying in more detail Bert's contributions in the realm of his conceptions of symbolization and desymbolization, with their reliance on the correlating of mental experiences with rhythmic and arrhythmic postural expressions discerned via videotape, that I have grasped the full enormity of Bert's achievements and of his triumph over adversity. To make so major a contribution in a realm so dependent on careful dissection of visual imagery can only make his many friends and admirers feel humble indeed. I feel honored to be one of those friends and admirers.

REFERENCES

Alexander, F. (1937). Five-Year Report of the Chicago Institute for Psychoanalysis: 1932–1937. Chicago, IL: Chicago Institute for Psychoanalysis.

Bucci, W. (1997). *Psychoanalysis and Cognitive Science: A Multiple Code Theory*. New York and London: Guilford.

Bucci, W., and Freedman, N. (1978). Language and hand: the dimension of referential competence. *Journal of Personality* 46:594–622.

Carmichael, H. T. (1956). Sound film recording of psychoanalytic therapy: a therapist's experience and reactions. In *Methods of Research in Psychotherapy*, ed. L. A. Gottschalk and A. H. Auerbach, pp. 50–59. New York: Appleton-Century-Crofts, 1966.

Coriat, I. (1917). Some statistical results of the psychoanalytical treatment of the psychoneuroses. *Psychoanalytic Review* 4:209–216.

Dahl, H., Kächele, H., and Thomä, H. (1988). *Psychoanalytic Process Research Strategies*. Berlin & New York: Springer Verlag.

Fenichel, O. (1930). Statistischer Bericht über die Therapeutische Tätigkeit 1920–1930. In *Zehn Jahre Berliner Psychoanalytische Institut*, pp. 13–19. Berlin: Internazionale Psychoanalytischer Verlag.

Fliess, R. (1942). The metapsychology of the analyst. *Psychoanalytic Quarterly* 11:211–227.

Fonagy, P., with Kächele, H., Krause, R., Jones, E., and Perron, R. (1999). *An Open Door Review of Outcome Studies in Psychoanalysis: Report Prepared by the Research Committee of the IPA at the Request of the President*. London: University College London.

Fonagy, P., and Target, M. (1996). Predictors of outcome in child psychoanalysis: a retrospective study of 763 cases at the Anna Freud Centre. *Journal of the American Psychoanalytic Association* 44:27–77.

Freedman, N., and Grand, S. (n.d.). *Before interpretation: on situating the listening process in psychoanalytic interaction*. Unpublished manuscript.

Freedman, N., Hoffenberg, J. D., Vorus, N., and Frosch, A. (1999). The effectiveness of psychoanalytic psychotherapy: the role of treatment duration, frequency of sessions, and the therapeutic relationship. *Journal of the American Psychoanalytic Association* 47:741–772.

Freedman, N., and Lavender, J. (1997). On receiving the patient's transference: the symbolizing and desymbolizing countertransference. *Journal of the American Psychoanalytic Association* 45:79–103.

Heinicke, C. M., and Ramsey-Klee, D. (1986). Outcome of child therapy as a function of frequency of sessions. *Journal of the American Academy of Child Psychiatry* 25:247–253.

Jacobs, T. (1991). *The Use of the Self: Countertransference and Communication in the Analytic Situation*. Madison, CT: International Universities Press.

Jones, E. (1936). Decannual Report of the London Clinic of Psychoanalysis, 1926–1937. London: London Clinic of Psychoanalysis.

Reich, A. (1966). Empathy and countertransference. In *Psycho-Analytic Contributions*, pp. 344–360. New York: International Universities Press.

Rogers, C. R. (1951). *Client-Centered Therapy*. Boston and New York: Houghton-Mifflin.

Rogers, C., and Dymond, R. F. (1954). *Psychotherapy and Personality Change*. Chicago: University of Chicago Press.

Seligman, M. E. P. (1995). The effectiveness of psychotherapy: the *Consumer Reports* study. *American Psychologist* 50:965–974.

——— (1996). A creditable beginning. *American Psychologist* 51:1086–1087.

Strupp, H. H., Schacht, T. E., and Henry, W. P. (1988). Problem-treatment-outcome congruence: a principle whose time has come. In *Psychoanalytic Process Research Strategies*, ed. H. Dahl, H. Kächele, and H. Thomä, pp. 1–14. Berlin and New York: Springer Verlag.

Target, M., and Fonagy, P. (1994). The efficacy of psychoanalysis for children: prediction of outcome in a developmental context. *Journal of the American Academy of Child Psychiatry* 33:1134–1144.

Wallerstein, R. S. (1986). *Forty-Two Lives in Treatment: A Study of Psychoanalysis and Psychotherapy*. New York: Guilford.

——— (2001). The generations of psychotherapy research: an overview. *Psychoanalytic Psychology* 18:243–267.

Wallerstein, R. S., Robbins, L. L., Sargent, H. D., and Luborsky, L. (1956). The psychotherapy research project of The Menninger Foundation. *Bulletin of the Menninger Clinic* 20:221–278.

Wallerstein, R. S., and Sampson, H. (1971). Issues in research in the psychoanalytic process. *International Journal of Psycho-Analysis* 52:11–50.

2

From Subsymbolic to Symbolic—and Back: Therapeutic Impact of the Referential Process

WILMA BUCCI

This paper continues the dialogue between Norbert Freedman and myself that began when I worked with him at Downstate Medical Center from 1974 to 1983. It was my good fortune to meet with his inspiring and generative influence and his love of ideas at the start of my career. Our interactions have continued, with disjunctions and transformations, since that time. The point of reference of my paper is Freedman's formulation of the emergence of the symbolic function, and the role of dialectic conflict in this process, as illustrated in the case of Mr T. (Freedman 1985). As I wrote this paper, I realized that it was taking its own dialectic form, with the processes outlined by Freedman as thesis, the theory of multiple coding and the referential process as antithesis, and a new psychological account of the therapeutic process as synthesis or transformation. This paper also gave me the opportunity to return to some of our earlier collaborative work and to examine its implications in this context.

In his 1985 paper, Norbert Freedman described a patient, Mr. T., who was suffering from ulcerative colitis and bronchial respiratory distress symptoms, and who had been through many medical consultations. His history was marked by experiences of terror and feeling abused, but these experiences were not readily represented in his verbal material.

Freedman describes three phases of the treatment of Mr. T. In the first phase, which Freedman terms "Thesis":

> . . . there was a restless running. He related how he missed the subway, tried to beat the traffic, couldn't stand waiting in line for tickets. He arrived at the session in a perspired, harassed condition. He dropped onto the chair and described his hectic trip. Then there was a long silence—he had nothing to say. (It was a blank silence, not one of contemplating new associations.) He then began to depict his various somatic problems—the cramps, the diarrhea, as well as mucous etc. [p. 321]

In Freedman's account, Mr. T.'s endless event recording indicates his difficulty in focusing on subjective experiences and representing affect in language. While this is a discharge state, Freedman says, it is an organization as well, that

> . . . signifies either via regression or fixation, a mental structure at the prerepresentational level of the body ego. For Mr. T., a very sophisticated man, it points to pockets of psychic functioning in which action or motor discharge is the primary mode of coping with stress, and where affect is concretized and registered in physiological rather than subjective terms. [p. 321]

In the second phase, the "Antithesis":

> . . . there was not only increased description of his somatic preoccupations and concern with the details in the immediate environment (items in my office), but the appearance of unintegrated sensations and perceptions. Notably he was bothered by the brightness of my lights. He also complained of itching, and was bothered by the hum of the air conditioner. (p. 322)

As Freedman explains this phase, "the therapist's presence is the agent of the antithesis" (p. 322). The environment of the treatment is necessarily regressive, evoking a "*disjunctive* experience," which he defines as referring to "conflict in primitive mental organizations." Freedman says:

> Even in a holding environment, dynamic conflict may be said to exist in a form of disjunctive experience. On the one hand, the patient has the primary libidinal wish for bodily care. On the other hand, the symbolic demand brings on diffuse, unassimilated, unencoded affective visceral reactions. It is the terror from below. At this point, what emerges is the dread of falling forever, a loss of bodily integrity, and unverbalized rage. [p. 322]

In the third phase, which Freedman terms "Synthesis," the patient began to tell stories about his father who was experienced as a torturer, and his boss who was seen as a murderous fascist, and also associated these experiences with the analyst:

> Once he came in in terror and rage saying, "This is a death camp. This analysis is torture. It is your office with the bright lights shining at me and your accent that gives me the shudders. How can you coming from Germany, help me?" [p. 323]

As the imagery emerged, the somatic disturbances disappeared, and this remission, as far as Freedman knows, was sustained. The patient had reached the stage of the symbolic process that Freedman has called the "symbolic equation."

> The experiences of the death camp and my accent had the property of a *symbolic equation*. Symbolic equations are phantom-like images which have the quality of immediacy and lack the property of psychological distance. . . . There is not an "as if" quality. It was not as if the room were like a concentration camp, but the room was a concentration camp. In that sense, it had the substitutive quality of symbolism (Jones 1938), but had lacked the properties of true symbol formation. [p. 323]

This symbolic equation is a transformation that involves both "consolidation of an image" and also communication of the image "affectively as well as verbally" (p. 324).

> The change observed fulfills the definition of a restructuralization in psychoanalytic terms. Not only do we observe a psychic organization at a higher level of structure, but we also find that the affects and drives are progressively carried by more complex vehicles of representation. One might think of this as a progressive process of assimilation of part processes so that the drives first carried by the body ego become assimilated into sensations and perceptions and then into images. [p. 323]

The transformation, as outlined by Freedman, requires an initial state of disequilibrium that unleashes dynamic forces and also requires an involvement of the analyst in "the turmoil of the patient's inner world," so that a symbolic equation "is not only a cognitive structure, but an object relations structure as well." The goal of the therapeutic work, in Freedman's terms, is "a restructuring of the patient's libidinal organization vis-à-vis his object world. From the experience of being regulated, he now seeks to regulate. What has been established is an intentionality to communicate" (p. 324).

Freedman then addresses the question of how this restructuring can be achieved in the therapeutic session. This occurs primarily through the analyst's "selective attunement to the dissociative perceptual and sensory experiences with the patient. In this way, the dissociated experiences can be seen within the patient's biography" (p. 324).

> Mr. T.'s sensitivity to the lights in my office (which, in fact, are not excessively bright) marked an important turning point in the treatment. It was precisely at the point of his complaining about the brightness that the sequence was initiated in which he experienced me as a concentration camp guard. He first linked the lights to a photographic session he had undergone as a 5-year-old, then to a cross-examination in South America, and finally, to the Nazi episode involving his father. It is this sequence that prompted me to say, "These are the bright lights of your past." [p. 325]

As Freedman describes it, the transformation from discharge to a symbolic equation, with its end point of communicative intent, is only a partial achievement in the symbolizing process. The next transition is "from symbolic equation to the formation of symbols" in which the end point is the "recontextualization of antagonistic images and with it, the attainment of shared reality." The patient needs to move from the stage of *symbolic equation*, in which the analyst *is* the object, equated, in this instance, with the concentration camp guard, to what he calls the *formation of symbols* in which the analyst may *represent* the object and in which there is a capacity for shared reality.

In accounting for symbolic transformation, Freedman applies Winnicott's notion of transitionality and also introduces Rapaport's (1967) hypothesis that "structure depends on the inhibition of wish, drive, or desire." He also goes beyond Rapaport in several ways, including identifying the analyst's activity and the analyst's presence as both providing the necessary inhibitory structure to contain the drives, and facilitating the subsequent development of new symbolic forms. "Like the mother who is the shaper of the drives, so is the analyst a shaper of the drives via language, always creating a differential or tension state leading to higher organization" (p. 336).

THE MULTIPLE CODE THEORY AND THE REFERENTIAL PROCESS

Freedman has outlined three basic phases in the process of symbolizing, which he terms thesis, antithesis, and synthesis, as illustrated above. He sees the patient as moving from an initial state of action or motor discharge to progressively higher levels of mental organization characterized by symbolic forms. The multiple code theory (Bucci 1997), developed in the context of current work in cognitive science, emotion theory, and neuroscience, brings a different perspective to the understanding of the symbolizing function as this occurs in all aspects of mental and emotional life, and in the therapeutic process as well. The two perspectives converge in interesting ways and the areas of difference raise questions to be explored.

Components of the Multiple Code Theory

The multiple code theory is a general psychological theory of the interaction among cognitive, linguistic, emotional, and bodily systems. The theory accounts for the integration of systems in adaptive functioning, their dissociation in pathology, and repair of dissociation in the treatment process.

Three basic modes in which humans represent and process information, including emotional information, may be distinguished; these are the *nonverbal subsymbolic*, *nonverbal symbolic*, and *verbal symbolic* modes. The three systems are connected by the *referential process*, which links all types of nonverbal representations to one another and to words. *Emotion schemas*—the psychic structures with which we are centrally concerned—are made up of components of all three systems. Change in the emotion schemas is what we mean by structural change. Change occurs through the bidirectional effects of the referential process in the context of the therapeutic relationship. I'll explain each of these concepts of the multiple code theory briefly here and then go on to show their application in the therapeutic process.

The Subsymbolic System

Subsymbolic processing is systematic processing that occurs in motoric, visceral, sensory form, as sounds, smells, feelings of many different sorts. In cognitive science, such processing is characterized as formally "analogic," processed as very fine variations on continuous dimensions, rather than generated from discrete elements. Such processing, modeled in cognitive science by what we call connectionist or PDP systems (McClelland et al. 1989), is hard to describe technically, but is most familiar to us in our daily lives. Subsymbolic "computations" underlie hundreds of common actions, from recognizing a familiar voice to entering a lane of traffic, and account as well for complex skills in athletics and for creative work in mathematics, sciences, and the arts. Subsymbolic processing also accounts for knowing one's own bodily states and responding to the facial and bodily expressions of others, without being able to measure them in discrete units or categorize them in symbolic form. We know this as intuition, the wisdom of the body, and in other related ways. The patient and analyst communicate profoundly in this mode. Reik's (1948) concept of "listening with the third ear" draws heavily on subsymbolic communication, as I have discussed in detail elsewhere (Bucci 2001).

In operating without explicit intention or direction, subsymbolic processes and representations may not be recognized and acknowledged, and may be experienced as in a sense "outside of oneself," outside of the domain of the self over which one has intentional control. In these terms, subsymbolic processing may be seen as a new and more precise formulation accounting for much of what has been characterized psychoanalytically as the unconscious mode, and also relates in part to the psychoanalytic concept of primary process thought, but with important differences as well. Subsymbolic processing is systematic information processing that is broadly applicable in many adaptive contexts, with particular organizational principles of its own, that may achieve high levels of complexity and that may occur in the conscious as well as unconscious mode. It is not driven by wish fulfillment any more than is any other form of thought, and is not inherently disorganized, infantile, or regressed.[1]

Symbolic Processing

Symbols as defined here in cognitive-linguistic terms have several formal properties that contrast with the subsymbolic mode. The major distinguishing features are as follows: (1) Symbols are discrete entities rather than continuous and analogic representations, that is, they chunk the representational field into finite units rather than representing infinite, continuous variation. (2) Symbols function as referring to other entities outside of themselves rather than as "things in

---

1. Terming this format "*sub*symbolic" is not intended to imply a lower or less complex level of organization, but one that underlies and provides a basis for the symbolic mode, in an information processing sense. The subsymbolic information is in some ways more extensive and complex than the symbolic format and can only be captured partially in the verbal mode, as will be discussed in the presentation of the referential process below.

themselves." (3) Symbols are generative, that is, they may be combined to generate infinite varieties of new forms. Such formal features are quite distinct from the psychoanalytic notion of symbols in the dynamic sense. Symbols may be images or words.

Nonverbal symbols, which we also know as *imagery,* exist in all sensory modalities. We are quite familiar with images in the visual system, but also have auditory images, as when a melody or a voice is represented in the mind. While most people may attend primarily to visual and auditory images, others have highly developed imagery of touch or taste or smell. Helen Keller (1908) vividly and evocatively described such images and their central importance in her mental and emotional life.

> A tangible object passes complete into my brain with the warmth of life upon it, and occupies the same place that it does in space; for without egotism, the mind is as large as the universe. When I think of hills, I think of the upward strength I tread upon. When water is the object of my thought, I feel the cool shock of the plunge and the quick yielding of the waves that crisp and curl and ripple about my body. The pleasing changes of rough and smooth, pliant and rigid, curved and straight in the back and branches of a tree give the truth to my hand. . . . The bulge of a watermelon and the puffed-up rotundities of squashes that sprout, bud and ripen in that strange garden planted somewhere behind my finger-tips are the ludicrous in my tactual memory and imagination. [pp. 10–11]

Images have all the properties of symbolic representation. A picture of a face is made up of discrete elements—eyes, nose, mouth—which may be recombined in various ways to create new forms, and the picture is not the thing in itself, as Magritte makes us know.[2] This

2. We may add here, since nothing in the field of semiotics is very simple, that nonverbal images may vary in a wide range of ways as to the degree to which these symbolic features are honored, as Magritte also shows us, and as the case of Mr. T. illustrates. All images in all modalities require some degree of firing of the same neurological apparatus used in perception. Thus the visual or auditory system is activated when imagery is experienced in one of those modalities; imagery in each sensory modality depends on specific physiological arousal of this nature.

applies in all sensory modalities, not vision only. "My fingers cannot, of course, get the impression of a large whole at a glance; but I feel the parts and my mind puts them together" (Keller 1908, p. 12).

The verbal mode: Language is the uniquely human symbolic system. Like all symbols, words are discrete entities that refer to other entities, including objects, images, and ideas, and that also refer to other words, in the complex networks of semantic memory. Language is systematically generative at multiple levels. Phonemes are combined to form morphemes; morphemes form words; words are combined to form sentences, following the generative principles of semantics and syntax. Thus from the limited set of phonemes, the infinite varieties of verbal expression are constructed.

Words also have the specific and crucial property, distinguishing them from nonverbal symbols, of being generally arbitrary and abstract, bearing no depictive relationship to the entities to which they refer, with few exceptions, as in onomatopoeia. This frees language from the concrete experiential mode but also limits its capacity to represent such experience. Language is the major medium of logical processing, with its capacity for differentiation and generalization, inclusion and exclusion. It is one, not the only one, but a major means by which the individual communicates inner experience to others, and by which the knowledge of the culture is transmitted to the individual. We use words to direct and regulate ourselves; it is the medium over which we have the most apparent control; we also use language to obfuscate and lie—to others and to oneself.

The Referential Process

The three systems, with different contents and different organizing principles, are connected by the referential links. The referential process is the major integrative process of the multiple code system; it enables organization of the nonverbal system, connection of subsymbolic experience to symbolic imagery, and connection of imagery to words, and underlies as well the reverse direction of connecting words to the nonverbal, including bodily modes. Through the referential process, one expresses emotional experience to others, understands and responds to the words of others, and uses language in self-regulation and direction. Images, with their transitional properties (modality-specific like subsymbolic processing, discrete and generative with properties of reference, like words), are pivots of the referential process, organizing the nonverbal system and facilitating connections to language.

The referential process operates in creative scientific work and in the arts, as well as in fantasies and dreams, and is a central aspect of the psychoanalytic process, as we shall see. It is often the case, however, that this interconnection of systems is only partial, leaving some concrete aspects of experience unexpressed and inaccessible to language, and some abstract verbal concepts without reference to the world of concrete experiences. This is the challenge for the use of language in the "talking cure."

Psychic Structures as Emotion Schemas

Our knowledge of the world in all its varied types—from the tastes of different wines, athletic skills, the skills of driving a car or riding a bicycle, and the abstract structures of philosophy and mathematics, to the specific memories of the episodes of one's life—are organized in what we term *memory schemas*. Schemas are the organizers of our representational worlds; they determine how we see each new event, and are in turn themselves altered with each activation. Emotion schemas are specific types of memory schemas built up out of repeated interactions with mother-other from the beginning of life. They incorporate one's knowledge of one's interpersonal world; they determine how one perceives other people, what one desires, expects, and believes about others, throughout life. Emotion schemas include components of all processing systems—nonverbal subsymbolic, symbolic, and verbal symbolic. They have the same properties as other memory schemas but are more strongly dominated by sensory and bodily representations and processes. The subsymbolic sensory, somatic, and motoric representations constitute the *affective core* of the emotion schema, the basis on which the organization of the schema is initially built. Thus, a schema of anger will consist of the characteristic clusters of somatic experience and representations of motoric actions or sets to act associated with that emotion, linked to the objects who figured in the anger schema (the persons toward whom the anger is directed) and the specific events and circumstances in which the schema was repeatedly evoked.

The objects and settings of time and place constitute the specific contexts and contents of the emotion schemas, which continue to be elaborated throughout life. The affective core is the constant that identifies or categorizes sets of emotion schemas across varying contexts and contents. Thus we may feel the same sort of feeling, the same emotion, with different people in different places and times. Schemas can be highly complex and interrelated with one another. Although shared emotion labels such as anger or joy or fear may be used, this clearly oversimplifies the nature of the schema. That is why it is not very useful if a patient comes in and says "I am angry." To communicate the emotion schemas requires communication of the specific content and structure of the schema in each individual's life.

The concept of the emotion schema corresponds generally to many familiar concepts from related theoretical domains such as Stern's (1985) notion of Representations of Interactions that have been Generalized (RIGs), Bowlby's (1969) concept of working models, Luborsky's concept of the Core Conflictual Relationship Theme (CCRT) (Luborsky and Crits-Cristoph 1990), and Dahl's (1988) measure of Fundamental Repetitive and Maladaptive Emotion Structures (FRAMES). The structure of the schema provides the conceptual basis for the process of transference, as we will discuss.

Emotion Schemas in Pathology

In normal development, emotion schemas, like all memory schemas, are continually being reconstructed and revised by new experience.

In pathology, this continuous reconstruction is blocked. If the arousal of a schema is experienced as painful, conflictual, or threatening, the individual will attempt to avoid and escape it, in thought or in reality. One generally does not have the power to control the subsymbolic activation of the affective core; one cannot directly control one's heart beat or blood pressure or skin response. Instead one turns attention away from the symbolic contents—the objects and contexts—of the schema. In effect, one says to oneself, "Don't go there," and this applies to internal representations as well as to external contexts.

While the impact of painful emotion may seem to be reduced by such turning away, the avoidance is spurious and the price is high. The sensory, somatic, and motoric tendencies continue to operate, but now without connection to symbols; thus without means of identification, self-regulation, or self-direction. The individual who is experiencing these dissociated sensory and bodily processes will generally attempt to contain or control them in some way, to provide meaning for them, to know "why I feel this way," but does this while avoiding the knowledge that would actually enable understanding. The attempt to establish substitute meaning is likely to be destructive in itself, appearing in such forms as somatization, displacement, or acting out. The nature of the pathology is determined by both the avoidant dissociation and the particular forms of substitute symbolizing that are imposed.

Treatment as Repair of Dissociation

The goals of psychodynamic treatment are repair of dissociation and change in the pathological emotion schemas. Change in the emotion schemas, including the connection or reconnection of dissociated subsymbolic experience to symbols, is what we mean by structural change. Ultimately, this involves changing the original expectations and beliefs about other people, once fulfilled and validated, now invalid in current life, that led to the pain and threat and conflict and caused the dissociation. But the nature of the pathology itself—the inherently threatening nature of the affective core, the dissociation from specific symbolic contents of the schema, and the establishment of spurious substitute meanings—restricts the taking in of new information. This underlies the "vicious circle" of which Strachey (1934) has written.

The process of repair requires maintaining the activation and regulation of the threatening dissociated affect while at the same time transforming its meaning. The patient comes to experience the painful affect in a new context, and eventually can disconnect from a maladaptive set of expectations to find more valid ones. The process depends on the patient's building or rebuilding connections between one's self and the other in the treatment, and at the same time building connections within one's own emotion schemas. The construction of connections within one's own schemas and the connection to the other occur interactively in the therapeutic process.

The Nature of Therapeutic Change: The Referential Process

The model of the therapeutic process that I propose is based on the concept of the referential process.[3] The problem for treatment is that the subsymbolic bodily information that makes up the affective core of the emotions cannot be represented directly in the discrete and arbitrary symbols of the verbal code. Yet the assumption of the "talking cure" is that change in the emotion schemas may be brought about through verbal interchange. The referential process is the means by which the affective core of the emotion schema, with its bodily components, may be represented to some degree in the verbal mode, and through which the words that are spoken in the treatment may contribute, ultimately, to change in somatic and sensory and motoric systems. The phases of the referential process occur repeatedly, within

3. Some aspects of this account have been described in detail elsewhere (Bucci 1997, 2001); some components, such as the concept of the protosymbolic phase, are introduced here.

a session and across a treatment. The operation of these phases may be illustrated in the case of Mr. T., as related to the phases identified by Freedman (1985).

Subsymbolic Phase

In the free association, the patient begins by expressing sensory and somatic components of a dissociated schema whose meaning he does not know. The restless running, the perspired, harassed condition, the blank silences that Freedman describes in the first period of the treatment of Mr. T. may be seen as expressions of this subsymbolic phase. As Freedman's clinical formulation suggests, the schema incorporates an intense activation of terror and rage, directed toward persons on whom the patient was dependent for bodily care. The schema is activated to some degree in relation to the analyst, and the patient seeks to avoid it here, as in its initial activation. The mode of avoidance may be characterized as dissociation rather than repression. Mr. T. is experiencing the bodily components of the emotion schema. They are not out of awareness, but are dissociated from the objects, the images of people, that provide the emotional meaning for the activated state.

Protosymbolic Phase: Transition to the Symbolic Mode

As patients begin to talk about their somatic and sensory experiences rather than to express them bodily, the transition to the symbolic mode begins. In Mr. T.'s case, his verbal depiction of his somatic problems would be the beginning of the movement toward symbolizing. He later expands this, in what Freedman terms the unfolding of the antithesis, with increased descriptions of his somatic preoccupations and details in the environment, including itching, bright lights, and the hum of the air conditioner. Here we see activation of additional components of the same emotion schema, but still dissociated from one another. Mr. T. is conscious of his itching and of the brightness of the lights and other sensations, but does not relate them to one another. They are indeed components of the same emotion schema, as initially formed, but the schema is dissociated.

In a formal sense, such representations of present feelings and events, which I term here *protosymbols,* have some but not all the features of the symbolic mode. They are like symbols in that they are discrete entities that chunk the analogic representational field into finite units; they have properties of generativity, capable of being combined with other contents in a variety of experiences; they also have the symbolic property of representing an entity outside of themselves, an emotion schema. On the other hand, they are in another sense "things in themselves," motoric or sensory components of the *presently activated* schema rather than representations of it, and are unlike symbols in this respect.

I suggest that the motoric expressions discussed by Freedman (1985) as expressions of meaning rather than as discharge may be seen as examples of such protosymbolic forms. Kanzer (1966) emphasizes "a motor sphere of transference" in which action has an integrative function. Balint (1968) describes a patient whose performance of a somersault in the session was an important step in reconciling the discrepancy between her infantile and mature views of herself. A patient described by Steingart (1983) became able to symbolize her fears of the associative process after she carried out a wish to sit on the analyst's desk. In instances such as these, as Freedman notes, motor activity functions not as discharge, but as an external symbol carrying meaning that may be shared. Yet the action is in the present, a "thing in itself."

Symbolic Narrative Phase

If the first phases are successfully negotiated, if the referential process is operating effectively, the arousal of an emotion schema will activate symbolic images that represent specific objects or contexts of the schema, going beyond the affective core. These may be displaced objects, but are nevertheless within the symbolic mode. The symbolizing in the referential process occurs in two stages: retrieval of symbolic imagery and its verbalization. The patient thinks of a fantasy, an episode, a memory, a dream, and tells it in narrative form. The narratives the patient tells in free association, which may appear to him to be trivial and irrelevant, and whose meaning he does not know, may now be seen as metaphors representing the emotion schemas; they are instantiations of the prototypic stories of one's life. The patient is engaged in the story and is communicating it in a way he could not have done in the first phase, but is unlikely to recognize its meaning as yet. Here we see the power of free association in the context of the relationship; the patient is able to communicate a threatening schema in a narrative whose meaning he does not recognize, while he could not verbalize the emotion directly. This relates in part to what Freedman referred to as the "symbolic equation." The symbolizing process enhances the patient's capacity for self-direction, but the patient has still suspended control to some extent in telling a story whose meaning he does not know or acknowledge. The story will include the analyst, sometimes explicitly, almost certainly implicitly.

For Mr. T., after about two years of treatment, themes of terror emerge. The patient moves on from his focus on sensory and somatic experience to a series of stories about his father as a torturer and his boss as a murderous fascist. He also experiences the analyst as a concentration camp guard. The bright lights figure regularly in these stories: a photographic session as a 5-year-old, a cross-examination, a Nazi episode involving his father. Mr. T. also speaks of his terror and rage at the bright lights in the analyst's office. The bright lights are an image linking past and present, as the analyst points out. The story and its enactments with the analyst have the power to reunite the subsymbolic somatic and sensory experience of the schema with its symbolic elements of context and content, thereby providing a potential basis for symbolic control, but this connecting occurs without the actual emotional meaning of the schema being known. Thus they constitute temporary repairs of the dissociation but generally without ownership or agency.

Reflection Phase

The schema that is represented in the story or enactment is the patient's vision of his current interpersonal world—a schema that is invalid and maladaptive. The stories and enactments whose meaning he does not recognize provide a potentially key to what this invalid vision may be. The analyst may see some of the structure of the emotion schema that the patient does not see. The opportunity for useful interpretation is here, to facilitate the patient's reflection on the meaning of the story that has been told or played out. The analyst will recognize that the patient is drawing him into his schema, as represented in the story or the enactment, and will use this opportunity as well. In the case of Mr. T., the analyst offers an interpretation that links the instantiations to one another and, by implication, to the current context, the analyst's presence.

In the reflection new meanings emerge. The reflection brings the logical powers of the verbal system to bear on the emotional contents. The patient identifies wishes, desires, expectations, beliefs; he reconstructs emotion categories in an interpersonal context that is new. The patient is active, able to view his emotion schema to some degree; he understands more, makes new distinctions. This phase adds the component of "mentalizing," in Fonagy's (1995) term, to the process of symbolizing that is the core of the referential or narrative phase. If this phase is effective, the words that are spoken will ultimately connect back to the somatic and sensory components of the affective core so that the person actually feels different, sees things differently. The danger of this phase is that the change will occur in the verbal or symbolic systems only, without impact on bodily systems.

SOME IMPLICATIONS OF THE MULTIPLE CODE ACCOUNT

The multiple code account of the therapeutic process has a number of significant and perhaps controversial implications that need to be elaborated in relation to the explanatory concepts of the metapsychology, and also in relation to Freedman's (1985) formulation. These include recognition of the endogenously organized and systematic nature of the multiple formats of representation; an emphasis on dissociation rather than repression as characterizing a maladaptive schema; and an emphasis on the activation of dissociated components of the emotion schema in the session, rather than the inhibition of desire or drive. I'll briefly examine each of these complex issues here, raising more questions than answers as I proceed.

Organization of Separate Formats

All components of the emotion schemas, subsymbolic and symbolic, carry organized information, but with different contents and in different formats. The subsymbolic information is not of a lesser or more primitive degree of organization, but of a different nature from the symbolic. Subsymbolic information is capable of complex degrees of organization, occurring in conscious modes, as in the art forms of music and dance. The difference lies in the structure of this information and the use that is made of it, not its level of complexity.

People are generally not well tuned into the channels that carry such analogic information and often fail to receive and register them. Perhaps this failure of attunement is intrinsic to the nature of the human information processing system; perhaps it is a product of the Western emphasis on language and other readily manipulable symbolic forms.

Freedman (1985) has emphasized the informational function of visual imagery, bodily experience, and movement, even in what he characterizes as the higher or more complex level of symbol formation, beyond the symbolic equation. In this light, he described an event in the case of the patient, Mrs. O. In a crisis of rage, Mrs. O. smashed the dishes in her sink. This was, in Freedman's terms, a concrete dramatic gesture that was "a thinly disguised aggressive act aimed at the analyst." She then calmed herself and, sitting with her son, produced a drawing that "depicted both her rage and affection. It was a compromise which synthesized the polarities. She was then able to drive off to face the unfamiliar with something familiar in her pocketbook. The drawing was a true symbol. It was a pictorial rather than a lexical symbol. It clearly had an independent meaning to her, to the boy, to me, and probably to the reader as well" (p. 328).

Thus, for Freedman, a drawing, a nonverbal symbol, may represent a transformation beyond the "as if" quality of the symbolic equation to true symbol formation with its capacity for shared reality. Motoric action, according to Freedman, may also represent a similar transformation to true symbol formation, as in the examples of Kanzer, Balint, and Steingart cited above. A movement or a sound may represent an internal state in a way that a word cannot, because it has the analogic structure of the state.

In this context, Freedman (1985) described some of our collaborative work, carried out about twenty years ago, on the structure of body movement, in relation to the flow of speech. In this work, we focused largely on the informational significance of movement, and its role in supporting verbal symbolization, rather than on the discharge function that is generally assumed. Freedman and Bucci (1981) identified a patterned sequence, which we termed a kinetic contrasting sequence, consisting of a large muscle movement, such as a foot kick, followed closely by a direct body-focused hand movement. This is a lateralized movement with one hand touching a specific body part, often the face, and often for a discrete and limited period—as in the characteristic rubbing of the cheek or chin associated with thought. The individual components of the sequence, particularly the body-touching movements, were concentrated in the pause, but occurred to some extent in speech periods as well. The patterned sequence, however, was always associated with a pause period, with no exceptions in this study. Through qualitative analysis of the contents of the speech, we showed a relationship of this motoric sequence to central planning operations in the encoding process, in particular the retrieval and inclusion of peripheral thoughts. As Gilani, Bucci, and Freedman (1985) have also shown, working silence may be differentiated from resistive silence through the presence of this sequence.

Freedman and Bucci (1981) discussed the patterned sequence as representing tension release through large muscle movements, followed by direct body-focused movements as the kinetic manifestation of information filtering. "Thus, the coordination of tension release and self-stimulation through the use of these movements provides the speaker with a means of regulating his own state of arousal and organizing his attentional field" (p. 238). Later, in analyzing the role of the particular bodily acts in contributing to transformation, Freedman (1985) discusses the transition from "discharge activity" to a "'narcissistic' form of body touching," to "a depictive form of gesture" (p. 335).

I would approach this motoric sequence today in terms of the referential process as representing an initial subsymbolic arousal, followed by protosymbolic forms, then eventually by imagery and verbal symbolic expression. I would also argue that the role of subsymbolic representation can be accounted for as providing emotional information without introducing the function of discharge, even in the first phase of large muscle movement. The notion of discharge introduces energic concepts that may or may not be applicable, but need to be verified in their own terms.

Dissociation vs. Repression

If it is the case that the several formats of representation all carry systematic information, needed for the overall adaptive functioning of the organism, then the fundamental goal of treatment may be characterized as the integration or reintegration of systems that have been dissociated, rather than as making the unconscious conscious, placing id where ego has been, or in any sense transforming more primitive representations to higher or more complex forms. In this sense, the multiple code model is, in effect, a return to a version of a structural model, but in a new form (Bucci, in press). All components of a dissociated schema may be accessible to awareness. Mr. T. was aware of his somatic symptoms and of the bright lights of the office, and aware of persons in relation to him, including the analyst, but lacked the thematic connection among these components. The fundamental point is this: What is lost in pathology and needs to be recovered in treatment is the synchrony of representations of self-states, including subsymbolic experience, in relation to the representation of the other within the emotion schema.

This formulation is similar to Freedman's emphasis on disjunctive experience as the basis of pathology, and the role of symbolizing as the linking of experiences from distinct spheres of the mind. I would add that while dynamic conflict may be the root of a dissociation, as Freedman argues (as in the rage or terror directed at the caregiver on whom one depends), the notion of dissociation is more general. It is not only that conflictual wishes directed toward the same object are dissociated from one another in the individual's representational system. The more general case is that dissociation occurs *within* each of these schemas; the somatic components of rage or terror or need for care may be dissociated from the objects that would provide the emotional meaning for them. I would also add that the emphasis on dissociation rather than repression applies for all forms of neurosis, not only for conditions of trauma and abuse.

Inhibition vs. Arousal

The painful expectations that drive the dissociation are primarily in bodily, motoric, or sensory form: how one expects to feel, how one acts or intends to act. It follows that the activation of the subsymbolic components of an emotion schema in the session itself is central to the therapeutic process. This is a different perspective from the metapsychological principle of Rapaport (1967), as explicated by Freedman (1985), that "structure depends on the inhibition of wish, drive, or desire." I would argue that the dependence on inhibition is a vestige of the energy model, in which change would proceed through the binding of drives via language, and is not applicable in the integrative model that has been presented here.

What I would also like to emphasize, in this context, is that whenever there is symbolic recreation of an emotion state, what is activated is not a representation of an emotion; it is the emotion itself. To say that an emotion is aroused means that the actual physiological components of the affective core are activated. In the session, the emotion may be activated in trace form in a memory of the past or a report of an event of the day, or in vivo toward the analyst. In whatever form, to greater or lesser degree, the physiological components themselves are present. In this sense, the level of "as if" does not apply for emotional experience. We may note that the same process occurs in emotional arousal through literature or music. Such arousal is not an "as if" function but a "thing in itself," in the sense of including the autonomic components of the emotion schema, not only images and words. Thus emotional experience will necessarily have the quality of immediacy. In that sense, for example, the patient's affective core as activated in the analyst's room was indeed equivalent to the experience of the death camp, but this could be distinct from his knowing, on some level, that the contexts were in reality different.

Here is where we see the crucial integrative nature of the psychoanalytic process. Our mental lives, memories, the emotion schemas that we construct and that form us, are composed of some elements that are symbols in the formal sense and some that are experiential "things in themselves," that have in a sense a life of their own, outside of intentionality and direct control. The images of objects that are described in the patient's narratives are symbolic, the affective core is subsymbolic, the whole is prototypic, representing the construction of the schema out of the events of one's life.

The reconstruction of the past as it occurs in psychoanalysis, or in literature, involves activation of subsymbolic somatic and sensory experience in a new integration. The actual physiological components of the schema need to be activated to be connected to objects; this in vivo connection provides the necessary basis for change in the affective core. The transference plays a unique role in this respect. The analyst may be recognized as "standing for" other objects, as the analyst of Mr. T. represented the guard or the father; but the person of the analyst is also present, and the power of the transference is in the evocation of the self-state of the emotion in relation to the present person in the here and now. (The question then arises of whether—and how—transference can ever be fully resolved.)

CONCLUSIONS: TO SYMBOLIZING—AND BACK

The challenge for psychoanalytic treatment is the bidirectional connection that is required—from the subsymbolic forms in which one's self-state is experienced to the symbols that are the vehicles for our interpersonal transactions—then most crucially, so that real change may occur, back to the motoric, somatic, and sensory bodily forms. The change is not complete until the somatic and sensory responses—

the turning of the stomach, the rapid heart beat—occur in new ways, in a wide range of life situations, and in what we may call emotional "real time," far more quickly and immediately than verbal cuing could possibly direct (even if we somehow knew how to use verbal interventions to direct such responses, which of course we do not). We can see the process in simple form in the attempt to change a motoric habit. The difficulty in incorporating verbal directives is apparent to anyone who has ever taken a dance lesson or a tennis lesson; how much more complex and difficult is this process for changes in the emotion schema.

Psychoanalysis—the "talking cure"—has assumed a privileged role for verbal language in bringing about change. We now know, however, that words are not the only symbolic forms, and that there are multiple systematic formats of representation and communication not only outside of the verbal but also outside of the symbolic mode. The analytic work uses many modes of communication in addition to words, as Freedman's work has shown. He points to images, drawings, and motoric actions as themselves facilitating not only the transitional stage of the symbolic equation, but also the formation of symbols, as I have described. This provides the cognitive basis for what has been characterized as a corrective emotional experience: an integrative function, dependent on the presence of the analyst in activating an emotion schema, operating in the nonverbal as in the verbal mode. I am not sure Freedman has fully addressed the questions these observations raise concerning the privileging of the verbal mode that is central in psychoanalysis. Beyond this, if we take seriously the endogenous organization of the subsymbolic process, we might carry Freedman's observation a step farther to examine to what extent subsymbolic modes of communication themselves may be effective in bringing about therapeutic change.

I can also argue from the other side. Even in a dance lesson, or a tennis lesson, it is usually the case that some verbal interaction is required to bring about change, to identify the difficulties, to make distinctions, to provide guiding metaphors. It is also possible that connection to the symbolizing realm is necessary to enable the individual to take over the direction and regulation of the self.

Rilke, in his semiautobiographical novel *The Notebooks of Malte Laurids Brigge*, which Freedman (1985) cites as part of Rilke's self-analysis, gives us not an answer, but a text to be explicated, concerning the relation between bodily experience and words. As Rilke tells us, one must have many experiences, accrue many memories, in order to write a poem. Yet it is not enough to gather memories: "For the memories themselves are not important. Only when they have changed into our very blood, into glance and gesture, and are nameless, no longer to be distinguished from ourselves—only then can it happen that in some very rare hour the first word of a poem arises in their midst and goes forth from them" (Rilke 1910, p. 20).

I suggest that the same must hold, in a limited and muted way, for the words that are spoken in analysis. If words can emerge from a source that is inherently nameless, they can also be connected back through such channels and to such a ground. I have pointed to some possible connecting processes in this paper. Freedman (1985) has emphasized the need, in analysis, for "a particular attunement to the vehicles of representation: the sensations, perception, images, enactments and revisualizations of the past" (pp. 336–337). Part of the answer may also lie in the mediating role of what I have termed *protosymbolic* forms, muscular movements, or somatic or sensory feelings that are discrete entities in what are largely subsymbolic domains and that may operate as cues in emotional "real time" where language cannot enter. Somehow, through interactions that include far-seeing attunement and that also make use of such mediating cues, change in one's "very blood, . . . glance and gesture" can eventually come about.

REFERENCES

Balint, M. (1968). *The Basic Fault: Therapeutic Aspects of Regression*. London: Tavistock.

Bowlby, J. (1969). *Attachment and Loss: Vol. 1: Attachment*. New York: Basic Books.

Bucci, W. (1997). *Psychoanalysis and Cognitive Science: A Multiple Code Theory*. New York: Guilford.

——— (2001). Pathways of emotional communication. *Psychoanalytic Inquiry* 20:40–70.

Dahl, H. (1988). Frames of mind. In *Psychoanalytic Process Research Strategies*, ed. H. Dahl, H. Kächele, and H. Thomä, pp. 51–66. New York: Springer Verlag.

Fonagy, P. (1995). Psychoanalytic and empirical approaches to developmental psychopathology: an object relations perspective. In *Research in Psychoanalysis: Process, Development, Outcome*, ed. T. Shapiro and R. N. Emde, pp. 245–260. Madison, CT: International Universities Press.

Freedman, N. (1985). The concept of transformation in psychoanalysis. *Psychoanalytic Psychology* 2:317–339.

Freedman, N., and Bucci, W. (1981). On kinetic filtering in associative monologue. *Semiotica* 34:225–249.

Gilani, Z. H., Bucci, W., and Freedman, N. (1985). The structure and language of a silence. *Semiotica* 56:99–113.

Jones, E. (1938). Theory of symbolism. *Papers on Psycho-Analysis*. Baltimore, MD: William Wood.

Kanzer, M. (1966). The motor sphere of transference. *Psychoanalytic Quarterly* 35:522–539.

Keller, H. (1908). *The World I Live In*. New York: Century.

Luborsky, L., and Crits-Cristoph, P. (1990). *Understanding Transference—The CCRT Method*. New York: Basic Books.

McClelland, J. L., Rumelhart, D. E., and Hinton, G. E. (1989). The appeal of parallel distributed processing. In *Parallel Distributed Processing: Explorations in the Microstructure of Cognition: Volume 1: Foundations*, ed. D. E. Rumelhart, J. L. McClelland, and the PDP Reasearch Group, pp. 3–44. Cambridge, MA: MIT Press.

Rapaport, D. (1967). Cognitive structures. In *Collected Papers of David Rapaport*, pp. 631–664. New York: Basic Books.

Reik, T. (1948). *Listening with the Third Ear: The Inner Experience of a Psychoanalyst*. New York: Pyramid, 1964.

Rilke, R. M. (1910). *Notebooks of Malte Laurids Brigge*, trans. S. Mitchell. New York: Random House, 1984.

Steingart, I. (1983). *Pathological Play in Borderline and Narcissistic Personalities*. New York: SP Medical and Scientific Books (Spectrum Publications).

Stern, D. N. (1985). *The Interpersonal World of the Infant*. New York: Basic Books.

Strachey, J. (1934). The nature of the therapeutic action of psychoanalysis. *International Journal of Psycho-Analysis* 18:127–159.

3

The Concept of Mind: A Developmental Analysis

JOHN S. AUERBACH AND SIDNEY J. BLATT

This chapter is devoted to a review of recent developments in the study of symbolic processes, particularly the development of the concept of mind. An essential component of the concept of mind is the capacity for self-reflexivity, the ability to make smooth transitions between subjective and objective perspectives on the self (Bach 1985, 1994). This reflexive self-awareness is central to the construction of self-representation. Self-reflexivity and self-representation emerge from, and in turn facilitate, the development of intersubjectivity. In this chapter, we review some recently developed procedures that assess systematically the capacities for reflexive self-awareness and intersubjectivity. These include the Adult Attachment Inventory (AAI; George et al. 1985), the Reflective Functioning (RF) Scale (Fonagy et al. 1991, Fonagy et al. 1998),[1] the Object Relations Inventory (ORI; Blatt et al. 1981, Blatt et al. 1979), and the Differentiation-Relatedness (D-R) Scale (Diamond et al. 1991, Diamond et al. 1990).

---

1. Fonagy and colleagues (1991) initially referred to this measure as the Reflective-Self Functioning Scale.

We demonstrate how these procedures enable us to understand the process of therapeutic change, as illustrated in the detailed analysis of changes in a patient's self- and significant-figure descriptions during the course of a long-term intensive inpatient treatment program for seriously disturbed, treatment-resistant adolescents and young adults.

SELF-REFLEXIVITY

Self-reflexivity, the ability to move easily back and forth between subjective and objective perspectives on the self, is a fundamental concept in psychology. As early as the late nineteenth century, and some years before Freud began to articulate a rigorous and systematic psychological theory, William James (1890) differentiated between self as subject (i.e., as knower and agent), which he termed the *I*, and self as object (i.e., as known and acted upon), which he termed the *me*. Although James's ideas were taken up by later psychological thinkers (e.g., Baldwin 1906, Cooley 1922, Mead 1934) and are foundational to modern discussions of issues of self-reflexivity in psychoanalysis (see, for example, Aron 1998, Auerbach 1993, Auerbach and Blatt 1996, 1997, Bach 1985, 1994, Fast 1998, Harter 1999, Modell 1993), this tension between subjective and objective forms of self-awareness was obscured in psychoanalytic discourse by Freud's (1914, 1923) use, as many commentators (e.g., Balint 1968, Hartmann 1950, Kernberg 1982, Laplanche and Pontalis 1967) have noted, of a single term, *das Ich*, to refer to both ego (i.e., the human subject) and self (i.e., the subject's self-conception). On the one hand, Freud's use of a single term to denote both ego and self reflected his dialectical conception of human selfhood—his positing of a tension, perhaps necessary and ineradicable, between the person as a subject (i.e., as a desiring but also potentially rational agent) and the person as an object of self-knowledge and narcissistic self-investment (cf. Lacan 1953, Laplanche 1970). On the other hand, because the term *das Ich* is officially translated into English as "the ego," the dialectical subtleties of Freud's conceptualizations are often difficult to grasp without careful reading.

Thus, for example, in "On Narcissism," the following quotation becomes much clearer if "ego" is read as "self" or "self-representation": "A unity comparable to the ego cannot exist in the individual from the start; the ego has to be developed" (Freud 1914, p. 77). Similar considerations also apply to this famous quotation: "The ego is first and foremost a bodily ego; it is not merely a surface entity but is in itself the projection of a surface" (Freud 1923, p. 26). Despite these difficulties with translation, it is clear that the tension between subjective and objective views of the self is central to a psychoanalytic understanding of human functioning. It is only with the developmental emergence of self-reflexivity, of the capacity for self-observation, in early childhood that psychic conflict (i.e., the tensions among the person who I am, the person I would like to be, the person I think I should be, and the person I fear I am or do not want to be) becomes possible at all.

REFLEXIVE SELF-AWARENESS IN NORMAL DEVELOPMENT

The process of self-representation requires reflexive self-awareness—the ability as a subject to reflect on oneself as an object. Thus, unlike object representations, which involve only what can one observe and infer about others, the self-representation has (at least) two sources (Auerbach 1993, Bach 1985, 1994, Blatt and Bers 1993, Broucek 1991, Damon and Hart 1988, Duval and Wicklund 1972, James 1890, Lewis and Brooks-Gunn 1979, Mann 1991, Mead 1934, Merleau-Ponty 1960, Modell 1993, Piaget 1924, 1926, Schafer 1968): (1) subjective self-awareness, or the experience of oneself as "a center of initiative and a recipient of impressions" (Kohut 1977, p. 99); and (2) objective self-awareness, or observations of oneself as an object among other objects, a self among other selves. Objective self-awareness includes an understanding that one is an object not only for oneself but also in the eyes of others. This division within the self, this capacity for reflexive self-awareness, first emerges between ages 18 and 24 months as, for example, an ability to recognize oneself in the mirror (Lewis and Brooks-Gunn 1979) or to comment on one's immediate actions and preferences through brief self-descriptive utterances (e.g., "climbing up," said while climbing on furniture) (Kagan 1981) and culminates in the abstract, systematic self-conceptions of adolescence and beyond (Damon and Hart 1988).

From a psychoanalytic perspective, however, the emergence of self-awareness in the second year of life is a mixed blessing. With the capacity for self-recognition, children also discover that they are objects in the eyes of others and, furthermore, that they are small and separate beings in a large world. The emergence of self-reflexivity between ages 18 and 24 months, then, is coincident with the rapprochement subphase (Mahler et al. 1975) and is accompanied by a potential upsurge in the child's experience of shame and embarrassment (Amsterdam and Levitt 1980, Broucek 1991, Kagan 1981), by a potential lowering of self-esteem that can be documented experimentally in adults' avoidant responses to the presence of a mirror or a camera (Duval and Wicklund 1972), although it should be added that under normal circumstances these dysphoric affects constitute a relatively minor part of a toddler's typical emotional experience.

SELF-REFLEXIVITY AND SYMBOLIC PLAY

Two-year-old children are faced, therefore, with a highly problematic psychological situation, but fortunately, the same symbolic capacity that led to the discovery of their separateness also enables them to cope with this difficulty. For it is in the next two or three years of life that children begin to develop a theory of mind (see Astington et al. 1988, Perner 1991, Wellman 1990)—that is, an understanding of how other people think, of the differences between beliefs and fantasies about the world on the one hand and realistic perceptions of the world on the other. In other words, coincident with the emergence of self-reflexivity in the second year of life is the emergence of pretend play (Piaget 1945)—of transitional object usage (Winnicott, 1953, 1971)—and two-year-olds are adept at distinguishing between pretense (i.e., make-believe) and reality (Bretherton 1989, Harris and Kavanaugh 1993, Leslie 1987).

Transitional object usage, as Winnicott (1953, 1971) proposed, is the means by which a child negotiates the dilemma of becoming separate and autonomous while remaining attached to caregivers. Alternatively, per Piaget (1945), the capacity for pretend play gives children an increased sense of control in a world that they have only recently discovered is separate from them. But if children at age 2 are quite capable of distinguishing pretense from reality and of using this distinction to cope with emotional dilemmas in their lives, they have much difficulty, prior to age 4 or 5, in grasping the distinction between appearance and reality, between how things look and how they actually are (Flavell et al. 1986), as well as in understanding the difference between their beliefs about the world and how the world actually is (Perner et al. 1987, Wimmer and Perner 1983). Alternatively, therefore, preschool children have difficulty in recognizing that their beliefs about the world are dependent on their perceptions of it and may be incorrect if their perceptions are incorrect. They also have difficulty in understanding that their beliefs may differ from those of others and that it is possible for people to develop false beliefs, to have secrets, and to lie (Astington 1993, Meares 1993). In short, although children come to understand the separateness of their bodies sometime in the second year of life, they do not come to understand that their minds are distinct from those of others until sometime in the fifth or sixth year (Mayes and Cohen 1996). The discovery of the separateness of one's mind is a crucial step in the development of self-reflexivity because it is then that children learn that their beliefs about the world can differ from those of others. It is with the discovery of the mind's separateness, therefore, that transitional object usage comes to be integrated with realistic cognition (Fonagy and Target 1996, Target and Fonagy 1996), at least under normal circumstances. In other words, the discovery of the mind's separateness places limits on the illusions of omnipotence and fusion that constitute the core of transitional fantasy.

SELF-REFLEXIVITY AND INTERSUBJECTIVITY

The capacity for reflexive self-awareness is a consequence of phylogenetic development; it is an ability that exists only in humans and, to some extent, in the great apes and the bottlenose dolphin, the only other animals in which mirror self-recognition has been found (Gallup 1977, Povinelli 1993, Povinelli and Prince 1998, Reiss and Marino 2001). But self-reflexivity is more than a consequence of higher cortical functioning. That apes raised as social isolates never develop the ability to recognize themselves in the mirror (Gallup 1977) tells us that the development of objective self-awareness requires a social milieu, certainly in the few infrahuman species that have this ability and, we can surely infer, in humans too.

The notion that self-reflexivity requires interaction with others is not a new one in psychology. Theorists like Cooley (1922) and Mead (1934) argued that one develops a self-concept from the reflected appraisals of others—from how others see one. These ideas were introduced into psychoanalytic discourse by Sullivan (1940). In developmental psychology, Piaget (1924) argued that objective self-awareness, the cognitive capacity upon which true self-knowledge depends, requires the overcoming of childhood egocentrism, the propensity to see the world from one's own perspective only. For Piaget, as for Cooley and for Mead, self-awareness depends on the ability to regard oneself as an object among other objects. In other words, contrary to the Cartesian tradition (Descartes 1637, 1641) that is predominant in Western thought, one develops a self-concept not via solitary introspection but by seeing oneself through others' eyes.

As important as these ideas are, however, they omit a psychological dimension that is central to a psychoanalytic understanding of the development of self-reflexivity. From a psychoanalytic perspective, a child's ability to understand the mind of another requires first being treated by others, specifically one's primary caregivers, as having a mind, will, and feelings of his or her own (see, e.g., Benjamin 1995, Stern 1985, Winnicott 1971). To understand the mind of another, one must first be regarded by that other as an independent subject oneself. This insight is also not new. Nearly 200 years ago, Hegel (1807) wrote, "Self-consciousness [Hegel's term for independent subjectivity] exists in and for itself when, and by the fact that, it so exists for another; that is, it exists only in being acknowledged" (p. 111). A child becomes an independent subject, a subject who can regard herself as an object, only by being regarded as such by her caregiver. Thus, although the ultimate consolidation of intersubjectivity will require a capacity for language (Cavell 1993), preverbal children start to become independent subjects, as Winnicott (1971, cf. Stern 1985) argued, when they see their spontaneous gestures reflected in mother's eyes. The independent subjectivity of the child, in other words, requires and is therefore limited by the independent subjectivity of the parents. Alternatively, as empirical infancy research suggests, a mutually interactive sharing of affective states between caregiver and baby is essential to the process of psychological differentiation, especially insofar as the caregiver's responses, while contingent upon the infant's affective displays, are not exact replicas of them (Beebe et al. 1997, Gergely and Watson 1996, Stern 1985, Tronick 1989). The baby starts to develop as an independent subject because the caregiver establishes an emotional communion with the baby while at the same time standing just outside of that communion. From the baby's point of view, therefore, early relationships with parental figures involve a dialectic between gratifying involvements (i.e., communion) and experienced incompatibility (i.e., separation; see Behrends and Blatt 1985, Blatt and Behrends 1987), a dialectic that is central to psychological development.

These ideas are commonplace in psychoanalytic theorizing, thanks to the classic contributions of Fairbairn (1952), Sullivan (1953), Lichtenstein (1977), Winnicott (1971), and Kohut (1977) on the centrality of affect mirroring and other preverbal affective processes in the formation of the self. At this point, however, the modern intersubjectivity theory that derives from Hegel's (1807) foundational analysis of the master–slave dialectic (e.g., Aron 1996, 1998, Auerbach 1993, Auerbach and Blatt 2001, Benjamin 1995, Kirshner 1991, Ogden 1994; cf. Lacan 1977, Winnicott 1971) introduces a more profound, dialectical turn. According to this variant of intersubjectivity theory, children start becoming independent subjects when regarded as such by their caregivers, but they do not complete this process until they can then recognize the independent subjectivity of their caregivers—more concretely, can recognize that their caregivers also have minds, wills, and feelings of their own, minds that are independent of their children. Only another independent subject can bestow the recognition that enables children to have minds of their own, and that recognition in turn becomes real only when the child recognizes the independence of the other's mind. In other words, this basic intersubjective situation, this mutual recognition by caregiver and infant of each other's independent subjectivity, is just as crucial as are phylogenetic processes to the child's development of reflexive self-awareness and of a theory of mind that enables a child to understand the beliefs and desires of others.

To put this argument in broader historical perspective, we are proposing a shift from a Cartesian theory of mind, in which the self stands transcendentally at the center of the universe, to a Hegelian perspective, in which self and other mutually constitute each other through dialogue (see, for example, Aron 1996, Auerbach 1993, Benjamin 1995, Orange et al. 1999). This shift has a certain parallel in the transition from Newtonian physics, in which the observer stands apart from the field of observation, to quantum physics, in which the observer is an essential part of the field (see Blatt 1999), although it must of course be acknowledged that Hegel's work predates quantum physics by a century and that his historicism and idealism are highly problematic. Nevertheless, Hegel's ideas have remained surprisingly modern and surprisingly relevant to psychoanalysis despite being 200 years old (see Marcuse 1941, 1955). In psychoanalysis, therefore, we have seen a progression from a focus on the development of an autonomous ego (e.g., Hartmann 1939) or of a unitary self (Kohut 1977) to a perspective in which a dialogue between self and other constitutes the basic unit of study (e.g., Aron 1996, Auerbach and Blatt 2001, Behrends and Blatt 1985, Benjamin 1995, Ogden 1994, Orange et al. 1999). It should be added that, although Freud's metapsychology is clearly derived from the world-views of Descartes and Newton, his clinical theory, with its focus on the self and the mind as loci of conflict, is most certainly consistent with the dialectical outlook that we are articulating.

INTERSUBJECTIVITY, ATTACHMENT, AND THEORY OF MIND

This intersubjective-dialectical model of psychological development is supported empirically by research documenting the link between attachment security and the development of a theory of mind. This connection was first noted by Main (1991), who, with her colleagues, developed the AAI (George et al. 1985), a semistructured interview measure of adult attachment status. The AAI inquires broadly about a person's relationship history, but it determines an individual's attachment status not by the content of his or her report but rather by that report's narrative coherence. Thus, a person who has had a traumatic past but who can describe his or her parents in a coherent, plausible fashion will be classified as securely attached, but an individual whose descriptions of his or her parents lack narrative coherence and plausibility will be placed in one of the insecure-attachment categories, preoccupied, dismissing, or disorganized, depending on the type and severity of the individual's deviations from coherent discourse. Main's (1991) argument is that insecure attachment on the AAI reflects failure in *metacognitive monitoring*, her term for awareness of one's own mental processes, with regard to one's attachment narratives. Insecurely attached adults fail to notice that their accounts of their childhood attachment experiences are incoherent or internally inconsistent, but securely attached adults, even those who have suffered developmental trauma, remain coherent in their descriptions of childhood.

Influenced by Main's ideas and by research on the development of a theory of mind in children, Fonagy and colleagues (1991, 1998) constructed an RF rating scale (see Table 3.1) that can be applied to AAI transcripts to assess the extent to which an individual has developed a theory of mind—an understanding of mental states, both one's own and those of others. Their scale ranges on an 11-point continuum from negative reflective functioning (scale point –1) through absent but not repudiated reflective functioning (scale point 1), questionable or low reflective functioning (scale point 3), definite or ordinary reflective functioning (scale point 5), marked reflective functioning (scale point 7), and, finally, full or exceptional reflective functioning (scale point 9). At the bottom of the scale, individuals either actively resist thinking about mental states underlying a person's behavior or else think about these mental states in an unintegrated, bizarre, or inappropriate way. At the top of the continuum, individuals display an organized, consistent, complex, often surprising understanding of the motivations guiding their own actions and those of others.

Fonagy and colleagues (1996) found that the AAI narratives of psychiatric inpatients are significantly lower in Reflective Functioning than are those of nonpsychiatric controls. Among psychiatric inpatients, RF was slightly better than questionable or low ($M = 3.7$) while among controls it was consistent with at least ordinary Reflective Functioning ($M = 5.2$). Among psychiatric inpatients, Fonagy and colleagues (1996) found that the AAI narratives of borderline personalities are significantly lower in Reflective Functioning than are the narratives of patients without borderline disturbance. For borderline patients, RF was just short of questionable or low ($M = 2.7$) and therefore indicated a highly limited ability to reflect on mental states. Similarly, in a different research tradition, qualitative analyses of the self-descriptions of borderline adolescent and young adult patients indicate that the ability of such persons to coordinate subjective and objective perspectives on the self is easily disrupted by intense affect early in long-term inpatient treatment but is much more stable at discharge from the hospital (Auerbach and Blatt 1996, 1997).

Still more important for our intersubjective theory of mental development, however, is research demonstrating that attachment security and reflective functioning in parents are linked to attachment security and symbolization in children. In a meta-analytic review of 18 studies involving 854 parent–child dyads, van IJzendoorn (1995) found that parental attachment status, as measured on the AAI, can predict infant attachment status, as measured in Ainsworth's strange situation paradigm (Ainsworth et al. 1978), with a classification accuracy of 75 percent. In other words, parental representations of attachment relationships with their parents predict the attachment behavior of their children.

As for how parents' attachment representations influence infant attachment status, it has been found that children of parents high in

Table 3.1. Reflective Functioning

Level/Scale Point	*Description*
−1 Negative Reflective Functioning	Responses that are distinctively anti-reflective, hostile, bizarre, or inappropriate in the context of the interview.
1 Absent Reflective Function	Responses either totally or almost totally lacking in reflective functioning, with little evidence that the person thinks about mental states. Accounts are barren, lacking in detail pertaining to mental states, or are egocentric and self-serving.
3 Questionable Reflective Function	Responses contain some evidence of consideration of mental states, but most references are not made explicit. The person's understanding of mental states is either banal and clichéd or diffuse and unintegrated.
5 Ordinary Reflective Functioning	The subject displays an ordinary capacity to make sense of experience in terms of thoughts and feelings and has a consistent model of mental states that requires little or no inference from the rater. The subject's model is limited and does not include understanding of conflict or ambivalence.
7 Marked Reflective Functioning	Responses contain numerous instances of full reflective functioning suggestive of a stable psychological model of the mind. Much detail about thoughts and feelings is present, and implications of mental states are explicitly spelled out. The subject is usually able to maintain a developmental (interactional) perspective and to arrive at original reintegrations of states of mind
9 Exceptional Reflective Functioning	Responses show exceptional sophistication. They are commonly surprising in their insights, are quite complex or elaborate, and consistently manifest causal reasoning with regard to mental states. The subject displays a consistent reflective stance across all contexts.

Note: Adapted from *Reflective-Functioning Manual, Version 5, For Application to Adult Attachment Interviews* (pp. 54–59), by P. Fonagy, M. Target, H. Steele, and M. Steele, 1998. Unpublished research manual, Sub-Department of Clinical Health Psychology, University College, London.

Reflective Functioning are three or four times more likely to be securely attached than are children of parents low in Reflective Functioning (Fonagy et al. 1991), and the relationship of high parental Reflective Functioning to infant attachment security is even stronger among mothers living in deprived circumstances (Fonagy et al. 1994). Mothers of securely attached children are more actively involved in their children's symbolic play than are mothers of insecurely attached children, and securely attached children are more responsive in their symbolic play to the contributions of others than are insecurely attached children (Meins and Russell 1997, Slade 1987). In addition, securely attached children acquire an understanding of false beliefs—that is, that beliefs about the world can be mistaken—earlier than do children who are insecurely attached (Fonagy et al. 1997) and therefore have a greater facility to reflect on their thoughts than do their insecurely attached peers. Furthermore, according to pilot data reported by Main (1991), securely attached children have a better understanding that thinking is private than do children with insecure attachments, especially those who are resistantly attached. Main notes that many resistantly attached children believe that their parents can read their minds.

In short, this research evidence supports the proposition that attachment, self-reflexivity, symbolization, and intersubjectivity are related developments. It is, in other words, by virtue of being regarded by their parents as having minds and feelings of their own that securely attached children develop the symbolic functioning necessary to reflect on their own minds and the minds of others.

SELF-REFLEXIVITY, EVOCATIVE CONSTANCY, AND DIFFERENTIATION-RELATEDNESS

The contributions of Main (1991) and Fonagy (1996, Fonagy et al. 1991, 1994, 1995) to the understanding of the role of relational processes in the development of self-reflexivity are paralleled by the efforts of Blatt, Diamond, and their colleagues (e.g., Blatt et al. 1998, Blatt, Stayner et al. 1996, Diamond et al. 1990, 1991) to extend the traditional psychoanalytic notion of evocative object constancy to include a capacity for intersubjectivity. Traditionally regarded as related to the Piagetian capacity for object permanence (Piaget 1937), object constancy has been conceptualized in the psychoanalytic literature as the ability to evoke a positive image of a significant other, or to maintain an integrated representation of that other, when the person in question is absent, unavailable, or frustrating (Blatt and Shichman 1983, Fraiberg 1969, Mahler et al. 1975). The development of stable object relations was thought to depend on the consolidation of object constancy, and borderline personality disturbances were thought to reflect an impairment of this psychological capacity (see Adler 1985, Blatt 1995, Blatt and Auerbach 1988, Blatt and Shichman 1983, Masterson 1981, Rinsley 1982, 1989). This model formed the theoretical basis of the Conceptual Level (CL) Scale (see Table 3.2) developed by Blatt and colleagues (Blatt 1974, Blatt et al. 1979, 1981, 1988) to rate descriptions of parents and other emotionally significant figures. According to this scale, representation of objects progresses from sensorimotor-preoperational through concrete-perceptual, external-iconic, internal-iconic, and, finally, conceptual levels of development. At the sensorimotor-preoperational level, objects are described in terms of gratification and frustration, and at the conceptual level, objects are characterized as psychologically complex, differentiated, and autonomous beings. Poor object constancy on this scale is therefore reflected in significant-figure descriptions dominated by sensorimotor-preoperational and concrete-perceptual modes of representation. That is, persons who describe significant figures in their lives primarily in terms of whether these figures provide gratification or frustration (sensorimotor-preoperational representation) or of how those figures look (concrete-perceptual representation) are unlikely to be able to evoke consolidated positive images of significant objects, let alone maintain positive ties to them, under conditions of stress or conflict.

It eventually became apparent to Blatt and colleagues, however, that the Conceptual Level Scale was too static, insofar as it rated descriptions of persons but not of relationships, and also insofar as it failed to capture certain intersubjective dimensions of object representation.

Table 3.2. Conceptual Level of Descriptions of Self and Other

Level/Scale Point	*Description*
Sensorimotor-Preoperational (Scale Point 1)	Persons are described primarily in terms of the gratification or frustration they provide. Others do not exist as entities separate and independent of their direct effect on the individual's pleasure or pain.
Concrete-Perceptual (Scale Point 3)	Persons are described primarily in concrete, literal terms, usually on the basis of physical attributes and features. Emphasis is placed on external physical characteristics and appearance.
Iconic (Scale Point 5)	External iconic level: Persons are described primarily in terms of manifest activities or functions.
(Scale Point 7)	Internal iconic level: Persons are described primarily in terms of their thoughts, feelings, and values, rather than their physical characteristics or activities. The description primarily involves psychological dimensions.
Conceptual (Scale Point 9)	Using a range of levels, the description integrates external appearances and activities (behavior) with internal dimensions (feelings, thoughts, and values). Apparent contradictions are resolved in an integrated, complex, coherent synthesis.

These intersubjective dimensions include the subtleties of how one comes to understand and describe the psychological uniqueness of significant figures in one's life, and they also refer to the notion that object constancy involves the ability to evoke the feeling that the other remains lovingly disposed toward the self, even under conditions of stress, conflict, or absence. Influenced, therefore, by Stern's (1985) account of the development of intersubjectivity, as well as by Mahlerian

(Mahler et al. 1975) separation-individuation theory and Blatt's (1974, Blatt and Blass 1990, 1996, Blatt and Shichman 1983) work on the interplay of relational and self-definitional developmental lines in normal and pathological functioning, Diamond and colleagues (1990, 1991) constructed the Differentiation-Relatedness Scale, with the following ten levels: a lack of basic differentiation between self and others (Levels 1 and 2); the use of mirroring (Level 3); self–other idealization or denigration (Level 4); and an oscillation between polarized negative and positive attributes (Level 5) as maneuvers to consolidate and stabilize representations; an emergent differentiated, constant, and integrated representation of self and other, with increasing tolerance for ambiguity (Levels 6 and 7); representations of self and other as empathically interrelated (Level 8); representations of self and other in reciprocal and mutually facilitating interactions (Level 9); and reflectively constructed, integrated representations of self and others in reciprocal and mutual relationships (Level 10). In general, higher ratings of differentiation-relatedness in descriptions of self and other are based on increased differentiation of the self-representation, increased articulation and stabilization of interpersonal schemas, and an increased appreciation of mutual and empathically attuned relatedness between the self and significant figures.

This scale, summarized in more detail Table 3.3, is based on the assumption that development moves toward (1) a consolidated, integrated, and individuated sense of self-definition and (2) empathically attuned mutual relatedness with significant others. Differentiation and relatedness, in this model, are interactive dimensions that unfold throughout development. The dialectical interaction between these two developmental dimensions facilitates the emergence and consolidation of increasingly mature levels of both self-organization and intersubjectively attuned empathic relatedness. The scale assumes that, with psychological development, representations of self and other become increasingly differentiated and integrated and begin to reflect an increased appreciation of mutual relatedness. In other words, the capacity for intersubjectivity is a central construct measured by the Differentiation-Relatedness Scale. Whereas the highest point of the Con-

Table 3.3. Differentiation-Relatedness of Self and Object Representations

Level/Scale Point	*Description*
1. Self/other boundary compromise	Basic sense of physical cohesion or integrity of representations is lacking or is breached.
2. Self/other boundary confusion	Self and other are represented as physically intact and separate, but feelings and thoughts are amorphous, undifferentiated, or confused. Description may consist of a single global impressionistic quality or a flood of details with a sense of confusion and vagueness.
3. Self/other mirroring	Characteristics of self and other, such as physical appearance or body qualities, shape or size, are virtually identical.
4. Self/other idealization or denigration	Attempts to consolidate representations are based on unitary, unmodulated idealization or denigration, with extreme, exaggerated, one-sided descriptions.
5. Semi-differentiated, tenuous consolidation of representations through splitting (polarization) and/or by an emphasis on concrete part properties	Marked oscillation between dramatically opposite qualities or an emphasis on manifest external features.
6. Emergent, ambivalent constancy (cohesion) of self and an emergent sense of relatedness	Consolidation of disparate aspects of self and other emerges in a somewhat hesitant, equivocal, or ambivalent integration. A list of appropriate conventional characteristics, but they lack a sense of uniqueness. Tentative movement toward a more individuated and cohesive sense of self and other.
7. Consolidated, constant (stable) self and other in unilateral relationships	Thoughts, feelings, needs, and fantasies are differentiated and modulated. Increasing tolerance for and integration of disparate aspects. Distinguishing qualities and characteristics. Sympathetic understanding of others.

Table 3.3. (*continued*)

Level/Scale Point	*Description*
8. Cohesive, individuated, empathically related self and others	Cohesive, nuanced, and related sense of self and others. A definite sense of identity, an interest in interpersonal relationships, and a capacity to understand the perspective of others.
9. Reciprocally related, integrated unfolding self and others.	Cohesive sense of self and others in reciprocal relationships that transform both the self and the other in complex, continually unfolding ways.
10. Creative, integrated constructions of self and others in empathic, reciprocally attuned relationships	Integrated reciprocal relations with an appreciation that one contributes to the construction of meaning in complex interpersonal relationships.

ceptual Level Scale reflected an appreciation of a significant other's psychological complexity, the highest point of the Differentiation-Relatedness Scale reflects an understanding that another's psychological complexity emerges and exists only within complex interpersonal relationships. Alternatively, the capacity for intersubjectivity—that is, the recognition that a person's independent subjectivity and the relationships in which that person participates are inextricably intertwined—is, in this model, the highest level of psychological development.

The ten levels of differentiation-relatedness were established on the basis of clinical and developmental findings and reflect what are generally regarded as clinically significant distinctions in the transition from grossly pathological to intact and even healthy object relations. The scale points are thus best regarded as discrete categories, not points on a continuum. In other words, the underlying logic of this measure is ordinal and not interval or nominal. The various levels of this scale, therefore, may not be equidistant from each other, and the specific number of scale points is to some extent arbitrary. That is, new levels of differentiation-relatedness can be added in light of new clinical observations, theoretical formulations, and research findings. Nevertheless, a clear implication of this scale is that higher differentiation-relatedness ratings reflect a greater degree of psychological health. In theory, differentiation-relatedness Levels 8, 9, and 10 are indicative of mental health, and differentiation-relatedness Level 7 (consolidation of object constancy) is regarded as a prerequisite for normal psychological and interpersonal functioning.

The Differentiation-Relatedness Scale was used systematically for the first time in a study of changes in significant-figure descriptions in severely disturbed adolescent and young adult inpatients involved in long-term, psychoanalytically oriented treatment. These significant-figure descriptions were obtained through a relatively unstructured interview procedure, the ORI, in which patients were asked, shortly after admission to the hospital and at six-month intervals thereafter, to describe mother, father, a significant other, therapist, and self (see Auerbach and Blatt 1996, 1997, Blatt et al. 1996, 1998, Diamond et al. 1990). Blatt and colleagues (1996), using partial correlations to analyze statistically the clinical changes resulting after at least one year of treatment, found that changes in Differentiation-Relatedness assessed from significant-figure descriptions were positively correlated with changes in level of psychosocial functioning, as independently measured on the Global Assessment Scale (GAS; Endicott, Spitzer, Fleiss, and Cohen 1976), rated from detailed case reports.[2] These

---

2. A unidimensional scale derived from from Luborsky (1962, Luborsky and Bachrach 1974), the GAS assesses functioning and severity of psychopathology. It has frequent, well-specified scale points for each of ten intervals, ranging from a high score of 91 to 100 for "no symptoms, superior functioning in a wide range of activities, life problems never seem to get out of hand, (person) is sought by others because of his warmth and integrity," through a score of 51 to 60 at midrange for "moderate symptoms or generally functioning with some difficulty (e.g., few friends and flat affect, depressed mood, and pathological self-doubt, euphoric mood and pressure of speech, moderately severe antisocial behavior," to a low score of 1 to 10 for "needs constant supervision for several days to prevent hurting self or others (e.g., requires an intensive care unit with special observation by staff), makes no attempt to maintain minimal personal hygiene, or serious suicidal act with clear intent and expectation of death" (Endicott et al. 1976). A slightly revised version of the GAS is included in the *Diagnostic and Statistical Manual of Mental Disorders*, 4th edition (American Psychiatric Association 1994) as the Global Assessment of Functioning (GAF).

positive correlations between change in level of object relations and change in level of clinical functioning were found in descriptions of mother, father, therapist, and self. Therapeutic gain was thus clearly associated with significant increases in the level of Differentiation-Relatedness of descriptions of self and significant others. Furthermore, Blatt and colleagues (1998) found that, over the course of treatment, this sample of seriously disturbed, treatment-resistant patients as a whole showed an increase in mean Differentiation-Relatedness from a predominance of polarization and splitting (D-R Level 5) to an emergent object constancy (D-R Level 6). In addition, those patients who showed the greatest clinical improvement, as determined by a median split of the distribution of differences between admission GAS and GAS after one year of treatment, initially described their therapists in a manner that was already approaching the emergence of object constancy, while those who were to show less improvement started at the level of polarization and splitting in describing their therapists. At discharge, those patients with greater therapeutic change had a consolidation of object constancy (D-R Level 7) in their therapist descriptions, whereas patients with less improvement had just achieved the emergence of object constancy (D-R Level 6)—that is, an emergent ability to tolerate and to begin to integrate contradictory aspects of significant figures—in their therapist descriptions.

Thus, the Differentiation-Relatedness Scale and the Reflective Functioning Scale are complementary efforts at assessing the relationship between intersubjectivity and psychological individuation. Whereas the Reflective Functioning Scale derives in large measure from research literature on attachment and the child's development of a concept of mind and was meant to be used with the AAI, the Differentiation-Relatedness Scale has its origins in the work of psychoanalytic developmental theorists like Mahler and Stern, in theoretical work by Blatt and colleagues (e.g., Blatt and Blass 1990, Blatt and Shichman 1983) on the dialectic of relatedness and self-definition in personality development and psychopathology, and in the tradition of research on the assessment of object representations (see Blatt and Lerner 1983); this measure was initially applied to descriptions of significant figures collected through the ORI. But despite these differences in origin, both approaches share an underlying theoretical assumption that intersubjectivity or, more broadly, interpersonal relatedness is a precondition for the development of an independent self, and both measures further hold that the development of an independent self requires first the development of a capacity to appreciate the psychological uniqueness of significant others—that is, a cognitive capacity for intersubjectivity. Thus, in both models, intersubjectivity as an interpersonal situation (i.e., a mutual recognition between independent subjects) and intersubjectivity as a psychological capacity (i.e., the ability to understand the thoughts, wishes, and feelings of another) are deeply interwined notions. Both models, then, are consistent with the growing emphasis in psychoanalysis on relational conceptualizations of the self and the mind (e.g., Aron 1996, Behrends and Blatt 1985, Benjamin 1995, Blatt and Blass 1996, Mitchell 1988). To demonstrate how these two models complement each other, we apply both of these scales to a case example, that of Patient C., who was a participant in the previously described study assessing changes in the long-term intensive inpatient treatment of seriously disturbed, treatment-resistant patients.

CASE EXAMPLE

At admission to our long-term psychoanalytically oriented hospital, C.,[3] a 15-year-old single white girl had been given diagnoses, in accordance with the *Diagnostic and Statistical Manual of Mental Disor-*

3. This case has previously been discussed by Blatt and Auerbach (2001), Blatt and colleagues (1998), and Diamond and colleagues (1990). It should be noted that the D-R scores to be presented are the same as those reported by Blatt and Auerbach and that these scores are by and large lower than those reported by Diamond and colleagues and Blatt and colleagues. The reason for this discrepancy is that the Differentiation-Relatedness Scale Manual (Diamond et al. 1991) has been revised for greater precision of scoring. The D-R scores presented in this paper and also reported by Blatt and Auerbach are consistent with current scoring procedures. Reflective Functioning in this paper was scored by Kenneth Levy, who had been obtaining RF training from Mary Target at the time that this paper was written and who noted that RF is usually scored on longer, more extensive interview materials than the ORI.

ders, 3rd edition (American Psychiatric Association 1980), of conduct disorder, undersocialized, nonaggressive; identity disorder; mixed substance abuse, episodic (alcohol, sedative-hypnotics, marijuana, amphetamines, and phencyclidine); and mixed personality features (dependent, antisocial, narcissistic, and histrionic). As this list of diagnoses suggests, she was considered to be functioning at a borderline level of personality organization. During her two-year, nine-month hospitalization, C. participated in multifaceted inpatient treatment that included psychoanalytically oriented individual and group psychotherapy, each three times weekly; milieu therapy, including a privileges-level system based on behavioral contingencies; involvement in community responsibilities and triweekly community meetings; weekly individual family and multifamily therapy; occupational and recreational therapy; attendance at an accredited special school run by hospital staff and specially trained teachers; and psychopharmacological evaluation and treatment.

C.'s admission GAS score was 34, and her GAS score at discharge was 47. C.'s self- and object descriptions at admission and discharge are presented in Table 3.4, and her Differentiation-Relatedness and Reflective Functioning scores for these descriptions are presented in Table 3.5. Also presented in Table 3.4 are C.'s self- and object descriptions after two years of treatment. This additional set of representations is included because, as the report of her clinical team indicated, C. became depressed at discharge as the prospect of separation from the hospital approached. Her clinical functioning in the hospital showed some regression as a result, and her verbal productivity in describing herself and significant figures also declined. The inclusion of her self- and significant-figure descriptions from two years into treatment, nine months prior to discharge, thus permits us to provide a better illustration of the changes in C.'s representational world than do her discharge self- and object descriptions alone. To focus the discussion, we have omitted C.'s significant-other descriptions and associated scorings. Thus, only mother, father, self, and therapist descriptions are presented here.

C.'s D-R scores at admission suggest that her psychological organization at that time was dominated by polarization and splitting,

Table 3.4. Patient C.: Self- and Object Representation at Admission, 2 Years, and Discharge

Admission	
MOTHER:	Looks or personality? 5'7", 135 pounds, brown hair, blue eyes. She's usually pretty cool but can be a bitch. Her voice is whiny, very piercing.
FATHER:	A dick. 6'2", heavy, short black hair. Real nasty, a real tyrant. Beady black eyes. *Inquiry:* (Why do you suppose he's like that?) Cause he's an asshole. Sucks dick for a living.
SELF:	Can be tough. Give no more than I expect to get. Get hurt a lot really easily, but I cover it up with a really tough front. *Inquiry*: (Why do you suppose you do that?) I don't know. Just like to help people.
THERAPIST:	Really nice, quiet, calm, pretty cool. Listens to what you say.
2 Years	
MOTHER:	She's—the way she is or the way she looks? (However you want.) Okay. She's kind of neurotic—she tries hard with her kids and her husband. She's basically a very nice person, and I'd say she's wise from experience, from all she's been through. She doesn't like to hurt people, but I think she can be hurt easily. She's organized, and she's very practical, but she's got phobias. She gets helped with [sic], though, and she verges on being very depressed sometimes. *Inquiry*: (Neurotic?) She can get pretty compulsive and stuff, like work—she'll work longer than she has to. Or like cleaning—she'll clean everything up. (Wise from experience?) After all the bullshit with me when I was running away and doing drugs and after my father was having trouble with drinking. She knows what's going on now; she's smart about people and things.
FATHER:	My father has a tough side to him which he uses as a front a lot. He's very sensitive, and I think he feels bad about himself 'cause he's had problems with drinking in the past. He's hard on himself, and he's got a very quick temper, but he's generous, and in his own way, he does care about his family. And he's really smart.

Table 3.4 *(continued)*

2 Years	
SELF:	I'm down on myself a lot. I think I'm fat and ugly, but I know I'm smart and I have potential to really make something out of myself if I put effort into myself and find out what I really want to do. I'm insecure of what other people think about me, and I can be shy.
THERAPIST:	She's straight out. She's trustworthy, and she's easy to talk to, and she's not stupid, and I can't fool her with anything. She's not the kind of person you could lie to and have her believe it. She's calm, and she doesn't get angry usually, but she also doesn't take anybody's shit. *Inquiry*: (Straight out?) She'll tell you what she feels—when she's gotta say something, she won't put it into other words; she'll tell you how she means it.
Discharge (2 years, 9 months)	
MOTHER:	Honest, basic, scared, natural, kind. Nurturing when she can be. *Inquiry*: (Basic?) Simple. (Scared?) Phobic. (Kind?) Nurturing. [Pt. C. had a flat affect but was thoughtful in choosing words.]
FATHER:	Depressed, personalizes things, angry. Reasonable at times. *Inquiry*: (Personalizes?) When someone is cold to him, he takes it personally.
SELF:	Goofy at times. Cold and appearing aloof. Smart. Personalizes things with people too much. Impulsive. Sometimes nice. [Refused inquiry.]
THERAPIST:	Calm, patient, extremely smart, caring. Easy to talk with. [Refused inquiry.]

Note: Examiner's questions appear in parentheses. Examiner's editorial comments appear in brackets.

Table 3.5 Differentiation-Relatedness and Reflective Functioning of Patient C. at Admission, 2 Years, and Discharge

	Differentiation-Relatedness		
	Admission	*2 Years*	*Discharge*
Mother	5	7	7
Father	4	6	6
Self	7	7	7
Therapist	6	7	6
	Reflective Functioning		
	Admission	*2 Years*	*Discharge*
Mother	2	6.5	3
Father	–1	7	5
Self	3	7	5
Therapist	1	7	1

although with some movement toward evocative constancy ($M = 5.5$). In particular, the Differentiation-Relatedness scores for her parent descriptions were indicative of polarization and splitting (D-R levels 4 and 5) whereas the Differentiation-Relatedness scores for her self and therapist descriptions showed that C. was beginning to be able to represent some of her significant objects in a constant manner (D-R levels 6 and 7). At discharge, after two years and nine months of treatment, representations of all her significant figures, as well as of herself, either approached or were at the level of evocative object constancy (D-R levels 6 and 7). These higher Differentiation-Relatedness scores ($M = 6.5$) indicated an increased capacity to tolerate and integrate affectively disparate elements in both herself and significant objects. Just nine months earlier, when she was at her best clinical functioning, her Differentiation-Relatedness was just marginally higher ($M = 6.75$) than it would end up being at discharge. Alternatively, C.'s Reflective Functioning at admission ($M = 1.75$) was midway between absent RF and questionable RF. Variability was considerable, with scores ranging from a low of negative RF for the father description to questionable RF for the self description. This pattern duplicated the finding at admission that C. had her lowest D-R score with her father description and her highest D-R score for her description of the self. After two years of treatment, C.'s RF scores ($M = 6.875$) approached the attainment of marked Reflective Functioning, but as C. approached discharge from the hospital, her scores regressed to a level just above low or questionable RF ($M = 3.5$).

Qualitative analyses of her statements meanwhile reveal that C.'s admission descriptions of her parents emphasized physical descriptors and polarized, negatively charged psychological features. In describing her mother, C. made a beginning attempt to integrate a depiction of her mother as supportive with a view of her as hostile and intrusive, but eventually the negative characterizations of her mother came to dominate the representation. Indeed, C.'s initial question, "Looks *or* personality?" (emphasis added), suggests that polarized, binary thinking was central to the manner in which she thought about significant others. A focus on concrete physical details helped C. to contain for a while her highly ambivalent feelings about her mother, but ultimately her concerns with her mother's intrusiveness overwhelmed this young woman's defenses.

In her admission description of her father, C. gave no indication of ambivalent feelings. Only anger and rage were present, as C. alternated between, on the one hand, concrete physical descriptors that once again served temporarily to mute and delay expression of her deeper concerns and, on the other, a hostility that was expressed through expletives involving primitive drive contents. C.'s regression from phallic to anal and, finally, oral themes suggest that she was unable to modulate her anger over what she regarded as her father's intrusive domination. These primitive drive themes also suggested the possibility that C. regarded her relationship with her father as inappropriately sexualized or perhaps that C. relied defensively on sexualized anger to ward off deeper concerns with nurturance and dependence. Nevertheless, for neither of her parents was there much indication that C. was able to think about their mental states, and in the case of the father description, there was an active repudiation of reflective functioning.

In marked contrast, however, to her depictions of her parents as intrusive and domineering were C.'s more nuanced and balanced descriptions of herself and her therapist. At admission, C.'s representations of these figures were consistent with the emergence of object constancy. In acknowledging the manner in which she deployed a tough facade to cover up her sensitivity and vulnerability, this young woman demonstrated a beginning capacity to overcome polarization and splitting or, alternatively, to integrate subjective and objective perspectives on the self—to recognize her own complexities. Her description of her therapist suggested that C. had finally found someone whom she could regard, unlike her parents, as supportive, empathic, calming, and nonintrusive. To be sure, C. had not yet begun to wrestle with the negative aspects of the therapeutic relationship, but neither was she unrealistically idealizing her therapist. Thus, these higher-level representations of self and therapist at admission (D-R levels 6 and 7) suggested C.'s potential for substantial therapeutic gain. But although C.'s view of her therapist was much more benign than her understandings of her parents, it was still lacking in reflection on her therapist's mental states (RF level 1). Only with her self description did she evidence a capacity for at least questionable or low Reflective Functioning (RF level 3).

After two years of treatment, C.'s descriptions of herself and her significant figures (parents and therapist) demonstrated a consolidation of object constancy and a movement toward the formation of a stable identity and mutual interpersonal relationships (D-R levels 6 and 7). By this point in treatment, C. had been transferred to a new therapist and had been working with her for approximately a year.

Although the opening utterance of her mother description ("She's—the way she is or the way she looks?") revealed her continuing propensity for cognition dominated by polarization and splitting, C. quickly advanced to a mode of thought in which she attempted in her statements to integrate some of the apparent contradictions in her parents' personalities. Gone at this point were angry depictions of her parents as predominantly domineering and intrusive, and in place of those angry descriptions were complex appreciations of their psychological struggles. In her emphasis on her parents' toughness, C. was still concerned about their attempts to control her, but now she was able to understand such behavior as motivated by a combination of psychological vulnerabilities and helpful intentions. This ability is reflected in an increase in scores indicative of marked RF in her parent descriptions.

In her self-description at two years, C. continued to display a capacity to recognize and integrate disparate aspects of herself into a cohesive representation. Less concerned at this point than she was two years previously with the maintenance of a tough facade, even as she now began to reflect on the toughness of the significant people around her (i.e., her parents and her therapist), C. spoke candidly of the tension between her psychological strengths and her many vulnerabilities. In speaking of her shyness and her appearance, she also revealed her continuing difficulty in integrating an objective perspective on the self, that is, how she thought she appeared in the eyes of others, with a subjective sense of who she was. Her D-R score for the self description was thus consistent with the consolidation of evocative constancy, and her RF score indicated the presence of marked Reflective Functioning. In describing her therapist, C. returned to the theme of toughness, but she integrated a somewhat veiled anger that she could not manipulate her therapist with a sense of her therapist's trustworthiness and emotional availability. Most surprising, given that C. knew much more about herself and her parents than about her therapist, was that she described her therapist at a level consistent with marked RF, as reflected, for example, in an ORI inquiry statement so clearly indicative of intersubjectivity and of the capacity to understand shared meanings, "She'll tell you what she feels. When she's gotta say something, she won't put it into other words; she'll tell you how she means it."

At discharge, with a decline in her verbal productivity, most likely the result of becoming depressed as she contemplated the prospect of leaving the hospital, C. displayed a decline in Reflective Functioning, down to the level of questionable RF. On the other hand, she maintained her capacity for evocative constancy, as manifested in the stability of her D-R scores, with the only changes being a one-point decline in the Differentiation-Relatedness of her therapist description. Thus, C.'s significant-figure descriptions continued to demonstrate her consolidation of evocative constancy and her movement toward the formation of a stable identity and reciprocal interpersonal relationships, but at the same time, C. had difficulty in maintaining her ability to reflect on mental states.

In particular, C.'s mother was no longer "a bitch" but instead a frightened woman who, despite her anxiety, still tried to be nurturing. Her father was no longer "a real tyrant" but instead a depressed, angry, and hypersensitive man who, despite his psychological limitations, was capable of being reasonable with his daughter. But despite her appreciation of the complexities of her parents' conduct, an appreciation reflected in her maintaining D-R scores consistent with the consolidation of evocative constancy, C. was having renewed difficulty, in her depressed state, in thinking about the mental states underlying her parents' behavior, as indicated in declines in her RF scores for her parent descriptions nine months earlier. Nevertheless, she did not regress in her Reflective Functioning to the levels recorded at admission. Thus, her mother description was still consistent with questionable RF, and her father description was consistent with ordinary RF.

In her self-description C. elaborated the many contradictions she felt about herself—for example, hypersensitivity versus aloofness, goofiness versus coldness—and demonstrated a greater integration of these various facets. In therapy, in the difficult, often shame-filled task of reconciling her subjective feelings with her objective self-perceptions, she was much less puzzled by her contradictions than she had been at admission and now regarded them as accepted parts of herself. Furthermore, she also seemed to recognize that, in her hypersensitivity, she was more like her father than she had previously known. Thus, even with her depression, she continued to display object constancy in describing herself, but in her depression, she had difficulty in thinking about mental states, as her refusal of inquiry and her decline to ordinary RF indicate. Finally, by discharge, C. had moved from regarding her therapist as a listener who provided empathic support, per C.'s admission therapist description, to viewing her as a truly caring figure. C.'s acknowledgment of her therapist's intelligence and patience, while perhaps indicative of her (C.'s) continuing propensity for self-criticism, meanwhile suggested that she (C.) was expressing gratitude for her therapist's help in her emotional struggles over the past two and a half years. Interestingly, although C.'s D-R score indicated her continuing ability to maintain a complex representation of her therapist, her RF score declined to absent Reflective Functioning, as if C., in her sadness over losing her therapist, were now too distressed to think about her therapist's mental states.

Thus, at discharge, C.'s representations had reached the more mature levels of the Differentiation-Relatedness Scale, in which there is a constancy of representation of self and others. She had achieved the realization that significant loving relationships can survive anger and conflict at a level of evocative (object) constancy. Additionally, her Reflective Functioning scores after two years of treatment indicated that she had begun to develop an ability to think about mental states, both her own and those of significant figures. On the other hand, the reduced verbal productivity in C.'s discharge descriptions and her decline at this point to the level of low or questionable RF suggest, in our view, that the emotional pressures of termination—most likely the depressive feelings and apprehensions associated with the loss of her therapist and the hospital—produced a degree of regression (we hope temporary) in this patient's ability to maintain complex, nuanced representations of the mental states of self and significant others. Thus, clinical observations of increased depression in this young woman at the time of discharge, associated with earlier depressive issues of loss and of guilt over aggression, paralleled the reduced verbal productivity with which she articulated increasingly sophisticated descriptions of significant figures. Her decline to absent RF in describing her therapist suggests that C. found the loss of her therapist and of the hospital especially painful. Despite her depression, however, C. was still capable of remaining at the level of evocative constancy (D-R levels 6 and 7) and did not return to a reliance on polarization and splitting (D-R levels 4 and 5).

DISCUSSION

Intersubjectivity is an increasingly prominent concept within psychoanalysis, and with the emergence of this concept has come the development of two complementary object-relations rating scales that are influenced by it: the Reflective Functioning Scale of Fonagy and associates and the Differentiation-Relatedness Scale of Diamond, Blatt, and their associates. These scales facilitate the development of psychoanalytic research by providing methods for assessing systematically an individual's capacity to represent the intersubjective world. A comparison of the two measures indicates that both of them are indeed inspired by the notion that the presence of others is required for the creation of the self, a notion that is the conceptual core of intersubjectivity theory. Nevertheless, there are clear differences between these two scales with regard to the aspects of intersubjectivity that they are measuring. One particularly important difference is that the RF Scale focuses on the cognitive aspects of intersubjectivity—that is, the ability to understand mental states, an ability that Fonagy and colleagues have termed *mentalization*—and the D-R Scale focuses on intersubjectivity's affective and relational aspects. That is, most of the points of the D-R scale pertain to how a person represents interpersonal relationships and his or her role in them. This is true even at the low end of the scale, where the main concept measured is the disruption of self–other boundaries. On the other hand, the D-R Scale lacks the sophistication and specificity in describing mental states that is the greatest strength of the RF measure.

A second important difference between the two measures is that the RF Scale focuses primarily on levels of evocative constancy, whereas the D-R Scale also assesses both more primitive levels of functioning, such as the disruption of self–other boundaries, and more advanced levels, in which a person comes to understand that his or her selfhood is defined by interactions with another. In other words, the RF Scale and the concept of reflective functioning generally have greatly advanced our understanding of evocative constancy. Evocative constancy is not just the ability to represent positive aspects of another in the other's absence or even to maintain an integrated view of a significant other when the relationship with that person is stressed; it is also the ability to think about the mental states underlying a significant other's behavior and to maintain a coherent, integrated view of them. Thus, as C.'s discharge descriptions indicate, it is possible to have D-R scores indicative of the consolidation of object constancy while at the same time manifesting a regression, on the RF Scale, in one's understanding of significant figures' mental states. The paradox of C.'s having high D-R scores and low RF scores at discharge is resolved if we understand that, per classical notions of object constancy, C. can maintain positive understandings of her relationships with significant figures, even if these persons are not always gratifying, but that C. has trouble coping with a more advanced aspect of object constancy, the constancy of another's mental states, while she is undergoing a clinical depression produced by significant losses. The discrepancy between C.'s RF and D-R scores at discharge highlights an aspect of evocative constancy that is particularly important in intersubjectivity theory—constancy in one's understanding of how the other views one.

In contrast, the D-R Scale, because its lowest points pertain to disturbances in self–other boundaries, makes possible the measurement of psychotic disturbances in intersubjectivity. This feature of the D-R Scale was not particularly important in the case presented here, but it would be important if we were assessing capacity for intersubjectivity in a schizophrenic patient, for whom the prospect of acknowledging others' minds is often terrifying (see Auerbach and Blatt 1996, 1997). The D-R Scale also makes it possible to assess higher levels of functioning, in which a person understands not just the complexity of the other's mental states, as measured by the higher levels of the RF Scale, but also the ways in which the person's own selfhood is constituted by relationships with others. Again, these higher levels of the D-R Scale were not relevant in the case of C. but might prove useful in the assessment of healthier patients and of normal individuals.

THERAPEUTIC ASPECTS OF INTERSUBJECTIVITY

All human interaction is intersubjective—in Aron's (1996) phrase, a meeting of minds—and it is by virtue of this intersubjectivity that psychoanalytic treatment has a therapeutic effect. That is, patients come to treatment with inadequate or problematic understandings of their own minds, as well as of the minds of significant others, understandings that they then use in trying to comprehend their actions and those of a new object, the therapist or analyst. Meanwhile, analysts, by recognizing aspects of their patients' independent subjectivity that were insufficiently or inadequately acknowledged in childhood, make it possible for individuals to heal from childhood wounds and to construct new understandings, not only of the analyst's mind but also of their own minds and the minds of significant others. These new understandings in turn permit patients to establish more satisfactory relationships in their lives. In other words, psychoanalysis involves a movement back and forth between how the analyst understands the mind of the patient, along with his or her own mind in relation to the patient, and how the patient understands his or her own mind and the mind of the analyst. In this respect, it is like all other human relationships. But analysis differs from all of those other human relationships insofar as the analyst, by recognizing the mind of the patient in a new way, enables the patient to recognize the mind of the analyst, and eventually those of persons other than the analyst, in new ways as well. It is through these new understandings of the minds of others that patients arrive at new understandings of their own minds too.

This process of mutual recognition takes place through the transference–countertransference matrix, a matrix that all psychoanalytic schools regard as central to the analytic process. It is through the transference–countertransference matrix that pathological modes of relating (i.e., the master–slave relationship, if we may return to Hegel's terminology) are evoked, enacted, and worked through, and indeed the transference–countertransference relationship can sometimes feel as if it is the kind of life-and-death struggle described by Hegel (1807) in his account of the dialectic between lord and bondsman. What makes it possible for pathological modes of relating to be transcended is that the analyst, presumably not needing to engage in relationships of domination with the patient, can create a potential space, to use Winnicott's (1971) phrase, in which the patient can play with the analyst's subjectivity—that is, with the analyst's mind—and can come to discover that the analyst sees him or her in new ways, in ways that both recognize and transcend conflict and regressive potential. It is in this spirit that we here briefly discuss *adaptive projective identification*, a phenomenon that we discovered in our research on patients' descriptions of self and significant figures (e.g., Auerbach and Blatt 2001, Blatt et al. 1996) and that we believe is a way in which patients play with—in a word, construct—the minds of their therapists.

Whereas classical conceptualizations of transference usually regard it as a displacement or projection of conflictual aspects of a patient's psyche onto the therapist or analyst, we have found patients also often identify in their therapists not only conflictual but also positive or adaptive aspects of themselves, aspects of themselves that they do not yet feel they can claim as their own. Attributing these positive aspects of themselves to their therapists, patients can then reappropriate these adaptive capacities by identifying with them. We believe that this phenomenon, *adaptive projective identification*, is most likely to occur in patients who have been traumatized or narcissistically injured and who therefore have learned to be frightened of their strengths, although it is certainly possible that higher functioning patients may exhibit such behavior as well.

In the case of C., this phenomenon manifests itself in her use of the dimension *toughness versus vulnerability* to describe not only herself but also, at various times, her parents and, especially, her therapist. Although she does not actually use the word "toughness" in describing her therapist, this quality is clearly the main theme of her two-year therapist description, and it is a quality that C. had attributed to herself, albeit in a poorly integrated way, in her self-description at admission. In her therapist description at two years, C. is using her therapist as an identificatory object so that she herself can find a way to be both tough and vulnerable at the same time. She unconsciously uses the therapist as a figure onto which to project positive aspects of herself so that she can then reappropriate these positive aspects of herself in a developmentally more advanced and integrated way.

ADAPTIVE PROJECTIVE IDENTIFICATION AND INTERSUBJECTIVITY

It is important, finally, to consider adaptive projective identification in terms of its theoretical relationship to intersubjectivity. As we have recently discussed (Auerbach and Blatt 2001), adaptive projective identification enables one to become more fully oneself by virtue of involvement in a relationship with a benevolent and caring other. It is this relationship that enables the patient to find in the other that which he or she wishes but is afraid to make more fully his own. The presence of a caring, benevolent other—for example, a therapist but also, in more normal developmental circumstances, a parent, a teacher, or a friend—is essential for this process to occur. Furthermore, it is likely that the aspects of the self that become involved in adaptive projective identification are themselves initially formed through the early relational matrix—that is, through the early identifications one makes with parental figures—and are therefore also intersubjective, once again in the sense of requiring an other if they are to be constituted at all. Alternatively, in human development, self-definition and relatedness are dialectically interconnected through the interplay of gratifying involvement and experienced incompatibility (Behrends and Blatt 1985, Blatt and Behrends 1987, Blatt and Blass 1990, 1996).

Thus, C. was able to use her therapists' relatively benign, caring, and nonintrusive presence to work out her own concerns with toughness and vulnerability and to make both of these aspects of herself more fully her own. It is likely that C. acquired this particular set of concerns as a means of coping with parents who (her father especially) were highly intrusive in order to cover over their own vulnerabilities. Thus, C. would have acquired her concern with toughness and vulnerability partly in reaction to her parents but also partly in identification with them. When her therapists made themselves available to her in a caring, nonintrusive way, C. was then able to use adaptive projective identification to begin to consolidate an identity in which she could be both vulnerable and tough and not regard these alternative modes of being as contradictory. This clinical movement is seen in her increased reflective functioning and differentiation-relatedness from admission to discharge, even when these functions were influenced by her depression at discharge. The changes in these functions over the course of treatment support the basic contention of intersubjectivity theory, perhaps stated best by Martin Buber (1923, p. 80): "Man becomes an I through a Thou" [translation altered].

REFERENCES

Adler, G. (1985). *Borderline Psychopathology and Its Treatment*. New York: Jason Aronson.

Ainsworth, M. D. S., Blehar, M. E., Waters, E., and Wall, S. (1978). *Patterns of Attachment: A Psychological Study of the Strange Situation*. Hillsdale, NJ: Lawrence Erlbaum.

American Psychiatric Association. (1980). *Diagnostic and Statistical Manual of Mental Disorders*, 3rd ed. Washington, DC: Author.

——— (1994). *Diagnostic and Statistical Manual of Mental Disorders*, 4th ed. Washington, DC: Author.

Amsterdam, B. K., and Levitt, M. (1980). Consciousness of self and painful self-consciousness. *Psychoanalytic Study of the Child* 35:67–84. New Haven, CT: Yale University Press.

Aron, L. (1996). *A Meeting of Minds: Mutuality in Psychoanalysis*. Hillsdale, NJ: Analytic Press.

——— (1998). The clinical body and the reflexive mind. In *Relational Perspectives on the Body*, ed. L. Aron and F. S. Anderson, pp. 3–37. Hillsdale, NJ: Analytic Press.

Astington, J. W. (1993). *The Child's Discovery of the Mind*. Cambridge, MA: Harvard University Press.

Astington, J. W., Harris, P. L., and Olson, D. R., eds. (1988). *Developing Theories of Mind*. Cambridge, England: Cambridge University Press.

Auerbach, J. S. (1993). The origins of narcissism and narcissistic personality disorder: a theoretical and empirical reformulation. In *Empirical Stud-*

ies of Psychoanalytic Theories: Vol. 4. Psychoanalytic Perspectives on Psychopathology, ed. J. M. Masling and R. F. Bornstein, pp. 43–110. Washington, DC: American Psychological Association.

Auerbach, J. S., and Blatt, S. J. (1996). Self-representation in severe psychopathology: the role of reflexive self-awareness. *Psychoanalytic Psychology* 13:297–341.

——— (1997). Impairment of self-representation in schizophrenia: the roles of boundary articulation and self-reflexivity. *Bulletin of the Menninger Clinic* 61:297–316.

——— (2001). Self-reflexivity, intersubjectivity, and therapeutic change. *Psychoanalytic Psychology* 18:427–450.

Bach, S. (1985). *Narcissistic States and the Therapeutic Process*. New York: Jason Aronson.

——— (1994). *The Language of Perversion and the Language of Love*. Northvale, NJ: Jason Aronson.

Baldwin, J. M. (1906). *Mental Development in the Child and the Race: Methods and Processes*, 3rd ed. rev. New York: Kelley, 1968.

Balint, M. (1968). *The Basic Fault: Therapeutic Aspects of Regression*. New York: Brunner/Mazel, 1979.

Beebe, B., Lachmann, F., and Jaffe, J. (1997). Mother–infant interaction structures and presymbolic self- and object representations. *Psychoanalytic Dialogues* 7:133–182.

Behrends, R. S., and Blatt, S. J. (1985). Internalization and psychological development throughout the life cycle. *Psychoanalytic Study of the Child* 40:11–39. New Haven, CT: Yale Unviersity Press.

Benjamin, J. (1995). *Like Subjects, Love Objects: Essays on Recognition and Sexual Difference*. New Haven, CT: Yale University Press.

Blatt, S. J. (1974). Levels of object representation in anaclitic and introjective depression. *Psychoanalytic Study of the Child* 29:107–157. New Haven, CT: Yale University Press.

——— (1995). Representational structures in psychopathology. In *Rochester Symposium on Developmental Psychopathology, Vol. 6: Emotion, Cognition, and Representation*, ed. D. Cicchetti and S. Toth, pp. 1–33. Rochester, NY: University of Rochester Press.

——— (1999). Object relations perspective on developments in the history of art. *Psychoanalysis and Contemporary Thought* 22:665–686.

Blatt, S. J., and Auerbach, J. S. (1988). Differential cognitive disturbances in three types of "borderline" patients. *Journal of Personality Disorders* 2:198–211.

——— (2001). Mental representation, severe psychopathology, and the therapeutic process. *Journal of the American Psychoanalytic Association* 49:113–159.

Blatt, S. J., Auerbach, J. S., and Aryan, M. (1998). Representational structures and the therapeutic process. In *Empirical Studies of Psychoanalytic Theories: Vol. 8: Empirical Studies of the Therapeutic Hour,* ed. R. F. Bornstein and J. M. Masling, pp. 63–107. Washington, DC: American Psychological Association.

Blatt, S. J., and Behrends, R. S. (1987). Internalization, separation-individuation, and the nature of therapeutic action. *International Journal of Psycho-Analysis* 68:279–297.

Blatt, S. J., and Bers, S. A. (1993). The sense of self in depression: a psychodynamic perspective. In *Self Representation and Emotional Disorders: Cognitive and Psychodynamic Perspectives*, ed. Z. V. Segal and S. J. Blatt, pp. 171–210. New York: Guilford.

Blatt, S. J., and Blass, R. B. (1990). Attachment and separateness: a dialectic model of the products and processes of psychological development. *Psychoanalytic Study of the Child* 45:107–127. New Haven, CT: Yale University Press.

——— (1996). Relatedness and self definition: a dialectic model of personality development. In *Development and Vulnerabilities in Close Relationships,* ed. G. G. Noam and K. W. Fischer, pp. 309–338. Hillsdale, NJ: Lawrence Erlbaum.

Blatt, S. J., Chevron, E. S., Quinlan, D. M. et al. (1988). *The assessment of qualitative and structural dimensions of object representations,* revised edition. Unpublished research manual, Department of Psychiatry, Yale University.

Blatt, S. J., Chevron, E. S., Quinlan, D. M., and Wein, S. (1981). *The assessment of qualitative and structural dimensions of object representations*. Unpublished research manual, Department of Psychiatry, Yale University.

Blatt, S. J., and Lerner, H. D. (1983). Investigations in the psychoanalytic theory of object relations and object representations. In *Empirical Studies of Psychoanalytic Theories,* Vol 1., ed. J. Masling, pp. 189–249. Hillsdale, NJ: Analytic Press.

Blatt, S. J., and Shichman, S. (1983). Two primary configurations of psychopathology. *Psychoanalysis and Contemporary Thought* 6:187–254.

Blatt, S. J., Stayner, D., Auerbach, J., and Behrends, R. S. (1996). Change in object and self representations in long-term, intensive, inpatient treatment of seriously disturbed adolescents and young adults. *Psychiatry* 59:82–107.

Blatt, S. J., Wein, S. J., Chevron, E. S., and Quinlan, D. M. (1979). Parental representations and depression in normal young adults. *Journal of Abnormal Psychology* 88:388–397.

Bretherton, I. (1989). Pretense: the form and function of make-believe play. *Developmental Review* 9:383–401.

Broucek, F. J. (1991). *Shame and the Self*. New York: Guilford.

Buber, M. (1923). *I and Thou*, 3rd ed., trans. W. Kaufmann. New York: Scribner's, 1970.

Cavell, M. (1993). *The Psychoanalytic Mind: From Freud to Philosophy*. Cambridge, MA: Harvard University Press.

Cooley, C. H. (1922). *Human Nature and the Social Order*, revised ed. New York: Schocken, 1964.

Damon, W., and Hart, D. (1988). *Self-Understanding in Childhood and Adolescence*. Cambridge, England: Cambridge University Press.

Descartes, R. (1637). Discourse on the method of properly conducting one's reason and of seeking the truth in the sciences. In *Discourse on Method and the Meditations*, trans. F. E. Sutcliffe, pp. 25–91. New York: Penguin, 1968.

——— (1641). Meditations on the first philosophy in which the existence of God and the real distinction between the soul and the body of man are demonstrated. In *Discourse on Method and the Meditations*, trans. F. E. Sutcliffe, pp. 93–169. New York: Penguin, 1968.

Diamond, D., Blatt, S. J., Stayner, D., and Kaslow, N. (1991). *Self–other differentiation of object representations*. Unpublished research manual, Department of Psychiatry, Yale University.

Diamond, D., Kaslow, N., Coonerty, S., and Blatt, S. J. (1990). Change in separation-individuation and intersubjectivity in long-term treatment. *Psychoanalytic Psychology* 7:363–397.

Duval, S., and Wicklund, R. A. (1972). *A Theory of Objective Self-Awareness*. New York: Academic Press.

Endicott, J., Spitzer, R. L., Fleiss, J. L., and Cohen, J. (1976). The Global Assessment Scale: a procedure for measuring overall severity of psychiatric disturbance. *Archives of General Psychiatry* 33:766–771.

Fairbairn, W. R. D. (1952). *Psychoanalytic Studies of the Personality*. London: Routledge & Kegan Paul.

Fast, I. (1998). *Selving: A Relational Theory of Self Organization*. Hillsdale, NJ: Analytic Press.

Flavell, J. H., Green, F. L., and Flavell, E. R. (1986). Development of knowledge about the appearance–reality distinction. *Monographs of the Society for Research in Child Development* 51(1, Serial No. 212).

Fonagy, P. (1996). The significance of the development of metacognitive control over mental representations in parenting and infant development. *Journal of Clinical Psychoanalysis* 5:67–86.

Fonagy, P., Leigh, T., Steele, M., et al. (1996). The relation of attachment status, psychiatric classification, and response to psychotherapy. *Journal of Abnormal Psychology* 64:22–31.

Fonagy, P., Redfern, S., and Charman, T. (1997). The relationship between belief-desire reasoning and a projective measure of attachment security (SAT). *British Journal of Developmental Psychology* 15:51–61.

Fonagy, P., Steele, M., Steele, H., et al. (1991). The capacity for understanding mental states: the reflective self in parent and child and its significance for security of attachment. *Infant Mental Health Journal* 12:201–218.

——— (1994). The Emmanuel Miller Memorial Lecture 1992: the theory and practice of resilience. *Journal of Child Psychiatry and Psychology* 35:231–257.

——— (1995). Attachment, the reflective self, and borderline states: the predictive specificity of the Adult Attachment Interview and pathological emotional development. In *Attachment Theory: Social, Developmental, and Clinical Perspectives,* ed. S. Goldberg, R. Muir, and J. Kerr, pp. 233–278. Hillsdale, NJ: Analytic Press.

Fonagy, P., and Target, M. (1996). Playing with reality: 1. Theory of mind and the normal development of psychic reality. *International Journal of Psycho-Analysis* 77:217–233.

Fonagy, P., Target, M., Steele, H., and Steele, M. (1998). *Reflective-functioning manual, version 5, for application to Adult Attachment Interviews.* Unpublished research manual, Sub-Department of Clinical Health Psychology, University College, London.

Fraiberg, S. (1969). Libidinal object constancy and mental representation. *Psychoanalytic Study of the Child* 24:9–47. New York: International Universities Press.

Freud, S. (1914). On narcissism: an introduction. *Standard Edition* 14:73–102.

——— (1923). The ego and the id. *Standard Edition* 19:12–66.

Gallup, G. G. (1977). Self-recognition in primates: a comparative approach to the bi-directional properties of primates. *American Psychologist* 32:329–338.

George, C., Kaplan, N., and Main, M. (1985). *The Berkely Adult Attachment Interview.* Unpublished manuscript, Department of Psychology, University of California, Berkeley.

Gergely, G., and Watson, J. S. (1996). The social biofeedback theory of parental affect-mirroring: the development of emotional self-awareness and self-control in infancy. *International Journal of Psycho-Analysis* 77:1181–1212.

Harris, P., and Kavanaugh, R. D. (1993). Young children's understanding of pretense. *Monographs of the Society for Research in Child Development* 58(1, Serial No. 231).

Harter, S. (1999). *The Construction of the Self: A Developmental Perspective.* New York: Guilford.

Hartmann, H. (1939). *Ego Psychology and the Problem of Adaptation,* trans. D. Rapaport. New York: International Universities Press, 1958.

——— (1950). Comments on the psychoanalytic theory of the ego. *Psychoanalytic Study of the Child* 5:74–96. New York: International Universities Press.

Hegel, G. W. F. (1807). *Hegel's Phenomenology of Spirit,* ed. J. N. Findlay, trans. A. V. Miller. Oxford, England: Oxford University Press, 1977.

James, W. (1890). *Principles of Psychology. Vol. 1.* New York: American Library, 1958.

Kagan, J. (1981). *The Second Year: The Emergence of Self-Awareness.* Cambridge, MA: Harvard University Press.

Kernberg, O. (1982). Self, ego, affects, and drives. *Journal of the American Psychoanalytic Association* 30:893–917.

Kirshner, L. A. (1991). The concept of self in psychoanalytic theory and its philosophical foundations. *Journal of the American Psychoanalytic Association* 39:157–182.

Kohut, H. (1977). *The Restoration of the Self.* New York: International Universities Press.

Lacan, J. (1953). Some reflections on the ego. *International Journal of Psycho-Analysis* 34:11–17.

——— (1977). *Ecrits: A Selection,* trans. A. Sheridan New York: Norton.

Laplanche, J. (1970). *Life and Death in Psychoanalysis,* trans J. Mehlman. Baltimore, MD: Johns Hopkins University Press, 1976.

Laplanche, J., and Pontalis, J. B. (1967). *The Language of Psycho-Analysis,* trans. D. Nicholson-Smith. New York: Norton, 1973.

Leslie, A. M. (1987). Pretense and representation: the origins of "theory of mind." *Psychological Review* 94:412–426.

Lewis, M., and Brooks-Gunn, J. (1979). *Social Cognition and the Acquistion of Self.* New York: Plenum.

Lichtenstein, H. (1977). *The Dilemma of Human Identity*. New York: Jason Aronson.

Luborsky, L. (1962). Clinicians' judgments of mental health. *Archives of General Psychiatry* 7:407–417.

Luborsky, L., and Bachrach, H. (1974). Factors influencing clinicians' judgments of mental health: eighteen experiences with the Health-Sickness Rating Scale. *Archives of General Psychiatry* 31:292–299.

Mahler, M. S., Pine, F., and Bergman, A. (1975). *The Psychological Birth of the Human Infant*. New York: Basic Books.

Main, M. (1991). Metacognitive knowledge, metacognitive monitoring, and singular (coherent) vs. multiple (incoherent) models of attachment: findings and directions for future research. In *Attachment Across the Life Cycle*, ed. C. Parkes, J. Stevenson-Hinde, and P. Marris, pp. 127–195. London: Routledge & Kegan Paul.

Mann, D. W. (1991). Some philosophical directions towards a simple theory of the self. *Theoretical Medicine* 12:53–68.

Marcuse, H. (1941). *Reason and Revolution: Hegel and the Rise of Social Theory*. New York: Oxford University Press.

——— (1955). *Eros and Civilization: A Philosophical Inquiry into Freud*. Boston: Beacon, 1966.

Masterson, J. F. (1981). *The Narcissistic and Borderline Disorders: An Integrated Developmental Approach*. New York: Brunner/Mazel.

Mayes, L. C., and Cohen, D. J. (1996). Children's developing theory of mind. *Journal of the American Psychoanalytic Association* 44:117–142.

Mead, G. H. (1934). *Mind, Self, and Society: From the Standpoint of a Social Behaviorist*, ed. C. W. Morris. Chicago: University of Chicago Press, 1962.

Meares, R. (1993). *The Metaphor of Play: Disruption and Restoration in the Borderline Experience*. Northvale, NJ: Jason Aronson.

Meins, E., and Russell, J. (1997). Security and symbolic play: the relation between security of attachment and executive capacity. *British Journal of Developmental Psychology* 15:63–76.

Merleau-Ponty, M. (1960). The child's relations with others, trans. W. Cobb. In *The Primacy of Perception*, ed. J. M Edie, pp. 96–155. Evanston, IL: Northwestern University Press, 1964.

Mitchell, S. A. (1988). *Relational Concepts in Psychoanalysis: An Integration*. Cambridge, MA: Harvard University Press.

Modell, A. H. (1993). *The Private Self*. Cambridge, MA: Harvard University Press.

Ogden, T. (1994). *Subjects of Analysis*. Northvale, NJ: Jason Aronson.

Orange, D. M., Atwood, G. E., and Stolorow, R. D. (1999). *Working Intersubjectively: Contextualism in Psychoanalytic Practice*. Hillsdale, NJ: Analytic Press.

Perner, J. (1991). *Understanding the Representational Mind*. Cambridge, MA: M.I.T. Press.

Perner, J., Leekam, S. R., and Wimmer, H. (1987). Three-year-olds' difficulty with false belief: the case for a conceptual deficit. *British Journal of Developmental Psychology* 5:125–137.

Piaget, J. (1924). *Judgment and Reasoning in the Child*, trans. M. Warden. New York: Humanities Press, 1952.

——— (1926). *The Child's Conception of the World*, trans. J. Tomlinson and A. Tomlinson. Totowa, NJ: Littlefield Adams, 1960.

——— (1937). *The Construction of Reality in the Child*, trans. M. Cook. New York: Basic Books, 1954.

——— (1945). *Play, Dreams and Imitation in Childhood*, trans. C. Gattegno and F. M. Hodgson. New York: Norton, 1962.

Povinelli, D. J. (1993). Reconstructing the evolution of mind. *American Psychologist* 48: 493–509.

Povinelli, D. J., and Prince, C. G. (1998). When self met other. In *Self-Awareness: Its Nature and Development*, ed. M. Ferrari and R. J. Sternberg, pp. 37–107. New York: Guilford.

Reiss, D., and Marino, L. (2002). Mirror self-recognition in the bottlenose dolphin: a case of cognitive convergence. *Proceedings of the National Academy of Sciences* 98:5937–5942.

Rinsley, D. B. (1982). *Borderline and Other Self Disorders: A Developmental and Object-Relations Perspective*. New York: Jason Aronson.

——— (1989). *Developmental Pathogenesis and Treatment of Borderline and Narcissistic Personalities*. Northvale, NJ: Jason Aronson.

Schafer, R. (1968). *Aspects of Internalization*. New York: International Universities Press.

Slade, A. (1987). The quality of attachment and early symbolic play. *Developmental Psychology* 23:78–85.

Stern, D. N. (1985). *The Interpersonal World of the Infant: A View from Psychoanalysis and Developmental Psychology*. New York: Basic Books.

Sullivan, H. S. (1940). *Conceptions of Modern Psychiatry*. New York: Norton.

——— (1953). *The Interpersonal Theory of Psychiatry*, ed. H. S. Perry and M. L. Gawel. New York: Norton.

Target, M., and Fonagy, P. (1996). Playing with reality: 2. The development of psychic reality from a theoretical perspective. *International Journal of Psycho-Analysis* 77:459–479.

Tronick, E. (1989). Emotions and emotional communication. *American Psychologist* 44:112–119.

van IJzendoorn, M. H. (1995). Adult attachment representations, parental responsiveness, and infant attachment: a meta-analysis on the predictive validity of the Adult Attachment Interview. *Psychological Bulletin*, 117:387–403.

Wellman, H. M. (1990). *The Child's Theory of Mind.* Cambridge, MA: M.I.T. Press.

Wimmer, H., and Perner, J. (1983). Beliefs about beliefs: representation and constraining function of wrong beliefs in young children's understanding of deception. *Cognition* 13:108–128.

Winnicott, D. W. (1953). Transitional objects and transitional phenomena: a study of the first not-me possession. *International Journal of Psycho-Analysis* 34:89–97.

——— (1971). *Playing and Reality*. New York: Tavistock, 1982.

4

Commonsense and Common-sense—From Ana-Alpha-Betism to Alpha-Betism

RICCARDO STEINER

"But can you prove it . . . can you prove it . . . ?" Some notes on the possible extranalytical evidence that can be used to support Klein's views concerning the depressive position and symbol formation. R. Jakobson's views concerning the importance of the first phonemic differentiation in the baby during the second half of the first year of its life.

"Oh how interesting, how interesting it is what you say and tell me a bit more, a bit more and tell me, tell me . . . what do you mean by that depressive position beginning of symbol formation . . . you know symbol formation is my main area of interest . . . but can you prove what you say, can you prove it . . . ? You know particularly today, we in America, need experimental evidence to prove what we are stating in psychoanalysis. . . . For me, M. Klein and even the post-Kleinians who are now visiting New York quite regularly, at times sound still a bit mystified in spite of their clinical seminars and their supervisions even at IPTAR. . . ."

My dear Norbert, forgive my naive verbatim of your enthusiastic verbal and physical *conversare*, as the Italians would say. I have in front of me the vivid image of you sitting at your favorite Italian trattoria, *Frascati*, in Hampstead, with a huge white napkin hanging from the neck of your shirt in front of your usual abundant portion of spaghetti with tomato sauce and something else, eating and at the same time speaking with me, constantly moving and protending yourself toward me, urged by your insatiably enthusiastic and voracious curiosity and at times your rather sharp and keen way of answering and questioning. Our discussion could go on for hours but we usually have to stop suddenly because you and your wife have to go back to your hotel or have to complete your explorations of London in between fitting in a meeting of those boring Committees of the IPA that you seem to like so much, because even there you manage to socialize, or a last-minute visit to some shops to buy something to take back to New York, or waiting for a matinée of a theater performance before flying back to New York.

Therefore, the notes that I have decided to write for your *festchrift* should be considered as an ideal intermezzo of our meetings, which have become quite regular during the course of these past fifteen years since you discovered me at a Congress on "Psychoanalysis during the Second World War" in Paris, the first International Congress organized by the International Association for the History of Psychoanalysis, founded by A. De Mijolla. It was at that Congress, after having heard my paper on what A. Freud called the "new diaspora" represented by the vicissitudes of the Central European Psychoanalysts during the Nazi persecutions, and what she called "Die Sorgen Kinder," that you invited me to read the same paper in New York under the auspices of the IPTAR of which you were sometimes President.

And "Can you prove it . . . can you prove it . . . ?" was the leitmotif that sprang to mind when I had to decide what to write about for your *festchrift*, recalling one of our latest discussions focused on Klein's (1930, 1940, 1946) and then H. Segal's (1957) views concerning the role played by the depressive position, the beginning of the so-called classical Oedipus complex that Klein, contrary to Freud, thought should be located, chronologically speaking, in the first year of the baby's life, and the repercussions all this has on the beginning of symbol formation and proper thinking. Indeed, it is in working through the persecutory and depressive feelings toward its external and internal objects, starting with the fourth and fifth months of its first year of life, that the baby is gradually able to achieve a whole object relationship. This whole object relationship is fundamental for the beginning of the classical Oedipus complex and for a more symbolic and less "concrete" way of thinking.[1]

Of course, my dear Norbert, I quite agree that to "prove all this" is not at all an easy task. It is not like what happens in front of your beloved huge portion of spaghetti and tomato sauce and whatever else! In this case one can apply the famous dictum: the proof of the pudding consists in eating it. One has only to watch the enthusiasm with which you eat to be persuaded of the reality and the correctness of the experiment, as if you had found a really good Kleinian breast, one would be tempted to say! Times have obviously changed in America. Even Klein and her followers' theories are no longer ignored or discarded today as eccentric or mad exaggerations even in your country, due to a complex series of cultural and social circumstances that have also affected the internal history of American psychoanalysis. That is also probably due to the increased importance and the formal acknowledgment from the IPA of the nonmedical pyschoanalytical societies during the last fifteen years and the IPTAR itself, which under your leadership has played a vital role in opening up America's psychoanalysis to the influence of the so-called object relations schools of which Kleinians are some of the main representatives in Great Britain and in Europe.

Furthermore, one could claim that even today some of the leading authorities in developmental psychology in your country, like D. Stern (1985, 1992a,b, 1995) for instance, seem to imply a way of considering the early months of the baby's life and of its relation to the mother that is not totally incompatible with Klein and her followers' views. By that I mean that at times it is possible to try to find

1. See Klein's (1930, 1935) and particularly Segal's (1957) notion of symbolic equations which characterize the first three to four months of the baby's life.

a sort of common ground, something that was much more difficult before. However, one has to say that Stern is perhaps a sort of special case in American developmental psychology, having been influenced by psychoanalysis himself. Nevertheless, I hope that my statements are not going to be misunderstood, because the problem is extremely complex, due to the different notions of conscious and unconscious psychic activity that exists in the baby according to Klein and her followers, who still remain deeply influenced by the structural model and the existence of the life and death drive of the late Freud and what D. Stern thinks about all this (Steiner 2000b).

Therefore, despite all those new interests in Klein and her followers' views and the possibility of further constructive developments in your country, it is understandable that even for a curious, open-minded researcher like yourself, Norbert, doubts and difficulties could still remain in accepting Klein's views. Why should it not be like that, one could incidentally ask oneself.

I do not know whether what I am trying to illustrate now is going to persuade you. Incidentally, even R. Jakobson's views concerning the first phonemic differentiations and all that follows—if one compares his discoveries with Klein's hypothesis concerning the chronology of the depressive position in the baby, which I am going to try to roughly summarize in a while in order to make my point—are not based on 100 percent empirical evidence, although the number of languages he quotes to prove his points proceeding from different continents and populations is at the very least astonishing.

What I hope to do is call to your attention the existence of some curious and significant analogies and at times close identities of observations and conclusions concerning what is happening in the mind of the baby, particularly during the second half of the first year of its life, which could provide further food for thought besides the pleasure of meeting you again to discuss all this at the *Frascati* trattoria in Hampstead or in some of your other most beloved restaurants in New York!

I have to confess that what follows is not completely new. Indeed my notes have to be traced back to my first interest in the work of Melanie Klein and the problem of symbol formation as she understood it. In 1969, I did a degree in psychology in Milan, the equivalent of a Ph.D., in which I discussed a dissertation based on Klein's theories and hypotheses, which I have just mentioned and which I later published in a book (Steiner 1975). The book, which has never been published in English, contained a long appendix entitled in Italian, *I correlati affettivi del fonema*, "The Relationship between the Phoneme and Unconscious Phantasies and Affects," where I tried to compare some of R. Jakobson's research on the genesis of the first phonemic differentiations in the baby with Klein's views concerning the depressive position and what the depressive position implies. If I am allowed a final autobiographical note, I would like to add that at the time I was also trying to counteract the fashion for Lacan in Italy and, in my opinion, Lacan's rather odd use of Jakobson and other views concerning linguistics. I was particularly trying to counteract Lacan's total lack of interest in the role played by affects in our unconscious life and in that of the baby, also due to his dismissal and belittlement of Klein and others' insistence on the importance of the preoedipal relationship between mother and baby or father, mother, and baby when mother and father are still perceived and phantasized as "partial objects."

Therefore, the following notes have never before been published in English and are also based on further data and observations that I have collected since 1975. Curiously enough, a recent study of mine on cultural sources, which I believe led Klein to establish her particular chronology of the unconscious psychic development of the baby during the first year of life (Steiner 2000c), has further stimulated me to choose this topic because, as I will try to show, the results of that study seem to me to confirm *a fortiori* the possibility and the validity of the analogies and at times similarities of the observations and conclusions of R. Jakobson and M. Klein concerning what happens in the mental life of the baby at a certain point of development. As I have already stated, I hope all this will at least stimulate further food for thought in this so fascinating and still mysterious area of research.

In order to understand what I would like to point out, one should contextualize both Klein's and Jakobson's thinking. By that I mean one should be able to show the development of their research. In the case of Klein we would start with the 1920s, and in the case of Jakobson even earlier, and relate their research to their personal events and movements from one country to another and the cultural context in which they were working and progressing in what could be considered psychoanalysis and in what could be considered not only linguistics but the human sciences in general, thinking of Jakobson's variety of interests during the first three decades of the twentieth century. Considering space restrictions and limitations, this would be obviously an impossible task. Therefore, as far as Klein is concerned, I have to refer readers to Segal's (1964) and to Grosskurth's (1986) work on Klein's life and intellectual development. As far as Jakobson is concerned, one can read one of the numerous studies written on his work, for example the excellent chapter on him written by Lepschy (1972) or the book by L. Waugh (1976) or the "Dialogue with R. Jakobson" edited by Jakobson and Pomorska (1983) or the extremely informative book written by Jakobson himself and Waugh (1987), and finally among others, the anthology edited by Waugh and Monville-Burston (1990), which contains Jakobson's most important papers, each of which is introduced and contextualized vis-à-vis his previous and later work.[2]

As far as Klein is concerned, I would like to remind you, as well as other possible readers, that everything I have already mentioned with regard to the depressive position, its chronology, and what it implies concerning the Oedipus complex and symbol formation, should be considered as one of the most important contributions made by Klein to the psychoanalytic theory of child development between the 20s and the 40s in the twentieth century, whatever one thinks about its validity.

One should also bear in mind that Klein accepted and developed in her own clinical way Freud's views concerning the life but also the

2. Incidentally, if one has just a look at the enormous bibliography of his work in this book, one realizes the gigantic and polymathic intellectual capacities of this scholar.

death drive and the fundamental role they play from the beginning of the baby's psychic life, which she believed to start if not before birth, certainly with the trauma of birth itself. For her, this trauma had a *psychological* meaning. Indeed, without reference to both drives and their role, even her views concerning the nonexistence of what Freud called primary narcissism and what she called secondary narcissism (due to her conviction of the existence of a primitive object relation since birth and her views concerning unconscious primary phantasies in the baby) would have been impossible. All this should also be contextualized, thinking of Klein's personal vicissitudes, her first analysis in Budapest with Férenczi and his influence on her, her second analysis in Berlin with Abraham, tragically interrupted by Abraham's death in the early 20s, and then from 1926, her decision to settle in England. One should also recall the interest that her views aroused in London and also the conflicts they created with the Viennese and particularly with A. Freud, conflicts that would culminate in the so-called Freud–Klein Controversies of 1941–45 in London due to the arrival of the Viennese in England because of the Nazi persecution of the Jewish analysts during the 30s and the death of Freud in London in 1939. However, what she noticed about the depressive position during the 1930s and the beginning of the 40s was not her final conclusion. After all, during the 30s, what she had called the normal phase of development, which precedes the depressive position, was the paranoid position, characterized by extreme splitting, partial object relationship, enormous libidinal idealization of mother breast and father penis, and extremely intense persecutory paranoid anxieties in the baby. It was redefined as the schizoparanoid position in 1946, when Klein started describing the schizoid fragmenting anxieties that according to her characterize even the normal development of the baby, without implying ipso facto that the baby is a psychotic, but insisting on the psychoticlike characteristics of those anxieties, even in the normal baby. Another extremely important clarification, even as far as the depressive position and symbol formations are concerned, come from her views on projective and introjective identifications, particularly through the way in which Bion, Rosenfeld, and Segal will use and further develop her views. Another important clarification comes from her latest research into the role played by primary envy (Klein 1957) in blocking the process of symbol formation and of thinking in general. Again, Bion (1967), Rosenfeld (1965), and Segal (1981) will further clarify all those issues (Steiner 1975). Yet if one looks at her work between the 1920s and 1940s, although Klein did not use the notion of projective and introjective identification, it is quite clear, particularly in "The Importance of Symbol Formation for the Development of the Ego" (1930) and the famous "A Contribution to the Psychogenesis of Manic-Depressive States" (1935), the paper in which for the first time she desribes very clearly what she meant by depressive position and when chronologically speaking, one has to assume its manifest appearance in the baby. If one links all those views and clinical observations to the paper "Love, Guilt and Reparation" (1937) and to "Mourning and Its Relationship to Manic-Depressive States" (1940), and finally to the paper Klein read during the Freud–Klein controversies in 1944 (King and Steiner 1992) entitled "The Emotional Life and the Ego Development of the Infant with Special Reference to the Depressive Position," one could clearly find in all this work the basic constitutive elements of Klein's thinking concerning the issues I am interested in and have touched upon in my notes. I have already briefly mentioned Klein's thinking on the problem of symbol formation. (Klein's paper of 1930 illustrates quite clearly the role played by the libidinal and the destructive phantasies, which according to her are related to the death drive in blocking or fostering the process of symbol formation.) This process is also extremely conditioned by the quality of the anxieties (more or less persecutive) of the baby and its projections and introjections. Particularly important is Klein's description of the sticking and blocking role played by primitive destructive phantasies, projections, and introjections in the baby, mixed with persecutive anxieties. This mixture does not allow the baby, and in this particular case, even the child Klein was treating, to play, to think properly, to move, to shift from one object to another, and to symbolize (Klein 1930). The child felt incapsulated in a deadly, rigid relationship or with his primary partial objects or their substitutes, which became enormously charged with violence and persecutory anxieties. Klein brought all this back, through her interpretations, to the earliest relationship the child had had as a baby with its mother's breasts or the content of her body and with his father's penis as phantasized by the baby. Using her own play technique and verbalizing the primitive unconscious phantasies and anxieties of the child, Klein managed to help it start playing and thinking again. It was in this paper that Klein called symbolic equations the nonsymbolized objects that the child confused with his original maternal and paternal partial objects: breast, penis, and so on.

Starting with her paper of 1935, in describing the role and the importance of the depressive position, Klein was then able to better clarify the role played by the libidinal and reparative phantasies of the baby toward its primary objects (mother and father), felt now as *whole objects*, even as far as the process of symbol formation was concerned. Indeed, this process started to be linked to the beginning of the so-called classic Oedipus complex, which, according to Klein, gradually starts prevailing during the second part of the first year of the life of the baby and substitutes for the primitive and more confusing oedipal constellation, represented by the combined figure of the parents as partial objects, which Klein postulated as characterizing the original paranoid position of the baby. This primitive version of the Oedipus complex still belongs to the realm of the symbolic equations that, one should not forget, are even part of the normal phase of development of the psychic apparatus of the baby to a certain point, if not too rigid and pervasive. The paper Klein read during the Freud–Klein controversies in 1944 did not add anything new to her theories and clinical observations but was an extremely rich and clear *mise au point* and description of the capacity that the baby acquires, particularly during the second half of his first year of life, to tolerate separation without becoming overpowered by persecutory anxieties and therefore, as in the paranoid position, attacking and trying at times to destroy in phantasy but even through actual biting its frustrating objects. This allows the baby to achieve a more symbolic, less "concrete" relationship with its external and internal objects, gradually displacing, in a symbolic way, its libidinal and destructive or aggressive impulses and phantasies. Incidentally, from the original to other objects, Klein was very careful in differentiating between aggression and destructive aggression.

If that, given the limits of my paper, is a rough attempt to condense and partially contextualize Klein's views on the depressive position and symbol formation during the first twenty years of her work, there is something else that should be added to all this. As I have already said, many years ago, when I first thought of a possible parallelism between Klein's and Jakobson's views on what occurs in the baby's mind, particularly during the second half of its first year of life, I did not know about the existence of the data that I am now going to illustrate. They seem to explain better the reasons of this possible parallelism and to prove *a fortiori* its validity and what one can further make of all this.

Klein was not a systematic thinker and very often she had been rightly or wrongly criticized for being too speculative and even ignorant of what was going on outside psychoanalysis as she understood it. Yet the research on the cultural background and the sources that could help to understand why Klein came to some of her conclusions, which I have recently published (Steiner 2000b,c), seems to show that even Klein was a daughter of her own age, to paraphrase a statement made by Freud to Fliess in a letter dated November 5, 1897, when he came across and read the work of the American psychologist J. M. Baldwin, "Mental Development in the Child and in the Race" in 1895 (Masson 1985). Indeed Klein was able to link her enormously powerful intuitive gifts to a tradition of empirically based research on the behavior of the baby from the last decades of the nineteenth century onward, a behavior that Darwin, Preyer, the Scupins, the Sterns, particularly W. Stern, and many others had started to describe, although in a nonsystematic and "nonscientific" way. Besides what had filtered through Freud's work from all those researches, Klein was able to know about them indirectly from Hugh Hellmuth's work (Steiner 2000c) and particularly, at that time, Bernfeld's classic book, which was originally published in German in 1925, *The Psychology of the Infant* (1929), a book she, S. Isaacs, and P. Heimann quoted with great respect also during the Freud–Klein Controversies. Bernfeld has reinterpreted all this nonanalytical literature, from a psychoanalytic viewpoint, insisting on the meaning of the changes one could observe in the baby during the first, third, fourth, fifth, and seventh month, and so on of the first year of life, giving as I have said, a psychoanalytic interpretation to the data and the observations of the scholars I have just quoted, as well as of others.

As I have tried to demonstrate, (Steiner 2000c), there is no doubt that Klein was supported by Bernfeld's observations in trying to fix a specific month for the beginning of the depressive position. Furthermore, Klein had constant discussions with her co-worker, the great educationalist S. Isaacs during the thirties, who could inform Klein about all the extranalytical literature available on the baby during that period. Just think of the extremely detailed study done by the American Shirley or the work of the Bühlers in Vienna, all discussed and critically evaluated by Isaacs, together with the work of Piaget (Steiner 2000c). All was reinterpreted according to the notion of unconscious primary phantasies elaborated by Klein. To this one should also add the research done by some British scholars, in particular the extremely interesting book by Lewis (1936), *Infant Speech*. All this evidence is indicative of Klein's hypothesis, supported by the scholarly work of S. Isaacs, and not only the result of her speculations. Although at times Klein could sound dogmatic and very single-minded, she was perfectly aware of the inferred and inevitably hypothetical nature of some of her observations. One has just to read what she stated during the Freud–Klein Controversies to be persuaded of that (Steiner 2000c). Nevertheless, the Freud–Klein Controversies were also the occasion whereby Klein and Isaacs had to focus on a detailed description of the baby's development and behavior during the first year of life and were compelled to demonstrate all that they knew about the extranalytical literature, in order to counteract the accusations and the criticisms coming from the Viennese and, in particular, from A. Freud and her British ally, E. Glover. They were all claiming that besides being a severe misinterpretation of Freud's views, Klein's claims concerning the earliest psychic unconscious and conscious development of the baby were unscientific and unsupported by proper empirical evidence.

With hindsight, one could say that both Isaacs and Klein could have made, had they known it, very good use of another very interesting and quite significant extranalytical source of possible evidence that their views on the intellectual implications of the depressive position were not a pure product of their eccentric minds. By intellectual implications, I mean the capacity that the baby is gradually showing, during the second half of the first year of its life, of relating more realistically toward the external world but also as far as its internal world is concerned and of starting to use some sort of more symbolic way of communicating.

It is on this source that I now want to focus Norbert's and the reader's attention. Indeed, exactly during those years, the late 30s, R. Jakobson became more and more interested in finding better evidence to clarify what was one of the main sources of his theoretical but also empirical interests and researches: the phoneme, its nature, its origins, its history, its function in possibly all the languages of the world (Jakobson and Pomorska 1983, Monville-Burston 1990, Waugh 1976). Jakobson had already had behind him an extraordinarily rich career as a linguist, literary critic, and theoretician, having been part of the formalist Russian school and the Prague Circle of linguists and having started to influence not only linguistics as such but the field of human sciences in general.

While in the process of emigrating to the United States during the late 1930s due to the Nazi persecution, becoming part of that cultural and sociopolitical diaspora that changed the cultural status of Central Europe, depriving it of some of its best scholars, artists, thinkers, scientists, and so on, while at the same time enriching the countries they ended up immigrating to, Jakobson spent a period in Sweden. The collection of notes and thoughts elaborated during the previous years led to Jakobson's decision to study the genetic aspects of the phoneme and, at the same time, what could be called its pathological outcomes and characteristics, which can be observed studying various types of aphasia. What Jakobson noticed and recorded in his book published in Germany in 1941 and entitled in the English translation that appeared in 1968, *Child Language, Aphasia and Phonological Universals*, was that, for instance, there was a strict parallelism between the kind of first phonemes and phonemic differentiations that the baby is able to produce and the way it is able to produce them at a certain time during its development, and the regressive destruction of the phonemic differentiations one can observe in various aphasic disturbances. The person who suffers from aphasia can regress to a kind of phonemic differentiation that can be observed in a baby who starts using language in a very primitive way.

The laws governing this regressive trend are the same that can be observed if one studies the way in which the baby gradually acquires more and more sophisticated phonemic differentiations, from the primitive to the more complex in the case of the baby and from the more complex to the more primitive in the case of the aphasic, but the order of acquisitions and the order in which the regression takes place *is the same.*[3]

However, what I think is still more interesting for us is what Jakobson observed about the relationship between the first phonemic differentiations as they appear in the baby, their functions regarding the use of language as a way of proper symbolic communication and not as pure expression of emotions, the moment in time when all this can be observed in the baby, and, of course, the universality of this phenomenon, that is, the possibility of claiming that the same first phonemic differentiations appear in all the world's languages more or less at the same time chronologically speaking, as far as the baby's development is concerned. Nevertheless, Jakobson's views turn up very complex issues related to the possibility to be objectively tested, in spite of the enormous wealth of information and data coming from so many languages around the world. Incidentally, the problem of the existence of universal patterns, that is, universal unconscious phantasies, the way they manifest themselves at various times in various cultures is, as we know, something that concerns psychoanalysis and its scientific status, too. Just think of the problem of the Oedipus complex!

---

3. Interestingly enough (and of course one could find analogies in order to describe all of this) Jakobson made use of Hughling Jackson's views on progression and retrogression as far as aphasia is concerned. It is well known that this Darwinian model also had an enormous influence on Freud (Solms and Saling 1990, Steiner 1982, 2000a). I am not only referring to the young Freud of the book on aphasia (Steiner 2000a).

Now in order to clarify better what Jakobson notices and in order to justify the importance of his observations for the issues I am discussing in these notes, I have to explain briefly what Jakobson meant by phoneme at that time and even later on. As I said, Jakobson's work paradoxically could nearly be identified with his study of the nature and function of the phoneme. There is a very clear paper that is the result of a series of lectures he gave in 1942 at the Ecole Libre des Hautes Etudes (attached to the New School for Social Research) in New York. This paper was not published until the mid 70s (Waugh and Monville-Burston 1990, pp. 217–241) and I refer the reader to it along with Jakobson's (1941) English version of his *Child Language, Aphasia and Phonological Universals* and many other works of his. Inevitably I have to restrict myself to a few statements that I hope will be sufficient to clarify the reasons the phonemic differentiations that first appear in the baby's communications are so important. Using mainly de Saussure's work but also that of other scholars, Jakobson reminds us of the double but intrinsically related nature of the linguistic sign that is composed of the signifier and the signified. The phoneme belongs to the signifier and, using Jakobson's analogic language that refers to the physics of the quanta (Jakobson 1942), is the minimal signifier deprived of any meaning in itself, which nevertheless is of fundamental importance to differentiate and to give meaning to the word. "Phonemes and words are related in different ways to the sign function of language. While every word, i.e., every grammatical form has its own particular and constant meaning, the phoneme performs only the function of distinguishing meanings without possessing any positive meaning of its own," says Jakobson (1941, p. 35) speaking about aphasia but obviously trying to clarify, through aphasia, the notion of phoneme and phonemic differentiation in themselves.

> It distinguishes every word which occurs from all other words which "ceteris paribus" contain some other phoneme. . . . The fundamental participation of the phoneme in meaning namely its distinguishing function is clearly demonstrated in the disturbance of sound comprehension as well as in the disturbance of meaning comprehension. A patient whose meaning comprehension is damaged and who has lost e.g. the distinction of the liquids, surely

> knows the meanings of Rippe and Lippe. Both words are homonymous for him, however he cannot identify the meaning of either words in any given case so long as the context of the situation does not supply him with any more information. On the other hand, patients with impaired meaning comprehension but uninjured sound comprehension can distinguish two words whose meaning they cannot understand but which are similar in sound by means of their non-significant phonological differences, and thereby perceive them as two different although enigmatic meaningful entities. [Jakobson 1941, pp. 35–37]

However, if that is an example taken from the pathological symptoms present in aphasia, let's take another example, a purely linguistic one, related to the nature and function of the phoneme, its role in distinguishing meanings without having any meaning itself. Jakobson (1941) writes, for instance, "The French nasal phoneme, ã, expresses simply the different words and types of words in which it occurs (as 'an,' 'allant,' 'enlever,' 'vente,' 'sang,' 'lent,' etc.) contrasted in their meaning with words containing a different phoneme in the same position (for instance 'sang' with 'saint,' 'son,' 'Ça,' 'sot' or 'lent' with 'lin,' 'long,' 'las,' 'laid,' 'loup')" (p. 43).

Of course, I could go on with other examples and technicalities because Jakobson constantly stresses the structural relationship of any single phoneme with the language system in which it operates, and as far as its nature is concerned he insists on the basic oppositional value that each phoneme creates and so on. I do not think it is important here to clarify what Jakobson observes about the relationship between the phoneme and the phonological unities because we would end up in an extremely complicated linguistic field (Waugh 1976, Waugh and Monville-Burston 1990).

What does matter is that in his seminal monograph of 1941, Jakobson tried to study, besides aphasia, as I have already mentioned before, how and when the first phonemic differentiations appear in the baby, which for him and modern linguistics is the "conditio sine qua non" of language as communication. Jakobson states that the first phonemic differentiations based on a wide vocal, usually an "a," and on a labial consonant as first consonant, usually a "p" followed then by an "m," appear "to be stable in its fundamental characteristics whether it is a question of French or Scandinavian children, of English or Slavic, of Indian or German, or of Estonian, Dutch or of Japanese children" (p. 47). In a note he adds all sorts of other languages, referring also to his astonishing bibliography on world language he collected at the end of the book. Although he points out that the speed in which successive phonological acquisitions take place is

> exceedingly variable and individual and two "newly added phonemes" which directly succeed each other in one child, can in another child, be separated by many months and even years, the first vocal and the first consonant are followed by the opposition of labials and dentals (e.g., after "mama papa" comes "papa tata" and "mama nana" . . .). These two oppositions form the minimal consonantal system of the languages of the world. These are the only oppositions that cannot be lacking anywhere, provided that there is no mechanical deformity of the speech apparatus (dyslalia labialis). [p. 47]

Jakobson gives examples coming from African and other languages where, for various reasons (ritual lip mutilations for instance) there is a lack of those primitive labial and dental phonemic oppositions.

I hope the reader will not think that the fact that we have, according to Jakobson, "mama" and "papa" or "papa" and "tata" or "mama" and "nana" as first phonemic oppositions and differentiations, implies that those words really mean mother and father in all or nearly all the languages of the world that he studied. Later on Jakobson wrote an extremely interesting paper called "Why Mama and Papa?" (1959). Those phonemic differentiations can mean and indicate mother and father but they can be used to indicate other meanings too. The important thing is that according to Jakobson they start being used in a meaningful way by the baby at a certain moment in time.

But when does this happen? I imagine that this question is lingering in the mind of all those who had the patience to follow my notes until now. Well, it is interesting that Jakobson comes to the conclusion that this happens i*n the course of the second half of the first year* of the baby's life and becomes more and more prominent toward the end of the first year. Of course, as we have already seen, Jakobson (who incidentally did not work directly with babies) does not refer to a *specific month*. He relied for his views mainly on what at that time was unanimously considered a masterpiece in the study of the language development of the baby, done by the Belgian linguist Grégoire (1937) on two of his children but taking into account all the available literature on the subject. Although Grégoire was very cautious in generalizing, insisting that one should know many languages to be able to come to some more precise conclusions. Jakobson, due to his unique polyglottism and his access to the most rare bibliographical references on this subject, had already an advantage over Grégoire, whom he nevertheless enormously admired and appreciated. It is interesting that Grégoire claimed that the passage from what he called physiological phonemes to linguistic phonemes, from the prelinguistic expressive stage of expression of the baby to the linguistic one, was a complex period embracing several months, starting with the fourth or fifth, but that the first possibility to observe the deliberate use by the baby of the first phonemic differentiations could be located between the seventh and the tenth month of its life. After the tenth month, the baby's efforts, which appear still tentative, gradually become much more evident and clearer (Grégoire 1937).

I would like to insist again on the fact that the phonemic differentiations do not imply only the wish to communicate, to have a conversation, which is already noticeable, according to Grégoire, after the first six months of the baby's life. They imply a primitive acknowledgment of the presence of the other or other objects, which then the baby gradually tries to differentiate, even linguistically. Therefore, the phonemic differentiations, according particularly to Jakobson, are *a sort of elemental logical operation* that helps the baby to give meaning and separate, individual existence to people and objects in the external world. Is it not at least interesting *that it is particularly during the second half of the first year of the baby's life* that Klein and her co-workers had started postulating more or less in the same years that Jakobson was working on his seminal researches and Grégoire had just published his findings, not only the existence but the working through of the depressive position, the beginning of the classical Oedipus complex, the acknowledgment of the parents as different, distinct persons, "whole persons," to use Klein's language (1940) and all that this implies, even in terms of symbol formations? And is not language, although still at such an elemental level, an extremely important aspect and moment of the symbolic process? One does not need to be a follower of Lacan to acknowledge that. Incidentally, in the case of Klein, more than the symbol of the father as far as language is concerned, one should speak of the symbol of the parental couple in which both parents collaborate in helping the baby to start using language symbolically and are symbolized by the baby itself.

Well, there is something else that I think needs to be added at this point. I emphasized more than once that some details concerning Jakobson's observations and the sources he relied on would confirm *a fortiori* the plausibility of my attempt to find a significant link between the views of such an illustrious researcher and those of Klein. It is important to stress that in relying on Grégoire, Jakobson curiously enough had to interact more or less directly with the whole literature on those issues used by Grégoire. Grégoire made use of Darwin, Preyer, Scupin, the Sterns and others' observations concerning the observable behavior of the baby, and there is no doubt that although using his own personal observations, and insisting particularly on the fact that many of those observers had only a rudimentary knowledge of linguistics, he nevertheless often used the same chronology they had used in observing changes and developmental issues during the first year of the baby's life. Klein, as I already said, was significantly influenced by many aspects of this literature too, particularly via Bernfeld's summary and research. It is therefore important to stress all those common links because despite the enormously different backgrounds of the various researchers, the different periods of time in which they made their observations or wrote about them, there is a sort of common ground among them that seems to constantly emphasize that particularly after the second half of the first year of the baby's life, *something extremely important seems to start to happen*. As I said when I first touched on this subject, I did not know about this common background. Of course there is nevertheless an enormous gap between what Klein stated and what all those other scholars and even R. Jakobson observed. If one studies Grégoire, one has the clear impression that he considered the first months of the baby's life a pure realm of chaotic sounds as far as language is concerned. Although those ideas are no longer accepted, according to Grégoire followed by Jakobson (Jusczyk 1997),[4] the baby has the potential to pronounce all the possible combinations of sounds of all the languages of the world and also uses sounds that do not appear in any language. Only gradually is there a normalization of this prelinguistic babbling phase and that happens from the fifth month onward. The image one gets from Grégoire's study of the baby's first months of life is that of a pure physiological, emotional baby, an image that was based on many of his sources' convictions.[5] Jakobson, too, seemed to be influenced by these views.

Yet, as I said, curiously enough, as far as the second half of the baby's first year is concerned it is possible to find the observations I mentioned. Incidentally, one could add that if properly understood, it is Klein who could also help to support Jakobson's views too. Indeed, in his need to stick just to the pure linguistic aspect of the discoveries, hypotheses, and observations, Jakobson lacks any discussion related to the emotions, both conscious and unconscious, of the baby toward his objects.

Besides focusing on many other points of Jakobson's research done during his long years spent in America during and after World

---

4. Jusczyk, to whom we owe the most detailed and recent summary on what he calls "the discovery of spoken language," to use the title of his book, stresses the enormous seminal importance of the work of Jakobson published in 1941. But he states that the idea of a sort of chaotic presence of all the possible sounds in the prelinguistic phase of the baby's development cannot be maintained. Furthermore, using contemporary research, he points out, and rightly so, the difficulties in claiming, like Grégoire and Jakobson, that there is a sharp distinction between a prelinguistic and a proper linguistic phase of development in the baby, something that Kleinians would agree with from their point of view, too!

5. It would be interesting to discuss the way Grégoire does not accept Cassirer's ideas concerning language and its function. Although he agrees that language helps the baby to give a unity to the object, and that this starts happening around the ninth or tenth month, he is not persuaded that the baby is so curious and in need to give a name to objects and things in order to ask, as Cassirer thought, but just to clarify things. Grégoire found Cassirer's view's concerning the mental state of the baby too speculative.

War II, which could be fruitfully integrated in a Kleinian perspective on the earliest phases of communication, at that time, although in a purely hypothetical way, I questioned Jakobson's conviction that there was such a sharp distinction between the prelinguistic and the proper linguistic period of the development of the baby when the interaction with its environment and the pressures coming from listening to and imitating its specific parental and national language gradually give a proper shape to his phonemic system (Steiner 1975).

Of course, I used Klein's hypothesis on the existence of a primitive object relationship between the mother and the father and the baby during the first six months of the baby's life, which I thought must have been reflected in the way they all relate to each other through *intonation*, repetition of particular words, and so on. This, I claimed, must have a sort of communicative meaning, too. *And some form of rough differentiations* concerning the intonative patterns and their affective but also their *primitive cognitive value* could perhaps be postulated as well.

I do not have enough space to report here and develop all that I wrote at that time. Nevertheless, what strikes me is the enormous attention that developmental psycholinguists, using the most sophisticated instruments of acoustic and data-testing analysis, have dedicated to the so-called prelinguistic phase of the development of the baby during these last thirty years. Those instruments were not available before or during the 1960s. One has only to study the enormous wealth of these important and revealing data and information contained in the researches of J. Amati and his co-workers summarized in a book not by chance called *What Infants Know* (Mehler and Dupoux 1997) to be persuaded that the baby interacts using a very sophisticated protolinguistic way of communicating with its environment since the beginning of its life after birth. I do not wish to touch on what happens in the uterus at this stage. Intonation plays an enormous cognitive and affective role in all that.

At this point I have to stop. Does all that I have tried to point out *prove* the validity of Klein's viewpoint? I am quite aware that there is and there will always be a gap between observations and interpretations, something that Klein pointed out very clearly herself during the Freud–Klein Controversies in discussing Bernfeld's extremely interesting data, which had pointed out the same (Steiner 2000c). Yet converging data and statements like those related to the logical cognitive aspects linked even to the first phonemic differentiations and the symbolic use of language as a method of communicating and discriminating, used in this particular context, often seem to have a certain meaning that can help bridge the gaps or at least make people aware that Klein was not working totally in isolation. I am particularly thinking of the intellectual stature of Jakobson who, incidentally, I have to confess, was extremely generous with me.

In the late 1970s, I met a distinguished linguist, G. Lepschy, and we both took part in a congress on Freud's theory of jokes held in Venice in 1981. Lepschy, listening particularly to what I was saying about the importance of intonation, an issue that interested him very much and on which he had written since he was a young scholar, insisted that I should contact Jakobson, whom he knew very well, and that I should send him my paper of 1975. To my great surprise, Jakobson answered me with two splendid letters showing a great interest in what I was trying to explain to him, particularly the convergence of some of his views and those of Klein, which I have also illustrated in these notes. I would just like to quote the final sentences of his last letter. He was over 80 years old, was still working with great energy, and had just finished the proofreading of the third volume of his *Selected Writings,* 900 pages long, a real titanic enterprise. He apologized for not yet having had the time to study properly what I had pointed out to him, although he felt greatly stimulated, and in the meantime he had sent me the book he had written on *Hölderlin's Schizophrenia from a Linguistic Viewpoint.*[6]

---

6. At that time, prompted by enthusiasm, besides writing a paper on jokes (Steiner 1982), those jokes based on phonemic distorsions, linguistic puns, which Freud, erroneously, I believe, called "innocent jokes," I had advanced a view, using Bion's (1967) ideas on the "attack on linking," that the so-called "salad of words" one can observe in certain communications of schizophrenic patients could be related to a paradoxical capacity of schizophrenics to perceive, attack, and try to de-

On December 18, 1981, he wrote to me, "What a pity that the unity of space and time is such a difficult question for our indeed fascinating mutual discussions. Let us believe in the new year." Unfortunately, Jakobson died in 1982 and I did not have the chance to continue with our discussions and to meet him as I had planned to do.

Well, my dear Norbert, in some way we have a problem with the unity of space and time too, but we met and we will go on meeting for many years. What I have written is simply an affectionate and personal tribute and interlude to our friendship, and for reasons that I cannot express in this paper openly, I hope you can understand how important it has been for me to have found such a friend like you. *Chi trova un amico trova un tesoro.* "Whoever finds a friend finds a treasure," so an old Italian proverb says. I hope we will go on treasuring our friendship, which does not need to be "proved" except for the pleasure it gives me, perceiving your enthusiasm for life and knowledge, even when you sit in front of your beloved "piatto di spaghetti con pomodora" instead of "pomodoro" (forgive me if I correct an incorrect "phoneme" of yours) as you call it, here in London or somewhere else in the world.

---

stroy phonemic differentiations, even the most primitive and elemental ones, in their attempt to attack and destroy their mental apparatus in all its functions, according to Bion and Rosenfeld or H. Segal. Of course, both in the case of jokes and in the case of psychotic communication, this was due to the confused interaction between life and death drives and their correspondent unconscious phantasies. Jokes have been compared very often to small psychotic episodes where the confusion, the emergence of the primary process's logic, is nevertheless still under control (Steiner 1982). In the case of schizophrenia there is no more of this kind of control. I advanced the hypothesis that schizophrenic patients project their attack of the parental couple and their intercourse, and of the maternal breast and paternal penis into the phonemic differentiations, breaking the links that allow them to function as "meaning givers" to the words. The phonemic differentiations became very concretely identified with the linking functions related to the parental intercourse or even more primitively to the breast or penis as partial objects. Language becomes charged even at a metalinguistic level, with all sorts of libidinal but also extremely destructive feelings, phantasies, and impulses. Jakobson had described the salad of words of the late and severely ill Hölderlin, studying his language and confusions from a purely linguistic point of view without any psychoanalytic input. My dear Norbert, please take this note as a pure personal extravaganza. I never developed any of this any further.

REFERENCES

Bernfeld, S. (1929). *The Psychology of the Infant*. London: Kegan Paul.

Bion, W. (1967). *Second Thoughts*. London: Heinemann.

Cassirer, E. (1933). Le langage et la constitution du monde des objets. In *Essais sur le langage*, ed. J. C. Pariente, pp. 39–68. Paris: Editions de Minuit.

Grégoire, A. (1937). *L'apprentisage du langue*. Paris: E. Droz.

Grosskurth, P. (1986). *Melanie Klein: Her World and Work*. London: Hodder and Stoughton.

Jakobson, R. (1941). *Child Language, Aphasia and Phonological Universals*. The Hague: Mouton.

——— (1942). The concept of phoneme. In *R. Jakobson on Language*, ed. L. R. Waugh and M. Monville-Burston, pp. 5, 218–241. Cambridge, MA: Harvard University Press, 1990.

——— (1959). Why mama and papa? In *On Language*, ed. L. R. Waugh and M. Monville-Burston, pp. 303–334. Cambridge, MA: Harvard University Press.

Jakobson, R., and Pomorska, K., eds. (1983). *Dialogues*. Cambridge, England: Cambridge University Press.

Jusczyk, P. W. (1997). *The Discovery of Spoken Language*. Cambridge, MA: M.I.T. Press.

King, P., and Steiner, R. (1992). *The Freud–Klein Controversies 1941–45*. London: Routledge.

Klein, M. (1930). The importance of symbol formation in the development of the ego. In *Love, Guilt and Reparation and Other Works 1921–45*, pp. 219–232. London: Hogarth.

——— (1935). A contribution to the psychogenesis of manic-depressive illness. *International Journal of Psycho-Analysis* 16:145–174.

——— (1937). *Love, Guilt and Reparation and Other Works 1921–45*. London: Hogarth.

——— (1940). Mourning and its relationship to manic-depressive states. In *Love, Guilt and Reparation and Other Works 1921–45*, pp. 344–369. London: Hogarth.

——— (1944). The emotional life and the ego development of the infant with special reference to the depressive position. In *The Freud–Klein Controversies 1941–45*, ed. P. King and R. Steiner, pp. 734–767. London: Routledge.

——— (1946). Notes on some schizoid mechanisms. In *Envy and Gratitude and Other Works 1946–63*, pp. 1–25. London: Hogarth.

——— (1957). *Envy and Gratitude*. London: Hogarth.

Lepschy, G. (1972). *A Survey of Structural Linguistics*. London: Faber.

Lewis, J. (1936). *Infant Speech* London: Kegan Paul.

Masson, J. M., ed. (1985). *The Complete Letters of Sigmund Freud to Wilhelm Fliess 1887–1904*. Cambridge, MA: Harvard University Press.

Mehler, J., and Dupoux, E. (1997). *What Infants Know*, 2nd ed. Oxford, England: Blackwell.

Rosenfeld, H. A. (1965). *Psychotic States*. London: Hogarth.

Segal, H. (1957). Notes on symbol formation. In *The Work of Hanna Segal*, pp. 49–65. New York: Jason Aronson, 1981.

——— (1964). *Introduction to the Work of Melanie Klein*. London: Hogarth.

——— (1981). *The Work of Hanna Segal*. New York: Jason Aronson.

Solms, M., and Sailing, M. (1990). *A Moment of Transition: Two Neuroscientific Articles by Sigmund Freud*. London: Karnac.

Stern, D. (1985). *The Interpersonal World of the Infant*. New York: Basic Books.

——— (1992a). *The prenarrative envelope: an alternative view of unconscious phantasy in infancy*. Paper presented at the symposium in memory of G. Moran, London, November.

——— (1992b). Considerations of unconscious phantasies from a developmental perspective. *British Psychoanalytical Bulletin* 11:140.

——— (1995). *The Motherhood Constellation*. New York: Basic Books.

Steiner, R. (1975). I correlati affettivi del fonema. In *Il processo di simbolizzazione nell'opera di Melanie Klein*. Torino: Boringhieri.

——— (1982). Es ludens . . . ? In *Il motto di spirito e Freud*, pp. 57–95. Firenze: Sansoni.

——— (2000a). *Einleitung S Freud: Die Psychopatologie des Alltagsleben*. Frankfurt-am-Main: Vischer Verlag.

——— (2000b). Introduction to *Clinical and Observational Psychoanalytical Research: Roots of a Controversy*: André Green and Daniel Stern. London: Karnac.

——— (2000c). The extra-analytical sources of the Freud–Klein Controversies. In *Tradition Change and Creativity in Psychoanalysis*. London: Karnac.

Waugh, L. (1976). *R. Jakobson's Science of Language*. Lisse: Peter de Ridder Presse.

Waugh, L., and Jakobson, R. (1987). *The Sound Shape of Language*, 2nd ed. Berlin and New York: Mouton.

Waugh, L., and Monville-Burston, M., eds. (1990). *R. Jakobson on Language*. Cambridge, MA: Harvard University Press.

5

Desymbolization in the Third Area

ALAN BASS

> *... every symbolic synthesis ... includes within itself spacing as difference.*
> —Jacques Derrida, "Freud and the Scene of Writing"

Norbert Freedman's work on desymbolization opens new approaches to psychoanalytic theory and practice. Always grounded in difficult clinical issues, Freedman demonstrates why they require fresh metapsychological thinking. He has shown that the basic question of therapeutic help—a question not often considered in terms of unconscious processes—has to be understood in terms of time and space. Winnicott, Loewald, and Laplanche, among others, have also found it essential to use notions of time and space as they think about the fundamentals of analytic treatment. Each has formulated a move into a "third area," an area outside conventional categories. For example, Winnicott famously calls transitional *space* a "third area of experiencing," which is neither subjective nor objective. Freedman himself has not specifically said that the clinical issue of desymbolization can *only* be resolved by "third area" thinking. My aim here is to synthesize his basic theory of desymbolization, and to show how it inevitably contributes to a "third area" metapsychology.

Freedman consistently starts with direct observation in order to make his basic point. Analysts automatically tend to assume that everything their patients say is meaningful, and thus interpretable. This prejudice, however, prevents thinking about processes whose aim is to defend against meaning and symbolization. In a fundamental article on desymbolized transference, Freedman and his co-author Berzofsky (1995) begin with a "theory-neutral" description of symbolization:

> Symbolization implies that aspect of communicated transference which signifies a *connection* [my emphasis] between two spheres of the mind and an effort to enhance shared meaning. In this sense, it represents an organizer of the treatment process in any dynamic system. . . . There is a consensus that the absence of symbolization (i.e. desymbolization) is a challenge to the unfolding transference and represents an obstacle to psychoanalysis or to psychoanalytic psychotherapy. [pp. 364–365]

By appealing to daily therapeutic experience, the authors are asking analysts to think harder about something as basic as "connection." Desymbolization actively prevents connection between spheres of the mind, and prevents the emergence of shared meaning—connection—between patient and analyst. This "theory-neutral" description already implies that "connection" is a "third area" question; it refers to a "place" that is both *within* the patient's mind and *between* analyst and patient. We are at the intersection of the intrapsychic and the interpersonal. Freedman and Berzofsky go on to say that "in a *help-seeking situation and in a talking cure*, it is the symbolized transference that provides the *framework* for analytic and therapeutic work" (p. 365, my emphases). Desymbolization, then, would affect the entire framework of treatment. The framework too, would be a "third area" question of intrapsychic-interpersonal connection.

Freedman and Berzofsky maintain their clinical-empirical focus by comparing the expression of aggression in symbolizing and nonsymbolizing patients. They state that despite major differences in presenting symptoms, some patients can articulate aggression while others cannot. The patients who cannot nevertheless discharge aggression through verbal and nonverbal means. From the Kleinian point of view, nonsymbolic discharge of aggression is closer to the paranoid-schizoid than to the depressive position (p. 368). In other words, symbolization-as-connection implies depressive position integration. In desymbolized transferences talking itself can serve as an inarticulate discharge of aggression. Its unconscious intent is to sever connection, without depressive position concern.

Although symbolization can *appear* to be simply an issue of depressive position integration (or of the resolution of rapprochement, or of the libidinally tinged positive transference), Freedman and Berzofsky think that we need a more metapsychological account of it. Patients from *any* diagnostic category can be desymbolizers, because desymbolization cannot be subsumed under a "linearly defined dimension of epigenetic development" (p. 371). This is a crucial point. There is a tendency in the literature to understand difficulties with symbolization either as psychic primitiveness (fixation to preoedipal or paranoid-schizoid organizations), or as cognitive primitiveness (fixation to Piaget's phase of concrete, sensorimotor operations). Freedman and Berzofsky state that symbolization is a relatively independent process of construction of meaning in the psychoanalytic situation, and is not simply an affective or cognitive competence. Symbolization moves from "the destruction of psychoanalytic space to the creation of psychoanalytic space" (p. 372). Desymbolization "must be considered as an *active process to destroy symbolization*" (p. 372), affecting the linking or connection necessary to therapeutic help.

Once one is speaking about therapeutic help in terms of the creation and destruction of intrapsychic-interpersonal space, one must include the analyst's unconscious dynamics. In an article on symbolized and desymbolized countertransference, Freedman and his coauthor Lavender (1997) examine the analyst's intrapsychic state when the patient attempts to destroy interpersonal connection. In order to sustain focus on the patient's inner world, the analyst, sometimes swamped by affects, "is challenged to achieve a state of *disembedding*. This inevitably demands the creation of an inner psychic *space* at the moment of onslaught" (p. 81, my emphases). In other words, if the analyst is simply "embedded" in the patient's intense affects, the analyst is not sustaining the space necessary to maintain the therapeutic framework. Freedman and Lavender give a metaphoric-metapsychological description of this idea.

> The basic assumption is that psychic content needs a space in which to live—we cannot move physically without a concept of space nor can we do so psychically. The inhabitants of such a space are inner objects, affects, and self-representations. . . . For an analyst to sustain an optimal state of listening, he or she will create a house, a container, that holds within it dimensions of listening space. [p. 83]

Freedman and Lavender have observed sessions with desymbolizing patients, and have found patterns of arrhythmic, shielding bodily activity by the *therapists* in these sessions. They observed the same therapist in sessions with a symbolizing and desymbolizing patient and found marked differences in the therapist's body language and facility of verbal expression. They call such an unconscious, uncontrolled response the "desymbolizing counter-transference" (p. 100). The analyst remains "embedded" in the patient's destruction of psychic space by unconsciously shielding him- or herself from the patient. The irregular and arrhythmic nature of this countertransference collapses the analyst's "listening space" because rhythmicity is the "kinesic *frame*" for empathy (pp. 89–90, my emphasis). But if the analyst grasps that rhythmicity is an essential preconcondition of listening, attention to bodily arrhythmicity can lead to a constructive use of the countertransference. The therapist can become aware that he or she is "embedded" in self-protective maneuvers, and can become more conscious of the transference–countertransference situation. Whether one looks at desymbolization from the side of the patient or of the therapist, there can be unconscious creation of space *and* unconscious destruction of it.

If rhythm is the "kinesic frame" of symbolization, then psychic space also has to be conceived temporally: rhythm is time. In some of Freedman's unpublished material, which he has generously made available to me, he offers descriptions of nonconscious processes in which space *is* time. I will refer to this material by chapter and page number in the manuscript. In Chapter III Freedman speaks of "temporal space," an arresting concept for a psychoanalyst. He writes:

> Organizers start with continuity and invariably or paradoxically create discontinuity. . . . Thus we must particularly emphasize *temporal* space and that is why sequential unfolding is so important. In development it is the unfolding time perspective which allows the symbolic functions to appear . . . the creation of *discontinuity* within a stable field of continuity is the very condition in which linking in the Loewaldian sense may take place. [p. 17, my emphases]

To think of temporal space as simultaneously continuous and discontinuous is to use conventional categories to describe an area in which continuity and discontinuity meet. Freedman refers to Loewald's conception of linking, which in fact is always conceived as a linking-differentiating process, simultaneously continuous and discontinuous (see, for example, Loewald 1980, pp. 167–168).

Expanding the metapsychology of therapeutic "temporal space," Freedman, once more like Loewald, situates symbolization in the preconscious. He revives the idea of preconscious processes, knowing that this early conception of Freud's has fallen into neglect for many reasons: it is part of drive theory, it is not "experience near," and it is not part of an object relations perspective. Freedman, however, reconfigures the preconscious as the "staging area" for the creation of psychic space, where differentiated links are formed. Following Freud, "staging" can be conceived as the transition from thing presentation to word presentation. It "occurs in moments prior to conscious awareness . . . [it] is the stuff we listen to especially within the frame of classical technique, although it is observable in all patients" (pp. 34–35). Desymbolization, then, is a "failure in the process of spatialization at the level of pre-conscious mental functioning" (p. 37). In the transition from thing presentation to word presentation, thing can be linked to word in a "non-spatialized" way. Words themselves can then be used to maintain dedifferentiation.

The clinical result is often temporal—a speeding up of associations, and a loss of rhythmicity. The loss of temporal regulation suggests an "arousal which is destructive to spatialization" (p. 45). In other words, the "arousal" expressed in temporally deregulated speech implies a nonconscious destructive-defensive response to nonconscious temporal space. In a later manuscript, "Toward a Descriptive Language of Clinical Discourse" (n. d.), Freedman essentially makes this point. Discussing desymbolization not simply as the absence of symbolization but as the destruction of a symbolic link, he writes: "Desymbolization, therefore, involves some kind of disavowal, that is, some potential symbol is registered and then repudiated" (p. 16). Temporal space is repudiated as its registration provokes destructive arousal. Desymbolization condenses "wishes to attack, not wishing to attack and wishing to attack oneself all at the same time. . . . It is necessary to recognize . . . a process of uncontained excitation" (III, p. 47).

In essence, Freedman has postulated a new kind of conflict, the conflict between incipient, registered symbolization, a repudiating attack upon it, and consequent desymbolization. As an inherently intrapsychic-interpersonal process it affects the very possibility of sustaining the framework of therapeutic help. Clinical aims have to be rethought in order to modify this kind of conflict: "the recovery of rhythmicity rather than the discovery of psychic content . . . is crucial in the treatment process" (p. 46). In other words, analytic technique must be revised when desymbolization attacks the differentiating framework of temporal space, when conflict and compromise occur in the "third area."

The technical revisions center on the conception of the analytic "surface." Freedman says that the dedifferentiated, arrhythmic, speedy surface must be modified in order to potentiate "those conditions which facilitate that *intermediary condition*, i.e. space, which makes re-symbolization possible" (p. 47, my emphasis). Here, Freedman overtly understands that theory and practice require a conception of an "intermediate" or third area, giving new meaning to the concept of "surface." The familiar analytic approach of "starting from the surface" usually means the observable "surface" of the patient's associations and defensive maneuvers. Here, the surface is conceived in terms of continuous-discontinuous temporal space. We usually think of the "surface" as what is most immediately observable. The "intermediate" surface of differentiating temporal space is, however, radically unobservable—like time and space themselves. In this intermediate area defense does not eliminate psychic content from consciousness, but rather serves to repudiate potential symbolization. Freedman has demonstrated how one can start from a readily observable phenomenon—desymbolization—and move toward a metapsychology of unobservable, preconscious processes, which themselves have to inform clinical technique.

In Chapter IV he deepens his analysis of destruction, space, and time. Both symbolization and desymbolization depend upon repetition, which, like rhythm, is intrinsically temporal. Creating or destroying space, he writes, has a history of its own. Freedman is asking us to rethink what we mean by a patient's "history" when we deal with desymbolization. History has to be expanded beyond the usual conceptions of development of id, ego, and superego, of psychosexuality, object relations, trauma, and so on, to include the history of all the patient's encounters with the "third area." Just as symbolization and desymbolization affect the entire framework of therapeutic help, so the history of the "third area" itself frames developmental history. When a patient needs to repeat the destruction of meaning and symbolization, the analyst is hearing derivatives of the repudiation of third area processes. These occur inevitably in everyone's history.

Because desymbolization tends to be insistently repetitive, Freedman refers to Lagache's idea that the transference manifests both repetition of need and the need to repeat. The repetition of need is guided by the pleasure principle, while the need to repeat "suggests dominance of destructiveness, the absence of organizing space, and the deadening of meaning" (p. 7). Thus, the compulsion to repeat would be linked to the death drive, as Freud thought. Freud famously claimed that it was difficult to find direct clinical evidence of the death drive, and that one could only observe it when it was fused with libido. Freedman provocatively offers the repetitive destructiveness of desymbolization as the clearest manifestation of the death drive. Because desymbolization is simultaneously an attack on oneself and on the other, Freedman's conception fits well with Freud's idea that the death drive is originally an inner destructiveness that *becomes* an outer destructiveness. The history of the operation of the death drive in the individual would be the enframing history of inevitable desymbolization, even in patients who are mostly "symbolizers." Just as Freud originally wanted to conceive of a nonconscious history of sexuality and repression, so Freedman opens up the possibility of a nonconscious history of incipient symbolization and defensive destruction of it—again, a history of the third area.

Freud postulated a primary masochism in relation to the death drive (1920), and Freedman, too, links desymbolization to primary masochism. This self- and other-directed aggression has a significant narcissistic component: Freedman cites Rosenfeld's conception of the idealization of destructiveness. The loss of rhythmicity, the failure to regulate stimulation, and the need to repeat an idealized destructiveness in the transference make primary masochism the "substrate" of all forms of desymbolization. (Clinically these are usually identified as the alexithymia and operational thinking studied by the Paris psychosomaticians and by Joyce McDougall; the perverse transference as delineated by Etchegoyen; symbolic equivalence as described by Klein and Hanna Segal; and the various forms of concreteness noted throughout the psychoanalytic literature.) In its relation to the death drive, primary masochism connotes what Freedman calls a "self imposed attack on psychic vitality" (p. 25). But why this defensive attack on psychic vitality?

This is the heart of the matter. Describing the trajectory from desymbolization to symbolization, from idealized destructive-masochistic wishes to more libidinal, pleasure-oriented activity, Freedman notes that the process is one of "enhanced differentiation. In desymbolization there is a condensed or fused undifferentiated state and symbolization by definition is a condition of differentiation" (p. 35). It is a question of understanding the relation between psychic vitality and differentiation. Freud actually provides the basis for understanding this relation when he describes the life drive, Eros, not only as a binding force, but also as the "introduction of *vital differences* into the organism" (1920, p. 55, my emphasis). (This is why Loewald [1988] understands the linking-differentiating basis of symbolism in terms of the binding-differentiating function of Eros.) But why the need to *destroy* the vitality of binding-differentiation? The answer, I believe, is an economic one. Freud consistently describes the economic function of Eros as one of raising tension levels within the psychic apparatus. Raised tension levels are the basis of trauma. Eros, as Freud came to understand, is essentially a vital disturbance of equilibrium (1940a). The unregulated, arrhythmic, self- and other-attacking "arousal" intrinsic to desymbolization manifests a traumatized response to a raised tension level, to the *vital* disturbance of binding-differentiation, of Eros, and of therapeutic help.

This is why I would modify Freedman's conception of symbolism under the dominance of the "pleasure principle." Freud himself (1920) noted the paradox that as a principle of tension reduction, the pleasure principle actually seems to serve the death drive. Eros, the life drive, becomes for him an intrinsic unconscious force of binding, differentiating, and increased tension. Therefore, I would say that the *unconscious* conflict between life and death often becomes the *preconscious* conflict between symbolization and desymbolization, a conflict intensified when there is a traumatized response to binding-differentiation. Unconscious, economic factors produce the preconscious process of active desymbolization. To describe the unconscious economic dynamics of the third area is not to propose a "one-person" model of the psyche because such processes are always intrapsychic-interpersonal. But neither is this a conventionally "experience near," two-person model, as Freedman always emphasizes, precisely because of its emphasis on drives, space, and time.

Further, if symbolization is the "kinesic frame" of analysis, then the unconscious conflict between life and death always concerns the entire analytic environment. Conflicts about symbolization potentially occur on the *surface* of every analysis. In "Psychoanalysis and Symbolism: Legacy or Heresy?" Freedman (1998) says that in general, the concept of spatialization is "the center of that which leads to analytic change. In the dynamics of the analytic interchange, as we create space in the encounter between, we are at the same time also promoting space within" (p. 94). By situating the essence of the analytic process in the intermediate, third area, Freedman changes what we mean when we think about making the unconscious conscious. In the third area we have to consider the unconscious dynamics of temporal space in terms of differentiation. This intermediate area is not only between and within, but also *on the surface* and *not conscious*. Again, Freedman's emphasis on preconscious processes has to be supplemented by the unconscious dynamics of life and death, creation and destruction of temporal space. The innovation is to understand that *surface* conflict may be radically unobservable, precisely because it manifests preconscious and unconscious processes. The clinical idea that interventions have to be geared to restoration of rhythmicity, and not to making "buried" repressed contents conscious, speaks to this conception of an unconscious surface.

Until now I have been describing an implicit dialogue between Freedman's work on desymbolization and my own thinking about life and death, differentiation and dedifferentiation, time and space, surface, frame, and the "third area" (Bass 2000). In his most recent work on desymbolization Freedman has made that dialogue explicit, referring to my own previous work on concreteness (Bass 1997). There my focus was on primary disavowal—registration and repudiation—of difference (in relation to Freud's late theory of fetishism). I have already cited Freedman's idea that desymbolization depends upon disavowal of incipient symbolization. He has contrasted my own work on nonsymbolic compromise formations to those who approach the same question in terms of mental evacuation (Freedman, in press). One important example is Bion, and his essential concept of "attacks on linking" (1967). Bion thinks that tension and "badness"—beta elements—are intolerable in early development, according to the pleasure principle. They are immediately ejected through action or the body, and become "thoughts without a thinker" or "unthought thoughts." Green (1993) has expanded Bion's conception in terms of "the work of the negative," in which one sees destruction of mental contents, leaving a "blank," a "nothing" in their place. Freedman (in press) cites my expansion of Freud on disavowal: There is only *ap-*

parent evacuation or destruction of whatever contradicts the pleasure principle. Thus, Freedman agrees that there is an unconscious process of creation of space, an anxious (or, I would say, traumatized) response, and then a destruction of the space—that is, a process of registration and repudiation of difference. In a footnote, Freedman grasps the essential idea that the concept of *unconscious* registration has to be enlarged in order to account for such processes. And he stresses that since desymbolization is an active process in a two-person clinical dialogue, the therapeutic object relation has to be included in any theory of desymbolization. This would mean that the therapeutic object relation itself has to be conceived in terms of registration and repudiation of difference, the unconscious and preconscious dynamics of creation and destruction of temporal space.

If one considers Eros an intrinsic, unconscious drive that introduces vital differences into the psyche *and* binds, then there is an intrinsic drive to register the differentiating function of the analytic environment. The symbolizing process, the "kinesic frame" of the therapeutic object relation, is a derivative of this unconscious process. As an attack on oneself and on the analyst, desymbolization *apparently* destroys the therapeutic object relation, just as there is apparent evacuation (Bion) or destruction (Green) of "badness" and "tension." But because desymbolization, as Freedman says, is a "motivated defense" (in press, p. 38), then there has to be registration of the therapeutic object relation wherever it is so repetitively repudiated. Repetition works in both directions—life and death, registration and repudiation, rhythmicity and arrhythmicity. This is why Freedman consistently concludes that every act of desymbolization is an act of potential symbolization. But symbolization can never be presumed—it can always be defended against by desymbolization.

In his last papers, Freud described registration and repudiation of reality as a splitting of the ego, with oscillation between registration and repudiation. He came to see such oscillating processes as intrinsic to the "process of defense" in general (1940b). Freedman's contention that symbolization and desymbolization always potentially oscillate to sustain and destroy the space of therapeutic help *in general* expands Freud's late thoughts. The *reality* registered and repudiated in desymbolization is the reality of differentiating temporal space. This is the reality of third area processes active in the unconscious and preconscious registration of therapeutic help.

SOME COMPARATIVE REMARKS

Winnicott (1951) describes transitional phenomena as "the third part of the life of a human being, a part that we cannot ignore, an intermediate area of *experiencing*, to which inner reality and external life both contribute" (p. 230). For him, this intermediate area is the place of "illusion," a place between a "baby's inability and growing ability to recognize and accept reality" (p. 230). In a related formulation Winnicott says that transitional phenomena are in the "intermediate area between the subjective and that which is objectively perceived" (p. 231). The transitional object itself is "symbolical of some part object, such as the breast," *but* "the point of it is not its symbolic value so much as its actuality" (p. 233). Thus, "the term transitional object . . . gives room for the process of becoming able to accept difference and similarity . . . there is use for a term for the root of symbolism in time . . ." (pp. 233–234). As the root of symbolism in *time*, transitional *space* would have to have a relation to desymbolization. And indeed, at the conclusion of the article on transitional phenomena, Winnicott envisions addiction, fetishism, lying, and thieving as "transitional" pathologies (p. 242). Ultimately, he thinks that the possibility and failure of transitional phenomena are the result of good enough mothering: "In infancy this intermediate area is necessary for the initiation of a relationship between the child and the world, and is made possible by good enough mothering at the early critical phase" (p. 241).

There is a marked contrast with Freedman's thinking here. When Winnicott speaks of "experiencing" and of "good enough mothering," he does not mean more than directly observable caregiving. For Freedman, one cannot envision pathology in the third area without a metapsychology of that which is not "experience near." The death drive, narcissism, and preconscious staging processes operate in the intermediate area where temporal space is created and destroyed. Freedman's is a more Freudian, psychodynamic approach to transitional phenomena. Clinically, Freedman's approach would not encourage the therapist simply to provide "good enough" experience in order to bring the patient into transitional space. His point that desymbolization can be modified by interventions that address rhythmicity, in both patient and therapist, certainly focuses on "experiencing" in the here and now of the session. But because Freedman objects to any exclusive value placed on the "experience near," he does not think that the replication of good enough mothering through consistent therapeutic care will modify the pathologies of transitional space. Interventions that aim to restore rhythmicity address the specific dynamics of third area, or transitional, compromise formations.

Winnicott, however, must be credited for his early attention to the therapeutic frame or environment. In "The Depressive Position in Normal Emotional Development" (1954) he revised Klein's understanding of the depressive position. Klein held that depressive position integration equals integration of the split images of the good and bad breasts. Winnicott holds that the mother has two functions: to be the object of "instinctual assault" and to provide environmental care (p. 266). The depressive position involves integration of these two functions. Winnicott wants to give equal weight to reality and fantasy in depressive position integration, where Klein's conception typically emphasizes phantasy. Crucially, though, Winnicott considers the relation of the infant to the "environment mother" in nonconflictual terms. The mother of "instinctual assault" is the object of the drives, while the environment mother is experienced in "quiet union" (p. 267).

For Winnicott, integration of the environment mother of quiet union with the mother of instinctual assault makes possible an "internal environment," where there can be "the acceptance of ideas and of fantasy related to fact, but not to be confused with fact" (p. 267). This, too, is an important way of thinking about the "root of symbolism in time," and possible desymbolization. Patients who have difficulties with depressive position integration will transferentially maintain a split between an "instinct" and "environment" analyst. When

Winnicott specifically addresses the function of the analytic frame he ramifies this point. In "Metapsychological and Clinical Aspects of Regression" (1954b) he states that Freud's invention of clinical psychoanalysis comprises two aspects: an interpretive technique and a particular setting in which interpretation takes place. He claims that the reliability, continuity, and basic rules of the setting replicate the function of the environment mother. This conception assumes, however, that there are no tensions or defenses in relation to environment or setting—the frame. Drive and defense compromises operate only in relation to the instinct mother or analyst.

Freedman's conception that symbolization *is* the frame of help seeking, and that it can provoke arousal, attack, and consequent desymbolization, means that environment cannot only be conceived in terms of "quiet union." Moreover, the linking-differentiating process intrinsic to interpretation would be an essential component of the analytic environment. Winnicott finally promotes an artificial division between interpretation and the setting. Both the setting *and* interpretation have differentiating functions and share complex dynamics. From Freedman's point of view, the rhythmicity of temporal space would be the split-off environmental factor wherever there are problems of depressive position integration. In treatment, the "process of becoming able to accept difference and similarity" depends upon registration of the kinesic frame.

In his last book, *Sublimation*, Loewald (1988) also debates with Winnicott about the nature of symbolization, the "location" of transitional space, and the dynamics of interpretation. It would be superfluous to give references to Loewald's emphasis on Freud's concept of Eros. Suffice it to say that throughout his work Loewald identifies Eros as a drive force that differentiates, binds, raises tension levels, and promotes integration with environment. Loewald's understanding of symbolization as simultaneous linking and differentiation—Eros—is as essential to Freedman as is Bion's idea of attacks on linking. (In fact, it seems that Loewald himself does not conceive of anything like attacks on linking. This is why Freedman had to complement his Loewaldian understanding of binding-differentiation with Bion's concept.) Once Eros is understood as an inherent drive force, then integration with reality or environment is also a question of interaction with the *dynamics* of reality. Interaction with such dynamics, says Loewald, necessarily affects "stimulus load" (p. 29). Like Freedman, Loewald thinks that one sees these economic factors at work in the linkage of word presentation with thing presentation. He uses the old Freudian term "hypercathexis" to describe this preconscious process. It is the essence of therapeutic *interpretation* and is intrinsically related to the question of transitional space:

> Winnicott's phenomena that have no climax [i.e., transitional phenomena] appear to show an "aim" that consists in a qualitative characteristic of the stimulation load. . . . The endopsychic binding of excitation can be seen as an equivalent of those nonclimactic phenomena that Winnicott describes as belonging to the experience of relating to objects but which . . . must not be challenged—also according to Winnicott—by the question "subject" or "object"? [p. 30]

In other words, Loewald brings energic and economic thinking to bear on the third area in order to grasp the dynamics of interpretation.

For Loewald, the economics of the third area require a third dynamic term, a term not confined to traditional conceptions of raised or lowered tension levels. He speaks of stimulation not only as "input" and "output" of energy, but also as "*resonance* with the 'wave length' of a neighboring system. Stimulation can result from an openness to the latter's level of binding or organization of activity. The neighboring system, in the case of such hypercathexis, is simultaneously open to, in tune with, the 'receiving' system" (p. 32, my emphasis). Such resonance would be another way of conceptualizing the frame or environmental function of interpretation. The "kinesic frame" would be a "resonating frame," in which the analyst must simultaneously register the desymbolizing patient's attack on the environment, but also "disembed" him- or herself, in order to sustain binding-differentiation. This is no mean feat for the clinician, given the inevitability of the desymbolizing countertransference.

It is very striking that Loewald, like Freedman, begins to think about interpretation and resonance in terms of time and rhythm: "As

Freud said of the qualitative characteristic of pleasure and unpleasure, so is resonance a phenomenon implicated with rhythm, with time, in ways that are not clear" (p. 32). Loewald, in fact, is referring to the passage near the end of "Beyond the Pleasure Principle" in which Freud says that pleasure and unpleasure themselves are the results of quantitative changes of cathexes within "units of time" (p. 63). The questions of rhythm and time that are not so clear to Loewald are perhaps clearer to Freedman, because he starts with clinical observation of arrhythmicity in desymbolization. Just as Loewald does not seem to envisage anything like "attacks on linking," so he does not seem to consider the clinical question of defense against the resonating, hypercathectic aspect of interpretation.

However, Loewald does raise a general theoretical question about the third area that Freedman does not raise. Again he is debating with Winnicott about transitional space. Loewald thinks that Winnicott's description of transitional phenomena in terms of "the infant's journey from the purely subjective to objectivity" is inaccurate, because transitional space is where "subjectivity and objectivity come into being" (p. 70). Loewald goes on to say:

> One faces a dilemma in that it is the hallmark of such states that they are neutral in respect to subjectivity and objectivity, but scientific language seems to demand or presuppose a decision one way or the other. Therefore, scientific language, as commonly understood, is inadequate here: descriptions and conceptualizations have to be couched in often self-contradictory circumlocutions and formulated with the help of analogies, metaphors, and negative terms. [p. 73]

Freedman's emphasis on simultaneously intrapsychic and interpersonal processes implicitly raises the same question. As an environmental or framing process, symbolization is the context out of which such traditional terms as intrapsychic and interpersonal arise. The economic aspects of interpretation as discussed by Loewald (resonance and hypercathexis) are also intrinsic to the conceptions of rhythm and time out of which pleasure and unpleasure themselves arise, as Freud thought. In a rigorous sense, this might be precisely where the language of consciousness has to be inadequate to unconscious processes. Even to use the term "*third* area" is the kind of analogy Loewald is speaking about. Intermediate space is the environmental condition of the other two (intrapsychic, interpersonal), and is not a "third" that simply comes after them. As an environmental factor, it is in a sense "first," just as symbolization is the precondition of therapy. Loewald makes just this kind of point when he questions Winnicott's idea that transitional phenomena are the "substance of illusion." He writes: "Experiencing, as exemplified in transitional phenomena, cannot be said to be either illusory or nonillusory. Because they exist *prior to or beyond* that dichotomy, transitional phenomena cannot be challenged with such an alternative" (p. 71, my emphasis). "Prior to or beyond" is another way of describing transitional or third area phenomena as "first" and "last," that is, as an enframing context. Freedman's metapsychology of space, rhythm, destructiveness, narcissism, and primary masochism provide critical insight into the *unconscious, surface, dynamics of symbolization as the enframing therapeutic context.*

In his recent work (1999), Jean Laplanche too has begun to elaborate a theory of the third area, and of surface unconscious dynamics. Laplanche's overriding concern, as he puts it in the title of one of his chapters, is to complete "the unfinished Copernican revolution" of psychoanalysis. Like Loewald, Laplanche thinks that a scientific conception of the unconscious, at its most rigorous, can never be couched in the language of consciousness, which is for him essentially "ipsocentric." The unconscious for Laplanche is essentially *other*, always decentering the narcissistic security of "my representations." Thus Laplanche rejects the idea of an unconscious as the "innermost depths" of one's *own* being. If it is essentially other, the unconscious is always a question of what is other than oneself, both internally and externally.

Laplanche thinks that the standard theory of sexuality, with its endogenous drives, can also lead to a "recentering" of the unconscious. Thus, he reconfigures sexuality, seduction, and trauma in terms of "otherness." In other words, while wishing to maintain the original emphasis on sexuality, Laplanche also sees that psychoanalysis needs a theory of unconscious processes that are intrinsically intrapsychic-interpersonal. Starting from the impact of the parents' *unconscious* sexual fantasies on the child, Laplanche's revised theory of seduction emphasizes what is "other to the other," that is, the parents' unconscious fantasies. He believes that these fantasies are transmitted unconsciously, implanting an essentially untranslatable "enigmatic signifier" in–or rather, on–the child's unconscious. In a summary statement, Laplanche writes:

> We propose to give full place, in metapsychology, to processes irreducible to autocentrism: those whose subject is quite simply the other . . . the other of originary seduction. . . . Central among such processes is *implantation* . By this I wish to indicate that the signifiers brought by the adult are fixed, *as onto a surface*, in the psychophysiological "skin" of a subject in which the unconscious agency is not yet differentiated. It is these signifiers, received passively, that are the object of the first active attempts at translation, residues of which are the primally repressed. [p. 136, my emphasis]

For Laplanche the primally repressed is not "'inside' the psychic apparatus . . . it would be on the contrary a surface entity . . ." (p. 255, n. 47). The most rigorous psychoanalytic thinking, which would help to complete its "unfinished Copernican revolution," is a question of otherness as a surface unconscious.

Remarkably, Laplanche conceives these unconscious, surface dynamics in terms of that which "resists symbolization" (p. 230). He contends that all development takes place "in the direction of a double closure to the message of the other . . . the closure on the side of what can be translated . . . and also closure through the sealing off, the repression of the . . . residue of messages, that is, of what resists symbolization" (pp. 229–230). In order to understand the *dynamics* of the resistance to symbolization, Laplanche has to take into account destructive defense against difference. He writes:

> In the face of the alterity of the other, the methods of defense are immutably the same: attempt at assimilation, denial of difference, segregation, destruction. These are quite clearly found again in attitudes to cultural and ethnic differences. But what is lacking in all the analyses of "racism" is any consideration of the internal split

> inherent in the other himself: it is this *internal alterity* which is at the root of the anxiety provoked by external alterity; it is this that one seeks to reduce at any price. [p. 230, n. 21]

From Freedman's perspective, Laplanche has expanded the theory of desymbolization. The registration of "otherness," which sustains the differentiating space of symbolization, is both the foundation of unconscious processes *and* inherently anxiety producing. It can always engender "denial," "segregation" (splitting), and "destruction." The very possibility of symbolization also produces resistance to symbolization. Laplanche therefore adds a fundamental anxiety about internal otherness to the dynamics of "that which resists symbolization." This kind of anxiety is a key component of the "arousal" that Freedman speaks about in relation to incipient symbolization.

Again like Loewald, Laplanche does not consider the specific clinical difficulties of resistance to symbolization, in Freedman's sense. But he does think that there are two basic kinds of transference. One is transference as usually conceived, what Laplanche calls the "filled in" transference of "my" wishes, fantasies, affects, and object relations. The other is the "hollowed out" transference of the original enigma of the other (p. 229). And the "hollowed out" transference itself demands a conception of a "third area" that is also "first." Laplanche contends that what is "originarily *from* the other, in the mode of the other . . . is only secondarily . . . split into good and bad" (p. 248). Neither Freud nor Klein, he thinks, had a "category which is neither external reality, real danger, nor the subjective, in other words the projected drives" (p. 248). Neither saw the "need of a third domain of existence" (p. 248). This "third domain" for Laplanche is specifically that of the "message," the enigmatic signifier of the other's unconscious fantasy. It has to be thought of in relation to time. Laplanche thinks that the "temporalization of the human being" is intrinsic to a decentered and decentering unconscious (p. 241). His model for temporalization is the one Freud developed in his original thinking about seduction, the model of "deferred effect," of *Nachträglichkeit*. For Freud, seduction always becomes traumatic after the fact, when early memories are connected to later sexuality. Laplanche expands the linkage of trauma and temporality, giving temporality both a "retrogressive" (present to past) and "progressive" (past to present) meaning. He alleges that the originary relation to the other *is* this temporal alternation, because unconscious transmission of the "enigmatic signifier" is always *to be translated*. The "hollowed out transference," with its intrinsic relation to that which resists symbolization, is a question of the temporality of the "to be translated." In other words, it concerns interpretation of that which resists symbolization.

Laplanche's theoretical emphasis on seduction and otherness brings him to the point of retheorizing transference and time in the third area. His insistence on an unconscious surface that is intrinsically "other" adds a critical dimension to symbolization as the frame of analytic help. It suggests that the "internal alterity" of the temporal space of differentiation, the basis of symbolization, can provoke fundamental anxiety. As an attack on the frame, desymbolization helps us to understand that the setting itself is a derivative of otherness. In fact, if one does not confine the third area of the "message" to the parent's unconscious fantasies, as Laplanche does, one can understand it in terms of the otherness intrinsic to interpretation. The "hollowed out" transference is for Laplanche always in relation to the "positive, creative conception of neutrality, productive of the enigmatic dimension," which depends upon the analyst's respect for and maintenance of "the other" in him- or herself (p. 228). This is another dimension of the "kinesic [temporal-spatial] frame," the disembedding differentiation of analyst and patient necessary for interpretation. As a message, interpretation, particularly when addressed to desymbolized compromise formations, helps to sustain the "otherness" of the analytic frame.

I would like to end with a clinical vignette, in order to show the necessity and vitality of this new area of psychoanalytic thought. A neurotic man is in the middle of his analysis. He is almost always the kind of patient Freedman would call a "symbolizer," and his traditionally interpretive analysis has so far had good results. In a recent session, following shortly upon some major moves forward in his life, he says that he feels overwhelmed. He is certain analysis cannot help him with it. He wants a referral for medication. We have moved into desymbolization—there is no reasonable indication for medication here, nor is there anything to make me think that his current distress cannot be handled interpretively. In fact the session proceeds as always, including transference interpretation of the *meanings* of his concrete demand for medication. The patient begins his session the next day by saying that upon reflection, it was surprising to him that he *really* did feel helped the day before, even though he *really* had not expected to be. Desymbolization has taken the patient into the third area. He is reacting to the entire interpretive framework of the analysis, to the basic conditions of the help-seeking environment. He goes on to say, "I had the most peculiar sensation as I was leaving to come here. Somehow I felt certain that you had changed the *time* of the session [I had not]. And then on the subway I kept thinking that the train was moving *in the wrong direction*. . . . But I had never felt in the same way before that I could really *change my mind*." Space and time change as the patient moves from desymbolization to symbolization. There is a disturbing otherness on the surface when the analyst maintains a differentiating, interpretive stance in response to desymbolization. A mind can be changed.

REFERENCES

Bass, A. (1997). The problem of "concreteness." *Psychoanalytic Quarterly* 66:642–682.

——— (2000). *Difference and Disavowal: The Trauma of Eros*. Stanford, CA: Stanford University Press.

Bion, W. (1967). *Second Thoughts*. New York: Jason Aronson.

Derrida, J. (1978). Freud and the scene of writing. In *Writing and Difference*, trans. A. Bass, pp. 196–231. Chicago: University of Chicago Press.

Freedman, N. (1998). Psychoanalysis and symbolization: Legacy or heresy? In *The Modern Freudians*, ed. C. Ellman, S. Grand, M. Silvan, and S. J. Ellman, pp. 79–97. Northvale, NJ: Jason Aronson.

——— (n.d.). *Toward a descriptive language of clinical discourse.*

——— (n.d.) *Manuscript, Chapters III and IV.*

——— (in press). *On desymbolization.*

Freedman, N., and Berzofsky, M. (1995). The shape of the communicated transference in difficult and not-so-difficult patients: the symbolized and desymbolized transference. *Psychoanalytic Psychology* 12:363–374.

Freedman, N., and Lavender, J. (1997). On receiving the patient's transference: the symbolizing and desymbolizing countertransference. *Journal of the American Psychoanalytic Association* 45:79–103.

Freud, S. (1920). Beyond the pleasure principle. *Standard Edition* 18:3–66.

——— (1940a). An outline of psychoanalysis. *Standard Edition* 23:144–203.

——— (1940b). The splitting of the ego in the process of defense. *Standard Edition* 23:275–278.

Green, A. (1993). *On Private Madness*. Madison, CT: International Universities Press.

Laplanche, J. (1999). *Essays on Otherness*. London: Routledge.

Loewald, H. (1980). *Papers on Psychoanalysis*. New Haven, CT: Yale University Press.

——— (1988). *Sublimation*. New Haven, CT: Yale University Press.

Winnicott, D. W. (1951). Transitional objects and transitional phenomena. In *Through Paediatrics to Psychoanalysis*, pp. 229–242. New York: Basic Books, 1975.

——— (1954a). The depressive position in normal emotional development. In *Through Paediatrics to Psychoanalysis*, pp. 262–277. New York: Basic Books, 1975.

——— (1954b). Metapsychological and clinical aspects of regression. In *Through Paediatrics to Psychoanalysis*, pp. 278–294. New York: Basic Books, 1975.

6

Symbolization, Multilingualism, and Countertransference

ISAAC TYLIM

ON SYMBOLIZATION

Symbolization is a process of mediation or transformation. This process is reflected in the psychoanalytic realm as an attitude that allows both analysts and analysands to expand on the multiple levels of meaning of actions and language. Although "psychoanalysis may have been born in the theory of dreams, and matured in the theory of transference and countertransference . . . these are all unthinkable without the concept of a process of mediation or transformation" (Freedman 1998, p. 79).

Symbols serve as bridges between experiences. These bridges condense a wealth of meaning that psychoanalysis is apt to translate. Hysterical symptoms, dreams, fantasies, artistic products in general, share their primary process source and the psyche's capacity to create a symbol capable of expressing and/or representing unconscious conflicts and contradictory wishes. When the analyst or the analysand speaks more than one language, the "other" language may be mobilized in the analytic process in ways that mirror the emergence of hysterical symptoms, dreams, fantasies, or artistic products in general. In other words, the "other" language appears as a bridge between different layers of experiences.

Multilingual analysands and multilingual analysts seem to navigate through a world of multilingual symbols that mediate experiences through something akin to what Cassirer (1955) called "symbolic form." Symbolic form is a sign that harbors both subjective and objective experience, feelings, and thoughts. The shift from one language to another during treatment may be considered a symbolic form that utilizes a different language to express a repressed conflict. The other language that erupts in multilingual treatments during a particular moment has the power to deepen and transform a complex process by conferring new dimensions of meaning. The eruption of a second language often appears as the signifier of a bridge between the repressed wish and the transferential juncture.

Wittgenstein regards language like a game or *Sprachspiel*. In Wittgenstein's system, to understand a word implies an understanding of the word's function and how it is used in the game. *Sprachspielen* must follow rules. They are embedded in an affective and sensorial landscape that transforms language into a *Lebensform*, a lifestyle. What happens then when a mind plays more than one game? In other words, what if the mind is inhabited by several languages at the same time, when one thinks, speaks, and dreams in more than one language? How many *Sprachspielen* can one engage at a given time? Every game has its rules.

A hierarchical pattern of languages in analytic treatment may reflect different degrees of the representation of bodily experiences. The body will be presented in a symbolic manner through the languages used. One may speculate that the mother tongue will be closer to the primitive body, the naked body, more visible and exposed.

Conceptualizing the symbol as a bridge or link between experiences has ignored the differentiating dialectic that attributes an opposite domain to symbolization—the process of unlinking (Freedman 1998). Applied to multilingual analysis, one language thus demarcates a territory within our psyche, and by definition it points to another one that is not covered by the symbol in question. The dialectic between the assertion and nonassertion of the referent is present every time a multilingual analysand shifts languages, that is, from the mother tongue to an acquired language or vice versa. The same may be applied to the associative word of the multilingual analyst in session. Moreover, the act and style of speaking varies from one language to the next. Loewenstein (1956) has alluded to speech as an objectification in bringing that which lies inside to the outside. Multilinguals accomplish this in pieces that may not necessarily be interconnected.

Javier (1989) has reported on the phenomenon of language independence. This is a condition in which an individual who speaks more than one language is able to maintain " separate representational mediation processes, each with its own lexical, syntactical, phonemic, semantic, and ideational components" (p. 88). Psycholinguistics studies have demonstrated that different cognitive and emotional activities can be activated by, and are associated with, more than one language. Ervin (1964) found that bilingual subjects fluent in both English and French verbalized different sets of responses to the Thematic Apperception Test (TAT) cards according to the language used. Ervin noted that in French achievements themes prevailed, while in English autonomy and anger through withdrawal were more common. She attributed these differences to behavioral norms in the English and French culture, which, in her opinion, were linked to language.

MULTILINGUALISM IN PSYCHOANALYSIS

The study of multilingualism and its influence on the psychoanalytic process remains underdeveloped and quite behind its counterpart within the social sciences. What is the reason for the apparent neglect of the subject of language by psychoanalysis? Should one be suspicious of this omission? Could it be that analysts tend to hold on to the proposition that the universe of discourse appropriate to the psychoanalytic experience is not that of language but that of the image (Ricoeur 1970), or that one image is still worth a thousand words? Must dreams stand alone as prominent representatives of analytic discourse?

The omission of multilingualism in psychoanalysis is filled with paradoxes. From its origins in the last chapters of the multilingual Austro-Hungarian Empire, psychoanalysis was embedded in a sociocultural milieu where polylingualism was customary. Although the German language ruled, the political realities of the late nineteenth and early twentieth century converted Vienna into a cosmopolitan city where people from different parts of the vast Empire, speaking a variety of languages and dialects, met. These facts stand in marked contrast to the lack of exploration of the phenomenon of multilingualism within the confines of our discipline. Do multilinguals constitute a neglected majority within psychoanalysis?

Psychoanalysis since its beginnings attracted individuals from different countries who spoke in a variety of languages and dialects. The early analysands brought the confusion of languages to their physicians. Bertha Pappenheim, after an initial period of mutism, began to respond to Breuer's hypnotic techniques. However, Bertha responded to her physician's power of suggestion not in German but in English. Perez-Foster (1996) reported how in psychotherapy patients' language switch is often accompanied by a concurrent shift in the transference–countertransference paradigm. Languages become associated with different modes of being that an in-depth analysis of multilingual patients cannot ignore. The use of a second or acquired language during treatment may be a symbolic referent to a lifting of a repressive barrier on one hand (albeit in a second, less threatening language), and to the manifestation of a process of mediation within the transference–countertransference paradigm.

At the turn of the century, Freud conducted analysis with multilingual patients who went to Vienna for that purpose. Although Freud was not too thrilled about substituting English for his beloved German, necessity forced him to do so. Freud valued the German language. For him, other languages seemed to serve ulterior motives. In a letter to Fliess of June 12, 1987, after quoting a joke about two schnorrers, Freud wrote, "I must confess that for some time past I have been putting together a collection of Jewish anecdotes of deep significance." In Freud's investigation of dreams he must have been struck by the frequency with which structures resembling jokes appeared in the dreams. Did Freud keep a record of Jewish jokes in Yiddish?

Early in 1933, when Nazism was threatening Western Europe, a group of Argentinean writers headed by Boveda extended an invitation to Freud to emigrate to Argentina (Garcia 1980). Freud, although deeply moved by the gesture, declined. In the foreword to the *Obras Completas de Sigmund Freud,* published in 1923, Freud declares: "I read and understand this beautiful language in which you write your poems, but don't trust myself in being able to write in it . . ." (p. 9). Language was the big deterrent to Freud's emigration to South America.

McDougall, cited by Sternberg (1985), offers an interesting alternative explanation to the relative neglect of the subject of multilingualism in our field. She states that analysts who were in training with German and Austrian refugees don't want to think that they weren't completely understood by their analysts. Are pedagogic transferences to be blamed for little evidence of multilingualism in psychoanalysis? Another reason for the paucity of papers on this subject may be related to Amati-Mehler's (1988) assertion that multilingual analysts are more prone to expose or reveal aspects of themselves than what the rules of abstinence and neutrality deem beneficial. Languages (and certainly accents) are not easily concealed.

MEMORY AND MULTILINGUALISM

Loewald (1980), elaborating on the intricate relations between memory and mourning, writes about the need to give up the unitary single-mindedness of instinctual life. The latter tends to preserve the state of primary narcissistic oneness, which must be relinquished in the development of conscious life and secondary process. Representational memory signals the departure from that unity prior to individuation. "Individuation is our human way of memorializing" (Loewald 1980) and thus re-creating the original unit.

Through the analysis, multilingual patients may recover lost links. Through memory encoded in language, a multilingual patient comes back to history, weaving past, present, and future in a new narrative that has the power to reconcile past and present languages. For the multilingual psychoanalyst, just as for the multilingual analysand, each language spoken during the psychoanalytic encounter is impure. Other encoding systems invade or intrude. When the boundaries between languages break in analysis, the languages betray an underlying networking of a communication system, a web of multiple references.

The psyche has its ways of recreating lost landscapes. Bollas's (1989) notion of "historical sets" seems to convey the meaning of these reminiscences. Historical sets imply that memories of past events recur in relation to one another in a cluster form that is bound by space and time. Bollas goes on to tell us that individuals who migrate frequently in childhood tend to have more potential historical sets than those who lead a more sedentary life. Historical sets are the common denominators of personal narratives where words, affects, and memory collude. The sets are the sedentary elements of one's inner world, offering a counterpart to the psyche's nomadic pulls. These sets constitute the psychological carry-on baggage of migrating individuals, the containers of multicoded memory traces.

A digression into the psychological bedrock of migration may shed light on the complexities of multilingualism. Balint (1968) coined the terms *ocnophilia* and *philobatism* to describe two types of migrating tendencies. Ocnophilics (from the Greek *ocne*: house, economy) tend to need contact with familiar people and places, holding on to what they know best, perhaps having trouble learning a new language upon migration. Philobatics (from the Greek *bato*: to walk) are in constant search of the new, the adventures of the road, tending to be more independent, perhaps learning foreign languages with ease. Do multilingual analysts reflect the dynamic tension between ocnophilic and philobatic tendencies? In other words, the shifting of language suggests at first glance a conflict between the familiar and the unfamiliar, the similar and the different.

Language is the inheritor of the transitional object (McDougall 1989). Transitional objects are the complex creation of the child's symbolic capacity. Can one reinvent oneself in a new language? Can one create new transitional objects? At the early stages of learning a new language, one may feel like a fake, as if words are used to create artifacts, tags to identify external objects. There is an inherent violence against words and communication. Signifier and signified lose each other, get separated or divorced, instilling a sense of futility and alienation. Spontaneity is lost and the words float in a land of ideas, devoid of the salt of the earth.

Acquiring a new language is often accompanied by its opposite, the abdication or renunciation of another language. Some people want to get rid of a language, declaring war against it, for example, Yiddish by those immigrants who were overly eager to assimilate to their adopted country. Trauma may lead to the silencing of a language, as was the case of a child of Holocaust survivors I treated who grew up in a multilingual family where Polish was banned from the household, but not German. In treatment it was shown that the banishing of language led to a sense of alienation from one language, which corresponded to the parents' conviction that the Polish people were more anti-Semitic than the Germans.

The question of the choice (unconscious choice) of language in regressive states or under traumatic circumstances is a crucial one. To Amati-Mehler and colleagues (1993), "The acquisition of a second language, in fact, not only determines an enrichment of the lexical and syntactical endowment, but also creates a minor internal revolution" (p. 120). Languages are capable of creating prisons as they invade and diminish the privacy of an individual (Gerson 1996). Languages may also provide a shield, a guardian angel that assists the individual to endure the unspeakable. For people facing extreme situations, language appears as a survival kit, in contrast to the tortured, broken body, a buffer against pain. Dorfman (1998), the Argentinean-born writer, tells about a woman who, while facing torture, kept repeating some lines from the poets Neruda and Machado. In this case, to hold onto language is to hold onto life, not unlike bilingual hospitalized patients who lose their acquired language and revert to their mother tongue during a regressive state. In the chaotic sea of madness, the delusions or hallucinations—voiced in the mother tongue—are a call for the forgotten or repressed, those old life supporters stored in the psyche.

Examining the fate of language in migrating individuals who became writers may open doors to the internal world of multilinguals. Eva Hoffman, Rosario Ferré, and the above-mentioned Ariel Dorfman are three writers who at one point or another in their lives, and due to different political events, immigrated to the United States. Although the circumstances of their immigration differ, they all had to deal with a struggle with languages, that is, a tension between languages that exerted a profound impact on their lives and work.

Eva Hoffman, in her memoirs *Lost in Translation: A Life in a New Language* (1989), states that when she emigrated from Poland to Canada in her early teens, telling a joke while learning English was like doing a linguistic pirouette. She declares that when writing in English, "My voice . . . does not seem to emerge from the same parts of my body as before" (p. 121).

Learning a new language is like putting something in one's mouth: strange, exotic, different food. The expression "eat your words" conveys the link between food and words. Hoffman is filled with nostalgia for the land that fed her primary language. She resists letting the new sounds in. Forced by her teacher to change her name, from Ewa to Eva, she feels as if an identification tag has been attached to her body. She experiences the loss of spontaneity, the lack of an interior language. The words in the new language hang in a Platonic stratosphere. She feels like a stranger to her own self. When confronted with choosing a language in which to write, she chooses English. She can write about the present only in the new language.

Rosario Ferré, a multilingual Puerto Rican writer, author of *The House on the Lagoon* (1998), has a different position regarding the shift from Spanish to English. She finds that something is gained in translation rather than lost. She writes novels in English and in Spanish, often translating her own work (from English to Spanish and vice versa). With English she discovered a psychological distance she couldn't achieve in Spanish. In Spanish she finds herself overwhelmed with words, tending to forget the point, so immersed is she in the narration of a story. On the other hand, English forces her to slow down, to consult a dictionary in search of the right word. Ferré translated *The House on the Lagoon* from its original English version to Spanish.

Rereading the text, she realized that the patriarch of the novel was less unpleasant, nicer, and more human in English than in Spanish. During an interview for *The New York Times* (Navarro 1998) Ferré recalled how her mother used to hold a belief that Americans make better husbands than Puerto Ricans. In her translation Ferré exposes how faithful she remained to her mother's belief with her version of American men.

The choreography between the acquisition of a new language and the renunciation of an old one is beautifully illustrated by Dorfman. In *Heading South, Looking North: A Bilingual Journey*, Dorfman (1988) tells the story of how he developed the capacity to renounce language. Shortly after immigrating to the United States, the 2½-year-old Dorfman suffered from pneumonia. He was hospitalized at a New York hospital, and for three weeks his parents were not allowed to visit him. Unable to communicate with the nurses, and feeling abandoned by his parents and by his mother tongue, Spanish, Dorfman suffered a "linguistic tantrum." When his parents "came to collect their son . . . I disconcerted them by refusing to answer their Spanish questions, by speaking only English . . . I did not speak another word in Spanish for ten years" (p. 29). Dorfman's separation and subsequent individuation was certainly quite dramatic and precipitous on all counts.

While attending college in California, Dorfman suffered another language tantrum. Forced to write papers in English, suddenly one day "it popped up into my thought without warning, a simple revelation. . . . What was I doing here, making believe I was a gringo, writing in this language that suddenly seemed an alien script?" Dorfman goes on to say, "I willed myself to become monolingual again" (p. 101), returning to Spanish, his mother tongue.

Amati-Mehler (Amati-Mehler et al. 1993) suggests that in polylinguals splitting and repression manifested in various languages are not recomposed along the line of fracture, but they can heal through the creation of alternative routes, new canalizations and new libidinal investments. Hoffman, Ferré, and Dorfman demonstrate how shifting languages, either in their writings or in translation, continuously rearranges the internalized experiences or historical sets. Nothing is ever lost in the internal world. As Freud stated it, repression is ultimately a failure of translation. The product is at times something fresh, new, unrecognizable, or puzzling, as shown in Ferré's comments regarding the patriarch of her novel translated into Spanish.

MULTILINGUALISM AND COUNTERTRANSFERENCE

Freud introduced the concept of countertransference in his 1910 paper "The Future Prospects of Psycho-Analytic Therapy." In this paper Freud asserts that the prospects for psychoanalytic therapy depend on internal as well as external factors. Symbolism and countertransference are those internal factors, the first at the theoretical level, the second at the technical one. While he regarded symbolism as an asset for psychoanalytic development, Freud viewed countertransference as an obstacle to be overcome. Contemporary psychoanalytic thinking has widened the significance of countertransference, considering it not an obstacle but an instrument for understanding.

The sudden shift from the language in which the analysis is conducted to a second or "other" language will significantly affect the transference–countertransference field. The other language may give access to the secrets and the mysteries of the early pregenital matrix. Understanding the second or other language and its nuances may unveil a new world of symbols hidden in its grammar or syntax. The other language is to the language in which the analysis is conducted as poetry is to prose. The other language may bring the analysis closer to primordial silence or to the poetry of the preverbal exchanges between mother and infant.

The other language opens worlds for both analyst and analysand. What position should multilingual analysts assume regarding the choice of language by multilingual analysands? How much initiative should these analysts take in the post-Babel scene? One must learn to wait for the spontaneous gesture, a crossover between the different codes, a slip of the tongue. The multilingual analyst is more than a tourist who happens to speak the language of the analysand's country. In multilingualism the analyst travels long distances, visiting his or her own old and new lands. While peeling the international onion, the analyst builds new bridges that connect and rearrange the borders of memories encoded in multiple tongues. The sudden or unexpected shift from one language to another introduces an element of surprise in the analytic process. This shift may be regarded as a simultaneous form of unlinking or uncoupling (Freedman 1998) of symbols in the transference and countertransference realm. When this occurs within the self-reflective mode of the psychoanalytic process, it strengthens differentiations between past and present, and between internal and external reality.

Speaking more than one language transforms the countertransference into a most sensitive instrument. Critical moments in the analytic multilingual process are bound to emerge around the use of one language over the other at a particular junction in the analysis. Omission of words, mistranslations, or the search for the right word in the other language are just a few examples of how the past is revived in a loaded symbolic moment.

Racker's distinction between two types of countertransference may prove helpful in attempting to elucidate the role of countertransference in the analysis of multilinguals. Racker (1968) distinguishes concordant countertransference from complementary countertransference. Concordant countertransfence expresses the analyst's identification with the analysand's ego, id, or superego; complementary countertransference implies that the analyst identifies with the analysand's internal objects. When the multilingual analyst speaks the same acquired or second language that the patient does, a concordant type of identification may be operating under which the analyst may convey his general empathy or capacity to understand the analysand's predicaments. However, when a second or other language erupts, the analysand may need to deal with the difficulties in filling the gap created by the shift of language. Under these circumstances the analyst may try too hard to understand, jeopardizing neutrality or contaminating the analytic process. A struggle for power and control may be enacted with an implicit idealization of one language over the other. Severe narcissistic and aggressive themes may be played out in the choreography of languages. Gedo (1996) believes that "it is the obligation of the analyst to master the various semiotic codes used by the analysand, no matter how eccentric they may be. . . . To forge a 'shared language,' both participants in treatment must take care to help each other as much as possible to grasp the intended meaning of their communications . . ." (p. 15), regardless of the language of the moment. It follows that analyst and analysand may have to work hard and carefully in order to attain an optimal shared language. A successful analysis of a multilingual analysand is one in which both parties are able to attain a version of a shared language. The analytic process often shows that the acquisition of a shared language between analyst and analysand is analogous to the acquisition of the mother tongue.

Gedo (1996) has expanded on the modes of communication encountered in psychoanalysis that rely not so much on words but, as he puts it, "the music of speech." The language of the body has also been incorporated into that list of languages that exert a profound impact on the treatment. To analyze in another language demands that the third ear listen as if listening to music. Each language has its own music.

From a different perspective, Gliserman (1996) attempts to combine semiotics, literary criticism, and psychoanalysis in his work. Gliserman's position is that language is embodied and embedded in the body, and the body is embodied and embedded in language. Language plays a central role in the integration of body and mind. The body evidences itself in the language, and the language in the body. In cases of multilingualism the question of the presence of the body in different languages may assist the analyst in getting closer to the meaning of the patient's communication in the language of the moment. Does the tone or the gesture that accompanies the use of a particular language by a multilingual analyst or a multilingual analysand change with the shift of language? Is a nod, or a slight variation in pitch or accent, a sensation, an indicator of meaning within a given language?

CLINICAL VIGNETTES

Jane

Jane is a rather articulate, bright young woman who has been undergoing a four-times-a-week analysis for the last two years. At the beginning of the third year of her analysis, I was summoned for jury duty by the New York State Supreme Court. Having to cancel a Monday morning session, and upon explaining the reason for my cancellation—a rare and infrequent event in my practice—the analysand, with a perplexed affect, said, "I didn't know you were a citizen of the U.S." Her comment had an immediate, unexpected impact on me. Reflecting on this exchange, I found myself thinking about early experiences of my immigration days, particularly those in which the quality of my English (or lack of it) distinguished me from my American peers. Not without hesitation, and somewhat aware of my curiosity about her perception of me, I asked Jane what made her think I was not a citizen. "Well," she replied, "I know you speak fairly good English [What a relief! I said to myself], it's your accent that made me wonder about your citizenship."

This brief exchange between the analysand and me is a reminder that languages do not escape politics. Speaking in English with an Argentinean accent introduced ambiguous demarcations in the analytic work, analogous to the not-so-well-defined borders between countries and cultures. Yet a twist of "imperialism" colors the analysand's remarks, perhaps a veiled allusion to her tendency to devaluate the analysis and the analyst.

Dov

Dov is a 45-year-old Orthodox Jewish man who came to analysis because of severe anxiety and multiple somatic complaints. When he was 9 years old, his parents emigrated from Europe to America. Dov spoke perfect English and Yiddish. From the beginning of the analysis Dov gravitated to Yiddish expressions, which he would invariably translate for me, his secular Jewish analyst, who he assumed was fully assimilated to the American way. Although the referral source had informed him of my South American background, the patient wasn't sure whether

> I was from Argentina or Brazil, being, as he put it, "deficient in sorting out accents." One early dream in the analysis has Dov arguing with a Sephardic Jew about some Talmudic portion. He associated to my last name, which to him didn't sound Ashkenazi. He was convinced that I was a Sephardic Jew, ignorant of Yiddish. He often contrasted what he considered strange Sephardic customs to Ashkenazi ones. The translations from Yiddish into English tended to elicit in me the feeling that Dov was looking down upon me, that he was convinced that I was unable "to grasp the richness of expressions, unmatched by English analogies." I was caught in an enactment: the analysand teaching the analyst what he already knew, the analyst pretending that he didn't know. Yiddish was used to devaluate the analyst, the treatment, and the Sephardis. The irony was that unbeknownst to Dov, I understood Yiddish quite well, since as a bona fide Ashkenazi I speak that language fluently.

The question as to whether analyst and analysand are better off when they share the same mother tongue is certainly an interesting one. I often get referrals of multilingual patients from colleagues who are convinced that patients should see someone who speaks their mother tongue. Resistances to confronting the other as other or different find refuge in a linguistic collusion between analyst and analysand speaking the same language. An analyst who understands a patient's mother tongue may stir up paranoid anxieties in a fragile patient who would rather hide in the acquired or second language. In this respect, the reactions to the language serve as a red flag to more severe pathology. I have worked with bilingual patients who became convinced that I could read their minds if they were to use the language we both shared.

Santos

> The multilingual analyst may be concealing countertransference elements linked not only to the language used by the analysand but also to the analyst's own history with languages. These not-so-obvious forms of countertransference, studied by Jacobs (1985) and others, may be camouflaged in sensations as well. Enactments or "actualizations" may

be the only outlets that allow the analyst to recognize certain forms of countertransferences in the analysis of multilinguals.

Santos, a demanding and intrusive bilingual male patient, needed constant reassurance about the appropriateness of his behavior both in session and in extratransferential situations. Although the analysis was conducted in English, he was fluent in Spanish as well. Despite his knowledge of my Latin-American origins, he would rarely speak in Spanish. On one occasion, after a lengthy description of an argument he had had with his boss the day before the session, he turned his head and asked abruptly in English, in a rather confrontative tone, "What do you think about this? Should I have done something different?" Caught by surprise, lost in my own polyassociative process in more than one language, Spanish sprang from my mouth: "*Que es lo que me esta preguntando*?" (What are you asking me?) Santos was startled by my little Spanish speech, remaining silent for a few minutes. Although my action betrayed my unconscious at work, I began to question the nature of this enactment. Was I reacting to the patient's conflicts with oedipal objects? Was I reflecting a hidden, hitherto unanalyzed aspect of the transference? Was my action an invitation to move to the language of the oedipal drama? Indeed, the patient, perplexed but also annoyed by my sudden shift to Spanish, replied, "*Por Dios Ud. debe creer que es mi padre*!!" (God! You must believe you are my father!) Only in Spanish did I sound like his father, the authority/ boss whose approval he often sought.

Julian

Masculine or feminine? In the realm of gender, the French feminist Luce Irigaray (1993) asserts that all language is sexed. To Irigaray, indicators of belonging to a particular sex are more significant than variables of context. Language is a product of the sedimentation of languages of former eras.

Julian is a married French man who moved to New York about ten years prior to the beginning of his analysis. He was referred to me by a colleague after Julian requested a French-speaking analyst. Although this appeared to be an important consideration in Julian's search for an analyst, once the analysis began Julian seldom used his mother tongue. In the third year of his analysis Julian reported a dream in which he saw a fly flying around his legs. Lacking English associations to the elements of the dream, he thought that perhaps in French it might be easier. He remembered that at home people used the word "*bête*" as a generic term for insects. Mother hated bugs around the house, spraying insecticides on a regular basis. Memories of seeing the open fly of his father reminded Julian that his mother used to refer to his penis as "*la bête.*" Julian expanded on the masculine and feminine character of words. "*La bête*" or "*la mouche*" in French sounded to him very different from the English fly. To Julian fly was a masculine thing, while "*la bête*" or "*la mouche*" threatened his masculinity, as if mother was invested in getting rid of that "*bête*" (insect) between his legs. Affect and memory linked to these words led to a commutation (Amati-Mehler et al. 1993) between languages rather than a real translation. "*La bête*" was to Julian "*une mouche*" that mother wanted to take possession of. In this context the "fly" seems to connote the interaction between two languages from which aspects of parental identifications were expressed.

CONCLUSION

> *. . . if you look at any wall spotted with various stains or different kinds of stones . . . you will be able to see in them a resemblance of various landscapes with mountains, rivers, rocks, trees. . . . With such walls and blends of stones . . . you may discover every name and word that you can imagine. . . .*
>
> —Leonardo da Vinci

Although the context of this quote refers to the creative process, it conveys the richness, texture, and allure that are the most salient features of multilingualism in psychoanalysis.

An inadequate theory of image formation and works of imagination may have forced analysts to rely on verbal language as the main reservoir of symbols. Languages unite but also divide. They point to various landscapes with different topography, distinct fauna and flora. The multilingual unconscious is like Leonardo's wall. A mother tongue and an acquired or second language blend. While the former evokes the original union with mother, the second may be regarded as a passport to distant countries, stamped with visas to foreign lands of symbols and meanings. Multilinguals travel from land to land, utilizing different tongues in the process of reaching distant lands that lie far and beyond the domain of the mother/tongue, that is, of the parent/child symbiosis.

REFERENCES

Amati-Mehler, J. (1988). Polylinguisme et polyglottisme dans la dimension intrapsychique. *Revue Francaise de Psychanalyse* 52(2):383–388.

Amati-Mehler, J., Argentierie, S., and Canestri, J. (1993). *The Babel of the Unconscious*. Madison, CT: International Universities Press.

Balint, M. (1968). *The Basic Fault*. New York: Brunner/Mazel.

Bollas, C. (1989). *Forces of Destiny: Psychoanalysis and the Human Idiom*. London: Free Association Books.

Cassirer, E. (1955). *The Philosophy of Symbolic Forms*, vols. I and II: *Language*. New Haven, CT: Yale University Press.

Dorfman, A. (1998). *Heading South, Looking North: A Bilingual Journey*. New York: Farrar, Straus and Giroux.

Ervin, S. (1964). Language and TAT content in bilinguals. *Journal of Abnormal and Social Psychology* 68:500–507.

Ferré, R. (1998). *The House on the Lagoon*. New York: Farrar, Straus, and Giroux.

Freedman, N. (1998). Psychoanalysis and symbolization: Legacy or heresy? In *The Modern Freudians: Contemporary Psychoanalytic Technique*, ed. C. Ellman, S. Grand, M. Silvan, and S. J. Ellman, pp. 79–97. Northvale, NJ: Jason Aronson.

Freud, S. (1910). The future prospects of psycho-analytic therapy. *Standard Edition* 11:139–151.

Garcia, L. G. (1980). *Oscar Masotta y el Psychoanalysis del Castellano*. Barcelona: Argonauta.

Gedo, J. (1996). *The Languages of Psychoanalysis*. Hillsdale, NJ: Analytic Press.

Gerson, S. (1996). A shared body of language. *Gender & Psychoanalysis* 1:345–360.

Gliserman, M. (1996). *Psychoanalysis, Language, and the Body of the Text*. Gainesville, FL: University of Florida Press.

Hoffman, E. (1989). *Lost in Translation: A Life in a New Language*. New York: Penguin.

Irigaray, L. (1993). *Je, tu, nous. Toward a Culture of Difference*. New York: Routledge.

Jacobs, T. J. (1986). On countertransference enactments. *Journal of the American Psychoanalytic Association* 34:289–307.

Javier, R. A. (1989). Linguistic considerations in the treatment of bilinguals. *Psychoanalytic Psychology* 6(1):87–96.

Jones, E. (1916). *The Theory of Symbolism: Papers on Psychoanalysis*. London: Bailliere, Tidall, and Cox.

Loewald, H. W. (1980). *Papers on Psychoanalysis*. New Haven, CT: Yale University Press.

Loewenstein, R. M. (1956). On the therapeutic action of psychoanalysis. *International Journal of Psycho-Analysis* 37:460–468.

McDougall, J. (1989). *Theaters of the Body*. New York: Norton.

Navarro, M. (1998). Arts in America: bilingual author finds something gained in translation. *New York Times*, September 8.

Niederland, W. G. (1976). Psychoanalytic approaches to artistic creativity. *Psychoanalytic Quarterly* 45(2):185–212.

Perez-Foster, R. (1996). Assessing the psychodynamic function of language in the bilingual patient. In *Reaching Across Boundaries of Culture and Class*, ed. R. Perez-Foster, M. Moskowitz, and R. A. Javier, pp. 243–263. Northvale, NJ: Jason Aronson.

Racker, H. (1968). *Transference and Countertransference*. London: Hogarth.

Ricoeur, P. (1970). *Freud and Philosophy*. New Haven: Yale University Press.

Rorty, R. (1979). *Philosophy and the Mirror of Nature*. New Jersey: Princeton University Press.

Shengel, L. (1991). "Father, Don't You See I'm Burning?". New Haven, CT: Yale University Press.

Segal, H. (1991). *Dreams, Phantasy and Art*. London: Tavistock/ Routledge.

Sternberg, S. (1985). The mother tongue and mother's tongue. In *Psychoanalytic Approaches to the Resistant and Difficult Patient*, ed. H. Strean, pp. 63–81. New York: Haworth.

7

Transformations in Psychoanalytic Treatment and Theory

ANDREW B. DRUCK

It is my honor to join in the salute to Dr. Norbert Freedman for his contributions to psychoanalytic theory and organizational psychoanalytic life. I will use one of his ideas as a springboard for thoughts about the nature of change in both clinical psychoanalysis and psychoanalytic theory. The topic is a grand one—I hope to explain how change occurs in work with patients at all diagnostic levels and in organized psychoanalytic groups—but Bert's ideas are always grand. His reach is far, but it rarely exceeds his grasp. I do not claim Bert's level of insight, but I have learned from him to think big. Thus this contribution to his *festschrift*.

What is the relation between transformations in individuals and in groups? There are several reasons these topics may be discussed together. For one, Dr. Freedman has made crucial contributions in both psychoanalytic theory and psychoanalytic organizational life, particularly at the Institute for Psychoanalytic Training and Research (IPTAR). Thus I would like to address at least two areas of his professional interests (I will actually bring in a third at the end of this paper). Second, if our ideas about psychoanalytic technique are, more or less, a function of our psychoanalytic theories, then the manner in which psychoanalytic theory evolves or does not evolve is crucial to our clinical work. Finally, and perhaps most important, to the extent that Dr. Freedman's ideas reflect a general principle of change, then it is useful to see how that principle is or is not valid with different phenomena. Therefore, I will discuss his ideas with regard to two different realms, beginning with change in psychoanalysis.

TRANSFORMATIONS IN PSYCHOANALYSIS[1]

Dr. Freedman, in an early paper (Freedman 1985), discusses factors accounting for "transformation" of psychic structures in psychoanalysis. He posits a dialectic between thesis (a wish), antithesis (a contradictory wish), and a synthesis of the two. Patients develop tolerance for contradictory wishes and insight into these "disjunctive experiences" acquired "under the hegemony of a libidinal object relationship" (p. 335). This experience leads to structural change. Following Loewald, Freedman discusses the analyst's dual role in this process.

> In the transition from thesis to antithesis, we noted the dual function of the analyst's presence as the inevitable provocateur of the antithesis at the prerepresentational level, and the facilitator of the synthesis at the representational level. Thus the analyst's activity can be thought to provide both the inhibitory structure as well as the facilitating structure. [p. 336]

I would like to use Freedman's description to attempt to identify a universal process operating in successful psychoanalytic or psychotherapeutic treatment with patients at all diagnostic levels. I begin with a preliminary remark: Freedman describes the contradictory elements (thesis and antithesis) as contradictory wishes. While this

---

1. Many of the ideas in this section were first discussed in Druck 1989, pp. 336–341.

is certainly accurate, the conflicts may also be between drive derivative and defense. The contradictory elements could also be thought of much more broadly. As Pine (1998) writes, one can be conflicted in different areas, such as ego, self, and object, as well as drive. Conflict can be intersystemic and intrasystemic. In my later discussion of change in psychoanalytic theory I will focus more on boundary conflicts. In clinical psychoanalysis, of course, these conflicts are expressed as conflicts over merger and separation. I want to stress, however, that I believe Freedman's remarks apply to all conflicts.

Freedman writes of helping the patient tolerate disjunctive experiences. He mentions two factors: tolerating experience of disjunction and insight into these experiences. Both occur "under the hegemony of a libidinal object relationship" (see also Akhtar 1998). Thus *every* successful psychoanalytic treatment, at the macro level, and *every* successfully mutative moment within an analysis, at the micro level, involves, first and foremost, a therapeutic relationship within which the patient feels safe, contained, and potentially understandable. Sandler (1960), for example, has described this as the experience of safety. In my opinion, the concept of therapeutic alliance addresses this issue, although it was conceptualized within the strictures of 1950s ego psychology, where analysts, reacting against ideas that focused on transference manipulation, shied away from directly addressing and exploring object-relations issues (see Lipton 1977). Emotional and cognitive closeness between patient and analyst, what Grunes (1984) terms *therapeutic permeability*, is the underpinning and center of the therapeutic alliance. Virtually every analytic writer makes one or another conception of the therapeutic alliance an essential aspect of an analysis, although they may use different terms that emphasize one or another of the analyst's roles within this analytic environment.

The analyst must enter the patient's psychological world within this overall context. The traditional concept of a transference neurosis captures such analytic closeness. While there is some controversy over whether a transference neurosis, defined as transference that recapitulates a childhood neurosis, is necessary, possible, or even meaningful as a criterion of psychoanalysis, certainly that aspect of the concept that describes an intense transference experience, one in which the analyst becomes central in his patient's inner psychological life, remains central. When a patient says that seeing me is the most important part of his day, he is telling me that I have become part of his inner world.

This experience of psychological connection is, of course, inevitably conflicted. What is affirmative and connecting for one person is intrusive and potentially merging to another. The way an analyst becomes experienced within a patient's inner world differs dramatically from one person to the next and is always the main subject of analysis. My point here is that the connection itself, conflicted as it is, even if it is primarily experienced as negative, is a necessary, if not sufficient, condition for a successful analysis. This is what Freud meant when he said that a patient must become libidinally invested in the analyst.

The connection is formed in different ways, usually dependent on a patient's structural level. In neurotic patients, the traditional psychoanalytic frame permits a patient's inner world to unfold. In a sense, the patient comes to the analyst, in the transference experience. Even here, the analyst's presence must be felt by the patient, often as a counterpoint to the analyst's interpretations (Loewald 1980, Stone 1961). By definition, neurotic transference is balanced between experience and reflection on that experience. More disturbed patients may require more active analytic involvement for the analyst to become meaningful in their analytic world. Sechehaye (1951) describes an extreme example of such involvement with a psychotic patient. Analyst activity may also be required to help with the opposite pole, helping a patient to feel connected to the analyst in a way in which he does not feel lost within the analyst or overwhelmed by him in a way that proves unanalyzable. Winnicott (1975), Balint (1968), Bach (1983), and Slochower (1996) describe creation of a holding environment with other kinds of patients, where the analyst allows an ambiguous murky transference, the analyst as environment rather than the analyst as object of conflicted wish, within which patients can allow themselves to unfold in what is seen as a genuine manner. Here interpretive restraint is essential. Kohut (1971) describes the kinds of narcissistic transferences that the analyst must allow with these kinds of patients. Kernberg (1975), in contrast, describes how one must confront the manner in which a patient almost pretends to use the analyst (primitive idealization) so that the patient begins to truly use the analyst. I could cite almost everyone who has ever written about psychoanalysis. Analysts disagree on the balance of activity and restraint (abstinence and gratification, to use other terms) and they disagree on what to interpret and what to refrain from interpreting. However, they all work to create an environment within which they become an aspect of their patients' inner lives, where they become psychologically meaningful, if not crucial, to their patients.

I want to emphasize that the patient may experience this connection in negative terms. When Kernberg (1984, 1992) discusses the process of interpreting with severely paranoid and narcissistic patients, his work could not proceed unless the patient was connected enough to Kernberg to tolerate and work with Kernberg's confrontations. I am not here discussing the kind of sadomasochistic enactment that sometimes develops between patient and analyst. That kind of transference is an enactment that is not an integral part of an analysis and that should be understood and analyzed. What I am emphasizing is a basic sense of connection and working alliance that must provide the underpinning to even the kind of analysis that Kernberg describes, where the patient, because of primitive envy and other dynamic issues, cannot allow himself to take help from his analyst.

Even as the analyst becomes part of his patient's world, he is also inevitably experienced as not part of the patient's world. This is Freedman's "disjunction." The disjunction occurs for several reasons. For one thing, the patient and analyst are, in fact, separate people. For another, the analytic sessions begin and end at prescribed times. Third, whatever the observable prescribed limits in the analytic setting, the patient and analyst are, in fact, involved in a professional helping relationship and are not primarily friends or lovers (even though they are certain to feel friendship and love toward each other). The patient with adequate reality testing will always know this. He will experience his analyst as separate from himself, whatever fantasies he has of closeness. The more neurotic the patient, the more this will be experienced as a matter of fact, and the feelings he has about such distance in the face of transference feelings will form much of the material for transference analysis. More disturbed patients will have more feeling around this disjunction, which will be between the experience of the analyst as part of themselves and the analyst as not part of themselves. They may feel relief that the boundaries between their selves and the outside world have become reestablished or they may feel lost because an aspect of what has become necessary for psychological survival has been lost.

Disjunctions also occur for dynamic reasons. Here the patient feels misunderstood. Sometimes the analyst has interpreted wrongly. Sometimes the analyst has acted in a way that disconfirms the patient's transferences wishes (or structural needs). Sometimes, because of conflict around closeness, the patient will engage in a series of defensive operations to protect himself from disappointment, closeness, envy, or other dysphoric feelings. At such times, the patient psychologically kills the analyst and then finds himself alone. Finally, there are those times when the analyst really does act in a way that confirms a patient's fears. The analyst may have to cancel sessions at times when a patient is most in need, or the analyst may become provoked by his patient and act as his patient wishes him to act (Katz 1998, Sandler 1976). Levenson (1972) has asserted that this is inevitable in any analytic situation.

It is repair of these disjunctions, however they occur, mostly through interpretation and sometimes through analyst action, that leads to what Freedman calls synthesis. The experience of thesis and antithesis, of junction and disjunction, becomes tolerated and tolerable through the interpretation, which makes the experience an understood experience and reestablishes the patient–analyst relationship at a higher level of psychological connection, one that is more symbolic in nature. It is through these interactions, repeated over and over, that the mutative effects of analysis take place.

INSIGHT AND EXPERIENCE

The alleged dichotomy between insight and experience, very broadly defined, has been a false way of dividing analysts. As discussed elsewhere (Druck 1998), there is no such thing as insight without experience. Part of the reason for our continued preoccupation with this issue is that we have been taught to think of insight as an issue of *content*. Here a patient *has* insight *into* the unconscious belief he carries that to become angry with his analyst will cause him to be subject to severe and castrating retaliation by the transferentially tinged analyst. Even in this definition, however, we see one difficulty of thinking of insight as content. To *have* insight must also mean to *become* insightful. Insight is ultimately a *process* variable rather than a *content* variable. We usually stress the content (the particular interpretation), but the particular content is really secondary in the interpretive process. One's capacity to consider certain contents (insights) about oneself, to work them through, and to integrate them is a function of their fluctuating capacity to be *insightful*.

That is why we term certain kinds of insights "intellectualized"; they express a particular content without the requisite process. At a given moment, for whatever reason, the patient is able to apprehend aspects of himself or others that he has been unable to see minutes before. The patient has made something of himself into something that is also not of himself. Something ego syntonic has become ego alien. To be and not be something simultaneously, to tolerate disjunction, as Freedman might put it, is *in itself* both mutative and the main goal of analysis. This is what is meant by the capacity to self-reflect. As these moments of capacity for self-reflection become greater, as aspects of one's personality become more and more ego alien, then one has greater mental capacity to reflect on the meaning of one's experience and one's life.

I am highlighting that aspect of psychoanalysis in which something ego syntonic is helped to become ego alien. This, in itself, is crucial for two reasons. First, as a process, it carries within itself what we strive for in psychoanalysis. Second, it is a necessary precondition to interpretation. Interpretation is an answer to an explicit or implicit question. When the analyst says something like, "You hold back your anger because you fear it will destroy me," the patient must first be noticing that he is holding back some anger and he must, explicitly or implicitly, be wondering why he is doing so.

Often an analyst interprets something and the patient "resists" because the patient is not asking about what the analyst is answering through his interpretation. Making some aspect of one's character ego alien raises questions that will be addressed through later interpretation. Insight, then, includes two parts: the patient asking himself something about an aspect of himself that troubles him, and the explanation that he gives himself for this troublesome characteristic. In a sense, the first part of this process—making something ego alien—provides the motive for a patient to consider various interpretive possibilities. The interpretation that "fits" most at a given time is satisfying because it closes the circle, in a manner of speaking. It answers the question that the patient, as well as the analyst, is now asking: "Why?"

The analyst's role in this process is complex. The patient must feel comfortable enough with the analyst to tolerate the inevitable anxiety that comes up when he and the analyst question ego syntonic aspects of character. Further, the patient and analyst together must come up with reasonable interpretations to address what is now being questioned. This is more difficult than it first appears because the patient is often considering these issues as they pertain to the transference. As Freedman states, when patient and analyst understand their own experience, the analyst functions as both provocateur and synthesizer, as participant and as observer. Traditionally, all this, from the patient's motivation to reflect upon himself to the patient's motivation to consider interpretations from an analyst who may be, at different transferential moments, experienced as a negative force, has been understood as part of the working alliance, depending on the patient's identification with the analyst's observing ego. In practical terms, this entire process is negotiated between patient and analyst. Such negotiation has always been referred to implicitly by Freudian analysts in concepts such as analytic tact, interpreting upwards and downwards, and interpreting unconscious material as it is almost conscious. Relational analysts, such as Aron (1996), discuss this negotiation process more directly. Whatever the theoretical rubric, the analyst and patient learn what is acceptable to each other, and how one can speak to the other in a way that will minimize disruptive anxiety and facilitate self-reflection and insight.

Two clinical examples may be relevant here.

Clinical Example 1

The patient is a man who is prone to psychotic transferences. He has been through times where he has sincerely believed that his therapist was sexually attracted to him and was planning on seeing him for an afternoon tryst. At the same time, the patient had the conviction that his therapist hated him and was critical of him. The therapist always walked a thin line. If he did anything that seemed rejecting (like inquiring into something the patient spoke about), the patient saw proof that the therapist really hated him. If, on the other hand, he did anything that seemed nice, like politely smiling at his patient when he walked into the room, the patient's sexual fantasy/beliefs became inflamed.

One day, soon after the therapist returned from vacation, the patient brought the therapist a gift. He said it was a small gift, not valuable, but one that reflected his thoughts about the therapist while he was away. The patient clearly expected the therapist to take the gift. The therapist felt himself to be in an uncomfortable situation. To reject the gift, even with explanation, would be disruptive. Based on experience, such disruption could lead to structural regression in this particular patient. Under other circumstances, the therapist would accept the gift. However, he believed that acceptance would encourage sexual fantasies that experience had taught led to transferential beliefs that would become hard for the patient to manage. The therapist felt caught between the devil and the deep blue sea.

The therapist responded by clarifying to the patient his dilemma. He described the situation as detailed above and suggested that, given the alternatives, they discuss the patient's motivation for giving the gift without the therapist accepting it. The therapist believed that this response would be acceptable to the patient in that the patient himself had felt out of control in previous psychotic transferences and would understand the rationale for the therapist's concern about inflaming positive transference fantasies. He also believed that explaining the rationale for his not accepting the gift would help mitigate the patient's inevitable feeling of rejection, with its own danger of structural regression.

The patient could not believe that the therapist refused the gift. He struggled with feeling rejected, but rationality did not quite take hold. He felt the therapist hated him and was critical of him for even thinking about giving the therapist anything. He vacillated between believing that the therapist was cruel and rejecting and that he himself was horrible for wanting to give the therapist something. Thus the idea that giving the gift might be, in some way, something to be discussed and understood was seen by the patient as a superego condemnation rather than as an ego aspect of the working alliance. At this moment, there was no working alliance. There was no truly ego alien aspect of the patient that an interpretation would address. There was only the patient's feeling that he had been caught with his hand in the cookie jar, so to speak.

The therapist understood that his first step had to be helping the patient stabilize so that the patient himself would become curious about the gift. He suggested that the patient leave the gift in the office while they thought about how to proceed. The patient grabbed at the suggestion. For the next two months, the patient would come to sessions, look at the gift on the shelf, and talk about whatever was on his mind. He would come back to the gift from time to time. Once he spoke about his conviction that the therapist had opened the gift box. He could not believe that the therapist had been able to contain his curiosity. The gift, in the therapist's office but not in his possession, became, over time, the concrete representation of how a thought and an action could remain provisional and examinable. As the patient talked of the gift and of the therapist's taking yet not taking it, he was able to himself ask about his motivation. He began to accept the thought (that is, the answer to what was now his own question) that he was trying to control the therapist and to make sure that the therapist would remember him. As he began to accept this idea, he took the gift and opened it in front of the therapist. The therapist and patient both looked at the gift and then the patient said, "Well, I might as well take it with me."

Clinical Example 2

The joining of concrete and symbolic meaning of a symbol under the overall rubric of a libidinal therapist–patient relationship can be seen in another example, this one in psychotherapy with a compensated psychotic patient. This patient had, in the past, become completely unable to work or perform daily activities when confronted by a disturbing thought, usually a thought prompted by some external event. For example, when she heard on the radio that the leader of a foreign country had died and that the country had declared a month-long period of mourning, the patient, who was not a national of that country and had, in fact, nothing at all to do with it, became immobilized for a month.

At this point in treatment, the patient was functioning in a tenuous way. She came in one day and said that she thought she had run over a rat with her car. This was quite disturbing to her and she feared that she would become lost in ruminations about the death and its connection to the many other losses in her life. She feared that she could not speak of the death without its taking over her life. The past and future would merge for her.

The therapist decided to do something quite unorthodox. She said to the patient that she was going to do something unusual, almost magical. She went to her closet and took out a three-foot wooden ruler. She placed the ruler on the office floor and said to the patient, "This ruler is a line between past and future. I want you to think of this side of the room as the past and the other side of the ruler as the future. Think carefully about the past and then, when you step over the ruler, you will be stepping over into the future. When you do it, the dead rat will be in your past and it will not take over your life. You will be able to talk about it but it will be something in the past that you are talking about."

The patient laughed, thought for a moment, and then stepped over the ruler. She then seemed calmer and said, "The magic trick is working." She said this several times over the next two sessions as she spoke of her feelings in running over the rat. She did not decompensate and was able to carry on with her life.

In this example, the therapist deliberately allowed herself to become a magical figure in a primary-process fantasy (that the rat's death would cause the patient to have to stop functioning but that the therapist's concretely represented magical strength could stave off such a plight). She did this because she knew that she was *also* a reality-based figure in a secondary-process world. She stepped into the patient's world believing that her predominance as a real figure in a secondary-process world would, in a sense, help the patient integrate the primary-process fantasy. It could have worked differently, with the therapist becoming experienced more and more as a primary-process figure, as one is seen in a psychotic transference. The act might also have proven unsuccessful. She risked looking foolish to her patient (and in the case report). Still, these were risks that she believed worth taking, given the potential for structural regression in the patient. We see here, in a momentary interaction, what I believe is true in overall terms about change in psychoanalysis and psychotherapy. In this moment, the therapist entered the patient's world and was simultaneously in it, in the patient's primary-process realm, and out of it, in the "real" world. The melding of these moments helps the patient move forward.

At these moments, and throughout an analytic treatment, subject and object move closer together. At times, they are empathically merged, "of the same mind." At others, they are separate, and feelings are clearly experienced from one separate object to the other. These moments, and gradations between them, are integral to an analysis. Analytic work cannot succeed unless patients feel understood by their analysts and connected to them. Patients must *experience* moments of connection and also of separateness.

Certain narcissistic patients cannot experience moments of separateness. They must feel that everything comes from them and revolves around them. For them to acknowledge being influenced by their analyst is too threatening and humiliating. It is understood that such a situation is something that is slowly worked on in an analysis. In other words, when we consider treatment of individuals, we understand that this mode of dealing with external influence—to essentially deny it and to believe that all truth and development come from within the patient—is problematic. When we consider the process of evolution in psychoanalytic theory, however, we move to the realm of group dynamics because theory is not formulated in splendid isolation. In this realm, for some reason, the denial of external influence that is problematic for the individual becomes the rule for the group.

TRANSFORMATIONS IN PSYCHOANALYTIC THEORY[2]

The motive for creative psychoanalytic work, the capacity to create this work, and the very nature of what kind of creativity is conceivable, are, in different ways, shaped by our overall intellectual and organizational environment and by personal relationships within this environment. Theory does not grow organically. It is shaped by conscious and unconscious systemic processes within the psychoanalytic community. Bion (1959) and Eisold (1994) describe such inevitable unconscious group anxieties and defenses against these anxieties that affect psychoanalytic training institutes and, by inference, the development of psychoanalytic theory. Eisold discusses unconscious factors that interfere with toleration of diverse opinions in analytic life (see also Aron 1999 and Lasky 1990). He writes that the analyst, working alone and with the anxiety that inevitably arises doing analytic work, looks to analytic theory to balance him- or herself and as a means of psychoanalytic identity. Theory helps the analyst identify

2. Parts of this material were delivered as a discussion at a conference celebrating the Freud exhibition at the New York Jewish Museum sponsored by the five psychoanalytic societies in New York City on April 19, 1999. This material was originally published as part of an article titled "Organizational Structure and the Establishment of Psychoanalytic Identification: Commentary on a Paper by Randall Lehmann Sorenson," *Psychoanalytic Dialogues* 10(6):889–907. Copyright 2000 by The Analytic Press, Inc.

with his or her teachers and with the larger psychoanalytic community. If one's theory is central in one's identity, then competing analytic schools may threaten that identity because they offer the possibility that one's sense of one's patient is somehow limited. Thus the social defense of adhering to one theory and dismissing others protects the analyst against anxieties of self-doubt in the analytic work (Eisold 1994).

Eisold also describes countervailing pressures between the training analyst–patient pair and the larger organization. He believes that rigidity in psychoanalytic organizations is partially a response to the anxieties posed to the organizations by this pair. Finally, Eisold discusses a historical detachment of analysts from their own institutions that leads analysts to have complicated relationships with their organizations' leaders, ones in which they covertly watch their leaders fail at tasks that Freud disdained. These factors are inevitable and lead to a sense of fragility in psychoanalytic organizations. Eisold writes that they can only be addressed "by our analytic institutions themselves taking up a self-reflective, analytic stance towards their own internal conflicts and defensive manoeuvres" (1994, p. 797).

Certain kinds of tension can interfere with psychoanalytic development. For Freud there was little distinction between theoretical difference and personal disagreement (Bergmann 1993, 1997). Once Freud no longer "owned" different aspects of a theoretical struggle, once the theoretical objection came from outside Freud, then disagreement was often personified, both on the part of Freud and the person who was disagreeing. In that kind of environment, change was dangerous. It was sometimes rebellion cloaked in theoretical disagreement and, other times, theoretical disagreement that was perceived as rebellion. To a greater or lesser extent, each particular psychoanalytic school continues, implicitly or explicitly, to define what kind of scientific developments are permissible. Certain kinds of ideas are received and welcomed into the evolving psychoanalytic corpus of thought; others brand one as an outsider and are seen as "not psychoanalytic" or "not Freudian" or "not relational."

This point can be made clearer if we recall Bergmann's (1993) important distinction among three kinds of psychoanalytic contributors: heretics, modifiers, and extenders. I will remind you of

Bergmann's definitions of these three groups. As you read, please note the extent to which the kind of contribution is defined both by its content and by its reception from the relevant surrounding psychoanalytic community. Bergmann writes that

> the heretics, rare in recent years but prevalent in Freud's lifetime, were typically close to Freud for some time, made important contributions, and then bolted to start their own schools. . . . Modifiers recast psychoanalytic theory or modified psychoanalytic practice, but did not leave the psychoanalytic field. A typical strategy for a modifier is to claim that his or her modification is implicit in Freud's writings or flows directly out of Freud's idea. While modifiers create controversy in psychoanalysis, they also keep it alive and protect it from stagnation. . . . Extenders, the third group, usually extend psychoanalysis into areas as yet unexplored, but their findings do not demand modification. Unlike modifiers, they evoke no enmity and their contributions are appreciated. [1993, p. 930]

Implicit in Bergmann's definitions is that new psychoanalytic ideas are almost immediately defined as more or less acceptable to the surrounding psychoanalytic movement, even as they are evaluated on their own merits. Expectations of how one's ideas may be received by the surrounding community can shape one's contribution in many ways. The expectation—often based on fantasy, sometimes not—may motivate someone, inhibit someone else, cause some to overemphasize the originality of their contribution, and cause others to disguise their originality.

Group pressures having to do with the definition of our psychoanalytic identity affect our reception of new ideas and also affect our individual creativity. We are all influenced, to a greater or lesser extent, by our sense of how our ideas will appear to define us within the larger psychoanalytic community. This, of course, is a vestige of Freud's overpowering presence and his defining which theoretical developments were "kosher" and which were not. In what follows, I will be using Freudian psychoanalysis as an example of how change takes place in a psychoanalytic group. I write about Freudians because

I know that particular school best. However, I believe that the process I am describing is similar in other psychoanalytic schools.

To some extent, Freudians have not adequately internalized Freud, so that they sometimes, more in the past than in the present, overly concretely link themselves with Freud by defining new ideas as Freudian or not. For example, concepts such as *drive* or *drive derivative* are important not only because they are believed to be crucial concepts but also because believing in them links Freudians to their psychoanalytic father. Other concepts are regarded ambivalently because Freudians may have theoretical doubts about them but also because acceptance of these concepts may appear to threaten their link to Freud. It is significant that modifiers such as Hartmann and Klein begin by citing Freud, albeit different parts of Freud. They then "engage in an irrational battle as to who is Freud's true heir. At times the argument resembles more a theological debate than a scientific discussion" (Bergmann 1993, p. 946). Disagreement about the value of new ideas turns into fights about the heart and soul of Freudian psychoanalysis. The more analysts do this, the more they repeat Freud's struggles with his followers.

We live in an era of multiple models in psychoanalysis. Freudians argue that new developments in areas of object relations, ego and superego development, narcissism and the self, and other such ideas can be integrated within a traditional Freudian theoretical rubric. They argue that early variants of these ideas are found in Freud's work. Others argue that emphases in psychoanalysis today were really not major elements in Freud's work. They reject the modifier's strategy and believe that a new organizing theoretical paradigm is necessary (see, for example, Greenberg 1996, Pine 1990, Tyson 1996, and the discussions by Mitchell 1999 and Richards 1999b). These are certainly legitimate differences of approach and opinion, but they also become the vehicle for an organizational struggle between psychoanalytic groups.

We all—as individuals, as organizations, as individuals inevitably affected by organizations, and as organizations inevitably affected by individuals—balance two trends: one of integration and assimilation of competing ideas, another of differentiation among these ideas.

Moves toward differentiation and sharpening of differences are more pronounced in psychoanalytic groups (and in individuals presumed to be speaking as representatives of groups) because of factors described by Eisold (1994). Synthesis, while perhaps benefiting psychoanalysis as a whole, inevitably threatens the distinct identities of the psychoanalytic subgroups. Nevertheless, there is always a concurrent move toward synthesis, particularly in individuals but also in the various groups. We form personal psychoanalytic theories based on our idiosyncratic synthesis of what we have learned from our texts, our supervisors, our analysts, our colleagues, our patients, and our psychoanalytic community. I am a Druckian, ultimately (see Aron 1999 for a thesis consistent with this point of view). This explains the variety of ways in which analysts understand their own particular theories (see Druck 1989 for a discussion of the "right" and "left" wings of Freudian psychoanalysis). It also helps us understand why there are sometimes very few differences between analysts on one end of the relational spectrum and analysts from another end of the Freudian spectrum. Finally, it helps us understand the old adage that experienced analysts of different schools often work more similarly than do experienced and inexperienced analysts of the same school.

To the extent that we can evaluate new ideas on their own merits, psychoanalysis is enriched. As ideas become assimilated and integrated, we are able to separate the wheat from the chaff, and both psychoanalysis and the "threatening" ideas evolve. One sees this in the way Freudian and Kleinian theory have moved closer (see the Freud–Klein "controversial discussions" [King and Steiner 1991] and compare it to Richards's [1999a] and Schafer's [1997] statements that the modern Kleinians are Freudians) and in the way that Loewald is regarded far more favorably today by Freudians than he was twenty years ago. To the extent that we react to new ideas symbolically, to the extent that acceptance of an idea from "someone else" is seen as threatening a school's basic tenet, then we see schisms and new schools. Once things become polarized on both sides, then both sides become extreme. As controversy swirls, however, something else occurs, much more quietly. For Freudians (again, this is my point of view) we engage in a process where we reexamine Freud and find the germ of these new ideas implicit in our own history. In a sense, we appropriate the most adaptable of heretics' ideas and then, in our own names, and as ideas that now seem to come from within our own tradition, we view them as modifications, or even only extensions, of our evolving theory. In this way, the best of the new, from within and without our traditional theory, is questioned, critically evaluated, and often assimilated into mainstream psychoanalysis. I am not arguing that this is the best way to assimilate new ideas. I am saying that I think it is the way Freudian psychoanalysis *has been able* to assimilate these ideas.

Again, other psychoanalytic schools engage in a similar process. For these schools, differences with Freud and with Freudians must be emphasized because to be linked to Freud threatens these schools' own sense of uniqueness and of their special contribution. These schools, like the early Freudians, also censor contributions within their own movements that are critical of their own founders and of their established premises. These other schools replay, in their own theoretical and organizational development, the struggles of the early Freudians, even as they criticize those same Freudians. My point is not that one group is as bad as the other. It is, rather, that *nobody* says to someone from another school who has a new idea challenging his or her central concepts, "You know, you're right, I have to rethink something in the face of your idea."[3] Every group must take the others' contribution and mold it so that it is their own. Through the filter of this group narcissism, what Rothstein (1983) has termed *narcissistic investment* in a particular theoretical paradigm, a theoretical group is able to integrate new developments while preserving its identity. Group anxieties are ubiquitous and cannot be defined out of existence by our good motives. They can only be repeatedly acknowledged, confronted, and worked through.

3. Also, nobody says, "I have this good idea that applies to one particular kind of patient but not to others." Instead, the idea is generalized to all patients and becomes the foundation of a new approach that supposedly supersedes other approaches.

CONCLUDING REMARKS

It seems that transformation in the clinical psychoanalytic situation works a bit differently than theoretical transformation. Psychoanalytic theory development seems to empirically depend on a theoretical group asserting that change comes from within itself. A group does not acknowledge that major tenets are incorrect. Rather, it seems to assert that the tenets can be understood differently, in line with contemporary advances, and that the newer ways of understanding are really implicit in the old theoretical hypotheses. In other words, preservation of a group's identity seems to always be paramount. Once this task feels complete, then a group gingerly addresses issues raised by other groups and begins to accommodate to them. In contrast, while an individual's identity concerns are certainly crucial in clinical psychoanalytic work, as we have discussed, change is perhaps more easily attained.

Why might this be? Let us return to Freedman's idea that opposing sides of conflict are both stimulated and then synthesized through the "hegemony of a libidinal object relationship" (Freedman 1985). It is that object relationship in analytic work that allows the patient to come to terms with anxiety-provoking material. The analyst is the object who both stimulates the conflict and serves to help the patient synthesize it. In tensions between psychoanalytic groups, conflict is provoked by new theoretical ideas that challenge ideas accepted by another theoretical system. However, there is no object to serve as a rubric within which synthesis between theoretical systems becomes narcissistically acceptable. While there are always trends toward synthesis, there are many more pressures toward increased differentiation.

What could serve such a function? The question brings us to one of Dr. Freedman's passions: psychoanalytic research. To what extent does empirical data affect the process of theoretical transformation? Good data, gathered in a way that seems relevant and acceptable to most practicing psychoanalysts, could serve a unifying function. This would not necessarily occur because the data answered controversial questions (although that would certainly help). The data would also serve as a narcissistically safe way for a group to begin to reconsider aspects of its basic tenets. They would concede to the *data* rather than to the *other group*. The data would become like the trusted and respected mediator in a boundary dispute between two nations. It would also, then, become the libidinal environment within which change could occur.

I have attempted to illustrate how Freedman's ideas about transformation are valuable in understanding change both in clinical psychoanalysis and in the evolution of psychoanalytic theory. I would again like to express my appreciation to Dr. Freedman for his pioneering efforts in so many areas of psychoanalysis.

REFERENCES

Akhtar, S. (1998). From simplicity through contradiction to paradox: the evolving psychic reality of the borderline patient in treatment. *International Journal of Psycho-Analysis* 79:241–252.

Aron, L. (1996). *A Meeting of Minds*. Hillsdale, NJ: Analytic Press.

——— (1999). Clinical choices and the relational matrix. *Psychoanalytic Dialogues* 9:1–29.

Bach, S. (1983). *Narcissistic States and the Therapeutic Process*. New York: Jason Aronson.

Balint, M. (1968). *The Basic Fault*. New York: Brunner/Mazel.

Bergmann, M. (1993). Reflections on the history of psychoanalysis. *Journal of the American Psychoanalytic Association* 41:929–955.

——— (1997). The historical roots of psychoanalytic orthodoxy. *International Journal of Psycho-Analysis* 78:69–86.

Bion, W. R. (1959). *Experiences in Groups*. New York: Basic Books.

Druck, A. (1989). *Four Therapeutic Approaches to the Borderline Patient*. Northvale, NJ: Jason Aronson.

——— (1998). Deficit and conflict: an attempt at integration. In *The Modern Freudians*, ed. C. Ellman, M. S. Grand, M. Silvan, and S. J. Ellman, pp. 209–233. Northvale, NJ: Jason Aronson.

——— (2000). Organizational structure and the establishment of psychoanalytic identification. *Psychoanalytic Dialogues* 10(6):889–907.

Eisold, K. (1994). The intolerance of diversity in psychoanalytic institutes. *International Journal of Psycho-Analysis* 75:785–800.

Freedman, N. (1985). The concept of transformation in psychoanalysis. *Psychoanalytic Psychology* 2:317–339.

Greenberg, J. (1996). Loewald's transitional model. *Journal of the American Psychoanalytic Association* 44:886–895.

Grunes, M. (1984). The therapeutic object relationship. *Psychoanalytic Review* 71:123–143.

Katz, G. A. (1998). Where the action is: the enacted dimension of analytic process. *Journal of the American Psychoanalytic Association* 46(4):1129–1167.

Kernberg, O. F. (1975). *Borderline Conditions and Pathological Narcissism*. New York: Jason Aronson.

——— (1984). *Severe Personality Disorders*. New Haven, CT: Yale University Press.

——— (1992). *Aggression in Personality Disorders and Perversions*. New Haven, CT: Yale University Press.

King, P., and Steiner, R., eds. (1991). *The Freud–Klein Controversies 1941–1945*. New York and London: Tavistock/Routledge.

Kohut, H. (1971). *The Analysis of the Self*. New York: International Universities Press.

Lasky, R. (1990). The influence of neurotic conflict on the analyst's choice of theory and technique. *Psychoanalytic Reflections* 1:110–134.

Levenson, E. (1972). *The Fallacy of Understanding*. New York: Basic Books.

Lipton, S. (1977). The advantages of Freud's technique as shown in his analysis of the rat-man. *International Journal of Psycho-Analysis* 58:255–273.

Loewald, H. (1980). On the therapeutic action of psychoanalysis. In *Papers on Psychoanalysis*, pp. 221–256. New Haven, CT: Yale University Press.

Mitchell, S. A. (1999). Reply to Richards. *The Round Robin* XIV(1):10–14.

Pine, F. (1988). The four psychologies of psychoanalysis and their place in clinical work. *Journal of the American Psychoanalytic Association* 36:571–596.

——— (1990). *Drive, Ego, Object, and Self*. New York: Basic Books.

Richards, A. (1999a). A. A. Brill and the politics of exclusion. *Journal of the American Psychoanalytic Association* 47:9–28.

——— (1999b). An intervention in the contemporary psychoanalytic debate. *The Round Robin* XIV(1):1, 6–9.

Rothstein, A. (1983). *The Structural Hypothesis: An Evolutionary Perspective*. New York: International Universities Press.

Sandler, J. (1960). The background of safety. *International Journal of Psycho-Analysis* 41:352–365.

——— (1976). Countertransference and role-responsiveness. *International Review of Psychoanalysis* 3:43–47.

Schafer, R. (1997). *The Contemporary Kleinians of London*. Madison, CT: International Universities Press.

Sechehaye, M. A. (1951). *Symbolic Realization*. New York: International Universities Press.

Slochower, J. A. (1996). *Holding and Psychoanalysis: A Relational Perspective*. Hillsdale, NJ: Analytic Press.

Stone, L. (1961). *The Psychoanalytic Situation*. New York: International Universities Press.

Tyson, P. (1996). Loewald as anticipator and integrator. *Journal of the American Psychoanalytic Association* 44:868–883.

Winnicott, D. W. (1975). *Through Paediatrics to Psychoanalysis*. New York: Basic Books.

8

Symbolizing as Abstraction: Its Role in Psychoanalytic Treatment

LAWRENCE FRIEDMAN

PURPOSE

Empirical research, such as that undertaken by Freedman and Lavender (1997), holds exciting prospects of substantive new knowledge about the connection between symbolizing and psychotherapy. The present essay does not purport to advance substantive knowledge. It is merely a way of rethinking symbolization and analytic procedure. In these terms, I simply rephrase familiar formulas of treatment rationale, sometimes altering the emphasis. Why should one bother to rephrase familiar concepts? I believe that the grasp of an elusive subject becomes firmer when we have different ways of cornering it. When assorted formulations don't actually confuse (as they frequently do), they help to clarify each other.

PSYCHOANALYSIS AS A FUNCTION OF SYMBOLIZING

Psychoanalysis has often been understood as a work of symbolizing. Treatment is thought to put into symbols what has been insufficiently or improperly symbolized.

As everybody knows, Freud's most explicit discussion of symbols was his account of the fluid primary process. According to Freud's theory, primary process ties one representation to another as each is visited in turn by a common drive in search of discharge. These representations may be considered symbols of each other, and ultimately of the original drive, which was, so to speak, "looking" to find an experience that is identical to a memory of satisfaction, or one that could re-create a whole nexus of urges. (Of course, Freud also referred to phylogenetically prepared symbols, and these were useful in dream interpretation, but they played only a small role in his theory of the mind.) More implicitly, Freud presented a general theory of symbolizing: language makes it possible to represent the relationships among things. Furthermore, there is a distant implication in Freud's topography that the "binding" of drive energies in the preconscious amounts to a kind of (temporary) surrogate satisfaction achieved by objective command of the world. One could argue that this general satisfaction in symbolizing explains the effect of treatment as it enhances the reality principle, increases self-responsibility, refines relationships among thing presentations, and provides sublimated satisfactions.

Freud's implicit theory of symbolizing gave it the job of sustaining hope in the presence of frustration. The real world we live in gets its flavor and human significance from the sometimes-indefinitely delayed satisfaction of the drives. Freud was interested in the satisfaction that was being delayed or sublimated, and so he dwelt more on symbols as disguising other meanings than as constructing the world via the reality principle. Ferenczi (1909) developed the latter implication, as did the Kleinian artist Adrian Stokes (see Friedman 1974). A typical Freudian symbol might be a phenomenon (a conversion symptom) substituted for a "mnemic symbol." Or a symbol might be a peculiar inborn representation of a vital meaning. Or it might be a representation upon which a number of primitive wishes converge. (Petocz [1999] has nicely outlined these uses by Freud.)

What are known as "Freudian symbols" have lost prominence in psychoanalysis. Interest in universal symbols has declined. Repression has yielded its hegemony over other defense mechanisms and interest has flagged in the dream work per se. Analysts aim less at unraveling mysterious symbols and more at freeing up processes—processes that form, transform, and liberalize symbolizing. In short, there is a new interest in the general process of meaning formation. It is a matter of emphasis. The old emphasis was on achieved knowledge (interpretation and insight), while in many quarters now the emphasis is on process.

No doubt the goal remains, as always, the achievement of better mental integration. But that phrase is too static to convey the sense of flow and process that many analysts have been describing as their goal. French analysts, in particular, see themselves as freeing up a flow of unconscious symbolizing. They also believe that what cannot be symbolized finds expression in bodily illness as well as disadvantageous behavior. That is a common theme in psychoanalysis, and the focus of interesting empirical research. "Postmodern" analysts lay special emphasis on the symbolizing process as an end in itself. On a more general level, the cardinal psychoanalytic notion of motivated, symbolic disguise is challenged or modified in some quarters (Bromberg 1998, Daniel Stern 1998, Donnel Stern 1997), or generalized to a universal function of all mental products (Brenner 1982).

In general, when the term *symbol* is used, its meaning has varied a good deal.

WHAT DO WE MEAN BY *SYMBOL*?

As Tzvetan Todorov (1982) says, symbols can be thought of in two ways. We can think of them as arbitrary designators. Those are the symbols that especially interest mathematicians and logicians. Or symbols can be thought of as sharing the quality or emotional significance of what they represent, these being the sort of symbols that literary people and psychoanalysts are interested in. "Freudian symbols" are examples of meaning-pregnant symbols. There has been much controversy over which of these notions best expresses the nature of language. At one extreme, Ferdinand de Saussure (1972) and some modern philosophers regard language as a kind of conventional calculus. On the other hand, Freudians, interested in wish and feeling, are naturally interested in speech that carries felt meaning. But no matter which way one looks at symbolizing, I will argue that its largest significance is the same: *It is a marker of abstraction.*

SYMBOLIZATION IS CONCEPTUALIZATION

It is unfortunate that the term *symbol* regularly focuses people's attention on a mechanism of coding, rather than on the all-important act that it crowns—the act of abstracting. When we hear the word "symbol," we are apt to picture a label or a logo (if we believe in meaning-saturated symbols), or perhaps tokens of a board game (if we are of the conventional calculus school). We think of a symbol as something that is put in place of something else (with which it may share resonance), as was true of the "Freudian symbol." We may think of a symbol as a useful tool. Or we may think of it as a member of a systematic collection. We may picture a coin shared or exchanged among companions, something that serves mainly as a means of communication. It can, indeed, be any one of these.

In fact, however, even the most formal system of typographical elements is noteworthy chiefly as the outcome of an act of abstracting. And in its most refined form, when it produces the examples we usually have in mind, it is coextensive with conceptualizing. That is true even when the symbols are sublinguistic. (The relationship of words to concepts is a controversial matter, of great speculative concern to philosophers and great practical concern to psychoanalysts. I touch on this later.)

THE ROOTS OF SYMBOLIZING

Our conventional symbol systems (words, mathematics) stand at an extreme end of a spectrum that arises from the organism's most primitive selection of a proper nutriment from the overall environment.

Does that seem far-fetched—word use and bird food on a par? But if we grant that a symbol, in its largest sense, is just a single figure that can somehow be repeated at other times and places, we must also grant that the bird lives in a world of worm symbols. The bird sees the moment's worm as representative of its historical eating mission. The bird's recognition of the worm's significance foreshadows man's infinitely elaborated tendency to see something as both itself (the momentary object, the wriggling worm) and as a representative of something more general (bird breakfast: the genus with its causal nexus). In that very general sense, we must say that symbolizing is what happens with every natural reaction to the environment. The organism "sees" everything as an *example* of something (see Uexkull, as cited in Cassirer 1944). For the bird, the symbolic representation of worm is an internal releasing mechanism, the ancestor of what is popularly referred to as procedural knowledge.

Nor does the primitive symbol lack a full system of its own. We must suppose that a bird sees a whole situation in every glimpse; otherwise it could not avail itself of its opportunities. (It knows enough about worms and earth to realize that the worm will burrow back into the earth unless seized promptly at one end and extracted.) We can translate the bird's awareness into a schema, or a programmed system of relations. But that translation should not be used to hide the complexity of the symbolism; to the bird, symbols present a worm substance and essence, cause (of the wriggling appearance), and relations (between worm and landscape), just as ours do, albeit in relatively simple and implicit form. Causal expectations are important ingredients in perception, from the earliest life forms upward. The bird has worm-dynamics and pecking consequences built into its little brain; it knows what will happen *if*. . . . One need only watch a bird at work to confirm this. Every organic movement, and certainly every perception, is an appraisal and an expectation. A perception is not the whole world coming into the organism; a perception is a selected symbol of something relevant. That point is made by Suzanne Langer (1972). It underlies the general phenomenology of Maurice Merleau-Ponty (1962). But it is no less present in the predictive meaning of scientific formulations. So when we speak of symbolizing, we are speaking of knowledge of objects and causality.

Why say that symbols represent objects and causality? Don't we associate symbols with emotion rather than cognition? That is our tendency, but we should not think of emotion and cognition as distinct faculties. John Bowlby (1969) pointed out that feelings serve to appraise a situation. We might consider the view of the philosopher Suzanne Langer (1972), who wrote that all mentation amounts to evaluation, the fine gradations of which are expressed as emotion. She locates the superiority of human intelligence in its elaborate development of emotionality, a thesis that finds recent biological support in Jaak Panksepp's (1999) evidence that a central brain mechanism (the periaqueductal gray matter) channels emotional appraisal in both lower and higher vertebrates. So we have reason to think that conceptual abstractions are defined partly by their emotional relevance. Or, reading it backwards, emotional relevance helps to define objects, elucidate cause-and-effect sequences, and predict the future.

Psychoanalytic theory encouraged speculation about the earliest infantile abstractions, suggesting that they centered on body functions and pleasures. In the twentieth century, there has been bitter argument about whether, in fact, there is such a single lineage of meanings, and whether one can know ahead of time the realm in which the most "basic" significance of a meaning (a symbol) will be found. According to Todorov (1982), psychoanalysis assumes that certain sexual significances are the basic elements that investigation will ultimately reveal. Agnes Petocz (1999) argues that at least all nonconventional symbol formation *must* be motivated in the Freudian fashion. (She assumes a sharp distinction between conventional and nonconventional symbols—a distinction that hermeneuticists dispute.) Robert Waelder (1930), a philosophically sophisticated Freudian, pointed out that meanings can relate to many universes, and it is a specialist *choice* that allows Freudians to select body, sex, and childhood meanings as primary. Marxists, Jungians, and others insist on their own ultimate "primitives." Lakoff and Johnson (1980, 1999) propose that all concepts derive from a sense of the body's orientation in space. On the whole, however, infant observation suggests that meanings are formed in more than one primary domain. One cannot ignore the evidence that infants distinguish all kinds of similarities and differences, as well as specific acoustic features, faces, self-generated contingent events, attachment expectations, and so on. The data suggest that at 3 months, infants can identify the music of conversation (see Stern 1994) and the infant brain seems to be programmed to hook together different sensory modalities (such as touch and sight), thus abstracting more and more creatively (Karmiloff-Smith 1994).

At issue, of course, is not just whether there is a knowable form and inspiration of the first abstractions, but whether, after numerous reconceptualizations, every contemporary meaning is *tinted* by its ancestry, an Ur-meaning, which can thus claim to be its "real" or "deep" meaning. Insofar as abstractions are created under the impetus of wishes. a Freudian might argue that the wish stays alive in all its later modifications (Petocz 1999). If that were true, knowledge of the vocabulary of primitive wishes would provide a key to the main interest concealed in each meaning. All these "methodical" theories are anathema to the newer hermeneuticists such as Hans-Georg Gadamer (1975), who holds that meanings are not constant in their contemplation or transmission, and that we cannot presume to know what will be found on examination. (But even Gadamer allows for unconscious meanings.)

Although abstractions have to start somewhere (as, for example, with sensory-motor schemas, or prepared brain-modules, or neural networks, or erotic zone excitement, or even archetypes or prehistoric memories), it seems pretty clear that they don't *end* anywhere. The hallmark of the human type of abstraction is that, once started, it has no limit. Farthest from the bird's simple abstraction of worm-food, we find human words, and still farther, mathematics. From abstractions achieved in words and numbers an always-receding abstractive horizon ceaselessly beckons forward to further abstraction. This is Ernst Cassirer's (1944) notion of symbolism, and it is the one I will favor. The availability of concepts to endless further abstraction is the achievement of human formal symbolism, speech, logic, and mathematics.

Language has many mysteries and a talking cure involves them all. But we should not forget that the psychoanalytic problem has to do not with language per se, but with the abstractions and the abstractive tendencies that language helps to form. Treatment has to do with what is being put into language, as well as how language facilitates the selection. When we say that psychoanalytic treatment creates or restores symbolizing we really mean that treatment fosters accurate abstractions and a fluid process of symbolizing. So our first question is how abstractions come to be formed, and the second is what influences their formation.

WHAT ARE THE ADVANTAGES OF CONCEPTUAL REPRESENTATION?

What does human concept formation add to primitive, organic readiness? Why isn't it sufficient to symbolize the world the way a bird symbolizes worms? First, let's list a few of the virtues that have been ascribed to conceptualization. Piaget (1978) says that concepts, even when unverbalized, allow a greater number of *coordinations* among a larger number of variables than is possible without concepts. And concepts enhance the ability to *predict* in more "worlds" than, for example, a bird lives in. The same power leads to a greater understanding of the expectable variability within a given field, that is, an understanding of the essential *nature of what's symbolized*. Furthermore, according to Piaget, symbolizing helps us control the world by understanding ourselves as actors in it. Abstractive symbolizing builds an understanding of the essential *nature of our own appetites and will* (they become less automated and reflexive). According to Gergeley and Watson (1996), a human mother's constant imagining "into" her baby helps him *objectivize his feeling states and emotions*, so that these can be used for *predicting his own and other people's reactions*. If, as maintained by Damasio (1999), consciousness is the awareness of the outside in relation to the inside, it would follow that a conscious, refined scanning of one's feelings will lead to a finer *appraisal of the outside world*. That principle is exploited in psychotherapy. It is supported by Piaget's (1967) argument that intentions and will are objectivized when children perfect their representations in play. Target and Fonagy

(1996) add that, first with the mother and then in other circumstances, the child rehearses two different modes of thinking: one where an idea is supposed to correspond to the real world, and another that is understood as just play. Distinguishing a play mode from objective reality allows the development of *reflective functioning* in which ideas are turned over and examined in their own right.

These are a few of the observations that suggest that concept formation involves picturing the self and the world as objects. As objects, the self and others endure through time and undergo predictable changes. Once seen as objects, more aspects of self and the world are abstractable. And, once abstracted, still more can always be abstracted from each of those abstractions. Each aspect can be examined in various ways and seen to have dependable features from which regular consequences are to be expected. Symbolizing has something to do with thinking objectively, that is, thinking about *things*, including feeling-things and emotion-things.

The great—indeed infinite—variety of available abstractions is a vast improvement over mere organic routines. But it is simply a capacity. It does not say how or why any particular abstractions are made. Human beings depend on abstractions that go way beyond preestablished abstractions like the bird's worm-food. Other mechanisms must decide which abstractions to make. Human motivation complicates the picture. How are wishes formed and how do they affect the choice of abstractions? The weight of this problem bears down upon us especially when we consider our inner hall-of-mirrors, the endless reflections upon our own reflections and reactions to our reactions that constitute the flow of mentation. The tension between organicists and cognitivists, to which I refer later, revolves around disagreement about how motives affect symbols, and vice versa.

TWO PARADIGMS OF TREATMENT

The reader may think it pointless to worry about the biological lineage of abstraction and its largest possible meaning. When psychoanalysts talk about symbolization, isn't it just linguistic symbolism they refer to? Historically, psychoanalysis has been single-mindedly dedicated to "putting it into words." Other sorts of expression were considered evasions. As noted above, many analysts believe that unwordable, conflicted feelings are automatically shunted over to maladaptive behavior, disturbed affect, and physical illness. (French analysts are particularly emphatic on that score.) I seem to recall that the nineteenth-century psychiatrist, Frances Maudesley, declared that "grief that finds no vent in tears makes other organs weep." It should be noted that the physiological function of symbolizing is sometimes taken for granted by contemporary analysts. Those analysts who no longer believe in energic cathexis have yet to say how strangulated symbolism is transformed into behavioral and physical phenomena. In this country, at least, indirect ("nonsymbolic," physiological) pathways tend to be incriminated, such as the adrenocortical system, the immune system, and so on. Perhaps the most interesting work on the relationship between symbolizing and physiology is in the area of alexithymia, which I refer to below. But much remains to be discovered about the health value of words and the penalty for wordlessness. We are a long way from solving this problem, partly because there is little philosophical, evolutionary, or psychological agreement about the function of language and how it relates to reality.

But not all analysts today are so single-mindedly devoted to words. It was metapsychology that married words to biology, as Paul Ricoeur (1970) pointed out. With metapsychology in disfavor, force and meaning have separated, each going its own way with a vengeance. Two divergent trends are to be found in current theory of therapeutic action, which I will caricature as organicist and linguaphile. The organicists appeal to the force of biological systems. Organicists wouldn't find it far-fetched to line up the meaning of worm to bird with the meaning of mother to infant and the meaning of analyst to patient. For these theorists, answers to the riddle of treatment will be found in the reflex nature of life, that is, that which we share with worm-abstracting birds. Organicists call attention to the broad function of symbolizing that extends beyond words. They are particularly interested in nondeclarative knowledge—knowledge in the form of competence, knowledge as action routines (including emotional action routines). To their eye, "procedural knowledge" is the substrate of effective psychotherapy, and they invoke neurophysiology, affect regulation, procedural memory, infant–mother-type interactions, and so on, where words may be useful but are not definitive.

Heading out in the opposite direction is the linguaphile road. It dwells on language and especially rhetoric even more exclusively than did the classical Freudians. Thus, Roy Schafer (1983) describes treatment as the critique of narratives. And analysts influenced by hermeneutics and postmodern deconstructionism exclude from their universe everything that isn't words. (I am not sure where the neo-Janetian contemporary dissociation school fits in, since it abandons the weakness of mind with which Janet explained the relation between biology and idea. I sometimes wonder whether the new dissociationists don't avoid the organicist strategy by making mental division and mental "weakness" each explain the other.)

Linguaphiles think they are the only ones who deal with genuine symbols. They argue against organicists that the pathological fault lies not with implicit knowledge, but with the psychic reality that implicit knowledge is called on to handle—the crabbed vision, the sick scenario, the flawed account of the situation. They fear that organicists will return psychotherapy to habit-training. In their turn, organicists view the linguaphile's "literary" program as an empty formalism, resting on air and begging the question of constancy and change. They argue that narrated scenes do not float into the mind but are deliberately tailored to the viewer's motivational program, and they argue that it is that action program, not the tendentious scene evoked to justify it, that can cause trouble. Organicists believe they can explain the *vitality* of the linguaphile's symbols by tracing them to *preferences*.

When it comes to treatment, linguaphiles tend to overlook the struggle between analyst and patient, since linguaphiles depict treatment as the offering and exchanging of ways of thinking. For their part, organicists have the problem of explaining why their chosen means of treatment (especially the verbal means) can be expected to foster the desired new skills. And neither organicist nor linguaphile seems to take full advantage of the clues afforded by the analytic set-up. I will return to that below. Each in its own way runs the risk of ignoring the stressful double dissociation that is involved in treatment.

Of course, this story of organicists and linguaphiles is a brash caricature drawn from tendencies that every analyst blends within himself in varying proportions. No psychoanalyst believes that speech is without impact on a person's functioning, and few hold that speech alone develops the human constitution. The older Freudian literature availed itself of the term *preoedipal* as a code word for a recognized, nonverbal foundation of words. Unconscious fantasies were thought to organize action and *also* find expression in words. For some time, John Gedo (1979) has explored a compelling epigenetic account that carries procedural knowledge into a worded world. And most research psychoanalysts investigate the effect of words on affect regulation. Indeed, two of the most popular ideas today are that words change brain proteins, and that a mother's ability to articulate her experience influences the child's attachment security.

Studies of alexithymia suggest that learned words actually manufacture feelings from a more primitive substrate (Taylor 2000). But that may not be the first abstraction that occurs. The first symbols may be organic, nonverbal abstractions, only partly susceptible to subsequent linguistic modification. (They may be temporal contours, as in music, as mentioned by Stern [1998].) In the framework of this paper, one might say that a mother's reactions generate neurological abstractions from inborn feeling states, and those abstractions are then utilizable by language for further definition. A good example is Peter Fonagy's (1991) description of mentalization that leads upward from automatic reflex to affect regulation by conceptualization. Wilma Bucci (1997) suggests that visceral and emotional schemata are first formed not as categorically labeled items, but as unsegmented spectra of quality. These continua of feeling are then subject to translation into more specifically delineated images, concepts, and ultimately words. Bucci supposes that those adults who continue to abstract internal signals only into primitive spectra, as just more or less of something, and are unable to abstract again from those into categorical representations, are likely to develop physical symptoms. There is much food for speculation in this. Does abstraction set limits to visceral reflexes? Do superimposed layers of categorical abstraction invite their own modulating, emotional reflexes as they are reflected upon? Is physical health enhanced by the cross-modal abstractions that abstractions make possible? Such ideas promise a liaison between organic ("habit") theories and cognitive ("literary") theories. More explicitly, the Boston group, especially as elaborated by Daniel Stern (1994), attempts to correlate habit and symbol by means of schemata that include both. It is to be hoped that a new union of habit and symbol can be achieved because we need to understand why inadequate words make people sick (if we are talking like linguaphiles), or (if we prefer an organicist formula) what special skills are taught in a talking treatment. My argument is that we can be assured at least that habits and words have something in common, since both are examples of abstraction.

Everything that has been said to this point might have been put in the more familiar terms of "representation." Abstraction, conceptualization, symbolization, and representation are all ways of approaching the same issue. Thus we could say that organicists and linguaphiles address themselves to different examples of representation. Organicists favor schematic representations that are revealed in even unthought action. For them, organized expectations qualify as representations. Linguaphiles look for thinkable concepts expressible in words. They would remind us that the term *symbol* should be reserved for the repeatable marker of organized expectations. Let us now turn to that subject.

THE ROLE OF VERBAL DESCRIPTIONS

What's the use of words? What do they add to implicit abstractions and unstated symbols? To begin with, of course, language is one way that attitudes are conveyed. In some situations, a whole sentence might amount to a mere phatic expression, for example, a fancy way of saying "ugh." J. L. Austin (1962) describes the pragmatics of words, that is, their use to get people to do things or to confer a status. Theodore Shapiro (2002) argues that psychoanalysts have participated in a generational shift of interest from the semantic to the pragmatic realm, that is, from the cognitive content of a statement to its effects on the receiver. Many nonanalytic therapies alter abstractions by means of paradoxical words that are not descriptions. (Haley [1963] argues that psychoanalytic therapy really works that way.)

That said, let us narrow the question to the descriptive content of words, and consider the cognitive content of interpretations, self-descriptions, and accounts of what's on one's mind (the constative meaning of descriptive sentences, in contrast to their illocutionary or manipulative meaning). What does the mere semantic power of words do that cannot be done without words? The linguist Ray Jackendoff (1997) notes that words allow people to think and feel *about* the abstractions they have made (and we should remember that feeling is a way of discriminating more closely). Moreover, he points out, language marks off items as objects, so they can be followed through more changes over time. (Jackendoff reminds us that our sense of a specific future depends on language: without language, there is no Thursday-a-week.) This extends the range of symbolizing by emphasizing the substantiality and causality of things. Steven Pinker (1994) reinforces that point by observing that the form of language uses analog representation, which provides an actual image of causality, as digital computing would not.

We can continue with the list. Language makes entities out of feelings so they can be identified later and used as a basis for prediction (see Gergeley and Watson 1996). Language allows one to separate from the moment. And we may say that words are ways of feeling out the possibilities of one's self. The basic principle is that language allows and fosters a *process* of abstraction—a continuous process, in principle (Gadamer [1975] is emphatic on that score). It is the *direction* of continuous abstracting that analysts are interested in.

What does a person miss if he cannot put his feelings into words? A person who cannot abstract cannot see the dimensions of his reactions, and therefore is at a disadvantage in observing his relationship with the world. Most people who cannot put their feelings into words are unable to abstract the features that would have gone into those words. To be sure, words are not the only way of articulating facets of experience. There are other symbol systems (see Arnheim 1969,

Goodman 1976, Langer 1953). In fact, when the word "symbol" is mentioned, most people think of the arts, not language. Music and dance abstract in ways that seem impossible for words. People who are unable to put into words even the kind of feelings that usually require words may have their own ways of distinguishing aspects of their experience. Nevertheless, it seems safe to say that if one cannot put feelings into words, though he may abstract some features in an implicit fashion, he will be hampered in his ability to reflect on his abstractions (for example, he will fail to observe that he is overgeneralizing), and have difficulty training his feelings onto those abstractions. (In line with this, we might speculate that traumatic memories are frozen abstractions—symbols that are relatively opaque to their owner because their aspects cannot be further abstracted. Traumatic memories may remain symbols of inadequacy that a patient cannot escape from into other aspects that would correct the overwhelming helplessness, such as active or adaptive aspects of the experience.) And, finally, the alexithymic person may be relatively lacking in an affective sensory system capable of abstraction.

THE CHOICE OF ABSTRACTIONS

Why do we abstract into the particular bundle or aspects that characterize our inner and outer worlds? Many contemporary philosophers claim that the choice of one's abstractions is not motivated at all but is dictated by one's language community. While that is largely true of language as a system, it is doubtful as regards speech. Speech is infinitely inventive and expressive (see Gadamer 1975, Pinker 1994). Analysts are in a good position to know that. They are painfully aware that patients must work hard to find a way of speaking their mind. As previously noted, when contemporary psychoanalysts say "symbolization," they usually mean verbalization of something that has been hitherto less verbalized, and they think of it as a transformation from depth to surface, not a translation from one symbol to another. (Theories of primary process and unconscious fantasy are equivocal on the issue.)

We are indebted to recent interpersonalists and intersubjectivists (Bromberg 1998, Hoffman 1998, Donnel Stern 1997) for reactivating the original Freudian question of how people form and transform their meanings. These writers prompt us to look beyond the relationship between already prepared meanings. They ask us to look anew at the state of relatively unsymbolized mentation and its relationship to perfected symbols. Unfortunately, in contrast to Freudians, these new theorists content themselves with very general sorts of motives to explain why a person abstracts as he does and not otherwise. Habituation and fear of novelty are frequently cited motives, and are no doubt worthy of more consideration than Freudians have given them (although nothing is more basic to Freud's system than the repetition compulsion). But Freudians demand something more specific to explain why a patient preferentially abstracts certain features of his mental scene, subordinates some abstractions to others, and consistently fails to abstract certain features altogether. Freudians answer those questions by a theory of defense and compromise. Interpersonalists and intersubjectivists deserve credit for alerting us to neglected phenomena of therapy that Freudians tend to relegate to an undertheorized preconscious. But I think that, like Freud, most psychoanalysts—indeed, most working psychotherapists—find few forces as formidable as the motives that *dictate* what a patient will and will not abstract from his thinking and feeling.

MOTIVATING AND MOTIVATED ABSTRACTIONS

If Freudians have elaborated in exquisite detail the general motives that shape expressions, they have not done quite so thorough a job on patients' motives for altering their abstractions as a result of treatment.

Useful hints on this subject may be found in Daniel Stern's (1994) model. In effect, he reminds us that abstractions are not confined to static items. Many symbols are symbols of sequences. One might say that symbolized sequences are abstractions characterized by a rhythm of effort and effect. (Stern is primarily interested in interpersonal experience, so he dwells on symbols that capture interpersonal sequences.) Symbols that refer to sequences are narratives. They have purpose, and therefore wish, built into them, and such is the essence of narrative. And we should bear in mind that narratives embrace many orders of both physical and moral experience, as Ricoeur (1988) demonstrates. Stern's model has the further advantage of allowing many dimensions to a single representation. A single representation has within it percepts, concepts, sensorimotor operations, and event sequences, all ordered into a single experience with an overall "temporal feeling shape," colored by effort. Stern is an infant watcher, and he persuades us that the earliest infantile forms of representation are probably protonarrational, having a dramatic or narrational—even musical—content that tracks interactions with the mother. Feeling and value help shape a representation into a complex symbol that orchestrates many components. Within one and the same envelope an assortment of varied emphases can be made, and the whole can be used as a fantasy, a memory, or a way of perceiving current experience. This complex object or schema has in it many levels of implicit and explicit knowledge, felt relevance, and speakable landscape. Thus Stern bridges the gap between organicists and logocentrists.

Therapists will welcome the implication of Stern's model that a motive packaged in such a schema can become a somewhat different motive within the same schema, as its relationship to other aspects of the schema is shuffled into the foreground or background. The orchestral schema can be played differently. For example, the emphasis might be on the experience as either a difficulty or an aspiration, a means to an end or an achieved success. (Piaget's model also permits us to imagine a patient focusing on means or ends, motive or situation.) The patient himself, according to Stern, runs through many versions of the momentary schema as he processes his current experience with the analyst. Perhaps most importantly, Stern offers a picture of a determinate something in the mind that can be rearranged and thus changed when it is regarded in a different light. In that way, he bridges the gap between narrational theories like Schafer's and substantialist theories like Freud's. (It is my impression that Stern does not take full advantage of that possibility.)

Viewed that way, psychological trouble might be thought of as inability to rearrange components of experience. Although Stern (1998) helps us with part of our difficulty by building motives into representations, I think he tends to neglect the motives for *rearranging* narrative schemas. As I read him, Stern (1998) contents himself with a general motive of being-with-another, and leaves undiscussed the particular wishes that act *on* schemas *of* motives. But Stern's general approach allows us the option of picturing hosts of different motives that might organize a schema this way and that from one time to another. The specific impetus for such a particular organization of a given schema might be one of Gedo's progressively unfolding motives, or one of Joseph Lichtenberg's (1983) modular, motivational schemas. These are possible motors of a particular act of abstracting *from* an established abstraction, in other words, styles of symbolizing a symbol.

To repeat, Stern builds motivation into symbols (of an interaction), and leaves us free to imagine impinging motives that change the representation of the preexisting motives. And he paints a truly beautiful picture of representations that do not just represent complex objects, but are themselves complex objects. Stern is therefore able to describe how a represented state of oneself can be seen in various lights, depending on what is highlighted. One might say that he shows how Donnel Stern's (1997) "unformulated experience" might get to be formulated.

WHAT IS THE PECULIARITY OF THE PSYCHOANALYTIC PROCEDURE?

In order to consider what symbolizing has to do with psychoanalysis, we must decide what to take as the hallmark of analytic treatment. It is not our objective to show how symbolizing is involved in psychotherapy generally. Life is probably not long enough to count those ways. Even in psychoanalysis, there may be ways that symbolism plays the same role as it does, for example, in voodoo healing. More to the point, an overall psychoanalytic experience almost certainly uses symbolizing in ways similar to religious counseling, behavior modification, gypsy dream interpretation, psychodrama, and the general practice of family medicine. Although a daunting and controversial task, we must locate something that is unique to the psychoanalytic situation in order to ask if symbolizing serves a *special* function in psychoanalytic treatment.

The easiest description of psychoanalysis portrays it as an investigative conversation. That is surely an accurate description, but it is also deceptive, at least as a description of the historical practice. For example, both the intimacy and the separateness of conversation are simultaneously exaggerated in a psychoanalysis. The field of forces thus set up, with all the suspended questions about the status, attitudes, affectionate and hostile bonds, and ultimate interests of the partners, must be factored into any account of analytic treatment. The slightest experience with psychoanalysis or psychoanalytic therapy reveals quickly enough that this charged atmosphere is what is special to the procedure. Since our task is to understand how symbolizing figures in psychoanalytic treatment, we must make sure that we have traced its relation to the uneasy uncertainties of the analytic relationship, and not just to the verbal conversation and the investigation that superficially seem to encompass the whole of the symbolizing work.

WHAT ABSTRACTIONS DO ANALYSTS WISH TO FOSTER?

Just as it is too broad a question to ask where symbolism is used in treatment, it is too broad a question to ask what inspires the making of an abstraction. It is the same as asking what calls a person's attention to something. We must be more specific. For one thing, psychotherapies are interested in directing a patient's attention in an especially unfamiliar direction. What prompts a person to form a truly *novel* abstraction? Two frequent answers given by infant and child observers are (1) observing something unexpected, and (2) wrestling with a problem. Following that hint, we might guess that all psychotherapies present the patient with an unexpected relationship and a new problem of some sort. I believe that therapies can be classified in terms of how and toward what they direct attention. In particular, therapies differ on the kind of problem their typical relationship poses. Some powerful therapies deliberately put patients in social predicaments. Disconfirmation of an expectation looms large in therapies such as Alexander's (1956) and that of the Mt. Zion group (Weiss and Sampson 1986). A patient might also be confronted with a discrepancy between his image of himself and the analyst's observation of his behavior, as in most psychoanalytic interpretations. In general, a psychoanalyst's socially aberrant behavior always poses a monumental problem for the patient, and one might say that transferences are part of his solution to that problem (see Macalpine 1950). The task that is set for both patient and analyst is vividly presented by Freedman and Lavender (1997) in their description of the detachment from automatic immersion and the need for inner mental space that is prerequisite for symbolizing.

What sort of abstractions do psychoanalysts want their patients to make? What do they want them to symbolize? Although some postmodem practitioners might demur, for the most part psychoanalysis is not aimed at just any new abstractions or symbolization. It is concerned with wishful views and the wishes embodied in actions. Characteristically, analysts want patients to take distance from their composite momentary wishes in order to abstract wish components from the overall effort. Because the patient's effort is a blend of motives (a compromise formation, as Brenner [1982] points out), disassembling them interferes with their blended implementation. We think again of the mental space that must be available for symbolization to occur (as discussed by Freedman and Berzofsky 1995 and Freedman and Lavender 1997).

That is why psychoanalysis is not a purely intellectual process. A patient might reflect quite usefully on his customary view of himself, abstracting various aspects in the process. He can do that any time in solitary introspection. But the abstraction that counts in analysis involves a personal self-alienation, a suspension of whole-hearted effort at satisfaction, and therefore an analysand must be trying for satisfaction at the time, not just thinking about it or remembering it. What one identifies with must be given up even while identifying with it, in order to appropriate its separate (i.e., abstract) aspects. It is not like turning a hammer to look at its head; it's like hammering while twisting the tool to see its head (and accordingly, an analysand may feel that he is hitting himself on the head instead of nailing down what he wanted). The patient must have his aim still in view if he is to examine it, and that means he must still feel the desirability of the very response in the analyst that he is jeopardizing by acknowledging his motives. Psychoanalysis is abstraction in the midst of action. That is what is so unusual about analysis and so painful for both parties.

HOW DOES ANALYTIC STRAIN FOSTER ITS PREFERRED ABSTRACTIONS?

For a patient to abstract his motives and their relevant world, we may suppose that he needs to draw them from sequences. Daniel Stern calls them "schemas of being-with-another," and he says that they can be resymbolized alternatively as memory, fantasy, or perception. The elements of each of those can, in turn, be abstracted in various ways, just as a tale can be told to illustrate various points or to highlight various elements, and be offered as history or as myth. Stern says this resymbolizing is determined by context. That may be only a partial account. Context provides opportunities for motives, but wishes do the deciding. Just as with static symbols, reabstractions (reflections) of narrative abstractions can be made during solitary introspection, remembering, or fantasizing. But it is only in interaction with another person that narratives can be experienced as perception. With a psychoanalyst, they are put into play more variously than can occur with ordinary companions who mobilize few such narratives, or whose response hems in the result. The analyst alone provides a context both passionate and nonconfirming that prompts new abstractions.

To say that the analyst provides a context for new abstractions is putting it mildly. After all, it is problems that orient attention, and attention is what guides abstraction. Thus, the direction of attention is partly determined not just by the analyst's explicit instruction, but by the problem that is set for the patient. One major way that an analyst controls the patient's attention is by creating tension (usually inadvertently and by custom). And one big tension-maker is the analyst's professional vision. The analyst is interested not just in what is happening at the moment but in the persisting principles that guide the patient. In other words, he reacts to a scene that is abstracted not just in the fashion of a narrative (with the patient as a dramatic figure), but also in a static fashion (with the patient as a theoretical object), that is, as a person who repeats customary ways of dealing with life because of his psychic make-up. That is not a comfortable way to be reacted to. To use Daniel Stern's term, the patient attempts to implement a schema of "being with another," and the psychoanalyst, instead of reacting with a Buber-like matching of that state, overlays his sense of the interpersonal drama with less dramatic abstractions of "human nature." There is a certain timelessness, a physicality in the analyst's view, underpinning his technique, rather at odds with the personal aspect of the relationship. Insofar as those abstractions color the analyst's reactions (and nonreactions), patients will see their dramas resymbolized in quite different terms. What will their response be? They may imitate that "objective" view, as Sterba described. They might hold up their narrative schema to the light and examine it as an *item* (of their nature) rather then as an interval (of their life saga). Analysts hope that patients will see the ethically neutral view as well as the social drama. I suspect, however, that patients always perceive the analyst's behavior toward them as an evaluative act in a current social drama, whether or not they also accept a view of themselves *sub specie aeternitas*. An analyst's most objective, arms-length response, for example, will be felt anyway as a particular narrative commentary, portraying the patient in some dramatic, and consequently ethical, light. My guess is that the best that can be asked of an analysand is a good faith *attempt* to purge ethical nuances from what the analyst intends as a nondramatic interpretation. I suspect it is the process of wrestling with that tension that gives rise to the patient's refiguring of himself that Daniel Stern refers to. Again, this is basically the thesis of Macalpine (1950), of Bird (1972), and of Sterba (1934) when looked at carefully.

But, as is often asked these days, doesn't a greater naturalness on the part of the analyst do more good? Don't the gains come about precisely when the strain is minimized? What about the beneficial effect noted by Daniel Stern and many others that issue from those turning points when the analyst emerges from his professional restraint with a risk-taking, informal, unpremeditated authenticity? What consequences might we anticipate if the analyst departs from a routine that, though painful, has been given an established transference meaning? Such unexpectedness would tend to challenge the abstractions that comprise the patient's transference. The result might be a frightening sense of the analyst's unreliability. It might be a reassuring sense of the analyst's mere humanity. It might be the affirmation of the patient's personal power or appeal. It might be the encouragement of a particular transference fantasy. In each case, the analyst's unexpected behavior would challenge the abstractions that comprised the patient's preexisting transference.

All in all, it seems likely that analysis depends on its agonistic aspect for its special abstractive force. One might say that the analyst's resistance is what's essential. The way a struggle fosters the special kind of analytic abstraction is suggested by Piaget's paradigm of the growth of knowledge out of action. Piaget (1976) argues that children learn how things work and what their own goals are by progressively reflecting on, and integrating, what they have found themselves doing that turns out to be successful and by trying to account for failure. He says that understanding moves from the periphery to the center, which means that, as regards acts on the world, understanding proceeds from the achieved goal to the strategies that achieved it. That process simultaneously reveals the inner laws of the object worked on and the nature of the will that set the strategies in motion. If we accept this as a general principle, we might assume that the patient's understanding of his own representations and narrative schemas will become more accurate as he sees himself struggling with the analyst for the desired response. In other words, the fullest elaboration of a patient's abstractions will be made when the actions they dictate are most fully activated. This, after all, is common sense. And it is a way of saying that a certain kind of frustrating tease might foster the symbolizing process. At a time when such a tease is often regarded as a purely noxious component of psychoanalysis, this possibility should be kept in mind.

REFERENCES

Alexander, F. (1956). *Psychoanalysis and Psychotherapy: Developments in Theory, Technique and Training*. New York: Norton.

Arnheim. R. (1969). *Visual Thinking*. Berkeley: University of California Press.

Austin, J. L. (1962). *How to Do Things with Words*, 2nd ed. Cambridge, MA: Harvard University Press.

Balint, M. (1968). *The Basic Fault*. London: Tavistock.

Bird, B. (1972). Notes on transference: universal phenomenon and hardest part of analysis. *Journal of the American Psychoanalytic Association* 20:267–301.

Bowlby, J. (1969). *Attachment and Loss*, vol. 1: *Attachment*. New York: Basic Books.

Brenner, C. (1982). *The Mind in Conflict*. New York: International Universities Press.

Bromberg, P. M. (1998). *Standing in the Spaces: Essays on Clinical Process, Trauma, and Dissociation*. Hillsdale, NJ: Analytic Press.

Bucci, W. (1997). Symptoms and symbols: a multiple code theory of somatization. *Psychoanalytic Inquiry* 17:151–172.

Cassirer, E. (1944). *An Essay on Man: An Introduction to a Philosophy of Human Culture*. New Haven, CT: Yale University Press.

Damasio, A. (1999). *The Feeling of What Happens: Body and Emotion in the Making of Consciousness*. New York: Harcourt Brace.

Ferenczi, S. (1909). Introjection and transference. In *Sex in Psycho-Analysis*, trans. E. Jones, pp. 33–93. Boston: Richard G. Badger, 1916.

Ferenczi, S., and Rank, O. (1925). *The Development of Psycho-Analysis*, trans. C. Newton. New York: Nervous and Mental Disease Publications.

Fonagy, P. (1991). Thinking about thinking: some clinical and theoretical considerations in the treatment of a borderline patient. *International Journal of Psycho-Analysis* 72:1–18.

Freedman, N., and Berzofsky, M. (1995). The shape of the communicated transference in difficult and not-so-difficult patients: the symbolized and desymbolized transference. *Psychoanalytic Psychology* 12:363–374.

Freedman, N., and Lavender, J. (1997). On receiving the patient's transference: the symbolizing and desymbolizing countertransference. *Journal of the American Psychoanalytic Association* 45:79–103.

Friedman, L. (1974). The nerves of the mind. *Contemporary Psychoanalysis* 10:511–521.

Freud, S. (1924). *Zur Technik der Psychoanalyse und zur Metapsychologie*. Leipzig: Internationaler Psychoanalytischer Verlag.

Gadamer, H.-G. (1975). *Truth and Method*. New York: Seabury.

Gedo, J. (1979). *Beyond Interpretation: Toward a Revised Theory for Psychoanalysis*. New York: International Universities Press.

Gergeley, G., and Watson, J. S. (1996). The social biofeedback theory of parental affect-mirroring: the development of emotional self-awareness and self control in infancy. *International Journal of Psycho-Analysis* 77:1181–1212.

Goodman, N. (1976). *Languages of Art*. Indianapolis: Hackett.

Gray, P. (1994). *The Ego and Analysis of Defense*. Northvale, NJ: Jason Aronson.

Green, A. (2000). The intrapsychic and intersubjective in psychoanalysis. *Psychoanalytic Quarterly* 69:1–39.

Haley, J. (1963). *Strategies of Psychotherapy*. New York: Grune & Stratton.

Hoffman, I. Z. (1998). *Ritual and Spontaneity in the Psychoanalytic Process: A Dialectical-Constructivist View*. Hillsdale, NJ: Analytic Press.

Jackendoff. R. (1997). *The Architecture of the Language Faculty*. Cambridge, MA: M.I.T. Press.

Karmiloff-Smith, A. (1994). Precis of "Beyond Modularity: A Developmental Perspective on Cognitive Science." *Behavioral and Brain Sciences* 17:693–745.

Kohut, H. (1977). *The Restoration of the Self*. New York: International Universities Press.

Lakoff, G., and Johnson. M. (1980). *Metaphors We Live By*. Chicago: University of Chicago Press.

——— (1999). *Philosophy in the Flesh: The Embodied Mind and Its Challenge to Western Thought*. New York: Basic Books.

Langer, S. (1953). *Feeling and Form: A Theory of Art*. New York: Scribner's.

——— (1972). *Mind: An Essay on Human Feeling*, vol. 2. Baltimore: Johns Hopkins University Press.

Lichtenberg, J. (1983). *Psychoanalysis and Infant Research*. Hillsdale, NJ: Analytic Press.

Loewald, H. (1960). On the therapeutic action of psychoanalysis. *International Journal of Psycho-Analysis* 41:16–33.

Macalpine, I. (1950). The development of the transference. *Psychoanalytic Quarterly* 19:501–539.

Merleau-Ponty, M. (1962). *Phenomenology of Perception.* London: Routledge.

Panskepp, J. (1999). Emotions as viewed by psychoanalysis and neuroscience: an exercise in consilience. *Neuro-Psychoanalysis* 1:15–38.

Petocz, A. (1999). *Freud, Psychoanalysis and Symbolism.* Cambridge, England: Cambridge University Press.

Piaget, J. (1967). The mental development of the child. In *Six Psychological Studies*, trans. A. Tenzer, ed., D. Elkind, pp. 3–73. New York: Random House.

——— (1976). *The Grasp of Consciousness: Action and Concept in the Young Child*, trans. S. Wedgewood. Cambridge, MA: Harvard University Press.

——— (1978). *Success and Understanding*, trans. A. J. Pomerans. Cambridge, MA: Harvard University Press.

Pinker. S. (1994). *The Language Instinct: How the Mind Creates Language.* New York: Harper.

Renik, O. (1998). Getting real in analysis. *Psychoanalytic Quarterly* 67:566–593.

Ricoeur, P. (1970). *Freud and Philosophy*, trans. D. Savage. New Haven, CT: Yale University Press.

——— (1988). *Time and Narrative*, vol. 3. Chicago: University of Chicago Press.

Saussure, F. (1972). *Course in General Linguistics*, La Salle, IL: Open Court.

Schafer, R. (1983). Narration in the psychoanalytic dialogue. In *The Analytic Attitude*, pp. 212–239. New York: Basic Books.

Shapiro, T. (2002). From monologue to dialogue: a transition in psychoanalytic practice. *Journal of the American Psychoanalytic Association* 50:199–219.

Sterba, R. F. (1934). The fate of the ego in analytic therapy. *International Journal of Psycho-Analysis* 15:117–126.

Stern, D. B. (1997). *Unformulated Experience: From Dissociation to Imagination in Psvchoanalysis.* Hillsdale, NJ: Analytic Press.

Stern, D. N. (1994). One way to build a clinically relevant baby. *Infant Mental Health Journal* 15:9–25.

——— (1998). The process of therapeutic change involving implicit knowledge: some implications of developmental observations for adult psychotherapy. *Infant Mental Health Journal* 19:300–308.

Target, M., and Fonagy, P. (1996). Playing and reality II. The development of psychic reality from a theoretical perspective. *International Journal of Psycho-Analysis* 77:459–479.

Taylor, G. J. (2000). Recent developments in alexithymia theory and research. *Canadian Journal of Psychiatry* 45:134–142.

Todorov, T. (1982). *Theories of the Symbol*. Ithaca, NY: Cornell University Press.

Tower. L. (1956). Countertransference. *Journal of the American Psychoanalytic Association* 4:224–255.

Waelder, R. (1930). The principle of multiple functioning: observations on over-determination. *Psychoanalytic Quarterly* 5:45–62.

Weiss, J., and Sampson, H. (1986). *The Psychoanalytic Process: Theory, Clinical Observation and Empirical Research*. New York: Guilford.

Winnicott, D. W. (1961). *Playing and Reality*. Harmondsworth, England: Penguin.

9

The Refractoriness of the Desymbolizing Function

DORIS K. SILVERMAN

Archaic mental life has a theory of the mind's own working space.
Wollheim (1984) in *The Thread of Life*, paraphrased by Lear (1990)

Norbert Freedman has delineated his view of the topography of the symbolizing and desymbolizing process (Freedman and Karliner 1999, Freedman and Lavender 1997, unpublished manuscript, Freedman et al. 1999a,b). The latter refers to unmentalized activity, or, when mentalized, symbolic thought is simultaneously disavowed so that experientially it is unmentalized. It is conceptualized as a loss of abstract functioning, a concreteness in thinking. The process of desymbolizing is a primitive defensive process, the aim of which is to destroy or negate symbolic thinking. Simultaneously thinking and feeling about issues close to one's traumatic past destroys symbolic thinking for such traumatized individuals. The pain associated with the maintenance of symbolic thinking is too difficult, too overwhelming, too disorganizing, too terrifying. The disavowal inherent in desymbolization maintains the experiences of the nothingness of the mind, its emptiness, a sense of a gap, the destruction of meaning.

Freedman discusses the "notion of the cycle as a recurrent unit in treatment," that is, experiences of symbolizing as well as desymbolizing occur during the course of individual hours and over the course of treatment. He suggests that "incremental symbolization," as treatment progresses, might be a gauge of analytic gain.

Freedman has developed a substantial, consistent body of work on symbolization and desymbolization. Such a body of literature offers the opportunity to organize one's thoughts about this subject as well as to consider variations and alternate possibilities. It is only after such a framework has been provided that subsequent innovations are possible. My hope is that my addenda to Freedman's ideas contribute to an increased understanding of the phenomena under consideration.

I want to describe a patient who sometimes "cycles" from the beginning to the end of a session, often presenting confused, disorganized feelings, sensations, images, and thoughts alongside of a coherent narrative about his experiences. The confused state is frightening and worrisome and is, at times, concordant with Freedman's description of a desymbolizing state. By the end of the hour his narrative is often clearer, more coherent, and less threatening to him. To continue with the use of Freedman's conceptual categories, we can say a symbolizing process has occurred. The problem, though, is that what is learned and symbolized evaporates. Blatt (1974) calls this a failure in evocative memory or loss of evocative constancy (Levy and Blatt 1999). This patient is unable to sustain the symbolizing process achieved during the course of an analytic session. Over the years of our analytic work, the patient experienced an increasing containment of the fear of the emptiness, the dread of vacant existence, the sense of the void, and the despair that such feelings bring. His fragmentation, sense of terror, overwhelming fearfulness, and intense panic have been mitigated. Nonetheless, the issue of recurrent desymbolization continues.

Whereas Freedman acknowledges the pathology of early object relations, he does not address psychogenetic factors in any detail. Freedman's focus is on a descriptive experience of thinking processes. I will delineate the precursors to the desymbolizing process as best as can be understood from a developmental perspective. With this in mind, I use a clinical case to illuminate a pathological early object relations experience and its negative effect on self-esteem regulation as expressed through the repetitive desymbolizing features reflected in the patient's commentary on his self-experience. In this presentation I demonstrate his need to preserve an internalized archaic relationship to a negative, hated, but essential attachment relationship to his mother. Any threats or potential disruptions to the attachment relationship readily set the stage for recurrent bouts of desymbolization, as reiteratively expressed in his verbalizations about his lack of self-esteem.

Freedman describes a continuum of stages from the concrete to the symbolic. I am elaborating on other variations, the nuanced stages of psychic experiences for a patient struggling with potentially severe mental anguish. Thus, my clinical description, I hope, will further contribute to an understanding of symbolizing and desymbolizing and other psychic states.

THE ATTACHMENT SYSTEM

There is now a burgeoning research literature on the attachment system. In recent years there has been an increasing emphasis on refining the various categories of attachment. With the recognition that the categories of secure and insecure attachments are insufficient to capture the complexities of early forms of relating between parents and their infants, these categories have been expanded. One of the additions is the disoriented/disorganized category. Children who are assigned to this category are lacking in strategies for dealing with their environment, showing disorientation and disorganization. They demonstrate an incoherent, inconsistent attachment pattern expressed by a combination of attachment-seeking behavior and immediate avoidance (Main and Solomon 1990). Such children exhibit what I have previously described as "apprehension, confusion, aggression, apathy, freezing, and stilling. They often exhibited dazed and trancelike facial expression" (Silverman 1998).

Main has repeatedly demonstrated the intergenerational transmission of attachment styles. Parents' attachment to their parents is similar to their child's pattern of attachment to them. Hesse and Main

(1999) suggest that parents who have had traumatic experiences of their own often respond to their child in a frightened, frightening, or threatening manner. They maintain that such disturbed maladaptive behavior on the parent's part leaves the child "in an irresolvable, disorganizing and disorienting paradox in which impulses to approach the parent as the infant's 'haven of safety' will inevitably conflict with impulses to flee from the parent as a source of alarm" (p. 484).

Such disorganizing episodes lead the child to experience a variety of potentially fearful, threatening, disorienting events with which the child is unable to cope. Aggressive fantasies, catastrophic reactions, feelings of emotional flooding, overwhelmed and negative feelings about the self, and a fear of a potential breakdown are likely accompaniments (Hesse and Main 1999).

Such tendencies toward chaotic, catastrophic reactions lead to a loss of symbolic functioning. In fact, infants labeled as disorganized have difficulty with concentration. It negatively affects their school performance, and there have been demonstrable decrements in their cognitive functioning apparent by 18 months of age (Lyons-Ruth 1992, Lyons-Ruth et al. 1991).

I have presented the disorganized/disoriented category of attachment because I see this style and its consequences as a relevant backdrop to the refractory aspect of self-esteem regulation in the patient that I will be presenting.

The patient is a high-functioning, articulate, sophisticated man. He handles himself easily and well in social and professional situations. He is cultured, widely read, enjoys the arts, literature, and theatre, and can skillfully engage with others demonstrating his knowledge, worldliness, humor, and clever repartee. However, he experiences this aspect of himself as the façade he presents to the world. He is troubled with bouts of annihilating anxiety, with confusional states, feelings of dissociation, hypochondriacal worries, and preoccupations with falling into a void, into darkness, into a black terror of despair, into a "purple room with a hum." Caught in such disorganizing experiencing he feels completely alone and helpless. He has always experienced himself as worthless, that something was wrong with him, that he was incompetent, not worth noticing. A quote from T. S. Eliot captures his feeling state: "I do not think they will sing to me."

His mother fit the pattern of a frightened and frightening woman. She suffered from a severe loss early in life and was marginally functional. She was easily confused and overwhelmed and would use clichés and repetitive religious phrases she had learned as solutions to complex issues. Although born and attended school in this country, she never learned to read or write, and as an adult mother was unable to leave her home. She was harsh and strict with the patient, often employing severe punitive responses for his mild boyish transgressions. She was unpredictable and, above all, felt unreal and robotic to the patient.

The father, who was capable of greater warmth and more genuine connection, was out of the home most of the time. A blue-collar worker, he endured long work shifts, and worked weekends and nights at a second job while struggling to meet the family's financial obligations. He was experienced as an unavailable figure in the young child's life.

First I present the descriptive features of the desymbolizing process as the patient discussed them. However, how I understand the mental process of this patient's desymbolization does not only reflect defensive processes. Using clinical data I try to characterize his various subjective states. I highlight, as well, his serious problem modulating his anxiety as a function of his disorganized attachment.

THE PHENOMENOLOGY OF SELF STATE EXPERIENCES

Desymbolization

In some instances the patient has recourse to desymbolization as Freedman describes it. For example, we had been talking for a number of sessions about the way his mind functions. I have talked with him about his compartmentalization. This arose from my recognition that we discuss feelings, emotions, fantasies, ideas, and so on, in his analysis and then he leaves it in the analysis. He never takes what he experiences and learns with him into his outside life. In addition, there is not the sense of accrual of meanings, that is, there is not an increase of symbolization. What he understands and feels in his session disappears when he leaves the session. He now recognizes that it is true that he compartmentalizes. He says, "I live in different states, or I have different grids. If I feel vulnerable and frightened I can't draw comfort from the experiences I have here or the experience I might have had yesterday. They are in boxes and I can't mix them or use them or, to use your word, integrate them. I am either in this box or that." Here the patient is describing an anxiety state that he is immersed in and his inability to cope. He cannot use language, narrative, or past understanding to help him bring new understanding or change to the experience.

Another time he described his mental state in the following way: "Intellectually I put these things we talk about on tape so I can use it. I can't do it emotionally. The stuff floats away. I become confused, unreal. I think nothing we say is definite. It could be this or it could be that. I have no conviction of what is true. Anything or everything could be true."

We have also understood that he has a "grinding machine" in his head. In his attempt to hold onto a helpful interpretation, he thinks about it repeatedly. It becomes something like a mantra. In this way he manages to reduce meaning to meaningless bits. Intellectualization (putting things on tape, use of his grinding machine) is a defensive attempt at managing his high level of stress.

Anxiety can rapidly escalate into overwhelming, annihilating, perilous trauma that is terrifying. Thus, various obsessive and compulsive maneuvers are used to create a sense of inner structure, control, and organization. His work-driven life, although punishing, allows little time for distraction. When he could tolerate some degree of anxiety, he could report:

> I can now look up from my work. I could pause and look out my window and not get anxious. I could stop my grind and it would be okay. I could stop without it being dangerous. There's comfort in this, also freedom, power, and competence. There are moments

> when I manage to step out of the box and there is a here and a there Being outside the universe [his special system of rules] and it's not such a terrible place. I can feel differently and feel safe. It's very unusual for me. It's having perspective. I normally live with a particular perspective and this was a different one. It was not based on my cognitive thinking. It's just feeling. In the past this kind of freedom meant it was my undoing and I will evaporate.

However, we saw even within this session his newfound perspective began to undergo a subtle shift and his anxiety increased. He thought the idea of his looking forward to seeing me is frightening. Something terrible might happen. He felt this new way of feeling and thinking was risky. A return to his defensive style was within short reach and felt safe.

His excessive reliance on disavowal helps maintain both his simultaneous or alternative use of symbolization and desymbolization. He maintains that he has created an illusion about the world that it is not as frightening and threatening as he knows it truly is. His illusion is "useful and workable and it helps. My illusions are safer than the underlying reality I know exists. I know that it came from my experience as a child. I know it ain't necessarily so that everyone is my mother, but I don't believe it." His incapacity, at times, to integrate his internal and external reality, to synthesize contrasting ideas about his mother, and to bear the anxiety associated with frightening, destructive merger experiences or the opposite pole of aloneness and disintegration produces defensive desymbolization. However, the patient would be labeled as a "segmental desymbolizer" in Freedman's (Freedman et al. 1999b) schema because he is frequently able to symbolize his anxious preoccupations.

OTHER SELF STATE EXPERIENCES

At times, he is not defensively coping, but is in the experience of trauma. For example, he describes his anxiety occurring in a particular mental landscape. "It feels like a location, a place. It's a place in my mind. I go there. I could go crazy. It's hell, where everything falls apart, I don't exist. I'm without hope." Here the patient appears to be in a state of retraumatization. In such an experience defenses and adaptive ways of managing anxiety are lost. Such a state can reoccur in analysis when he no longer experiences the analyst as providing understanding, intervening to open an area of exploration, or offering new ways of looking at an issue. Rather, the analyst has induced anxiety because she replicated, in her interpretation, the experience of the terrifying mother. Then, retraumatization occurs. I understand this as different from desymbolization. Desymbolization, concretization, or frozen old ways of looking at an issue is not his experience. He is in a state of overwhelming trauma.

The patient has a profound sense of dislocation and feelings of alienation. He is communicating what his existential state often feels like to him. He says:

> It's temporal or event-bounded. My life is chopped up into events. My emotions are fragmented. The stuff in between the events is meaningless. Time is oscillating across a line. Experiences don't accrete. It's as though I'm in a different universe day to day. I live in different worlds and none of them feel quite right. And I'm not part of them. I'm lonely and the world feels alien. I live compartmentalized lives. When I was a kid, I had a school life and then I had a home life and they were completely different. It was creating a world apart from each other.
>
> I sense a more three-dimensional world. Being there with other people is what I want instead of my two-dimensional world. I am in this scene that passes before me and I interact with my left hand. People are cardboard figures and then the cardboard figures leave. Then I have a profound sense of loneliness when I am with people.
>
> There are times when I am reconnected with you. Sometimes I have this sense outside of this room as well. It feels different. It feels good. They are not profound moments; they are ordinary, but different. I am saying what I feel and feeling what I say. It is vexing and troublesome because I have an inability to sustain the feeling of connection. That's what makes these little vignettes with you unusual. A lot of my interactions are not of the moment. I've learned how to interact with people, but I don't feel it. I'm never spontaneous.

Here he is describing profound dislocation, sprinkled with occasional connection and genuine feeling. The former, which is his predominant experience, at times may reflect desymbolization. It is akin to what Grotstein (1981) has called ego syntonic dissociation and Goldberg (1987) has suggested is a subtle and disguised "splitting of the subjective experience of the 'I'" (p. 516). However, I would venture that his description is not only one of desymbolization. It is not concrete or regressive. His analytic experience has allowed him to be an increasingly acute observer of his inner states and he can symbolize them. He is experiencing controlled anxiety (Hurvitz, personal communication). However, he cannot alter such a state. His symbolic functioning typically is intact but it does not induce growth and change.

Potential growth experiences, that is, new ways of being in the world, are often seen as frightening because they threaten the tie with his internal object and leave him feeling frightfully alone and abandoned. This too, while not retraumatizing, is existing in a state of anxiety, one that may be potentially uncontrolled. It prevents any movement, any thoughts about new relational configurations or potentiality for growth. Here, he is attempting to ward off feelings of trauma.

LOW SELF-ESTEEM—THE DEFENSIVE AND REPARATIVE FEATURES—AS A WAY OF FENDING OFF ISOLATION AND ALONENESS

The patient has a high-salaried position and is valued for his expertise, creativity, and productiveness. He has a superior position, with important managerial responsibilities. He is sought out for his advice, his competent assessment of situations and employees, and his moderating and fair evaluative judgments. Nonetheless, he describes his frequent preoccupation with other people and their negative thoughts and appraisals of him. He is always thinking that people are noticing that he is failing short, that he's not doing enough, not thought of highly, not recognized or acknowledged. Such thoughts about his professional work experiences occur, for example, when he has come late to work, failed to get a memo out quickly, not immediately returned a phone call, lacked a quick response to a client's needs, and so on. We discussed how such a focus was putting himself in the center of lots of people's thoughts. I commented that they are preoccupied with him, not with positive thoughts, but with negative ones. "You want to be admired, to be responded to and be appreciated. In your mind lots of people are paying attention to you, but it's negative attention." This idea surprised him. He commented that I was talking about his narcissism. He doesn't think of himself as narcissistic, saying, "That's because for me it's associated with feeling arrogant, superior, sure of yourself, none of the things I associate with myself." Yet, he says, what I was talking about feels right. His hidden sense of superiority derives from his maintaining a belief in his own independence, his wish not to rely on anyone. He also idealizes his critical, frequently negative, and cynical thinking processes. His view of his powerful destructiveness belies his sense of inadequacy. It is here that one catches glimpses of his narcissistic self-idealization (Rosenfeld 1971). However, his narcissism is in the service of filling an empty void that he constantly feels is close to engulfing him. I suggest he might feel that if he could people his world, the threat of isolation and aloneness that accompany his anxiety might diminish.

He comments, "I was such a lonely, isolated kid. I had no friends, I was always alone. My mother didn't let me out of the house, so I played alone." He considers the way he has led his life and he recognizes its relationship to warding off the lonely, empty feeling. He comments, "I fill it with work. I have a long list of 'to-dos.' It occurs to me if I wasn't involved with these to-dos I am alone, desolate." (He had described his work experience, of being inundated with the long line of people waiting at his office door, the steady phone calls, e-mail messages, and so on, a constant demand on his time.) "It's the same as the to-dos and the need to be effective. I believe people are making harsh judgments about me. I need to be vigilant to fend off these judgments. If I don't have that then I am alone. If I'm worried about what other people can think about me I'm connected. I'm interacting. I created the fiction [of interacting] because

I feel alone, cut off. Ironically, I make myself feel better. I'm connected. The world is judging me negatively but I have control of the world."

There is an ironic quality to his painful position in the world. He feels potentially inundated by overwhelming anxiety and desolation. This is accompanied by wretched feelings of being completely unconnected from everyone, existing alone in a darkling field of hellishness. His preoccupation with all those people thinking about him and commenting negatively and harshly about him at least fills up his landscape. It is this feature of his preoccupation with the evaluative views of others that reflects his reparative attempts at connection when he is frightened by feelings of isolation.

SOURCES OF NEGATIVE SELF-WORTH

His negative self-worth has complex roots and serves a number of purposes. In his fantasy, he can use his inadequacies to connect himself to others. He also remains attached to a mother who felt threatened by her son's competence and intellectual abilities. He grasped her clear message that he shouldn't be too smart. In addition, his negative self-view connects him with her inadequate, marginally functional behavior. Thus, he was aware that at times he pursued experiences of worthlessness. "When I'm doing well, although not great, that allows me to focus on little errors and then I feel less worthy. If I don't do that I'll never be loved or cared about."

His mother was unloving, harsh, and judgmental. She physically punished him, sometimes using an old-fashioned leather cat-o'-nine-tails. Such excessive force made him feel he was very bad. He was not only offending her but she invoked his behavior as killing the Virgin Mary.

> "My mother made me feel bad so I understood it as I'm worthless and it led to feeling bad about myself." Her praise of him had equally serious repercussions. "When my mother said I was such a good boy I got frantic. I traded my self-esteem, my self-respect,

> in order to get her love. Even positive regard is insidious. I read it as positive regard for being enslaved (as I was by my mother). I mistrust positive regard. It was there in my relationship with my mother. It was an element of connection, but when she said positive things about my being a good boy I knew it was all bullshit, a lie. She didn't genuinely love me. She didn't have the capacity. Her being nice to me I knew was not genuine. It was a lie."

DEVELOPMENT

Disorganized/Disoriented Attachment and Its Affective Component

His confused, sometimes chaotic state has existed since childhood. There are a number of early traumatic memories of being abandoned, left alone in a strange, isolated environment, which he experienced as terrifying. He remembers himself as a lost soul in school, without any comprehension about its rules and regulations and being completely at sea with the academic work. A new, young, enthusiastic fourth grade teacher recognized him as smart, acknowledged and appreciated him, and transformed his school life. However, he never formed a deep attachment to her and in his early and subsequent life he was emotionally isolated and alone. His early disorganized/disoriented attachment at times alternates with extreme insecure attachment. This style of atttachment does not provide for the development of adequate affective regulation. His mother was often frightened and frightening to him. She felt unreal, artificial. Even her hugs seemed simulated. He never felt she was authentic. "If she responded it wasn't to me. Her gestures were so hollow. She was embracing some likeness of me. She was a two-dimensional image and I was a cardboard image. She never saw me or felt me." There were repeated feelings of a nongenuine responsiveness on his mother's part. "I have the idea that I discovered my mother was a robot, a machine, not like me, and that everyone else may be robots. My mother was not real. It's scary, it's unsafe. I can't experience people as being a person like me. She's like the figure in the Wizard of Oz. If you pull back the curtain you realize there's no one there."

His mother was frightened and overwhelmed when his mischief or misdemeanors confronted her. She apparently could not make judgments about normal noncompliant behavior. In her overwrought, confused state she punished, abused, and frightened him. Given her own threatened and disoriented state in these circumstances, she was unhelpful in modulating his anxious states. He remembers many situations when he was filled with overwhelming anxiety and her sterile, ritualized ways of coping with them.

When the patient experiences stress-filled states as chaotic and overwhelming, we can see his identification with his mother's inability to cope. Neither mother nor son had adequate ways of managing anxiety states. For him, nascent anxiety can quickly become full-blown and he finds himself in the traumatic experiences that dominated his early life.

His tie to the world of reality is linked to some discomfort, an optimal level of anxiety that is within tolerable limits. His search is for a mild anodyne, one that doesn't preclude some painful feeling. A negative self-image is also an essential condition for ensuring his hold on reality. His conviction about his badness and worthlessness feels real to him. He would rather feel miserable about a lowly self than feel he doesn't exist. His tie to his inner conviction of unworthiness gives him the feeling of being in the world. He says,

> I would rather have bad feelings than no feelings at all. I need to feel that I'm not cared about because I need to think of myself as loathsome or else I don't exist. This was given to me by my mother. This is the only reality and sense of myself I have. If I lose that there is nothing else. I need to hate myself. I can't believe I'm saying this. It's important to me. Caring about me, seeing value in me. It's a threat to my ability to loathe myself and then I'm left with nothingness. It's crazy that I'm saying this but it feels true.

At another point he said, "I need the illusion that I am bad, deserving of punishment, unworthy of care, without this [illusion] I am alone. She needed me to be weak, dependent, needy of her. I didn't quite believe they were real needs from a real person. It was a crutch to believe this and I seized upon it."

The importance of his disavowal helps him to stave off what he fears is a tenuous connection to the world. He has negotiated an inner bargain with his internal object. He will maintain a hateful connection to his mother, maintain a disorganized/disoriented attachment to her, utilize her defensive style and adopt her negative view of him. He has, at times, acknowledged that his vague thoughts, his sense of disorganization, his lack of real conviction about issues that we discuss, "is like my mother." He loathes the bargain he has arranged and maintains, but in doing so he feels he is not wretched, terrified, and alone.

Vengeful Destructiveness

The legacy of his bartered soul is also massive ragefulness. "I don't want to give up hating my mother. I don't want reconciliation. I have an interest in hating her. I can't get even, be satisfied. I want to punish her." I comment that his statement "I'll never forgive you" is also saying, "I'll never move away from you." "I do persist stubbornly in wanting to hate her. I don't shift. I can't forgive or I won't. It feels like I can't. The rage is there. If I hate at least I'm feeling the hating. I can't love her, I can only hate her, so if I hate I'm connected to her. It's the defining experience of my life. I can't step back. It runs so deep the hate and rage. The by-product is I'm connected." I say, "When you don't feel yourself as being in the world you are in combat with your mother." He says, "It's right when I wake up in the morning. I'm a child again with my mother as if I were back being a child. A sense of things being unresolved and searching for a different ending for the story. Searching for a perfect relationship, benevolent, benign, loving, looking for a loving mother."

Transference

In the transference as well, it is difficult for him to maintain the symbolizing function of our relationship. When he insists on some idealized version of an all-powerful, beneficent, ever-loving and ever-hovering mother, he loses sight of the benefits that might accrue from our relationship. His splitting and concretization, at these times, lead him to feelings of disillusionment and despair about his treatment. Positive feelings that might emerge from our connection are troubling, alien, and potentially traumatizing. He says, "Something about me that resists our connection, a more basic mistrust. It could be real but I don't trust it. Also, I am in danger of feeling overwhelmed. It's dangerous, chaotic. It's the fear of being too happy, too stimulated, and too intense. I know what to do with feeling miserable." I question him about too intense feelings. He says,

> I could explode, I could feel overloaded. It is easily something dangerous. I often seek out stimulation which is intense. It has to do with freedom. I took away the idea [from my childhood interactions with her] that maybe if I'm too happy, it will have a terrible destructive result. If I'm too happy, happiness will cause suffering on some grand scale. I will destroy mother, myself, the world. I have that kind of power and it's related to my being happy. If I'm happy the world will end. Things will get out of hand if I'm too happy. I'll go crazy, overstimulated and overwhelmed. It's like a wave at the beach and I'll drown. The logic of feeling good is not reinforcing.

His disorganized/disoriented attachment provides minimal tools for modulating his affect. There is inadequate capacity to self-soothe. He might benefit from a reliance on the analyst's calming and soothing presence. However, this idea is fraught with feelings of helplessness and experiences of humiliation.

> When I'm feeling that I need other people, when I fantasize about it, it makes me feel like a loser. It negatively affects my self-esteem. So the very task I'm supposed to have negatively erodes my self-esteem so I can't accomplish the task. It creates another problem—a sense of unworthiness, a loss of self-respect. I feel I'm pandering, like I did with my mother. I'm ashamed of my neediness. If I start to feel needy I suddenly withdraw. I don't go further with relationships. I retreat. [I talk about a recent experience with a friend, and how helpful and good it had made him feel.] I

> could use such an experience in a way that occurred to me after the last session where we talked about it. I could say to myself when I am anxious I'm not alone in the world. There's always Doris, I can count on her. There is something profound about our relationship that I never want to admit to myself and it can be useful and comforting. At least I know that Doris is there for me. However, such an insight is short-lived. What is frequently substituted is the worry that I (his analyst) am unreal and robotic.

When I point to aspects of his experience that belie this, he comments, "There's a denial. Truth can exist in another box. I've adopted my mother's defensive apparatus. It's the same with our relationship. It's in another box even though I know the relationship has depth and importance. It is profound." What he would prefer is a more insistent, intrusive relationship between the two of us, one with sadomasochistic features. "I want you to be more intrusive, direct, tell me things. If you're not I feel you are cool and detached and not connected. I feel it as a flight from me. You're nice to me. I don't trust positive regard. I got praise for being a good boy, but it was for being a good slave."

I have used this case as illustrative of the tenacious hold that a negative sense of self can have even though its maintenance causes significant unhappiness. The experience of a traumatic early childhood that led to a disorganized/disoriented attachment experience can stamp the personality of the child. Such patients appear to have an essentialist, foundational view of themselves. Even in positive, reasonable interactions, for example, functioning as competent professionals, they do not forgo the entrenched negative and hateful self-view. Thus, there is a static quality in their perception of themselves over time and in different contexts. The patient I have been describing can alter historical events in his life to fit his view of himself as rejected and loathsome.

Emde (1999), a psychoanalytic developmental researcher, has a position that is consistent with my own point of view. He suggests that those self schemas that are "resistant to change over the course of development . . . [occur] because of the strong influence of subsymbolic input in the early linkages with interpersonal experience" (p. 328). Emde is positing, along with other developmentalists (e.g., Lyons-Ruth 1999) that pathology is not necessarily linked to specific phases in the infant's development, for example the oral or anal stage. Rather, it is function of a broader, more characteristic interaction between the parent and the child that has an early initiation and then has endured over a lengthy period of time. Even the traumatic experiences that the child has suffered at a particular stage of development must be understood in the context of the ongoing dialogue between parent and child in relation to this event. The nature of such interactions can mitigate or intensify subsequent understanding and behavior in the child.

I am trying to enlarge on the concept of desymbolization. I do so because clinically I wish to capture more of the ingredients that produce a refractoriness to change. Whereas the patient has recourse to defensive use of concretization and there is a frozen quality to the organization of his experiences, other features can be detailed as well. I have described his free-floating anxiety, his more controlled anxiety, his escalating fears of retraumatization, the experience of being traumatized, as well as the anxiety that growth and change produces.

As a result of analytic work, many of his self-state experiences can be symbolized. However, symbolizing for this patient does not enhance his psychological well-being. We now understand that he feels best when he feels he is connected to me, when I understand his experiences, when he feels safe and secure in our sessions. He has learned a great deal about himself and it has been helpful. However, it has not sufficiently freed him from his states of unrelatedness. He maintains that what he has learned about himself, although useful, has not been facilitating. This is significant, because it emerges from a man who relies on intellectual, cognitive, and symbolic functioning. Nonetheless, this level of functioning does not relieve him of his internal terrors. Such a realization has led me to think more about the nonsymbolic in the analytic experience.

Freedman (Freedman et al. 1999a) recognizes the cyclic nature of symbolization and its loss. In this way he is addressing activities in all of us that circulate back and forth. Acknowledging the oscillating tendency toward the nonsymbolic allows for a connection to various vague, ill-defined states that we grapple with and cannot formulate. These can be anxiety-filled or not, and they offer the opportunity for exploration, play, and expansion of our unformulated experience (Stern 1997). It may lead to symbolization and creative enlargement. Such nonsymbolic experiences, however, may remain on the level of the unmentalized but increasingly permitted, even though not comprehended verbally. This line of reasoning suggests the possibility that tolerance for the tacit in emotional life can be rewarding and enriching.

As Freedman (Freedman et al. 1999b) suggests, the unmentalized can be considered from the vantage point of primitive defense and it can also be conceptualized as a mode of communication. I plan to build on the latter aspect of Freedman's thinking because it may be additionally relevant to what is potentially curative in the analytic experience. In addition, I stress it because it includes ideas from contemporary research. The developmental researcher Lyons-Ruth (2001) comments:

> The older dichotomy between rational and irrational thought or between secondary and primary process, a dichotomy that assigned privileged status to logical, symbolized or self-aware systems of knowledge, is being replaced by a more complex multileveled model of what it means "to know." Recent developmental and cognitive research has made clear that there are other forms of knowing that do not require self-reflective awareness and so have not played a large part in our previous theories of what constitutes meaning or knowing. [p. 90]

What this researcher is referring to is procedural knowledge or what other researchers (Stern et al. 1998) have referred to as implicit relational knowing.

In a previous paper (Silverman 2001), I described implicit relational knowing in the following way:

> I am pointing to the non-verbal, non-symbolic system that characterizes not only initial infant–parent interactions, but a

> coding system that continues unabated throughout our lives. A great deal of emotional signaling and cueing takes place outside of our conscious awareness. Much of our social interactions, which include our use of space with others, our leaning toward or away from the other in discourse, our expressive body, face, and hand movements, head shaking, gazing, etc. are governed by our implicit knowledge. [p. 329]

It is through such a medium that the mother is able to communicate a tapestry of her rich imagistic-fantasy life as well as her feelingful-physiological sensations and psychological meanings. Analogously, I believe that such implicit relational knowing occurs between analyst and analysand. On the analyst's part, it is in her greetings, her sober and/or playful facial qualities, her movements, the emotional timbre and tone of her voice, her inflections, the language she employs, and the implicit gaps in her discourse. It is apparent as well in the readiness to understand, or the foreclosing of interactive discourse. It is there in the spontaneous gesture, or, in more formal responses, in her capacity for surprise and unpremeditated response. It is what I believe Hoffman (1998) is trying to capture when he talks about the necessity at times of "throwing away the book" and responding in an impromptu manner. These forms of implicit communication may open unforeseen and unanticipated ways of being together that can alter the predictable and expectable in the patient's view of relational experiences, that is, the possibility of breaking up frozen constellations. Ideally, of course, such interactions may be transformed into symbolized meanings. However, ultimately, it is an empirical question about what facilitates growth and change in patients. Is it a focus on the nonverbal, or the development of the symbolizing process, or as I suspect, the intermingling of the nonverbal with the symbolization of the dynamic processes within the patient?

By stressing the empirical, I once again show my concordance with Freedman, who above all appreciates the knowledge derived from empirical findings. The enlargement of our psychoanalytic expertise emerges from the richly rewarding interaction between the findings from the clinical experience and the testable hypotheses that such findings can produce.

REFERENCES

Blatt, S. J. (1974). Levels of object representation in anaclitic and introjective depression. *Psychoanalytic Study of the Child* 29:107–157. New Haven, CT: Yale University Press.

Emde, R. (1999). Moving ahead: integrating influences of affective processes for development and for psychoanalysis. *International Journal of Psychoanalysis* 80:317–340.

Freedman, N., Berzofsky, M., and DeMichele, A. (1999a). *On transformation cycles: the symbolization of a frozen constellation*. Paper presented at the Annual Meeting, Division 39 of the American Psychological Association, New York, April.

Freedman, N., and Karliner, R. (1999). *On incremental symbolization: clinical and empirical definition*. Paper presented at the annual meeting of Division 39 of the American Psychological Association, New York, April.

Freedman, N., Karliner, R., and Lavender, J. (1999b). *Desymbolization: pervasive and segmental*. Paper presented at the Annual Meeting, Division 39 of the American Psychological Association, New York, April.

Freedman, N., and Lavender, J. (1997). On receiving the patient's transference: the symbolizing and desymbolizing countertransference. *Journal of the American Psychoanalytic Association* 45:79–103.

——— (unpublished manuscript). *On desymbolization: the concept and observations on anorexia and bulemia*.

Goldberg, P. (1987). The role of distractions in the maintenance of dissociative mental states. *International Journal of Psycho-Analysis* 68:511–524.

Grotstein, J. S. (1981). *Splitting and Projective Identification*. New York: Jason Aronson.

Hesse, E., and Main, M. (1999). Second-generation effects of unresolved trauma in nonmaltreating parents: dissociated, frightened and threatening parental behavior. *Psychoanalytic Inquiry* 19:481–540.

Hoffman, I. Z. (1998). *Ritual and Spontaneity in the Psychoanalytic Process*. Hillsdale, NJ: Analytic Press.

Lear, J. (1990). *Love and Its Place in Nature*. New Haven, CT: Yale University Press.

Levy, K. N., and Blatt, S. J. (1999). Attachment theory and psychoanalysis: further differentiation within insecure attachment patterns. *Psychoanalytic Inquiry* 19:541–575.

Lyons-Ruth, K. (1992). Maternal depressive symptoms, disorganized infant–mother attachment relationships and hostile-aggressive behavior in the pre-school classroom: a prospective longitudinal view from infancy to age five. In *Rochester Symposium on Developmental Psychopathology: Vol. 4: A Developmental Approach to Affective Disorders*, ed. D. Cicchetti and S. Toth, pp. 131–171. Rochester, NY: University of Rochester Press.

——— (1999). Two person unconscious: intersubjective dialogue, enactive relational representation and the emergence of new forms of relational organization. *Psychoanalytic Inquiry* 19:576–617.

——— (2001). "I sense that you sense that I sense. . . ." Sander's recognition process and the specificity of relational moves in the psychotherapeutic setting. *Infant Mental Health Journal* 2:85–98.

Lyons-Ruth, K., Repacholi, B., Mcleod, S., and Silva, E. (1991). Disorganized attachment behavior in infancy: short-term stability, maternal and infant correlates, and risk-related subtypes. *Developmental Psychopathology* 3:377–396.

Main, N., and Solomon, J. (1990). Procedures for identifying infants as disorganized/disoriented during Ainsworth strange situation. In *Attachment in Preschool Years: Theory Research, and Intervention*, ed. M. T. Greenberg, D. Cicchetti, and E. M. Cummings, pp. 121–160. Chicago: University of Chicago Press.

Rosenfeld, H. (1971). A clinical approach to the psychoanalytic theory of the life and death instincts: an investigation into the aggressive aspects of narcissism. *International Journal of Psycho-Analysis* 52:169–178.

Silverman, D. K. (1998). The tie that binds: affect regulation, attachment, and psychoanalysis. *Psychoanalytic Psychology* 15:187–212.

——— (2001). Sexuality and attachment: A passionate relationship or a marriage of convenience? *Psychoanalytic Quarterly* 70:325–358.

Stern, D. B. (1997). *Unformulated Experience: From Dissociation to Imagination in Psychoanalysis*. Hillsdale, NJ: Analytic Press.

Stern, D., Sander, L., Nahum, J., et al. (1998). Non-interpretive mechanisms in psychoanalytic therapy. *International Journal of Psycho-Analysis* 79:903–920.

10

Some Thoughts on Symbolization and Transference

JEAN SCHIMEK

Freud's famous statement about the goal of psychoanalysis, "where id was, there shall ego be," has been interpreted in many ways. It implies a process of transformation, not only making the unconscious conscious, but, more broadly, raising mental processes to a higher level of organization. Freedman's (1999) concept of incremental symbolization specifies and clarifies some of the main dimensions of this process of transformation.

In the first part of this paper, I comment on some of the main features of Freedman's concepts of symbolization and desymbolization. Following this, I compare briefly some of the symbolizing and desymbolizing aspects of the transference. Finally, I put the concept of symbolization into the broader context of changing trends in psychoanalytic theory, particularly the contrast between the classical view of transference and transference interpretation and the current American emphasis on the intersubjective and relational reality of the treatment situation.

Symbolization primarily involves the linking of different aspects of experience, integrating them into larger units and allowing for multiple perspectives. Freedman distinguishes three levels of incremental symbolization. First, there is incipient symbolization, involving the connection of bodily feelings and thoughts. The second level, discursive symbolization, includes the building of some coherent narrative of self and other experiences. At the final and most specifically psychoanalytic level, dynamic symbolization, one sees an increasing awareness and integration of previously unconscious and conflicted impulses and fantasies.

Symbolization is contrasted with desymbolization, where a narrow, concrete, and rigid perceptual focus dominates. Desymbolization is not viewed as a general lack of cognitive competence but rather as a motivated defensive process, often involving broad and primitive defenses such as disavowal or a need to discharge rapidly and ruthlessly any tension and conflict. It is more than an absence or decrease of symbolization but an active drive to destroy connections and meaning. Symbolization is expressed through language and verbal signifiers, but its level and range depend on many clinical factors, including, among others, the dynamics of the interaction with the analyst, the specific areas of conflict involved, and the status of defenses.

As I understand it, symbolization refers here primarily to the articulation and reflective awareness of inner experience, not to the capacity to use concepts and abstraction in the handling of external reality. Scientists and technicians can be prime models of desymbolized lack of self awareness, and "pensée operatoire." We can assume an interactive spiraling effect among increase in symbolization, decrease of resistance, and effectiveness of interpretations (Freedman and colleagues [2000] provide a detailed description of these concepts with clinical illustrations and criteria for a rating scale.) While increased symbolization can be seen as a major goal of successful treatment, Freedman makes clear that this does not occur in a steady linear fashion; his clinical and research data show that we find repeated cycles of symbolization and desymbolization.

It is important to keep in mind that symbolization involves a linking of mental experiences but also a new and sharper differentiation and separation of various contents, objects, and situations. Ideally, differentiation and integration go together, and one requires the other, both developmentally and in ongoing mental functioning. Linking at a global undifferentiated level may amount to a defensive desymbolization, closer to what Hanna Segal called symbolic equations. Higher levels of symbolization can remain split off from lower levels and lack anchoring in the more physical and affective aspects of experience; here we would have the familiar defenses of intellectualization, isolation of affect, doubt, and inhibition of action. Conversely, if we do not limit desymbolization to its most rigid and narrow defensive manifestations, it may be seen as providing some immediacy of concrete lived experience, as a necessary building block for symbolization. Freedman, on the basis of clinical data, shows how episodes of desymbolization can be part of a cycle leading to higher symbolization.[1]

TRANSFERENCE AS EXPERIENCED AND SYMBOLIZED BY THE PATIENT

It is evident that transference, as a core aspect of the clinical interaction, is a prime area where the concept of symbolization can be applied. As part of that, I think it is useful to contrast the transference as experienced and expressed by the patient with that as constructed and experienced by the analyst.

In a study a few years ago (Freedman and Berzofsky 1995), Freedman defined the symbolized and desymbolized transference from a descriptive, empirical point of view. His focus was on the level of observable communication of the patient's experience in the therapy interaction. He used a broad, relatively content-free definition of transference. In the communicated, symbolized transference, the patient's language indicates "a capacity to represent subjective experiences, articulate ambivalent promptings, create a relatively cohesive narrative, and in-

1. As I understand Freedman, he tends to see symbolization and desymbolization as two separate factors, the latter mostly defensive and the former as levels of integrative linking. I feel more comfortable seeing them as a continuum, which would include incremental symbolization as well as incremental desymbolization, depending on the direction and emphasis.

voke the relationship between the therapist and the patient in the here and now" (p. 367). By contrast, desymbolized transference states are more likely to be inferred by the therapist and expressed through blocking, behavioral enactments, or somatization, and, not surprisingly, they are characteristic of more "difficult" patients.

I think one could add a dimension of transference that is at a higher dynamic level of symbolization, and that is quite relevant to the classical analytic process. It is, of course, also much more inferential and harder to objectify. I am referring to the degree of a patient's reflective awareness of transference, the capacity to observe what he contributes to his experience of the relationship. For the patient, awareness of transference requires a certain level of symbolization, a reflective awareness of one's own thought processes. At a fully desymbolized level, there would be no awareness of transference; the contents of the transference are experienced as coming from outside, as actual perceptual characteristics of the analyst and of the situation. The patient believes that he simply perceives and reacts to what is objectively out there. Thus, in a desymbolized state, there is likely to be maximum enactment and minimal awareness of transference. With increasing symbolization, the patient becomes aware of his contribution to his experience, of the way it is shaped by his subjectivity, his motives and feelings, rather than simply by the external input. Or, to put it differently, the patient is able to differentiate his impressions, his thoughts, and his fantasies from his perceptions.

This requires some capacity, even if momentarily overshadowed, to feel the discrepancy between one's more subjective reactions (e.g., rage at the analyst) and the more objective judgment of the situation (e.g., the analyst being a few minutes late)—an objectivity that often needs the maintenance of a positive identification with the analyst and trust in his judgment. Interpretation of the transference by the analyst, but ultimately by the patient, can be seen as a royal road to higher symbolization and as well as to the unconscious; but this is probably only possible if a certain degree of symbolization and reflective awareness (the old "observing ego") is already present to begin with.

Freedman's findings about communicated transference may be extended to inferences about levels of incremental symbolization in the patient's awareness of the multiple meanings and perspectives of the transference. At the first level, there would be increased awareness and ability to communicate the immediate experience, including the feelings and bodily sensations involved. At a higher level, the patient would be able to link the unique, present experience with other relationships, real and imagined, in broader areas of his life, past and present, and find common patterns in them. And finally, at the dynamic level, there would be greater awareness and integration of previously unconscious conflicts and fantasies. One may add that with many analytic patients, any of these levels can become dominant at certain stages of the treatment, and can coexist and interact within a single session.

Symbolization of the transference can also function as a defense; for some patients, everything remains "mere" transference, pure subjectivity, and the immediacy and objectivity of the present moment are minimized or denied. This can be particularly true when the patient needs to disavow unwelcome realistic perceptions of the analyst, which may damage a certain image of the analyst that both patient and analyst may collude in maintaining.

Ideally, the transference experience has to have enough emotional impact and vividness to provide convincing material for interpretations; on the other hand, if it is experienced as full perceptual reality, it will no longer be open to interpretation and new perspectives. Loewald (1975) uses the metaphor of a play. A spectator may be fully involved in the play while still knowing that it is only acting in the theater. Using this metaphor, concrete desymbolization would be the spectator who feels compelled to participate in the action on the stage, and a defensive oversymbolized level would be the spectator who acts like a theater critic, remaining detached and merely interested in the technical aspects of the performance.

It is probably a distinctive and most valuable aspect of the psychoanalytic situation that it allows for the patient, and to a lesser extent, for the analyst, the shifting expression and exploration of different coexisting constructions of psychic reality, with cycles of the merging and differentiation of the subjective and objective dimensions of experience.

THE ANALYST'S CONSTRUCTION OF THE TRANSFERENCE AND THE ROLE OF THE COUNTERTRANSFERENCE

Transference is not a clearly delineated and self-evident clinical phenomenon. It is first and foremost an inference and an interpretative construct of the analyst. It is the analyst who judges which aspects of the patient's behavior are primarily expressions of transference and which are mostly reactions to the real (as seen by the analyst) immediate situation. Such selected here-and-now transference elements can then be interpreted and linked to various aspects of the patient's life, present and past, as well as to underlying themes in his dreams, associations, and fantasies. Which aspects of the patient's present behavior are seen as transference, and how these get interpreted, is bound to be heavily influenced by the analyst's concepts and theory, as well as by his personal reactions and beliefs (Schimek 1983)—what is now broadly labeled as countertransference. The analyst's countertransference will shape his interaction with the patient and thus influence the patient's behavior, but it will also be reflected in his judgments as to what in this behavior constitutes transference.

As with the patient's transference, one may see the countertransference as more symbolized when more open to critical awareness and reflection, and as more desymbolized when unconscious distortions and biases intrude in the analyst's judgment. Traditionally these desymbolized aspects of the countertransference were emphasized, but now countertransference is usually considered as a major avenue to the understanding of the patient's transference, through the reactions that it induces in the analyst. This assumes a complex process of self-reflective symbolization, of linking and differentiation between one's own perspective and what is observed in the patient.[2] But we may consider desymbolized and symbolized aspects of the countertransference as intrinsic features of the clinical interaction.

---

2. The present approach also tends to focus more on the passive reactive part of the countertransference than on the active and mostly unconscious initiating and shaping role of the analyst's personality, beliefs, and conflicts.

A similar distinction between symbolized and desymbolized aspects can be applied to the contemporary use of the now-popular concept of enactment. Enactment has come to refer to any behavior of patient or analyst that is spontaneous and unplanned, without immediate awareness of its meaning or motives. Enactment is essentially unreflective and desymbolized, at least initially, even if its manifestations are primarily verbal rather than major motor actions disrupting the analytic frame (the old-fashioned "acting out"). Present rationale assumes that such enactment will lead, after the event and if all goes well, to higher symbolization, through reflective analysis and dialogue by both analyst and patient. Such a process may be looked at as another cycle from desymbolized enactments to higher symbolization.

Enactment is usually contrasted with neutrality. Neutrality has become a confused and controversial notion, which would require a whole discussion in itself. I believe that while the analyst cannot be totally neutral, he can and should strive for neutrality, in the sense of maintaining, with varying degrees of success, a symbolizing attitude open to changing multiple perspectives and a constant reflective monitoring of his countertransference.

TRANSFERENCE AS SYMBOLIZATION OR ENACTMENT

In the classical model, the transference is to be interpreted and partly "dissolved" (deconstructed, to use a modern term); its analysis can provide essential and powerful material for increased dynamic symbolization.

But there is another way of defining and using the transference that is currently becoming more dominant, especially in the United States; it has a long history (going back to Ferenczi and the cure through love) and has always been an important, though often only implicit, component of the analytic situation. The focus here is no longer on the interpretation of the transference as a core aspect of the analytic relationship. To put it in a somewhat oversimplified manner, the transference is used and fostered rather than interpreted and analyzed. A symbolic enactment of the uninterpreted transference, partially shared and validated (coconstructed) by the analyst, may become the key aspect of the analytic relationship.

As symbolic enactment, the relationship acquires and embodies the affective power and psychic reality of what it symbolizes. The lived interactive experience with a "new object" is seen as the primary therapeutic factor. The analyst is a new object, not primarily because of his technique and professional role but because of what the patient's transference has made of him and the way the analyst is selectively responding to the patient's demands and expectations. Of course, this confirmation of the patient's transference demands and fantasies is only partial and symbolic, more omission than commission. At times the analyst's enacting a mixture of transference and countertransference roles is probably involuntary and unconscious; at other times it may be deliberate and conscious when it fits the analyst's image of his role (for instance, playing mother to the patient's infant) and what he experiences as his attunement to the patient's needs.

For many current authors, the primary therapeutic reality is a merged intersubjective interaction; trying to separate out the transference, countertransference, and realistic aspects of the relationship has become rather irrelevant, or even counterindicated. The transitional reality of the analytic relationship, with its unique shared mixture of fantasy and reality, is not to be questioned, to paraphrase Winnicott.

At this point, interpretation of the transference, and even the term itself, may cease to have much specific meaning or relevance. The emphasis is no longer on making links between various parts of experience more conscious, explicit, and integrated; nonverbal affective communication leading to some "implicit relational knowing" (Stern et al.1998) has become the main goal and rationale. With the dominance of such a model, the importance of increased symbolization as a therapeutic goal may become minimized.

Much of this contemporary approach can be seen as a toned-down version of what Sechehaye (1951) long ago described as "symbolic realization" as the power of symbolic acts (feeding her psychotic patient apples as a symbolic realization of breast feeding, and a repair for presumed traumas of early oral deprivations). Lévi-Strauss's (1949) discussion comparing the shaman and the psychoanalyst within their respective cultural contexts and of the quasimagical "effectiveness of symbols" may also be relevant here; he saw this effectiveness as mostly based on formal similarities in the shared cultural symbols and belief systems of the participants in the therapeutic relationship. With all this, we are back in the realm of unconscious symbolic meanings as manifested by the compelling power of concrete and often ritualized actions.

One can readily accept that the analytic relationship involves *both* the enactment and the interpretation of its symbolic aspects. The emphasis on the intrinsic power of the relationship does not exclude interpretations (if only to defuse the negative transference), and the classical approach needs the power of the unchallenged aspects of the positive transference to reduce resistance and make interpretations effective. But still, there are major differences in rationale and primary emphasis; these are bound to influence the kind of therapy offered and the kind of patients who can use it. One approach stresses the ongoing support of a relationship, in many ways more and less real than those offered in ordinary life. If and when such a relationship has to be given up, the analyst, as a selectively validated transference figure, may become internalized as a good object—a process that usually does not wait for termination of the treatment. On the other hand, the model of increasing symbolization uses the unique analytic relationship as a starting point for exploring broader and more lasting underlying patterns, meanings, and motives; the goal is mostly to help the patient acquire a more solid and generalizable sense of self-understanding and mastery.

Maybe, in a broad sense, cycles of symbolizing and desymbolizing can be found not only within the therapeutic process but also in the history of analytic theories and techniques.

Freedman has reminded us of the enduring importance of symbolization for psychoanalysis and has enriched the concept by applying it to theory, clinical process, and empirical research data.

REFERENCES

Freedman, N. (1999). *On incremental symbolization: clinical and empirical definition*. Paper presented at the Annual Meeting, Division 39 of the American Psychological Association, New York, April.

Freedman, N., and Berzofsky, M. (1995). The shape of the communicated transference in difficult and not-so-difficult patients: the symbolized and desymbolized transference. *Psychoanalytic Psychology* 12(3):363–374.

Freedman, N., Karliner, R., and Kagan, D. (2000). *Scales of Incremental Symbolization*. Unpublished manual.

Lévi-Strauss, C. (1949). The effectiveness of symbols. In *Structural Anthropology*, pp. 186–205. New York: Basic Books, 1963.

Loewald, H. (1975). Psychoanalysis as an art and the fantasy character of the psychoanalytic situation. In *Papers on Psychoanalysis*, pp. 352–372. New Haven, CT: Yale University Press, 1980.

Schimek, J. (1983). The construction of the transference. *Psychoanalysis and Contemporary Thought* 6(3):435–456.

Sechehaye, M. (1951). *Symbolic Realization*. New York: International Universities Press.

Stern, D., Sander, L., Nahum, J., et al. (1998). Non-interpretive mechanisms in psychoanalytic therapy. *International Journal of Psycho-Analysis* 79(5): 903–921.

11

Action in Psychoanalysis: On the Symbolization of Peremptory Motor Discharge

STANLEY GRAND

Current concern with the actual relationship between patient and analyst in the analytic situation has stimulated renewed interest in the role that action plays during analytic sessions. Action, in the sense I refer to here, is the behavioral expression of the patient's unconscious fantasy, as distinct from the more usual verbalized elaborations of these fantasies via dreams and associations. For some (Summers 1999) action has assumed increasing importance because of the emphasis being placed upon what is real and actual in this complex situation. For others, an extension and elaboration of our psychoanalytic understanding of action as enactive communication, or "pathological play" (Steingart 1983), has been useful for the understanding and treatment of the concrete preoperational, or iconic imagery of certain borderline, narcissistic, and desymbolizing (Freedman 1998) patients (Bass 1997, Frosch 1995). For the most part, however, psychoanalytic interest continues to center on the sort of action formerly referred to as acting out or acting in, more contemporaneously referred to as the dramatization, actualization, or, to the extent that it engages the analyst's participation, mutual enactment of unconscious transference fantasies. Such behavior is considered to be an important part of the analytic work (Busch 1995, Chused 1991, Katz 1998, McLaughlin 1991), and interesting because of its role as "an alternate to response in the psychic field" (Loewald 1971, p. 88).

Despite its importance, psychoanalysis, as currently understood, has no explicit theory of such action, in the sense called for by Hartmann (1947) as "an accepted or at least generally known body of facts and hypotheses." This, despite the fact that for Hartmann "a theory of action based upon knowledge of the structural aspects of personality and its motivations is the most important contribution psychoanalysis will one day be able to make" (p. 38). Boesky (1982), underscoring this current situation, says that the question of "why a patient substitutes action for verbal communication" is one "we least understand" (p. 50). Within the context of our present concerns with enactment, Boesky's question can be expanded to include the analyst's participation in such action as well.

Boesky's observation about the lack of theoretical clarity with respect to *why* patients oscillate between the intra-psychic/introspective reporting mode and the sphere of action does accurately reflect our current state of theoretical understanding. It also underlines the importance of efforts to systematically explore the *functional significance* that this oscillation may have for the analytic process itself. In the present paper I am going to consider a limited aspect of this issue through a consideration of the role of action in defending against the dangers of peremptory discharge of unconscious fantasy, and illustrate this with some clinical examples. Given the ubiquity of action in the analytic process, its function in regulating the expression of fantasy material needs further clarification.

Historically, action within the psychoanalytic situation has always been considered to be part of the transference. It is, as Sandler and colleagues (1973) have suggested, "the vehicle for acting out and may be the *only way in which repressed memories may initially find their way to the surface*" (p. 96, emphasis mine). Thus, when Freud's patient Dora (1905) broke off treatment, he attributed this to his failure to notice the transference:

> In this way the transference took me unawares, and, because of the unknown quantity in me which reminded Dora of Herr K., she took her revenge on him, and deserted me as she believed herself to have been deceived and deserted by him. Thus she acted out an essential part of her recollections and phantasies instead of producing it in the treatment. [p. 119]

Dora's action reflected a transference resistance.

Or, when, in describing his reasons for wanting to be analyzed, the Rat Man (1909) began to tell Freud the story of the rat punishment, he rose up from the couch and pleaded with Freud to allow him to discontinue. Rather than comply with the Rat Man's wish to avoid describing the rat torture, Freud explained to him that "the overcoming of resistance is a law of treatment." Freud viewed the Rat Man's act of rising from the couch as a transference resistance to telling him something terribly shameful. The Rat Man's action, in place of his words, revealed to Freud a resistance to speaking of a series of unconscious sadistic fantasies related to his father.

This view of action, as a resistance to the awareness of unconscious transference fantasies, was to become a defining attribute of the concept of acting out. Seen from the early perspective of what might now be called a topographical model of action, namely, as an interference with conscious remembering, it was a resistance to making unconscious fantasies conscious. A rather different model for action was presented in Freud's (1914) paper on "Remembering, Repeating, and Working Through." There, action was seen as a form of remembering. That is, it was seen to be in the service of making transference a more vivid and compelling experience, and providing the patient with a sense of conviction that his transference was a repetition, or a way of remembering an earlier, original relationship with a parental figure. Thus, action was a necessary aspect of transference *and enabled the patient to grasp the significance of the distortion he imposed on his relationship with the analyst*. Here, action was not simply a resistance to remembering, that is, in the service of unconscious transference gratification, but like transference itself, a form of making memory actual and real. "The patient does not remember anything of what he has forgotten, but acts it out. He reproduces it not as a memory but as an action. He repeats it, without, of course knowing that he is repeating it" (p. 150). In this sense, action is a mode of representing what has been repressed—a more vivid expression of the unconscious. These two modes of conceptualizing action in the psychoanalytic situation have provided the basis for our contemporary understanding of the concept of acting out, or, more generally, our conception of action in the psychoanalytic situation.

In his reconsideration of the concept of acting out, Boesky (1982) raises the unanswered question of why patients shift to action at all. "Why does a given patient choose acting as a way of resolving or expressing his conflict? Who is it that would rather enact than think? Why discharge instead of delay?" (pp. 50–51). A partial answer is given by Freud's observation that when resistances are at a maximum patients are most likely to act out. When transference becomes unduly intense, "verbalization and introspection" give way to action, but, according to Boesky, not simply as a resistance that represses the transference fantasy, but as a compromise formation that expresses that fantasy—a compromise necessary because of the closeness of the original fantasy to being actualized in relation to the analyst and therefore, a fantasy that has become increasingly dangerous:

> It is the tendency toward actualization that promises to make transference wishes come true. The pain and poignance of transference is the tension between the actuality of the experience of the affects in the transference and the futility, danger, or both of ever fully realizing or actualizing the transference wishes. Any tendency toward actualization is a signal to the ego that a transference fantasy is about to be gratified in reality. Action at this point facilitates a compromise formation, which is required because of this defensive imbalance. Actualization means immediate danger of a defense imbalance requiring compromise formations. [p. 51]

Further, Boesky says, action heightens the reality force or reality quality of an event, and the shift to the action mode creates an illusory reality that serves the purpose of defense in that it creates verisimilitude. It serves to prove that a false reality is true, that is, that the defensive action is true, not the underlying fantasy. According to Boesky, it is defensively necessary for most patients at one time or another to supplement their defenses by shifting to the realm of action and behavior when an excessive imbalance occurs.

Viewing action as a compromise formation for frightening transference fantasies dangerously close to actualization in the reality of the analytic situation enables Boesky to compare acting out to the hallucinated images of vivid manifest dreams. In a way similar to how the unacceptable dream wish is transformed, via secondary revision, into acceptable manifest dream narratives, acting out is the defensive transformation of an unacceptable transference wish into a rationalized bit of overt behavior with verisimilitude. And, just as most patients can grasp the distinction between the vividly hallucinated internal reality of their dream images and external reality, the acting out patient, whose sense of reality remains relatively intact, can be helped to understand the difference between the apparent external reality of his/her compromise formation and his/her actual unconscious wishes toward the analyst.[1] Both the dream and acting out satisfy the structural constraints placed upon the expression of unacceptable unconscious transference wishes. It is, however, the action component of acting out that imbues it with verisimilitude. Thus, as Sandler and colleagues (1973) have suggested, acting in the transference, for some patients, "may be the only way in which repressed memories may initially find their way to the surface" (p. 96). And, along with Boesky, it is the action component of the compromise formation that makes it seem real.

George Klein's (1970) model, attempting to account for the power of an idea to take hold of behavior and influence perception, imagery, symbolic construction, gesture, and action, is consistent with these ideas. According to Klein, action is part of an ideomotor struc-

1. Steingart (1983) has used this distinction between patients who can recognize the difference between transference and the real relationship to their analyst, and those who cannot, or do not, as a defining attribute of "pathological play," a form of preconceptual thinking characteristic of preoperational children as well as certain borderline and narcissistic adults.

ture, that is, "a train of thought involving receptive, affective, and motor components in relation to which environmental changes are produced and experienced" (p. 336). In Klein's model, actions are an aspect of the organized sequence of thought and vice versa. What is of interest here is that for Klein a train of thought caught up in conflict and repression may be especially intense and motivating. Under such circumstances, unrelieved unpleasurable affect produces an urgency for peremptory "switch-off" behavior, that is, terminating feedback, which can result in acting out "whose aim is not to gratify the wish, but to mitigate the negative affect itself" (p. 391). Klein suggests that the unique requirement for "switching off" a repressed train of thought is that

> it must occur without endangering repression. Conditions that will cancel out the initiating excitations without allowing direct approaches to, perceptual contact with, action upon, or gratification from a wished for object are sought. . . . Terminal events must be similar enough to the wished for activity to make possible the switch off, yet dissimilar enough to allow perceptual experience without release of anxiety. This is a prescription for displacement. [p. 389]

In Boesky's terms, there is a powerful tendency to correct the imbalance. Successful defense alleviates imbalances without threatening to undo repression, and action is often the most compelling way to regulate such threats. As Boesky suggests, action enhances the verisimilitude of the defensive compromise formation.

But action also turns a passive experience into an active one. It not only heightens the sense of the reality of the compromise formation, it strengthens the experience of mastery that derives from reversing a potentially dangerous and passively experienced wish into an actively experienced expression of it in a less dangerous form. Klein (1976) reminds us that action in the transference is more than a compulsive repetition operating on the basis of the pleasure principle. It is a "recreation with the aim of resolution or mastery." He says, "The principles of repression and active reversal are not contradictory but coordinate, and both are critical in accounting for what Freud dealt with as the repetition compulsion" (p. 264). Thus action, which makes a compromise formation seem more true and real, also turns a passively experienced displeasure into something acceptable and ego-syntonic through its contribution to the active aim of mastery.

SOME CLINICAL ILLUSTRATIONS

As a way of illustrating these points about action in the transference, I would like to present two clinical examples of the way action adds both verisimilitude and an experience of ego-syntonic mastery to the compromise formed to express a transference wish in a form acceptable to the patient's ego. In the first example, action is circumscribed and limited to a brief moment in a long analysis. Despite its brevity the meaning of the action resonated to the very core of the patient's pathology. In the second example, action was generalized to the entire conduct of the treatment. Here, the patient's manner and style of presentation constituted the action and reflected a well-integrated characterological defense against anger. In both cases, action was in the service of both repetition and active mastery of passively experienced trauma.

The first patient, a 42-year-old civil engineer who was severely obessive and compulsive, had come to treatment with serious doubts that he could ever feel truly alive emotionally, or would ever be capable of having what he considered a real relationship with a woman. At the time of the incident that I am going to describe, Mr. Y. had already been in the analysis for eight years. Despite serious difficulties in his capacity to experience the analysis in an emotionally meaningful way, the work had carried him to a point where his angry disillusionment with an ungiving and unloving mother was beginning to surface in an unusually intense way. In this particular hour the patient was bemoaning his fate as a lonely and isolated man devoid of the comfort of human attachments, and lacking even the most basic warmth and affection that might come from a relationship with a woman. Divorced for the past ten years, after an unhappy marriage that had lasted but two short years, the patient had retreated from social contact with others, maintaining a tie only with his 9-year-old son, a tie that was deeply loving but also highly narcissistic. The only area of his life that provided some pleasure and self-esteem was his work, at which he was competent and capable of steady advancement. The years of his analysis had made him aware of the enormous distrust and rage he felt toward a mother who seemed ungiving yet seductive in her promises of eternal bliss if he would be what she wanted. In this session, the patient recalled a memory from age 8, in which he saw himself racing home from school with an enormous need to defecate. On his arrival home he found a note from his mother, pinned to the locked apartment door, saying that she would be back soon and that he should wait there for her. He recalled the anxiety and pain attached to the need to defecate and the fear of doing so in his pants. After what seemed like hours of waiting, he let go of the movement with a mixture of relief and sadistic pleasure at the thought that now she would have to clean up the mess in his pants.

In the session that I have been describing, one could hear the angry complaints of the little boy of 8, suffering a painful sense of aloneness and abandonment at the hands of his absent mother. I was silent in the session as he described his painful trauma, and in this sense I, too, was absent and abandoning. The pitch of the patient's upset increased until a point in the session was reached at which he shouted angrily, "I don't want to talk about this any longer." He then turned on his side to face the wall and remained in his angry silence for many minutes. In childhood, when frustrated and angry with his mother, he often assumed a similar position on his living room couch. So, in the session, the patient enacted with me the particular compromise formation that served, so often in his childhood, to protect him from the danger of allowing his rage toward his mother to be openly expressed. His silent turning away from his mother as a way of expressing his rage was repeated in the transference where it symbolized a similar rage toward me. And further, his refusal to speak to me about this behavior was his way to actively reject me, just as his angry silence with his mother served to reject her. It was as if he were saying, "It is not I who have to endure this painful and lonely abandonment. I will make you the pained and abandoned one." His turning to the wall and his refusal to speak in the session combined, as Klein suggested, the expression of both his compulsion to repeat and his attempt to actively master the passively experienced and frightening rage toward his abandoning mother-analyst. While the moment seemed right for an interpretation of this transference enactment as resistance to the analytic, self-reflective process, his refusal to speak indicated that verbalization had become implicated in the transference, and silence was being actively used to both express and master his overwhelming rage and passivity. It seemed to me that what was needed at that moment was not only an interpretation of his action as a repetition, but as an indication of the particular way silence had become implicated in managing the enraged relationship that existed between this child and his mother. I commented to him that his frustrations with the analysis and with me caused him to react much as he did in his childhood when his mother was not able to provide the bliss she had promised. "In a way," I said, " your angry and silent turning to the wall in here is your way of expressing your sense that I, too, have failed a promise to you." I then added, "Rather than openly claim what you wish, you retreat in angry silence." The patient began to sob quietly and repeated over and over, "I can't do it, I just can't do it." I believe that by holding up my view of this patient's conflicted and neurotically inhibited expression of anger, and his claim for the love and attention of his mother, I had reflected back to him an image of the possibility that he might one day freely ask for what he wanted so intensely. While his plaintive cry that he couldn't do it reflected his ambivalent struggle in the transference, it also heralded the return of verbalization and, as such, a hopeful rejoining of the analytic enterprise.

For this patient, the act of turning to the wall in angry silence was a complex yet circumscribed action that both expressed and defended against rage at a mother who was unable to satisfy his urgent and compelling needs. His action in the transference, triggered by the memory of the abandonment by his absent mother, was an old compromise formation, displaced onto the analytic situation, in response to similar feelings of abandonment and fear of retraumatization stimulated by my silence in the session. This repetition in the transference, resulting from intense conflict over destroying me, as well as the treatment, served to defend against a passively experienced dangerous impulse by actively initiating behavior that not only reversed the expression of his rage but imbued this reversal with verisimilitude.

The second patient that I will present illustrates a more generalized use of action to repeat as well as to master passively experienced and overwhelming rage. Here, defiance in both the manner and style of the patient's presentation was a highly integrated characterological defense that served as a compromise formation, both expressing and defending against dangerous rage toward a mother who seemed unable to acknowledge the independent existence of her child.

Ms. B. came for analytic treatment following an unsuccessful and prolonged psychotherapy of five years duration, complaining about the frustration she experienced with her previous therapist. Apparently, the last few years of her treatment were spent discussing frivolous details of her current life, rather than the serious problems caused by her depression. An avid bridge player, she complained that her therapist would engage her, almost exclusively, about her bridge game, and she felt that she was getting nowhere with respect to her depressed feelings. A woman in her early forties, unmarried and significantly overweight, she described herself as hopeless about her prospects for marriage and family, and helpless to bring her weight problem under control. Despite her negative feelings about her future, she held out a glimmer of hope that an analysis might help her to go beyond her present sense of hopelessness about her life. However, her intense ambivalence about starting was underscored when she informed me that the idea of analysis loomed as futile in her mind. It appeared to her as an impossible undertaking because she had already told her previous therapist everything there was to know about herself and she still felt as depressed and helpless as before. Thus, she began her analysis in a subtly defiant way, challenging me to prove to her that analysis could help her to change.

As might have been expected, the beginning of Ms. B.'s treatment consisted almost exclusively of complaints about frustrating and uncertain relationships with men and complaints about her weight. That is, she externalized all of her difficulties. The essential message seemed to be that she felt neither able to control the men in her life, nor her ego alien impulses with respect to eating. In addition, the concreteness of her complaining and the intensity of her upset about the conditions of her life appeared to be her way of telling me that she could not change anything about the way she felt. It also suggested that anything I might say to her that could be helpful for understanding her difficulties would be useless. Her manner of speaking expressed an underlying rejecting attitude that prevented any productive use she might have made of my efforts to help her explore the issues of which she complained. Even empathic resonance with her plight was rejected; she experienced it as a threat to her self-esteem. Clearly, her communicative stance had cut her off completely from any help that I might have been able to offer.

However, while my patient was unresponsive to my many efforts to help her explore her dilemma, these efforts did not go unnoticed. Rather, she used them to reinforce her defiance. In this regard, a shift in her complaining began to occur. She now began to complain directly about me. Ms. B. blamed the treatment, and me in particular, for not being able to help her overcome her social difficulties or control her overeating. "If," she said, "I could not help her to stop overeating she was hopelessly doomed to failure." She would never achieve her lifelong yearnings for a husband and family. She wanted me to do something other than talk. She wanted action from me, not understanding.

Her pessimism about relationships and her externalization of responsibility were now being directly expressed in the transference and thus served as a new level of defense and resistance to the exploration of the meanings of her complaints. Rather than reflect upon the meanings of these complaints, Ms. B. attacked the analysis and me for not doing anything to help her. It was I who was seen as causing her pain insofar as it was I whom she experienced as both incompetent to help her and a witness to her inability to be in control of herself. She defiantly consulted her physician for diet pills and began to express the wish to end the treatment. Leaving treatment was the only way she knew to rid herself of her angry feelings and avoid the humiliation of her failure.

The quality of the transference had turned adversarial as Ms. B. transformed her struggle to control her men and overeating into a battle to control me and the analysis. It was the treatment that was depressing her, not her social difficulties or her impulse control. In this transferential context I began to interpret Ms. B.'s externalizations and wishes to stop treatment as a way of protecting herself from the pain and anxiety she felt about simply having to tell me about her difficulties. It seemed, I said, as if she was experiencing this aspect of the treatment, that is, talking about her problems, as an unreasonable demand for her to do something to change. I told her that it seemed to me that whenever I attempted to help her understand some aspect of the difficulty she found herself in, she felt either that I didn't really understand what she wanted or that I was being critical of what she had said or done. I said, "You react as if I were telling you that what you've done is wrong or bad and that you should have done things differently. I think you want something from me but it doesn't seem like you want me to help you understand the things that upset you." I asked, "What is it that you would like from me?" After a long pause, and with strong emotion, she said, "All I ever wanted was for someone to recognize that I always get the dirty end of the stick." I said, "And is this what you feel you want from me here, and is this what you feel you never got from your mother?" Ms. B. moaned in agreement. "She didn't validate your complaints and seemed to always expect something more from you. And when I try to help you understand your difficulties you feel I am also saying that you're not good enough." Ms. B. remained silent for some moments. Because we were close to the end of the session I asked her what she was thinking about. She said, in a somewhat resentful tone, "Well, where do we go from here?" I said, "We will have to see where this road takes us."

My articulation of the difficulty she felt being in the analysis apparently had touched her because in the following session she acknowledged that what I had said about her reactions to my efforts to help were true. She said that she felt humiliated talking to me about her problems and she hated having to talk about her fear of being out of control. But most important for our work together in the transference, Ms. B. now acknowledged her lifelong, secret defiance of her mother, who frequently expressed wishes that her overweight daughter be thin and self-controlled like everyone else in the family. Being obese was being different, and therefore, bad and unacceptable. At the age of 8, in what was for Ms. B. a catastrophically decisive moment in her life, she made up her mind that she would defy her mother's wishes and be fat until her mother accepted her as she was. She would not be what her mother wanted her to be, and in this way would punish her mother for the pain she caused her. Remaining obese and unacceptable was a way of getting even and hurting her mother, just as Ms. B. had been hurt by her mother's critical complaints. Similarly, in the analysis, her anger at me was a reflection of her feeling that I, too, would not accept her as she was, and remaining obese and unacceptable to men reflected her wish to get even with me and defy the implicit demand of the treatment that she change. To bring her oral impulses under self-control, and to succeed in achieving her lifelong goals of marriage and family, was to give in to her mother's wishes and lose the battle that her defiance had served. Thus, she continued to overeat in order to destroy me as she had, throughout her life, attempted to destroy her mother.

For Ms. B., defiance, in thought and action, was a compromise formation that both expressed and actively defended against the rage and humiliation she felt at the hands of a mother who could not accept her as she was. It also served a similar function in regard to her analyst, whose implicit demand for her to change repeated the early traumatization she experienced at the hands of her mother. In a way, the entire analysis had become an enactment of this childhood traumatization. Her defiant stance formed a powerful compromise that defended against the rage she felt toward her mother and me by giving reality to her feelings of victimization. It also mastered this rage by reversing the humiliation of having to endure the mother's complaints (and the analytic demands) through turning passive humiliation into active, defiant, and ego-syntonic retribution.

DISCUSSION

Earlier in this paper I cited Boesky's (1982) cogent observation that the question of why a patient would substitute action for verbal communication is relatively poorly understood in our psychoanalytic literature. Beginning with Freud's dual notions about the functions of action in the psychoanalytic situation, as both an expression and as a resistance to expressing unconscious conflict, and up to the present concerns with enactment, a precise theoretical understanding of why a patient enacts rather than verbalize his conflicts has eluded us.

It was the purpose of this paper to explore an aspect of this question by considering clinically the role that action plays in regulating the danger of direct discharge of instinctual wishes. Boesky's understanding of the use of action to make defensive compromise formations seem more true or real than their underlying wishes served as an orienting point from which to consider this issue. George Klein's consideration of action as part of an ideomotor structure placed action on a par with verbalization as a means of representing the compromise formation. But, the mechanism of reversal of passive into active seems to complete the necessary (although perhaps not sufficient) conditions for patients to resort to action in place of verbal expression. Thus, by making the ego-alien experience of being passively overwhelmed by a frightening wish into an ego-syntonic experience of self-controlled action, reversal makes the compromise formation seem more true and real. From this perspective, the question of why a given patient chooses action as a way of expressing or resolving conflict seems more understandable.

Both cases reported here illustrate the operation of these forces of repression and mastery, emphasized by Klein. In the case of Mr. Y., the gradual intensification of the possibility of fully activating the anger that he felt toward his mother signaled a danger of being passively pulled toward a state of frightening and uncontrollable rage. His breaking off the associative process was the first level of defense against this rage. Turning to the wall dramatically enacted the reversal of the frightening wish to kill, not only by inhibiting action, but by fully eliminating the sight of the object toward which his rage was directed. Thus, both the silence and turning toward the wall prevented the actualization of murderous rage, and, indeed, reversed its impact by "turning tail," so to speak. It was as if he were saying, "It is not that I want to kill you. I am a coward, you see, and wouldn't hurt anyone." But, turning his back on both his mother and me expressed his rage, as well, via his rejection of us. This rejection expressed, in a more ego-syntonic and actively controlled way, the rage that underlay his compromise formation. By turning to the wall in angry silence, Mr. Y. symbolized his feelings of self-justified victimization, which fit better with his masochistic character and made his sense of victimization feel more true and real to him.

Whereas Mr. Y.'s action in the transference was brief and circumscribed, Ms. B.'s action was a thoroughly integrated aspect of her character structure, and was revealed in the analysis from the beginning, in the form of her defiant style of communicating her difficulties. Right from the start, Ms. B. seemed to be challenging me to prove to her that analysis would be helpful. On the one side, she tried to induce me to reassure her that I could help her overcome her difficulties. But on the other side, she rejected everything I tried to do to help her understand her complaints. Defiance, in thought and action, was her way of enacting the compromise formation she evolved as a way to defend against the dangers of actualizing rage at a mother who seemed to be demanding that she be someone other than who she was. Her defiance made this rage ego-syntonic by expressing it in a form that she could control and that she believed was more true to her character structure. Not until her defiant stance could be addressed interpretively in the transference as a reaction to her feeling that the analysis and I, like her mother, were rejecting the very essence of who she was and demanding that she change, was it possible for her to begin to reflect on the original trauma and her fateful decision to defy her mother in this self-destructive way. In the case of Ms. B., the medium of her communicative action was her message. When the medium is used to symbolize the underlying dynamic struggle and can be understood as such by the patient, then analysis of that underlying struggle becomes possible.

Considering the question of who would rather enact than think, the clinical illustrations presented above suggest that acting occurs across a broad spectrum of psychopathology and across a range of time periods during treatment. The clinical vignettes highlight the fact that acting in the transference is more pervasive for patients who exhibit more primitive levels of psychopathology. Among more integrated patients acting tends to be more circumscribed and verbal communication appears to predominate. It is true, as Freud indicated originally, that when conflict is intense, acting out is most likely to occur. But as Klein has suggested, the tendency to action is an intrinsic aspect of the representational process, that is, all representations are ideomotor structures. Here I think that Norbert Freedman's work linking communicative structures to psychic structures (Freedman and Grand 1976) is quite relevant in pointing to the importance of both the discharge and structuralizing aspects of motor action to the representational process. Freedman and his colleagues have collected a wealth of data highlighting the structuralizing role of motor accompaniments to verbal communication, as well as the functional significance of motor discharge under conditions of desymbolization. With respect to the latter, desymbolized action occurs as a *sign* of an object relationship, rather than as a *mode of symbolic representation.* As such, it defines moments of psychoanalytic impasse. Such moments may occur in any analysis but frequently dominate the clinical situation during the analyses of more primitive types of psychopathology. While such forms of action must surely be considered in a general psychoanalytic theory of action (Hartmann 1947), within the context provided by the present work such concrete behavior reflects an effort to destroy meaning rather than create it. From a psychoanalytic (i.e., meaning-creating) perspective, when the sign function of action predominates over its symbolic meanings it signals the approach of the treatment to the outer boundaries of psychoanalytic interpretive work.

Finally, we come to Boesky's last question: "Why discharge instead of delay?" Here, I think the question links directly to Freedman's (1998) concerns with desymbolization. To the extent that discharge of impulses is peremptory and brooks no delay, action bypasses the defensive function and operates in opposition to the symbol-making function of the mind. Here, as in the case of Ms. B.'s defiance, action is opposed to self-knowledge. There are many structural conditions of the mind that contribute to such an impasse in analytic self-reflection and symbolization: strength of the impulses, weakness of ego functions, or lacunae in superego development. These are the typical ways we have traditionally understood the concept of acting out. In the present paper I have tried to emphasize more positive symbol-making processes that are involved in the use of action as "an alternate to response in the psychic field." Action in the service of defensive compromise formations makes an unacceptable and dangerous impulse less dangerous and more ego-syntonic. It does so by reversing the passive experience of being overwhelmed by the wish and making it an active, believable compromise formation that seems to be true.

REFERENCES

Bass, A. (1997). The problem of "concreteness." *Psychoanalytic Quarterly* 66:642–682.

Boesky, D. (1982). Acting out: a reconsideration of the concept. In *Enactment: Toward a New Approach to the Therapeutic Relationship*, ed. S. J. Ellman and M. Moskowitz, pp. 37–61. Northvale, NJ: Jason Aronson, 1998.

Busch, F. (1995). Do actions speak louder than words? A query into an enigma in analytic theory and technique. *Journal of the American Psychoanalytic Association* 43:61–82.

Chused, J. F. (1991). The evocative power of enactments. *Journal of the American Psychoanalytic Association* 39:615–639.

Freedman, N. (1998). Psychoanalysis and symbolization: legacy or heresy? In *The Modern Freudians: Contemporary Psychoanalytic Technique*, ed. C. S. Ellman, S. Grand, M. Silvan, and S. J. Ellman, pp. 79–97. Northvale, NJ: Jason Aronson.

Freedman, N., and Grand, S., eds. (1976). *Communicative Structures and Psychic Structures: A Psychoanalytic Interpretation of Communication*. New York: Plenum.

Freud, S. (1905). Fragment of an analysis of a case of hysteria. *Standard Edition* 7:7–122.

——— (1909). Notes upon a case of obsessional neurosis. *Standard Edition* 10:153–249.

——— (1914). Remembering, repeating and working through. *Standard Edition* 12:147–156.

Frosch, A. (1995). The preconceptual organization of emotions. *Journal of the American Psychoanalytic Association* 43:423–447.

Hartmann, H. (1947). On rational and irrational action. In *Essays on Ego Psychology*, pp. 37–68. New York: International Universities Press, 1964.

Katz, G. (1998). Where the action is: the enacted dimension of analytic process. *Journal of the American Psychoanalytic Association* 46:1129–1167.

Klein, G. S. (1970). Peremptory ideation: structure and force in motivated ideas. In *Perception, Motives and Personality*, pp. 357–412. New York: Knopf.

——— (1976). *Psychoanalytic Theory: An Explanation of Essentials*. New York: International Universities Press.

Loewald, H. W. (1971). Some considerations on repetition compulsion. In *Papers on Psychoanalysis*, pp. 87–101. New Haven, CT: Yale University Press, 1980.

McLaughlin, J. T. (1991). Clinical and theoretical aspects of enactment. *Journal of the American Psychoanalytic Association* 39:595–614.

Sandler, J., Dare, C., and Holder, A. (1973). *The Patient and the Analyst*. New York: International Universities Press.

Steingart, I. (1983). *Pathological Play in Borderline and Narcissistic Personalities*. Jamaica, NY: Spectrum.

Summers, F. (1999). Psychoanalytic boundaries and transitional space. *Psychoanalytic Psychology* 16:3–20.

12

Symbolization and the Development of Interpretable Transference

STEVEN J. ELLMAN AND MONICA CARSKY

In this chapter we focus on those aspects of the analyst's activity that are designed to help the patient develop and sustain the capacity to symbolize and reflect upon intrapsychic experience. We include helping the patient to develop a capacity to tolerate feelings that have been considered intolerable, and to use words to sustain such experience and nurture self-observation, because being overwhelmed by affect tends to interfere with symbolization (Ellman and Weinstein 1991).

These developments are important because we posit that transference can be interpreted to the patient in a useful way only when the patient has some capacity to symbolize the transference. This capacity includes the idea that the patient does not (primarily) believe that her perceptions of the analyst are due to external reality. That is, the patient has some sense of the difference between her perception and the idea of representation of inner reality by means of symbolic words and other actions. This representation may be consciously or unconsciously intended. We see these developments as intertwined with the fostering, by the analyst, of the development of analytic trust (Ellman 1991, 1998).

Historically, analysts have stated that only patients already capable of adequate symbolization are analyzable. From this requirement follows the familiar idea that mostly neurotic patients can benefit from analysis, as they are presumed to have intact reality testing, and are thus able to hear and believe the analyst who tells them that their perceptions of him are due to unconscious fantasies. They can play with (or consider) abstract concepts and deal with the simultaneously real and "unreal" nature of the transference.

Yet not all patients (even excluding psychotic patients) can do this all the time. In fact, although we speak of intact reality testing in neurotic patients, or in borderline patients under certain conditions, these seem to us to refer to global percentages rather than dichotomous variables. We know that a neurotic symptom contains a kernel of rejection of some aspect of reality in it, and we posit that the same is necessarily true of transference. We hope, however, that our patients will still be able to hold in mind the complex nature of the transference relationship and their transference feelings. This capacity is important whether one speaks of the transference as playground (Freud 1914), transitional object (Winnicott 1971), cocreation as analytic third (Ogden 1994), joint construction (Hoffman 1994), or simultaneously real and unreal, with an as-if quality (Ellman 1998). Bird (1972) refers to the way in which the patient makes the analyst part of her neurosis. All these terms point in a similar direction, toward the patient's capacity for abstract thought and symbol formation while simultaneously having intense experiences. At the same time, many authors have made suggestions for dealing with lapses in symbolic abilities.

From this perspective, the question of timing of interpretation is partially an issue of the patient's capacity for awareness of reality and for symbol formation, which vary with level of pathology but also with many other moment-to-moment factors, regardless of diagnosis. Paradoxically, we hope that patients *will* develop intense transference states, because it is through this that they come to believe in the power of their unconscious fantasy to shape their lives. However, the capacity for symbolic awareness and self-reflection is at least temporarily lost during intense transference states.

We are proposing that a distinction between transference and interpretable transference is crucial to psychoanalytic technique. It is not the patient who is analyzable or not; it is the patient's transference at a given time that is interpretable or not. The development of analytic trust makes transference gradually interpretable and meaningful to the patient, and it is through this process, we believe, that the patient becomes able to tolerate and address the symbolic representation of difficult realities.

A healthier patient, with better reality testing and object relations and a stronger capacity for self-reflection, will tolerate errors in the analyst more easily. So mistakes about whether the transference was really interpretable may do less harm to these patients, particularly if the error is not persistent. Nonetheless, to interpret before the development of interpretable transference can lead to unwelcome developments even in these patients, such as compliance to authority rather than the development of freedom to explore one's thoughts and feelings.

In this chapter we will briefly review some other authors' recent experiences with patients who are unable to tolerate interpretive efforts. We will then present one developmental model that underlies the concept of analytic trust. The third and longest section of the chapter presents both the concept of analytic trust and clinical examples of symbolization and desymbolization. We end with a brief concluding section.

BACKGROUND

A number of authors have put forth ways to deal with patients' varying capacities for symbolization, especially in nonclassical/nonneurotic patients. For example, Carsky and Selzer (1994) observed that the most severely impaired patients who seek psychotherapy need more clarification of reality before they are able to use interpretation. Fonagy (e.g., Fonagy and Target 1996), in describing analytic work with more impaired patients, believes that the crucial aspect of the treatment is the development of mentalization, the capacity to think about the facts of one's own and others' minds. While we agree with Fonagy it is our view that this is only one factor in developing the capacity for hearing another perspective.

Gibeault (2000) presented a definition of analysis that focuses on the patient's capacity "to experience formal and topographical regression," with interpretation aimed at opening up new areas of association. Patients who lack this capacity "are often unable to imagine a situation that they are not actually experiencing. This leads to a wish to create a situation . . . in order to be able to imagine it" (p. 380). In such a case, the analyst's task is different, until the patient becomes able to handle shifts in modes of thought rather than continuing to be concrete. Our reading of Gibeault's statements is that the French (in this description) have recognized the need to develop analytic trust before interpretation is possible. Later in the chapter we will try to develop this theme more convincingly.

A contemporary Kleinian, Britton (1997) talks about patients who cannot bear the analyst's objectivity for a long time because of its dreaded oedipal implications.

> If the link between the parents perceived in love and hate can be tolerated in the child's mind, it provides him with a prototype for an object relationship of a third kind in which he is a witness and not a participant. A third position then comes into existence from which object relationships can be observed. This provides us with a capacity for seeing ourselves in interaction with others and for entertaining another point of view whilst retaining our own. . . . This is a capacity we hope to find in ourselves and in our patients in analysis. There are analyses when for some time, or at certain times, this seems impossible. . . . It was also intolerable for them to feel that I was communing with myself about them independently of them. . . . [pp. 245–246]

Britton found that the only way to manage such an analysis, for lengthy periods, was to think and observe and experience, but to share only an understanding of the patient's point of view (rather than making the oedipal interpretation suggested earlier).

All of these authors are referring to what Freedman has described as the nonsymbolizing patient. In Freedman's (1994) descriptions the capacity for symbolization is the necessary requisite for utilizing interpretations. The remainder of the chapter talks to the development of the capacity for symbolization in both the child (developing infant) and the analytic patient.

DEVELOPMENTAL CONSIDERATIONS

In this section we could appropriately include aspects of many developmental theorists from Freud (1905) to Bion (1967) to Stern (1985). For the purposes of the present chapter we will utilize Winnicott (e.g., 1951, 1960, 1963, 1971) to provide a developmental framework. Winnicott was one of the earliest psychoanalytic theorists to write meaningfully about the continuum from early development into adult life. He gave meaning to the ego (self) as the integrator of both exogenous experiences and endogenous experiences (the drives). In healthy development, with the help of the mother's ego, the drives are experienced through object relations, so that id impulses (experienced as affect) come to seem part of the baby, not intrusions. In infancy the baby's separate identity and eventual sense of self are only gradually developed, with the mother serving many different, crucial functions at the various stages in this process. A great deal of early anxiety, aggression, and trauma can be integrated into the ego by "good enough" mothering.

New experience in a safe setting is central to Winnicott's ideas about development and how analysis cures. It is clear that although Winnicott aims to eventually work in a way that resembles "standard" psychoanalytic treatment (1954, 1962, 1963), he did not feel that he should sacrifice flexibility in his responses to patients because of this aim. Rather, he seems to have done many things to help patients feel safe or responded to or not traumatically overwhelmed. There is a definite similarity between the roles of the good enough mother and the analyst. Winnicott did not distinguish sharply enough between the holding environment and other phases of analysis but this will be discussed later in the chapter.

Winnicott also states that the analyst has some characteristics of a transitional object (1962). In this analogy the analyst is thought to be felt as partly under the patient's control and partly having independent life and movement. If the beginning of treatment is holding, too much awareness or a preoccupation with the analyst indicates a problem. Gradual use of the analyst as a transitional object would be the goal: the patient develops an awareness of the analyst as partly me, but also a reminder of the not-me—a part of me but with particular connotations.

However, the reality and goodness of the child's transitional object depend on the reliability and goodness of the real mother; if she is not good enough, or leaves for too long for the infant to bear, the transitional object no longer comforts and serves its functions. This would imply that the analyst must be sufficiently real, alive, and good, in the perception of the patient, for the patient to sustain the use of the analyst as a type of transitional object.

In infant development, the transitional object precedes the development of reality testing. In analysis, therefore, the patient needs to have the experience of believing in the transference, feeling it as real and as part of her, a creation of her mind. However, the actual awareness that the patient has created this out of the analyst's presence and her own internal world is a later development. The patient who cannot think symbolically about the analysis has no capacity to play and simply experiences everything as real, without any awareness of how her inner life affects her perceptions of experience. Thus, the initial task of the analyst, according to Winnicott, would be to teach her to play.

For Winnicott as for Klein, the use of the denotative symbol, the word based on consensual reality testing, requires the achievement of the depressive position (Carsky 1978). To be able to call something by a name implies the idea that there is a thing that might not be there, and that therefore might need to be called. The idea of an absent breast or mother is an actively held idea. At first, the idea is of an absent object that is longed for and loved, or rejected and hated, but it is the target of feelings. To hold both sets of feelings requires tolerance of ambivalence, regret, and guilt about one's feelings toward the object, and implies a capacity for mourning. The transitional object is partway to this goal. Thus, the analyst must help the patient to bear various affect states, as well as help the patient to tolerate fantasy derivatives. Eventually the patient will symbolize affects and ideas that are involved with the loss of cherished or needed images or hopes. As reality testing develops, the child becomes able to think about loss, to think about "what's behind the wall," to consider possibilities, initially in a concrete fashion. Busch's (1995) work on how the analyst attends to the nature of the ego's functioning in analysis builds on this point. It is only with this development that the patient can begin to accept that the analyst may have a different point of view, based on his status as having a separate reality.

Winnicott (1960) states that "Changes come in analysis when the traumatic factors enter the psycho-analytic material in the patient's own way, and within the patient's omnipotence" (p. 37). This gradually leads to confidence in the analytic setting and to experimentation, where the patient may develop direct whole object (that is, instinctual) ties to the analyst that are less disguised and defended (1962). We see this development of interpretable transference as necessary for change to occur; the corrective emotional experience of the setting is not enough unless it is processed in some way. Some symbolic representation of the experience of the relationship is necessary. Then, some action by the analyst can serve as an implicit transference interpretation ("You may notice I am not your mother, I do X not Y"), underlined by a statement about it. Even when the analyst may have enacted something, it is important for the analyst to point out that she is having a reaction about an event. Thus it is crucial for the patient to see that the analyst actually looks sad or angry, not because the patient is unmanageable and bad, as he may have felt and imagined in the transference, but because of an event that is going on inside of the analyst.

In the process of using the analyst to create scenarios from her internal world, the patient allows the analyst more of a role, though still under her control. At some point, even if the analyst is accepting, the patient will find a way to hate the analyst for the original environmental failures. When these first occurred, they were impingements, felt as outside the baby's (omnipotent) control. Now, they are "staged in the transference" but by the patient. These impingements occur not because the analyst can manipulate or consciously choose when to disappoint the patient, but rather as inevitable disappointments that the patient produces in a transference that she can tolerate. This a point similar to Kohut's (1971) idea of the inevitable empathic failure of the analyst, which leads to structural growth in the analytic situation. The point at which it is possible to interpret the projective and introjective processes in the patient, as she reacts and creates the trauma, occurs when holding can continuously occur in the background transference.

If there is a need to pay attention to the mother, because the infant senses the mother's anxiety or distress too often, the holding environment necessary to the development of the spontaneous gesture and the experience of omnipotence is destroyed. Instead, the infant experiences distress and must prematurely develop a sense of the other, an alertness and a watchfulness, to deal with an environment felt as impinging. Rather than developing a "true self" from the experience of omnipotence, the infant develops a false self to protect what spontaneity is left and to ward off the feelings of impingement.

The parallel in analysis is a compliant or distressed patient who watches the analyst carefully. In Libbey's (1996) example of a nonsymbolizing patient, when the analyst overtly addressed the transference these transference concerns led to tension and seeming disorganization in the patient, who therefore began to ignore her and simply continued talking. When she stopped interpreting, she gradually found herself free to think and fantasize about his and her experience, and by the third year of treatment the patient began to reflect upon some of what he said and reported a dream that he could associate to in a manner that seemed meaningful to the analytic pair.

If the mother is unable to meet the baby's gesture, either due to her or his limitations (frustration tolerance, inability to communicate), the baby does not develop the sense of security and pleasure in the world necessary for spontaneous gestures and the maintenance of a true self. Instead of an experience of omnipotence, there is an early need for vigilant attention to the other, eventually giving rise to the development of a false self. The mother's response is felt as an impingement, and the required reaction, or compliance to the felt demand, replaces the spontaneous gesture. The world is then felt to be impinging, something to be dealt with, a source of demands for compliance. Without the pleasurable period of omnipotence, it is harder to give up the wish for omnipotent control to compensate for the sense of frustration and not-me-ness, even though the baby may comply and appear to be "behaving."

However, if all goes well, there is a capacity to play with reality, and transitional space and transitional objects in this space are the beginning of a cultural world for the infant/child. Since the transitional object has a link to the mother, via sensation and love, it is the beginning of symbol formation. It is space where the mother can exist but does not impinge on or change. The loving link is a necessary part of the experience of the world as a place to which the baby feels a positive connection. Things can also be destroyed in transitional space and be re-created over and over again. Eventually, the infant/child can think about the world and use language, albeit in a primitive (sensorimotor) way.

When the patient lacks the ability to tolerate the as-if qualities of the transference, she cannot play with it. Then, the analyst needs to first work on creating an atmosphere where play is possible (Winnicott 1954, 1971). The condition of mutual play is necessary for the success of an interpretation. This play takes place in transitional space and permits the patient to receive from the analyst in a manner that allows the patient the experience of creating, while simultaneously keeping the experience intensely real for both.

Nonetheless, as Winnicott consistently implies, the task of reality acceptance is never completed and the adult as well as the child absorbs culture via transitional space. The intermediate, transitional space, which becomes the space for creativity in art, culture, and shared myth, and the space for play, is necessary in part as a relief from this everpresent strain. In analysis, the patient needs to be able to make use of this space in order to experience interpretable transference, and part of the analyst's role is to help create this space if the patient has difficulty with it. As a last parenthetical point, reality for Winnicott is created in healthy individuals. If reality is experienced as an impingement (rather than a creation) it is impossible to develop a true self and the capacity to receive from others.

PHASES OF DEVELOPMENT OF INTERPRETABLE TRANSFERENCE AND SYMBOLIZATION

It is our view that we have generally overestimated the ability of patients and analysts to tolerate transference and to understand its irrational aspects (Ellman 1998). Compliance has been mistaken for acceptance of transference interpretation because we have underestimated the extent and the impact of even the neurotic patient's loss of reality sense in the transference.

We have described the concept of analytic trust and its development elsewhere (Ellman 1991, 1998) but briefly, analytic trust follows Winnicott's ideas that the analyst must "hold" the patient, by creating a particular atmosphere and type of relatedness. We have described this relatedness as being a product of the analyst entering the patient's world (Bach 1985). This is done, in part, by allowing the patient's affective states to penetrate the analyst's consciousness and subsequently through allowing the analyst's emotional responsiveness to interpenetrate the analysis. Consistency, reliability, and acceptance are among the methods analysts use to establish trust. The analyst should also intervene in ways that foster in the patient the development of tolerance for his experience of his unconscious as it gradually is manifest in the analysis. This is particularly true for the patient's experiences of negative transference. Bion's (1967) concept of containment is particularly relevant for this aspect of trust.

Certain types of disturbance in the patient, such as narcissistic and borderline conditions, make analytic trust more difficult to establish. Its early stages may require the analyst to tolerate a certain level of meaninglessness, or nonsymbolic communication (Freedman 1994), in which he is not perceived or related to as anything like a whole object. Such patients often have limited ability to self-reflect, or none at all. For this type of nonsymbolizing patient (Freedman 1994, Steingart 1995) what the analyst perceives as transference is seen by the patient mainly in realistic terms.

To put it as does Bach (1985, 1994): to be able to fully use interpretation, the patient must realize there are two people in the room, and she must be ready to hear something from outside her self and process it. Implicitly, she must experience it as a symbolic communication. Otherwise, the interpretation may be felt as an attack, a demand for compliance with the analyst's view, or a traumatic impingement. It may be ignored except for the tone of voice in which it is delivered, or heard as validating the patient's distorted reality. It may force the patient to pay attention to the analyst's existence in present reality, at a time when the patient is trying to explore her internal world, and it can interrupt the patient's creative use of the transference relationship.

What are the phases of development of interpretable transference? First of all, the patient must be able to be with the analyst. The analyst needs to allow the patient space to begin this process in her own way, within what the analyst considers the conditions of the work. The patient may have trouble allowing herself the experience of another being (with needs and ideas) sharing the same room. Such a patient may need an analyst to be relatively silent or purely reflective, using only words the patient has used, not even synonyms. Getting used to hearing the analyst's voice, becoming accustomed to the setting, may be very anxiety provoking for some patients, and the process may be akin to behavioral exposure therapy: allowing the patient to expose herself to the setting and the analyst's responses at a slow pace to allow her to unlearn the anxiety or at least become aware of it as a topic for discussion. One analyst learned that even repeating the patient's words back to him too early in the session was disruptive, and seemed to cause increased anxiety and disorganization.

For some patients, at the beginning, even questions for information or comments reflecting what the patient has just said are felt as intrusive and disruptive (impingements, in Winnicott's terminology), so the analyst limits comments to reflection. Later, as the patient feels more secure and can begin to notice elements of the other (something about the office, or the analyst's appearance), more complex remarks that add to what the patient has said may be offered.

Lacking the ability to objectively (or consensually) represent and observe themselves, these individuals are not aware of how they attempt to get rid of their states, or of fantasized parts of the self, by putting them in others. Because such patients usually also lack the ability to see the analyst as a separate whole object, the analyst can only slowly begin to describe to the patient how this is occurring. A separate whole object can have opinions of her own, but some patients cannot use this fact. The relative inability to take what the analysis offers can be the expression of unconscious fantasies of many types from many stages, including a scenario where for some reason the very existence of another is felt as threatening. With such patients, it seems to be more effective to begin to interpret extra-transference material. This enables the analyst to be part of the patient's world and not too painfully separate (in the patient's experience), in that analyst and patient are looking out at this world together.

This is the point where the analyst can comment about the patient's sequence of material or implied concerns, or fairly evident affects, such as anxiety. This is laying the groundwork for clarification of defenses. It is important at this stage that the analyst be sure the patient understands his words in the way he means them, and that he can specify why he made a remark. This is particularly important with patients for whom the concepts of self and other are constantly or transiently affected by significant distortions. Beginning awareness of the otherness of the analyst makes it more likely that projections and distortions will become evident, at least to the analyst, as the two begin to communicate in more involved ways. There is a risk that some of the analyst's remarks could reinforce an unconscious fantasy that he can read the patient's mind, which may be a fantasy necessary to the patient. However, if the two are at the stage of trying to clarify some of what goes on between them, the analyst should be prepared to explain his observations.

After the opening phase of treatment the analysand shows signs that she believes (and has demonstrable reason to believe) that the analyst understands her subjective states as these have arisen at the beginning of the treatment. The patient will then demonstrate that she can tolerate perspectives that are separate from her former purely subjective reactions. For example, there may be indications of less splitting directed toward others in the patient's life, as when the patient starts to genuinely wonder about a parent's life experiences and their impact on that parent's inner world. Or, an aspect of the analyst's stance or a position the analyst has taken may be appreciated or partially understood. This may occur about meaningful matters or trivial issues such as the lighting in the room or the temperature.

Example

> A borderline, alcoholic patient who generally treated others, including the therapist, with a kind of bullying contempt, called one day, after some years, to share a realization she felt the therapist would understand. "I asked them to change something for me at work, and they wouldn't," she said. "Now I know what it is to be blown off like you say I do to you. Then I called my grandfather, who was drunk, and I think I see now why you won't talk to me when I'm drunk." She went on to thank the therapist for the session earlier that day.

When the patient begins to include the analyst in his object world, we see the patient as able to tolerate some aspects of the other without needing to dismiss him. It becomes possible to take in aspects of the other without feeling disrupted or feeling as if a fragile sense of self has been attacked. A space has been created for interpretation to serve a therapeutic function, rather than being experienced as an impingement. Eventually, the patient can play with the analyst's and her own ideas, responding creatively and experiencing the transference and the relationship most fully, with increasing ability to reflect on them. This implies an ability to see the object as separate from oneself, but also as one who has needs that are separate from one's self.

Example

> Ms. D. was able to tolerate certain aspects of interpretive efforts when she started showing that she could allow another to exist in her presence. However, the trust broke down when her analyst was unable to understand her inability to tolerate the entire interpretation. She then felt alone in the treatment situation, but she was able to reflect on this. She began to consider why she is unable to tolerate differences between her and her friends.
>
> "If someone argues with me or crosses me I am superficially nice to the person but I cross them off my list forever," she says. "I consider myself lucky to have survived with any friends at all." She laughs a bit and then asks herself whether or not she has survived with some friends. I am internally taken aback and wondering about her peculiar use of language. Then I realize that in this phase of treatment Ms. D. was pondering my fate, after the break in analytic trust. She somehow knows that I now understand her and she goes on to say that she doubts that she would have stopped coming but she feels that she would have made treatment useless. "Empty," I say. She laughs and says that she feels she can allow me some differences, "but not too much," she cautions.

Actually, she was underestimating herself, for she had moved to the extent that she could begin to tolerate an exploration of her envy in and outside of the transference. When she laughed and said that she could allow me some differences, she was implicitly saying that I no longer had to reflect her feeling states in the way that was previously a necessary function that I had to perform. She was laughing self-consciously, remembering the extent to which she had needed an almost purely reflective stance from me. This had been necessary for her to be able to stay securely in the room.

Transference interpretations typically draw the sharpest divisions between analyst and patient. This involves not merely the act of providing a different perspective, but one that brings forth the intensity of experiencing a conflict in the here and now ("in the flesh"). Often, under these conditions, the separation between patient and analyst increases, which can be an indication that the interpretation was premature—perhaps the interpretation is given because the analyst needs to make a transference interpretation to create some distance.

Thus, prior to making a transference interpretation, the analyst must make a complex set of judgments about the patient's state as well as the patient's conflicts. The analyst's conclusion should be that the transference, and the analyst's separateness, can be tolerated enough to be talked about by the analyst with some of the analyst's own words and ideas. A usable transference interpretation enables the patient to remain in the therapeutic interaction while simultaneously enduring some feeling of estrangement from the analyst (although sometimes a usable transference interpretation is so clarifying emotionally and intellectually that the patient experiences relief and even gratitude). One way to look at the interpretability of transference is the level of object relatedness manifested in the treatment relationship. If, for example, the patient is dealing with the analyst as an extension of himself, or like a piece of furniture in the room, the same remark will impact this patient very differently than it will another patient who has a reliable concept of the analyst as having a separate existence and separate thoughts not necessarily identical to those of the analysand.

THE INTEGRATION OF OBJECT, AFFECT, AND DRIVE

One of the major tasks of the analyst is to begin to understand the experience of bodily states of the analysand. In our theoretical matrix this entails an understanding of the drives, and particularly the intensity of the drives. The experience of the drives (defined as endogenous stimulation [Ellman 1992, Freud 1915]) is potentially overwhelming, causing the infant to feel annihilated or in danger of "falling to bits." Before the drives or other bodily experiences are integrated and felt to be one's own, they, too, may be experienced as "impingements" or traumatic not-me experiences. By providing stimulation, gratification, and soothing, the mother aids in the regulation of the drives so that they gradually come to feel under the infant's control. But libidinal factors must predominate over aggression for there to be a secure ego integration of id experience.

The patient is always having drive-stimulated experiences of affect-laden fantasies related to transference, but these are not always interpretable, because of the factors we have noted. The actual experiences with the analyst and the contemporary transference also codetermine the affects the patient has in the sessions in and around transference states. However we feel that the intensity of the drives (usually but not always reflected in affect states) is something that the analyst has to be able to experience and reflect to the patient. Often patients who experience intense states are more likely to defend against these states by attempting to externalize their affect states. Sometimes this is done without the patient consciously experiencing the affect.

Analysts perceive the level of danger or safety the patient feels by noting the patient's defensiveness, spontaneity, and openness, and particularly, the patient's affect intensity and its impact on the analyst. We hope the patient will become able to tolerate affect previously experienced as unbearable because of its intensity and/or its association with dangerous fantasies or feared results. Helping to verbalize and being with the patient while she experiences this affect are important activities of the analyst toward this goal. A similar process goes on with patients who do not experience affect but rid themselves of it through action (activity) or projective mechanisms (experiencing the affect in the other).

Thus, the analyst begins to talk about affect, and to label and use words that refer to emotions, even if these cannot be precise at first. The idea is to generate a way to talk about these experiences together as a means to help the patient expand his tolerance for his emotional states and the conflicts and impulses connected to them. Simply being with a patient in his emotional states, offering a word to describe, asking a question, saying "this seems hard for you," are ways to enhance analytic trust so that the patient begins to feel safer and less despairing or frightened of his feelings. Then one can show the patient the sequences of painful anxiety, affect, avoidance, and so on, as these take place in the sessions. Clarifying these processes is akin to clarifying a defense, although here we may be speaking also of ego defects or of characteristic ego states.

With patients who often need to rid themselves of distressing affect it is the analyst's task to reintroduce these affect states gradually. If this can be done in a tolerable way it is an example of how we use the term *containment*. It is an expression of the interpenetration of states that is central to analytic trust, and it is often accomplished by forms of reflection and synthesis of affect states.

Example

> A patient relates that it seems almost impossible to deal with his drug use when he is trading stocks, because he must get relief from his frustration either through alcohol (when he can't relax) or cocaine (when he needs energy). The analyst comments that his frustration feels overwhelming to him, at work and at home. He talks about trading, and the pressure he feels knowing that his wife hates his addictions, and his belief (fear) that she will leave him. "I want to tell her everyone takes drugs in the market and that there is no other way to stand the pressure, except she knows B (another trader) and he's clean. I want her to understand." "And to allow you to do this," the analyst says.
>
> "Yeah, I want her to stop being so critical—it reminds me of stealing, as a kid, and thinking that it was macho and I could get anything I wanted to and do anything I wanted to. . . ." "And your wife wants you to come home clean and be with her and your son," the analyst says. "I don't want any constraints and yet I love them." [Here, he begins to feel something.] "There is no way out of this except divorce." The analyst asks what he was thinking before divorce came up. "I was beginning to feel down, to think about what it would be like without them." "And you wanted to get rid of those thoughts. . . ." "Perhaps I did but I'm beginning to hate being here," the patient says. The analyst responds, "It feels frustrating in here now, as if I'm oppressing you too."

Prior to this point, six months into the analysis, the patient could only tolerate direct reflections of what he said. Then he began to tolerate the analyst's reminding him of other situations where he had similar affect states (synthesis), and he could listen to some explanations of his states. It took several years for him to be able to hear direct transference interpretations, which obviously included interpretation of unconscious fantasy.

> Three years later: "I've been coming here so long, and I find that while you've been helpful I need to leave the treatment. I can't keep coming here, my wife wants me home, and then I have to be with her and my children, and now I no longer have cocaine to help me out (he laughs). But I'm not kidding, I need to get out. I had a dream (he tells a long dream where many of the places from childhood are represented). There is also my brother there and I see all this water around and my mother is going swimming. Here we have a dream with no meaning, and of course you won't agree, you won't agree about my stopping treatment either. It's either my coming here or my going home." "It seems as if I'm keeping you from your wife and you can't have both of us in your life," the analyst comments.
>
> "Maybe I can't have either of you. I feel that even though things are going well on the outside—I'm on the verge of collapse, no maybe not collapse, but at least I'm not doing as well as you and my wife think I'm doing. I don't know why I dreamt about the beach and why my mother was in the dream. I just remembered that I had a dream about my old room. It was the night before, and I was in my room after my brother was switched into the playroom. My mother was there and she was saying something but I couldn't hear her—I just felt that I was hanging out there." "You had returned home to be the center of your mother's attention and no one else was there. You feel as if you will collapse unless you are allowed back into this state or this room."

This led the patient to his resentment not only of my intruding on his life, but more centrally, there being other children in his present and past homes. His narcissistic wishes intersected with the idea that there could not be a triangulated situation where he would not collapse, or be brought down from, his fantasized exalted position in his family. His wishes to possess everything for himself had a more central meaning in a wish to be the only one allowed to plunder the riches of his mother's body. This material could emerge in interpretable form only after he could tolerate another; even if he hated the existence of the analyst, he had to consider the analyst's existence. He could tolerate another because at this time he had developed sufficient trust in the analysis to allow him to endure his destructive wishes to end the treatment. He could also tolerate his anxiety-provoking fantasy that the analyst wanted to interfere with his attempts to possess all that is valuable. Of course this session followed years of work, and there were subsequent periods when this patient could not endure interpretive material. But the interpenetration of states had allowed for a reflection and synthesis of the patient's states, which enabled the patient to develop meaningful fantasies in the analysis.

NEGATIVE TRANSFERENCE AND AFFECT

Giving words to and empathizing with negative transference is part of fostering its symbolization and interpretability. Negative transference is contained and commented on in a way that takes into account the level of the patient's current relationship and trust in the analyst, so that the patient can bear the intervention. For example, the analyst makes comments that indicate her willingness to hear more about negative transference material. She repeats the patient's complaints about the analysis or her, to be sure she understands them and to encourage the patient to continue with this train of thought, and points out when he becomes anxious about doing so. At other times she simply reflects what he is saying, or offers a word that may help express what he seems to be trying to say.

Example

> A patient had been trying for weeks to describe the terrible anxiety that overtook her on the way to her sessions and continued during the sessions so that it was difficult to talk. She made efforts, obviously labored, to say what was in her mind, including various references to therapists who have sex with their patients and to child abuse cases in the news. When the analyst suggested that such fantasies about him were the source of her fears, she began shrieking at him. She finally explained that she could hardly bear to say these things, and that to have them repeated back

> to her in such form felt assaultive and humiliating. When not in that moment, she was not psychotic and knew the analyst was trying to help.

For this patient, her conviction was of bad things happening inside of her. When these bad things got out via her words, then they got into the analyst. When he repeated and interpreted her fantasies, she experienced the event as the analyst throwing back these bad objects in an attacking way. The intensity of her affect, stimulated by this fantasy experience, made her feel the sequence as a real attack. She was unable to perceive the analyst's attempt at being helpful. Of course the analyst's motivations were more complex then just the desire to be helpful. However at that moment, because of various conflicts and transference fears, she was so overwhelmed by the feeling of fear that she lost the ability to reflect in a meaningful way. It would take extra effort on the part of the analyst to help the patient learn to tolerate this fantasy, in order that she could hear an interpretation in this conflict area without immediately moving into the sequence of reactions described.

After such a disruption, however, the analyst first had to reestablish analytic trust, at first by simply clarifying and reflecting the patient's experience: "This seems to have been a terrible experience for you" or "This is so difficult for you when I say things like that; you seem to feel attacked." Whether the analyst would even use the pronoun "I," or I as having independent volition, as in, "You felt that I wanted to attack you," would depend on his assessment of whether the patient could tolerate even this reminder of otherness. Since this patient's particular transference at this time was not interpretable, the patient experienced the interpretation concretely, as an attack. This response of "desymbolization" is one indication that the interpretation was premature, even if its content was correct.

Example

> After years of treating a very masochistic woman patient for a low fee, the analyst noted that the patient's work situation had improved. The

> analyst said that he had come to collude in the patient's need to deprive herself to care for her ne'er-do-well relatives, and said he was raising his fee for her evening hours. Initially, the patient responded with insistence that she would deprive herself in some other area of her life or come less often, and this type of concrete comment was all she would say when asked about her feelings or fantasies about the request. The analyst continued to clarify the request and remained calm, repeatedly pointing out how difficult it was for the patient to even think about it.
>
> Several weeks later, before the fee increase was scheduled to take place, the patient came in and linked her immediate reaction to the fee increase to the way she reacts to her mother, who was alcoholic and abusive, currently as well as throughout the patient's childhood. "I see now my mother is bad, really a mix of good and bad, but mostly bad, flawed to the core. Maybe that's why I always kept coming back. I hoped that if I were perfect she'd love me and we'd be close again. And my brother [who was also chronically abusive and exploitative of the patient, who was currently supporting him and his common-law wife] keeps going back to her too. He's like an orphan baby elephant I saw on a show that's rejected by the herd, but it keeps going back until they kill it and hyenas come." "What about you?" the analyst asks. "I wouldn't like being alone, but I'd live," the patient says finally.

In this case, the patient's initial response was concrete, as she was overwhelmed with affect. As the transference became real to her, she was unable to symbolize and play with the material. The analyst's steadiness and continued clarification of the patient's reaction eventually brought her to a point where she spontaneously introduced a metaphor for her realization that the analyst's action was not identical to the mother's abuse or the brother's exploitation of her. She was then able to work out a plan for her sessions. More important, this was the beginning of the process of separating from and mourning her hope for a close, warm relationship with a giving mother of her own.

In this section we have tried to give examples of some of the more difficult times in analytic treatment, using the theoretical idea of combining the object, affect, and drive. We were particularly concerned with this combination in terms of patients' transference reactions. We tried to give examples where the patient was able to symbolize and where desymbolization occurred. Clearly, negative transference has given analysts more dramatic difficulties but in each transference state there are always both sexualized and aggressive (or destructive) elements that are combined.

CONCLUDING COMMENTS

Clearly the analyst's ability to tolerate nonsymbolizing moments is crucial in developing analytic trust. After the patient has experienced the interpenetration of affective states, developed the capacity to self-reflect, and begun to utilize the analyst as a transitional object (in symbolic play) the analyst must also be able to tolerate seeing herself in a manner that is often unfamiliar. The analyst's ability to tolerate this situation and to engage in what Ogden (1997) has called *reverie* is crucial in order for the pair to engage in analytic play. This is often difficult to do and Ellman (1998) has described how the analyst is often unable to tolerate the transference that results in a state of narcissistic disequilibrium. When the transference becomes too intense for the therapeutic pair to contain the intensity in symbolic terms, a state of narcissistic disequilibrium exists. This may occur in either party but the result is that one or both of the analytic pair no longer have the ability to exist in transitional space. In other words, the ability to see the transference (by either analyst or analysand) as both real and unreal (fantasy) has been disrupted. For the analyst this frequently results in some type of action that is designed to protect some aspect of the self. The analyst may need to inject an aspect of himself in the treatment to establish himself as real or he may become distant and try to reduce his involvement in the analysis. In either of these scenarios the ability for reverie and symbolic play is obstructed. When these states continue for a period of time, analytic trust is also disrupted.

Analytic trust is frequently disrupted for short periods of time when the transference is interpreted. This is more frequently the case in the earlier parts of the treatment but can occur at any point. When interpreted, intense transference states ask the patient to absorb a point of view that is different than her intensely experienced conscious state.

This type of interpretation always involves ideas and affect in conflict. Thus there is a heightened probability that following these interpretations the patient will feel impinged upon, violated, or embarrassed. This may temporarily lead to a break in analytic trust. In corresponding fashion the analyst may feel unappreciated after he has offered what he considers to be an important (and self-valued) insight to the patient. This may create a sense of narcissistic disequilibrium in the analyst. There may be some defense of his interpretive efforts or he may turn away from the patient for a period of time. Our assumption is that breaks in analytic trust normally occur during the course of an analysis and that the survival of these ruptures is beneficial to the analytic pair. There is also an assumption that periodically the analyst, as well as the analysand, becomes temporarily incapable of symbolization and sees the patient as unanalyzable, or less dramatically as being temporarily unreasonable. Thus the analyzing instrument is blunted for a period of time and the analyst is feeling injured in parallel fashion to the patient.

We have spoken about the difficulties in interpretive efforts but it is our view that the benefits of interpretation are crucial to a successful analysis. An interpretation that is utilized by the patient means that the patient is able to tolerate a perspective that is different than her own. It is important to recognize that we are not implying an intellectual ability to understand another viewpoint; rather we are talking about the ability to adopt another view around material that involves longstanding conflict. Moreover, a successful interpretation involves the analysand's being able to increase her symbolic capacities around issues that most frequently inhibit the person's ability for reciprocal object love. From our perspective this almost always means understanding an aspect of oneself that involves unconscious fantasy. This usually means a shift in defensive balance and frequently the utilization of more benign defensive alignments.

It is our hope that we have helped explicate the transition that Freedman has so eloquently described from the nonsymbolizing to the symbolizing patient to, at times, the desymbolizing patient. We have not strictly utilized his terminology but have implicitly referred to breaks in analytic trust as periods of desymbolization. Clearly, his work has described and is stimulating us to try to describe how the analysand gains and holds the capacity for symbolization in the analytic situation.

REFERENCES

Bach, S. (1985). *Narcissistic States and the Therapeutic Process.* New York: Jason Aronson.

——— (1994). *The Language of Perversion and the Language of Love.* Northvale, NJ: Jason Aronson.

Bion, W. R. (1967). *Second Thoughts.* London: Karnac.

Bird, B. (1972). Notes on transference: universal phenomenon and hardest part of analysis. *Journal of the American Psychoanalytic Association* 20:267–301.

Britton, R. (1997). The missing link: parental sexuality in the Oedipus complex. In *The Contemporary Kleinians of London,* ed. R. Schafer, pp. 242–258. Madison, CT: International Universities Press.

Busch, F. (1995). *The Ego at the Center of Clinical Technique.* Northvale, NJ: Jason Aronson.

Carsky, M. (1978). *An elaboration of Bion's group theory.* City University of New York unpublished dissertation for doctoral program in clinical psychology.

Carsky, M., and Selzer, M. (1994). Technical implications of impaired reality testing in the psychotherapy of schizophrenia. In *Psychotherapy of Schizophrenia,* ed. G. Benedetti and P. M. Furlan, pp. 129–141. Toronto: Hogrefe and Huber.

Ellman, S. (1991). *Freud's Technique Papers: A Contemporary Perspective.* Northvale, NJ: Jason Aronson.

——— (1992). Psychoanalytic theory, dream formation and REM sleep. In *Interface of Psychoanalysis and Psychology,* ed. J. W. Barron, M. N. Eagle, and D. L. Wolitzky, pp. 357–374. Washington, DC: American Psychological Association

——— (1998). Enactment, transference, and analytic trust. In *Enactment; Toward a New Approach in the Therapeutic Relationship,* ed. S. Ellman and M. Moskowitz, pp. 183–204. Northvale, NJ: Jason Aronson.

Ellman, S., and Weinstein, L. (1991). REM sleep and dream formation: a theoretical integration. In *The Mind in Sleep,* ed. S. Ellman and J. Antrobus, pp. 466–488. New York: Wiley.

Fonagy, P., and Target, M. (1996). Playing with reality: I. Theory of mind and the normal development of psychic reality. *International Journal of Psycho-Analysis* 77:217–233.

Freedman, N. (1994). More on transformation: enactments in psychoanalytic space. In *The Spectrum of Psychoanalysis: Essays in Honor of Martin S. Bergmann*, ed. A. K. Richards and A. D. Richards, pp. 93–110. Madison, CT. International Universities Press.

Freud, S. (1905). Three essays on the theory of sexuality. *Standard Edition* 7:135–243.

——— (1914). Remembering, repeating and working through. *Standard Edition* 12:135–146.

——— (1915). Instincts and their vicissitudes, *Standard Edition* 14:117–140.

Gibeault, A. (2000). Brief communication: in response to Otto F. Kernberg's "Psychotherapy, Psychoanalytic Psychotherapy and Supportive Psychotherapy: Current Controversies." *International Journal of Psycho-Analysis* 81:379–383.

Hoffman, I. Z. (1994). Dialectical thinking and therapeutic action in the psychoanalytic process. *Psychoanalytic Quarterly* 63:187–218.

Kohut, H. (1971). *The Analysis of the Self*. New York. International Universities Press.

Libbey, M. (1996). *The emotional position of the analyst with the non-symbolizing patient*. Paper presented at The Freudian Society Scientific Meeting, New York, March.

Ogden, T. (1994). The analytic third: working with intersubjective clinical facts. *International Journal of Psycho-Analysis* 75:3–19.

——— (1997). *Reverie and Interpretation*. Northvale, NJ: Jason Aronson.

Steingart, I. (1995). *A Thing Apart: Love and Reality in the Therapeutic Relationship*. Northvale, NJ: Jason Aronson.

Stern, D. N. (1985). *The Interpersonal World of the Infant*. New York; Basic Books.

Winnicott, D. W. (1951). Transitional objects and transitional phenomena. In *Through Paediatrics to Psycho-Analysis*, pp. 229–242. New York: Basic Books, 1975.

——— (1954). Metapsychological and clinical aspects of regression within the psycho-analytical set-up. In *Through Paediatrics to Psycho-Analysis*, pp. 278–294. New York: Basic Books, 1975.

——— (1960). The theory of the parent–infant relationship. In *The Maturational Processes and the Facilitating Environment*, pp. 37–55. New York: International Universities Press, 1965.

——— (1962). The aims of psycho-analytical treatment. In *The Maturational Processes and the Facilitating Environment*, pp. 166–170. New York: International Universities Press, 1965.

——— (1963). Dependence in infant-care, in child-care, and in the psycho-analytic setting. In *The Maturational Processes and the Facilitating Environment*, pp. 249–259. New York: International Universities Press, 1965.

——— (1971). *Playing and Reality*. London: Tavistock.

13

The Analytic Treatment Relationship: Reflections upon Neutrality, Intersubjectivity, and Classical Views of the Treatment

MARK GRUNES

The past fifteen years have seen increasing emphasis upon open and explicit dyadic interaction in analytic treatment, particularly by the orientation often called relational intersubjectivity. This trend has involved a movement to abandon entirely the concept of neutrality and make interpretation subordinate to a "healing" relationship (Mitchell 1988, Renik 1996).

Among classical analysts, despite attempts to soften and liberalize the traditional stringency of neutrality, the idea of a treatment relationship separable from the transference is vigorously rejected by many as parental, hypnotic, and suggestive.

It is the purpose of this paper to present a view of the treatment relationship that is not only consistent with the essential meaning of neutrality, but that is a systematic, explicitly defined, and necessary component of any effective analytic treatment. By effective I refer to the inevitable ego and identity destabilizations that occur with thorough transference analysis.

In the course of my discussion I examine a paper entitled "Finding the Neutral Position" (Baker 2000), which is an example of current attempts by some classical analysts to find common ground with relational intersubjectivity. In the course of my comments I also touch upon intersubjectivity and the classical resistance to the idea of a treatment relationship that appear in Baker's paper.

I begin my discussion of the analytic treatment relationship with Loewald's (1960) paper "On the Therapeutic Action of Psychoanalysis" for several reasons. I consider it to be the earliest and most systematic conceptualization of the subject. It continues to retain its pertinence and relevance to this day. I believe that for a paper of its importance, it has been relatively neglected and insufficiently understood.

Loewald begins, "If structural changes in the patient's personality mean anything, it must mean that we assume that ego development is resumed in the therapeutic process of analysis. And this resumption of ego development is contingent on the *relationship* with a *new object* (my italics), the analyst." The preceding sentence is perhaps the most crucial one in the entire paper. Loewald continues, "Psychoanalytic ego psychology based on a variety of investigations concerned with *ego development* (my italics) . . . deals with the central problem of the relationship between the development of psychic structures and interaction with other structures and the connection between ego formation and object relations" (p. 16).

Loewald warns against the tendency that has taken the "relationship between a scientific observer and his subject of study as the model for the analytic relationship. The objectivity of the analyst in regard to the patient's transference distortions should not be confused with the neutral attitude of the pure scientist toward his subject of study" (p.18).

Speaking of the ideal image of the analyst as a detached scientist, Loewald says, "It is not self-explanatory why a research project should have a therapeutic effect on the subject of study" (p. 19). The optimal psychic position in relation to the patient "requires an objectivity and neutrality the essence of which is love and respect for the individual and for individual development. This love and respect represents that counterpart in reality in interaction with which the organization and reorganization of ego and psychic apparatus take place" (p. 20).

For Loewald, the question of whether relationship or interpretation and insight cure simply does not arise. The interpretive process itself—the spirit, feeling, and content with which it is conducted, and the belief in the psychic reality of the new object relationship—all create the therapeutic action.

Loewald makes the point that the real and new object relationship with the analyst makes possible the patient's willingness to risk the identity and relational destabilization of the regressive transference. In a similar way neutrality on the analyst's part is only helpful to the patient when the patient experiences the deep support of the intimately interpsychic treatment object relationship.

Space does not allow me to go into further detail with regard to additional specifics of the new object relationship, particularly with regard to developmental analogues, and I have also not elaborated the interpsychic force field of identification in the mutual activity of guided self and other scrutiny between patient and analyst. I briefly describe the former and elaborate the latter in a later section of the paper.

The developmental analogues are: (1) the analyst's focus on the patient's rudimentary core, (2) the patient's experience of being centered upon as a unit self, (3) the analyst's structuring of the patient's productions, analogous to the mother's differentiation of the child's undifferentiated urges, and (4) the analyst as a higher level of psychic organization mediating what in the patient is in need of reorganization.

Despite the fact that many of the features of Loewald's new object relationship have helpful applicability to narcissistic problems, he recognizes that important differences would occur in the patient with more serious ego defects. A more complete account of the treatment relationship would therefore have to include such matters.

In order to depict the nature of the treatment relationship in instances of more regressive functioning, I will selectively quote from and comment upon a 1993 paper by the Dutch analyst Nikolaas Treurniet, "What Is Psychoanalysis Now?" The paper is a comprehensive summary of the changes in theory and technique involved in analytic treatment of narcissistic phases of treatment, with particular focus upon an earlier form of transference that he calls the primary transference. Ultimately he designates it as the primary *relationship* that is the core of the preoedipal, more narcissistic treatment relationship to which the analyst must adapt his interpretive activity and therapeutic stance. Treurniet notes the increased importance of this "second" form of transference and its numerous designations under various names: Greenacre (1954) the basic transference, Stone (1967) the primal transference, Kohut (1968) the narcissistic transference, and Modell (1990) the dependent-containing transference.

Like Loewald, Treurniet is "profoundly convinced that a relationship by itself, without insight into that relationship, can never set an analytic process in motion. Interpretations are indispensable for this purpose" (p. 888).

It should also be pointed out that Treurniet assumes that the primary transference or relationship with the analytic patients he is discussing exists within and alongside capacities for an object transference. He has isolated the two only for purposes of exposition.

Treurniet first quotes Winnicott and Balint with regard to the patient in a regressive state:

> In this way both analysts [i.e., Winnicott and Balint] stress the importance of the patient's actual experience in the regressed state, the importance of sharing the experience with the patient, the importance of not interpreting, particularly the transference, during these phases and the importance of interpreting after the regression. Balint thought of it as the difference between the agency of interpretation and the agency of object relationship (between analyst and patient) in the process of psychic chance, with both being essential.
>
> In such states an analysand has moved to a level at which the analyst is experienced as a pre-verbal memory that cannot yet be known in a language able to use words, but in an idiom that requires that certain highly specific conditions are satisfied: non-intrusiveness, holding, wordless understanding, the use of intuitive and symbiotic knowledge and the promotion of thinking in feelings. A patient once shouted at me: "You are an idiot, you want

> to know how things are and how they arose, but I just want you to feel what I feel; the other will come later, and you are a fool if you cannot see that." [p. 880]

Treurniet continues: "The patient was of course, absolutely right; interpretations only become appropriate later. The correct technique is to accept the acting out as a valid means of communication" (p. 880). He goes on:

> The post-classical analyst, as a new object, has both a more difficult, and an easier time of it than his classical forbear. He must preserve the primary relationship; which means contain, survive and detoxify the projections, receive and absorb the regression, be present as a supplier of time and environment, but not as a person, lovingly promote, but also interpret the process of disillusionment and separation, and in all this he must resolutely but flexibly preserve the limits of analytic space while at the same time ensuring that this space does not degenerate into a vacuum in which the patient can lose his boundaries and evaporate. This is not to say that his classical forbear did not need to do all this. I am convinced that very many analysts of that school did do all these things in those days, although it was not then permissible to use such terms, and when they did so they had a guilty conscience about it. In this respect things are easier for the post-classical analyst. . . . Owing to the communicative and controlling functions of the patient's projective identifications, some acting out by the analyst inevitably occurs. [p. 882]

All of these factors described by Treurniet constitute the primary relationship between analyst and patient. This relationship is variably interwoven with object transference factors. But more and more, the real maternal-like developmental aspect of such stages of treatment are described as relationship because they do reflect residues of early narcissistic ties to which the analyst in reality regulates his connection to and separateness from the patient in a variety of ways. The primary relationship may be simply described as analogous to Winnicott's environmental mother of maternal provision, in contrast to the more differentiated object mother.

For Treurniet, affective sharing does not mean that the analyst explicitly shares his deepest feelings with the patient. Brief single-word responses, silence, spontaneous breathing, physical changes in position that bring the analyst a little closer to the patient can indicate to the patient—if it is actually the case—that the analyst can feel some real version of what the patient is feeling and approximate what Treurniet means by wordless feeling and thinking in feelings. Affective sharing restores real contact and brings relief from despair about ever resuming human communication. This type of interaction, including holding, containing and detoxifying projections, and absorbing and allowing the regression preceding which a patient may feel totally alone with his deepest feelings, is also an example of what Balint has called, in contrast to interpretation, the agency of object relation. It alone cannot do the work of analysis, but without it interpretation can become parched, overly neutral, and empty. Why does Balint, in a patient's regressive phase, advise against interpretation and particularly transference interpretation? It is because interpretation often introduces a separational you and me where there was a fusional communion. The use of language is a secondary process of development that may create disruptive distance as well as connection with the literal object mother. Patients in what Winnicott calls the regressive new beginning may need to linger for a while in the state of fusional communion from which they have often been torn away too abruptly and prematurely. Treurniet's patient screams, "I need you to feel what I am feeling." The transference interpretation, when it refers to the past and early object, acts similarly to interpretation itself. The patient is, so to speak, sent back to where he came from, the fusional communion with the analyst ruptures, and transference interpretation should probably have been made later when the fusional phase had run its course. At this point I will return to Loewald and a very important quotation from his 1970 paper "Psychoanalytic Theory and Psychoanalytic Process." Interestingly, like Treurniet, the quotation bears upon affective communication, implicit and intuitive knowledge, and primal, mutual identification. In many respects he is describing a core aspect of the new object relationship between patient and analyst.

> In contrast to physics or biology for instance psychoanalytic knowledge and explanation depend not so much on the difference between the processes obtaining in the scientist and those obtaining in his subject, but on their similarity and inter-relatedness. It is commonplace that introspection and empathy are essential tools of psychoanalysis and that we can analyze others only so far as we have been analyzed ourselves, and understand ourselves. To this there is the corollary: we understand ourselves psychoanalytically by seeing ourselves as others (objectivating introspection), and our self-understanding is greatly enhanced by analyzing others. . . . This is not only because in the external other we can see ourselves more clearly, but also because in this concentrated, in this specially focused and heightened field of forces, the analyst's intrapsychic field gains in vitality and vivid outline. The analysand in this respect can be compared to the child who—if he can allow himself that freedom—scrutinizes with his unconscious antennae the parent's motivations and moods and in this way may contribute—if the parent or analyst allows himself that freedom—to the latter's self awareness. Internal communication, on which self-understanding is based, and communication with another organization of the same rank of reality—the psychic reality of another individual—are inextricably interwoven. [pp. 47–48]

The intense force field of affective, mood, and mutual identificational interpenetration between analyst and patient described by Loewald is a core aspect of the new object relationship. It is what enables the patient to tolerate neutrality and to risk the regressive transference phases of destabilization of familiar object ties and identity formations, which occur in every analysis. (Norbert Freedman et al. [1999] has described such periods of destabilization in terms of treatment cycles of desymbolization and resymbolization.) Without any extra-analytic measures, the intense interpenetrative force field decreases the sense of distance between analyst and patient and is a resource in ego restabilization. It increases the sense of equality since the interpenetration that Loewald describes underlines the treatment's need for mutual accessibility and identification. Interpsychic interpenetration and communication decreases the analyst's anonymity for the patient without recourse to explicit self-disclosure, although this will occasionally occur where needed. This force field of emotional interpenetration also creates a unique and high level of gratification for the analyst and patient. Without this gratification little useful work gets done. It is this mutual process, in its contribution to the analyst's psychic vitalization and expansion, that enables him to love his work and gradually his patient, who makes this work possible, as well. It is the process of progressive emotional interpenetration that in turn moves the patient to love the analyst and the treatment process itself, which is an intrinsic part of the analyst himself. I think it becomes evident how this therapeutic object relationship changes the meaning of neutrality and allows it to fulfill its own role and function in the treatment.

I have called the point of view in which I locate Treurniet and Loewald *developmental psychoanalysis* for the following, as well as other reasons. (These are some of the features of what I have termed the *therapeutic object relationship* [Grunes 1984, 1998].) It focuses upon mother–child interaction and attempts to apply this material to adult analysis. It concerns itself with the structuralization of the self and the ego in childhood. It attempts to adjust technique to the patient's tolerance level, developmental ego strength, and personal coherence.

The analyst needs to be able to vary his interpretive stance from no interpretation, to empathic location inside the boundaries of the patient's perspective, to transitional emotional positions in which the analyst is partly inside the patient's subjective perspective and partly outside as separate object, to a more fully defined otherness who is available for the rageful collisions that the patient may enact at such times, but that the patient needs developmentally.

The quotation from Loewald deals with matters I have called *interpenetration* and *empathic permeability* (Grunes 1984). They show how seriously Loewald takes interpsychic interaction in human development and in the treatment process itself. The quotation deals with one aspect of what Loewald calls the new (and real) object relationship in treatment. It reflects, I believe, a good part of Loewald's own solution to the neutrality, abstinence, and anonymity problem.

The picture he gives us of treatment conveys an essential quality of equality with his patients. Intense levels of involvement seem to be reached by the analyst as he feels himself, feels the patient within himself, feels himself within the patient, and feels the patient as he, the analyst, allows himself to be immersed as well in associative memory and emotional recollection. Such involvement is not neutrality as we have come to know it. But it is very essentially neutral, characterized as it is by nonintrusiveness, nondirectiveness, and concern for the preservation of the patient's individuality and autonomy.

The issue of gratification of analyst as well as patient also becomes less of a problem. When empathic, permeable interpenetration occurs, the sensation of intimate communication can be incredibly high. Both participants also often experience a vivid sense of an unusually open state of human communication, and often each seems to sense what is in the other's mind and what he or she will say next. Patient and analyst often experience such moments with a feeling of exhilaration and a sensation of loving connection. These features of the analytic treatment relationship are some of the constituents of the centrality given by Ellman (1998) to the concept of analytic trust.

In the remainder of this paper I discuss a number of aspects of Ronald Baker's (2000) paper, "Finding the Neutral Position." It contains many features that are pertinent to the issues I have raised about the analytic treatment relationship. Baker is a classical ego psychologist, and his attempt is to introduce an element of flexibility and liberalization to the traditional stringent and noninteractive classical conception of neutrality. Thus "neutral position" is a location from which the analyst departs and returns, following intersubjective transference–countertransference disruptions. In this way neutrality is not a steady state, but a variable one, and in accord with postmodern relational-dyadic views, subject to intersubjective influences. My own view is that Baker's approach provides little modification of the noninteractive character of the classical view of the analyst's neutrality. The intersubjective episodes he describes are mainly distinguished by the analyst's need to bring them to a close as soon as possible. Intersubjectivity has no positive or therapeutic role. Neutrality, although redefined as the *neutral position* (my italics), has a negative connotation because it is not supported by any interactive paradigm between patient and analyst, except the disruptive one.

Baker's effort to build a bridge between Freudian and relational perspectives upon neutrality is an interesting attempt. But I do not think it will impress many relational theoreticians and practitioners. Baker underestimates the differences between the two schools. These are some of the major differences between relational and Freudian practice that make bridges difficult to achieve:

1. The absence of any comprehensive theory of personality development makes it difficult to see how the analyst can grasp the nature of progression and regression.
2. The intersubjective concentration upon the here-and-now dyadic interaction is linked to a weak or nonexistent interest in the patients's past.
3. The discrete intrapsychic entity of the individual person is lost in the concept of coconstructionism. The individual is not discovered and released but cocreated by analyst and patient.
4. The concept of transference seems to have been entirely discarded. How does the individual discover his own history and biography without a serious concept of transference?
5. Does the ubiquitous presence of the interactive matrix with the analyst as object ever give the patient the chance to become directly reacquainted with his parents and resolve early pathological relationships?

Baker, I believe, underestimates the way in which the entire theory and technique of relational psychoanalysis inevitably supports the near-unanimous rejection of neutrality because of the preponderant focus upon the here-and-now relations between analyst and patient. I believe Baker also understates the degree to which contemporary structural technique and theory of therapeutic action hold to the old view of neutrality, and here the body of clinical theory and theory of technique also lead inevitably to an *adherence* to neutrality in the old sense, because certain features of orthodox classical theory limit the depth of treatment and operate to create and keep excessive distance between patient and analyst.

There are two streams in Baker's paper. One is his argument, particularly with the more extreme relational analysts like Owen Renik, who would abandon neutrality, anonymity, and abstention rather entirely. But somewhat more ambiguously, Baker is attempting to revise the traditional orthodox classical view of neutrality, particularly in the United States, in a more flexible direction. He avers that the traditional views of neutrality by Freud, A. Freud, and Hartmann were excessively rational, objective, and lacking in human flexibility. But he says no traditional analyst works that way anymore: ". . . the idealization of a method in which neutrality was central, and in which objectivity, detachment and rationality are absolute became the perennial focus of dispute and today that scientific view enjoys little support" (p. 130). I do not think that the view enjoys little support. Although in general I do not agree with many of Owen Renik's positions, here I am in some agreement with him when he writes, "We may have our doubts about the ideal of the analyst as a reflecting mirror and want to feel we have left it behind . . . but we have just made it more user friendly by not entirely taking it seriously" (p. 498).

Let me try to demonstrate that some very influential Freudian writers and theoreticians of the classical structural school preserve the essential features of the original concept of neutrality as a result of their body of clinical theory and theory of technique. Paul Gray (1982), Dale Boesky (1988), and Charles Brenner (1982) emphasize oedipal-level conflict resolution and exclude structural change from the analytic process. In Boesky's words: ". . . structural change is better left to nature" (p. 305). All three also attempt to exclude internalization of the analyst as part of the treatment process. This is a neutrality-influenced distancing. They consider the reality of the therapeutic relationship between analyst and patient to be an undesirable suggestive influence that derives its therapeutic results from the hypnotic action associated with technique in the early history of psychoanalysis. All three attempt to reduce as much as possible the analyst's function as empathic participant-observer. Blum (1986) cites Brenner as stating: ". . . eighty years of psychoanalytic data gathering from free association have repeatedly demonstrated that empathy is regularly subject to falsification, self-deception, and disguises" (p. 309). All three emphasize the analyst's roles as an external, objective natural-science observer. Patient and analyst have no business getting inside of each other. The basic and central unit of treatment is analysis of the ego's resistance to the emergence into consciousness of id derivatives. Ego developmental needs and object needs are at best secondary. All three attempt to minimize the facilitative operation of the positive transference because of its presumed suggestive hypnotic action.

Gray (1982) views developmental paradigms such as the one I have defined as providing "parental" roles, which share a reliance on suggestive, interpersonal influence. There is no reason to assume, however, that the model to which he subscribes is less parental than the one I describe. It may simply constitute a different kind of parent.

In his interest in building the neutral position bridge to relational psychoanalysis, Baker commits himself to a number of positions which, from my perspective, can be questioned. For instance, he places Greenson and Loewald in the like-minded position of standard analysts who have been able to retain the concept of neutrality within a liberal and flexible perspective. Yet the two positions differ radically with regard to the nature of the real relationship, the use of parent–child paradigms to illuminate problems with and promote regression, the rebuilding of psychic structure, the intimacy and contact built into the concept of the interpenatrative empathic force field, the possibility for therapeutic activation of early ego states, and what is meant by the new object relationship between patient and analyst.

Greenson's (1971) real object analyst stops being an analyst and engages the patient in friendly, somewhat social dialogue. Greenson dichotomizes the real and the transference relationship, and as a result the deepest intensities of the analyst–patient interaction are consigned to the pathological transference. Thus, Greenson's real object relationship does not interpenetrate the analysis proper.

Baker does not easily open the field of therapeutic ego regression with his patient in anything like Loewald's terms and some of this appears in a possibly overly cautious and traditional approach to problems of acting out, countertransference developments of high emotional intensity, and in his stance on the analyst's enactments, countertransference, and acting out. I think his position may create too much restraint and consideration of reality factors for the risk-taking loosening of old structures that is needed for optimal analytic ego regression. Bion (1970), for instance, states that for certain patients (and in some stages of treatment for all patients), despite the satisfaction of symbolic communication, to be obliged to speak in order to be understood and have wishes granted constitutes a continuing narcissistic wound in everyone's unconscious. Fusion and communion are sought versus separateness and communication.

In Baker's account of countertransference factors, acting out, and enactment, there is no reference to the extensive amount of work that has been done by McDougall (1980), Chused (1992), Bach (1985), and Steingart (1983), for instance, on the primitive communicative and contact functions of nonverbal forms of action and enactment that can occur characteristically with some patients and at certain stages in any analysis. Whereas his points regarding the present trend, particularly in relational treatments, to actively promote and engage in enactments and acting out are well taken, his theoretical positions and parts of the clinical vignettes contain some indication of the maintenance of the old ideal of only striving to achieve maximum reduction of countertransference reaction, enactment, and acting out. He states, "The point is that when an enactment occurs, however minute or subtle, there is always a degree to which the analyst has failed his patient and the patient feels let down even when the skilled analyst can turn this to the patient's advantage" (p. 132). The point is that in patients with impaired symbolization capacities, or in obsessional patients in whom the verbal dimension is overly and rigidly developed in defenses against more primary process productions, acting out may be the only way they can communicate certain essential aspects of more primary process experience. Extreme exclusion of these vehicles of contact and communication, or even the tacit ambition to limit them severely, inevitably leads to impasse, premature termination, or a false-self analysis.

I also believe Baker has a tendency to move as rapidly as possible into the neutral position via the object transference of the patient's past parental images. This may be true in his first vignette of the patient Mary, who reacted to a few minutes of silence on his part as a punitive withdrawal and remonstrated sharply. The analyst, seemingly very rapidly, tells the patient, "When I was silent you seemed unable to experience me other than as your absent withdrawn father." My impression is that this interpretation may deflect the patient away too quickly from the here-and-now transference as well as aspects of the incipient object relationship with the analyst. The quick shift to the past may lead the patient to feel that the analyst wants to reduce her anger as quickly as possible. The patient could quite possibly be a sadomasochistic character and experience the interpretation as a rejection of a masochistic overture to the analyst. Also the seemingly rapid introduction of a separate-whole object transference may be beyond this patient's level of ego tolerance. Baker seems to rely exclusively on interpretation of transference distortion to promote the emergence of the analyst as a new object. For Loewald, this aspect of the development of the new object is only one of numerous long-term processes in the establishment of the new object relationship. Pertinent here is my previous quotation of Loewald in which he states that the patient can "dare to take the plunge into the regressive crisis of the transference only if he can hold on to the potentiality of a new object relationship." For many patients this requires shorter or longer periods of abstention from transference interpretations going back to the past. The patient needs to spend time with the analyst in the present in order to begin to experience a potentiality for a new object relationship.

Something similar to the process with the patient Mary, with some additional features, takes place with Baker's patient Greta, who appears to be sexually provocative from the start of treatment, and increasingly so as time goes on. In one session she asks Baker what he would do if she exposed her nipples. "I interpreted," says Baker, "that she was very worried that I might be seduced by her because if that were to occur it would mean the end of the analysis." Baker's interpretation seems to be consistent with the evidence of his caution and restraint. Alternatives to such caution and restraint are not limited to responses that would necessarily encourage the patient to act out.

It is reasonable to infer that the patient assumed the analyst's answer to her question was that if in fact she exposed herself he would have to end the analysis. I am aware that Baker qualified this by saying to the patient that the analysis would have to end if she succeeded in seducing him. Such distinctions, however, would be unlikely to be processed with linguistic precision by the patient. I imagine she would hear mostly, "It would mean the end of the analysis," and this would signify to her a threatened course of action. I would think other forms of intervention would be desirable alternatives to the one made, which seems to run the risk of prematurely suppressing the patient's sexual feelings and fantasies in relation to the analyst. Why would she want to take such an action? What were her thoughts about what would ensue if she took such a step? Was it possible that for some reason at this point she had to prove to herself that she could seduce the analyst? Baker's several interpretations might have been based upon material about trust and sexualized parental betrayal that was known to him. Or he may have had access to material that told him the patient was developing some intense anxiety about trusting him and deepening the treatment. Nevertheless, the implied threat to end the treatment seems to be a potentially serious restriction, not just of the patient's behavior, but also of inner psychic freedom to develop not readily verbalizable sexual affiliation feelings toward her analyst, as well as verbalizable sexual fantasies and more regressive expressions of object need as well.

SUMMARY

I have attempted to depict a contemporary version of the analytic treatment relationship, demonstrating that analytically conceived, such a relationship need not in any way conflict with the central role of interpretation, the maintenance of analytic neutrality, and the goal of bringing into consciousness the deeper unconscious, through the development of insight and the analysis of transference. In addition, I have emphasized that effective analytic therapy *requires* the establishment of a treatment relationship if the ego and identity destabilizations of transference regression are to be successfully negotiated by the patient. A treatment relationship is *necessary* to allow the patient to make integrative use of the analyst's neutrality. Narcissistic and regressively dependent transferences can occur in all patients, and a well-established treatment relationship helps to stabilize such stressful and deeply anxious periods of analysis.

In my discussion of Ronald Baker's paper, "Finding The Neutral Position," I have indicated some skepticism that attempts to find common ground between relational intersubjectivity and more standard forms of analysis may be premature. I have also indicated my belief that the vigorous rejection of the idea of an analytic treatment relationship by some classical analysts restricts the depth of analytic work, and leads to preservation of traditional, noninteractive forms of neutrality.

REFERENCES

Bach, S. (1985). *Narcissistic States and the Therapeutic Process*. New York: Jason Aronson.

Baker, R. (2000). Finding the neutral position. *Journal of the American Psychoanalytic Association* 48:129–154.

Bion, W. R. (1970). *Attention and Interpretation*. London: Heinemann.

Blum, H. (1986). Countertransference and the theory of technique: discussion. *Journal of the American Psychoanalytic Association* 34:309–328.

Boesky, D. (1988). Comments on the structural theory of technique. *International Journal of Psycho-Analysis* 69:303–316.

Brenner, C. (1982). *The Mind in Conflict*. New York: International Universities Press.

Chused, J. F. (1992). Interpretations and their consequences in adolescents. *Psychoanalytic Inquiry* 12:275–295.

Ellman, S. J. (1998). The unique contribution of the contemporary Freudian position. In *The Modern Freudians*, ed. C. S. Ellman, S. Grand, M. Silvan, and S. J. Ellman, pp. 237–268. Northvale, NJ: Jason Aronson.

Freedman, N., Berzofsky, M., and DeMichele, A. (1999). *On transformation cycles: the symbolization of a frozen constellation*. Paper presented at the Annual Meeting, Division 39 of the American Psychological Association, New York, April.

Gray, P. (1982). "Developmental lag" in the evolution of technique for psychoanalysis of neurotic conflict. *Journal of the American Psychoanalytic Association* 30:621–656.

Greenacre, P. (1954). The role of transference: practical considerations in relation to psychoanalytic therapy. *Journal of the American Psychoanalytic Association* 2:671–684.

Greenson, R. R. (1971). The real relationship between the patient and psychoanalyst. In *Explorations in Psychoanalysis*, pp. 425–440. New York: International Universities Press.

Grunes, M. (1984). The therapeutic object relationship. *Psychoanalytic Review* 71:123–143.

——— (1998). The therapeutic object relationship—II. In *The Modern Freudians*, ed. C. S. Ellman, S. Grand, M. Silvan, and S. J. Ellman, pp. 129–140. Northvale, NJ: Jason Aronson.

Kohut, H. (1971). *The Analysis of the Self*. New York; International Universities Press.

Loewald, H. (1960). On the therapeutic action of psychoanalysis. *International Journal of Psychoanalysis* 41:16–33.

——— (1970). Psychoanalytic theory and psychoanalytic process. In *Papers on Psychoanalysis*. New Haven, CT: Yale University Press, 1980.

McDougall, J. (1980). Countertransference and primitive communication. In *Plea for a Measure of Abnormality*, pp. 247–273. New York: International Universities Press.

Modell, A. H. (1990). *Other Times, Other Realities: Toward a Theory of Psychoanalytic Treatment*. Cambridge, MA: Harvard University Press.

Mitchell, S. A. (1988). *Relational Concepts in Psychoanalysis*. Cambridge, MA: Harvard University Press.

Renik, O. (1996). The perils of neutrality. *Psychoanalytic Quarterly* 65:495–517.

Steingart, I. (1983). *Pathological Play in Borderline and Narcissistic Personalities*. New York: Spectrum.

Stone, L. (1967). The psychoanalytic situation and transference: postscript to an earlier communication. *Journal of the American Psychoanalytic Association* 15:2–58.

Treurniet, N. (1993). What is psychoanalysis now? *International Journal of Psycho-Analysis* 74(5): 873–891.

14

Integration and Splitting of Symbol Systems in Dreams with Illustrative Manifest Content

JOHN ROSEGRANT AND IRVING STEINGART

We intend in this presentation to investigate dreams in which the manifest content illustrates, rather than disguises, the clinical issues that are most relevant for the patient at that moment. We believe that such dreams are not uncommon in clinical practice, and have been at least implicitly recognized since "The Interpretation of Dreams," but that their theoretical and clinical implications have not been thoroughly thought through.

That the manifest content of dreams in general can be highly informative has been explicitly recognized at least since Erikson's paper of 1954. Erikson described several ways in which the manifest content can complement or add to the information transmitted by the latent content. We begin our presentation by making the case that there is a type of dream in which the manifest content complements the latent content in a very specific way—not by carrying additional information, but by carrying the same information in a different form.

A version of this paper was presented at the Scientific Meeting of the Institute for Psychoanalytic Training and Research, New York City, January 25, 2002.

These are dreams in which the manifest content *pictorially illustrates* the same clinical issues that the patient *verbally describes* in his or her associations leading to the latent content. We make the case that clinical analysis of such dreams serves not so much to provide new cognitive insight as to help the patient integrate pictorial understanding with verbal understanding, and that this can be an important aspect of working through.

We then shift our presentation to a brief discussion of the theory of dream formation. We believe that our understanding of dreams with illustrative manifest content requires a shift in the emphasis of this theory, so that the compromise formation motive for dreaming, emphasized since "The Interpretation of Dreams," is more strongly supplemented by a motive to illustrate key clinical issues without disguise in the manifest content. (We want to make clear from the outset that we recognize that standard compromise formation contributes to creating the type of dream we are discussing—more on this below.)

Finally, we turn our attention to dreams in which the manifest content illustrates the clinical issues that are most relevant at that moment, but that the patient does not accompany with verbal associations leading to a latent content. Our shift in emphasis in the theory of dream formation makes it easier to recognize a particular defense operative in these dreams: the patient is using clear pictorial understanding to defend against verbal understanding of his or her issues. The operative defense is not a repression of crucial meanings, such as we typically think of in dream formation, but a splitting off of pictorial understanding of crucial meanings from verbal understanding. Both the expressive and the defensive aspects of self-state dreams can be clarified by understanding this dynamic.

So let us begin investigating dreams in which the manifest content illustrates, rather than disguises, the most clinically relevant aspects of the latent content arrived at by verbal association. We will present two vignettes of analysis of this type of dream. The dreamer is a man in his late twenties. Peter's reasons for seeking analysis included a generalized inhibition against asserting himself, so that he had been unable to select a career and had great difficulty asking women on dates or moving his few dating relationships beyond a platonic level. He was unhappily employed in retail sales, and his avocations were sports and the arts. In recent sessions, he had been discussing his ambivalence about asking women out and his ambivalent fantasies about training as a therapist.

> *Dream 1*: I was looking at the Eiffel Tower, but its foundation was weird, brick instead of metal, then it twisted up and up and as I looked up I felt very dizzy. Then I was on top of the tower in Seattle, and then I was on top of the Empire State Building, and I was very dizzy and afraid I would fall. Then I was with some women, and I was a woman too, although that didn't really matter, what mattered was that everyone was the same. If they knew someone was different they would kill him. We were high up a building. All of a sudden they jumped off and floated down; I was scared because I couldn't do that, so I knew they would find out I was different. I started running down the stairs, and heard one of them making excuses for me, saying . . . [Here the patient momentarily interrupts himself. In response to later exploration, he stated that the women had said he was more delicate and fragile than they.] Near the bottom I skipped off and found I could fly down. The women are no longer dangerous.

Peter's first association is that he had asserted himself to a woman manager at work regarding a scheduling issue, and his fear of a major confrontation turned out to be unfounded, as she accepted his request as a reasonable one. He is also somehow reminded of a friend of his who asked him for advice about a complex emotional issue, to which Peter responded by "acting like an analyst and not giving a straight answer." The brick foundation of the Eiffel Tower makes it less sturdy, and is reminiscent of a wall on which Peter played with friends as a child and from which he actually fell at times. Peter muses about how in both parts of the dream he is afraid of falling from a building, and says that being up high is getting a girl, a career. He is scared of trying this and prefers not to stick out from the crowd. The dream is about fitting in. The analyst says it seems something is scary in thinking about fitting in by turning himself into a woman. Peter says his first reaction is anxiously to think that the analyst thinks he really wants to be a woman, but in fact that's true in some ways, and maybe not surprising, since he always thought his sisters had it better than he. The analyst mentions that Peter had interrupted himself when telling that a woman in the dream made excuses for him, and Peter clarifies that the excuses were about his greater delicacy and fragility. He then associates to a man at work who is aggressively soliciting for a charity. The manager told him not to do this at work, but Peter decided to donate anyway, so that this man would not sabotage Peter's work. It's really better to be able to fit in like that, and this is part of what the dream means. The analyst points out that what Peter had hidden in his first telling of the dream was that the deadly women excused him because he was more delicate and fragile than they; it seems that something makes Peter anxious about recognizing that he is willing to fit in even if it means making himself the most feminine person around. Peter then talks more about being afraid of sticking out from the crowd. The analyst reminds him how he had "acted like an analyst" with his friend, and interprets that he fears there is room for only one of them in the high building of being a therapist.

> *Dream 2* (a few sessions later): I was on the express train, and realized it was going to take me too far, all the way to Connecticut. I wanted to get off at the halfway stop. Finally I got off at the West 4th Street station and switched to the local. Then I dreamed I had a complaining customer and protested to him that he must want me to read his mind.

Dream 2 was one of a series of what Peter calls "train dreams," which have the manifest content of his being in a vehicle that is moving too fast and/or too far. Peter tells the analyst that he never had such dreams prior to starting analysis. It has been easy for them to recognize that the dream occurs when Peter experiences the analysis as moving too fast or too far, both because he is feeling increasingly close to the analyst and because he is becoming more conscious of an important conflict.

In this instance, Peter begins by saying that getting off halfway reminded him of the boxing class he was taking, because he is at the halfway point but is feeling overwhelmed by it and is thinking of quitting. In his class yesterday, he was paired with a woman who doesn't hold back her blows the way she should in practice. She hit Peter in the face twice, and then he told her, "Watch it." He then refers back to previous dreams in the series, musing that each time they had to do with a feeling that he is going too far in the analysis; last time it had to do with fantasies of dating a woman. The station he got off at reminds him of the station where he got off the train yesterday; on that ride, a woman had smiled at him three separate times, and he returned each smile, but was too anxious to speak to her even though he rehearsed an opening line having to do with the book she was reading. Also it was 4th Street—the next smile would have been the fourth. The analyst wonders out loud in what way Peter feels he is going too far in the analysis now. Peter states that he feels the analyst is pushing him to move too fast in getting involved with women. To pick up a woman on the train would make it too obvious that he wanted sex eventually; he was too afraid to expose himself like that. The analyst has recently been asking why Peter feels that way when Peter states that he cannot ask out or flirt with some woman, and Peter finds he cannot defend his position. He feels like the analyst has him up against the ropes. The part about the customer wanting him to read his mind reminds him that a couple of days ago he asked if the analyst thought he would make a good therapist, and not receiving a "yes" or "no" answer left him feeling he was supposed to read the analyst's mind. He knows that he could handle the work well; the analyst says that then his asking whether the analyst thinks so too is asking for permission. Peter then associates to a "hard guy" in his boxing class with whom he dislikes being paired because his movements are stiff, rigid, and violent. He thinks struggling with this hard guy represents struggling with his problems. The analyst interprets that Peter is frightened by his thoughts that the analyst is a hard guy with whom he must struggle.

THE DREAMWORK IN PETER'S DREAMS

Let us examine the import of Peter's recurring dream. The elements that recur are that Peter is in some kind of vehicle that is taking him either too far or too fast. In the example presented, he is in a train that is taking him too far. He remembers the meaning of such material previously identified—generally, that the vehicle symbolizes the analysis, so his dream means that he fears he is going too far too fast in the analysis; specifically, that the previous time he had the dream it was because talking about dating made him feel that way. He then associatively links this meaning to the current analytic context: The analyst is pushing him too fast to get involved with women. This is connected to a day residue of when he was consciously aware of this set of feelings (flirting with a woman on a train but holding back from doing more lest he expose his longing for sex). Other associations indicate the feared outcome of going too far: being hurt by a woman, or being hurt by a man who appears to symbolize the analyst. The recurring element expresses the wish to go far, both sexually and on a career track. It also expresses the fear of the ensuing punishment.

Here is the curious part: The recurring meanings of the dream that Peter discussed in the session—the wish to go far sexually and in his career, the fear of punishment—although spoken of in a network of verbal associations, were also obvious from the manifest content. The manifest dream had already been interpreted and explored when it occurred previously, and was already comprehensible to the preconscious ego. This was not merely an intellectualized understanding, as Peter easily produced the network of affectively alive, confirmatory associations. The dreaming ego, which ordinarily censors the latent thoughts and unconscious wishes, must be positioning itself differently in this example. Indeed, the dream seemed more like a pointer than a disguise. It is as though a partygoer wore the same costume to his friends' house every Halloween; the first time it might fool them, but after being seen through, every subsequent use would make it obvious who was behind the mask.

Recognizing that this dream was not censoring certain important latent issues does not imply that the censorship was inoperative regarding other latent issues. For example, the dream appears to defend against and express a homosexual transference wish: that the analyst, the "hard, stiff, rigid guy," would push the patient fast. The analyst judged from the clinical context that this meaning would be too anxiety-provoking to interpret at the time. Later in the analysis, material consistent with this dream interpretation was explored. Therefore, this latent wish (and presumably others) appears to have been disguised according to the mechanisms described by Freud.

Now let us return to Dream 1 and consider the similarity between its manifest and latent content. The latent dream thoughts on which we focused were that Peter would like to have a girlfriend and be successful in his career, but the assertion this requires is very dangerous, perhaps resulting in deadly conflict. A woman he woos might hurt him, or the analyst might hurt him for challenging him. Even more minor self-assertion is dangerous; although his manager did not get angry at him and supported him over his co-worker, it is still best to submit to his co-worker's demand and fit in, despite it costing him money. After all, he knows from his childhood about dangerous falls and the need to fit in with women. Two wishes and the defenses against them organize the dream. The wish to be a successful, phallic man is defended against by the wish to be a woman; both wishes are defended against by dreamwork and by Peter's manner of reporting the dream, saying that being a woman "doesn't matter," and leaving out a part of the dream relevant to this wish.

And what is the manifest content? In sum, Peter is terrified of being in a high building, must become like a woman in order that he not be killed by women, is nevertheless at risk of discovery and death because he cannot get down from the heights as rapidly as they, but finally becomes safe due to having greater fragility and delicacy than the women. This manifest content does not disguise the above set of latent dream thoughts, but depicts them in a transparent manner. The verbal associations to childhood memories and the day residues were thematically related and affectively alive, but the manifest content expressed the same theme in vivid images. In this dream, too, the dreaming ego must be positioning itself differently in relation to the latent thoughts and wishes than it does when censorship produces opaque dreams. It is as if our Halloween partygoer had selected a costume that vividly depicted one of his forbidden wishes, as indeed Halloween partygoers often do, thus not so much disguising themselves as achieving a normally forbidden degree of self-expression. This self-expressive quality may be noted even though, again, the homosexual transference wish appears to be disguised in this dream according to the mechanisms described by Freud.

These dreams were also transparent in that they included obvious manifest symbols. Both the train and the high buildings are iconic representations of their latent meaning. For the patient, the train and high buildings were iconic representations of certain dream thoughts that were immediately apparent to him: progress, speed, and achieving too much (train); success, prominence, sticking out from the crowd (high building); lack of confidence and safety (stone foundation to the Eiffel Tower). They were also iconic of more body-related dream thoughts and wishes—fast trains and high buildings are obvious phallic symbols.

So once again we see that the dreaming ego must be positioning itself vis-à-vis the latent thoughts and wishes differently than it does when the dreamwork produces opaque dreams. The recurring train dream was transparent not only because it previously had been understood, but also because it incorporated a culturally universal symbol. The latent content of Dream 1 was openly manifested not only in private symbols but also with a culturally universal symbol. We now have our Halloween reveler attending parties repeatedly in the identical costume that depicts with socially familiar symbols some of his forbidden wishes. Since other dream meanings, including a homosexual transference wish, were effectively disguised by the mechanisms described by Freud, we may more precisely say that our Halloween partygoer has chosen a costume to vividly express some of his wishes, although he is simultaneously expressing and hiding other wishes outside of his awareness.

Other analysts, especially if from a different theoretical orientation, might have perceived latent meanings in the dream that did not come out in the work described, but that could have been helpfully addressed with the patient in the sessions in question. To consider our Halloween reveler one last time, it may be that the analyst looked most closely at the texture of the mask, whereas others in the audience might have looked more closely at the color. This would actually support our argument, however, because any such latent meanings, if readily apprehensible to the patient, would provide additional examples of dreamwork not producing disguise.

There is a very important sense in which the manifest content of these dreams, even though transparent to aspects of the latent content, may be assumed to have been motivated by the censorship. By so vividly depicting one set of conflictual issues, the dreams could serve to divert our attention from other issues. For example, by leading us to focus our attention on homosexuality as a defense against phallic heterosexual strivings, the dreams defended against recognition of homosexual wishes as drives in and of themselves. Considered from this point of view, the transparency of the manifest content was in fact another strategem of the censorship, a form of displacement.

But the identical problem is ubiquitous in clinical work. How do we decide if the conflict being explored is the important conflict to explore at that moment, rather than being merely the defense side of another conflict that would be more important to explore at that moment? We can imagine a situation in which a conflict is repetitively depicted in dreams, and the supportive associations take on a stereotyped, lifeless quality, which might lead us to the conclusion that the defensive aspect of the manifest dream's transparency had become its primary motivation. Freedman (1998) could describe this as a species of what he calls a "frozen constellation" (p. 84) with respect to any possibility of forward movement in the symbolization process. But considering the dreams we presented, we believe that the overall context of the analysis and transference, together with the network of affectively alive associations, indicated that the conflicts on which we focused were in fact the appropriate ones.

Therefore, the transparency of this patient's manifest dreams cannot adequately be explained as defensive in the same way as is opaque manifest dream content. The dream ego shaped the dream images—plenty of dreamwork occurred, so that blatant drive material was not directly depicted and anxiety was not high. But the dream ego appears to have positioned itself differently in relation to the latent thoughts and wishes than it does when creating more opaque—or more direct—dreams. In more usual dreams, whether anxiety dreams with directly depicted wishes or more opaque dreams, the dream ego shows less tolerance for awareness of the latent thoughts and wishes. In Peter's dreams, his preconscious dream ego was more aware of the latent thoughts and wishes.

This type of dream is not uncommon in clinical practice. However, we think that what actually goes on during analyis of these dreams has not been well understood. Dream analysis is usually conceptualized as leading from manifest to latent content, and thus as serving to uncover unconscious dynamics. Since the manifest content of Peter's dreams illustrated the same material that was arrived at when the patient gave verbal associations leading to a latent content, analysis of these dreams did not uncover unconscious dynamics. Instead, it is as though we were presented with both an illustration and a verbal description of the same set of conflicts, and this set of conflicts was one that we already knew was alive in the analysis. The dreams did not provide much in the way of new cognitive understanding, but both analyst and patient experienced them as a meaningful part of the process. What was going on here?

We suggest that an important aspect of the analysis of such dreams is the *integration* of the pictorial and verbal representations of a conflict. Because of the vivid pictorial nature of dreaming, a patient may feel that a conflict can be more genuinely understood if it is experienced and described in dream form as well as in verbal secondary process form. Associating to and interpreting Peter's dreams served most prominently not to increase verbal secondary process understanding, but to create linkages between the preexisting verbal secondary process understanding and the dream manifestations of the clinical material, making the material more alive and genuine. Such a repeated integration of these two symbolizing systems can be especially achieved with dream analysis, and can be considered a special variant of "working through." Grand and Pardes (1974) found evidence for an increased integrative working-over of dream imagery in successive REM-awakening dream reports obtained from subjects in a sleep laboratory. They speculated that in the clinical situation, such integrative working-over occurs during effective dream analysis done in dialogue with the analyst.

Greenson (1970) referred to a similar dynamic as a central reason for "The Exceptional Position of the Dream in Psychoanalytic Practice." He stated that the patient experiences the dream as irrevocably his own creation, and as particularly evocative of childhood and the drives because of its pictorial form. The first dream that Greenson discussed in this paper, from a patient in the sixth week of analysis, is a good example of a manifestly transparent dream. The dream included manifest content of vomiting, which was understood as signifying out-of-control free association, and manifest content of a salesman trying to force acceptance of ill-fitting clothing, which was understood as signifying the analyst forcing ill-fitting interpretations. Greenson indicated that he focused therapeutically on relatively transparent material in order to give the patient clarity and conviction.

A REVISION OF THE THEORY OF DREAM FORMATION

Freud's most fundamental idea about dreaming is that dreams are formed by a process of dynamic conflict between wishes and repressive forces. "A dream is a (disguised) fulfillment of a (suppressed or repressed) wish" (1900, p. 160). According to this basic model of dreaming in Freudian psychoanalysis, dreams are a compromise formation between unconscious wishes pressing toward consciousness and a preconscious censor, motivated by the wish to preserve sleep, which represses the unconscious wishes.

This model of dreaming sensitizes the analyst to search for repressed material behind dreams even more than behind most psychic productions, because the explanation for dreams being dreams rather than secondary process formations is that dreamwork has been wielded in the service of defense. The most important meanings of a dream are by definition latent, repressed. It is true that dreams also serve to illustrate in this model, but the dream can *clearly* illustrate only if the dream thoughts are clinically trivial (such as in simple childhood dreams or dreams about fulfilling nonconflictual wishes, such as wishes to eat or sleep), or if the defensive process has failed, as in anxiety dreams.

Peter's dreams do not fall into either of those categories. Although, as we have indicated, typical dreamwork mechanisms must have disguised other latent thoughts, the most clinically relevant latent thoughts were illustrated by the dreams. To account for this, our theory must recognize that latent thoughts can be altered by the dreamwork for motives other than defense.

We believe that this revision of theory only requires a slight shift in emphasis. Although Freud's dynamic psychology of dreaming was more prominent, he also developed a state psychology of dreaming: The processes of the dreamwork, with the exception of secondary revision, are not created by the censorship; they are the form of thought typical of the sleep state, and are harnessed by the censorship for its own purposes. Secondary revision, truly created by the censoring agency, is the one aspect of the dreamwork that makes dreams *less* dreamlike. In describing why it is precisely primary process forms of thought that the censorship must utilize to disguise dreams, Freud (1933) uses the metaphor of an occupying army imposing its own laws rather than submitting to the laws of the land occupied; analogously, the unconscious wish imposes its form of thinking on the dream rather than submitting to the secondary process. It is a very small step from here to recognizing that the dreamwork can shape a dream even if the censorship is not its only motivation.

In particular, the hallucinatory/perceptual quality of dreams is a quality of the dreaming state that can be independent of conflict and censorship. Freud described two sorts of dreams that occur outside a context of conflict: simple wish-fulfilling dreams that are typical of early childhood but may continue to occur at any stage in development (1900), and traumatic dreams (1920). Therefore, the hallucinatory quality of such dreams cannot be conceptualized as a conflict-driven regression in the psychic apparatus such as is described in Chapter VII of "The Interpretation of Dreams." (Adams-Silvan and Silvan [1990] have argued that traumatic dreams do involve typical conflict-driven dreamwork, in addition to their specific motivation for mastery of trauma.) Furthermore, even in Chapter VII, Freud differentiated the regression in dreaming from pathological regressions in that the former is partly due to the cessation of external perception during the state of sleep. Freud made the independence of the hallucinatory quality of dreams from conflict even clearer in "Metapsychological Supplement to the Theory of Dreams" (1917). There, Freud argued that the hallucinatory quality of a dream cannot be due to regression, stating:

> If the secret of hallucination is nothing else than that of regression, every regression of sufficient intensity would produce hallucination with belief in reality. But we are quite familiar with situations in which a process of regressive reflection brings to consciousness very clear visual mnemic images, though we do not on that account for a single moment take them for real perceptions. . . . Hallucination must therefore be something more than the regressive revival of mnemic images that are in themselves unconscious. [p. 231]

Freud concluded that hallucination results from a cessation of reality testing that is caused by the ego withdrawing a cathexis from the system *Conscious*. He then stated that, unlike pathological states in which such withdrawal of cathexis is motivated by conflict, the hallucinatory quality in dreaming results from "voluntary renunciation [of this cathexis because] the state of sleep does not wish to know anything of the external world" (p. 234).

Freud (1900) tells us of people who are aware of their dreams while dreaming and can consciously direct them, and of another person who wished to observe his dreams and to enjoy them. He further points out that anyone who becomes interested in dreams will remember more of them. For Freud, all these examples showed the action of other preconscious wishes that were consistent with the wish to sleep. The dreaming ego may also be relatively aware of latent content because of particular unconscious wishes. Freud (1923b), in a passage discussing his observation that more of the repressed is brought to light during analysis of dreams than by any other method, writes, "What is here in question cannot well be any factor other than the patient's compliance towards the analyst which is derived from his parental complex—in other words, the positive portion of what we call the transference; and in fact, in many dreams which recall what has been forgotten and repressed, it is impossible to discover any other unconscious wish to which the motive force for the formation of the dream can be attributed" (p. 117). We believe that in this passage, Freud is discussing manifestly transparent dreams, for what else can we understand him to mean when he describes a dream that reveals what has been repressed and has as its only unconscious motivation the positive transference? Freud is telling us that love for the analyst can lead the dream ego to be more aware of the latent content.

Kanzer (1955) and Bergmann (1966) described the wish to communicate as an additional motivation in dreaming. Kanzer and Bergmann were not writing only about manifestly transparent dreams, and gave examples that vary from relatively transparent to relatively opaque. It is probable, however, that an urge to communicate could influence a dreamer to create a relatively transparent dream.

We may summarize these theoretical considerations as follows: Just as pictorial imagery and the dreamwork are available during the sleep state to be harnessed by the censorship to fulfill the preconscious wish to sleep, they are available for other motivations that will let the dreaming ego be more aware of the latent content. These motivations can include both unconscious and preconscious wishes.

SPLITTING OF SYMBOL SYSTEMS IN DREAMING

Now let us turn our attention to dreams in which the manifest content illustrates the most important clinical issues of the moment, but which the patient does not accompany with verbal associations, leading to a latent content. We believe our emphasis that dreams may be motivated to illustrate crucial aspects of the latent content facilitates understanding the defensive process that is involved when such dreams are not accompanied by associations.

In the two examples of his dreams that we have cited, Peter associated to his dreams cooperatively and effectively, a patient in a moment of solid alliance. At other moments in his analysis, this patient's typical use of dreams was to report them, usually early in the session, then make no direct associations or only perfunctory ones, before moving on to other material. A clinically familiar oedipal transference inhibition often contributed to Peter's limited associations: Peter was hoping for the analyst to interpret the dream without Peter himself directly acting. This served both to create the analyst as an idealized, wise father figure, and to avoid self-assertion that has competitive, aggressive implications; Peter stated that he did not want "to go too far," or to suggest meanings at which the analyst might sneer.

But at other times, Peter used the illustrative form itself of his dreams to defend against verbal exploration. At these times he was reluctant to associate to his dreams because he was using them as illustrations of his psychic state, which he believed would function less well if given direct associations, just as illustrations in a book can lose part of their power if given verbal captions. Consider the following dream, related on the first session following the analyst's summer vacation:

> *Dream 3*: While the analyst was gone, Peter dreamt a sad dream, that he was in the city where he lived as a child, looking for his house, but couldn't find it. Then he dreamt that he came into the analyst's office and was criticized by a suitemate for having phoned ten times while the analyst was gone; Peter denied this but knew that it was true.

Peter gave no associations to the first part of the dream. To the second part he gave the day residue, that he had read of a patient calling her absent therapist repeatedly, and that this book also talked about how a therapist could be the only stable figure in a patient's life. Peter said that this described his relationship with his analyst. He had no other direct associations, but said the dream was interesting even without them. He agreed when the analyst said it was hard for Peter to talk about how much he missed him.

Although the first part of the dream presumably contains much undiscovered meaning behind the image of the childhood house, it also functions well as an illustration of Peter's state of longing and sadness while the analyst was gone. The second part of the dream is an even clearer illustration of this state, together with a feared punishment for his longing. But beyond briefly putting into words that the second part of the dream described their relationship, Peter's verbal associations were descriptive of the manifest content rather than leading to a latent content. He would not talk about his longing and sadness during that session. His finding the dream interesting in itself, without verbal elaboration, parallels a way he had communicated with a woman with whom he had lived previously: he would make collages for her out of magazine photos, which reflected his mood about the relationship. It was clear that vivid nonverbal communication was achieved. But it was equally clear that this served a defensive purpose, in that it saved Peter from putting his feelings into words, which he found very scary because he expected severe narcissistic wounding (rejection).

This is a splitting defense, rather than the repressive defense found in dreamwork as traditionally conceived, or in the oedipal inhibition of associations described above. Freud pointed out that thinking in imagery, whether during dreaming (1900) or conscious thought (1923a), cannot easily represent causal, temporal, logical, spatial, and so on, *relations* among symbols. We will term a matrix of such relations a *contingency-structured* reality, which will thus qualify and limit one's experience, and also will subject all of one's own experience (narcissism) to a significant, relational contextualization having to do with the perspective of a significant other(s). We believe it is a movement toward such a contingent reality that occurs when one verbally free associates and secondarily elaborates dream experience which, itself, only possesses perceptual (hallucinatory) quality. At the same time, we want to hold onto a distinction between such an idea of a contingent reality and a notion of rationality. Such a contingent reality may be seriously pathological as is evident, for example, with a systematized, paranoid delusion. Nevertheless, verbal, secondary process language is the medium of *some kind* of reality of relations and separation, and using this language presupposes that such contingencies are real (Bach 1994).

This contrast between imagery and words allows images to defend against contextual, relational understanding at the same time that they promote vivid, expressive understanding. What Peter was doing in the current example was defending against understanding a conflict in verbal terms by substituting understanding in pictorial terms. He was defending not against awareness of a conflict per se, but against a certain form of awareness of this conflict. Peter resorted to this type of defensive splitting because he was in a temporarily heightened state of narcissistic vulnerability that he and his analyst had come to recognize as a typical reaction to his analyst's vacations. They knew that Peter often experienced discomfort about accepting the world of realistic limits because he expressed frequent regrets that growing up, choosing one woman, choosing one career, meant the loss of all other possible lives and women and careers. His need to escape a reality of limits was especially strong when vacations confronted him with limits on his relationship with his analyst.

Some twenty-three years after "The Interpretation of Dreams," Freud appears to have come to some understanding of dreams with this split between illustration and verbal description, although he never systematically followed up on the idea. In "Remarks on the Theory and Practice of Dream Interpretation," Freud (1923b) wrote as follows:

> A number of dreams which occur during analyses are untranslatable even though they do not actually make much show of the resistance that is there. They represent free renderings of the latent dream-thoughts behind them and are comparable to successful *creative* writings which have been artistically worked over and in which the basic themes are still recognizable though they have been subjected to any amount of re-arrangement and transformation. Dreams of this kind serve in the treatment as an introduction to thoughts and memories of the dreamer without their own actual content coming into account. [pp. 110–111, italics added]

Just what is Freud saying here? And what justifies our using the term *split*? Perhaps an imagined, concrete illustration of Freud's simile that this kind of dream is like creative writing will provide clarification. Let us suppose that Ernest Hemingway is in psychoanalysis and that he is associating to the contents of various of his novels. It would be easy enough for his analyst, Hemingway, or indeed any literate reader, to discern phallic masculine themes having to do with bravery, potent force, willingness to risk in the face of danger, and so on (or the opposite of such qualities). But let us also suppose that Hemingway would not or could not associate further into a more personal reality of experience (e.g., some significant childhood memory or transferential fantasy about his own sense of maleness) that is so vital for a productive analysis. It is such a clinical circumstance that supports our use of the term *split*, and we believe it is this kind of insight that Freud (1923b) had achieved in his addition to dream theory and practice.

Freud may also have been trying to account for dreams with this split between illustration and verbal understanding by his conceptualization of dream symbols. It is our impression that most psychoanalysts define symbols semantically, as images that refer to certain ideas. Freud (1900, 1916, 1933), however, also defined symbols in terms of clinical process, as images to which the dreamer produced few or no meaningful personal associations. Any dream image to which a dreamer did not associatively arrive at some personal past or present experience, even after it could be accepted that the dreamer was not resisting, was assumed to be a symbol. This is a curious idea, which, to our knowledge, has not been taken seriously and explored in the literature.* Why does Freud think that by definition one cannot produce personal associa-

*It has been our experience that some individuals find it difficult to accept that Freud formulated such a process definition of a symbol; this is likely due to difficulty accepting the concept of a general (universal) symbol intrinsic to such a process definition. Freud certainly was wary about the concept of a general symbol, as well as how to approach such symbols in clinical work with deams. In his introduction to "The Interpretation of Dreams," Strachey documented that almost all of the material on symbolism was added subsequent to the first addition. Freud first composed a separate section on such general symbols in dreams in the 1914 edition, where he cautioned "They [general symbols] frequently have more than one or even several meanings . . ." (p. 353). But Freud nevertheless understood that whatever general symbolic meaning might attach to a dream image was of an entirely different order than meanings shaped into a dream image by primary process thinking and obtainable through the analysand's free associations. And despite his caution, Freud continued to add to the section on general symbols in subsequent editions.

It will be useful for us to document Freud's process definition of symbols in his ongoing writings. He first presented this idea in a section on symbols that he added to "On Dreams" in 1911: "A knowledge of dream-symbolism . . . afford[s] the most valuable assistance to interpretation precisely at points at which the dreamer's associations are insufficient or fail altogether" (pp. 684–685). In the above-mentioned section on symbolism added to the 1914 edition of "The Interpretation of Dreams," Freud stated: "As a rule the technique of interpreting according to the

tions to a symbol? It is commonplace for patients to give personal associations to symbols if "symbol" is defined semantically; for example, Peter associated to his dream symbols of trains and high buildings. And what sense does it make to say that the patient is not resisting when the patient is unable to associate?

One way to answer these questions is to suppose that Freud was encountering dream contents that he knew were not censored in the ordinary way, since they transparently manifested latent issues, but that served a defensive function in the sense of the patient's refusing to accompany them with verbally associative elaboration. This explanation could not apply to symbols that had been co-opted by the censorship so that their meaning was opaque. But Freud believed that there were certain people for whom symbols were not co-opted by the censorship, who could immediately intuit the meaning of their own symbols.

Current thinking about narcissism provides a theoretical background for understanding these observations of splitting in dream dynamics. These dreams result from a felt need to protect some fundamental organizational status of the personality, so it is not surprising to see them occur in narcissistic personality disorder. However, it also would not surprise us to find such a protective use of splitting off the domain of a verbalizable, contingent reality of separate self-object perspectives in any clinical condition wherein such contingent

---

dreamer's free associations leaves us in the lurch when we come to the symbolic elements in the dream content" (p. 353). Freud maintained this idea throughout his career. For example, in the "Introductory Lectures on Psychoanalysis" (1916) he stated that "it does sometimes really happen that nothing occurs to a person under analysis in response to particular elements of his dreams . . . an association fails to emerge or, if it *is* extracted, does not give us what we expected from it . . . we eventually discover that this unwished-for event regularly occurs in connection with particular dream elements [symbols] . . ." (pp. 149–150; italics original). In the "New Introductory Lectures on Psychoanalysis" (1933) Freud similarly stated, "If in general and primarily we are dependent, in interpreting dreams, on the dreamer's associations, yet in relation to certain elements of the dream's content [symbols] we adopt a quite independent attitude, chiefly because we have to, because as a rule associations fail to materialize in their case" (pp. 12–13). We conclude that Freud continued to find this conceptualization of dream symbols useful as he continued to accumulate clinical experience.

experience is felt to be unbearable (e.g., at least in some individuals who have addictive personalities). It is characteristic of patients with certain narcissistic organizations to have difficulty integrating various self-states in such a way as to allow comfortable transitions between these states, or to have vertical splits between self-states that make simultaneous awareness and integration of different self-states difficult (Bach 1985, 1994); it is reasonable to hypothesize that these qualities would make such patients less amenable to switching from the pictorial idiom of the dream to the verbal idiom of association and interpretation, and more likely to relate to the dream in such a way that direct linkages to the secondary process are not made. It is also characteristic of certain narcissistic organizations that they find the abstract verbal symbol less adequate (Bach 1985, 1994), and are more in need of enacted symbols to express core issues (Steingart 1995). Steingart has further shown that a patient may use words themselves as enacted symbols, but that in this situation the patient is treating words as things that function as part of a concrete, imagistic symbolic system, rather than as part of the usual, consensual, verbally symbolic system. It is reasonable to hypothesize that such patients would be less likely to find verbal association and interpretation meaningful, and more likely to find illustrative or manifestly expressive uses of the dream meaningful.

From a different theoretical perspective, self psychologists have examined what appears to be a subset of illustrative dreams, which they have called self-state dreams (Kohut 1977). These are conceptualized by self psychologists as dreams that in manifest imagery depict the state of the self, and are not accompanied by associations to a latent content; the patient may talk about the dream, but in a way that broadens rather than deepens the images. From a self psychology perspective, other kinds of dreams may be accompanied by associations to *latent* content dealing with the self, but these are not self-state dreams (Tolpin 1983); in a self-state dream, content relating to the self is formally expressed via transparent *manifest* content unaccompanied by associations to latent content. The classical Freudian rejoinder has been that the concept of self-state dreams reflects a misunderstanding of the dreamwork and the relationship between manifest and latent content, so that the *product* of defense against wishes, rather than the conflictual *process* between wishes and defense, is taken as the core motivational issue (see Richards 1981, Rothstein 1980), and rote allegorical interpretation is substituted for open-ended, deepening exploration (Reed 1987).

Recognizing that in the very act of illustrating, the dreamwork may serve the purposes of defense against verbalization creates room in contemporary Freudian theory for an understanding of self-state dreams that takes into account both illustrative and defensive functioning. A self-state dream may be conceptualized as a type of dream in which an illustrative function, focused on the state of the self, is especially important, and in which the patient needs to defend powerfully against integrating the dreaming state with verbal, secondary process discourse, so that the patient cannot or will not meaningfully associate in a way that leads to a latent content. This suggests that it could be clinically reasonable and helpful in these situations to understand the manifest dream as an illustrative creation, rather than focusing on defensive aspects.

This is exactly what occurred in Peter's dream about having "phoned ten times while the analyst was gone." We consider this to be a self-state dream that highlights experience of early narcissistic injury and object loss, linked to the absence of the analyst over the summer break. The emergence of such a dream later in his analysis also implicates latent narcissistic meanings for Peter's earlier dreams, which we handled at the time by focusing on oedipally colored dynamics, as they were both manifestly illustrated and arrived at by association. We believe not that these oedipally colored dynamics represented the whole meaning of Peter's earlier dreams, but that they were what Peter could handle most productively at that moment in his psychoanalysis.

CONCLUSION

We have examined two very different dynamics that are involved in the formation of illustrative manifest dream contents. In the first dynamic a dreamer who is both preconsciously and unconsciously motivated to provide vivid understanding of conflicts produces a manifestly illustrative dream accompanied by verbal associations leading to latent content—latent content that has been illustrated by the manifest content. Such relatively transparent manifest dreams are created by a process of rather easily integrating verbal with imagistic forms of thought and experience. We recognize that such relatively transparent dreams can at the same time serve as a resistance against consciousness of other dynamic material that an analyst judges is best left latent at the moment. When working with such dreams, the analyst may choose not to interpret this rather special sort of resistance, and instead to work with the issues that are illustrated by the dream. (Here we touch on the general technique problem of when, and with what associational platform, an analyst should elect to interpret some new dynamically unconscious experience; an examination of this topic is beyond the scope of this paper.) Analysis of illustrative dreams from this perspective serves to integrate pictorial symbolization with verbal symbolization. We see this integration as an aspect of insight and "working through."

In the second dynamic a dreamer who needs to defend against verbal comprehension of his or her inner life produces a manifestly illustrative dream that is not accompanied by verbal associations leading to latent content. Such dreams are created by a splitting process in which the dreamer uses the pictorial symbol system of the dream to simultaneously illustrate his or her conflicts and defend against verbal elaboration of those conflicts. Such a dream dynamic is indicative of either a temporary or characterological state of narcissistic disturbance. Self-state dreams appear to be a subtype of such dreams. It may often be clinically helpful to work with such dreams as illustrative creations, rather than focusing on defensive aspects.

Our approach to manifestly illustrative dreams shows them to have a crucial locus of insight or defense at the juncture of the pictorial and verbal symbolizing systems, rather than at a line of censorship against particular mental contents. This point of view highlights the always significant matter of the status of integration between these two symbolizing systems within the human mind.

REFERENCES

Adams-Silvan, A., and Silvan, M. (1990). "A dream is the fulfillment of a wish": traumatic dream, repetition compulsion, and the pleasure principle. *International Journal of Psycho-Analysis* 71:513–522.

Bach, S. (1985). *Narcissistic States and the Therapeutic Process*. New York: Jason Aronson.

——— (1994). *The Language of Perversion and the Language of Love*. Northvale, NJ: Jason Aronson.

Bergmann, M. (1966). The intrapsychic and communicative aspects of the dream. *International Journal of Psycho-Analysis* 47:356–363.

Erikson, E. (1954). The dream specimen of psychoanalysis. *Journal of the American Psychoanalytic Association* 2:5–56.

Freedman, N. (1998). Psychoanalysis and symbolization: Legacy or heresy? In *The Modern Freudians: Contemporary Psychoanalytic Technique*, ed. C. S. Ellman, S. Grand, M. Silvan, and S. J. Ellman, pp. 79–97. Northvale, NJ: Jason Aronson.

Freud, S. (1900). The interpretation of dreams. *Standard Edition* 4/5.

——— (1911). The handling of dream interpretation in psychoanalysis. *Standard Edition* 12: 89–96.

——— (1914). On narcissism: an introduction. *Standard Edition* 14:67–102.

——— (1916). Introductory lectures on psychoanalysis. *Standard Edition* 15.

——— (1917). A metapsychological supplement to the theory of dreams. *Standard Edition* 14:217–235.

——— (1920). Beyond the pleasure principle. *Standard Edition* 18:1–64.

——— (1923a). The ego and the id. *Standard Edition* 19:1–66.

——— (1923b). Remarks on the theory and practice of dream interpretation. *Standard Edition* 19:107–121.

——— (1933). New introductory lectures on psychoanalysis. *Standard Edition* 22:1–182.

Grand, S., and Pardes, H. (1974). The transition from sleep to wakefulness: implications of a study of the organization of laboratory dream reports for the psychoanalytic situation. *Journal of the American Psychoanalytic Association* 22:58–82.

Greenson, R. (1970). The exceptional position of the dream in psychoanalytic practice. *Psychoanalytic Quarterly* 39:519–549.

Kanzer, M. (1955). The communicative function of the dream. *International Journal of Psycho-Analysis* 36:260–266.

Kohut, H. (1977). *The Restoration of the Self*. Madison, CT: International Universities Press.

Reed, G. (1987). Rules of clinical understanding in classical psychoanalysis and in self psychology: a comparison. *Journal of the American Psychoanalytic Association* 35:421–446.

Richards, A. (1981). Self theory, conflict theory, and the problem of hypochondriasis. *Psychoanalytic Study of the Child* 36:319–337. New Haven, CT: Yale University Press.

Rothstein, A. (1980). Toward a critique of the psychology of the self. *Psychoanalytic Quarterly* 49:423–455.

Steingart, I. (1995). *A Thing Apart*. Northvale, NJ: Jason Aronson.

Tolpin, P. (1983). Self psychology and the interpretation of dreams. In *The Future of Psychoanalysis,* ed. A. Goldberg, pp. 255–271. Madison, CT: International Universities Press.

15

Symbolization, Desymbolization, and Annihilation Anxieties

MARVIN HURVICH

A major focus of Freedman's work in recent years has been on symbolic processes and their relevance for psychopathology. In line with his interest in combining theoretical, clinical, and empirical facets of psychoanalysis, Freedman has been progressively elaborating and refining an understanding of symbolization, working out ways to measure it, and applying it to clinical issues. In their empirical work, Freedman and his collaborators have assessed symbolization in associative monologues, and their measurement scales can also be applied to dreams, early memories, and TAT stories.

In this chapter, I explore relationships between symbolization and anxiety, specifically annihilation anxiety, with the goal of enriching both concepts and their empirical assessment. The Freedman, Karliner, and Kagan (2000) Scale of Incremental Symbolization (SIS) is utilized to aid the understanding of a patient's panic attack report.

I would like to thank Wilma Bucci, Annette DeMichele, and Denise Kagan for their contributions to this paper.

SYMBOLIZATION

Symbolic processes are central to ego functioning (Aragno 1992, Kubie 1958), and are fundamentally interconnected with all other facets of human development. Symbolic progression, especially language growth, is correlated with desomatization of responses. While essential for maximal mental performance, symbolic functioning also makes neurosis and psychosis possible. Symptoms as compromise formations can be seen as symbols that have been constructed in part to serve defensive functions: phobias, obsessions, and so on, have unconscious symbolic meaning.

Disturbances in symbolic functioning have been seen as central to all psychopathology (Aragno 1992, Kubie 1958). These can be the result of failures in the development of the symbolic capacity, as well as losses of symbolic functioning. A key distinction can be made between psychopathological symptoms that have symbolic meanings, which serve to disguise the connection between the symbol and what is symbolized, and those that are directed toward obscuring meaning altogether (Bass 1997). In psychosis, a regression or breakdown of the capacity for symbolization may be experienced as the death of the mind (Lifton 1979).

Of the many definitions of symbolization and the symbolic process, the approach of Kubie (1958) is relevant for our purposes. He has identified three interrelated processes that conceptualize symbolization as a "multivalent tool." The functions he specified can be characterized as literal, allegorical, and unconscious symbolism. The first reflects concept formation, the second, metaphor (where the connection between symbol and symbolized is apparent), and the third, following Jones, where the tie between symbol and underlying symbolized has become dynamically unconscious.

Through theoretical formulations refined by attempts to measure these phenomena empirically, Freedman and his colleagues have defined the manifestations of symbolization and its levels. He has focused on desymbolization (a failure of mentalization and a defensively motivated attempt to discard meaning), as well as on incipient and then dynamic symbolization. In the latter, different points of view, which may be contradictory, can be simultaneously entertained and integrated, leading to the discovery of novel meanings.

DESYMBOLIZATION

Freedman and his colleagues hold that desymbolization, a mode of communication, may be manifest in perceptual concreteness, in apparently unmentalized tension states, and as a primitive defensive effort to destroy meaning (disavowal). It can also be seen in the insistence on a single meaning, maintaining a frozen position, and losing body rhythmicities. Two major techniques here are labeled by Freedman and colleagues as *shielding* or *immobilization*. Shielding is a pattern of self-stimulation that breaks symbolic links among meanings. Immobilization is a freezing of the musculature in an effort to evacuate meaning by adopting an inert state.

Freedman and colleagues have elaborated the dimensions of symbolization in terms of levels, degrees, and motivations. Levels are defined as desymbolized, incipient, discursive, and dynamic (psychoanalytic symbolization proper), and can be understood as transitions that may constitute transformations. For Freedman (1985), the process of transformation is central to human functioning, and change is made possible through the dynamic force released by a state of disequilibrium. Desymbolization has been further defined in terms of degree, going from segmental to pervasive. Consistent with psychoanalytic symbolization, Freedman holds that true desymbolization must involve an active underlying motivation. Finally, Freedman and colleagues (1999a) have defined transformation cycles, which may go from a frozen constellation, to its modification, to the achievement of new symbolic functions, and a return to the frozen configuration, with lowered intensity.

Central to symbolization is that one thing stands for another. In desymbolization as Freedman conceives it, one thing must not stand for another (Bass 1997). In desymbolization, the patient has difficulty with symbolization per se. With regard to the attempt to destroy meaning, the defensive aspect of desymbolization is a palpable example of a defense against anxiety. Psychic trauma, failures of symbolization, alexithymia, and a tendency toward somatization are all related. More about this after a delineation of annihilation anxiety.

In this paper I attempt to demonstrate that a more explicit consideration of annihilation anxieties will enhance the understanding of desymbolization and its variants, namely perceptual concreteness, segmental and pervasive degrees, and the dynamics of transformation cycles. The features of annihilation anxieties that are especially relevant here are the distinction between levels of annihilation anxieties, the quality of uncontrolled vs. controlled anxieties, the threat or presence of mental disorganization, and the issue of secondary anxiety. Some clinical material is presented to illustrate relationships between annihilation anxieties and desymbolization.

ANNIHILATION ANXIETIES

Annihilation anxiety is here defined as the dread of imminent psychic or physical destruction: mortal terror, apprehension over physical and/or psychological survival. Major dimensions under which virtually all survival-related concerns can be grouped are identified as fears of being overwhelmed, of being merged, penetrated, or abandoned, fear of loss of the self representations, and concern over survival and the presence of a catastrophic mentality (Benveniste et al. 1997, Hurvich 1989). Doris Silverman, in her paper "The Refractoriness of the Desymbolizing Function" (Chapter 9, this volume), independently includes each of these subfunctions of annihilation anxieties in the delineation of her desymbolizing patient. Her description reflects underlying annihilation anxiety as a basis for the desymbolization: "The pain associated with the maintenance of symbolic thinking is too difficult, too overwhelming, too disorganizing, too terrifying" (p. 231).

Factors that increase the likelihood of annihilation anxieties are proposed to be traumatic experiences, ego function weaknesses, and threats to self-cohesion (Hurvich 1989), as well as prevalence of disorganized and insecure attachment styles (Diamond 1999). Correspondingly, the presence of annihilation anxieties may increase the likelihood of these very factors.

Apprehensions voiced by patients that often are derivatives of underlying annihilation anxieties are fears of being engulfed, invaded, fragmented, suffocated or drowned; of losing mental, physical, or bodily control and/or of going insane. There may be concerns about dissolving, coming unglued, being absorbed, crushed, shattered, or mutilated, of exploding, melting, leaking out, fading away, or falling endlessly.

In another paper (Hurvich 2000b), I have proposed that annihilation anxieties appear developmentally early, are triggered by survival threat, are residuals of psychic trauma, may occur in presymbolic form or be associated with fantasies in conflict–compromise formation, may arise with or without anticipation, be accompanied by controlled or uncontrolled anxiety, constitute motives for defense, and be associated with particularly recalcitrant resistances. Three levels of annihilation anxieties have been proposed (Hurvich 1991): basic, intermediate, and higher level.

Both desymbolization and annihilation concerns are universal, and under certain conditions, both can be found to reflect varying degrees of psychopathology. It is consistent with clinical experience to hypothesize that the more pathological the annihilation anxieties, the more primitive the symbolization processes. That is, manifestations of basic annihilation anxieties are seen to occur along with pervasive desymbolization. This kind of connection is amply illustrated in the panic attack account below, as well as in Freedman and colleagues' material. In the cases used to illustrate pervasive symbolization (Freedman et al. 1999b), the clinical descriptions include a number of annihilation anxiety markers (Hurvich 1991, 2000b). The association of annihilation anxieties with pervasive desymbolization is a general tendency, with individual differences, and there is a need to take account of other variables.

UNCONTROLLED AND CONTROLLED ANXIETY

Freud (1926) formulated the basic distinction between *traumatic* and *signal* anxieties in the same publication where he asserted that the ego is the seat of anxiety. This statement applies most validly to signal anxiety. Traumatic anxiety is uncontrolled and is not under ego command. It is both a marker of compromised ego control and a contributor to decreased ego mastery.

Desymbolization reflects a regressive-defensive reaction to anxiety, often to annihilation anxieties. Massive psychic trauma can interfere with the capacity to symbolize. Evidence here comes from reports on people subjected to extreme situations, such as concentration camps. Schizophrenia, where desymbolization also is often an issue, has also been seen as a response to extreme situations and to terror (Bettelheim 1956, Karon and VandenBos 1981, Teixeira 1984).

In concentration camp survivors, it was found that living under the continuous peril of death had a desymbolizing effect on inmates (Grumbrich-Simitis 1984). Associated with this desymbolization was a regressive dedifferentiation, deverbalization, and somatization of affects.

Annihilation anxiety as a psychic content may occur in the context of *controlled* or *uncontrolled* affect. When the affect is controlled (low amplitude), it is not disruptive to the mental organization or to specific ego functions, such as reality testing and synthesis. This allows a more accurate identification of the specific feelings involved, which increases the possibility for utilization of this information as a self signal, that is, signal anxiety. Desymbolization accompanied by low affect amplitude is more reflective of segmental desymbolization. Here, the annihilation fantasy tends to be based on earlier traumatic experience, but the person's substantial capacity for taming and for affect tolerance has resulted in the fantasy being engendered or triggered without disruptive, uncontrolled anxiety.

The clinical and theoretical significance of annihilation anxiety is underscored when the affective component is *uncontrolled*. Such status changes the therapeutic atmosphere, affects the therapeutic frame, and can influence the psychotherapeutic process (Silber 1989). This is also true for mutual influences between uncontrolled anxiety and desymbolization.

On the more pathological side, the desymbolization-concretization of experience due to arrest or to regression can leave the patient with the sense of a two-dimensional world, which tends to be experienced as terrifying. There is an absence of the capacity for abstraction and for synthesis. The patient can comprehend words, but finds it hard to understand sentences. The patient may also experience perceptions as a series of separate still photographs that do not take on the feeling of movement in time (Hurvich 2000a). This has also been described (Mitrani 1995) as unmentalized experience, reflecting early somatosensory functioning that did not achieve mental representation, and thus did not advance to the symbolic level. It is what Tustin (1981) called the world of the encapsulated child, where there is limited potential for distinguishing self from object, and restricted tolerance for separateness.

With regard to any desymbolized experience, the relative extent of uncontrolled vs. controlled anxiety, primary vs. secondary process, disorganization vs. organization of mental functioning plays a consequential role in the desymbolized experience. The panic attack described below will illustrate these points.

SECONDARY ANXIETY

Secondary anxiety (Schur 1953, 1971) has been discussed as a response to regressive reactions, including resomatization. When anxiety cannot be limited to an ego-controlled signal, it tends to disorganize psychic functioning, This and the associated ego regression often engender more anxiety, new psychic danger, and further defensive efforts. Here, anxiety, resomatization, and the other manifestations of desymbolization (perceptual concreteness, apparently unmentalized tension states, and meaning destruction) may become psychic dangers themselves. Schur (1971) pointed out that the patient who experiences a nightmare or an anxiety attack is not only afraid of the danger of a disguised instinctual demand, he is also afraid of his own ego regression, which could result in the *uncontrolled* anxiety in the situation of traumatic helplessness. This anxiety can be more disruptive than the original response to the danger situation. It is the threat of reexperiencing helplessness in a framework of low anxiety tolerance that results in the patient's becoming afraid of being frightened. The person may thus feel overwhelmed from the initial failure of defense, and/or from the disorganizing results of the defensive efforts following the first defensive and adaptive attempts to contain the anxiety. When the patient becomes frightened by the symptom that was the compromise formation from the initial conflict, additional anxiety may be generated. With regard to desymbolization specifically, Bass (1997) has hypothesized that concreteness and the need for sameness serve as defenses against differentiation, which is associated with overwhelming tension, and which we find often to be associated with annihilation anxieties.

CLINICAL EXAMPLE OF ANNIHILATION ANXIETY: A PANIC ATTACK REPORT

A 28-year-old female patient reported the following panic she experienced the previous evening after apparently feeling ignored by someone important to her.

> At the beginning of the attack I felt inundated from my head and body, bombarded, my body felt bigger, my wrists throbbed and felt cut, I was extremely aware of my heart and other parts of my body, my hands began to tingle, different parts of my body got tense, my stomach knotted up and I felt cramps in my muscles. Everything was going very fast, and when she [the person by whom the patient had earlier felt ignored] began to talk, the words were cut up into little pieces and scattered around. The sound of her words made me feel more shaky; they hurt because they added to the inside noise. At that point I felt threatened, like someone was going to assault me, and that I had to get away from the words because if I didn't I would get hurt. Then I felt I was really losing control, and it snowballed and I got panicky and started to shake and pant. There was nothing clear on my mind, pure panic, like adrenalin rushing, like a sound getting louder and louder. It's not anything like a thought. But it's like the feeling you'd have if you were about to get raped or mugged, and you can't get away. At some point it got into such a salad that I wanted to scream or throw things. There were a million things going on at once.

> It was like if someone would hook you up to a machine and jumble up your thoughts, like print that's not clear, parts of words taken out, or like a newspaper that's been underwater and you can't read it. It's big and chaotic. Like words are on an assembly line and it's going so fast I couldn't select any in time. And if I could select some, this would stimulate the whole crazy process again and activate it even more.
>
> I felt like a victim watching it all and being helpless to straighten it out. It was beyond me, and the more it went on, the more helpless I felt, and stupid. At that point, any kind of mental exertion would make it worse, any noise, movement, or activity, by me or others.
>
> It reached some kind of peak and then I got exhausted. It started to decrease, like a car slowing down that's been going very fast. I felt depressed. The jumble began to sink away, like something going under water, receding into the background, and few sentences came out like generalizations: "I can't do it." The emotions went up to a peak then broke, and there was some relief. When I start to feel any fear, even a little, I start to feel I'm going to have an anxiety attack. I have to push it away, get away from it. I'm so afraid of fear.

COMMENTS ON THE PANIC ATTACK

This panic attack was triggered by disappointments with a significant person, which likely meant for her some combination of loss of love, loss of the object, and a self-esteem slight. As with other panics she has reported or I have witnesssed, anger played an important role. My conjectures about this material are as follows: Feeling bombarded and inundated reflects a turning on the self of the activated anger. Regressive sensations of a large body put her in a better position to defend herself. The throbbing wrists that felt cut recalled in a concrete feeling the actual wrist cutting during previous anxiety attacks. It was "to let the poison out," as she had earlier said, referring to the ego-alien anger and hateful fantasies associated with negatively toned internalized object representations.

The racing thoughts suggest a loss of cognitive control and the weakening of various inner boundaries as the defenses are unable to keep order in consciousness. The words being described as cut up and scattered around reflect her anger toward the frustrater and a regression in synthetic-integrative functioning. There is also an inability to tolerate any additional stimulation, a feeling of threat, and a fear of being ineffective. Boundaries are weakening; there is a threat of being overwhelmed by stimuli and an externalization of anger.

The friend's attempt to talk to the patient when she can bear no further input and the anger generated by both are followed by a sense of increased loss of control, accompanied by panic, shaking, and panting. Now the annihilation experience is central, with a sense of helplessness and no way to escape the danger. The awareness of cognitive functioning is like a TV screen showing static, and there is a sense of thoughts being jumbled and fragmented, while the racing sensation continues, and feelings of chaos and helplessness pervade.

Typically for this patient, the regression is time-limited, and she describes the jumble receding into the background. The build-up and release also suggest sexual arousal, orgasm, and relaxation. The patient is nonorgasmic. The final comment about her fear of fear points to how the anxiety signal can lead to panic and underscores the vulnerable defense organization, where an anxiety signal, rather than aiding in the protection against a traumatic state, tends to usher it in.

When I later inquired about her self-experience during the panic attack, she answered as follows: "My sense of self was hollow, like I didn't have a self, like it was outside myself. Like a ghost—I'm watching like I have absolutely no impact on what's going on. I felt like I was being literally ripped apart. There are all these characters that feel separate, not part of me, and they start fighting. I can't stop them or integrate them."

The ingredients of overstimulation, threat of disorganization, and fragmentation of the self are all there. The panic attacks began after a suicide attempt while she was in treatment. There were traumatic experiences in her past: the father had a volatile temper and sometimes broke things when he was angry. The patient was very frightened of him and believed on several occasions that he would kill her in the course of a beating for misbehavior. She was the oldest child in a large family of closely spaced children, and it appeared that her attachment to the mother was repeatedly interfered with by the arrival of each successive sibling. She has had panic attacks of decreasing frequency and intensity during the psychotherapy, a number of them in the office. She shows intense separation anxiety, weak ego boundaries, vulnerable integration of self and of object representations, and a tendency to regress deeply, though reversibly. She has regressed to a psychotic state on a number of occasions. There are indications of failures throughout the separation-individuation subphases, beginning with an unsatisfactory symbiotic attachment.

A Kohutian formulation would stress that a less-than-optimal self–object merger has resulted in a weakness in affect-taming capacity, in the presence of defective structures. This would suggest a primary disorder of the self with protracted breakup, enfeeblement, and serious distortion of the self, with some defensive covering that is easily incapacitated (Kohut 1979).

Such reactions as a blocking of emotional awareness, temporary motor paralysis, a loss of will, a constriction of cognition, and a decrease in the capacity for pleasure have been found in concentration camp survivors and other victims of adult psychic trauma (Krystal 1988). These are characteristics of this patient during regressive periods.

ANALYSIS OF THE PANIC ATTACK IN TERMS OF DESYMBOLIZATION

In Freedman's terms, there is here a direct transformation of tension states into motor or somatic channels. This formulation fits the patient's account of the panic attack. With the panic attack protocol, it is possible to further elaborate on this process when, in this instance, the material is centrally reflective of annihilation anxieties.

The panic attack description can be seen to constitute an organized nonverbal emotional schema, split off from the verbal system, a mental representation that includes intense and massive somatic, visceral, physiologic, and motor images. It thus reflects the somatization and deverbalization that have been found associated with desymbolization.

Nonverbal emotional schemas have been described as including images of objects, actions, and bodily states (Bucci 1985). The formulation of a nonverbal anxiety schema provides the basis for assuming desymbolized, concrete, autonomic imagery as precursor signals for annihilation anxiety. This autonomic imagery would bear the same relation to the perception of an actual traumatic state as a memory image bears to the perception of an object. This would be similar to a representation having some relation to the perception, but distinguishable from it in structure, content, and intensity.

The panic imagery does indeed reflect the tension being shunted into somatic channels, and while a concreteness prevails, the colorfulness of the somatically based imagery is noteworthy. Missing from the patient's account of the annihilation anxiety, which characterized the panic experience, is reference to or depiction of specific objects.

Now to a more detailed consideration of the panic description. The patient begins with general somatic imagery ("my body felt bigger, my wrists throbbed and felt cut"), then goes on to use autonomic and visceral imagery ("I was extremely aware of my heart . . . my hands began to tingle, my stomach knotted up," etc.) and action ("everything was going very fast"). While the therapist assumed the feeling of being rejected by her friend was the proximal trigger of the panic episode, there was no indication that the patient made this connection. This apparent absence of seeing such a connection with the triggering event is a marker of lower level symbolization in the Freedman and colleagues approach.

A description of her anxiety experience in terms of somatic imagery and action reflects a regression from a portrayal in more directly verbal terms, words and feelings, and occurs in the framework of uncontrolled anxiety. We note especially that the perceptual concreteness and the apparently unmentalized tension states constitute two of Freedman's three main criteria for desymbolization.

The patient then reports an image that appears directly to concretize the severing of the referential connections between nonverbal representations and words: ("the words were cut up into little pieces and scattered around"). This concrete perceptual imagery depicts a destruction of meaning in Freedman's terms, as well as suggesting

Bion's (1959) "attacks on linking." Through this splitting or "cutting," the words become concrete physical entities, reduced to their sound, losing their connection to meaning. This considerably intensifies the experience. The imagery becomes more intense and seems to move out of the domain of mental representation ("Then I felt I was really losing control, and it snowballed and I got panicky and started to shake and pant"). Here, the imagery gradually activates an arousal state.

The mental experience ("There was nothing clear on my mind, pure panic, like adrenalin rushing, like a sound getting louder and louder") is recognized by the patient as very different from symbolized thinking ("It's not anything like a thought"). At this point, underlying dynamic issues are suggested, in a context of abject helplessness ("it's like the feeling you'd have if you were about to get raped or mugged, and you can't get away"). The patient's description of her panic experience reflects a general failure to use words to regulate and direct herself. Language comes from the outside and takes control over her: she wards off the connections to words.

The disorganization of mental processes is graphically reported by the patient at this juncture, where the defenses are unable to maintain order in consciousness ("it got into such a salad" . . . [as] "if someone would hook you up to a machine and jumble up your thoughts"). In the earlier example of words being cut up, the active destruction of meaning as Freedman and colleagues have specified, was clearer than in the examples just cited. Here, it is a question of the extent to which the loss of meaning is on a dynamic basis, and to what extent the jumble is more directly a result of the ego function regression.

The patient further details the phenomenology of the regressively disorganized thought functions ("like print that's not clear, parts of words taken out . . . like words . . . on an assembly line . . . I couldn't select any in time . . . helpless to straighten it out"). There is some movement toward incipient symbolization here, and above ("hook you up to a machine") where symbol making begins, reflected in the metaphorical and "as if" qualities.This awareness is connected to concrete bodily experience.

Now the patient illustrates what Freedman calls immobilization ("At that point, any kind of mental exertion would make it worse, any noise, movement, or activity, by me or others"). This patient regularly uses immobilization as a defense against anxiety, especially in an effort to stave off a panic attack she feels is brewing.

Intelligible language comes back only after the panic experience has peaked, and the anxiety has become more *controlled* ("The jumble began to sink away, like something going under water, receding into the background, and a few sentences came out like generalizations . . ."). This increase in the level of functioning can also be seen as a transformation, in Freedman's terms, which, together with the previous material, constitutes part of a transformation cycle. Such a development underscores the relevance of the earlier emphasized distinction between controlled and uncontrolled anxiety. As hypothesized below, the decrease in the extent of uncontrolled anxiety facilitates the progression of the transformation toward a more full transformation cycle. At this point the patient expresses her feelings of powerlessness, lack of control, and inadequacy. As she said: "I can't do it."

The patient's many images are not of specific things, people, or events. Even when she talks about actions upon her, such as being raped, mugged, and assaulted, there are no specified agents. She uses nonspecific object words or the passive tense: "*someone* was going to assault me . . . you were about to *get raped or mugged*." She maintains this schema apparently without objects; she concretizes the somatic aspects of the emotions to link to words. The imagery the patient uses in the description of her panic experience can be understood as based on a nonverbal, nonsocial interactional representation of somatic memories from the first few years of life. This is generally consistent with my characterization of annihilation anxiety at a basic (primitive) level (Hurvich 1991), and with Freedman's depiction of a lower level of symbolization, most notably, desymbolization.

The panic attack description ends with a reflection of her low anxiety tolerance and the fear of reexperiencing a traumatic situation ("When I start to feel any fear, even a little, I start to feel I'm going to have an anxiety attack . . . I'm so afraid of fear"). This latter statement also implies an incipient level of symbolization because she names the fear, reflects on her reaction to fear, describes it in relation to herself, and gets some degree of distance from it. But the stated concern that any degree of fear/anxiety leads to panic apprehension underscores the absence of a well-established signal function, and suggests the ready regressive reversion to uncontrolled anxiety, and, likely, desymbolization.

Thus, the move from desymbolization to incipient symbolization does not necessarily herald further movement toward higher levels of symbolization. This is very much of an individual difference issue, reflective of ego function strengths and weaknesses of the defense organization, of the integrity of the signal function, and of the vulnerability for uncontrolled anxiety.

This panic attack material illustrates the relevance of Freedman's components of desymbolization: perceptual concreteness, apparently unmentalized tension states, defensive effort to destroy meaning, and loss of body rhythmicities, as well as the relation of the latter to annihilation anxieties. It also raises the question of a possible further elaboration of the Freedman and colleagues scale. Freedman and colleagues have developed a scale that details an incremental process going from desymbolization to higher levels, as described earlier. But the very primitive imagery found in the reported panic attack description suggests that there are different levels of desymbolization, beyond the quantitative segmental and pervasive that appear to be consequential enough to be dimensionalized. And do their criteria reflect different levels of desymbolization? The panic attack examples of primitive concreteness and allegedly unmentalized tension states in the visceral, somatic, physiologic, and motoric images may deserve separate subcategorizing, since they may account for unique variance to the results. The panic attack data may be seen as reflecting a level of regression that goes beyond the therapy session material Freedman and his associates have been considering, and is more like the data derived from eating disordered patients. I agree with Freedman and colleagues' (2000) decision to include, under perceptual concreteness, a separate subcategory for somatic, visceral, physiologic imagery. This is consistent with the view that not all desymbolization is associated with annihilation anxieties, but that relevant markers are useful. Somatic imagery suggests a tendency to resomatization, which has been seen as an unfailing accompaniment of a traumatic situation (Schur 1971).

To underscore the extent of the regressive, desymbolized mode in the above example, I now include a description by another patient of an experience that would also score high for annihilation anxiety content, but that is formulated on a higher level of symbolization.

> I fear at any moment that my life will become a catastrophe. I feel I will explode because I can't contain the turmoil. If I take a risk, something bad will happen to me. When the catastrophe happens, it will destroy me because I can't overcome it. I will become so emotionally overwhelmed, they will have to commit me. Everything with me is life and death, I don't know why. When I tell myself all the rational things to calm my fears, it does not help. It even makes me feel I'm going insane, because I *think* one way and *feel* another.

This anxiety-laden statement, while focused on survival issues and the dread of being overwhelmed, does not centrally reflect desymbolized processes, as did the panic attack protocol. Also, while the patient anticipates catastrophe, the anxiety accompanying her report is controlled anxiety, and indicators of ego function regression are limited. In the panic attack report, there was evidence for uncontrolled anxiety, and signs of ego function regression were substantial.

In the panic attack report, we saw repetitive somatic, visceral, and physiologic imagery, and the body was used to express feelings in a concretized form. In this second anxiety sample, the material is more consistent with an incipient level of symbolization, where feelings are expressed in a verbal mode, and there is a sense of an internal life that is differentiated from physiological arousal. There is an awareness of conflict, which implies the presence of symbolic functioning. Additionally, there is an "as if" quality to the narrative, and a sense of cause and effect among events. One indicator that this narrative falls short of the discursive level is the absence of an interpersonal component.

In these two clinical samples, annihilation anxieties are central. But the levels of symbolization and desymbolization contrast sharply. This underscores the earlier stated proposition that annihilation anxieties can be found in conjunction with different levels of personality functioning, and with different degrees of controlled and uncontrolled anxieties.

SOME HYPOTHESES RELATING DESYMBOLIZATION TO ANNIHILATION ANXIETIES

When desymbolization involves the effort to eject meaning and to curb elaboration, it is often to reflect a defensive effort against unbearable (annihilation) anxiety. Freedman and colleagues (1999b) point out that the purging anorectic is displaying a defensive need to expel. I add two more specific hypotheses in this regard: the need to expel is sometimes related to fears of penetration, or the wish/fear of merger, via ejecting the food-mother. Freedman also relates desymbolization to alexithymia. We have empirical evidence that alexithymia is correlated with annihilation anxieties (Hoffer et al. 2002).

Freedman and colleagues (1999b) note that both segmental and pervasive desymbolizers defensively expel meaning and limit elaboration. These authors distinguish segmental desymbolizers from pervasive ones in that the former are able, for example, to pause in a moment of blankness following the expulsion of meaning, to allow sadness. The pervasive desymbolizers, on the other hand, can allow no mental space. The paradox described by the authors that the two kinds of desymbolization are embedded in such different contexts is clarified with the hypothesis that an important aspect of the difference is that between controlled and uncontrolled anxiety and the structural underpinnings in the given case.

I believe that segmental symbolizers have more controlled anxiety, which is associated with greater affect tolerance. In the case of the pervasive desymbolizers, allowing mental space becomes terrifying for some patients because it threatens the relaxing of controls, which the patient fears will lead to intolerable and overwhelming thoughts and images. I also believe that a transformation cycle is facilitated by lowering the level of uncontrolled anxiety, such that the annihilation content is less disruptive, less terrifying, allowing a reversal of ego regression and reinstituting higher levels of ego functioning. Under these conditions, the likelihood of secondary anxiety reactions is decreased. *Desymbolization involves a variable degree of ego regression; the more ego regression is associated with desymbolization, the more likely it will be accompanied by annihilation anxieties.*

REFERENCES

Aragno, A. (1992). *Symbolization: Proposing a Developmental Paradigm for a New Psychoanalytic Theory of Mind.* Madison, CT: International Universities Press.

Bass, A. (1997). The problem of "concreteness." *Psychoanalytic Quarterly* 66:642–682.

Benveniste, P., Papouchis, N., Allen, R., and Hurvich, M. (1997). Rorschach assessment of annihilation anxiety and ego functioning. *Psychoanalytic Psychology* 15:536–566.

Bettelheim, B. (1956). Schizophrenia as a reaction to extreme situations. In *Surviving and Other Essays*. New York: Knopf, 1979.

Bion, W. (1959). Attacks on linking. *International Journal of Psycho-Analysis* 40:308–315.

Bucci, W. (1985). Dual coding: a cognitive model for psychoanalytic research. *Journal of the American Pyschoanalytic Association* 33:571–607.

Diamond, D. (1999). *Attachment disorganization: the reunion of attachment theory and psychoanalysis*. Paper presented at the International Conference: Freud at the threshold of the 21st Century. Sigmund Freud Center, Hebrew University, and the International Psychoanalytic Society, Jerusalem.

Freedman, N. (1985). The concept of transformation in psychoanalysis. *Psychoanalytic Psychology* 2:317–339.

Freedman, N., Berzofsky, M., and DeMichele, A. (1999a). *On transformation cycles: the symbolization of a frozen constellation*. Paper presented at the Annual Meeting, Division 39 of the American Psychological Association, New York, April.

Freedman N., and Karliner, R. (1999). *On incremental symbolization: clinical and empirical definition*. Paper presented at the Annual Meeting, Division 39 of the American Psychological Association, New York, April.

Freedman, N., Karliner R., and Kagan, D. (2000). *Scales of Incremental Symbolization Scoring Manual*. Unpublished manuscript.

Freedman, N., Karliner, R., and Lavender, J. (1999b). *Desymbolization: pervasive and segmental*. Paper presented at the Annual Meeting, Division 39 of the American Psychological Association, New York, April.

Freud, S. (1926). Inhibitions, symptoms and anxiety. *Standard Edition* 20:87–174.

Grumbrich-Simitis, I. (1984). From concretism to metaphor: thoughts on some theoretical and technical aspects of the psychoanalytic work with children of Holocaust survivors. *Psychoanalytic Study of the Child* 39:301–319. New Haven, CT: Yale University Press.

Hoffer, N., Hurvich, M., and Vorus, N. (2002). *Alcohol consumption and annihilation anxieties.* In preparation.

Hurvich, M. (1989). Traumatic moment, basic dangers and annihilation anxiety. *Psychoanalytic Psychology* 6:309–323.

——— (1991). Annihilation anxiety: an introduction. In *Psychoanalytic Reflections*, ed. H. Siegel et al., pp. 135–154. New York: New York University Press.

——— (2000a). Fears of being overwhelmed and psychoanalytic theories of anxiety. *Psychoanalytic Review* 87:615–649.

——— (2000b). *The place of annihilation anxieties in psychoanalytic theory.* Accepted for publication, *Journal of the American Psychoanalytic Association.*

Karon, B. P., and VandenBos, G. R. (1981). *Psychotherapy of Schizophrenia.* New York: Jason Aronson.

Kohut, H. (1977). *The Restoration of the Self.* New York: International Universities Press.

Krystal, H. (1988). *Integration and Self-Healing: Affect–Trauma–Alexithymia.* Hillsdale, NJ: Analytic Press.

Kubie, L. S. (1958). *Neurotic Distortions of the Creative Process.* New York: Noonday Press.

Lifton, R. (1979). *The Broken Connection: On Death and the Continuity of Life.* New York: Basic Books.

Mitrani, J. (1995). Toward an understanding of unmentalized experiences. *Psychoanalytic Quarterly* 64:68–112.

Schur, M. (1953). The ego in anxiety. In *Drives, Affect and Behavior*, ed. R. Lowenstein, pp. 67–103. New York: International Universities Press.

——— (1971). Metapsychological aspects of phobias in adults. In *The Unconscious Today*, ed. M. Kanzer, pp. 97–118. New York: International Universities Press.

Silber, A. (1989). Panic attacks facilitating recall and mastery: implications for psychoanalytic technique. *Journal of the American Psychoanalytic Association* 37:337–364.

Teixeira, M. A. (1984). Annihilation anxiety in schizophrenia: Metaphor or dynamic? *Psychotherapy* 21:377–381.

Tustin, F. (1981). Psychological birth and psychological catastrophe. In *Do I Dare Disturb the Universe?:* A Memorial *to W. R. Bion*, ed. J. Grostein, pp. 181–196. London: Karnac.

16

Survival, Symbolization, and Psychic Space

ALLAN FROSCH

INTRODUCTION

From a particular perspective psychoanalytic theory is elegant in its simplicity. The infant or child, and perhaps fetus, has certain needs and wishes that constitute desires. Depending on how the environment responds to these desires we begin to form certain ideas and expectations of others and ourselves. We develop strategies to maximize pleasure and minimize unpleasure. These expectations, strategies, and desires are organized into an unconscious construction of the world that represents the personal meanings we give to events and actions in the past and present (Schafer 1985). These constructions are organized according to the laws of the primary process and are understood to be affect-laden sensory motor images that are primarily, but not exclusively, visual in nature. Freud referred to these unconscious constructions as "psychic reality" and believed that new editions of psychic reality were reprinted throughout one's life (1912), and in psychopathology the person had a greater investment in psychic reality than in material (i.e., external or "actual") reality (1917).

In the psychoanalytic situation the analyst begins to develop certain ideas about the patient's psychic reality. That is to say, the analyst may believe that a certain pattern of organizing experience imbues the patient's life with a meaning that transcends any particular situation. The analyst's ideas are informed by what the patient brings to the situation and by how the analyst reacts to the patient. In this paper the reciprocal relation between transference and countertransference is referred to as the transference/countertransference matrix. The analyst's ideas about the patient's psychic reality are understood to be compromise formations that reflect conscious/unconscious and symbolized/desymbolized aspects of this matrix.

At particular times and with a reasonable amount of tact and empathy, the analyst offers up these ideas to the patient in the form of an interpretation, hypothesis, or conjecture, depending on one's style and belief system. At certain times these clinical conjectures are offered up as psychic reality unfolds in the heat of the transference. The idea is that with sufficient trust and safety the patient can look at the transference and see past, present, and future in an emotionally meaningful way. This can allow for the possibility of some alteration of psychic reality in terms of a modification of the relationship between wishes (desires) and defenses (strategies), and/or some modification of the emotional investment in psychic reality vs. material reality.

We know only too well, however, that our interventions are not always experienced by patients in a way that has therapeutic value. Sometimes patients can feel overwhelmed when asked to self-reflect, or, alternatively, feel that they understand exactly what the analyst says but this understanding is so devoid of affect that it is meaningless. The person feels the same. We also know from our experience on both sides of the couch, as well as from our research efforts (Freedman et al. 1999b), that over time patients do feel helped by the therapeutic experience, and this feeling of being helped is very much tied to the nature of the therapeutic relationship. How then do we understand the process that goes on between therapist and patient that facilitates the transformation of a meaning structure based on the primary process to one based on the secondary process? This is exactly the kind of transformation we talk about as we move along the continuum of the symbolic process.

The purpose of this paper is to discuss the symbolic process in relation to the therapeutic relationship. It is in the transference/countertransference matrix where issues of psychic survival can play a crucial role in the emergence of a more symbolized therapeutic relationship. The term *psychic survival* refers to the analyst's ability to remain a reliable object in the face of the patient's desymbolized transference. This will be discussed further and illuminated by case material where particular attention is given to the therapist's recognition and working through of countertransference issues as a necessary condition for the emergence of a symbolic process in the patient.

SYMBOLIC PROCESS

The symbolic process is seen as an ego function or general capacity of the mind, which may be used by the primary or secondary process (Rycroft 1956). When the symbolic process is dominated by primary process activity the perceived object (e.g., the analyst) stands for an archaic object but is not well differentiated from it. The affects directed toward the contemporary object are the same as those associated with the archaic one (Segal 1957). In this situation self and object, past and present, and internal and external are not well differentiated. The object does not exist as an independent entity. There is no psychic space between self and other.

When the symbolic process is dominated by secondary process activity the affective charge toward the contemporary object is not the same as it was toward the archaic one. When a substitute in the external world is used as a symbol infused with secondary process activity it can be distinguished from the original object. It stands for the archaic object but is also recognized as an object in itself (cf. Segal, p. 43). There is greater differentiation along all of the dimensions I have just touched upon. In this situation the person can go beyond the immediacy of the moment and begin to view contemporary experience from a number of perspectives. This is not the case when symbolic activity is organized according to the laws of the primary process. In this case the immediacy of the moment is "frozen" so that it cannot be decentered. It can *only* be seen from the person's subjective experience. Rycroft (1956) argues that when the symbolic process is infused with primary process activity the relationship to the object is "fundamentally autistic," whereas symbolic functioning organized around the secondary process leads to "communication, contact and interaction with the external object" (p. 139). This latter kind of symbolic functioning will be referred to as *symbolization*. Symbolic functioning that is organized along the lines of the primary process will be referred to as *desymbolization*. Desymbolization is characterized by a lack of secondary process activity that can be a result of developmental issues and/or a shift away from a more symbolized position. Desymbolization, like symbolization, is considered a compromise formation with multiple functions.

Movement along the continuum of the symbolic process toward a more optimum level of symbolization is marked by a number of transformations in the patient's relationship to the analyst as well as in the level of symbolic functioning. These are best understood as cycles of incremental gains and have been discussed in some detail by Freedman (1994, Freedman et al. 1999, Freedman and Karliner 1999). In this paper I will show the cycles of transformations of fantasy/enactments as they occurred in the treatment of an adolescent boy. These enactments occurred in the fifth and sixth years of David's twice-weekly treatment when he was 12 to 14 years old, and were related to shifts toward a more optimum level of symbolization. The term *fantasy/enactment* refers to the content of the patient's fantasies that sometimes became dramatized between the two of us. That is to say, sometimes I actively participated in the drama. The phrase "a more optimum level of symbolization" refers to a particular use of the therapist by the patient.

CLINICAL MATERIAL

Brief History

David was referred for treatment when he was 8 years old (Frosch 1998) because he was verbally abusive at home and seemed on the edge of losing control physically. He threatened people, had trouble engaging in activities unless he was assured of being the best, and seemed completely distracted in school. David had difficulties with both of his parents, but these difficulties were particularly pronounced in relation to his mother. I saw David as a youngster with narcissistic vulnerabilities related to early, primarily maternal failures. He compensated for these early failures with aggression. In the treatment situation David expressed his anger through a barrage of verbally abusive comments, devaluations, and provocations, as well as physical threats. I felt I had to prepare myself for these onslaughts and I often did not look forward to our sessions. In short, David's behavior and my feeling state reflected what was going on in his family and, to a lesser extent, in school and with friends. Over the years there has been a gradual shift in how David experiences the psychotherapeutic situation, and my experience of it as well. I conceptualize these shifts as consisting of a number of transformations in the transference/countertransference matrix and in David's capacity to utilize secondary process thinking, which is a necessary condition for the emergence of symbolization. The shifts do not follow a clear linear progression. They are part of oscillating cycles that move between desymbolization and symbolization with corresponding affective states of hate and love.

Treatment

When he was 12 years old David told me about a game he was playing on his computer called "The Age of Explorers." The point of the game was to capture a city. David decided to do this by taking control of the surrounding countryside and eliminating the city's food supply. When the people were nearly dead from starvation, David's forces, which were hidden in the city, slaughtered everyone. During this period of time David talked about his own relationship to food. Because his mother often worked late during the week David sometimes cooked for himself at home. He excitedly described the wonderful meals he would make and took great delight in telling me how he had second or third helpings at his school cafeteria. Food has always played a crucial role in David's life and in a previous paper (Frosch 1998) I have discussed David's experiences at his mother's "less than optimal breast" as both fact and metaphor. During the first few years of our work together David viewed me as a decidedly less than optimal breast. I could give him nothing. What I did give him was devalued to the point of turning it into shit, which is how David described it. His whole manner of relating to me was along the lines of an intense power struggle in which David was always in the driver's seat. The content of the fantasy in the "Age of Explorers" game could be seen as a symbolic representation of David's early experiences with his mother. These early memories have been transformed so that now David is the sadist who deprives others of food and then slaughters them. In this sense the sadomasochistic dynamics organized around early feeding experiences with mother were very much active at this time. The feeling tone of the sessions, however, was of a more positive nature and I had the distinct impression that David's pride in telling me his strategy and skill at playing this game was a reflection of a different use of me as a transference object. With David's entrée into puberty and the need to disengage from the archaic mother, I became the symbolic father that David could use in his struggle against the regressive pull of the early maternal object. David's need to turn me into shit and his intense competition organized around issues of castration diminished in intensity and a more positive transference developed.

Over the next few months David began to bring his laptop computer into the sessions and played car-racing games. He wanted me to actively participate and use the computer. He responded to my anxiety about my ability to play these games with a certain amount of contempt and scorn, but also with patience and support. The emotional tone was weighted toward David's being a benevolent teacher.

A more wishful reversal in fantasy between parent and child was now enacted with me.

The use of the computer ushered in a new phase of the transference cycle. Shortly after my hands-on experience with the computer, David began bringing in his CD collection of "Gangsta Rap" music and playing it on the computer. A short time later he brought in a CD player and one set of earphones. David gave me one earphone and he used the other. There we sat with an earphone plugged into one of David's ears and the other plugged into mine. And a common wire joining each of the earphones with the CD player connected us. The CD player eventually gave way to a tape deck, but the common earphone set that joined David and me remained. The shift to the tape deck was significant. Now David could play tapes that he mixed. He told me he wanted to be a DJ and he enthusiastically explained the many technical skills he had learned and was continuing to learn. The earphone enactment represented a very important shift in the transference cycle. The structure of our sessions at this time could be seen as a regressive reenactment of the early mother–child relationship, which was so traumatic for David. A qualifying comment is needed here. If I had been unable to view David's presentation of his music in a less than positive way it could well have led to a replication of the early trauma of the less than optimal breast, now enacted with a contemporary object. Fortunately this was not the case and I was able to view David's presentation in a more symbolic way. My distaste of gangsta rap music very quickly gave way to an appreciation of David's interest in it and his burgeoning technical skills, including his ability to create his own lyrics and, most important, I understood how important it was for David to show me this. I believe a necessary component in David's increased capacity to use symbolization was my own capacity to anchor my reaction (i.e., my distaste) in a secondary process context so that a "working space" (Freedman and Lavender 1997) could be created within me that allowed for a particular kind of focus on the other.

As an infant David nearly fell into the category of a failure-to-thrive child because his mother's milk was not nourishing. As mentioned earlier, I view this as both fact and a metaphor for David's very difficult relationship with his mother, particularly during his early years. In the transference I became a more narcissistically gratifying mother. More accurately, of course, I became a symbol that David could use in the process of working through some of the early trauma. What I am describing is a secondary process context that could facilitate a particular form of thinking called symbolization. It is a repeated observation of analysts interested in the adolescent process that the regressive swings of this period can lead to greater structuralization (what Blos [1979] refers to as the second individuation process) only when these regressions occur in the context of a relatively healthy ego. David had been in therapy for four years at this point and the therapeutic gains complemented the consolidation of ego functioning that characterized his latency period. His ego strength, conceptualized here as the use of secondary process thinking that could support symbolization, served David well. I came to represent aspects of his parents that David could symbolically use to work through early trauma. I believe the preparatory work for this was accomplished during the previous four years of therapy where David often experienced me as a more direct representation of a negatively cathected parental imago. Where David's early years were characterized by a struggle for psychic survival, I felt our early years of working together were characterized by my own struggle for psychic survival in the context of David's rage, and the shifts in my countertransference between relative states of symbolization and desymbolization.

The Wanna-Be-Rapper and the Lyrics of Psychotherapy

David's transformations from "The Age of Explorers" to the earphone enactment can be seen as a series of incremental risks. With each shift he puts more on the line. How will I respond to his desire that I think well of his talents, his interest in "gangsta rap" music, and his wish to be a DJ?

In the fantasy/enactment of the earphones the analytic relationship was characterized by an increased ratio of libido to aggression. Love more than hate. From my side of the dyad I looked forward to my sessions with David and could well remember a time when I did not. From

David's side he often did not want to leave when the time ran out. And he talked more about pressing issues in his life. He spoke of girls—his libidinal interest in them as well as his sadism. David wanted to provoke and humiliate older women as well as girls his own age. Sometimes I could comment on this in terms of his relationship with his mother as well as his relationship with me. In the past David might simply curse me out if I did this, but at this point he usually would not curse or yell at me. At times he would smile and agree. These moments of "interpretive work" were actually few and far between, and the major topic of conversation was David's relationship with Jimmy.

Jimmy was the biggest kid in David's class and clearly the strongest. He was also the leader of a clique that David belonged to. As I understood the relationship between David and Jimmy, the most important thing for David was to be Jimmy's good friend. David was also frightened of passively submitting to Jimmy. On the one hand David wanted to feel protected, loved, and admired by Jimmy, but, on the other hand, he fought with him, sometimes physically, a good deal of the time. This was a not-so-thinly-veiled repetition of the dynamic between David and his father as well as with me. David might call his father at the office two or three times a day to ask some questions about music. At the same time he would denigrate his father's taste in music and aggressively provoke him. With me David would clearly want me to listen to his mixing of music and to recognize and admire the various techniques he had perfected. And just as he often left after the hour was up, he would sometimes announce that he had enough and leave before the hour was over. A barrage of provocations and angry insults often accompanied this. Thus with his father, with me, and with Jimmy, this pattern of moving toward the object and then moving away through aggressive and sometimes sadistic behavior was played out repeatedly.

It was with Jimmy, however, where we could most often talk about these conflicts. When I say talk about them I mean exactly that. We would talk about what went on between David and Jimmy. What I said was informed by my understanding of David's unconscious dynamics. Our conversations took place in the context of my thinking in an interpretive mode. What I would like to emphasize here is that these were my private thoughts that went beyond the immediacy of the moment and, for the most part, they remained private. I found that the closer I could stay to the concrete issues—what happened and who did what to whom—the more the dynamic issues could be represented.

Two factors were clearly associated with the series of fantasy/enactments culminating in the "earphone enactment": (1) there was a clear shift in David's ratio of libido to aggression and (2) there was an increased capacity for David to move beyond the concrete "realities" of the therapeutic situation. Psychotherapy was still something that David consciously did not want to come to. But this feeling did not determine his sense of reality as completely as it had in the past. (See Frosch 1995 for a discussion of the relationship between a person's sense of reality, affects, and archaic thinking.) David came and was eager to talk about things that were going on in his life that had meaning for him. And he wanted to communicate these things to me. Language began to share the stage with action. I thought that David was moving toward a new level of symbolization, a level that Freedman and Karliner (1999) call *discursive symbolization*. He was developing self-awareness in connection to others, a nascent self-reflectiveness in the context of relationships. Incremental gains in symbolization and the complexity of the therapeutic relationship go hand in hand.

Symbolization and Complexity

In the elements of betrayal and sadism that characterized "The Age of Explorers" David may have been repeating what he felt had been done to him while simultaneously expressing the sadistic things he would like to do if the parent–child situation were reversed (cf. Klein 1932). In the earphone enactment David also remembers the early trauma through repetition but this time the compromise formation has been shifted. The wish for a more narcissistically gratifying relationship with mother is represented by the earphones, which join us together. I listen to David. I am tuned into him—after all, we share a common cord. The verbal associations to the fantasy represent David's longings toward his father who, in point of fact, is extremely knowledgeable about music. The movement between "The Age of Explorers" and the earphone enactment may be viewed as an attempt to integrate love and hate. In this sense the cycles of love and hate may be "regarded as an attempt at cure, an endeavor to reconcile the divided Ego—divided by the trauma—with the rest and to unite it into a strong whole that will be fit to cope with the outer world" (Freud 1937, p. 97).

The integration of love and hate has led to a shift in the complexity of David's objects. They are no longer either all good or all bad. David can see the relationship with Jimmy from multiple perspectives. He is better able to decenter himself from the immediacy of the moment and put himself in Jimmy's place. David's transference to Jimmy is tempered by David's secondary process thinking. Jimmy stands for the archaic object, but he is not that object. David can also see Jimmy as a person in his own right. This is also happening in David's transference to me. I am not only the person who forces David to come and, therefore, deprives him of instinctual gratification, that is, of an opportunity to go home, eat, and watch TV. I am beginning to become someone David wants to talk to about things that feel important to him. David has made an incremental gain along the continuum of the symbolic process.

TRANSFORMATIONS: THE MODIFICATION OF TEMPORAL PARAMETERS

In the first year of our work together David played out an elaborate fantasy with Legos where he killed all of his friends and became king of everyone. Two years later David was very interested in drawing super heroes in sessions. In my previous report (1998) I described a particular session with David.

> [T]he session was colored in a distinctly positive, I would say libidinal, tone. David wanted to show me his card collection and clearly valued my interest in it. He was in no hurry to leave the session, and I did not feel a great need to *do* something with the

> material. As the session drew to a close and David collected his things and started to leave, I noticed that he had left his baseball cap on the couch. I mentioned this to him as I picked it up and flipped it to him. He dropped it, picked it up, and left. . . . In the next session he threw a bottle of Wite-Out at me: "Because you threw my baseball cap at me." [pp. 271–272]

This oscillating pattern of sadism and libido has been described in the present paper. A computer replaced Legos and Gangsta-Rap super heroes replaced comic book super heroes. What I would like to emphasize here is the notion that the temporal parameters of these new editions of earlier dynamic representations have been modified. This is most clearly presented in the earphone enactment where David's confidence in the analyst's capacity to survive his sadism allowed David to take greater emotional risks. David talked about his conflicts with Jimmy, his wishes and insecurities with girls, and a variety of other emotionally significant issues. He began to represent his inner world through language and began to stretch the temporal parameters of the cycles of love and hate. That is to say, he spent longer periods of time in a more libidinized transference and his *recovery* from his sadistic attacks toward me was more rapid. It is not that David's aggression disappeared. His aggression was always a part of the ongoing process and would present intermittently in a session or completely color the emotional tone of many sessions. I highlight the word "recovery" because it is often easier to see the therapeutic value of a patient's positive feelings, which do seem associated with a greater capacity for symbolization. My emphasis in this paper, however, is that love and hate both represent necessary aspects of repeating cycles of transformation associated with incremental gains in symbolic functioning.

SYMBOLIZATION AND THE CAPACITY TO USE AN OBJECT

To "use me" in a therapeutic sense, David must recognize me as existing independently of him. In the process that leads to my existence as an independent object, David's sadism is crucial. If I can survive

David's destructiveness, his fantasies as well as his overt behavior, something new is created. Winnicott (1971) puts it as follows: "A new feature thus arrives in the theory of object-relating. The subject says to the object: 'I destroyed you,' and the object is there to receive the communication. From now on the subject says: 'Hullo object!' 'I destroyed you.' 'I love you.' 'You have value for me because of your survival of my destruction of you.'" (p. 90). For Winnicott the patient's destructiveness and the object's survival is crucial to placing the object outside of the self. Winnicott's discussion of the patient's destructiveness focuses on the object's "liability not to survive" (p. 93). Survival in its broadest sense means not to retaliate. However, it also refers to the therapist's overall feelings toward the patient that color the quality of the therapeutic relationship.

Here the question of David's sadism is not how to overcome it through interpretations, which David might (perhaps correctly) see as defensive. Hate and love coexist. Without the hate David cannot love and, ultimately, integrate the two. And I do not survive the hate in any absolute sense. I survive from moment to moment, from session to session. The ongoing quality of the relationship, that is, my attitude toward David and my overt behavior, are indices of survival/nonsurvival. Put into the language of this paper, they are indices of symbolization or desymbolization. Over time the individual moments blend into cycles of transference, which are characterized by a particular event that stands out. The particular eye-catching event should not obscure our view of the similar micropatterns embedded in the daily work. David plays his latest mix and in the middle of a piece he turns the volume up full blast. At this moment the earphone is not in his ear but it is in mine! David and I talk about his work and he tells me that I don't even know what he is talking about. "You're pathetic." And then he goes back to the music and excitedly points out the technical skills that he has developed.

SURVIVAL AND DESYMBOLIZATION

David's desymbolized experience is a communicative act. "I dislike you because you force me to come here, and you tell me I am crazy.

If you say anything to me I will devalue it and you. I negate your therapeutic function. You don't exist. I have killed you off. Are you still alive?" The analytic task here is to remain alive, interested, and in the mode of symbolization. The task is to be able to go beyond the moment and believe that a receptivity to David's sadism will facilitate the potential for transformation. By receptivity I do not refer to a masochistic submission. There must be an acceptance on the analyst's part, however, that David's immersion in this primary process mode of the symbolic process is the only way he can maintain and tolerate the therapeutic relationship at this point. The analyst's receptivity must also include a willingness to carry on the analytic process internally rather than communicate his understanding before the patient is ready to take in new meaning.

One does not forget David or take him lightly. He makes his presence known through his desymbolized experience of the transference. As an infant David was "forgotten." In other words, he may have experienced his mother's less than adequate milk and a variety of other experiences in his early childhood as if he was forgotten, as if he did not exist. David's sadomasochism compensates for this by doing to others what was done to him and by making the kind of impression where he cannot really be forgotten. This is the adaptive aspect of a compromise formation that is easily seen as pathological.

The Analyst's Inner Space

David's aggression in the form of his devaluing comments about me and the time we spent together was an important stimulus for my own self-reflections. Am I, as David so often told me, worthless to him? Is there any value to what we do together? David has spent nearly half his life in psychotherapy with me. How many of my interventions has he actually been able to make use of? Over time I have been able to formulate some idea of how our time has been useful to David. The word "formulate" may be misleading, because this has not been an entirely intellectual process for me. I often feel that I would like to jump up and scream when he turns the volume up and the music feels like it's going to crash through my eardrum. When David pours his potato chips all over the couch and floor I have had fantasies of opening the door and telling him to leave. When he tells me to "shut the fuck up" after I have made what I think is a sensitive and thoughtful intervention, I have wanted to say something equally nasty to David. In retrospect I can recognize that these impulses to do something have been a prelude to my construction of an inner space—a more secondary process level of symbolization in relation to David. In short, David has a profound impact on how I think about myself and how I think about him. At some point this process allows me to sink into the moment with David without worrying what to say or how I can formulate something and offer it up to him. When this happens I believe there is a greater chance that my own unconscious can, so to speak, be inspired by the moment. I speak or I do not speak; I listen to the music and may say something about it, about Jimmy, or about David's latest attempt to provoke his mother into losing her temper.

The Patient's Inner Space

David's need to feel omnipotent through devaluing or controlling me by ridding himself of unwanted parts and attributing them to me is a way of creating a space between us. It is as if David says, "Look here, I provoked you and you did not retaliate. I killed you and you are still alive. You contain me but are not me. I have filled you with these unwanted parts but you do not act like I think I would act if you did this to me. When you act this way it must mean that you love me. Now I can risk having different feelings toward you."

By creating a space between us David can begin to create an inner space. Now something can happen, in the sense that Herzog (1996) uses this phrase. That something has to do with the availability of David's inner world, which can now be presented to me in the form of a verbal narrative. For this something to happen there must be an overlap between David's availability and mine. Neither is static or to be taken as a given. This is the meaning of Winnicott's notion of survival. It is a moment-to-moment proposition. Survival and overlap mean that the analyst must be emotionally present, involved, and willing. His or her feeling state is of critical importance here. It is only then that David can begin to take more emotional risks. This is certainly not a conscious process on David's part. What begins to happen in such a situation is that we have increased the potential for a range of optimal linking of past and present, self and object, symbol and what is symbolized. This optimal linking is called *symbolization* and is marked by a capacity to experience the past in the presence of the other in such a way that the experience itself becomes an object of one's thoughts. The visceral lived-through present is a representation of the past and a template for the future. The present moment can be seen from a variety of perspectives and its emotional coloration is not the same as it was in the past. The new experience is imbued with secondary process activity and is part of a psychic space between the analyst and patient and within the patient as well as the analyst. We have moved toward a dialogue between two symbolizers (Freedman 1988). The cycle of the analytic process has shifted and, at some point, it will shift again in the direction of the primary process level of desymbolization. This is the very nature of the work.

SURVIVAL, SYMBOLIZATION, AND PSYCHIC SPACE: A RECAPITULATION

Although hate and love both represent an investment in the therapist, they are not equivalent. Hate may be a prerequisite to love but it is only through the patient's love for the analyst that a certain kind of investment can be made in reality, that is, in the person of the analyst, that can lead to a broadening of perspectives and a shift in the relationship of wishes and defenses. On the other side of the dyad it is the analyst's commitment to the patient or, as Steingart (1995) puts it, "the analyst's steadfast devotion *only* (italics added) to understanding the analysand's psychic reality" (p. 113) that is at the very center of the therapeutic relationship. This devotion, conceptualized as a working through of action-oriented impulses in the countertransference, is a necessary component for the actualization of David's inner space.

Actualization, rather than construction, may be a more accurate way of approaching the whole issue of psychic space. Actualization means that something is potentially there. This brings the idea of psychic space into the realm of a general ego function—like the symbolic process. They are not independent concepts. It is hard to conceive of one without the other.

Freedman (1998) talks about a relational space or a potential space that is anchored by the therapist's creation of his or her own symbolizing space. I believe this is what I am describing with David. Based on my experience with David I would say that the therapist must do the lion's share of the work that goes into actualizing this relational space. David creates (actualizes) meanings within me and only then is it possible for me to create (actualize) meanings within him. I am describing a reciprocal relationship between patient and therapist that is directly related to incremental gains in symbolization.

INCREMENTAL GAINS, COMPLEXITY, AND THE ACTION OF PSYCHOTHERAPY

David is doing significantly better in all aspects of his life, including our work together. Given the fact that at David's age we would expect an increased capacity for secondary process thinking (Blos 1979), a reasonable question to pose before ending this paper has to do with the efficacy of psychotherapy. Are we seeing advances in symbolic functioning that are part of the developmental process and relatively independent of our psychotherapeutic endeavors? Of course there are major advances in cognitive functioning at David's age. But David has spent nearly half his life in psychotherapy. Psychotherapy is an integral part of the complex system that *is* David's life. We know that duration of therapy is associated with incremental gains in symbolic functioning and in the capacity for a more meaningful psychotherapeutic relationship (Freedman et al. 1999b). In a system composed of many variables in interaction we would expect incremental gains (or small changes) to have potentially profound effects (cf. Moran 1991). The question of whether psychotherapy "caused" the shifts in

David's life implies a linear relationship between cause and effect, which is not the case in complex systems. Something has happened in David's psychotherapy. We have "survived" each other and reached a point where for extended periods of time the work takes on the quality of two symbolizers in dialogue. That this is happening in David's life as well enhances the potential for his continued success. To say that psychotherapy caused these shifts to occur is like saying that David's mother's increased (and now extraordinary) capacity to be a true symbolizer in the presence of her often desymbolized, aggressive, and physically threatening son, caused the shifts in psychotherapy. This argument does not diminish the importance of our psychotherapeutic efforts at all. We hope it gives us pause to think about the complexity of people's lives and the potential for impact that we really do have.

Right before our summer break David missed his last session. I called him and he said, "Oh my God. I forgot. I'm sorry." Here David is able to express an awareness of self in relation to another. That is to say, *I* did this to *you* and *I* have a *feeling* about it. David is able to connect his feeling of being sorry with an action. He is more reflective and can see the event from a different perspective than before. In the past David might have denied that we had a session, or said that I had simply forgotten that we had cancelled. Now he can be less than perfect and not feel obliterated. He can go beyond the immediacy of the moment.

SUMMARY AND CONCLUSIONS

In this paper I have emphasized the therapist's capacity to experience in the transference/countertransference matrix aspects of the patient's feeling states without losing the capacity to remain in a relative state of secondary process symbolization. It is this capacity that is constantly lost and regained throughout the analytic endeavor that can act as an agent that transforms the patient's potential for symbolization into an actuality. A concrete example of this was presented in the nonverbalized internal dialogue of the therapist's sense of worthlessness actualized through David's projective mechanisms. It is the ongoing process of the therapist working through these emotional storms that represents the symbolized countertransference.

As analysts we have certain expectations about our work. We expect to be able to make interpretations and we expect that patients will be able, to a greater or lesser extent, to make use of these interpretations. This is basically how I began this paper. The bulk of the paper, however, has been devoted to a discussion of a patient who, by and large, could not do this for a number of years. David's ability to do this even now is still limited.

Some of the issues around David's capacity to self-reflect are confounded by his age. Although adolescence is a time of movement toward more secondary process thinking, the narcissistic vulnerabilities of this period make it a less than optimal time for self-reflection (A. Freud 1958). I believe it is David's heightened narcissistic vulnerabilities and the accompanying defenses that contribute the lion's share to his desymbolized experience in the transference. These narcissistic difficulties are readily generalized to many of our adult patients whose capacity for self-reflection is also less than optimal. This presents the analyst with a dilemma: How do we continue to feel like analysts if we cannot make interpretations? Are we doing psychoanalysis when the bulk of our work is similar to what I have been describing with David? Even though David is not in an analysis, a variation of these questions play an important role in how I feel about myself and how I feel about David. These issues go to the very core of our work with all patients at one time or another and, for some patients, for an extended period of time.

Freedman (1998) tells us that an expected part of the analytic process consists of the analyst's being (feeling) marginalized and disregarded, and then at some point becoming the focus of the patient's experience. Suppose the analyst does not become the center of the patient's experience? Suppose, in other words, the patient is not able to experience the transference and/or talk about it?

Here I believe the concept of incremental gain is crucial. Using my work with David as an example, I felt less marginalized and better able to be emotionally available to him when I became aware of how a small change could have significant implications. At some point in our work together David could lose a game of "Spit" without throwing the cards at me. Incremental gains in David's capacity for symbolization allow the game of "Spit," or a touch football game, to be a game, rather than a castrating humiliation of his budding manhood. These examples demonstrate the shift in the relationship of wishes and defenses and David's increased investment in reality. His narcissistic vulnerabilities do not have to be so energetically defended through aggressive grandiosity. This allows him to actively place himself in situations where he can be less than perfect and still feel good about himself.

Incremental gains in psychotherapy can have profound consequences in a person's life. In this paper these gains were viewed along the continuum of the symbolic process and David's capacity to form a meaningful relationship with the therapist.

REFERENCES

Blos, P. (1979). The second individuation process of adolescence. In *The Adolescent Passage*, pp. 141–170. Madison, CT: International Universities Press.

Freedman, N. (1994). More on transformation: enactments in psychoanalytic space. In *The Spectrum of Psychoanalysis: Essays in Honor of Martin S. Bergmann*, ed. A. K. Richards and A. D. Richards, pp. 93–110. Madison, CT: International Universities Press,

——— (1998). Psychoanalysis and symbolization: Legacy or heresy? In *The Modern Freudians: Contemporary Psychoanalytic Technique*, ed. C. Ellman, S. Grand, M. Silvan, and S. J. Ellman, pp. 79–97. Northvale, NJ: Jason Aronson.

Freedman, N., Berzofsky, M., and DeMichele, A. (1999a). *On transformation cycles: the symbolization of a frozen constellation*. Paper presented at the Annual Meeting, Division 39 of the American Psychological Association, New York, April.

Freedman, N., Hoffenberg, J., Vorus, N., and Frosch, A. (1999b). The effectiveness of psychoanalytic psychotherapy: the role of treatment duration, frequency of sessions, and the therapeutic relationship. *Journal of the American Psychoanalytic Association* 47:741–772.

Freedman, N., and Karliner, R. (1999). *On incremental symbolization: clinical and empirical definition.* Paper presented at the Annual Meeting, Division 39 of the American Psychological Association, New York, April.

Freedman, N., and Lavender, J. (1997). On receiving the patient's transference: the symbolizing and desymbolizing countertransference. *Journal of the American Psychoanalytic Association* 45:79–103.

Freud, A. (1958). Adolescence. *Psychoanalytic Study of the Child* 13:255–277. New York: International Universities Press.

Freud, S. (1912). The dynamics of transference. *Standard Edition* 12:97–108.

——— (1917). Introductory lectures on psycho-analysis, Part III. *Standard Edition* 16:243–496.

——— (1937). *Moses and Monotheism.* New York: Vantage, 1969.

Frosch, A. (1995). The preconceptual organization of emotion. *Journal of the American Psychoanalytic Association* 43:423–447.

——— (1998). Narcissistic injury and sadomasochistic compensation in a latency-age boy. In *Narcissistic Disorders in Children and Adolescents: Diagnosis and Treatment,* ed. P. Beren, pp. 263–280. Northvale, NJ: Jason Aronson.

Herzog, J. (1996). The therapeutic action of play in the curative process. In *Understanding Therapeutic Action: Psychodynamic Concepts of Cure*, ed. L. Lifson, pp. 187–200. Hillsdale, NJ: Analytic Press.

Klein, M. (1932). *The Psycho-Analysis of Children*, 3rd ed. London: Hogarth.

Moran, M. (1991). Chaos and psychoanalysis: the fluidic nature of mind. *International Review of Psychoanalysis* 18:211–221.

Rycroft, C. (1956). Symbolism and its relationship to the primary and secondary processes. *International Journal of Psycho-Analysis* 37:137–146.

Schafer, R. (1985). The interpretation of psychic reality, developmental influences, and unconscious communication. *Journal of the American Psychoanalytic Association* 33:537–554.

Segal, H. (1957). Notes on symbol formation. *International Journal of Psycho-Analysis* 38:39–44.

Steingart, I. (1995). *A Thing Apart.* Northvale, NJ: Jason Aronson.

Winnicott, D. W. (1971). The use of an object and relating through identification. In *Playing and Reality*, pp. 86–94. London: Routledge.

17

A Mind of One's Own: Some Observations on Disorders of Thinking

SHELDON BACH

Then felt I like some watcher of the skies
When a new planet swims into his ken
Or like stout Cortez when with eagle eyes
He star'd at the Pacific—and all his men
Look'd at each other with a wild surmise—
Silent, upon a peak in Darien.
John Keats, "On First Looking into Chapman's Homer"

I believe that we in the Western world find ourselves in the midst of a change of viewpoint that will become increasingly important in this second millennium and that is bound to affect us in every field of endeavor. For almost a hundred years now we have slowly been coming to understand that we can no longer separate the object we observe, whether an atom, a virus or a patient, from the person doing the observing and the means employed to make that observation. In our own field this has led to a profusion and confusion of theories about intersubjectivity and transference-countertransference that will take decades to think through, understand, and sort out. Just to give one simpleminded example: while thirty years ago I might have ventured a strong opinion when asked to evaluate the analyzability of a patient, today I find this question more difficult to answer without also taking into account who the proposed analyst might be, that is, the total system, including both what the analysand brings to the encounter and what the analyst brings.

In physics this has led to a similar imbroglio, typified by the impassioned debate between Bohr and Einstein, which has produced theories about other worlds and nonlocal action that seem to surpass in fantasticness both science fiction and the fantasies of even our most psychotic patients. The field of medicine is undergoing a corresponding evolution so that our view of disease, typified by the germ theory, is also giving way to a larger field view in which the host and the host's immune functions and mental attitudes become as relevant as the attacking virus or bacteria. Because allopathic medicine and the germ theory have contributed to extraordinary advances in medical care over the past century, the medical establishment tends to emphasize these past successes while ignoring those chronic health problems, including mental health problems, that are less susceptible to this approach. The practical consequence has been the rapid expansion of alternative medicine such that Americans apparently now spend more money on alternative medical services than on allopathic medicine.

Likewise in the humanities and social sciences, this evolutionary change in our thinking has led, in literature, for example, to deconstructive readings that question whether the author is really the authority on the meaning of his text and, indeed, may go so far as to claim that a text has no inherent meaning whatsoever but is simply the container for whatever meanings a particular reader or society chooses to impute.

As we try to grasp the far-reaching implications of these changes both for our field and for others, we sense that there are at least two opposing visions of the world, proponents of each of which have staked their claim to absolute truth at the expense of the other. On the one hand there are those who emphasize subjectivity, relativism, contingency, and the deconstructive mode and who view all situations as mutual coconstructions of the involved participants. To return to my example about analyzability, such people might feel that nothing at all can be said about a patient's analyzability unless we know who the analyst is and the parameters of the analytic situation.

On the other hand there are those who lay claim to realistic, empirical, objective, and so-called scientific observations and who, in the extreme, might claim that any patient can be equally well analyzed by any well-trained analyst, regardless of the degree of fit, the social context, or the analyst's personal peculiarities. While there are many gradations between these two extremes, for convenience I will call the first group, who believe in the mutual coconstruction of reality, the "constructionists," and the second group, who believe in the absolute existence of an independent reality, the "essentialists." In certain ways this controversy historically resembles the nature–nurture controversy, with the constructionists emphasizing nurture and the essentialists emphasizing nature.

At the risk of caricaturing these extreme positions, which not everyone holds, let me remind you of some of the heated debates they have engendered in our own field. Constructionists, for example, because they believe in cocreation, tend to feel that analyzability is primarily a function of the dyad, that mutual enactments and self-disclosures are inevitable and even desirable, that socially instilled values, developmental deficits, and implicit behaviors are fundamental, and that holding, mirroring, and moments of meeting are the primary engines of psychotherapeutic change. Essentialists, on the other hand, feel that one can say a great deal about analyzablity apart from the therapist because the pathology is structurally inherent in the patient. They tend to believe that enactments should be interpreted and self-disclosure avoided, that endogenous drives and conflicts take precedence over deficits, and that the primary or even the sole engine of psychotherapeutic change is verbal interpretation, and especially transference interpretation.

While I find myself at neither of these extremes, I do believe that eventually most of this will probably sort itself out with the adoption of a larger point of view that may synthesize both positions and incorporate ways of thinking about thinking that are more sophisticated than we are able even to imagine at this time in our history.

Now patients, whose conflicts often resemble those of philosophers, can also be either constructionists or essentialists; that is, they can feel that their thinking and sense of self are completely field dependent and relative to the people and context they find themselves in, or they can feel that their thinking and sense of self are completely field independent, an essential truth that depends not on context or other people but on some innate sense of reality. Bearing all of this in mind, I want to show you how these issues affect our clinical work by telling you of some experiences I've had in the past several years working with patients who complain that they have difficulties with thinking.

In former times, of course, difficulties in thinking were categorized as thought disorders and were labeled as one of the primary symptoms of the schizophrenias or psychoses. Later on, under the influence of David Rappaport and the psychological testing movement, it became clear that each and every personality category implied a specific and idiosyncratic way of thinking, so that one might categorize a hysterical thinking disorder, an obsessive kind of thinking disorder, or even a narcissistic thinking disorder. Indeed, diagnostic psychological testing is based on the assumption that the psychologist, using tests, will be able to pick up and specify the particular kind of thinking disorder that is characteristic of each diagnostic syndrome.

But in the changed intellectual climate of this second millennium, we have come to understand in a profounder way not only that the observer and the observed are part of one system but that the mind and the body are also one, so that any thinking disorder is also a disorder of the chemical environment and the synaptic architecture of the brain; that is, a thinking disorder is by definition also a brain disorder, and vice versa. The artificial distinction that we have maintained for so long between thinking, emotions, and bodily regulating functions is no longer viable, and it makes more sense to see even such apparently disparate professions as neurosurgery, psychopharmacology, psychotherapy, and parenting as all engaged in related efforts to alter brain functioning by direct or indirect interventions that will ultimately change the neurohormonal environment and the brain architecture.

In a similar way, whether the patient complains of a disorder in thinking, such as obsessive thoughts, or a disorder of emotions, such as self-esteem fluctuations or mood irregularities, or even a disorder of bodily functioning, such as the irregular breathing of panic attacks or parasthesias or a paralyzed limb, he is complaining of a disorder in self-regulation of body or mind or feelings, and we understand that to influence the one is to influence all the others because they are in effect different parts of one and the same system.

Thus thinking and brain disorders may be initiated by apparently endogenous internal events such as the genetic endowment, the hormonal surges of adolescence, menopause, or a stroke, or apparently exogenous environmental events such as negligent parenting, traumatic shocks, or even a sharp decline in the stock market. Fortunately, there is now considerable evidence that the chemical and structural changes of a brain disorder, which may sometimes be reversed or modified by the direct intervention of neurosurgery or psychopharmacology, can also be reversed or modified by certain kinds of talking and social contact; that is, that psychotherapy can change brain chemistry and brain architecture just as psychopharmacology and psychosurgery can, but perhaps in different ways and often with fewer side effects.

What I am maintaining is that thought, emotions, and the body that contains them are all different aspects of an interrelated system. Thus, if you consistently respond to your infant child with a frozen face every time she smiles at you, you may eventually induce in her not only a deviant emotional development but also a deviant thought development and a deviant brain development. To the extent that these developments are reversible, they may be changed either through early intervention in the dyad by teaching the parent to respond more appropriately, or through later psychotherapy, psychopharmacology, or perhaps yet unimagined interventions, although each modality may produce different kinds of changes.

What I want to discuss are some general principles involved in reversing or modifying such an early induced thought, brain, body, and emotional disorder in adults. While this may seem like a tall order when conceptualized in this way, it is really nothing more than some therapists have been doing all along, just as Molière's bourgeois gentleman was amazed to discover that he had been talking prose all of his life.

Let me descend from the heights of theory to give you a simple clinical example.

A patient of mine named Bob once casually mentioned that as an adolescent whenever he borrowed the family car his father insisted that he never move the seat adjustment. Since the father at that time was a good head taller than Bob, Bob learned to drive while barely able to see over the hood of the car and he continued to drive like that for many years. Naturally, this story is emblematic of the many ways in which Bob's father couldn't really allow his son to be in the driver's seat or to be different from himself in thought, feeling, or even bodily configuration, and this zero tolerance for differences resulted in distortions of Bob's own life in all of these areas. In fact, it wasn't until Bob was in analysis and his wife remarked on his peculiar way of driving that this distortion became conscious and Bob was finally able to adjust his seat to fit his own bodily dimensions. I will later give some examples of how Bob's position of being scrunched down in his driver's seat was also a model for how he was scrunched down in both his emotional life and in his thinking. Most of this had been completely out of Bob's awareness before he came into analysis, and yet, constructive forces were also unconsciously at work trying to undo some of these constraints.

It turned out that for a long time Bob had been a devotee of a particular form of yoga that emphasized unrestricted breathing and stretching and that he had become quite expert at it. I took this to be an unconscious attempt on the part of his body-mind to counteract the constrictions of the scrunched-down position his father had imposed on him and to which he had acquiesced in one way, but struggled against in another. From Bob's point of view he learned to drive in the same way he had learned so many other things, by going along with the family system. An outside observer might have thought that he seemed strangely compliant to a rather unusual demand, but it might have taken a psychoanalyst to note the life-affirming rebellion inherent in his practice of yoga. This is a simple example of an observation that has so often amazed me: that the mind and body work together in attempts to self-regulate the system and that the analyst can note this and encourage it without violating parameters if he can only find a larger perspective from which to view the patient's dilemma.

Finding a larger perspective is, of course, not easy, particularly since so many different schools of analysis proclaim that their own perspective is the only truth. Experience suggests that what patients talk about is highly correlated with what they think interests the analyst, so that Freudian patients feel they should talk about sex and aggression, Jungian patients feel they should talk about symbolism and religion, and Kleinian patients see their projections and reparations as the essentials of psychic life. Meanwhile, some of the research suggests that a major factor for therapeutic success is the warmth and availability of the therapist and the congruence of the therapeutic couple, regardless of what theories the therapist or patient might hold. Other research insists on the importance of frequency and continuity, as well as on the ability of the therapy to promote self-observation. Of course, all of these apparent disparities make more sense from a systems perspective, and to me they make particular sense if we view the therapeutic dyad as a reworking of the original dyad in which the continuing goal of each participant was to understand how the mind and the body of the other person really worked.

From one perspective, good parenting, as well as good therapy, entails a lively interest in how one's own mind and body work, *both separate from and in conjunction with the mind and body of another person*, and often the fewer preconceptions that we bring to the task, the better it goes. Both parenting and therapy are good examples of on-the-job-learning, where some preparation may be helpful but can never substitute for the real thing. So mother and baby, when facing each other for the first time, are both novices at this particular dyad and indeed, the infant, unencumbered by theory, is often a much faster learner than the mother.

We know that the mother is trying to find out how the baby works: how and when it wants to eat, sleep, and eliminate and what it thinks and feels about her ministrations. And the baby is equally trying to find out the complementary information about the mother, and to somehow balance out this information about what the mother wants with its own often uncontrollable urges of hunger, fatigue, and the other endogenous forces that drive it on. The mother, too, is struggling against her own endogenous forces: her fatigue, her shifting hormones, or perhaps her resentment against her husband or against a hated sibling with whom she might identify the baby. Thus, from the beginning, the learning situation is disturbed by dark unconscious and preconscious forces that both participants bring to the drama and that complicate it immensely.

Bob's scrunched-down position driving his father's car was emblematic of the distortions the field had induced in both his mental and bodily functioning. But it turned out that Bob's acquiescence to the Procrustean bed his father had laid for him meant even more than a surrender to his oedipal fear or guilt. Up until this point, about a year into analysis, I had formed only a vague picture of Bob's mother, until one day, when complaining about his confusion and difficulties in thinking at work, he casually mentioned that as a child he could never find the forks for dinner. I asked, "What do you mean, never find the forks?"

"Oh, you know, there wouldn't be any forks and I would ask Mom where they were and she would say 'Go look in the drawer.'"

"And so . . ."

"Well, the drawers would be all messed up and I couldn't find the forks . . ."

"How do you mean, all messed up?"

"You know, old rubber bands and paper clips and recipes and all kinds of stuff you had to look through to find the forks . . ."

"You mean the silverware wasn't organized in some kind of way?"

"No, everything was just thrown in the drawer . . . I was surprised when my wife insisted on buying a special holder to put the silverware in. That was the first time I had ever seen such a thing. . . ."

By now, of course, it had dawned on me that we were somehow talking about the internal organization of Bob's mother's mind and, by extension, of his own mind, and about his own confusion and difficulties with thinking. It would take many months before this became clear to Bob and many years of work before he could rearrange the configuration of his own mind to make things more logical and easily accessible.

Now of course not every caregiver whose child complains of a thinking difficulty is disorganized in the same way as Bob's mother. Others may appear quite organized in some ways and chaotic in others, and a pattern of erratic or intermittent inattention or disorganization is quite common. But in this case Bob's mother's difficulty in separating her silverware was emblematic of her difficulties with separation in general—with mentally separating from anyone, with taking distance on her own opinions, or with seeing her child as a separate entity.

Children who are not seen as separate entities remain enmeshed in the early dyadic state of consciousness; they have difficulty in seeing themselves or others as separate and at the deepest level *they do not feel entitled to have a life or a mind of their own*. Even when these children are able to *physically* separate they often continue to feel guilty about it, and they find mental separation frightening to achieve.

So whatever the particular state of maternal or familial organization or disorganization, if the child cannot separate himself from it he will be unable to gain any perspective on it. Thus the mother's mental processes and often the family processes remain impenetrable to the child who feels in a continual state of confusion. If Bob's mother had been able to say, "I know the drawer's messy but I'm sure the forks are there somewhere," it would have made all the difference, because this would have meant that she was able to take some perspective on her own behavior and she might then have allowed him some room for his own perspective. But she was unable to view herself reflectively, and therefore unable to allow Bob to see her objectively or to see himself reflectively. Children like this cannot figure out how their caregivers' minds work and consequently cannot understand how their own minds work or, eventually, the minds of other people. Patients whose minds have not been legitimized by their parents feel confused and frantic. One of them, speaking of his mother, said, "She is this dark, brooding, amorphous cloud of secrets. Is she selfish or is she scared? Does she love my father or does she hate him? You just can't tell . . . she'll drive you crazy . . . I don't want to think about her . . . If I think about her then I can't think. . . ."

Thus, many of these patients remain, throughout their lives, consciously or unconsciously obsessed in a very concrete, literal way with questions of epistemology: Do other minds exist? How can you know the mind of another person? Can I trust a person to reveal his mind? How can I tell if he's lying? Am I dealing with a human mind or just a computer simulating a mind? Is my mind human? Am I really alive? Does death really exist? And so forth. These patients live in a constant state of ontological insecurity, which they experienced as infants and which they reexperience in the analytic transference.

This, then, was Bob's dilemma, and it is characteristic for people with disorders of thinking. The patient is confused and anxious about having a mind of his own that exists independent of other people's minds. Sometimes this confusion pervades all areas of life and sometimes only selected areas, depending upon the caregiver's specific deficiencies and prohibitions. Sometimes the patient doesn't know what he's feeling and doesn't even know how to think about what he's feeling. Often he can't describe anything about himself or his family except the facts, so that you don't get a real feeling for the people involved. Being factual about relationships may give the appearance of objectivity, but it may also indicate a repression of the emotional context of events and, often, an actual deficiency in the area of relationships with people and with things.

I recently came across an excellent description of this deficiency in the autobiography of the distinguished British literary critic Sir Frank Kermode (1999), called, interestingly enough, *Not Entitled*. Here he describes how, as a child, he was so totally inadequate in both interpersonal and motor skills that his teachers all believed he was purposely trying to make fun of them and they repeatedly punished him. Let me quote:

> Since nobody any longer can compel me to carve or draw, or even hang a picture straight, it may be supposed that my incapacity became a trifling problem once the pains of childhood humiliation had faded. But it has persisted, and may be related to some of my difficulties in dealing with other people, especially women. I lack what appears to be in others a perfectly ordinary skill or tact in handling not only things but persons. I notice this ability among children in playgrounds and people in pubs; or when somebody draws a sketch map, peels an orange, assumes an attitude obviously correct but not in my repertoire, or embarks on a seduction. They all seem to know what it takes; where and how they found it out is a mystery to me. My lack of qualities so natural to others that they never needed even to congratulate themselves on having them was emphasized by my being a fat boy. . . . [Kermode 1999, p. 54]

Now Kermode's complaint of deficiency in "what appears to be in others a perfectly ordinary skill or tact in handling not only things but persons" has often been noted by psychoanalysts. John Gedo has for years described it as a deficiency in a learned skill, and I myself and the infant researchers have often referred to it as a deficiency of self- and mutual regulation or as a defect in narcissistic equilibrium or procedural knowledge. This has most recently been given extensive attention by the infant researchers in Dan Stern's Boston group (Stern 1998), who label this ability "implicit relational knowing" and connect it with the ongoing preverbal proceedings between mother and infant. Now Kermode, who is a professional intellectual, does not complain of difficulties with thinking, but he does note that the deficiency of skill he describes is profoundly implicated in his rather tenuous relations with both people and things.

It is worth noting that patients who do complain of confusion or difficulties with thinking also often have difficulties with implicit relational knowing and vice versa, if only because you cannot feel implicitly awkward or physically uncomfortable in the presence of people and not have this affect the way you listen, understand, and speak with them. The Stern group suggests that there are two modes of therapeutic action: verbal interpretations acting in the domain of *explicit* knowledge, which can alter conscious or unconscious processes, and what they call relational or behavioral "moments of meeting" where "the *implicit* knowledge of each partner gets altered by creating a new and different intersubjective context between them—the relationship has changed." They believe that "this process requires no interpretation and need not be made verbally explicit" (Stern 1998, p. 302).

But I am trying to suggest that these two domains interpenetrate and are not really separate, or, if they indeed seem separate, that this is a pathological outcome that needs to be understood. For the baby is interested in finding out how his own mind and body work *both in conjunction with and separate from the mind and body of his caregiver*, and the later distinctions that we make between explicit and implicit, conscious and unconscious, verbal and nonverbal, and one-person and two-person are meaningless to him.

Of course, one very important aspect of combining *explicit* representational thinking with *implicit* relational knowing is that this is a fuller way of acknowledging another person's mind. But under good-enough circumstances the child develops both a mind of his own and the ability to accept the mind of another person without surrendering his own mind. And that is why those of us who were lucky enough to have been adequately parented as children can enjoy ontological security as adults without being constantly persecuted by worries about whether we or other people actually do exist, are only pretending, or can really be trusted.

The ontological security that leads to a basic trust in life and trust in the analytic situation (Ellman 1991) is most often disturbed by splitting in the areas that I described: splits between mind and body, between implicit and explicit knowledge, between intersubjective and intrasubjective processes, and so forth. Let me give you a simple example to illustrate what I mean.

During one session Bob recounted a day he spent taking his mother, who had chronic arthritis, to the doctor, and sitting with her while she complained bitterly to the doctor about her pains and also about how her son Bob had repeatedly and persistently neglected her throughout all the years of her illness. Although Bob knew this to be untrue and tried to correct her, his mother never even acknowledged him and he found himself becoming quite upset and even beginning to doubt his own clear memory of the facts. Later, at the end of the day, his mother had turned to him with a winning smile and told him what a lovely day it had been, how much she had enjoyed spending this pleasant time with him, and how much she loved him.

I asked him how he had felt inside and he told me he had been confused, distrustful, angry, and upset, not really knowing what was happening or what to believe—his mother's loving words or the terrible turmoil in his gut. Eventually we established that this had been going on throughout his childhood; at times his mother would praise him to the skies and at other times denigrate or abuse him, and he could never really understand why she did the one rather than the other and he couldn't really believe the praise any more than he could understand the abuse.

Here we have a simple example of discordant reality in which Bob's bodily perceptions of anger and loathing are totally at odds with the loving words he hears coming from his mother's mouth, words that at other times have led to warm and positive emotions. He feels confused because he can't understand why his mother would have been so abusive to him in the presence of the doctor and yet now so loving at the end of the day. Should he believe what she's saying now or what she said then? On top of this confusion about the workings of his mother's mind, he feels confused about the workings of his own mind and body, for he cannot reconcile the loving feelings he sometimes felt when she spoke those words with the violent loathing he now feels as she talks to him. Much later we learned that he was having unconscious fantasies about being physically violated and about mutilating her in return. Consciously, he now becomes uncertain about the actual facts of their relationship, how many times he has visited her in the past month, or whether indeed he had ever done anything to help her or ever really loved her.

Even in this simple example we can see the complexity of the processes involved and we can grasp more clearly the existential confusion of the many patients who have grown up with such parents, who quite literally do not feel sure that their minds and bodies are their own, are functioning properly, or can be relied upon. These patients are often unable to trust their relationships or the analytic situation because in order to trust we must first have some abiding faith in the coherence, constancy, and continuity of our own minds and bodies and the world in which we exist.

If, for example, we were meteorologists and our weather predictions were frequently incorrect, we might doubt either our instruments or our theory, but we would probably still retain our faith in the predictability of the weather. The patients I am describing are convinced from experience that their instruments are faulty; some also feel that their theory is defective, and the most unfortunate have altogether given up hope that the world is predictable at all.

A young woman, who had the misfortune to grow up with a psychotic mother but who through great effort had begun to create a rich and enjoyable life for herself, came in and told me the following story with great excitement. On entering my office yesterday, she had noticed a bag in the closet that belonged to the previous patient who was still in session, and she had the passing thought that the patient would forget her bag when she left. And sure enough! When she left after her own session was done, the other patient's bag was still in the closet and she had forgotten it just as predicted!

For clarity's sake I will omit all the other meanings that this little enactment entailed and focus simply on her great enjoyment at finding that her prediction, or ESP, as she jokingly called it, was accurate. In the course of trying to understand the meaning of this, she described to me a game that she used to play as a child.

"Our windows were on the second floor and I would pull the shade halfway down so I could only see people's feet and lower body and I would watch them walk along and I would imagine some image of the whole person and then when they got close I would pull up the shade and check to see if I was right. That was my favorite game!"

I asked her what that was all about.

"Well, I was desperate to know. I just didn't think I understood all of the multiplicity of things I observed and it was like an exercise in teaching myself to see if I could learn . . . I would make this image of the person and then check to see if I was close to it . . . like a training . . . I wanted always to know, to understand, to make sense of . . . I don't understand that feature in myself."

I said, "Maybe you were trying to make sense out of the disconnected parts of your mother, trying to see if you could get them to match each other or to match your image of reality . . . ?"

She said, "Well, I certainly couldn't make any sense of my mother's irrational rages or her unpredictability. It was continually upsetting to me . . . and I think that there's something about knowing or understanding things that I find very soothing or consoling."

Indeed, this young woman who had been raised in such an unpredictable and largely psychotic environment was absolutely thrilled when she could find or create something logical, organized, and coherent around her and, in fact, she later went on to become a professor of philosophy. But it turned out that her playful attempts to put together the chaotic and fragmented parts of her mother and of her perception of reality were only part of the story.

It seemed that the mother had been engaged in a lifelong effort to destroy her daughter's reality by attacking all the links that could make her life meaningful. Thus all the daughter's attempts to study, to work, or to make other relationships were ridiculed, harassed, and actively interfered with. But the patient herself, until the analysis, had just as actively denied her mother's psychosis and maintained the illusion that she might yet win her mother's love if only she could find the proper way to do so. Hence, by her denial, the patient was also attacking the links in her own thinking that would otherwise have led to the inevitable but frightening conclusion that her mother was crazy. These attacks on linking had resulted in a generalized feeling that she didn't understand people and couldn't figure out what made them tick.

Thus the game she had loved as a child turned out to be not only an attempt to reconstitute the fragmented reality that her mother had bequeathed to her, but also a restitutive attempt to bind together those parts of her own thoughts and objects that she had defensively split apart. Here we may note again the unconscious attempts of the body-mind to heal itself, for just as Bob practiced yoga in order to counteract the constrictions that were imposed upon him, so this little girl played a game trying to rejoin the meaningful links that her mother had torn apart, a process in which she had defensively colluded.

Although I have spent many years working with patients whose parents were thought-disordered and relationally disordered, I have found it uncommon for the patient to broach this or even to be consciously aware of it. More usually, it is in the course of relating some familiar incident that the patient may suddenly realize that what was accepted as ordinary in his family was really quite strange indeed. In this respect the situation reminds me of those puzzle pages one finds in children's magazines that show a large illustration with the question: What's wrong with this picture? Often the analyst's intervention can be confined to a simple question such as: "You mean the silverware wasn't organized in some way?"

Out of such little cracks in the cosmic egg may then emerge a familial world-view or state of consciousness that might have had a totally shattering impact on the child. I recall in this connection a patient who even as a young child was accustomed to waking, dressing, and feeding herself and then trying to awaken her drunken mother before going to school. It came as a great surprise for her to learn, many years later, that other children didn't have to shake their mothers awake but were instead awakened and cared for *by* their mothers. Similarly, another patient, when asked how he got to sleep as a child, insisted that it was just like everyone else. Whenever he happened to feel tired, he went up to his room, turned on the TV, and watched till he fell asleep. When he awoke in the morning, the TV would still be blaring. He was quite surprised to learn that most small children of his background were put to bed by their parents at a regular time, often with a book or a song.

My point is that these disturbances of regulation in the family system often go unrecognized by the child and are usually accompanied by disturbances of implicit relational knowing and of thinking, as well as disturbances of reality testing, because the child is so often enmeshed in the family pathology. So it may take a very long time before a clear and useful representation of the patient's early years can be established, because when the patient fully understands what is wrong with this picture of his childhood he has already emerged from the pathological family state of consciousness in which he had been embedded.

Let me pause here to explain what I mean. Just as individuals have a "normal" state of consciousness and altered states such as intoxication, and just as these states develop in complexity over time, so certain groups can engender mutually shared states of consciousness. The examples that immediately come to mind are mother–infant dyads, couples in love, and jazz combos, but larger groups can also share states of consciousness, for example, symphony orchestras, families, and lynch mobs. Observing the clinical phenomenon of the patient who regresses dramatically when he returns to his family over the holidays, we are witnessing a regressive shift in a state of consciousness, that is, the patient feels pulled back toward the shared state and the old parameters that were the norms in his family. This is especially true if the parents have separation issues and are, like Bob's parents, unable to accept differences. Then the family's way of being becomes the only possible way of being, and the child is faced with threats of abandonment should he try to be different or to grow up and find his own way.

In such cases, although the child cannot *make sense* out of his parents' mental functioning, he learns that any questioning of their attitudes is forbidden and that there is indeed a prohibition on thinking about thinking. This makes it doubly difficult for the child to feel at ease with his own thinking or to achieve reflective self-awareness, unless he is lucky enough to find a book, a friend, or a teacher outside the family who, in one way or another, may raise questions about the premises of the family system. Although this may sometimes happen explicitly, often enough it occurs in an implicit manner as it slowly dawns upon the child that he feels very different being with this neighbor or with that friend's parents than he does being in his own family. As if a miracle has taken place, a brave new world suddenly comes into view.

But in life as well as in therapy, I have found that the child or patient must first be able to recognize what happened and to understand what interfered with his ability to think before he can fully resume the interrupted developmental path and start to resolve the conflicts that this detour has helped him to avoid. Simply to substitute a more benign therapeutic environment for the pathological family environment is a very big step indeed, but without also being able to question even the more benign therapeutic system, the patient will never be able to achieve the evolved self-awareness that will ensure him true independence.

That is why, in matters of technique, I find it especially important with these patients not to conceal my thinking processes from them, but rather to engage in a mutual effort for us both to think together about each other's thinking. I try, whenever possible, to explain the reasoning behind my comments and interpretations and, better yet, I allow the patient to witness my mind at work in the process of free associating or making formulations, so that the interpretation becomes a mutual endeavor and is thereby much improved. It is especially useful for such patients to experience the analyst as he tries to deal with doubt and ambiguity, or as he tries to hold two ideas or two roles in mind at the same time, for it opens the possibility of their doing the same. Most important, because I am implicitly asking my patients to trust me with their minds, I struggle to attain a position where I can trust them with my mind and feel that I have nothing to hide from them.

The feeling that one has a mind of one's own is the complex outcome of a long developmental journey, some disturbances of which I have tried to touch upon. The contradictory elements involved were dramatically underlined for me by a man I once worked with, a professor who, after several years of analysis, revealed his conviction that I used the same paper napkin for each patient all day long. We knew that his psychotic mother had collected burned matches and little pieces of string, but the principal dynamic behind this fantasy was an oceanic state of consciousness that kept him sadomasochistically attached to his mother and to the symbiotic family system. He once told me:

"I feel that the world is seamless, that we're all connected by a sticky ocean of glue, and I can't allow any cracks or ruptures or breaks in this medium which holds us all together."

His mother's death had not ruptured this medium nor had the desertion by his first wife, whom he still continued to support. *Indeed, to help such patients recognize the parental pathology and to separate from it is one of the most difficult clinical problems we face.* Interestingly, this timid-appearing professor was in fact an intrepid mountain climber who sought, by scaling the highest mountains, to place himself in a position where he could identify all the peaks, passes, and mountain chains and to orient himself in relation to them. At this supreme moment he would experience a feeling of well-being and sexual satisfaction and, indeed, when this first occurred at age 11 he had been surprised by a spontaneous sexual orgasm. As it became clearer and clearer that his entire personal and professional life had been one enormous attempt to understand his mother's mind and to separate from her without losing his own mind or destroying hers, he said to me one day:

"You remember how I used to complain that I can't make any judgments, that I don't know where I stand, that I'm dumb? That was a lack of overview, a lack of placement relative to other landmarks. When I'm on top of the mountain, I know that *I'm* exactly here and that *that other mountain* is over there. There's a fantastic pleasure in seeing how it all hangs together, in knowing what is what!"

It was fascinating to observe how this very intelligent man, who had difficulties with both explicit and implicit thinking, began to work his way out of the defensive maternal symbiosis, which he compared to an ocean of glue, by climbing alone to the peak of a mountain from which he could observe the lay of the land and experience his separateness.

Freud, as we know, always maintained that the ego was first and foremost a body ego. And it turns out that thinking, that proudest achievement of our mind, is also coupled to the body so that disorders of thinking are isomorphic with disorders of the body ego, with disorders of the ego's self-regulation, and especially of its boundaries, that is, with the attachment and separation of one body from another.

This wouldn't have surprised the professor, who in some sense had spent his life trying to separate his body from the body of his mother without losing his grounding in the reality that the body of the mother first represents.

It seems that both the philosophers who believe in coconstruction and those who believe in essentialism are, like the rest of us, still trying to deal with the paradox of how it is possible both to be born of someone's flesh and yet to be separate from her, or how it is possible both to live in one's own experience and yet also to observe oneself from the outside.

I hope that in this paper I have opened some perspectives on the varieties of disturbed thinking and how we can deal with them in ourselves and in our patients. It was a great honor to be asked to contribute something to this *festschrift* for Dr. Norbert Freedman who, in the course of our long association together, has opened up so many new perspectives for me.

REFERENCES

Ellman, S. (1991). *Freud's Technique Papers: A Contemporary Perspective*. Northvale, NJ: Jason Aronson.

Kermode, F. (1999). *Not Entitled*. New York: Farrar, Straus & Giroux.

Stern, D. (1998). The process of therapeutic change involving implicit knowledge: some implications of developmental observations for adult psychotherapy. *Infant Mental Health Journal* 19(3):300–308.

18

Missing in Action: The Enacted Dimension of Analytic Process in a Patient with Traumatic Object Loss

GIL A. KATZ

This paper will present a clinical illustration of the *enacted dimension of analytic process*, a second dimension of analytic treatment that evolves alongside, and in concert with, the verbally symbolized dimension (Katz 1998). Its evolution is a function of the unique, unconscious transference–countertransference fit of each analytic dyad, an outgrowth of the unconscious connection that develops between analyst and patient as the analytic process deepens and unfolds. Within the enacted dimension, without awareness or intent, a patient's enacted transference can activate a countertransference (defined broadly) in the analyst that is experienced by the patient as an actualization of the transference, creating an analytic version of the patient's conflicted object relationship. Such processes, when they become conscious and brought within the verbally symbolized realm, provide valuable experiential insight into core conflicts.

In my 1998 paper the context was standard analytic treatment, treatment characterized by a reliance on verbally symbolized processes as the normative communicative mode and by a relative absence of gross behavioral action. In that paper I attempted to demonstrate that even in such "standard" analytic treatment an ongoing enacted dimension—more than we may have realized or acknowledged—regularly forms an integral part of the treatment process, contributing to its therapeutic action. In the present paper I would like to further illustrate these ideas by describing the treatment process of a patient with a history of traumatic object loss. Analytic treatment of patients with object loss or significant early trauma illustrates the enacted dimension of analytic process with particular clarity, as it often centers around dramatic behaviors that are the manifestations of an elaborately developed, enacted transference (and countertransference) process. Despite the fact that these "enactments," due to their disruptive nature, may occupy the foreground of the treatment process and become its conscious focus, they tend to remain inaccessible to verbal symbolization and unresponsive to interpretative work. The treatment of such patients typically requires an extensive period of time for the trauma to achieve symbolic actualization within the transference–countertransference matrix, during which time patient and analyst may remain unaware of crucial aspects of the re-creative meaning and analytic significance of the patient's (and the analyst's) behavior.

I will describe a segment in the treatment of a 23-year-old man,[1] who, for unpredictable periods of time—weeks, and on one occasion, three months—did not attend his sessions. He never formally stopped his treatment nor did he ever indicate that he would not be coming. Rather, he would simply not show up. Attempts to analyze with him the meaning of his absent behavior had little effect, and at times produced an intensification of the enactment. The absent behavior had its roots in the death of his father, who died while away for six months on business when the patient was 15 years old. Through a splitting of

1. The treatment segment reported is the initial two-year period of a psychoanalytic psychotherapy that enabled the patient to later enter a traditional psychoanalysis. It is not intended as a full case history. This case was first presented at the Division of Psychoanalysis (39) Spring Meeting, New York City, 1993, under the title, "A Death in the Countertransference: A Patient's Unconscious Enactment of Object Loss in the Analytic Relationship" (Katz 1993).

the ego, the loss had been consciously acknowledged but, simultaneously, denied. In the enacted dimension of the treatment, the patient re-created the absence and loss, over time, through an identification with his father as abandoner. An interpenetrating countertransference receptivity allowed the patient's actions to engender within the analyst the patient's disavowed experience of the trauma—the uncertainty and anxiety of waiting, the deprivation and despair of loss, and finally the immutability and finality of death. The analyst's eventual giving up on the patient's return—the culmination of this treatment-long, unconsciously negotiated transference–countertransference process—created an analytic version of the original traumatic death. As the enacted dimension of the treatment was gradually brought within the verbally symbolized realm, the patient began the initial stages of mourning for his father, now more in consciousness instead of action.

CLINICAL VIGNETTE

Jimmy walked into my office two weeks before the anniversary of his father's death eight years earlier. I was to remain unaware of this connection for some time. Jimmy was 15 when his father died, and while he appeared in my office at the age of 23, in many ways he had not aged—he had a chubby, boyish face; his clothes were unkempt; and his manner was halting, shy, and insecure. He carried with him a large cup of soda from which he sipped regularly. While he did mention his father's death during that first consultation session, it was not his primary preoccupation. He came to therapy because he was unemployed and still living with his mother and sister, his girlfriend was breaking up with him, and he suffered from vaguely described symptoms of alienation, depersonalization, and dysphoria. His affect was flat, and he seemed lost and unfocused, a character unformed. He stated that he could come to treatment only once a week because he had little money. I recommended twice a week and offered to see him for a modest fee. He agreed to my recommendation, but overslept and missed our next session, a prelude of what was to come.

Jimmy was a middle child, with an older and younger sister. His father was an architect and contractor who designed and built large housing developments. He was on-site on a long-term project in California when he died of a massive coronary. Jimmy revered his father but was also terrified of his volatile and sadistic temper. He was a stern disciplinarian and ran the household with what Jimmy described as "the strict rule of law." Jimmy longed for his father's pride and love but felt he received derision and criticism from him instead, making him feel inadequate and unworthy. Jimmy's mother was a needy and narcissistic woman who was overprotective and seductive in her attentiveness to her only son, an attitude that intensified after the father's death.

Over the course of the first nine months of treatment, a picture emerged of Jimmy as a young adolescent boy struggling to achieve a secure masculine identification with a father perceived as powerful and dangerous on the one hand, and loved, idealized, and desperately needed on the other. He described his father's temper and the many occasions when he felt criticized and ridiculed by him; and he also described his idolization of his father along with fears of being homosexual. These fears had begun when he developed a dependent relationship with a male mentor at college, although he had never had any conscious homosexual desires or actual experiences. He felt anxious and overwhelmed living with his mother and sister, describing both the seductive pull of his mother's nurturance and sexuality—they watched television together in the evenings on her bed—and his own conflicted and confused feelings. His girlfriend broke up with him shortly after he began treatment because of his dependency on her, and he was unable to decide on a career or get interested in any job. He wanted to become a stand-up comic but could not take any steps to implement the desire. (I must add that he was in no way funny.) He began living an itinerant existence, alternately living at his mother's house and at the homes of friends and relatives until they asked him to move. He was passive and dysphoric, staying up late into the night, overeating, smoking cigarettes, drinking beer, and watching old movies on TV, and then sleeping late into the afternoon, allowing whole days at a time to pass him by.

The transference during this early phase was silent but intense. I gradually became aware that he felt quite afraid of me, attributing to me sadistic and sexual motivations. His own anger and homosexual wishes were rarely brought directly into the treatment. They were instead projected in this fashion, causing him to feel painfully constricted and blocked, often unable to articulate his thoughts. Most important, from the beginning of the treatment Jimmy often came late, missed sessions without calling, paid erratically, and bounced checks. His attitude toward this behavior was one of chagrin, self-blame, and helplessness. He could not understand why he kept doing it or how to change it. His responses to my attempts to interpret the motivation in his behavior were contradictory. At times, he seemed to understand that his actions were provocative, re-creating the relationship with his critical and angry father. At other moments, even within the same hour, he seemed genuinely confused and disoriented, unable to comprehend what I was saying, unable to organize or articulate his thoughts. What did not vary, though, was the behavior. It persisted and intensified, despite my attempts to keep it in the forefront of our work.

Toward the end of the first year Jimmy's debt to me had reached an unmanageable level. He was impulsively spending any money he earned on indulgences and acquisitions—junk food, alcohol, cigarettes, a second-hand car—and he was unable to attend sessions on any consistent basis. I felt that the treatment could no longer be sustained productively as long as his indebtedness continued. I discussed this with him and he appeared to understand and agree with my assessment. We agreed to suspend the treatment until he could repay what he owed.

He did not, however, respond to my bills for several months, and I felt I had to inform him that I might have to pursue legal recourse. This counteraction on my part quickly produced a phone call from him and a desperate plea for my patience. I received a check shortly thereafter. Unbeknownst to me it arrived on the anniversary of his father's death, which was also the anniversary of the start of our work together a year earlier. I received a check from him approximately every other week for three months until his bill was fully paid. I did not hear from him again until the summer, a month later, when he called to ask if he could resume his treatment. We had five appointments scheduled prior to the August break. He missed the last two.

When we resumed in the fall, Jimmy decided on his own to use the couch, and to regulate his finances by paying me after each session. I commented on his effort to be responsible and to safeguard our relationship and agreed to his suggestion, keeping my questions about this procedure on the back burner.

This second phase of the treatment lasted from that September until the following more July. It was characterized by a general, but far from complete, diminution in the frequency of his missing sessions and a greater involvement in the treatment. Over the first several months he attended consistently and paid me regularly. Gradually, he began missing about a session every other week. Over the four months preceding the August break, he missed sessions more frequently, up to half of his appointments, but he paid me his entire debt when he did come.

The content of the sessions during this phase centered more consistently on his relationship with his father and with father-substitutes at work. During his seven-month absence from treatment, he had worked full-time in an established restaurant as a waiter and bartender. He expressed ambivalence about being a waiter, but he was liked by both the owner and the maître d' and was being groomed for a more responsible position. He spoke often of his desires and his confused feelings toward these two men—his need for their approval, his feelings of intimidation, his confusion and inability to assert himself—which led us to various facets of his relationship with his father while growing up.

However, he still found it almost impossible to talk about his feelings or reactions to me. He seemed to understand and benefit from my interventions, yet alternately and even simultaneously seemed to be completely perplexed and disoriented. In addition to his steady employment and the displaced transference arena it provided for our work, there were other improvements in his life. He stopped his drinking and he moved into his own apartment, ceasing his itinerant living arrangements.

Jimmy's depressive symptoms, however, continued unabated—feelings of despair, meaninglessness, suicidal thoughts and fears—along with fears of losing control of what he called "a powerful rage," which he did not understand and could not further articulate. I gradually began to pay more attention to the fact of his father's death and to his apparent incomplete mourning, and to the ways in which this intersected with the adolescent conflicts with his father prior to his death. But attempts to connect his feelings and symptoms to his father's death, while never rejected, did not go anywhere either. Moreover, as these issues began to emerge more in the treatment during the early spring of that year, he began to miss sessions again.

The increasing irregularity of our meetings made it difficult for me to maintain the continuity of the process, but Jimmy, in contrast, seemed to be able to easily pick up where he had left off two or three sessions earlier. I struggled with frustration, with doubts about the viability of the treatment relationship, and with continual technical quandaries about whether and when to call him when he disappeared for two or three sessions at a time, and how to bring this up without engendering an intensification of his absences. I became aware that he was making me wait for him as he had been forced to wait for his father when he was away in California, and was making me feel the frustration of not being able to do anything about it, as he too had no doubt felt. My interpretations along these lines had the same effect as before: he seemed to understand, but his behavior did not change. Indeed, his absences were about to increase exponentially. He did not show up for any of his appointments during the month prior to the August break.

A Dramatic Enactment

I called him toward the end of the month to let him know I would be away. He apologized for not attending his sessions, said that he wanted to come, asked for an extra appointment, then did not show up. After he missed his first session following my return in September I called him again, at which point he once more apologized and assured me he would come next time. He did not come then and I continued to wait, session after session, as three more weeks passed.

It was now late September, almost three months since I had last seen him. I had gradually become less preoccupied with the treatment and with what I should do, although I continued to hold his time. Then one evening as I was closing the office, I was startled to realize that I still had one more patient scheduled—Jimmy. As I reflected on my lapse, I realized that I had given up hope in the treatment. "It's about time," I admonished myself. "This has clearly never been any kind of viable treatment." I decided that I would wait out this last session and then write it off as a failed case. After thirty-five minutes I was about to leave when the doorbell rang. When I went out to the waiting room Jimmy greeted me with a slightly self-conscious but nonetheless warm and familiar "hello." It was as if he had returned from the grave, come back to life. He entered the office, took his place on the couch, and picked up where he had left off.

He was contrite and apologetic about not coming for so long, said he had some of the money he owed me, and asked if it would be okay if he paid me the remainder in installments over the next few weeks. He then went on to consider, without being asked, why he had not come for three months. He stated, in his halting way, that it was perplexing to him because he had thought of coming all the time, planned on it every evening prior to a session, but never seemed to be able to make it. I was stunned to hear this as I had so irrevocably lost all sense that there was any connection at all remaining between us. He asked how long it had been. He reflected on the time period of three months and said, "Now that I'm thinking about it, three months was how long it was between the last time I saw my father and when he died." As I continued to listen in amazed silence, he went on to inform me, for the first time, that his father had been away for a total of six months. He had left for California in September, Jimmy visited him three months later over Christmas, and he died three months after that in March. There had been two three-month absences. Jimmy then reflected on the fact that it was now the end of September, the time of year his father had first left him. Aware now of the induced source of my countertransference experience of having given him up for dead,

I commented to him that he returned on this day to undo his father's departure, and that perhaps he had not come for three months to recreate his father's absence and that he returned to undo his father's death. I also commented on how he "thought of coming all the time." I told him that it was quite striking—and quite meaningful—that despite our not seeing each other for so long, his experience of our relationship did not change, that despite the fact that he did not come or call, he never doubted that I would be here waiting for him. He nodded his agreement, and so ended our ten-minute reunion.

Jimmy did not come for his next session. In the following session, he stated, with much difficulty, that he was angry at me. He was angry, first, because I did not seem to sufficiently appreciate his efforts at setting up a payment schedule—he had wanted more approval and support from me; second, because I seemed not to have known that his father had been away for six months—it didn't seem possible that he had never told me; and third, because of my comment about his never doubting I would hold the time for him—he experienced this comment to mean that I might not have held the time and that I had doubted his commitment. I commented that he seemed to fear that, in one way or another, I would not be available to him, that I would fail him in some way or abandon his treatment. He agreed, comparing it to the time the treatment had been suspended, in his words: "the time you kicked me out for six months." He described how hard that period of time had been for him, how painful it felt to be "cut off" that way. I asked him about the "six months," since the time period had been closer to eight months, and he again associated to the six month period when his father was away. I commented on how powerful and important his relationship with his father had been during that six-month period, how intact and vivid it was in his mind then and now, and how present it had always been with us in the treatment.

Aftermath

In the phase of the treatment following the time the enacted process became conscious, about a year, Jimmy still did not come regularly to his sessions, sometimes not showing up for weeks at a time, sometimes showing up twenty or thirty minutes late for the session. During the periods of waiting, I continued to struggle with the countertransference fantasies of abandonment and loss, although my greater understanding of Jimmy's need for this enactment, and my own reactions to it, made it easier to sustain faith in the presence of an ongoing and meaningful treatment relationship. In the sessions Jimmy did attend, memories of his father's death and its psychological sequelae emerged, and his life outside the sessions steadily improved.

On sporadic and discontinuous occasions, Jimmy described his sense of abandonment when he missed sessions. He imagined that, like his father, I, too, must feel critical of him for owing me money and that I should kick him out of treatment, "cut him off," as his father had done by taking leave of him. At the same time, he felt his father still owed him and that he should not have to pay for a father now. Other poignant enactments became verbally accessible: he mentioned that on his way to work now he often drove out of his way to pass through the housing developments that his father had built. He would park his car and sit looking for people he had known through his father. I commented on his efforts to keep his father alive and with him. In a later session, he told me of a time he had come late for our appointment and sat in his parked car across the street from my office for the duration of the session, looking at the light shining in my window. I likened this to his vigils in the housing developments, and asked him if he ever visited his father's grave. He said he had not been there since the funeral.

Midway through this year, after an absence of nearly a month, he called to say he wanted to "get back into the swing of things," pay me what he owed me, and that he would attend his next session. Two days later my own father died. I called him and told him that there had been a death in my family and that I would not be in the office for the week. With emotion in his voice he said, "I'm very sorry to hear the news. I hope you're all right—as well as anybody could be under the circumstances." I was struck by the immediate connection he made with me, in such contrast to his usual halting, frightened, and blocked manner. I called after the week to confirm our next appointment, but Jimmy did not come for another two weeks.

When he did return, he stated that he felt like a liar for being in therapy but not coming. I suggested that perhaps he felt that I was the liar. I was his therapist, but I was unavailable to him for a week. He repeated his concern about the death in my family. He imagined it had been my father, and feared I would not be able to deal with my patients and would cut him off as a result. He worried whether his expression of consolation had been appropriate; he wanted to convey how much he felt for my loss. I told him that what he had conveyed had been heartfelt, and that he seemed to understand something about loss very deeply. After a pause, he went on to say that he had been doing better—he had given up smoking, lost weight, and was becoming more confident at work—and that he had been able to think about his father with more love and with less anger. At the session's conclusion, he paid me and said, again with more feeling than usual, "Thanks for being patient and for letting me be a patient."

Over the next several months, Jimmy was able to carve out a position as wine steward at the restaurant, and to free up time for a social life. He also felt more assertive in his interactions with his mother. His grandfather died, his father's father, arousing his ambivalent feelings toward both paternal figures. He received a financial inheritance, which he felt was a direct line from his grandfather through his father to him, but receiving money rather than love and support also made him angry. He related this to his unexpressed anger about wanting more from me, and yet was also able to express gratitude that I had not given up on him.

DISCUSSION

I will first describe the elaborately developed enacted dimension of this patient's transference—how his object loss was enactively symbolized in the treatment. I will then describe the process by which this dimension of the transference gradually came to be integrated within the verbal dimension of the treatment. I will show how an unconscious, enacted countertransference process inadvertently intertwined with the patient's enacted transference to form a therapeutically necessary analytic version of the trauma, an experience that made possible the emotionally based, experiential insight (see Chused 1991, 1996, Jacobs 1991, 1993, 1997, Steingart 1995) necessary for a resumption of psychological growth. I will conclude with some comments about enacted processes and analytic technique.

The Enacted Dimension of Jimmy's Transference

The process of mourning is a most difficult one, a process that even under the most favorable conditions is perhaps never fully completed (Freud 1917). When the task of mourning must be accomplished by an immature ego, one that is still dependent on the object, the task may be nearly insurmountable and may take a long, circuitous route (see A. Freud 1958, Jacobson 1961, 1964, Lampl-de Groot 1960, Wolfenstein 1966, 1969).

Jimmy's father died at a crucial time in his adolescent development, at a time in his life when positive and negative oedipal issues were active, a time when his developmental need to have a father was vital (Blos 1979). As an adolescent who had not yet consolidated his identification with his father, he lacked sufficient superego structuralization to do without the external presence of his father (Deutsch 1937, Laufer 1966). As a result, he was unable to accept the death and mourn his father's loss, remaining in many respects a 15-year-old boy, arrested in his psychological development in the midst of an unresolved negative oedipal struggle (see Altschul 1968, Fleming and Altschul 1963). Many of Jimmy's presenting symptoms reflected this arrest: his frozen affect, his stunted level of object relations, and his infantile ego ideal that resulted in pervasive vocational indecision, lack of initiative, and aimless dysphoria.

Jimmy's pathological solution to his dilemma was to deny his father's death, altering his ego's perception of reality along the lines described by Freud in his discussions of fetishism (1927, 1940a,b), a process wherein he maintained *both* contradictory beliefs simultaneously, the beliefs that his father was both alive and dead (see Altschul 1968, Blum 1983, Fleming and Altschul 1963). In the treatment, this split was evident in the erratic nature of his ego functioning within any given session: the way he could talk poignantly and thoughtfully about his father at one moment, and then seem detached and perplexed an instant later; and also the way he reacted to his behavioral enactments as if they were being done by someone else. Attempts on my part to connect his distress and his enactments with his loss were accepted only in one sector of his ego, that sector that contained intellectual knowledge of his father's death, but then were immediately denied in the other, more powerful sector of his ego, that sector upon which he acted and lived out his life.

When the inability to mourn a death results in such denial, ego splitting, and developmental arrest, the experience of the trauma does not get encoded into representational memory but is encoded instead on the sensorimotor level (what Dowling [1982] referred to as "motor recognitions") or in primitive forms of enacted behavior and enactive language (Busch 1989, 1995, Loewald 1975), where it continues to organize psychic life side by side with higher forms of symbolic functioning. Bereaved individuals will tend to support the denied reality by living out circumscribed segments of their lives as if the love object were not dead. When they come for treatment, they re-create aspects of their unmourned trauma in the enacted dimension of the treatment, regardless of whether or not they talk directly about the death.

The enacted dimension of Jimmy's transference served to maintain the denial of his father's death and to reestablish the six-month relationship-in-fantasy that preceded his father's death. His behavioral enactments—missing sessions and then showing up again, disappearing and reappearing—sustained and actualized an ongoing unconscious fantasy that his father was absent but still alive, transforming the treatment process and its participants into a living memorial of his unmourned trauma. Specifically, I will elucidate the latent meaning of

Jimmy's behavior in terms of the following: (1) denying time, (2) alterations in identity, (3) reversing the trauma, and (4) undoing the trauma.

Denying Time

When Jimmy's father died, the movement of time became dangerous. To be aware of time meant to acknowledge the end of waiting for his father, to acknowledge his death. Holding time still, on the other hand, meant he could remain waiting for a father who might return. So Jimmy stopped the clock and put his psychological growth, and indeed his whole life, on hold. He tried to reverse time—sleeping during the day and staying up through the night—in an effort to reverse the trauma. He was unable to adapt to the conventional demands of time such as maintaining a schedule or keeping appointments. No appointments kept, no date with death. He stayed up all night watching old movies on TV, involved in "reruns" of earlier times in his life.

Thus, in the treatment, each absence represented a retreat in time to the relationship he had with his father in fantasy during the six-month absence—a "waiting relationship" with an absent but, most important, a still living object. As it had been with this relationship-in-fantasy with his father, his relationship with me was most intense and most safe when he was *not* in sessions, when it remained a fantasy in his mind. Thus, after having been away for a long period, he was able to easily pick up where he left off because in *his* psychic reality, time had stood still and we had never really been apart. In *his* mind, we were alive and well and together. It was only I, keeping one eye on the external structure of the treatment, who experienced absence and the reality of time passing when we did not meet.

Put another way, Jimmy stayed away from his sessions because he could not yet tolerate his transference to me as the father of his adolescence who would die. The danger of abandonment and death was too real and imminent. Every vacation, every holiday, every weekend was a death waiting to happen. By absenting himself from treatment he could avoid a relationship with me that would, by definition, move forward in time, and therefore ultimately, in his mind, eventuate in death.

Alterations in Identity

Many facets of Jimmy's identity became concrete embodiments of preserving the pre-death "waiting relationship" with his father. Having been forced to "wait" for his father, in anger and unrequited longing, Jimmy became a "waiter" by profession. He "waited" in the restaurant, in boredom, impatience, and anger, on the chance that his father would reappear, establishing relationships with the "regulars," the ones who did come back. Unable to experience the loss of his father, Jimmy not only became one of those individuals who continually misplace or lose their belongings (A. Freud 1967), unconsciously repeating the loss, he became, from that moment on, the personification of loss: he became a "loser," a young man unable to accomplish anything with his life, stuck in a "loser" job, waiting on tables. And he became a "lost soul," lonely, alone, and unable to feel emotionally whole.

Reversing the Trauma

Jimmy sustained his fantasy of a relationship with an absent but living father by reversing the passively experienced trauma and identifying in action with his father, becoming reunited with him in the act of abandoning and depriving. As his father had abandoned him, so he abandoned me; as his father had deprived him of a needed relationship and an object for identification, so he deprived me by not allowing me to work and by not paying his bills. This "identification with the doer" (Segel 1969) enabled him to re-create the trauma but avoid the suffering of being abandoned and deprived himself. His actions engendered in me his own disavowed experience of the waiting that eventuated in death. He turned me into the "waiter" and the "loser," and I experienced the same questions, doubts, and feelings about Jimmy and our work together as he had no doubt experienced toward his father and their relationship: Did I have a patient? Was this a treatment? Was he coming back? Was the treatment over? Had it died? On an unconscious level, in the treatment's enacted dimension, he was testing the safety of the process and my capacity to endure his trauma. "Can you tolerate absence? Can you tolerate interminable waiting? Can you tolerate death?" he was challenging. "If you can, perhaps I will be able to risk the pain of it also."

Undoing the Trauma

Jimmy's enactment also actualized his fantasy of a reunion with his lost father. Throughout the treatment, in addition to missing sessions, Jimmy was repeatedly *returning* to sessions, his attempt to cheat death of its victory. Identifying with the aggressor and absenting himself from his sessions was an act of revenge and hostility; returning and reappearing was an act of reparation, restoration, and renewal. It was as if we were playing hide-and-seek, or an elaborate game of peek-a-boo (Frankiel 1993). "Look," his absences were saying to me, "I am away and gone like my father, you can't get anything from me now"; but then, unexpectedly reappearing, he would add, "Peek-a-boo! Here I am."

From Enacted Symbolization to Verbal Symbolization

I will now focus on that day I so irrevocably gave up on Jimmy's return and he in turn reappeared. Although transference fantasies (and countertransference fantasies, as I will presently describe) were being actualized from the treatment's inception, it was on that day that they finally became conscious in a way that allowed them to be symbolized on the verbal level. That day's dramatic events signified that an important shift *had already taken place* in Jimmy's intrapsychic balance—from the denial of his father's death toward its acceptance, from enacted symbolization toward verbal symbolization. As is often the case (see Katz 1998), dramatic behavioral enactments, as distinct from the underlying unconscious fantasies being actualized, are "lagging indicators" of psychic change that has forged ahead of both the patient's and the analyst's awareness. They are a wake-up call that summons the analyst to recognize that the enacted and verbally symbolized dimensions of the treatment are ready for integration.

All through the early phase of this treatment, although it was not recognizable at the time, Jimmy's abandoning and depriving behavior had actually been proceeding beyond the actualization of his fantasy that his father was absent but alive, toward the actualization of the very trauma he was trying to deny—his father's death. Through increasingly longer periods of absence, he was coming ever closer to letting the treatment die.

Over the same period of time, I was involved in an anticipatory mourning process for my own ambivalently held father who was in the advanced stages of Alzheimer's disease. In a sense, my father too was both dead and alive: present in body but absent in mind. This idiosyncratic parallel led to a countertransference disposition to the patient's unconscious fantasy, and an availability to be enlisted in his playing out of this fantasy. That is, I may well have been, in my unconscious identification with him, inclined to wait for Jimmy when he was absent in order to deny the impending loss of my own father. Or, from another viewpoint, I may have been reluctant to let go of Jimmy and become the depriving and abandoning father. Without being fully aware of it, the interpenetration of this countertransference disposition (connected as well to other issues at deeper levels) with Jimmy's transference press—what Sandler (1976) termed the analyst's role-responsive countertransference, what Tower (1956) called a countertransference structure, and what Boesky (1990) calls an unconsciously negotiated resistance—had made me increasingly able to tolerate the idea, far longer than I typically would have, that absence and waiting could be part of a viable relationship.

Within the enacted dimension of the treatment created by this shared[2] unconscious fantasy of denying death, Jimmy extended his absence toward the symbolic three-month time period, just beyond the period of time he must have unconsciously gauged would be the

2. By "shared" I do not mean "co-created." While the overt form taken by our transference–countertransference *interactions* was co-created, the underlying transference and countertransference themselves were different (see also Boesky 1990, Chused 1991, Smith 1993). We each had our own unique version of the fantasy, each with its own genetic roots, unconscious dynamics, and subjective experience. In effect, two separate intrapsychic dramas blended to look like one interpersonal play (Chused 2000).

limit of my patience, thus moving the treatment toward the re-creation of a death, his father's death, represented in the countertransference by the day I so conclusively gave up on his return.

Jimmy then returned on that day, to fulfill his unconscious fantasy of reversing death—both the death of his father and its enacted re-creation in the treatment. But his return also signified a readiness to allow the disavowed trauma a measure of conscious, verbal representation. In Loewald's (1971) terms, the enactment had moved toward a "re-creative repetition" of the trauma in the sphere of the ego's organizing activity, as opposed to a compulsive reproduction of it. The analytic version of the trauma played out in the enacted dimension of the treatment constituted, in Freedman's (1994) terms, a "nonverbal transformation" of Jimmy's experience that served as a precursor to the alteration of his internal representational space. Further, the "shared fantasy space" created between us (see also Bach 1994, Winnicott 1971) now made transformational dialogue possible, leading to higher levels of symbolization.

These developments were evident at the outset of that session, when Jimmy spontaneously brought up the symbolic meaning of his three-month absence, as well as new information about the six-month absence that preceded his father's death. I had temporarily experienced the loss he was trying to disavow in my reaction of giving up on the treatment. But when Jimmy unexpectedly returned, my recognition of the event's meaning, in interaction with Jimmy's readiness to understand and accept it, allowed my verbal representation of the enactment—the interpretation of his unconscious fantasy of undoing his father's death—to finally have mutative effect.

My comment to Jimmy during this sequence—that there was something to be understood about his never doubting that I would still be there—implied that important relationships *can* end, and that it may not make sense to assume that an abandoned relationship can always or so easily be resurrected. I implied in it that I had doubted—that I had not shared his denial of reality and unreciprocated commitment to a relationship—I had doubted, and by implication had despaired and suffered when he had not returned for so long. Not surprisingly, confronting his denial of death had made him angry, but he tolerated this affect without having to disavow it. Specifically, for the first time Jimmy was able to talk about his anger with me over the earlier "six-month" hiatus in the treatment, and he was able to relate this experience to his father's six-month absence and death.

This shift from enactive symbolization to verbal symbolization marked the beginning of a process of integrating experience that had previously been disavowed. This process may be seen as a *formative* psychic activity, one in which new representations and concepts were constructed and an ego split gradually integrated, rather than one characterized by an undoing of a repression followed by the recall of a once-conscious representational memory. It had been made possible by the unwitting creation of an analytic version of the patient's trauma in the enacted dimension of the treatment, a treatment experience that was crucial to making it accessible to verbal symbolization and meaningful insight. Jimmy's ensuing process of working through the trauma was predictably slow and uneven. Despite a growing capacity to experience his father's death through introspective thought, the fantasy that his father was alive persisted, as did his need at times to continue to express this transference fantasy in action and behavior. During this phase of treatment I continued, now consciously, to contain the awareness of the disavowed trauma on his behalf and bear his absences without rushing to comment or interpret.

As this phase proceeded, time began to move again in Jimmy's life. He brought in a large appointment book one day—his attempt to acknowledge the reality of time and to invest in the reality of living in the present. He began to look physically older and more mature, as if the aging process had resumed. Relationships with people began to deepen and he started a serious relationship with a new girlfriend. When he thanked me for "letting him be a patient," he was acknowledging that he *was* a patient, as opposed to an abandoned boy or an abandoning father. He began allowing himself more memories of his father and, in his dreams, the psychic representation of his father's age was no longer fixed at the age he had been when he died. During sessions, he began to feel pressure and itching in his eyes—the physical sensations of grief. And he visited his father's grave for the first time since his death, the symbolic action of acknowledging death.

CONCLUDING COMMENTS

I have illustrated the enacted dimension of analytic process as it occurred in this dramatic case of a patient traumatized by the loss of his father in early adolescence. The patient's necessary task of completing the mourning process required a preliminary period during which he literally re-created absence and waiting within the transference–countertransference relationship. In short, he replaced one external reality—death—with a less traumatic external reality—absence—and then created concrete experiences of absence and waiting to support his fantasy that his father was alive. His effort was to enlist me as a witness to this new reality (see Boesky 1982) and for it to remain an unalterable "fact," unamenable to interpretation, for a symbolically meaningful period of time. An ongoing countertransference receptivity to the enactment ultimately allowed the death itself to find symbolic actualization in the treatment, following which it could begin to be symbolized verbally and integrated into conscious experience.

With patients who are less traumatized and more able to symbolize verbally, such dramatic behavioral enactments do not typically form the ongoing foreground of the treatment. Nevertheless, unwitting actualizations of transference (and countertransference) wishes and defenses are continuously woven into the fabric of the analytic process, emerging into awareness in the form of seemingly discrete "enactments" as developing psychic transformations in the treatment allow or demand. Such processes within the enacted dimension of the treatment fashion an attenuated, symbolic version—a living analytic version—of the patient's central conflicts. As lived-in experience, these "original creations" (Poland 1992) between patient and analyst infuse the patient's core conflicts with the immediacy and affective vitality necessary for effective interpretation and ultimate integration within the verbal sphere.

As I have discussed previously (Katz 1998), our increased awareness of the ubiquity and importance of the enacted dimension of analytic process does not, in and of itself, justify the recent calls for the abandonment of the basic treatment model or the principles of relative neutrality and abstinence (see, for example, Renik 1993). Enactments are not a component of technique; they are the observable aspect of an unconscious process—a transference–countertransference process—that is continuously evolving. Enactments are *unintended departures* from the optimal analytic attitude that technical discipline, however defined, is intended to promote. They will occur regularly in every treatment, regardless of the analyst's conscious technical stance, whether it be strict adherence to "standard" technical principles, or abandonment of these principles in favor of a more spontaneous and deliberately interactive style. Any technical approach can be psychically appropriated and organized by enacted transference–countertransference processes.

To illustrate, both technical approaches I took with Jimmy—setting a limit on his disruptive behavior by suspending the treatment (as in the early part of the process), and then allowing these behaviors to continue (as in the process leading up to the dramatic session)—had an additional level of meaning, for each of us, in the enacted dimension of the treatment. Jimmy experienced my suspending the treatment as an actualization of his father's leaving him for "six months" and then, later on, he utilized my tolerating the absences to enact a reversal of this trauma (leaving me for the symbolically significant period of time) until he could re-create the death itself and then undo it (by returning that fateful day). On my end, neither technical approach was a simple matter of conscious or rational technique. Each was shaped, in significant degree, by enacted processes. Each was an unconscious compromise formation, fashioned out of Jimmy's pressure toward transference actualization and the press toward actualization of my own interpenetrating countertransference, tempered by my work ego and analytic conscience. Each technical decision, as well as its timing, was part of an unconscious transference–countertransference drama that was unique to our particular unconscious fit. They were part of the enacted dimension of the treatment.

Yet, as with any advance in our understanding of clinical process or the therapeutic action of psychoanalysis, appreciation of the enacted dimension of the treatment will affect how we listen and to what we attend. Such awareness expands the array of data available for analytic investigation to include the world of transference actualizations that are unconsciously created and communicated, through verbal and nonverbal action, by both patient and analyst. Further, the analyst's awareness of the inevitability and ubiquity of his or her own unwitting participation in enacted processes can help moderate concern and self-criticism regarding minor lapses in technique and intrusions of countertransference, allowing the analyst not only to include these as well in the data to be investigated, but also to consider how they may be forming an essential and facilitating part of the analytic process. Such expansion of the analytic purview can help sustain a treatment when little seems to be going on, or when resistance seems to be overwhelming. In cases of dramatic and even disruptive behavior, as in the case presented here, it can fortify the analytic patience needed to treat the behavior as an integral part of the treatment and to tolerate not being able to fully understand it or usefully interpret it for long periods of time. In any treatment, the analyst can be assured that significant developments are continuously taking place, outside of awareness, in the enacted dimension of the treatment.

REFERENCES

Altschul, S. (1968). Denial and ego arrest. *Journal of the American Psychoanalytic Association* 16:301–318.

Bach, S. (1994). *The Language of Perversion and the Language of Love*. Northvale, NJ: Jason Aronson.

Blos, P. (1979). *The Adolescent Passage: Developmental Issues*. New York: International Universities Press.

Blum, H. (1983). Splitting of the ego and its relation to parent loss. *Journal of the American Psychoanalytic Association* 31(Supp.):301–324.

Boesky, D. (1982). Acting out: a reconsideration of the concept. *International Journal of Psycho-Analysis* 63:39–55.

——— (1990). The psychoanalytic process and its components. *Psychoanalytic Quarterly* 59:550–584.

Busch, F. (1989). The compulsion to repeat in action: a developmental perspective. *International Journal of Psycho-Analysis* 70:535–544.

——— (1995). Do actions speak louder than words? A query into an enigma in analytic theory and technique. *Journal of the American Psychoanalytic Association* 43:61–82.

Chused, J. (1991). The evocative power of enactments. *Journal of the American Psychoanalytic Association* 39:615–639.

——— (1996). The therapeutic action of psychoanalysis: abstinence and informative experiences. *Journal of the American Psychoanalytic Association* 44:1047–1071.

——— (2000). Panel presentation, *Contemporary Freud–Klein Controversies: Clinical and Technical Implications*, Institute for Psychoanalytic Training and Research (IPTAR), New York, April.

Deutsch, H. (1937). Absence of grief. *Psychoanalytic Quarterly* 6:12–22.

Dowling, S. (1982). Dreams and dreaming in relation to trauma in childhood. *International Journal of Psycho-Analysis* 63:157–166.

Fleming, J., and Altschul, S. (1963). Activation of mourning and growth by psycho-analysis. *International Journal of Psychoanalysis* 44:419–431.

Frankiel, R. (1993). Hide-and-seek in the playroom: on object loss and transference in child treatment. *Psychoanalytic Review* 80:340–359.

Freedman, N. (1994). More on transformation: enactments in psychoanalytic space. In *The Spectrum of Psychoanalysis: Essays in Honor of Martin S. Bergmann*. ed. A. K. Richards and A. D. Richards, pp. 93–110. Madison, CT: International Universities Press.

Freud, A. (1958). Adolescence. *Psychoanalytic Study of the Child* 13:255–278. New York: International Universities Press.

——— (1967). About losing and being lost. *Psychoanalytic Study of the Child* 22:9–19. New York: International Universities Press.

Freud, S. (1917). Mourning and melancholia. *Standard Edition* 14:237–258.

——— (1927). Fetishism. *Standard Edition* 21:147–157.

——— (1940a). An outline of psycho-analysis. *Standard Edition* 23:141–207.

——— (1940b). The splitting of the ego in the process of defense. *Standard Edition* 23:271–278.

Jacobs, T. (1991). The interplay of enactments: their role in the analytic process. In *The Use of the Self: Countertransference and Communication in the Analytic Situation*, pp. 31–49. Madison, CT: International Universities Press.

——— (1993). Insight and experience: commentary on Morris Eagle's "Enactment, Transference, and Symptomatic Cure." *Psychoanalytic Dialogues* 3:123–127.

——— (1997). In search of the mind of the analyst: a progress report. *Journal of the American Psychoanalytic Association* 46:1129–1167.

Jacobson, E. (1961). Adolescent moods and the remodeling of psychic structures in adolescence. *Psychoanalytic Study of the Child* 16:164–183. New York: International Universities Press.

——— (1964). *The Self and the Object World*. New York: International Universities Press.

Katz, G. (1993). *A death in the countertransference: a patient's unconscious enactment of object loss in the analytic relationship*. Paper presented to Division 39 of the American Psychological Association, New York, April.

——— (1998). Where the action is: the enacted dimension of analytic process. *Journal of the American Psychoanalytic Association* 46:1129–1167.

Lampl-de Groot, J. (1960). On adolescence. *Psychoanalytic Study of the Child* 15:95–103. New York: International Universities Press.

Laufer, M. (1966). Object loss and mourning during adolescence. *Psychoanalytic Study of the Child* 21:269–293. New York: International Universities Press.

Loewald, H. (1971). Some considerations on repetition and repetition compulsion. *International Journal of Psycho-Analysis* 52:59–56.

——— (1975). Psychoanalysis as an art and the fantasy character of the psychoanalytic situation. *Journal of the American Psychoanalytic Association* 23:277–299.

Poland, W. S. (1992). Transference: "an original creation." *Psychoanalytic Quarterly* 61:185–205.

Renik, O. (1993). Analytic interaction: conceptualizing technique in light of the analysts's irreducible subjectivity. *Psychoanalytic Quarterly* 62:553–571.

Sandler, J. (1976). Countertransference and role-responsiveness. *International Review of Psycho-Analysis* 3:43–47.

Segel, N. (1969). Repetition compulsion, acting out, and identification with the doer. *Journal of the American Psychoanalytic Association* 17:474–488.

Smith, H. (1993). Engagements in the analytic work. *Psychoanalytic Inquiry* 13:425–454.

Steingart, I. (1995). *A Thing Apart*. Northvale, NJ: Jason Aronson.

Tower, J. E. (1956). Countertransference. *Journal of the American Psychoanalytic Association* 4:224–255.

Winnicott, D. W. (1971). *Playing and Reality*. New York: Basic Books.

Wolfenstein, M. (1966). How is mourning possible? *Psychoanalytic Study of the Child*, 21:93–123. New York: International Universities Press.

——— (1969). Loss, rage, and repetition. *Psychoanalytic Study of the Child* 24:432–460. New York: International Universities Press.

19

From Somatizing to Analyzing: The Psychoanalytic Treatment of a Female Patient with Peptic Ulcers

NAAMA KUSHNIR-BARASH

Many patients who come for psychological treatment suffer from psychosomatic illnesses. Some present the well-known psychosomatic diseases such as bronchial asthma, peptic ulcers, ulcerative colitis, and dermatological disorders. Others at times manifest marked sensitivity to infectious diseases or gum problems, or proneness to accidents. These are common phenomena found not just in our consultation rooms, but in the population at large as well.

The reciprocal relationship between mind and body has been an area of interest since the time of ancient Greece and is a counterpoint to the dualistic concept, namely, that mind and body are two separate entities. The goal of the present paper is to explore the ways in which unconscious material is transformed from being discharged physically to being elaborated and experienced psychologically. After presenting some general characteristics of most psychosomatic patients, I examine the shifts that occur in the course of treatment in the ways one individual patient experiences and processes the world outside her and the world of her emotions. The clinical material illustrates the process.

Freud maintained that the instincts are the source of energies, which give the mind–body interrelationship the specific characteristics of each individual. Freud described two major types of somatizations: conversion hysteria and actual neurosis. In hysterical conversion, there is a leap from mind to body. Primary process thinking gives to certain parts of the body particular symbolic meaning. In actual neurosis, very strong affect is consciously experienced, but this affect is not attached to an idea. Freud's concept of the actual neurosis included both neurasthenia and anxiety neurosis. Neurasthenia is marked by symptoms such as headaches, constipation, diminished sexual activity, and digestive difficulties. Anxiety neurosis is marked by symptoms such as palpitations, sweating, and trembling. Freud attributed the origin of the actual neurosis to a blocking of the libidinal affect due to a lack of sexual satisfaction. McDougall (1978) attributes the activation of these tension states not only to unrecognized sexual tensions but to aggressive tensions and unintegrated sadism as well. According to Alexander (1950), every organic symptom has emotional significance for the individual. The ego takes advantage of physical pain for the relief of emotional conflicts. Illness allows a person to be regressed. More is expected of a person when he or she is well. Theoretically, every disease is psychosomatic because emotional factors influence all physiological processes. The ego utilizes physical symptoms in creating and modifying compromise formations. The psychosomatic solution serves partially to discharge more regressive emotions and partially to defend against the direct expression of such emotions.

Although Alexander (1950) developed the idea of specificity in the development of psychosomatic illness, the consensus today is that the relationship between psychological variables and the creation of a physical symptom is a highly complex one. The fact that stress situations cause gastric problems in some individuals does not tell us why this actually happens nor does it explain why some individuals never develop gastric problems in response to stress. In order for a psychosomatic problem to develop there must exist psychological stress, a vulnerable or weak organ or system (from birth or from later accidents), and a complex way in which the two interrelate. The fact that there is a continuous relationship between somatic processes and psychic ones does not mean that the two sets of processes are the same or are governed by the same principles. This idea was emphasized by McDougall (1978), who claims that psychosomatic transformations are not necessarily symbolic products in the same sense that neurotic symptoms are considered to be. The capacity to symbolize, or rather the lack of such a capacity in many psychosomatic patients, will be discussed later on.

In the past, many psychoanalysts were discouraged from treating psychosomatic patients. A major factor responsible for the reluctance to use analytic treatment in such cases is the appearance of psychotic episodes following the disappearance of the somatic symptoms during treatment. Hogan (1989) states that there are relatively few trained psychoanalysts with interest in, experience with, and techniques for the treatment of psychosomatic diseases. His own experience with the psychoanalysis of psychosomatic patients has been facilitated by his participation in a long-term study group led by Melitta Sperling in New York. Today many analysts believe that psychoanalysis is not only possible but in most cases the only long-term solution for the chronic sufferer. For analysts working with psychosomatic patients, the first phase of the treatment is crucial. During this phase patients are invited, instructed, and helped to move from a somatic way of dealing with life to a more mental one. By the time they are able to somatize less and analyze more, they begin to resemble neurotic or narcissistic patients in analysis.

THE CLINICAL PICTURE OF THE PSYCHOSOMATIC PATIENT

Most psychosomatic patients seek psychological treatment after having endured a long history of physical pain and uncomfortable medical procedures. They present themselves as basically content and practical people who suffer from crippling medical conditions. They tend to deny conflicts, psychic pain, or anxiety. They cannot acknowledge their own aggressive feelings, especially irrational anger, and present themselves as helpless victims of their physical illness. Most of these patients disregard substantial physical discomfort for long periods of time until it reaches an intensity they no longer can ignore. It is not uncommon to see such patients dressed in light clothes on a freezing day, denying being cold. Anorexic patients frequently deny hunger pains when they starve themselves.

In 1963 the French psychoanalysts Marty and de M'Uzan described their clinical experience with a wide variety of physically ill patients. They reported that many of their patients were unable to produce fantasies and during interviews the content of their associations was mundane, unimaginative, and rigidly tied to reality. They named the experience *pensée operatoire* (or operational thinking) and introduced the idea of a specific psychosomatic personality. In 1970, the American analyst Nemiah began to investigate the communicative style of psychosomatic patients. Based on their observations, patients with psychosomatic diseases frequently show a specific disturbance in affective functions that renders their communication style sterile and colorless. They coined the term *alexithymia* (from the Greek *a*=lack, *lexis*=word, *thymos*=emotion) to denote this disturbance. Although further studies have shown that an alexithymic communicative style is not specific to patients with psychosomatic diseases, Nemiah and Sifneos focused attention on an aspect of contemporary psychoanalysis that is of central importance. By emphasizing the communication style, they anticipated a direction in psychoanalysis soon to blossom: the study of communication between patient and analyst.

According to McDougall (1978), psychosomatic patients do not like to discuss the real problems that they struggle with in their daily lives and instead talk about their physical problems, or they speak with very little affect about a topic that is emotionally meaningless, yet provides a screen that ensures their not touching upon vital issues. The need to avoid emotional references is a very powerful one. One reason is that admission of feelings implies that they are weak, vulnerable, or out of control. Since many psychosomatic patients feel that they have relatively little control over their lives, they shift the control toward their body functions. They actively, yet unconsciously, control a part of their body. As Sperling (1968) suggested, these are not passive victims of their ills. Their active need for control is directed toward their body. In this sense it is a form of acting out: the patient cannot tolerate the tension and has the urge for immediate discharge. The inability to wait and the tendency toward hyperactivity characterize psychosomatic patients. I am reminded of a patient I treated who told me in the initial consultation that she had recently divorced her husband of twelve years. She mentioned in passing that her ex-husband was engaged to be married to her best girlfriend. When I asked her how she felt about it, she replied, "Fine, we're divorced." It took three years of analysis for her feelings of betrayal and rage to surface. During that first consultation and during the months that preceded it, she experienced violent stomach pains, diarrhea, and nausea. She presented herself as a normal, reasonable, logical, and practical person. Emotional responses were very few and mild. She expected me to provide her with a list of the things that I could do for her. Because she was referred to me by her gastroenterologist, she expected me to do something and not just to listen and talk. She looked at me with scorn, contempt, and disbelief when I told her that the psychological treatment would consist of talking. She claimed that it was childish to just talk and reassured me that she was strong and tough and could benefit from aggressive treatment. Unconsciously, she was asking for more physical pain.

One of the major difficulties of many psychosomatic patients is their inability to symbolize. When a person verbalizes emotional experience and is able to elaborate it in fantasy, there is less chance for somatic manifestations. In that sense the psychosomatic patient uses the body in the same way an addict utilizes the external agent in order to fulfill the function that is missing because of the inability to symbolize.

Wurmser (1978), who examined the psychodynamics of compulsive drug use, claims that drug users cannot articulate important and bothersome feelings. They project affects into somatic complaints. Krystal (1975) states that in alcoholics and drug-dependent individuals emotions are only dimly perceived and are unverbalizable. To put feelings into words or other symbolic means (such as music or picture) means at least their partial acknowledgment and not complete denial.

Bion (1962) pointed out that prior to symbolization, there must be a state of "no breast," a state that is differentiated from the purely "good" and "bad" breast. According to him, symbolic thought begins in moments of "no breast." If mother does not allow moments of "no breast," instinctual impulses run the risk of not gaining psychic representation. The early fragmented elements of fantasy that accompany aggressive and libidinal impulses are not stored in ways that allow them to evolve into the fabric of neurotic fantasies. The lack of "no breast" experience leads to a tendency to somatically discharge and not to psychically bind impulses through fantasy.

In her 1978 formulations, McDougall claimed that psychosomatic phenomena, in contrast to neurotic manifestations, were completely devoid of any repressed fantasy material. She said that the symptoms had no symbolic meaning whatsoever. In her later work (1985), she somewhat modified her point of view, stating that very primitive body fantasies did exist in the psychosomatic patient. She claimed that the somatic symptom was a form of preverbal communication.

At times, psychosomatic symptoms may acquire, in addition to their primitive symbolic quality, a secondary symbolic manifestation, as well as secondary gains. The major mechanisms that are at work, however, usually do not contain the more complex symbolic meaning that one finds in neurotic symptoms. The psychosomatic symptoms are attempts to cure oneself by repudiating from psychic awareness any form of psychological pain. Many psychosomatic patients appear on the surface to be very normal. They do not manifest any neurotic symptoms nor do they exhibit the psychopathology of everyday life. They seem to cope extremely well even in traumatic situations. Since their associations sound coherent, they may fool the analyst for a while in the clinical situation, until the analyst begins to realize that the associations are leading nowhere and that something is not working right.

McDougall (1978) considered the psychosomatic personality as both nonneurotic and nonpsychotic. (She actually used the terms *antineurotic* and *antipsychotic*.) These patients are nonneurotics in the sense that they are not able to create neurotic defenses that contain complex symbolic meaning of repressed affect. They are nonpsychotic in the sense that they are overadaptive to reality and to the difficulties of life, and most of them cannot escape to delusional constructions.

The psychogenic conflicts that provide the basis for the somatic reactions date back to the preoedipal phase of development. For most psychosomatic patients, to be ill means to be taken care of as well as to have the opportunity to discharge destructive impulses through bodily symptoms. The punishment for the dependency cravings is built in. There are no overt guilt feelings. The punishment is provided somatically.

Psychosomatic patients run away from painful situations. They do not try to solve their problems by creating mental solutions that are realistic or distorted. They only reject the signs of pain. However, the more they repudiate the emotional side of life, the greater is the possibility for somatic illness to occur. The early channels for somatic expression were never replaced by more adequate mental structures.

The events that usually precede the outbreak of psychosomatic reactions are loss of love, abandonment by one's love objects, a sudden loss of self-esteem, and similar painful separations. On the surface these patients act as if they were the Rock of Gibraltar, yet they become physically ill. It is not unusual to see psychosomatic patients become annoyed with body parts. This is but another indication of the split. According to Sperling (1955), the patient does not feel that his body belongs to him. It is someone else's property. The illness is frequently an unconscious link to the mother and is often a secret weapon that is directed toward the destructive parts of the maternal imago. By destroying a part of one's body, one destroys what is hated in mother. To own one's body and to be in charge of one's life is equivalent to a total destruction of mother. Maintaining the physical symptom ensures the feeling of being at one with mother. It serves the functions of staying connected to mother, making sure she is not abandoned, and punishing her—all with the same preverbal act.

In presenting the following case, I hope to illustrate how, as a result of analytic work, the patient transformed her somatic ways of dealing with life conflicts into increasingly more mental ones. This case will also illustrate the close relationship between somatic problems and addictions.

CASE

Miss W. was 27 when she was referred to me by her gastroenterologist following a hospitalization for a bleeding ulcer. The history revealed various manifestations of psychosomatic difficulties as well as periods of bulimia and drug and alcohol abuse dating back to her adolescence. Miss W. is the only child of Jewish upper-middle-class parents. A few months after the patient was born, her mother was diagnosed with breast cancer that later metastasized to her lungs and to her brain and eventually led to her death when Miss W. was 8 years old. Early in her treatment, the patient had very few memories of her mother and her childhood. She remembered periods prior to her mother's death when her mother would ask for oxygen. There were times that her mother would scream with terror, frustration, and pain. Miss W. responded to the painful situation by being helpful and very adaptive. She was partly aware that she was tuned into people's needs and tried to please them in order to keep them around. When her father told her that her mother had died, her first reaction was "Why didn't you tell me? I could have helped." After her mother's death, her father had a number of girlfriends. Some of them acted very seductively toward Miss W. in order to gain her father's affections. She became quite attached to a few. But once they stopped seeing her father, she lost them as well.

The area of academic accomplishments and professional advancement has always been relatively conflict free for Miss W. She has worked hard, is very ambitious, and is doing very well. From the time she began to work for the corporate world (her work has included both artistic and business skills), she was very sensitive to corporate politics and became integrated into this world with ease, skill, and charm. Her father is a successful businessman who always shared with her his life at the office and his own struggles and successes within the corporate world. When Miss W. discusses her work she often uses her father's words and intonations, such as " this is a b-i-g job" or "he is no dummy." She articulates these expressions in a tough manner that implies she knows it all. She feels comfortable boasting about her success at work. It is not pride but arrogance that cements her identification with her father. Like her father, she has a profound fear of being vulnerable, weak, inferior, not in control, or embarrassed.

Miss W. is a small woman. Very often she enters my office carrying bags that make her look overburdened. These bags usually contain volumes of work that she takes home.

During our first consultation Miss W. told me that she had been living with a man for three years. Since she did not love him, she was not surprised when she became very infatuated with another man whom she met briefly prior to her last ulcer attack. She said that she felt really in love for the first time in her life. She stated, "For the first time in my life I realized that there is something stronger than reason. He made me face my life." She felt that this second lover has been her mirror image, her twin." I looked at him and I saw myself. We are both quite manipulative. We could not do it to one another. We were the same."

During that first interview we explored her feelings about being hospitalized, and Miss W. stated that she loved being in the hospital. She felt like a baby being cared for. She did not want to be discharged from the hospital and was surprised that when she expressed suicidal ideas to her physician, her doctor recommended psychotherapy. Her response is quite typical for psychosomatic patients who are not able to make the connection between suicidal wishes, which indicate a certain emotional state, and the idea of being assisted psychologically.

From the way she described her life during the first few consultations, it became clear that Miss W. had worked very hard building her career, being a disciplined and brave soldier on the work front. She lived with a man she did not love and who was very ambivalent toward her, but she convinced herself that he was a good catch because he was rich and cultured. She was unaware of how offended she felt by the fact that he never asked her to marry him. Miss W.

acted as his cook and maid but she avoided sexual relations with him because she felt repulsed by his body. She hated him for her feelings of dependence on him.

Miss W. had no idea that she had difficulties caring for herself in a consistent and sensible manner. During her growing up years, she lacked the presence of a caring parent. Her absence of sound judgment was manifested in her inability to anticipate danger. For example, she would drive while drunk or high on drugs. A few minor car accidents did not frighten her. She invited to her home strange men whom she met only briefly in bars or in the park. She discussed the details of her personal life with various people and without any discrimination. This difficulty in anticipating danger is frequently observed in psychosomatic and addictive personalities. Danger is not so much welcomed (consciously or unconsciously) but rather is never anticipated, perceived, or appreciated.

In assessing the clinical picture that she presented in the first few consultations, I had the impression that she had no idea what went wrong in her life and how psychological treatment might help her. I felt that her intelligence, her capacity to work hard over long periods of time, and her ability to maintain relations were factors in favor of psychoanalysis. At the same time, it was clear that she would need help in becoming introspective and reflective. My initial attempts in engaging her in such a way were encouraging. She tried to be responsive and cooperative. Some of it was defensive, but it was a beginning. She had some understanding that her "logical" way of living, which was basically an operational way of dealing with life, was failing. When I recommended psychoanalytic treatment, she responded with relief. Unconsciously, being in treatment allowed her not to force herself out of the regression that began during her hospitalization. She was allowed to express her longings to be cared for. I felt that the first task was to increase her awareness of her inner psychic life. When we reanimate the psyche, the somatic symptom becomes milder.

Her initial reaction to treatment was crying. She cried for months. The bleeding stopped and she was not experiencing much stomach pain. It was at that time and as a result of the development of transference feelings that she left her boyfriend of three years and moved to an apartment three blocks away from my office. As she began to cry less and to talk more, it became clear that her verbalizations were used as a mask. She was superficially friendly, telling me about restaurants that I should try and about local shops that were having sales. At the same time, she reported feeling as if she was not a part of this world. She knew that she fooled people with her appearance of being talkative and engaging. Her false-self adaptation was that of a lively, somewhat childish person who is easily and falsely enthusiastic about things. She would talk about different topics in a pseudo-insightful way, keeping me at a distance and keeping her feelings hidden. Since she is very bright and has years of experience acting in this fashion, it came very easily for her. Miss W. is smart, articulate, funny, quick, and superficially clever.

I focused on her tendency to escape from feelings, especially feelings and reactions toward me. Her answer was that she had read about the concept of transference, but she had no transference. She told me she had made up her mind early in our work together not to have any transference. When I told her that her transference was her belief that she had none, we began to move forward. She told me that the only thing she ever said about me to her friends was that I was "young, Israeli, and brilliant." She reassured me she never felt anything else, nor did she ever fantasize about my life. She concluded the discussion one evening by stating, "You are not a real person and therefore feelings are irrelevant, not important; you are not a real-life person." I wondered if that is what she did with the memory of her mother.

As the treatment continued, the theme of guilt over the wish to be left alone surfaced. She experienced people as a burden that she needs to carry. "You have to entertain them in order to keep them around." The patient would often invite people to dinner parties and cook elaborate meals for them, all the while not really wanting to be there and wishing they would all disappear. She would often say, "I don't care if I never see them again. It is like changing channels. I'm going from person to person. I don't care about them, I'd rather be alone."

In the first year of treatment, Miss W. often experienced guilt over being in treatment. She felt that since the stomach pains and the bleeding were gone, she did not deserve such luxury. It was acceptable for her to be in treatment only as long as she was suffering from physical pain. Guilt became a new conscious experience. Until the pain was gone, she was unable to experience guilt as a psychological state. It was at that time that the risk of leaving treatment became noticeable. The wish to avoid becoming more mentally attuned and further explore painful feelings, combined with the disappearance of her physical pain, made it very difficult for her to attend four sessions per week. She was frequently late and occasionally missed sessions. She complained that I took away all her free evenings, and that because of treatment she could not afford to have a maid. Slowly, and as a result of increased verbalization, a new form of transference configuration emerged. She came to the sessions in order to unload her feelings and daily tensions. She would mention names of many people whom she had encountered in the course of the day. She became like her father, who used to unload his burdens in her presence when he came home from the office. I found myself uncomfortable listening to all these empty details. I also sensed that it was a very loaded issue. Finally, when I pointed out to her that she was repeating with me what her father had subjected her to, she became overtly furious with me. She felt that I humiliated her and that I did not allow her to say what was on her mind. She felt manipulated and trapped and became suspicious that I was playing with her feelings. She took it as an indication that she needed to be alone. It frightened her to realize she could feel things so strongly. Miss W. told me that even if I was right, my timing was off. She accused me of being unsupportive and mocked my technique. At some point she started to talk with great frustration and anger about the many hours she used to sit obediently and listen to her father. Actually, she was listening only occasionally. She developed a technique of pretending she was there. During her adolescence she would get high before he came home. She recalled wishing that he would be more interested in her. Whenever she asked him for something, he told her that her timing for asking was off. He was always too tired, too hungry, busy on the phone, and so on. Miss W. felt that my timing was off, too. She felt that I should have waited for a more appropriate opportunity. During that stage of treatment I felt the way she felt with her father: inadequate, having a faulty sense of timing, somewhat bored, confused, and walking on egg shells.

After this first stormy period, I became more confident that the treatment was evolving into a more mental and solid frame. Miss W. still occasionally exhibited some somatic symptoms such as skin rashes, headaches, and backaches, but her stomach pains were fewer and milder. Her verbalizations reflected a wish to bridge the physical and the mental. She had internalized my attitude and took it as her own goal. While in the first few months of treatment she would talk about stomach aches as "spikes going through me," she would now say, "I'm trying to impose order; my inside is insane."

During my first summer vacation she suffered stomach pains and had blood in her stool. Upon my return, she blamed the analysis for making her dependent upon me. As it turned out, when I was away she became ill. I pointed out that her calm manner prior to my leaving was a surface one and that she was protecting me from her violence by attacking her stomach again. I told her that she resented being dependent and hated me for reminding her that other people matter after all. Her reaction to this interpretation was a physical one: she was trembling, kicking on the couch with her feet, pulling on her hands, and screaming that she is frustrated with herself, with me, with her father, and with her inability to know what she feels. During such moments, I often needed to name feelings, to give them a title and context.

Her superego was highly perfectionist, demanding perfection from herself and from the world. She claimed that if she were to stay in treatment, she had to do it "right" and to finish. She was attempting to extract from me a "map of free associations," as she called it. She felt that I was depriving her by not telling her what kind of free associations she should produce. She was trying to control me and asked me to extract all the bad feelings from her insides. As she was recalling times she was given enemas as a child, she fantasized that one day I would make her clean. Being clean was associated with being drug-free, thin, and angelic. She expressed her willingness to suffer physical pain for the sake of purification.

During the second year of treatment, the symptomatology changed from being expressed primarily through medical problems to addictions and endless attempts to control some of the addictions. She knew that she drank too much and indeed she became drunk a few times a week. When she went on business trips, she was unable to resist the cocaine parties. Miss W. had difficulty controlling her eating and had put on about fifteen pounds, which she was unable to lose. She had a few episodes of bulimia.

In her attempts to control the various addictions, she moved from total deprivation to binges. She experienced similar feelings toward the analysis: she would move from periods of intense involvement in the treatment to a wish that I would release her from the obligation of having to come to sessions. It was during that time that she was promoted at work to a new position that involved frequent traveling. Again, she wished to abruptly leave the analysis. A part of her was still tempted to avoid dealing with mental areas. At the same time she felt that she could not go back to her old ways of coping with life. She stayed in the analysis and arranged her trips in such a way as to minimize the number of sessions she would have to miss.

It was during this period and in the context of exploring addictive behavior that Miss W. began to discuss her relationships with men in a more introspective manner. She confessed that since adolescence she was compelled to be a sexual champion. She felt that she was the best lover and could lead any man to the heights of sexual ecstasy. She was particularly ambitious in her encounters with married men. She believed that in her sexual performance she surpassed their wives and was surprised when the men did not stay with her. She rarely reached orgasm. Sex was like work: a place to perform and to be the best. Miss W. could not relax during her sexual encounters. She never masturbated and said she could not fantasize. Whenever she tried, nothing happened. From dream material it became clear that the unconscious fantasies were incestuous in nature and she felt much shame and guilt whenever we moved in that direction. Although Miss W. showed only minimal signs of anxiety while explicitly discussing her sexual activity, she was easily embarrassed and uncomfortable when exploring her feelings in relation to sexual matters. With great difficulty she began to associate to dream material. It was no longer a logical and well-prepared explanation to the manifest content.

It is of interest to note the physical manner in which Miss W. responded to interpretations. When anxiety was evoked in response to something I brought up, she immediately shifted her posture into the fetal position. She stayed in that position for a couple of minutes, often covering her face with her hands. Then, still in the same position, she scratched her feet, sometimes tried to remove her shoes, and scratched her head. She was physically very active and discharged some of her anxiety in this manner, prior to engaging in any mental way with the interpretation. Very often, after physically discharging some of the anxiety, she would agree with my statement in a compliant way and give an intellectualized "talk" about the subject matter. This was her way of distancing herself from its possible emotional impact. However, there had been an increase in times of true emotional insight and integration. She became upset when she realized that she had forgotten yesterday's insight. She was trying to hold onto gains and at times repeated my words as a way of holding onto them in a concrete way. Sometimes she repeated my words so often that they became empty and devoid of significance.

Another typical response to an interpretation was a change in her state of consciousness. This is a narcissistic mechanism described by Bach (1985). She entered a semihypnotic state during which her speech was slurry, much softer than otherwise, and it seemed that she was about to fall asleep. She emerged from these states a few seconds or a few minutes later, unsure of what had happened.

As we entered the third year of treatment, the clinical picture increasingly resembled that of the narcissistic personality disorder in treatment. There were conscious and frequent fluctuations in self-esteem. Miss W. observed herself as she blocked out feelings and wondered what she was missing. She discussed feeling empty and depressed. She was able to see the connection between these feelings and her impulsive pull toward the various addictive agents. Miss W. stated, "When I'm getting close to feeling something, I get a sensation that I need a quick fix." She was in constant need of mirroring and quickly moved from grandiose postures to total despair. She was increasingly able to differentiate between feelings such as anxiety, depression, envy, emptiness, guilt, and shame. Whereas in the first couple of years of treatment she experienced every hour as a discrete experience and unrelated to previous sessions, she began to have a sense of continuity and progression in the analysis. She associated to previous hours and past insights through the thread of feelings and not through logical figuring out. She became very excited when during one session she realized that even painful feelings can transform into something new and surprisingly pleasurable and that she could be angry and still care and preserve an emotional tie with another human being.

In the transference there was a growing curiosity about me as well as a wish to protect me and to take care of me. She became frightened by her occasional anger at me and handled me as if I were a fragile woman, like the sick mother of her childhood. There were also more conscious longings for her mother. The growing capacity to verbalize her feelings enabled her to begin to mourn the death of her mother. For months she was involved in collecting pictures and letters of her mother and was wearing her mother's jewelry. She contacted people who knew her mother and tried to get a sense of who her mother was. She no longer accepted her father's evasive descriptions and asked him more complex questions about her early relationship with her mother. At the same time, she was talking about not being clear on what it means to be a woman. She found herself staring at women on buses and in the street, trying to imagine how they act at home with their men. The material was rich with homosexual longings. She was curious about women, yet was frightened of getting close to a woman. In one dream she was trying to lock all the doors of a hotel room where she was staying. An Arab tried to push his way in. From her associations and reactions to the dream it was apparent that she was the Arab, intruding upon the Israeli analyst. Miss W. felt ashamed of her curiosity about me and guilty over her envy and strong competitive strivings. She felt that she was the sneaky and toxic Arab who caused her mother's death and could destroy me as well. On the session before the Thanksgiving holiday she asked me what I was doing for the holiday. When I invited her to explore her fantasies, she exploded. "I don't want to play this game. I'm ugly and fat, I'm disgusting." I pointed out to her that it was me she was annoyed with and she replied, "I get myself in the corner and now I have a headache." She was quite clear about how she created a psychosomatic symptom. First she trivialized the analysis, then she verbally attacked herself, and finally she created a psychosomatic symptom.

It was at that juncture in the treatment that I became pregnant. During the first trimester of my pregnancy Miss W. must have perceived something on an unconscious level. She dreamed, "I was pulling Sarah's hair and yelling, 'What kind of friends are we if you didn't tell me that you're buying a new apartment?'" Sarah is one of her closest friends, a married woman who has a baby. In associating to the dream, she talked about feeling left out by Sarah and her husband who are private about their lives. She said that they kept secrets from her and did not always include her in their plans. When I pointed out that she did not know many details about my life and that she may have felt left out or betrayed, she experienced me as teasing and humiliating her. The following week she reported another dream. "I was in bed with a woman who had a huge penis. She entered me, but then refused to move and told me not to move. She enticed me but left me unfulfilled. She said she'd be back, but she did not come back." In her associations she said, "It started as a dream of promise. She'll fill the hole in me. I was looking for men to fill the hole, but you are the one who fills the holes. From men I get pathetic discharges that make me feel sick." She talked about her longings for her father and then continued, "The woman promised me and then tortured me. She could be really tender. But she could be teasing. She promised to give me the deepest fulfillment and then she left." I told her that she may have felt that I wanted her to act a certain way and in return she will be fulfilled. Her response was, "I feel you don't want me to miss sessions. I'll miss six sessions starting next week. I'm not going to California for Passover, not to miss sessions. In the dream I obey you. I loved the dream and wanted to continue the dream." After a short silence she continued, "I'm not your blood relation . . . I have no siblings." For a while she moved between seeing me as the phallic woman who could control and manipulate her the way her father used to, and seeing me as the sick mother who is nice but fragile.

When she consciously realized that I was pregnant (during my fifth month of pregnancy), she cried for a long time and wondered why she was crying. At once she expressed intense curiosity about my life. She wondered how old I was, where I lived, whether it was my first child, and why I came to the United States. She fantasized that my parents were survivors of the Holocaust and that my family had suffered a great deal. There were no questions or thoughts about a husband or the father of the baby. Unconsciously, she was the father, the man, like her father who married a fragile woman who became sick and died following the birth of her child. She wondered if the pregnant analyst would become irrational, repulsive, and strange looking like her mother, who became very fat, then very thin, then lost her breasts and her hair. The strong identification with her father, which was apparent in the first phase of the treatment, reappeared. She talked about being one of the boys at work. "All the men know they can tell dirty jokes in front of me and it doesn't faze me." She boasted, "I'm funny, I'm serious, and I'm as close to perfection as possible." On another occasion she said, "I love when people discover how smart I am. I'm just like my dad."

During that time it became extremely difficult to engage Miss W. in any reflective or introspective work. When I asked her about her feelings, she replied she did not want to play my games any longer. She was hostile and distant. She felt that the only way to be in control with me was to stay away from me, even if she hurt herself in doing so. In order to protect me and the baby I was carrying from her aggression and agitation, she drank more during her evenings at home. She talked about wanting to terminate the analysis before I started my maternity leave. I confronted her about her increased use of alcohol and her answer was, "Maybe I want the worst confirmed . . . maybe I want to be sick like my mother."

I gave birth six weeks earlier than expected and therefore my maternity leave began suddenly and sooner than I had planned. The week prior to the delivery, she spoke of the possibility of joining Alcoholics Anonymous. She was preparing herself for my absence through this substitute. She was not able to discuss her feelings or to reflect in any meaningful way on what she was planning. During my leave she phoned me twice. In the first phone conversation she told me that she had joined A.A., that she was free of alcohol, and that it had been a wonderful experience. She called me a second time to ask me whether she should go to a famous residential treatment facility for alcoholics. I replied that we needed more time to discuss it and I suggested we do that when I returned. Her response was, "By then I wouldn't need it." She was searching for a way to feel maintained and contained during my absence.

My pregnancy challenged her fantasy that I will always care for her. As my belly grew larger, she had to give up the notion of the analyst as the omnipotent parent. It forced her to touch upon her own needs for omnipotence. When I went into the hospital and delivered the baby early, she was overwhelmed with anxiety and fear that her childhood trauma had recurred and that she was wrong to have depended on me. She joined a group to depend on. There are many members and they are anonymous. If one leaves, there are others. In line with her pattern of mental functioning, which had been that of immediate discharge, she found a way not to have to experience her emotional reactions to my absence.

When I returned to work after three months, Miss W. seemed dramatically different. She was in a state of paranoid regression. She was angry with me and suspicious of all my statements. She talked about A.A. with great idealization and warned me that if I did not support A.A. she would not be able to continue the analysis. At the same time, she tried to extract criticism of A.A. from me. She was furious with me for not referring her to A.A. earlier and accused me of being irresponsible. She expressed the wish to reduce the frequency of her sessions in order "not to put all my eggs in one basket." Miss W. was trying to control and avoid the expression of her rage related to the interruption of her treatment. She attended A.A. meetings every day and at times twice a day. It became a new idealized and powerful addiction. In this state of paranoid regression, she often twisted my statements, attacked them out of context, mocked Freud and psychoanalysis, and even saw me as a poor victim of psychoanalytic thinking. She hated and envied me in the most Kleinian sense and continuously brought up the topic of termination of treatment. She acted like an infant who had waited too long to be fed. She had waited so long that by the time the food arrived, she refused to eat it even though she was hungry. My pregnancy, my sudden delivery, and my maternity leave made her wait too long. In her mind she was replaced by the new baby. In joining A.A. Miss W. communicated to me that she found an anonymous breast that would not disappoint her. She found a breast that is free of charge, that is always available, and that does not go away. With me she was provocative and testy. She frequently tried to change analytic hours in order to attend A.A. meetings.

Because of her strong dependence on me, I became a powerful threat to her. To continue the analysis meant challenging the maintenance of the narcissistic structure. She was in a panic and wished to escape and free herself of me. This wish mobilized intense separation anxiety. The conflict contributed to her need to test my commitment by increased provocation and acting out. The paranoid regression continued for about three months. She was constantly late and once she missed an appointment. As she began to reestablish the connection to me and to the analytic work, she grew more reflective and introspective. However, she was late for every session and began every hour by threatening to leave treatment. In so doing, I sensed she was reminding me of how she felt when I left her, when I was not around. I constantly interpreted how betrayed and hurt she felt by my pregnancy and by my absence. I discussed her lack of trust in me and her lack of clarity in regard to where I stood vis-à-vis A.A. I pointed out that she needed to create a conflict between me and A.A. This was a repetition of the past in which she was placed between two antagonistic forces: her father on one hand and her maternal grandparents on the other. She was often caught in the middle feeling confused and trapped. Greenacre (1963) states that a multiplicity of authoritative figures in childhood, especially when tension exists among these adults, can contribute to serious acting-out tendencies. Following this interpretation she had a dream: "I was supposed to tell my story at A.A. We were all sitting in this huge hall. A woman was sitting behind a desk and was talking about her baby, who was born with handicaps. I thought, poor woman, but this is not a drinking problem, she should get help elsewhere. I wanted to feel sorry for her, but she does not belong here." Her initial associations were to me and to my baby, who was born early and may be ill. She rejected the idea that she had wished to harm me and the baby and to see us all suffering. Later on, she was associating to herself as the handicapped baby as well as the woman, and that the dream reflected her own recent doubts about whether A.A. was indeed the appropriate place for her problems. This dream helped her to discuss how terrified and left out she felt when I had interrupted the process of her analysis. She cried, "When I realized that you were pregnant, it was like losing my mother again." She grew more comfortable describing her experiences at A.A. "It's like fourth grade again. We meet and we discuss a topic such as drug abuse or alcohol. . . . There is no dating and no desire to date. We only have crushes like in fourth grade. I have a crush on D., so after the meeting we go out for soda."

As the paranoid regression lifted, she returned to a more narcissistic way of relating. Again, there were frequent fluctuations in self-esteem, angry outbursts at the world and me, feelings of deprivation, and revenge fantasies. She did not develop somatic symptoms and was able to use more mental channels.

During that period there were many conflicts with her father. It was the first time in her life that she did not allow him to manipulate and control her. She moved from feelings of anger to guilt and a need to be his little girl again. She sought his company only to discover time and again how empty their contacts were. She was upset to realize that in spite of all the changes in her, he had not changed. Somehow, in the middle of the storms she expressed a desire to have a good life. She felt she had the right to have a place in the world. She was imagining her future home as a peaceful place, where the sun comes through the curtains and there are flowers in the garden. She fantasized about having room for her thoughts, her books, and her friends. She actually bought a small country home on the beach, which she furnished with great care. It was my impression that, unlike her dead mother, she saw me as having a life, which freed her to want to have her own life.

Strong oedipal feelings surfaced with a wish to see her father divorcing his "selfish, stupid, and manipulative [present] wife" and fantasies that I told my husband about her and that he was fascinated by her. She was able to understand how she was drawn to the position of an oedipal winner, which ultimately left her feeling guilty, empty, and unfulfilled.

Throughout the treatment, although she continued to attend A.A. meetings, she was attending fewer meetings and the initial enthusiasm and appreciation subsided. However, it continued to be a meaningful place. While her initial attraction to A.A. was to be held and contained, later on it became a place where she reenacted family romance fantasies in a safe environment. It was also, of course, a strong message to me—she was not ready or willing to rely only on me.

Her decision to terminate the treatment was abrupt. She was offered a position in another city and was considering it. She thought she needed to move on and to test her ability to be on her own. She was also aware of her need to leave me. She fantasized about returning to analysis with the birth of her child. After she left treatment, I often wondered about her. She touched me in a very profound way and taught me a great deal about psychosomatic illness, as well as about how problematic situations in treatment can ultimately generate growth and development.

CONCLUSION

Psychosomatic difficulties are always the result of both physiological and psychological factors. From birth on (and probably even earlier), the baby is exposed to the home atmosphere and personalities of the parents. Certain families tend to emphasize the somatic channels as a means of expressing and organizing experience. At times, the somatic solution is the most adaptive response to a difficult family situation. This solution may at times substitute for a psychotic disorganization.

Miss W. grew up with a very ill mother and was exposed to her physical pain, medical procedures, and preoccupation with bodily functions. Her father could not tolerate passivity or regression in either himself or his daughter. He expected Miss W. to be independent, self-reliant, and well functioning. Signs of sadness, neediness, or difficulties were discouraged and not respected. This situation reinforced the creation of psychosomatic disorder.

I often asked myself what in the analysis helped the patient move from a somatic and addictive way of being to a more mental and introspective one. I believe the answer has to do with her capacity to enter a deep regressive transference state. This is not self-evident with psychosomatic individuals, who commonly avoid such states. It is more typical for them to leave the treatment as soon as the physical symptoms clear up.

Psychosomatic individuals usually begin an analysis during the somatic crisis. If they form a good connection with the analyst during this initial period, there is a better chance that they will stay in treatment after the somatic crisis ends. On the other hand, if the physical symptom subsides due to medication, the individual has no motivation to continue further in treatment.

The role of the analyst is to introduce the goals and methods of the treatment as they are relevant to the specific issues of the patient. In the case of Miss W., her regression began while she was hospitalized for the bleeding ulcer. She loved being taken care of by her female physician and then by me. On the couch, she cried for months. We understood the internal bleeding to be a form of internal crying that stopped only when she actually sobbed. When the physical problem subsided, the emotional difficulties surfaced. She became ambivalent toward me and wanted to both run away from me and cling to me. I felt that I was containing her intense anxiety, neediness, hunger, and anger, her wish to push me away and hold me tight. There were periods of intense frustration, despair, chaos, and confusion. Throughout her analysis I admired her courage and commitment to improving her life. In spite of her frequent desire to escape the analysis in order to avoid pain, she stayed and internalized my respect for her life and my trust in her capacity to grow.

REFERENCES

Alexander, F. (1956). *Psychosomatic Medicine*. New York: Norton.

Bach, S. (1985). *Narcissistic States and the Therapeutic* Process. New York: Jason Aronson.

Bion, W. R. (1962). *Learning from Experience*. London: Heinemann.

Greenacre, P. (1963). Problems of acting out in the transference relationship. In *Emotional Growth, Vol. II*, pp. 695–717. New York: International Universities Press, 1971.

Hogan, C. C. (1989). Inflammatory disease of the colon. In *Psychosomatic Symptoms: Psychodynamic Treatment of the Underlying Personality Disorder*, ed. C. P. Wilson and I. L. Mintz, pp. 367–399. Northvale, NJ: Jason Aronson.

Krystal, H. (1975). Affect tolerance. *Annual of Psychoanalysis* 3:179–219.

Marty, P., and de M'Uzan, M. (1963). La "pensée opératoire." *Revue Française de* Psychanalyse 27:345–356.

McDougall, J (1978). *Plea for a Measure of Abnormality*. New York: International Universities Press.

——— (1985). *Theatres of the Mind*. New York: Basic Books.

Nemiah, J. C. (1970). Psychosomatic illness: a problem of communication. *Psychother. Psychosom.* 18:154–160.

Sperling, M. (1955). Psychosis and psychosomatic illness. *International Journal of Psycho-Analysis* 36:320–327.

——— (1968). Acting-out behavior and psychosomatic disorder. *International Journal of Psycho-Analysis* 49:250–253.

Wurmser, L. (1978). *The Hidden Dimension*. New York: Jason Aronson.

20

The Relationship between Empathy and Symbolic Communication

ELAINE SCHWAGER

Psychic maturity is not possible without optimal symbolic development, and one of the central manifestations of this is the capacity for empathy. Empathy both facilitates the development of the symbolic attitude toward experience and is a developmental achievement, not possible without differentiated symbolic evolution. The spectrum of pathology to health is viewed here as inextricably intertwined with the developmental process of symbolic communication, from the most concrete or functional use of language to playful, creative communication that is resonant with multiple levels of meaning. Many theorists of early infancy (Beebe 1985, 1988, Bick 1986, Bion 1959, 1962, Mitrani 1996, Ogden 1989, 1994, Winnicott 1971) have shown that the early lack of a containing, holding, empathic environment results in an inability to separate from the maternal object. This results in a fused self/object sense of self, and catastrophic anxieties that can derail the evolution of the symbolic process. Where there is genetic vulnerability along with substantial failure on the part of caregiver in providing a containing or empathic environment, symptoms of concreteness, perseveration, and adherence to hard external objects, often associated with autism (Tustin 1986), can result.

In this paper I illustrate how the severe derailment of symbolic functioning in a 7-year-old boy with some autistic-like symptoms, was facilitated through the empathic relationship with the therapist over a three-year period.

Parallel work with the parents, helping them engage their son more empathically, reinforced Michael's progress. When Michael first started treatment his interactions were marked by verbalizations that were concrete and perseverative. This state reflected "a collapse of the symbolizing space," a state of desymbolization, a "frozen constellation" (Freedman et al. 1999a, p. 2), where there was no space or ability to reflect or play in a way that would allow for creative elaboration of his own meaning and feelings. If one looked at Michael's symptoms as primarily neurological or genetic (as symptoms of autism often are), one would tend to view this state of desymbolization as meaningless, that is, not making sense except as a disorder of his biological condition. This would essentially be taking a position of despair in regard to reaching Michael on a relationship level and would be viewing him as having little capacity to grow from the robotic desymbolized state of denying meaning into a self that can participate in evolving into a separate self through the development of a playful, creative, symbolic capacity, capable of creating coherent meaning out of his experience.

The symbolic/empathic attitude of the therapist views this desymbolized state as having meaning in terms of Michael's experience and history. From interviews with the mother and observations of Michael and his mother, it appeared that most often his symptoms were viewed as signs with fixed meanings. In addition to symptoms described above, Michael's disruptive behavior in nursery, his tendency to isolate himself, and his outbursts of anger were for the mother (1) signs of her disturbed brother, who had serious psychological problems throughout his life and tended to live a very isolated existence, (2) indications of her not being a good mother (experienced as a narcissistic injury), (3) a source of shame in terms of how he appeared to others, and (4) signs of Michael being bad. She didn't doubt the meanings she held, nor did she inquire of Michael, or empathically try to sense what underlying motivations he might have. She responded in fixed ways based on her fixed meanings. She tended either to deny his problems or symptoms, or react punitively or self-referentially (how they affected her rather than what they meant for him). The two of them were locked in a frozen, fixed interaction. It was necessary to loosen this interaction, both through my work with Michael and by helping the mother see how she could respond differently.

Freedman and colleagues (1999a) go on to say that

> the very process of being engaged in a dyadic interchange facilitates the transformation of the de-symbolized. . . . The listening therapist becomes the recipient of the patient's verbal and yet to be encoded non-verbal memory. It is the therapist's reception, the ability to absorb and use these communicative aspects of the de-symbolized that matters in the ensuing clinical course. [p. 6]

In working with Michael, I utilized the therapeutic process to facilitate the empathic connectedness that would mobilize the symbolic process. This allowed Michael's frozen desymbolized state to evolve into a symbolizing process. I also tried to help Michael's parents advance in their own symbolic/empathic stance so as to nurture his development at home.

THE INTERTWINING OF EMPATHY AND THE SYMBOLIC

Empathy is described by Rycroft (1968) as "the power of projecting one's personality into (and so fully comprehending) the object of contemplation. . . . The concept implies that one is both feeling oneself into the object and remaining aware of one's own identity as another person" (p. 42).

The essence of the symbolic process is described by Susan Deri (1984) as a capacity to unite opposing categories within one gestalt. Initially, one aspect of the symbol may be conscious while another is not, as in the manifest and latent content of a dream image. The emergence of the symbol provides an opportunity to discern the unconscious meaning and link it with the conscious one. Meaning in symbols is never fixed, always to be discerned and revised through multiple ways of linking the known with the unknown. This is different from signs where the meaning is agreed on, established, or supported by convention or the culture, as in the fact that green is a sign to go or crying is a sign of hunger.

The empathic stance reaches for what is not known or is hidden in the symbol, and may be too threatening to integrate into consciousness; it is the vehicle for reaching the invisible, the intuitively sensed. Empathy is needed to grasp the hidden meaning of symbols but not the literal or absolute meaning of signs. Empathy epitomizes the symbolic attitude; that is, it assumes the difference of the other and the desire to know the other from its own meaning generating core. Therefore every psychic product is viewed symbolically, not with fixed, predetermined meaning, and assumes that the manifest leaves a lot to be known. The symbol invites the empathic response and the empathic response helps unfold the symbol. In one image, the symbol can express the unity of polar opposites and convey the oneness of elements that logic regards as paradoxical. It is through symbols that we go beyond our logical, rational, narcissistically invested selves and get in touch with what is missing. It is through symbols that we can master and order the unruly feelings and chaos that accompany venturing into the unknown. The empathic discernment of the symbol thus helps the process of wholeness, of integrating the forbidden and feared into one's self image.

This stance thus becomes a facilitating bridge to the yet-to-be-explored, as well as an invitation to the other to contribute actively to the dialogue of unfolding meaning. It is the only stance that allows for an authentic evolving relationship between the mother and child, or the analyst and patient.

Empathy is integral to all phases of the symbolic process. Freedman and Karliner (1999) delineate these phases as progressing from the concrete insistence on a single meaning (desymbolization), where empathy is not at all possible, followed by incipient symbolization, when affects spark images and allusions. This leads to a form of sensed knowing, allowing for some form of feeling for the other. In discursive symbolization "a crucial attribute . . . is . . . the coherent telling of relationship episodes in which there is the recognized presence of self and other interacting affectively, perhaps with mutual recognition" (Freedman and Karliner 1999, p. 6). This form of symbolization allows for increasingly greater inner coherence and a self able to feel for the other without losing its own sense of self and integrity. Finally, there is dynamic symbolization, which Freedman and Karliner (1999) define as "not just dealing with the linking of affects or relationship episodes which can be quite conscious, but with experiences that are conflictual, incoherent, or chaotic. These experiences are brought into line with experiences that are rational, coherent or bound . . . here we are concerned with the symbolization of the dynamic unconscious" (p. 6).

This more evolved form of symbolization involves self-reflection, an ability to bring together opposites, known and unknown, and a progressive integration of denied and unconscious aspects of the self, so that there is a diminishing of denied unconscious material being projected on the other and an optimal integration of opposites within the self. What results is a state in which one can be openly receptive to the other without being biased toward one side of an issue, and one can participate in contacting the other's unknown self without imposing one's own opinion or narcissistic needs. Differentiating levels of symbolic development in analysts may, in some ways, bridge the current dichotomy between an objective or neutral stance and a subjective one, by identifying the quality or capacity for listening and communicating in both analyst and patient. In analyzing symbolic and empathic capacities in analysts with professed subjective or objective stances, one may find convergence in both categories in analysts with highly developed empathic and symbolic capacities as well as convergence in both categories with analysts who are not as empathic or have certain narcissistic or underlying traumatic issues that lead them to be overly concrete or defensive. Commonalities on the continuum of symbolic development in both objectively and subjectively oriented analysts might help determine what is harmful and beneficial to patients, regardless of the professed orientation.

An essential beneficial effect of both a parent's and an analyst's developed symbolic capacity is the ability to simultaneously hold a consistent but flexible sense of himself with an openness to the other and thus allow the patient (or child) the experience of being simultaneously securely connected to a consistent and reliable other, while feeling free to play with being different than the other without punitive, hostile, or anxiety-provoking consequences. This capacity is needed by the parent (therapist) at every stage of the child's (patient's) life. It is the moral core of the relationship that allows the child (patient) from birth (the start of analysis) to be responsive to her own creative inclinations and needs and not merely exist in compliance with the other's (parent's or analyst's) imperatives. This kind of responsiveness evolves in the presence of an other who has successfully separated him- or herself from internalized objects and so developed the separate subjectivity that allows for a space of difference, where one can mediate between one's perceptions and the thoughts about which one is perceiving, and so not be overly identified or attached to one's perceptions. Ogden (1986) describes this as "the experience of oneself as subject who has created one's symbols" (p. 213). It is in that space that a capacity for ambiguity, uncertainty, and freedom to play with ideas can develop. Here one no longer sees the other in terms of one's need, or in terms of one's fixed meaning or understanding, often determined by a rigid, nondifferentiated fusion with a parental imago and thus with one's own ideas and affects related to that imago. In this more differentiated space, one can play with possibilities of who the other really is, without feeling a threat of loss of self when feeling one's way into another's self experience different from one's own.

In Bion's (1959) idea of healthy projective identification, the mother, in being able to make herself psychologically available to the infant, can elicit from her infant thoughts that cannot be thought and feelings that cannot be felt. "Projective identification makes it possible for him (the infant) to investigate his own feelings in a personality powerful enough to contain them. Denial of the use of this mechanism . . . leads to a destruction of the link between infant and breast and consequently, to a severe disorder of the impulse to be curious on which all learning depends" (p. 314). This destruction can lead to what Bion (1962) calls "nameless dread" (p. 116).

Ogden (1994) explains that "it is nameless because it lacks the shape and definition afforded by the mother's containing/creative response to the infant's projective identification including those provided by her conscious and unconscious symbolizing functions" (p. 46).

A highly developed symbolic capacity is the one factor most likely to provide the healthy projective identification that facilitates empathic connection rather than projective identification, which imposes disowned aspects of oneself on the other. Parents who have achieved facility with symbolic functioning are likely to have a more integrated sense of self; to pay attention to how the symbolic productions of mind reveal themselves through dreams, reverie, and creative pursuits; to acknowledge disowned and dissociated aspects of themselves; and to flexibly revise their sense of reality as new data about themselves and the world expand their consciousness. Knowing that symbols are rich with un-gleaned meaning and may evoke conflict as they become more conscious, symbolically developed parents respond to the symbolic productions of their child with respect, gentleness, and care.

The flexibility, creativity, and willingness to contact and integrate disavowed aspects of the self make symbolically developed parents less likely to project dissociated aspects of themselves onto their children and unconsciously attempt to control them or bind them to rigid self-constructs without some reflection—that is, make their offspring victims of their negative projective identifications. These unconscious negative projective identifications are perhaps the biggest impediment to empathy.

Empathy is both an activity and a state of mind on the part of a parent. As a state of mind it is receptive, capable of deep "empty" listening, without a need to impose values and self-states on the other. As an activity it refrains from manipulating the child so that he conforms to the parent; it is poised with no predisposition to react in one way rather than another. It is not identified with itself as reality, but allows itself to be disorganized and changed as it attempts to bring parts of self into being that may not yet exist. It is a mode in constant opposition to stasis, the existent; it is an energy that keeps things dynamic and in motion, involving imagination that expands the limits of what is. A truly creative, intimate relationship seeks the wholeness of the other person through empathic facilitation of what is hidden, unknown, and not yet part of the self. Revelation of what is innermost occurs through the unconscious production of symbols. It is in the warm, empathic attention of the other that symbols unfold to reveal most deeply what lack of empathy first made the person hide.

CASE MATERIAL

I first met Michael when he was 4½, shortly after he had been asked to leave a private nursery school. The reasons given were that he had been wandering around aimlessly, did not involve himself in interactions with either peers or staff, exhibited poor eye contact, demonstrated echolalia-like repetitive communications, and showed no interest in toys or any kind of creative symbolic play. The parents reported that he avoided other children, any kind of skin-contact activities like rough-and-tumble play, preferred to be alone, and tended to be very shy and fearful with strangers.

Michael's parents reported normal milestones in terms of motoric and verbal development. His father described him as being "a strange kid," particularly in the past two years, who would involve himself with vacuum cleaners and broken phones, or rock to the sound of the dishwasher. He rarely threw tantrums, but when he was a problem, his mother said, "The only thing that helped was getting mad at him." His mother reported having no awareness of anything being wrong with Michael until he was dismissed from nursery school.

The mother's denial of Michael's problems during his first three and a half years seemed to stem in part from her need to perpetuate a symbiotic tie, to not threaten her own positive self-image as a mother, to avoid feelings of pain or narcissistic injury that noticing his difficulties might arouse, and her fear of seeing him as being in any way like her two younger brothers, who had a history of psychiatric hospitalizations. Her denial cost Michael the empathy he needed in difficult times. The extent to which Michael's problems in symbolic development were related to genetic and neurological factors, as opposed to deficient empathy, is not certain. But the consequences of his often odd behavior on social interactions and on his self-esteem suffered further as a result of environmental empathic deficits. Michael's mother was not able to value the child's inner experience over how he appeared to others. She did not sufficiently help him feel that she understood his behavior from his own perspective, and she induced guilt for his hurting her with his behavior. This served to "freeze" further the child's inner life and ability to express himself. An example of the mother's denial and empathic lapse was illustrated when she was asked about how he reacted to his sister's birth when he was 2. She said he had no trouble at all with her arrival and that he was an exemplary brother, though she did notice he ignored the baby's existence for some time.

He was tested by a school psychologist shortly before coming to see me. In the test report questions were raised as to whether there was a psychotic process, an autistic syndrome, an organic component, and/or a pervasive developmental disorder. The examiner reported that Michael would become unproductive and distracted because he missed his mother and would perseverate on this throughout the session. She found his language confused, poorly organized, and lacking logical thought. He would produce bits of unrelated monologues like, "I just don't know you. I'll never know you. I'll always never know you." He tried to control his anxiety with stereotyped, concrete responses, and when presented with affect-laden stimuli he would regress, communicating that he felt endangered and threatened. When asked to name the people in his family he mentioned his mother and father, but no sister, and could produce no opposite for brother.

He was tested again, by a child analyst, a few months after he began to see me for therapy. The examiner reported that initially he paced around the office and spoke in "a fragmented, often illogical, and sometimes incomprehensible manner. What finally emerged in his fragmented narrative was the fact that he believed the examiner was to replace Dr. Schwager as his therapist. Once this misunderstanding was clarified and Michael understood that he *would* be seeing Dr. Schwager again, he settled down and was easier to engage." This behavior illustrated how Michael used a regression to desymbolized thought to defend against anxiety evoked by the anticipated loss of a significant object. This anxiety kept him fused with the missing object and did not allow him to fully attend to tasks. This was true in the first testing situation as well, where the missing object was his mother.

The second examiner reported:

> First, his thought and perceptual processes lack sufficient flexibility. This rigidity of mind fosters thought that is essentially descriptive, functional, factually based or temporal-sequential in nature. It does not permit insightful, intuitive leaps from the facts to the overall meaning of a situation. Thus, although Michael has a good—even superior—mind, he cannot use it to think creatively or adaptively. . . . In contrast, when a problem involves the processing of concrete, factual, or serial information, Michael fares remarkably well.
>
> Just as Michael is unlikely to "get the picture" when the elements of the picture are abstract or when they must be meaningfully analyzed and synthesized, so too he fails to "get" the meaning of situations when the content is emotional or interpersonal in nature.
>
> He is prone to experiences of diffuse and overwhelming anxiety, which at times further impair the quality of his thought processes. His sense of himself is vague, blurry and, as yet, indistinct from his mother. He has little sense of himself as a definite, separate individual person in the world. . . . He has an infant-like experience of himself that is absolutely dependent on others for survival. . . . He tends to perceive the world outside his immediate family as a threatening place . . . himself a guileless soul who has been pre-maturely thrust out into a dangerous and unpredictable jungle. Like a "baby tiger without a mom" (his response to a Rorshach Card).

In an interaction I observed in the waiting room, Michael expressed to his mother that he had been very angry at me and hated me, to which his mother responded, "Michael that's not nice, you don't hate Dr. Schwager." This made him even angrier, so he hit his 2-year-old sister and said he hated her. His mother again said, "You don't hate Teresa, Michael, you love your sister." This exemplified his mother's need to impose her perceptions and needs on Michael.

I saw Michael twice a week and the parents every two to three weeks. In the sessions with the parents I tried to help them understand the meaning behind what Michael said and did; to help them be more curious and open to his feelings; to make them more aware of the effects of their punitive, denying, and guilt-provoking behavior; and to help them diminish these responses to him. In one session the mother reported Michael telling her, "I don't think you love me." She responded, "Well, I'll tell *you* that I don't think *you* love *me*. How does that feel? It hurts, doesn't it?" Responses like these, along with her reporting being punitive or withholding love in response to his anger or inappropriate behavior, illustrated her tendency to deny or even punish Michael's feelings, especially those that led to differentiation and movement away from her. This seemed to be a factor in Michael's difficulty knowing what he felt, differentiating inside and outside, separating his feelings from her, knowing what he needed, and his painful inner disorganization. When I pointed out that she was turning the focus on her hurt feelings, while Michael was coming to her with hurt feelings that needed her attention, she was responsive and able to reflect on the effect this kind of response might have on Michael. Slowly, she seemed able to shift to a more sensitive, less narcissistic, and at moments even empathic response to him.

After the first year of treatment, Michael went into a Special Ed class in the public schools with only seven other children. The teachers there seemed understanding of and responsive to his problems. The shift in his family and school environment augmented the work in therapy. Examples of Michael's communication in the first few sessions follow.

In the first session one of the things Michael said was, "I'm afraid of dark things, spooky things, shadows. Sometimes I imagine scary things."

I responded that it must be awfully lonely to feel like that and asked him what he did when he felt that way. He said, "Tell Mom and Dad." Then he looked at the cactus plant in my office and said, "Feels sharp and pointy. Are you real? Red is the water. Mom and Dad told me that." He took out a checker game to play and said, "You be black because you have blond hair. I'll be red 'cause I have black hair. I could stand to laugh. Bonzi is a good joke."

In this first session Michael fleetingly but clearly expressed his terror. When asked what he does when he feels that way, his response, "Tell Mom and Dad," disorganized him. One could speculate that the response he gets from them—"Forget it, there's nothing there." makes him feel he has to deny what he feels, confuses him about what he feels, disorganizes him and makes him feel frightened, not only of what initially scared him but also about sharing what scares him and the response he will get in response to expressing himself. He then becomes additionally frightened of the perception and feeling that his parents tell him is not true or is not in response to something really there. In the session with me he lost contact with me and turned away from his inner life to a plant on my table. He exhibited the derailed interaction that perhaps goes on with his parents. His subsequent communication exemplified desymbolization, rooted in fear and a need to hide. It resulted in disorder, naming, and use of words as things or signs. This retreat into meaninglessness also served Michael's need to separate himself from the painful feelings of his inner life and the dangers of sharing them. Revealing his worst fears made him vulnerable to their nonempathic negation.

In the next session I asked Michael what he would want if he had three wishes. He said, "I wish for my mom to come here. You mean my command? Would you like to see my baby browns? My mom calls them baby browns. I came to see you 'cause of my feelings. I lost my feelings. I feel sad about something that my mind happened."

He was unable to get beyond wishing for his mom to be there. He then took up a pencil and with two hands started drawing a face with two vacant eyes and said, "Something got me angry. Leave me alone and get lost. Everyone's crazy. Crazy means you're not good.

You're naughty. My mom calls me Bigaboo. Dad calls me Michael. Everyone calls me Bigaboo. It means you're a big boy." He made a face. I asked him if something was bothering him.

He said, "My goldfish is calling me. Mom's angry at yourself. Something that's not me. Would you like to come to my house? I have a mother, father, sister, and brother."

I asked about his brother, since I knew in reality he had no brother.

He told me his brother's name was Adam and that he was 4.

Michael's communication here seemed to stem from perceptions arising from a fused self–object representation. His mother's perceptions of him were fused with his perceptions of himself. His perceptions of them were fitted into their Procrustean bed, and only those that fit their own self-image were allowed. Michael's difficulty separating internal and external made it hard for him to know to what extent the goldfish was in his fantasy or memory or actually in the room, or whether the imaginary brother he wished he had really existed or to what extent his perception of scary, negating, rejecting parents is really them or something he makes up. At this point in Michael's life there was very little self or subjectivity apart from the fused self–object experience that could allow him to reflect, wonder, pretend, or play, so as to test out the validity of his perceptual world.

In the first months of treatment with me he showed an absolute aversion to all imaginary play material like puppets, a dollhouse, or play figures. When shown these objects, he would become visibly anxious, reject them, and tell me he had no time for them.

What he showed most interest in was the computer. At first this involved repetitive listing of words and numbers. I slowly extended this ritualistic, mechanical procedure by helping Michael write sentences about what he had done that day in school or simple declarative sentences about what he felt. These lists would typically be called "Class News" and he would mirror precisely and robotically what he remembered, like "Today is Friday. It is winter. It is cloudy and cold. Five boys are here today. Tomorrow is a special day." After some time it was expanded to lists of declarative sentences with a little more content, feeling, and relatedness like

1. I'd like to have fun with the five kids in my class.
2. Why is there 48 miles in Dr. Schwager's house?
3. I'd like you to see something.
4. I am hungry and want to eat my snack.
5. I was angry about my father.
6. He made a mean face at me.

Eventually this expanded into writing short stories. The computer was, in some way, a first transitional object for Michael. While not invested with warmth or giving him back the cuddliness of a blanket or stuffed animal, it was invested with a need for some accurate mirroring. It gave him back exactly what he put in, undistorted by its own narcissistic needs. The computer, and other mechanical devices he was drawn to, often provided greater safety, reliability, and accurate response to his self than did the interpersonal world he lived in.

A similar interest in a tape recorder evolved into his making recordings of himself talking and singing. He showed pleasure in playing back and listening to the exact replica of what he recorded. I sometimes stopped the tape and asked him what he meant by something he said. This was with the intent of helping him begin to reflect on his own communication and so develop a margin of experience outside of the fused self–object perception.

At this point, he showed a preference for mechanical things and manifested repetitive behaviors, but he was also beginning to exhibit a greater range of affects. At first they appeared to be random and often inappropriate. I would attempt to match his affect state with similar expressions of my own, or repeat in words what I experienced him feeling.

A ritual that went on each session for over a year was Michael's telephone call to his mother. About a year and three months after starting treatment, Michael brought in his own black phone because he said he didn't like my phone. He pretended to call me from his phone. I picked up my phone. He said there was static and he couldn't hear me, and hung up quickly, unable to sustain a conversation. He then asked me for the tape recorder and said the connection was loose. I said, "There seem to be a lot of bad connections today."

In looking back, I see that this remark was an empathic failure on my part. I reflected only the manifest communication and did not pick up the deeper meaning. He told me he was trying to connect to me and not just his mother, whom he had always called on my phone in the sessions. He also showed me he could play and pretend, and that it was all very scary and difficult for him to sustain a connection to me and to this new creative way of trying to communicate.

His response reflected not only his disappointment in me, but also seemed to be an attempt to clarify what he meant. Perhaps because we had a basically good empathic connection for over a year, my empathic failure at this point served in some way as an optimal frustration and pushed Michael to draw on his own resources a bit more.

He said, "Too bad, Elaine. I'm being sad. I think I can't come here for Valentine's Day. I have to go to somebody else's house. What's the matter, Elaine? I'm afraid for you. When you cry, she feels blue. You look like you feel blue. I feel green, yellow, red—that's happy. I'm going to make you feel green, orange, blue, red, black. . . . I'm very sad that you're sad. . . ."

Michael expressed confusion as to who feels what, but he also was saying that he wasn't going to give up, that he wanted me to feel everything he felt and wanted me to know what's inside of him. He showed more indications of a longing to be in contact with me, as well as attempting some of the matching of affect states that I had been doing with him. Here one can see the emerging of what Freedman and Karliner (1999) call *incipient symbolization*, where the patient "gains access to the pre-linguistic stirrings of primary emotions in the body and links them to spoken language" (p. 4).

In the next several weeks, his work on the computer expanded from lists to stories. One of the first he wrote was titled, "A Story of a Duck Named Donald," which he dictated to me.

> He talks like a duck. He takes his car. (I'm making up the story now.) A bee stings him. He gets his cooley pinched. He tries to make it feel better. He puts some Neosporin on it. He puts it on

> himself. The bee comes back. He stings Donald again. Donald feels scared and I think sad. He's mad at the bee. He blows him away back into the honey tree. The bee always bothered Donald.

This story moved from incipient to discursive symbolization, continuing to use language to more meaningfully link his feelings to another, other than the mother imago, who had been his primary audience. His remark, "I'm making up the story now," also suggested the beginning of a separate subjectivity where he was developing the ability to discern the symbol from the symbolizer and to have a sense of himself as the creator of his symbols. A few weeks later he wrote the following story on the computer.

> A little white duck lives far away in Buffalo. He made corn pie for all the other little ducks to come over. When all the ducks came over they threw up. Davy duck was white. All the other ducks were yellow. He felt different. He had a pond. The yellow ducks come to swim in his pond. The little duck's oven broke. The toilets broke. The pond broke. The filter broke. He goes to swim at one of the yellow duck's house. Davy lives all alone. He's 17. He doesn't have a family, only friends. His favorite duck is Donald Duck, a yellow duck.

Here Michael tried to represent symbolically latent fantasies that were difficult to express: concerns about being different, fears that the mechanical things (ovens, toilets, filters) he counted on may not be as safe and reliable as he thought. In the story he created a new form of comfort—a friend. He even went so far as to risk it being a yellow duck, who was different from himself. Stories such as these became more frequent and reflected a transition to an ability to make use of discursive symbolization that Freedman and Karliner (1999) describe as "the coherent telling of relationship episodes in which there is the recognized presence of self and other interacting affectively, perhaps with mutual recognition" (p. 6).

About a month after writing this story I took out some hand puppets and for the first time Michael didn't say he had no time to play with them. He put one puppet on his hand and called it Daniel and the other on my hand and called it Lambchop. Later in the session he wrote on the computer, "Daniel and Lambchop are friends." In subsequent sessions he asked for Daniel and Lambchop and used them to carry on dialogues or talk for his feelings. These pieces of cloth were now beginning to be invested with his thoughts and feelings.

Soon after this change in Michael, his mother gave birth to her third child, another baby girl. In a session the evening after his sister was born, he told me about the birth of his sister and then immediately went to the phone to call his mother. When he got the answering machine he started to cry, realizing his mother was still in the hospital. He then told me he was angry that he didn't get a brother. He said, "I got to go up there and tell God I want a brother. Girls are a problem. I'm gonna chop her foot off."

"What else?" I asked.

"I'm not going to chop her foot off. You know what I'm going to do if it's really a girl? I'm going to make her knees bend both ways."

He went to the computer, typed some words quickly on it, and told me that he wanted the words to disappear. I said, "Like you want your sister to disappear." He then took a pencil and wrote in one of my notebooks, " I love you."

My response gave Michael the feeling that I was as interested in his angry feelings as I was in any other feelings. He could be angry without my rejecting him, or being angry back at him, or him sensing I did not want that anger to be a part of him. This seemed to be a powerfully liberating experience for him, evoking feelings of being loved and loving. It was also markedly different than how his mother reacted to his angry feelings when his first sister was born and subsequently.

Following this session there was a marked increase in Michael's ability to express anger freely and in imaginative play. He played school, railed at me for being a no-good disgrace of a child, or acted out the movie *Home Alone* with the doll house, sending Kevin to his room as a total disgrace. The relationship with me gave him the margin of safety to express scary feelings in symbolic play, particularly anger and fears of being bad and crazy, which his mother had a hard time allowing. He also began to play out family scenes with a doll house. He would do to me what he experienced was done to him, and also revealed to me the diminished way he perceived himself as a result of how he was treated. In the doll house play there were occasions when he would have one of the children express anger at the mother or refute what she said.

Simultaneous to these strides in his development, Michael developed an uncanny phobia of shipping peanuts—the white styrofoam pieces that are used for packing to protect merchandise. During an arts and crafts project in school, where these styrofoam pieces were being used for a string chain, Michael screamed in terror and ran out of the room into a guidance counselor's office. There was a similar panic reaction when he spotted some of these peanuts in my office. His parents confirmed that he had developed a phobia to these white peanuts.

While I was never able to get clear associations from Michael as to what these shipping peanuts symbolized, I was aware of this terror occurring as he was making remarkable strides in his symbolic and expressive development. My intuitive sense was that these pieces, airy and without substance, yet used to protect, symbolized for Michael the terror of his own hard protective covering falling apart around him, as well as his reliance on hard surfaces (like machines, computers) failing him as sources of comfort. This seemed to be foreshadowed in the story where the ovens and toilets and pond break down. This shift from reliance on the hard, mechanical to the human seemed to be a terrifying one. Unconsciously, he was beginning to perceive these hard things as having so little substance they could just scatter to the wind, leaving him absolutely vulnerable to the changeable, less reliable human world and so to annihilation, and "nameless dread."

The juxtaposition of these two states suggests as well that contained in the story telling, the puppet play, and imaginative play were experiences of dynamic symbolization, where Michael was attempting to integrate painful, conflictual, incoherent, and chaotic experiences into the self. Both the story and play with the puppets seemed to indicate as well that there was an internalization of a more comforting other. This may have been a combination of me, a change he sensed in his parents, and perhaps the more tolerant school environment. A school report summarizing his behavior in a special education class at this time said:

> Michael has shown steady progress in areas of peer relationships and adaptation to new situations. . . . Although initially seen as a negative behavior, Michael did show some acting-out behavior when he would "stand up" to some of his classmates in some minor altercations. During the course of an annual review meeting with the parents, this was seen as a positive quality because for the first time, Michael was seen as not retreating from a conflict, but learning to deal with it! Consequently Michael's peer interactions were actually improving.

Indications of having internalized a more comforting other were evident in his having the courage to encounter painful and conflictual unconscious feelings and his expressing forbidden negative feelings like anger. This also reflected an emerging self apart from the fused, symbiotic relationship with his mother.

In one session during this time I told Michael his time was up and he said, "I don't want to go, I want to play." Following this, he brought in two soft Winnie-the-Pooh bears. He threw the little one on my couch and said, "This one is the stuffed animal." He picked up the big bear, held it close to him, looked it in the eyes, and said, "This is the real live one. I give him honey. He talks to me. I love him and snuggle with him every night. He's my best pal. He watches *Home Alone* with me. He's afraid of that guy in the movie with the shovel, that I'm not afraid of. He's a bear with very little brains."

I asked if I could hold Winnie. He said, "I would never let you hold him. He doesn't even know you. You can hold the little one; he's just a stuffed animal."

DISCUSSION OF THE DEVELOPMENTAL PROCESS OF SYMBOLIZATION IN MICHAEL

During the course of therapy Michael passed through all levels of symbolic development. One could safely hypothesize that in addition to any inherited component, his fixations and derailment of the symbolic process had roots in early infancy and interventions initially had to address this early impairment.

The first attempts at symbolization arise when the infant longs for something that is not available, and attempts to create an image of the absent need-gratifying object. Freud referred to this as primary hallucinatory wish fulfillment. This may be thought of as the first presence of an absence. True symbolism evolving from this primitive desire is seen by Deri (1984) as always taking place in the context of longing. Desymbolization, on the other hand, is rooted in the need to repress, to remove from consciousness that which is wished for because it creates too much anxiety or dread. It thus results in the need to conceal or obscure, rather than bring into being and clarify, and thus further results in disorder and loss of meaning. In the first few months of life the mother's mediation or lack of mediation is experienced as a part of the self. In this preobject state, the infant's primitive internalizations of its experience of the infant–parent relationship pattern lay the foundation for perceptual and self-experiences as well as where there will later be developmental arrest.

Bick (1968) proposed the concept of a "psychic skin." This psychic skin develops from the "continuous interaction between a physically and emotionally 'holding' and mentally 'containing' mother, and the surface of the infant's body as a sensory organ. . . . " It serves to bind together experiences of the infant's early self in the direction of integration and cohesion." Bick saw its function as "giving rise to phantasy of internal and external space" (p. 484) and becoming the basis for idealization and separation. She also believed that the lack of development of this function resulted in unintegration and catastrophic anxieties. Tustin (1986), in discussing problems of autistic children, found that in the absence of this containing presence, these children were "chronically unintegrated" (p. 127). They dealt with this terror and feeling of falling apart by creating boundaries and safety through the sensation of adhering to the surfaces of hard objects. In some cases of autism, she observed, children would become addicted to this as a means of survival. She saw autistic children as being fused with the mother in ways that made them feel the same as the object and with no space between them. She referred to this as the "adhesive equation" as opposed to the "adhesive identification," where "the subject feels similar to the object and there is space between them." (p. 19). In both these states the capacity for true empathy is limited.

While it is hard to know what the mood and interplay between Michael and his mother was in infancy, some of the mother's remarks such as, "He was a perfect baby, no trouble, hardly cried," and as a small child, "He's a good boy, never difficult to manage," are consistent with her later denial of his negative emotions and her responding negatively to what was troublesome or unacceptable to him. On child development assessment forms and checklists done by social workers when problems in nursery school first appeared, Michael's mother said he was never left with anyone but her, checked "never" for being restless, upset, crying excessively, or showing intense reaction to new experiences, foods, or places.

The capacity for symbolism has been thought to evolve from the oscillations of intense longing and disappointment in the infant. The infant longs for someone he has experienced with great pleasure. The good enough empathic relationship provides the basis for the longing and the hope of the return of satisfaction. But as the child gets older, moments of need result in an object who is at times not available or optimally satisfying. Early in life an oscillation of empathic connection and nontraumatic frustration is essential for optimal development. Winnicott (1951) emphasized that "If all goes well the infant can actually come to gain from the experience of frustration, since incomplete adaptation to need makes objects real, that is to say hated as well as loved" (p. 238). If delay is optimal, not too frustrating, it facilitates the child's turning more to his own resources, an important capacity in developing separation of the fused self–object imago, and critical for his further development. The innate capacity for symbol formation is in some important ways influenced by the strength given to the child in the empathic connection to overcome the rage and hate that emerge from frustration. The infant resolves the intense tension that comes from this by creating an image of what is missing. In the creation of this initial image, the baby also experiences the capacity for hope that even in absence there is presence of the object and the possibility of its return. Contained in this early protosymbol as well are the rudiments of separateness and autonomy.

The description of Michael as a baby does not show these fluctuations in intense desire and disappointment. He is described as good, never crying intensely, always with the mother. The conditions of optimal empathy and optimal frustration seem to be missing. Michael's mother's needs to see Michael as a "good" baby and to see herself as a "good" mother. These narcissistically driven needs seemed to interfere with an optimal empathic response as well as optimal frustration.

Winnicott (1971) referred to this presymbolic phase as *the holding stage*. It was later empirically studied by Beebe and Lachmann (1988), who describe experiences of matching or derailed interaction between mother and infant that contribute to presymbolic representations. Winnicott hypothesized that the empathically attuned mother has the breast or arms there at the right moment, giving the infant the experience that his wish has magically created its own fulfillment. Her empathy more or less accurately senses what is missing and allows the infant the experience of being a participant in bringing about what he gets from the mother. With poorly attuned mothers, the infant may give up wishing or become excessively demanding, rageful, or inconsolable, or else withdraw, experiencing a sense of inner emptiness resulting from the destruction of his wishes. The consistent "goodness" that Michael's mother described may have been related from her side in part to an empathic withdrawal, resulting in that inner emptiness and destruction of his wishes.

For the infant at this stage of development, symbol, object, wish, and fulfilment are inextricably fused. The symbol does not represent anything but is equated with the symbolized and used to deny the separateness between subject and object. The image of the breast is no different from the breast itself. The empathic requirement of the mother in early infancy is to provide the reliable, accurate attunement that promotes this fusion and sense of omnipotence.

Fixation at this level interferes with mediating between one's perception and the thoughts about which one is perceiving. This allows for limited subjectivity or I-ness. The fusion with the primary object makes differentiation difficult, and later in life concreteness, rather than the symbolic attitude, is likely to prevail. When fused representations of early life dominate perception, it is difficult or impossible to separate self from others. Projections dominate perceptions and it is also difficult to disentangle the self from the projections of others.

The emerging capacity to symbolize, to hold an image of an object in its absence, facilitates separation of the fused self–object imago. If one has the symbol, one doesn't need the object all the time. As Hanna Segal (1957) stated, "as the symbol is acknowledged as a creation of the subject, unlike the symbolic equation, it can be freely used by the subject. When a substitute in the external world is used as a symbol it may be used more freely than the original object, since it is not fully identified with it. Insofar, however, as it is distinguished from the original object, it is also recognized as an object in itself. Its own properties are recognized" (p. 42). One could see an impairment in this capacity with Michael's constant preoccupation with his mother and his need early in the treatment to stay connected by his regular phone calls in the session.

This capacity for symbol formation proper allows for the experience of ambivalence and loss and the capacity for depression. This was evident in Michael as he began to touch on the capacity for dynamic symbolization. His ability to contact anger and dysphoric feelings through symbolic play and stories brought up fears of the loss of love of his mother, ambivalent feelings toward those he loved, more conscious feelings of being different, and expressed feelings of being alone. In a school report around the time he was developing this capacity, he was described as emitting "a sad tone." This sadness, as well as the anger emerging around this time, was progress from the flat, automatonlike affect he primarily displayed at the onset of treatment.

These optimal lapses in empathy in an otherwise attuned parent have a very different effect than the chronic frustration caused by lack of empathy, mirroring, and accurate responsiveness that is the result of narcissistically wounded and wounding parents. These parents, who most often have not achieved true symbolization themselves, can contribute to freezing the child's symbolic development and individuation process by denying the child's feelings or perceptions and overriding the child's needs by their own. The healthy, dynamic oscillation of the child's responsiveness to his own needs and desires with responsiveness to a responsive other, the capacity to feel joyful in being both agent in bringing about desired results and receiver of the love he has elicited, is short-circuited by a nonempathic response in whatever form it takes—indifference, coercion, punitiveness, manipulation, deprivation, or abuse. Instead, an unhealthy symbiosis develops in which the child tends to label his own needs and perceptions negatively in favor of preserving some image of a good parent. This pathological dynamic dampens the child's spontaneous aliveness and creativity, necessary for ongoing symbolic differentiation and self-definition. In Shengold's (1989) words, it creates the kind of soul murder where "one person absorbs the life of another" (p. 20).

If the child has had sufficient empathic mirroring and responsiveness in infancy, that is, according to Winnicott, is alive enough, real enough, and good enough, he is able to blend the basically non-persecutory inner object world with an object in external reality to create the transitional object. It is what Winnicott (1951) calls "an intermediate area of experiencing to which inner reality and external life both contribute" (p. 230). The blanket may be symbolic of the breast, but it's not being the breast, its actuality, is as important as the fact that it stands for the breast. When this type of symbolism is employed, the youngster is distinguishing between fantasy and reality, inner objects and external objects, and creativity and perception.

The ability to create and make use of a transitional object is the beginning of the ability to play. Play involves the ability to trust both the external object world and spontaneous internal productions. In the child's play one can observe where he is in his symbolic development, the degree of self/object differentiation, the projection of good and bad internal objects, the capacity for illusion, how he handles disillusionment, his own capacity for empathy—how he feels his way into experiences and characters unlike himself. Michael came to inhabit and invest the puppets, which had initially evoked feelings of revulsion and aversion, with formerly forbidden feelings and thoughts. He was ultimately able to create a transitional object out of a bear who was warm and cuddly and fuzzy and could love him unconditionally, a monumental feat for a little boy who rocked to the sound of a dishwasher and sought hard surfaces to establish his boundaries and give him his sense of self.

CONCLUSION

The level at which the mother functions symbolically and empathically will influence the child's symbolic development, and the child's capacity and manner of expressing himself will often enhance the mother's responsiveness or exacerbate her difficulties in relating. What is cause and effect can be difficult to discern. From observations of Michael and his mother and reported data, there was evidence that the mother tended to respond from a rigid, overly narcissistic, nonreflective, nonsymbolic attitude. The mother's style and level of empathic/symbolic development both exaggerated whatever organic/genetic predisposition Michael had and interfered with his ongoing symbolic development. In turn, Michael's innate difficulties and limitations in expressing himself worsened his mother's narcissistic, punitive style, affecting her attunement to him. Each advancement in Michael's symbolic capacity increased his empathic capacity, his receptiveness to empathy, and his ability to reveal his inner world and to be responsive to the subjectivity of the other. Michael's improved symbolic development helped make his mother a better mother. She felt less narcissistically injured, less blamed, and so more available to him emotionally. Slowly, this more responsive mother was able to replace the earlier harsher internalized one and, together with the internalization of his therapist, create a more benign inner environment.

Viewing Michael's desymbolized productions as meaningful allowed him eventually to internalize an interested empathic other. Michael was confined to a psychic space where he had to be like the other to be loved by her. He could not express the rage and protest that this confinement evoked in him. He had to deny negative feelings, so could not link them with words in ways that would allow him to begin accessing and owning these forbidden feelings and images. He was, in fact, frozen in this desymbolized space. The empathic/symbolic attitude takes the stance with the other that one is open to what is to be known about any particular psychic product without assuming beforehand what it means. Slowly this attitude became internalized, and he was able to open up internal space where he could wonder and take in "good" external otherness that would allow him to play in the world as well as in his mind.

It was through Michael's beginning to glean meaning from his own symbolic productions that he started to develop a self that was truly his own. I will never be able to hold Michael's bear in the way he holds him, because that particular creation of his self has a meaning and existence it can have for no one else. By this point Michael knows there is a part of himself that is not his mother, and not me, that only his bear knows.

REFERENCES

Beebe, B. (1985). Mother–infant mutual influence and precursors of self and object representations. In *Empirical Studies of Psychoanalytic Theories*, Vol. 2 , ed. J. Masling, pp. 27–48. Hillsdale, NJ: Analytic Press.

Beebe, B., and Lachmann, P. (1988). The contribution of mother–infant mutual influence to the origins of self and object representations. *Psychoanalytic Psychology* 5:305–337.

Bick, E. (1968). The experience of the skin in early object relations. *International Journal of Psycho-Analysis* 49:484–486.

——— (1986). Further considerations on the function of the skin in early object relations. *British Journal of Psychotherapy* 2:292–299.

Bion, W. R. (1959). Attacks on linking. *International Journal of Psycho-Analysis* 40:308–315.

——— (1962). *Learning from Experience*. New York: Basic Books.

Deri, S. K. (1984), *Symbolization and Creativity*. New York: International Universities Press.

Freedman, N., Berzofsky, M., and DeMichele, A. (1999a). *On transformation cycles: the symbolization of a frozen constellation*. Paper presented at the Annual Meeting, Division 39 of the American Psychological Association, New York, April.

Freedman, H., and Karliner, R. (1999). *On incremental symbolization: clinical and empirical definition*. Paper presented at the Annual Meeting, Division 39 of the American Psychological Association, New York, April.

Freedman, H., Karliner, R., and Lavender, J. (1999b). *Desymbolization: pervasive and segmental*. Paper presented at the Annual Meeting, Division 39 of the American Psychological Association, New York, April.

Mitrani, J. (1996). *A Framework for the Imaginary* Northvale, NJ: Jason Aronson.

Ogden, T. H . (1986). *The Matrix of the Mind*. Northvale, NJ: Jason Aronson.

——— (1989). *The Primitive Edge of Experience*. Northvale, NJ: Jason Aronson.

——— (1994). *Subjects of Analysis*. Northvale, NJ: Jason Aronson.

Rycroft, C. (1968). *A Critical Dictionary of Psychoanalysis*. London: Nelson.

Segal, H. (1957). Notes on symbol formation. *International Journal of Psycho-Analysis*, 38:391–397.

Shengold, L. (1989). *Soul Murder*. New Haven, CT: Yale University Press.

Tustin F. (1986). *Autistic Barriers in Neurotic Patients*. New Haven, CT: Yale University Press.

Winnicott, D. W. (1951). Transitional objects and transitional phenomena. In *Collected Papers*, pp. 229–243. New York: Basic Books, 1958.

——— (1971). *Playing and Reality*. London: Tavistock.

21

When Words Will Not Suffice

JEAN B. SANVILLE

INTRODUCTION

Norbert Freedman (1998) has posited the concept of symbolization as the centerpiece for understanding a quality of mind crucial to analytic process and outcome. Like Goethe, he disagrees that "in the beginning was the word." Instead, he asserts that "in the beginning was the act." Our concepts of the symbolic today are no longer tied to the basic assumptions of Freud (1900, 1915) early in the last century. So drastically different now is our thinking about the language that goes into the "talking cure" that Freedman voiced a somewhat humorous apprehension that he might be accused of heresy. But his solution was a good one, a recommendation that concepts could best be improved if we could but allow a dialectic between legacy and heresy. I hope to follow that prescription.

I will be drawing on some recent research into infancy and early life as it sheds light on the unfolding of the symbolizing capacity. And I will also play with the applicability of the theories of Matte Blanco as they may facilitate our understanding of the domains of the unconscious and of the conscious and their interactions in thinking, feeling, and being. Finally, I will be using clinical material from two patients, one at the beginning of treatment and the other in the process of termination. The first was a young man who, in spite of a marked spelling disability, had for years kept a diary, and as we began our work together, he shared several volumes with me. I will cite from those, as they also reveal his need at the time he wrote them for acts as well as for words. The second was a middle-aged woman, a college professor, who supplemented words with drawings and paintings that she brought to her sessions. For both, language was something of a double-edged sword, a way of attempting integration of self-experience, but complicating self-with-other experiences. As Stern (1985) once noted, it has the potential for driving a wedge between two simultaneous forms of interpersonal experience. It can move relatedness away from the personal immediate level toward the impersonal and abstract. Many of our patients sense that and find it therapeutically useful to draw also upon preverbal modes of expression.

TREATMENT OF CHILDREN AND EXPANDING RESEARCH INTO EARLY LIFE

Children, of course, always draw upon these preverbal modes. Words are rarely enough. Depending on the age and level of development of the child patient, the mode of treatment is usually play therapy—*acts* with toys and things. The interaction between child and therapist is accompanied by words when these are part of what the little patient can bring, and when not, we who treat children may make commentaries in our own words, as much to register what we are seeing and guessing about the themes of the play as to interpret deep meanings. Whether verbal exchange ensues depends on the child's experience of the therapist and his own capacities with verbal language. So this is a seemingly different situation from traditional psychoanalysis with adults. In the latter we generally have invited the analysand to take the couch, hence to use bodily motion minimally, and to assume most of the responsibility for putting out words. We have set the stage and played our parts in such a way as to evoke transferences that we believe would afford us clues about the quality of past relationships as these may have contributed to the problems and complaints the person was bringing. Apart from initial greetings and postsession partings, we usually occupied a space behind the couch, not immediately visible to the patient, and we kept more or less quiet until we felt we had some important interpretations to offer.

Unlike the philosophy of Freedman and his researchers (Freedman et al. 1998) that choices about frequency and duration are integral to the therapeutic process itself, it is likely that since many analysts' preferences are for greater frequency and longer duration, they are inclined subtly or not so subtly to influence their patients' choices. And, since their ICC (IPTAR Clinical Center) study offers us statistical evidence that effectiveness does increase with greater frequency and duration, we may be even more inclined not to defer so completely to patients' own choices! As the researchers write, the facts of greater intensity and extensivity may be physical ones, but they facilitate the experience of a meaningful relationship that may be internalized. That is also what we hope good enough parenting from early life might accomplish.

OBSERVATION OF NEWBORNS AND YOUNG INFANTS

We could be provoked by the ICC data to review findings from research on early development, particularly to focus on how all of the senses play roles in the unfolding of symbolization. If we begin with recent data about the newborn, we may constructively confuse ourselves and have to ask afresh when and how the baby begins to develop symbols. Bruner (1977) views the infant as having an innate and central tendency to form and test hypotheses about experiences, to evaluate whether this is the same as or different from that. It would seem the infant is a born researcher! What equipment does the newborn bring that enables him to perform the needed tasks and experiments?

Because I am a teacher who often finds that words are not enough to impart to students certain concepts and ways of thinking, when I teach courses on infancy I show Hack's film, *The Amazing Newborn*. Made at Case Western Reserve, it shows the newborn in the first moments, hours, and days after birth. It is so moving that it often brings tears to the eyes, and not only in those of female viewers. What we see is the baby emerging from the body of the mother, and the physician, after making sure that all is well, delivering it into the arms of the mother. The two, now *in touch* outside the womb, gaze soulfully into each other's eyes for quite a few minutes. The infant's attention span, we later learn, is longer at this time than it will be again for quite a while. He does turn away briefly, but then returns to this eye-to-eye contact with mother. Both appear manifestly entranced.

In one instance, a mother seems to do a bit of research on her own; she puts out her tongue, and to our amazement, the baby, after looking intently at this act, does likewise. When I first saw this film, I felt I had found an additional clue as to why the word *language* derives from the Latin *lingua*. I imagined that both participants were unconsciously sensing that future meetings of the minds would entail "speaking in tongues." As I was writing this paper, there appeared in the Science File of *The Los Angeles Times* (Hotz 2000) an article about the imitation instinct. It cited the "brain mapping" being conducted at UCLA by neuroscientist Marco Iacoboni and his colleagues in Italy and Germany. Using functional magnetic resonance imagery, they located the built-in mechanism that allows us, from birth onward, to imitate movements and facial expressions that we see in other people. Two areas of the brain are especially active: the right parietal cortex involved in physical movement, and Broca's area, a key language center. So already researchers are trying to locate the literal spaces in our heads where these behaviors originate.

This tendency to imitate unconsciously can be seen to stem from what Matte Blanco (1988) calls the "region where asymmetrical relations are non-existent or almost non-existent, and where symmetrical relations prevail" (p. 86). He calls it the region of "the basic matrix of introjection and projection." Later, the human being will "clothe . . . indivisible being with happening," thus replacing the whole by the part. Seen in this way, "consciousness—which is built upon the physiological model of vision/hearing/touch/smell and as such is suitable for 'seeing' spatio-temporal phenomena—is really a deceit which replaces indivisible being by happening!" (p. 186). In this matter he sees himself allied with Freud, who called the innermost nature of the unconscious the "true psychical reality."

In later scenes in *The Amazing Newborn*, we see infants being tested for reactions to certain visual patterns and manifesting marked preference for those that resemble the human face, fixing their eyes on them when presented choices. And in other moments we are shown the baby lying on a table, moving ecstatically in rhythm to the sounds of an adult speaking with him in marked cadences, as though in a dance of oneness with the other. It seems impossible for us analysts to see those scenes and not imagine them to depict innate propensities for empathic response, for identification with the other. Yet, only a decade before this film, Spitz (1965), who must surely have viewed such scenes in his own studies, was still agreeing with Freud (1923) that there is no ego at birth and that "language is nonexistent during the whole of the first year of life" (p. 5). Nevertheless I often quote Spitz to the effect that "dialogue" (and he does keep that word in quotes, perhaps lest he be accused of heresy?) is established from the start between infant and mother. Or at least it is established when there is a good enough mother and a good enough infant. And in that circumstance, we cannot be talking of projective identification, if by that we designate attempts to rid oneself of unwanted feelings. Rather, we seem to be witnessing bodily manifestations of the human being's inborn inclinations to resonate with others.

Today we have researchers who would examine the world of the fetus, "a secret universe inaccessible to human sight" (Piontelli 1987, p. 453). Through the advent of ultrasound techniques it has become possible to show the perceptive and motor apparatus of the baby-to-be. Long before birth the fetus "can hear, respond to pressure and touch, swallow and taste, react to pain, choose its preferential position and also have some kind of primitive dream experience and show the beginning of some form of learning" (p. 454). Piontelli's interest in fetal life was provoked by the frequency with which she heard very young children describe fantasies of life before birth, and by her puzzlement that several of her little patients showed a "severity of withdrawal and regression" in spite of having parents who seemed warm and devoted. This confronted her with the old question: Is it genetic or is it environmental? As her observations expanded, she was struck by the individuality of movement of each fetus, its preferred postures and reactions. So her research interest led her to explore with certain pregnant mothers whether her impressions would find further confirmation in subsequent development of the child, and she did find that was possible to detect early markers of character in utero. From only two cases, however, she was not ready to answer questions as to what is genetic and what is environmental.

Piontelli later studied twins before and after birth (1989). She notes that the intrauterine environment is not identical for both; one often has a more favorable position than the other, so the sensations reaching each twin can be quite different. But she was struck by the individual reactions of each toward the other. She specifically reports in this article on two pairs of dizygotic twins, each couple consisting of a male and a female fetus, where she observed clear individual temperamental differences. In the first pair, the little female was the more lively one, albeit smaller than the male. The latter conveyed to Piontelli the impression of being disturbed by any stimulation from his sister, burying his face deeply in a far corner of the placenta. If his sister didn't give up attempting contact, he would violently kick her! In the second pair, it was the little male who was the more active, turning and kicking and stretching, and the little female seemed comparatively sluggish. Follow-up after birth revealed the persistence of these idiosyncratic features in the children. Apparently the *act* that characterizes the beginning is also descriptive of early life outside the womb, for follow-up visits to the homes revealed each child's inclination to continue preferences either for connecting or for being left alone. And of course, Piontelli observed these temperamental differences being seen and responded to by the mothers in ways that reflected their own inclinations.

The dialogues from infancy of which Spitz (1965) wrote were of course primarily affective exchanges, with all their "coenesthetic" aspects. They are "gut feelings" that will constitute components of later meetings with others, including that between analyst and potential analysand, which may or may not find validation in language proper. Affect and cognition are never altogether separable. Brenner (1982) writes that "any affect includes (a) sensations of pleasure, or unpleasure or a mixture of the two, plus (b) thoughts, memories, wishes, fears—in a word *ideas*. Ideas and sensation together constitute an affect as a psychological phenomenon" (p. 41). But there are persons who have great difficulty getting these components together. Clinically we are interested in the question as to how reversible are affects. In early childhood there is a tendency to "externalize," to tie feelings of good and bad to others or objects. Later, perhaps in the so-called latency period, some reversibility becomes possible, with distinctions between "self" (inner) and "external reality" (Thompson 1985). Ideally, as we mature, we human beings become increasingly able to think "thoughts about thoughts," to step back a bit from feeling, and to monitor self and others as affect experiencers. The whole psychoanalytic approach tends to be concerned with creating a new affective/cognitive domain.

NONSYMBOLIZERS AND THEORIES

Freedman and colleagues (1999) have written about desymbolization, but this word makes an assumption that there was symbolization that has been undone. Some of us, however, have worked with autistic children (Tustin 1981, 1984) in whom evidence of their having achieved much of the symbolic in the first years of life is scarce indeed. Once upon a time mental health professionals assumed that such children had very inadequate or even schizophrenogenic mothers. I have never subscribed to that way of thinking and have thought it iatrogenic in our therapeutic work. I assumed that some as yet unknown innate factor was centrally involved. I often heard from the mothers of autistic children that even the infant's crying was not communicative, that touch was not welcome, that eye contact was lacking or seemed actively avoided. So the early relationship between infant and mother had not been of the quality that leads infants to develop signs, signals, and symbols. Although, like all babies, the autistic one at first lacks language proper, if by that we mean words, these unfortunate ones seem not to make use of what we call "organ language" (Jacobson 1964, Kris 1953), or affective communication. They are indeed the patients who need intensive and extensive therapy, for they cannot readily engage in the play mode that we generally employ with young children. Over ten years of my treatment of little autistic Katie, she slowly, and with regressions at times, did acquire words and some capacities for play and playfulness (Sanville 1991). Mothers of such children and therapists who take them as patients do need abundant stamina, once defined by Schafer (1982) as the capacity for "empathizing sturdily, steadfastly, and patiently" (p. 48), if there is to be even partial repair.

RECENT ANALYTIC VIEWS ABOUT EARLY UNFOLDING OF SYMBOLIZATION

Clearly, affect plays a central role in the development of symbolization. Slade and Wolf (1994), in their writings on developmental approaches to meaning and representation, have emphasized the role of play, drawing on their own research on the interplay of children with their mothers or with their clinicians. They and the authors in their book are among those remodeling our theories in ways that show that human beings are profoundly affecting and affected by their social surround. When, for whatever reasons, interplay is in short supply, there results a paucity of mental representation; imagery does not coalesce into organized units, language is sparse or remains at descriptive levels, fragmented. In her own chapters, Slade presents clinical material on children from disorganized families; their play manifests such a quality of incoherence that it precludes meaningful interpretation. Indeed, Slade believes that when the picture is of the child's very primitive mode of organization, we have to question a disguise theory of repression and symbolization. The healing element may reside in *acts*, in playing itself. So she, as therapist, was both "in" the play and outside, encouraging expansions and elaborations that led to discovering and creating meanings. Under such an approach, as in Freedman's (1998) project, narratives did develop with emotions guiding the plots, and gradually a sense of being, of identity, was evident in these little patients.

MATTE BLANCO ON THINKING, FEELING, AND BEING

A Chilean analyst, Matte Blanco (1975, 1988), has provoked many of us to rethink former analytic concepts—maybe even to risk accusations of heresy?—if we begin to conceptualize somewhat differently what Freud called the unconscious. Drawing on mathematical theory, which is perhaps not very familiar to many of us clinicians, he sees mind not only as dynamic, involving energies that cause action or change, but also as *discriminator* and *classifier*, inclined to organize data into sets, that is, collections or aggregates that share certain constituents. He has developed ideas about the modes that mind employs to do this.

The *symmetrical* is one in which the converses are identical and wholes are the same as the parts. Individual items belonging to a set are not distinguished from one another. When thinking is dominated by emotion, the symmetrical mode is the one that is prominent in the thought. The symmetrical has all the aspects of the unconscious: timelessness, replacement of external by internal reality, condensation, displacement, and absence of mutual contradiction. But "the quality of being unconscious is not inherent in or essentially inevitable to symmetrical being. It is, instead, a consequence of the nature of consciousness, which cannot contain within itself the symmetrical being" (1975, p. 97), and this is because the dimensions of the latter are infinite. Having no asymmetrical relations within it, this concept is incompatible with space and time.

The *asymmetrical* or classical logic is a discriminatory mode in which converses are not identical to one another and individual items in a set may be discerned as not identical. Thinking and consciousness demand asymmetrical relations, and the asymmetrical is spatiotemporal. Yet Matte Blanco proposes, "It is the nature of man that appears to be constituted by a generalizing part (i.e., the symmetrical) which leads to symbols, and a constricting part which leads to precise (asymmetrical) thinking" (1975, p. 106). And he agrees with a much earlier writer who, in describing the first cognitive principle, declared that "any lived experience tends to evoke immediately a knowing of its direct attributes and its experience" (Spearman 1927, p. 342). In psychoanalysis we cannot *make* conscious what is unconscious but it can *become* conscious.

If we return to reimagine the *dynamic* scene of the newborn in that first act—meeting with the mother—we harken to Matte Blanco's (1975) development of a general concept that comprises both thinking and feeling. In both modes of being there is a "psychical movement toward a psychical object. To put it in a symbolical way (because words are insufficient to express it directly) both modes of being illuminate the object, bring it from an external obscurity into an internal clarity; and both bring it from an external cold into an internal warmth" (p. 286). (I presume he recognizes that in calling his terms symbolical here, he is acknowledging that his language implies space, a feature of the asymmetrical.) I have imagined in that initial profound eye-to-eye contact that there is an intensification of emotional warmth, and that perhaps in the infant's turning away (which is spatial) he assimilates that warmth to his sense of self, and briefly (a time concept, albeit that of the observer) samples something of the asymmetrical. Then he returns for more. There is already bilogical thinking, differentiated from the bilogical thinking of later life only in that the symmetrical is as yet predominant.

Although Matte Blanco does not address infancy and childhood much in his writings, he does tell us that Klein's *The Psychoanalysis of Children* (1932) played an important role in his analytic training, that it brought him into contact with the mathematical concept of the infinite. He also credits her, especially for her footnote in *Envy and Gratitude* (1957) on "memories in feelings," phenomena from early stages of development before language proper, that is, the language of the unconscious. As he later deals with the notion of internal world

(1988), he refers to Rascovsky (1960) who, even before Piontelli, was impressed that before birth internal perceptions are already occurring, preceding those of the external world. Matte Blanco defers to the child analyst Paula Heimann (1952) about how fantasies and realities contribute to the infant's symbolizing. "The infant feels that there are objects, parts of people and people inside his body, that they are alive and active, affect him and are affected by him. *This inner world of life and events is a creation of the infant's unconscious phantasy, his private replica of the world and objects around him*" (1988, p. 127, italics in original).

Would he differentiate the identification that I have described between mother and child as depicted in *The Amazing Newborn* from Klein's projective identification? I think so. He seems somewhat bemused by what he views as the Kleinians being "bewitched" by that concept (1988, p. 146). He points out that when Klein says the child "becomes" the mother, she is indicating process, which in Matte Blanco's terms would be the asymmetrical. But Klein (1946) also features the infant as making a "fantasied onslaught" on the mother, as having the impulse to "suck dry, scoop out, rob the body of its good contents" (p. 300), and to expell dangerous substances (excrements) into her. His intent is to injure, control, take possession. So the mother is felt not to be separate but bad self. Clearly that is not the image we get in the film, which of course Matte Blanco never saw, or it could have helped him to develop further his conceptualizations, especially his inclusions of the positive impulses and motives that go into identifying with others. He called this latter the "gift component," when we delegate aspects of our own ego ideal to others. He did conceive of a "Simmasi" psychic structure, one in which there was both symmetry and asymmetry. It seems not to have altogether satisfied him, and he acknowledged that there was much more to be understood. He allows for the imperfections of our theories when he writes, "Scientific writings are not free from bi-modality, and often manifest the bi-logical, a mode in which there is both affect and intellect" (1988, p. 161).

In their theory making, very young children clearly play in both modes. Elsa First (1994) describes this in what she terms *the leaving game*, which some 2-year-olds play. She sees this pretend play as an example of what Winnicott described as *cross indentification*, that is, putting oneself in another's place and understanding another's experience. I see this as evidence for the unfolding of a cognitive and emotionally novel mode of symbolic expression. It seems not to have arisen as a reaction to current external trauma; it was played with pleasure. The toddler initiates the play with a reversal of a common experience, directing the mother, "I'm leaving and you cry." Then there is a phase of protodrama, the child pretending to be a creature somewhat *like* herself, while instructing mother to be someone *like* herself. In phase three, there is a reversal of roles; the child plays a character who is the mother and the mother is instructed to play a character who is the child. The meaning of the game depends on what occurs between the two; missing and independence both become playable. But some later conflictual themes involved in symbolizing self and other can be difficult to play out.

SEPARATIONS AND INDEPENDENCE IN LATE ADOLESCENCE

These themes, of course, recur throughout our lifetimes, and in later life there are likely to be complications far beyond those in the imaginative play of those 2-year-olds. So playing out may be sometimes closer to what psychoanalysis has called *acting out*. But the intent is similar: to maintain good feelings about the self even if "left" by the other, either literally or emotionally, and—ideally—not to trash the one who was once the object of affection, since one thereby demotes oneself in demoting the other.

I am going to draw here upon the journals of a relatively new patient, Aron, a man in his mid-twenties, struggling with both social and sexual identity. After the first few sessions, he found a way of imparting something of his history by bringing to me three big books that he had used as journals beginning in his college years and continuing until the present. One of the facts he confided early in our meetings was that he had a learning disability and still needed to exert special effort to overcome it. It was clear that he was very sensitive about this felt deficiency, feeling considerable shame about it. I would like to think that he experienced my empathy with that piece of his history; in my earlier professional life I had been a consultant to the Frostig School, one that served school-age children who suffered various forms of learning disability, and I had treated a number of them. So I experienced Aron's sharing his diaries with me as an expression of trust that at first had seemed dubious, especially since at the time he was voicing an intense put-down of the whole feminine gender (his symbolizing of females ruled by Matte Blanco's symmetrical principle). The journals contained many misspellings of even the most common words. But I found the stories well told, interesting reading, illustrating this young man's efforts to manage his rageful feelings as he tried to construct bearable images of self and of others and of interrelationships. I thought it was an indication of courage to acknowledge that writing those words to the "self" of journals was not enough; he was reaching for their use in human dialogue, which had not always been easy to come by. An element of admiration went into my countertransference.

The first diary begins shortly before he is to depart for his second year of college, when some of his thought-to-be good friends had been accusing him of appropriating part of the moneys they had entrusted to him. At first he hoped that they would call and talk things over in a better way than they had in their initial confrontation, but he heard from none of them. He was especially wounded that his girlfriend, Lisa, had not stood by him, and was evidently leaving him for Dan, one of the men in this little group. "If she's really my friend, she will stand by me. If she won't, I learn an extremely important lesson, and at a small price." At least he was trying to keep it a small price, trying to reduce his own pain, attempting some wry humor about his sorry predicament. "I swear that the universe is one huge practical joke. One big Broadway comedy. We're not laughing because we're playing the role of the fool."

By the next entry, Lisa had called and had left a message that she'd been kicked out of her house. Why was she calling, he asked himself. "Is she calling to apologize or just to get support now that she needs it? What do I do? I can't leave her hanging, but she was willing to disappear without a word. I hate being compassionate." I was struck by this hating of his own inclination to be sympathetic there; it was as though if he were, he would forego feeling compassion for himself. The diary goes on: "I'm having problems leaving because I still care for her. So will I forgive her? I probably will because I'm a sucker, but who knows?" He seems in conflict over whether he should see himself as magnanimous or as a fool.

He was working at the time in a restaurant, and got furious with a fellow employee who didn't do her share of the work. She even bragged, "I didn't bus one table today!" It was as though the suppressed rage at Lisa spread (in the symmetrical mode) to another woman who at the moment seemed to be taking advantage of him. Then Lisa herself came in with Dan. "I was very false and nervous for a while. Lisa started to cry about being kicked out of her house, and I didn't know what to do. My posture was so cold and false. I was stymied. I ended up hugging her but she didn't hug me back. Needless to say, it was weird and uncomfortable. Finally we sat down and started to talk of that fateful night when they accused me. *In their eyes* (my italics) they had come that time just to make sure I had accounted for everything, but when I got pissed they reacted and started all that crap." He rejects the self-image that would be entailed by seeing himself in the mirrors of their eyes. In this new scene, though, he finds himself in conflict. On the one hand, emotionally he identifies with Lisa's plight, which moves him toward giving comfort to her. This could be seen as an example of Matte Blanco's (1998) "gift component" of projective identification. On the other hand, he is moved to continue to enact his own aggressive feelings about her abandoning him. We could say that his empathy with Lisa was a manifestation of the symmetrical, while the latter was the kind of aggression that requires a good amount of asymmetry (Matte Blanco (1988). His solution could be seen as a compromise, and not very satisfying: he hugs her, but coldly. The act is walled off from the feeling. As Matte Blanco (1975) might put it, "All human beings have a great many impulses which though easily coexisting within the self are incompatible in terms of action. It is up to the ego-functions to exercise the various defense mechanisms in such a manner that each impulse receives a discharge which will not interfere with that of other impulses. Syncretism provides this to a certain extent" (p. 429).

In his next writing, Aron still is thinking of the previous night, remembering that Dan slipped and said these words, "That's when we thought you were lying about the money." Aron wrote, "I don't know how to be friends with people who think of me as a person capable of stealing money from his friends. The answer is I can't . . . I'm tired and have a hard day ahead." He did call Lisa that night. "She said 'Hi,' knew it was me. I said I was leaving for college the next day, and I wished her a happy and great year. 'Ok,' she said. 'Well I'll see you . . . next summer. 'Bye.' So that does it. In my mind we are no longer friends, nor will we ever be again. I'm not sure why I called her, maybe to say, 'Hey, last chance—if you come to see me off or something.' I'm really going to miss her. But hey, look on the bright side. I won't be spending hundreds on phone bills." So he attempts to console himself, but it doesn't help much. He adds, "But I will miss the email that the two guys and I used to exchange." That night he went out to a bar with another male friend, drank a glass of beer and four shots of tequila. "We were talking about everything deep in our hearts and our minds. He and I really got along. I'd consider him one of my very good friends. I can't wait to write him. I hope he keeps in touch . . . I hope my suitemates are cool. It would just suck if I was living with two assholes. As for my grades, I will do great this semester no matter what it takes, simple!" But those reparative efforts were not altogether successful.

His bleak mood persisted well into the next day, which he declared "once again horrible." It began with his mother banging on his door to wake him. "The noise didn't get me to wake; it just irritated me, so I went back to sleep. She banged again, still louder, and this time I said, 'Please don't bang on my door!' And that was the incident that ruined the entire day." We could see Aron's fury here as a manifestation of what Matte Blanco has called "the law of either positive or negative infinite sets" (1975, pp. 144–145). He viewed his mother that morning not as an individual but as the whole class of females, seeing her not as manifesting infinite positive potentialities but with infinite negative powers. And his outlook seems to have been rather contagious. He writes, "She smoldered for about an hour and got into a fight with my dad. They both got mega-stressed, and Mom got full-blown pissed. She went back into the house when the van was ready, and Dad went in and talked with her. . . . She was quiet then the whole trip, as was everyone else. I imagine the trip wasn't bad for her because she had so much to read. But Dad, on the other hand, had only the road and the driving, so I suspect his ride was rough. When we stopped to eat, the three of us had it out. At some points, I felt like saying, 'Fuck this!' but I didn't." By then Aron was manifesting a degree of resilience, and was able to put some brakes on his negative impulses. "It helped to some extent. Fortunately Mom and I worked it out, but I don't think my parents did."

One of the early entries after he is back in college shows ongoing restiveness about self, others, and relationships. "I admit I'm happy about being here, but I don't feel complete; I think the reason is that I haven't shown anyone the real me. I'm hoping I warm up to Chester and Helen and let my guard down eventually. . . . Last night I left my last big secret behind me. Ches and I were discussing our homosexuality.—I can't believe I'm writing this!—I told him that I'm attracted to women somewhat, but when I masturbate I love to fantasize about men. We started talking of the fronts we both put up to stay in the closet. Ches had ordered *Playboy* last year, and all the things he's looked at and cut out are the pictures of men. To be honest, some were very hot. We eventually moved on, and I decided to tell him about my first homosexual experience. After I finished spilling my guts, he told me about his homosexual encounters with a guy in his home town . . . I can't tell whether this sharing was a good idea or not, but you can't unring a bell."

There was an entry the next morning in which he again addressed his diary as "you," someone in whom he could more safely confide than Ches. "For the record, yesterday's notes may have made you think I have no or very little sexual attraction to women. This is not true. But it is true that I am more attracted to men. . . . On a more depressed note, I'm starting to feel that type of loneliness I felt last year. I don't have the close friends I'm used to having. But the funniest quirk about my whole problem is that I'm perpetuating it. I'm playing 'the role' here, and that's how I've made my friends, not as my self. In addition, I won't drop that mask and let someone in. What if they don't like me? That's the question I'm always asking. But, on the other hand, I do like Aron better." He is having difficulty symbolizing both his sexual and his social self, and with liking his representations.

We glimpse here the admixtures of Eros, Thanatos, symmetry, and asymmetry, and the problems with finding suitable words to symbolize them. As Matte Blanco puts it, "In hate as well as in love, one can see the operation of the principle of symmetry" (1975, p. 105). He points out that the verb "to love" denotes action (asymmetry), and hence designates a more superficial level, while "love is a way of being in which the individual who loves is loved as being one with the beloved" (p. 198). Hate, in his schema, presupposes movement, that is, asymmetry, while love, being ecstatic, is more in keeping with profound symmetry. He concludes, "It is the nature of man that appears constituted by a generalizing part, which leads to symbols, and a restricting part, which leads to precise (asymmetrical) thinking" (p. 106). Aron was having difficulty loving himself when he could not feel the love of others, and his depression was close to self-hate. As he tries to draw upon the generalizing principle as it operates to create language categories, he cannot include both his heterosexual and his homosexual inclinations, or his being unpopular with others and yet liking himself. But he manages tentatively what could be seen as a constructive split: an observing ego that lets him sense both heterosexual and homosexual features and lets him think more positively about his self. That self hasn't yet taken definite shape, if by that we mean to conform to one or the other of the words heterosexual or homosexual.

In the second journal he writes on huge black pages in either white or silver ink. Bothered at first by there being no lines (which I took to be both literal and metaphorical), he soon sketched them in. He describes a new girl friend, Tessie, who "reawakened my sex drive, but now I want to share and not just have good sex . . . I want to be part of her easygoing life. Who could I have more to share with than another bisexual person: cool, pretty, intelligent . . . It's not the puppy love I had for Lisa. I'm thinking of her and dreaming of her. The dream was of she and I sleeping side by side, head to foot, in a big white bed. We were close and I was happy. But the telling part of the dream was I saw mother sitting on a bench, watching us in disapproval."

A few days later, he writes, "My roller-coaster is beginning to destroy me." He describes a second date with Robert, how he was having problems talking and maintaining conversation. After a movie, they went to Aron's place and, because his friend had a headache, Aron massaged his head. He wanted to kiss Robert, but the latter would not look at him, and told him, "I'm seeing somebody else." But soon they were kissing and for several hours. They "never touched skin below the belt," but fell asleep in each other's arms. Early in the morning Robert woke Aron, and they both "got naked," saw each other's "dicks." "His was impressive, but I'm bigger. . . . This time I blew him and swallowed! I was very panicked by this stupid move; and the panic was compounded by having had blood drawn for an AIDS test the day before. We fell asleep and woke the next morning to jerk each other off. I panicked because of the homosexual guilt, and was upset that Rob seemed a 'taker.'" Nevertheless, he confronted his partner, who promised to break off with his girlfriend.

However, when he called him the next night Robert was with his girlfriend, and Aron found himself in intense pain. "How can life be so cruel? Happiness is disappearing. It was beautiful, tempting, fulfilling from a distance, only to disappear into sand and rocks as I moved close. . . . What is wrong with me? How could he do this? I would have loved him with all my heart . . . given him my prize, my secret self which I share with no one." He went to Robert's house to try to persuade him not to end this relationship, but Robert told him that they could not see each other; he had decided to stay with his girlfriend. Aron demanded to know whether he had kissed her, in spite of the last night's promise never to do so, and was told yes. "I left after that, wanted to burst into tears but only one fell. . . . Here I've broken up with Tessie and lost Robert all in one week. How can I bounce back? To whom? Who's there? No one." He attempts poetic expression: "Will I ever find someone special, or will I forever be the foot-blistered traveler of a sand-scorching desert, mouth filled with sand and dust, body aching for water and comfort?"

For some months the entries in the journal were bleak, but he gradually began to ask himself some questions. "Was I in love or was I in love with being in love? Very difficult question to answer. . . . Did I care for Robert? I believe I did. Can I honestly answer my question with a simple response; absolutely not. . . . Through the pain I feel more alive than I have in months, years; it is a higher level of existence than my emotional coma. . . . But I will not embrace it so as to kill my emotions and feed my starving cynicism. I will move toward openness to people and to love . . . I see my loneliness as testimony to my awakening. I am alive once again." But he was fighting suicidal impulses; words of resolve were not enough. He did then shortly apply for a part in a musical, did well in the audition, was even able to bear not getting the part because everyone praised his performance. He rejoined his dance group. In spite of the fact that he has tended to feel incompetent there, the bodily expression seemed helpful.

In my early sessions with Aron, I would mention that I had been reading his diaries. I told him that I had a sense of relating to two Arons: the younger one he had shared in the writings and the one in today's session. He liked that, and I believe it let us work over some old scenes while primarily attending to the here and now.

Later there were times when Aron expressed his sense that adult life is much harder than the college years, when one shared ambience with one's agemates and making connections was easier. Now he was working in a highly technical field, twelve hours a day for five days a week, so social life was virtually nonexistent, but not only because of his schedule. He reported discomfort at having anyone visit his apartment, found himself attending more to what was not in good order rather than to any of the rare visitors who came. Occasionally he would have a gay date, but reported reticence to share much of his thoughts and feelings with the other. Weekends he mostly just holed up, preferring to be alone. At some point I recalled aloud that in his diary he had reported some periods of relative withdrawal, but that the word "lonesome" would creep in, and he would then seek out some company. He seemed surprised at that, but reported that his immediate superior at work had asked why he didn't tell his fellow workers the reason he left for several hours each week (these times for his appointments with me). He then did tell them, finding it painful to do so, but they responded empathically. Perhaps like his boss, I found myself at times with countertransference inclinations and once shared with him an image that had come to me of an impulse to somehow dig him out of his "stuckness." I told him that as a child, I used to make trips with my physician father out into the countryside where he had patients. At times, in those days when roads were not paved, they became very muddy in rainy weather, and occasionally our car would be stuck in the mud, and we'd have to dig out enough mud to place rocks under the wheels so that there could be traction. Aron was amused by that and shortly was saying that he has thought of looking into pursuing tango as soon as he finds an interested partner. No doubt my sharing with my patient something of my personal life would be seen by the orthodox as acting out. But retrospectively I would now defend it. After all it was my father who was the car's driver, as Aron is the driver of his life. I am only the "other," willing to help if I can.

Aron sees himself as full of rages, and is finding it difficult to love. And, as Matte Blanco writes, "when somebody does not love, this amounts at the deepest levels to the non-recognition of the existence of the other, either within the self or outside: a non-presence" (1988, p. 198). This is the predicament that Aron brings to his analyst.

A MATURE WOMAN WHO ALSO FINDS WORDS NOT ENOUGH

I have selected some clinical notes from the last year of analysis of Clare, a woman who, although adept at language proper, often communicated in media other than words. I think she would have liked the Prologue from Goethe's *Faust*, which Freedman (1994) cited in introducing his paper on "Enactments in Psychoanalytic Space." In many ways, like Goethe, she felt stopped by the word, and, in her effort to create shared fantasy space, she supplemented logos with acts, and then play could ensue between the two modes of representation.

She was a frequent dreamer, and interested in exploring the images that came to her mind at night. Of course to relate them, she had to use our common tongue, but sometimes she chose to supplement words by bringing in drawings or paintings of her dream. This seemed partly to master content about which she had had no conscious choice, but also to share with me more explicitly the idiosyncratic senses its imagery connoted for her. If I could but glimpse her images too, I might better comprehend her intrapersonal domain. For example, we had been working on her tendencies to conform rather strictly with what she deemed right and permissible, to be pretty conventional in her outlook. In one session she had related a dream in which she was driving across a bridge but failed to make a sharp turn of the road on the other side. Her car went off the bridge, descending to the deep water below, and she woke in terror. To the following hour she brought a visual version of this dream, but with modifications made while awake: she had painted a colorful parachute over the car. She thought the dream might have been saying that, in avoiding a turn to the left and staying on the straight and narrow, one could nevertheless find oneself in jeopardy, miss important turns. In waking life, her growing insight into her own predilections could considerably diminish her sense of drastic danger and lead to greater flexibilities about directions to be chosen.

Several years ago Clare had come to a conference at which I was a speaker, and she purchased a recording of my talk. Over time she found it quite useful on occasions when she would have some trouble falling asleep. She would play the disk, not attending particularly to the words or the message I was trying to communicate; simply hearing my voice was sufficiently soothing that she could allow herself to relinquish consciousness. When she saw me at the Mark Taper Theater, as she often did, she would report it with some satisfaction. It was clearly evidence for us both of certain common cultural interests: a symmetrical component in our relationship. There are many ways in which she reaches for that.

One holiday season, she brought me a present, a large collage that she had made. Like Freedman's (1994) patient who brought him an audiocassette, Clare was communicating something of her transference at the time, her perceptions of me, and their fit with my book *The Playground of Psychoanalytic Therapy* (1991), which she had purchased and studied. (We who write books clearly do reveal something of our selves to patients who read professional literature.) I could employ Freedman's (1994) analogy of her creation to arpeggio in music; her notes too were sounded in rapid succession yet constituted a chord. She had made a number of small colorful drawings adhering to the large white background, and, separately, little rectangles somewhat randomly placed with quotes from authors who have dealt with play and playing. Some of the names were among those I had quoted, such as Huizinga and Winnicott; others were new to me, a special aspect of this gift, announcing that she could give, not only this object, but additional ideas. So, like Freedman's patient, she was teaching and informing me, and I was receiving. She too wanted to make sure I heard the intermingling of these notes, and needed later to know that I had framed and would recurrently look at the composition. But otherwise this "enactment" had nothing of the coercive; it stayed close to the wish for both separateness and union, coexisting in shared fantasy space.

In a recent session, Clare came in with a folder containing a drawing. It was the kind of situation that could make us wonder what the analysand may know of the analyst but does not immediately share. She sat up on the couch, and, though not facing me, turned her head at times to look directly at me. She handed me her drawing of Joel, my late husband. She told me that she had done it several years ago. She had not known of Joel's death at the time he died, but about a year later someone told her. She had been troubled not to have known. She dealt with her own distress by taking out his book and drawing a picture of him, partly based on the photo therein and partly on how she remembered glimpsing him, in a sweater vest, wearing a beret (which he did only after chemo had rendered him bald). Over the top of the portrait she put in big letters, WORK, LOVE, and PLAY, the title of his book (1992), and, on a scarf over his shoulders, she wrote those letters in smaller capitals. We could now talk of why she had never discussed with me her reactions to learning of my loss of a loved one. When Clare had come for analysis, death was "entering the analytic door" (Redding 2000), for her mother was critically ill and subsequently died. Her grieving was acute, continuing for years, finally subsiding only recently. That loss, followed by a separation and divorce from a traumatic short-term marriage, was unbearable. So, she told me now, that may have been the reason I had not shared with her that my husband had died; she had made a tacit assumption that death would represent to me what it had to her. On the feeling level, Matte Blanco's symmetry was in evidence in her unconscious assumption that I would react as she had to such a loss. She had not thought she could bring it up with me if I had not brought it up with her. We both thought that her reason for venturing to share the sketch with me now was her beginning contemplation of termination (which will entail more of the asymmetrical).

On one occasion Clare told me that the previous week when she came to my office (which is in my home) she had smelled something cooking. That night she had an olfactory dream: "I was in a session and I smelled that same thing. I was aware that I had phlegm in my throat; it came up on my hands. Washing wasn't enough; I decided on a shower, and I took it." Here she laughs, "I can't imagine taking that liberty! . . . came back, thinking you'd wonder where I was. You were on the couch resting or sleeping or not feeling good." She pronounced it a strange dream, coughing up disgusting stuff. Her father had allergies, was always blowing his nose. But it was she who was the one not feeling good just now. "I have stuff inside that I don't like. Yesterday I saw my gynecologist for a second Pap, because the other wasn't totally normal." (Strong negative affect leads to a certain symmetrization between the substances from one part of the body and from another.) She liked better the physician she used to see when she lived in another city. (Asymmetry prevails in her images of the doctors.) The one here made her write answers to pages and pages of questions. "To reduce the essence of me to a piece of paper!" (Until quite recently, she had made it clear I was not to write about her.) "I wanted a while ago to put you on paper, but I could not capture your liveliness." She observed that she does not convey her own liveliness in real-life situations. She associated to several persons who had so deeply irritated her that she "became explosive." Now her stomach growled, and she wondered if I'd heard it. And, as often, she became aware of the ticking of my clock and of the abstract characters in a painting above the couch, "where monsters are creeping in today." As with many abstract pictures, one can see different things at different times, and on that day the images seemed to symbolize for her the grotesque, ugly, unnatural.

She has lately been reworking a painting of a little girl attempting unsuccessfully to crawl over a fence into a playground where boys are engaging in a ball game. This was partly based on a memory of being deprived of using her excellent athletic capacities, which now she does enjoy, especially on the tennis court, where she even wins at times in games with men.

Recently Clare has arrived at a state in which she is no longer feeling speechless when faced by a man whom she finds attractive. She has lost weight, feels attractive, and has a busy and interesting life both professionally and socially. She recently reported a dream: I am traveling. It has a magical quality, as though I'm in a plane or car or a scooter. I can't see how I'm moving but I have a sense of wonderment, enjoying the ride, not even worrying where it's to." When she woke, she felt this had to do with feeling changed but not knowing how that had happened.

But in waking life, as she has contemplated termination, she wanted more clarity about how she got where she feels herself to be. "I am more in a playing mode, but at times I have to explain this change. It's as if a voice says, 'Now, let's get serious!' It's a hangover from childhood, being a responsible child. Mother had two voices. She did teach me games, but the other side was heavy: 'You must do well, be independent.' At summer camp, I'd have two months of free play, and I loved that. But the playground shrank when I got home." Clare now explored how she sees me. "Sometimes I think you play at working. Again, I think you need more vacations. I hear your playful voice more than I hear mother's." She thought she had benefited from my love of the profession, so great that I didn't retire at 65. She asked herself, "Why might I think you play too much?" I ventured, "Maybe because I don't seem to worry that you can't explain intellectually how you got to this greater playfulness?" She knows that she does sometimes feel at a loss for words, and she dislikes that. She observed that nothing with me is ever black and white. She experienced me as saying, in effect, "Look into your own eyes." For her, she reflected, while growing up, there was a time for play and a time for work. Here, she saw me as mixing them together. Her mother, she said, always worried lest Clare might make mistakes, didn't seem confident one could learn from them.

She reviewed the collage she had made for me. "I put together people's words with *my* images, but now my words are important too. . . . I felt not on the same playing field as mother with words. But I'm not bad at words; and I can write." I observed, "You've intermingled words, dreams, drawings, paintings, sports." She nodded, "It's rich; I don't want to give up any of it." She'd noticed the book *Visual Thinking* (Arnheim 1969) on my coffee table, and wondered about it, since vision is so important to her. I observed, "When you feel frustrated that you are not able to say how you got to where you feel yourself to be now, you are speaking only of words, but you have all these other modes of thinking too, and we've drawn on them all." She quietly thought about that a few minutes, and then agreed. She'd spotted a book, *The Passion of Watercolors*, in a bookstore. She had bought it, read it. But she contrasted her own processes with the series of prescribed exercises that the author was promoting, "a way I didn't do it." And she concluded, "Now I like who I am."

In reflecting back on this analysis and its ending period, I find myself in imagination back with someone very dear to me, Marion Milner. She wrote that if there is to be a new creation, there must be "a plunge into no-differentiation, which results (if all goes well) in a re-emerging into a new division of the me–not-me, one in which there is more of the 'me' in the 'not me' and more of the 'not me' in the 'me'" (1987, p. 223).

SOME REFLECTIONS ON WORDS IN PSYCHOANALYTIC THINKING

Recent researches are informing us that creating representations of self, of other, and of relationships begins from earliest life, even within the womb. We find ourselves in awe when we witness the protosymbolic impression of emotional import in that first gaze between newborn and mother. The impact of that visual connection would seem to fuel the epistemophilic instinct (Sanville 1997), and the infant is powerfully motivated to know more, to utilize all of the bodily senses to make further discoveries about self and social world. His innate capacities for empathic response enable him to imitate the behaviors of others as he builds up representations of self, of others, and of possible relationships. Affect and cognition are forever inseparable, although their proportions in thinking may vary in different persons and in different situations for any of us. In a favorable social surround, preschool children tend to engage in interplay with parents and caregivers, using capacities for identifications with both self and others to manage affects of connectedness and of separateness. In the process, they hone modes of symbolic expression that will subsequently be expanded and reshaped. Those shapes will be influenced both by inherent predilections and by particular experiences with family, school, friends.

For none of us are words sufficient. The ubiquity of dreaming in the mammalian species is testimony to this. Words do inevitably become decontextualized; their formal structure is implicitly antifantasy and antiplay (Bruner 1972). Although Freud's attempts at metapsychology can be viewed as ways to free his thinking from dependence on actual clinical observation, all such attempts at abstraction can go too far, become too separate from the world of action. So Freud recurrently returned to actual clinical experience. He would, I think, have agreed with one of my models, Erik Erikson (1972), who wrote that "if reality is the structure of facts consensually agreed upon in a given state of knowledge, actuality is the leeway created by new forms of interplay" (p. 703).

REFERENCES

Arnheim, R. (1969). *Visual Thinking*. Berkeley, CA: University of California Press.

Brenner, C. (1982). *The Mind in Conflict*. New York: International Universities Press.

Bruner, J. (1972). Nature and uses of immaturity. In *Play: Its Role in Development and Evolution*, ed. J. S. Bruner, A. Jolly, and K. Sylva, pp. 28–64. New York: Basic Books, 1976.

——— (1977). Early social interaction and language acquistion. In *Studies in Mother–Infant Interaction*, ed. H. R. Schaffer, pp. 271–289. London: Academic Press.

Erikson, E. H. (1972). Play and actuality. In *Play: Its Role in Development and Evolution*, ed. J. S. Bruner, A. Jolly, and K. Sylva, pp. 688–704. New York: Basic Books.

First, E. (1994). The leaving game, or I'll play you and you play me: the emergence of dramatic roleplay in 2-year-olds. In *Children at Play*, ed. A. Slade and D. P. Wolf, pp. 111–132. Oxford, UK: Oxford University Press.

Freedman, N. (1994). More on transformation: enactments in psychoanalytic space. In *The Spectrum of Psychoanalysis: Essays in Honor of Martin S. Bergmann*, ed. A. K. Richards and A. D. Richards, pp. 93–110. Madison, CT: International Universities Press.

——— (1998). Psychoanalysis and symbolization. In *Contemporary Freudian Perspectives*, ed. S. Ellman. Northvale, NJ: Jason Aronson.

Freedman, N., Hoffenberg, J. D., Vorus, N., and Frosch, A. (1998). *The effectiveness of psychoanalytic psychotherapy: the role of treatment duration, frequency of sessions, and the therapeutic relationship*. Paper presented at the Annual Meeting, Division of Psychoanalysis of the American Psychological Association, Boston, April.

Freedman, N., Karliner, R., and Lavender, J. (1999). *Desymbolization: pervasive and segmental*. Paper presented at the Annual Meeting, Division 39 of the American Psychological Association, New York, April.

Freud, S. (1900). The interpretation of dreams. *Standard Edition* 5.

——— (1915). The unconscious. *Standard Edition* 14:159–216.

——— (1923). The ego and the id. *Standard Edition* 19:3–66.

Hack, M. (1975). *The Amazing Newborn*. Film made at Case Western Reserve University, Ohio.

Heimann, P. (1952). Certain functions of introjection and projection in early infancy. In *New Directions in Psycho-Analysis*, ed. M. Klein, P. Heimann, and R. E. Money-Kyrle, pp. 134–136. London: Tavistock.

Hotz, R. (2000). Imitation instinct is more basic than just flattery. *Los Angeles Times*, p. B2, May 8.

Jacobson, E. (1953). Affects and their pleasure-unpleasure qualities in relation to psychic discharge process. In *Drives. Affects, Behavior*, ed. M. Loewenstein. New York: International Universities Press.

——— (1964). *The Self and the Obiect World*. New York: International Universities Press.

Kris, E. (1953). Discussion remarks on L. S. Kubie's paper, "Modern Concepts of the Organization of the Brain." *Psychoanalytic Quarterly* 22.

Klein, M. (1932). *The Psychoanalysis of Children*. London: Hogarth.

——— (1946). Notes on some schizoid mechanisms. In *Developments in Psychoanalysis*, ed. M. Klein, P. Heimann, S. Isaacs, and J. Riviere. London: Hogarth, 1952.

——— (1957). *Envy and Gratitude*. London: Tausfoen.

Matte Blanco, I. (1975). *The Unconscious as Infinite Sets: An Essay in Bi-Logic*. London: Duckworth.

——— (1988). *Thinking, Feeling, and Being*. London and New York: Routledge.

Milner, M. (1969). *The Hands of the Living God*. New York: International Universities Press.

——— (1987). *The Suppressed Madness of Sane Men*. London:Tavistock.

Piontelli, A. (1987). Infant observation before birth. *International Journal of Psycho-Analysis* 68(4):453–464.

——— (1989). A study of twins before and after birth. *International Review of Psycho-Analysis* 16(4):413–426.

Rascovsky, A. (1960). *El Psiquismo Fetal*. Buenos Aires: Paidos.

Redding, K. (2000). *When death knocks at the analytic door*. Unpublished Ph.D. dissertation, Los Angeles Institute and Society for Psychoanalytic Studies.

Sanville, J. (1991). *The Playground of Psychoanalytic Therapy*. Hillsdale, NJ: Analytic Press.

——— (1997). *Epistemophilia and theories of thinking*. Address at the Sixth National Clinical Conference of the National Institute of Psychoanalytic Education and Research in Clinical Social Work, Seattle, WA, September 25–28.

Schafer, R. (1982). *The Analytic Attitude*. New York: Basic Books.

Shor, J. (1992). *Work, Love, and Play*. New York: Brunner/Mazel.

Slade, A., and Wolf, D. P. (1994). *Children at Play: Clinical and Developmental Approaches to Meaning and Representation*. New York: Oxford University Press.

Spearman, C. (1927). *The Nature of Intelligence and the Principles of Cognition*. London: Macmillan.

Spitz, R. A. (1965). *The First Year of Life*. New York: International Universities Press.

Stern, D. (1985). *The Interpersonal World of the Infant*. New York: Basic Books.

Thompson, A. E. (1985). The nature of emotion and its development. In *Event Theory: An Integration of Piaget and Freud*, ed. I. Fast. Hillsdale, NJ: Lawrence Erlbaum.

Tustin, F. (1981). *Autistic States in Children*. London: Routledge & Kegan Paul.

——— (1984). Autistic shapes. *International Review of Psycho-Analysis* 11:279–290.

22

My Personal Tiresias: A Geographer of the Inner World

JESSE D. GELLER

"Let man's soul be a sphere."

John Donne

INTRODUCTION

This essay is concerned with the spatial properties of the representational world. It was inspired by the intimate privilege of reading a valued friend's works in progress. Last year I began reading two of Norbert Freedman's (1997a,b) unpublished essays. The ultimate aim of these essays is the development of a model of the intricate and constantly changing ways in which varying kinds of space are experienced, particularly in the therapeutic situation.

Taken together, these essays are an invitation to think systematically about the network of relations that link the representations of the spaces that separate self and others, the representations of the spaces within the body, the representations of the spaces within the mind, and the overall physicality of a situation or event. Bert assumes that these three domains of experience, which he refers to as "object relational

The author wishes to thank Maggie Scarf for her enormously helpful editorial comments.

space," "body-self space," and "symbolizing space," are in constant dialogue with one another and with the physical actuality of the forces and spaces outside of our bodies. He reserves the term "inner psychic space" to refer to an inclusive framework, or functional composite, within which are arranged the interrelations among these representational domains. At the center of his still provisional model is the hypothesis that "psychic content needs a place in which to live—we cannot move physically without a concept of space, nor can we do so psychically. The inhabitants of such a space are inner objects, affects, and self representations" (Freedman and Lavender 1997, p. 83).

Bert's innovative ideas about the spatialization of the representational world are a dazzling synthesis of psychoanalytic thought (Anzieu 1989, Bion 1963, Grotstein 1978, Lewin 1946, Viderman 1970, Winnicott 1971), body-image theory (Fischer and Cleveland 1968, Schilder 1950, Wapner and Werner 1965), anthropological studies of variations in personal space (Hall 1959, 1966, Sommer 1969), and Susanne Langer's (1948) philosophical perspective on symbolizing. These ideas represent an extension of his keenly observed kinesthetic-linguistic studies of the nonverbal facilitation of verbalized symbolic thought (e.g., Freedman 1983, Freedman and Bucci 1981). Bert's insights are also a product of his efforts to understand what his blindness can teach us about the origins, nature, functions, and modifiability of the psychological experience of inner space.

Here, the fate of Tiresias might be recalled. Legend has it that Hera, Zeus's wife, blinded Tiresias because he saw too clearly and spoke the truth about female and male sexuality. Then, according to the myth, Zeus compensated Tiresias for his loss by giving him the gift of "inner sight," which Tiresias, in turn, called upon to foresee and reveal to Oedipus the King the true origin of the tragedies confronting Thebes (Sophocles 1971). Like Tiresias, Bert has unflinchingly gazed upon the truths that are revealed when the eyes are open, and those that are revealed when the eyes are closed. It is only because of knowing Bert personally that I have come to appreciate, and now write about, the psychic geography of the inner world.

First I will address the question "What does the notion of psychic inner space actually mean?" Next I will present what my therapist colleagues have been revealing to me about their own experiences of inner space. Then, I will present the broad outlines of Bert's theorizing about the emergence and evolution of the spatial qualities of the representational world. And finally, I will discuss how Bert's ideas have led me to new kinds of thinking about the therapeutic action of the processes of introjection.

WHAT IS INNER SPACE?

Consider the following modes of self reference: "My mind is racing." "I couldn't put the thought out of my mind." "I must have been out of my mind." "I couldn't keep my mind on my work." "My mind plays tricks on me." "I couldn't wrap my mind around it." "Thoughts of suicide entered my mind." "I am of two minds about that." "I'm losing my mind." "You've been on my mind." "My mind feels like a sieve."

These common expressions point to two deeply ingrained human inclinations: the tendency to objectify processes by transforming them into autonomous things or thing-like entities, and the tendency to conceive of the mind as its own "place," as if it were an imaginary container in which thinking, remembering, feeling, fantasizing, and other mental activities take place.

The idea that the mind actually has an "inside" is basically the concretization of a metaphor. Modern philosophers of knowledge agree that substantive designations implying that the mind actually has an inside that exists within a person are not a sound basis for thinking, theoretically, about psychological processes and events. Bert concurs. At the same time, he recognizes that it is legitimate and desirable to retain phenomenologically based uses of the terms "internal" and "external." In other words, he does not confuse the subjective differentiation of the experiential field into inner and outer regions, and the localization of psychological activities in physical space.

In order to differentiate Bert's own phenomenologically based investigations of psychic inner space from the idea that the mind has an actual inside, I will hereafter speak of "the experience of inner psychic space." My primary focus will be upon that quality or activity of mind that Bert has named "symbolizing space."[1]

REPRESENTATIONS OF INNER SPACE

Some aspects of Bert's evolving understanding of what constitutes psychic inner space find expression in the following definition: "a *mode* of spatial *representation* that exists side by side, or is coordinated with mental content but is not reducible to this content" (1997a, p. 11, italics added). The meanings and implications of this working definition reside in the convergence of a network of ideas. As a whole, the statement can be read as an answer to the question "What [activity or quality of mind] remains when you have eliminated the emotionally charged self-representations, representations of the other, and representations of interactions with him or her that comprise an internalized object relationship?" Bert's notion of representation applies equally to words, pictures, postures, gestures, sounds, tastes, and odors; and the term "mode" can be understood as a synonym of "form," which in this context refers to the distinct and constantly changing representational configurations that structure and organize the experience of inner space.

Bert's working definition leaves open the question of whether one can sever psychic contents and the inner spaces in which they reside. The phrases "side by side" and "coordinated with" suggest that inner space can be likened to the file icon on the computer screen before items have been added. So conceived, inner space exists as a potentiality, a virtual space. An alternative view, and the one to which I subscribe, is that one cannot exist without the other, and that inner spaces both shape and are molded by their contents.

The distinction I am making is comparable to the difference between a bottle of water and a drop of water.[2] A bottle of water is a

---

1. At times, Bert appears to use the terms "listening space," "associative space," and "representational space" as synonyms of symbolizing space.

2. The idea of a drop of water and the notion of inner space are both examples of what Whorf (1956) refers to as "container-ingredient metaphors."

"real" container. It does not change its shape when emptied of its contents. It can stand alone or apart from its contents. A drop of water cannot. The "drop" and the "water" do not exist independently of one another. Their relationship is one of codetermination.

The connection between moods and feelings, as experienced qualities, provides me with yet another model for thinking about the ways in which varying types of psychic contents and inner spaces mutually influence each other. As I have discussed elsewhere (Geller 1984), moods permeate and envelop our existence, whether experienced for shorter or longer periods of time. To a lesser or greater degree, they provide the background against which other contents of consciousness stand out. It is as if we were embedded in our moods. When the subject of introspection pertains to bad moods, we speak of being "in a black cloud," or "down in the dumps," "surrounded by a fog." Styron (1990) described his depression as resembling "the diabolical discomfort of being imprisoned in a fiercely overheated room" (p. 2). In other words, moods are experienced as happening *around* us in a contextual surround but not necessarily *within* us.

Consequently, insofar as they are enduring, moods provide the frameworks or contexts that anticipate and modify the manner in which emergent feelings are experienced and expressed. I believe this is what Kundera (1984) had in mind when he wrote, "The sadness was form, the happiness content. Happiness filled the space of sadness" (p. 314) to describe his hero's feelings about returning home, in *The Unbearable Lightness of Being.*

The Gestalt psychologists' conceptualization of the relations between figure and ground resembles in almost every respect what art critics refer to as the relations between "positive shapes and negative space" (Blom and Chaplin 1982). In graphic works of art, negative space is defined as the surrounding areas created by, around, and in between the spaces formed by images (i.e., positive shapes). The interaction between these design elements can be clearly seen in the optical illusion of the vase/face profile drawing.

As can be seen in Figure 22–1, the viewer has a choice of perceiving either the black or white as the positive shape and designating the opposite color the negative space. Focusing attention on the negative

Figure 22–1

or empty spaces reveals that they are not, in fact, "dead spaces." Rather, negative spaces are as important as positive images, for they, too, occupy and mold a given amount of space, and are malleable, as well. Moreover, any change in the foreground or background results in a specific and accommodating change in the other. In a similar vein, I am proposing that the thoughts and feelings a person is capable of experiencing and the shapes taken by the inner spaces that contain his or her thoughts and feelings are inseparably related.

Most people seem to be unaware that inner space is an integral and omnipresent aspect of their subjective experience. For a variety of reasons, we are interested in the "what" or content of our experiences. Unless we're specifically asked about them, there is no obvious reason we should pay attention to the spatial attributes and qualities of our thoughts and feelings. Doing so requires shifting attention away from the symbolic content, or explicit function, of an experience and bringing into focal awareness its structural or formal properties. This would entail a reversal of foreground and background.

Furthermore, without access to a vocabulary that permits one to speak about the structure of sensory experiences, it is extremely difficult to tell others about the ways in which one experiences psychic inner space. I anticipate that if introspective investigations were conducted with individuals who were disciplined and refined observers of their own subjectivity, the results would reveal that the forms taken by inner space are capable of being apprehended and described in terms of the same spatial dimensions and orientations that are used to perceive and describe physical spaces: size, height, distance, up/down, front/back/left/right, and here-in-the-center.[3]

Psychoanalytic therapists are trained to pay attention to and talk about experiences that do not readily lend themselves to description. I have been asking colleagues who are also friends to tell me about their experiences of inner space. With varying degrees of skill and anxiety, they have been able to "know," "sense," and "recognize" how they experience inner space. In an informal experiment of my own, I provided colleagues who were unfamiliar with the notion of inner space with Bert's working definition (see pp. 513–514). If they had difficulty grasping it or were resistant to performing the task, I asked them to relax, close their eyes, and imagine a painting or a photograph and the frame that surrounds it.

Decorative frames can draw one toward or away from the works of art they contain. Unadorned picture frames fade into the background of experience as attention is brought by the work of art to itself, while other frames are experienced as an integral part of the subject matter portrayed. I presume that the cognitive structuring functions performed by psychic inner space are comparable to the unnoticed organizing influence unobtrusive picture frames have upon the viewing of a painting or photograph, that is, frames, whether real or imaginary, provide the windows, lenses, perspectives, and points of view that arrange the information presented to the mind. They contain, limit, and direct one's attentiveness, and do so at a prereflexive level of symbolic functioning.

To date, I have conducted approximately twenty introspective inquiries. My preliminary findings suggest that (1) the human head is the primary, but not necessarily the exclusive, site of psychic inner

3. Theoretically, time can be added to these dimensions, making inner psychic space time, a single continuum within which movements and directions could be perceived and described. The common expression "I need space" carries two meanings: "I need to increase the distance between us," which is equivalent to "I need time away from you," and "I need to expand the sense of space within my mind."

space, (2) the fundamental constituents of psychic inner space are constellations of visual, kinesthetic, proprioceptive, and auditory representations, and (3) discursive explicitness about the sense of inner space inevitably requires the use of metaphors.

SOME PRELIMINARY FINDINGS

Innumerable mental activities take place within the brain, and most of the sensory apparatus is high up on the human face. The head probably owes its special status as the most frequently chosen landmark for the location of inner space to these facts. Objectively speaking, adults know that the brain is a material substance. Nevertheless, according to Bloomer and Moore (1977), it is represented, in many people's imaginations, as more of a void than a filled entity.

The notion of physical space, as most of us understand it, refers to voids; that is, to those portions of a place that are empty of solids. We see the walls, or objects between which empty space exists. Space itself is not directly perceived. It is mostly apprehended and emotionally felt in relation to ourselves as standing, sitting, walking, lying down (on the earth, which holds us down). All of these forms of movement are tacitly thought of as domains separate from their existence in space.

Theoretically, mental activities are describable in terms of the spatial and temporal dimensions that are used to describe the directions and magnitude of movements in physical space. When someone moves in and through physical spaces, two changes can be observed: change in the *shape* of the body, and change in the *place* where the body is located. That the flow of thought is not unlike the paths the body travels in movement, or the route the eyes take when scanning the landscape, is for Bert an experiential reality. In recognition of this phenomenon, William James coined the phrase "the stream of consciousness" many years earlier (1890). While reading or thinking about James's phrase, I am apt to see in my mind's eye images of a river's flowing dark waters moving across, within, and beyond. When she is reading novels, my wife imagines the words "snaking through my right ear and going out through my left ear like a pen-and-ink Saul Steinberg cartoon of a moving train." The poet Lux (1997) tells us that he hears his voice speaking, while reading silently in the "dark cathedral of his skull" (p. 15).

A colleague told me, "When I can't retrieve a memory, or even the words for something, I feel suspended in space, ungrounded. But when I am feeling organized, focused, motivated, I experience my thoughts as moving through a circle that is moving in on itself. It's like I can picture the hole in a powdered donut." Another colleague envisioned his brain as "full of stuff," but as attached at its base to an "empty bubble where thoughts go and play with one another." He associated the image of a bubble to the ways in which thinking and dialogue are portrayed in comic books and cartoons.

Inner space is not necessarily experienced as located within the confines of the head. A Jungian therapist described her experience of inner space as located in her chest, as oval in shape, and as varying in the extent to which it felt "full, busy, and crowded." In order to convey the feeling of a "crowded mind" that is "not big enough to hold all of my ideas," a social worker told me it "feels as if a vise is attached to my temple and is squeezing my mind narrower and narrower." As this and the previous example suggest, the psychological experience of inner space can expand and contract, like the postures taken by the body, and can vary in the extent to which it is hospitable to memories, fantasies, and the attributes of the reflective self.

To be sure, that which encloses can also exclude. Schizoid patients speak of feeling trapped inside "a plastic bubble" or a "cocoon," or behind a "sheet of glass," allowing nothing of emotional importance to leave or enter. One can feel supported and comforted—or confined and shut-in—by an embrace, or by the current status of one's sense of psychic inner space.

A SCENE FROM *FIVE EASY PIECES*

I consider the following scene from *Five Easy Pieces* (Rafelson 1970) a fine illustration of the failure to separate a "container" from that which it "contained" (Bion 1963). The character portrayed by Jack Nicholson (JN) is speaking to a waitress in a diner (W).

JN: I'd like a plain omelet, no potatoes, tomatoes instead, a cup of coffee, and wheat toast.
W: No substitutions.
JN: What do you mean you don't have any tomatoes?
W: Only what's on the menu. You can have a number two—a plain omelet. It comes with cottage fries and a roll.
JN: I know what it comes with but it's not what I want.
W: I'll come back when you make up your mind.
JN: Wait a minute. I have made up my mind. I'd like a plain omelet; no potatoes on the plate. A cup of coffee, and a side order of wheat toast.
W: I'm sorry, we don't have any side orders of toast. An English muffin or a coffee roll.
JN: What do you mean you don't make side orders of toast? You make sandwiches, don't you?
W: Would you like to talk to the manager?
JN: You've got bread and a toaster of some kind?
W: I don't make the rules.
JN: O.K. I'll make it as easy for you as I can. I'd like an omelet, plain, and a chicken salad sandwich on wheat toast, no mayonnaise, no butter, no lettuce, and a cup of coffee.
W: A number 2. A chicken salad sandwich. Hold the butter, the lettuce, and the mayonnaise, and a cup of coffee. Anything else?
JN: Yeah, now all you have to do is hold the chicken, bring me the toast, give me a check for the chicken salad sandwich, and you haven't broken any rules.
W: You want me to hold the chicken, huh?
JN: Yeah, I want to hold it between your knees.
W: You'll have to leave, sir. I've had enough of you.

If we focus on the waitress in the above scene, we can see that her insular and rigidly held view that a menu contains immutable descriptions of what constitutes a meal makes it impossible for her to separate the bread that surrounds a sandwich from the sandwich's ingredients. She is embedded in her own narrow point of view, without being aware that she has a point of view. This raises the question: Do narrow- and broad-minded people differ in the structure of their symbolizing spaces?

FORMS TAKEN BY INNER SPACE

Visual images are the predominant mode of representing the spatial attributes of physical reality. It also appears as if individuals rely heavily on visual images and metaphors when asked to describe their sense of inner space. If an interviewee included visual images in his or her description, I asked, "Do the shapes taken by your visual images of inner space resemble anything?" Invariably the answers came back to me in metaphoric form. The metaphors chosen by my sample of therapists were drawn from a wide variety of domains: architecture, mathematics, anatomy, geography, astronomy, and so on. Some likened their sense of inner space to the visible properties of the land forms found in nature (such as caves, craters, and the hollow habitats animals create by burrowing into the earth). Others characterized the shapes taken by their sense of inner space as resembling the shelters and structures created by humans (like houses, rooms, molds, scaffoldings, tunnels). For several respondents, the notion of inner space brought up images of the proscenium arch or film screens of which we are vaguely aware in the semi-darkness of a theater. I would not be surprised if the shapes taken by inner space have, in our culture, come increasingly to resemble television and computer screens with their four sides at right angles. Did Lewin's (1946) clinically based finding that dream images, especially if they are visual, tend to be experienced as if they were being projected onto blank surfaces, anticipate this trend? Still earlier, Proust (1913) opined that "When a man is asleep, he has in a circle round him the chain of the hours, the sequence of the years, the order of the heavenly host" (p. 5).

THE UNIVERSE AS CONTAINER

Space (and time)[4] on a cosmic scale are commonly conceived of as immense containers of a universe, in which all of nature and organic life exist and move. For several members of my informal sample, the notion of inner space evoked immediate associations to the universe. These people tended to be individuals for whom inner space is more felt than seen. A music therapist told me that as a boy he was haunted by two questions: "If the universe is bounded, what is on the other side? If it is unbounded (infinite), what does it mean that it can go on forever?" Whether conceived as infinite or finite, his questions about the unknown immensities of the solar system left him feeling small, weak, and vaguely terrified.

He then described the essential constituents of his adult sense of inner space as a "matrix of psychophysical or body-centered sensations" and translated these sensations into an image of inner space that was not radically different from his boyhood thoughts about interplanetary space. "I have the feeling that I am standing in the center of a circle that turns above and around my head and body. It seems to radiate axes in all directions that extend outward into a vast darkness." In comparison to his childhood view of his place in the universe, he feels at home in this enclosure; he experiences himself as the center of his cosmos. His image reminded me of the comforting

4. Bert takes into account the fact that while time is usually regarded as an aspect of reality, differing from space, they are experienced and described in much the same way. A moment in time is analogous to a point in space. A time span can be subdivided infinitely, as a line in space can be. Time includes such relations as before and after. We speak of the distant future and of temporal schedules that are long or short. By analogy with rising and falling in space, successive musical tones can be interpreted as rising and falling. Silence, as a period of time without noticeable sounds, is somewhat analogous to empty space. Neither silence nor empty spaces are merely absences of stimuli; they provide the frames of reference within which actions, perceptions, and thoughts start, continue, or stop. For these and other reasons, the temporal ordering of auditory events that are bounded by the onset and cessation of stimulation—that is the "open spaces" that separate sound and silence—provide yet another model for the creation of "inner spaces."

idea of an earth-centered cosmos and of the mandala, in Jungian psychology a symbol representing the effort to reunify the self.

Another respondent, a dance therapist, recognized that her experience of inner space was fluid and its changeable characteristics seemed to depend upon how centered or grounded she felt. At her best, this person feels as if she is "standing in the middle of my circle." Here we see that the visualization of what is at first experienced kinesthetically and proprioceptively does not always yield descriptions of inner space that are limitless or indeterminate with respect to their form or shape. On the other hand, when under stress, she could discern that her kinesthetic experiences of inner space yielded images of "being unhinged and floating through eternity, or of falling through a black hole." She also observed that "good and bad introjects seem to be experientially located in different parts of my body—the bad ones are in my stomach and the good ones in my chest."

ORIGINS OF INNER SPACE

Bert's theorizing about the emergence and evolution of the representational capacities required to create and maintain symbolizing spaces that are hospitable to those forms of mentation that aid in adaptation takes into account the contributions of geography, biology, culture, and psychology. He assigns fundamental importance to the fact that psychological experience always takes place within the context of two physical actualities: the ever-present body and the environmental surround. Being *in* a body is always also about being located *in* a place.

Following Schilder (1950), Bert would characterize an adult's confrontation with the world outside his body as the simultaneous encounter of an inside world occurring within an outside world, each dependent on the other for its existence and complexity. As a developmentalist, Bert presumes that the most primordial source of our representations of space is the body itself. As Adrienne Rich (1984) has so beautifully phrased it, the body is "after all, the geography closest in" (p. 33).

Surely long before infants reach any degree of articulate visual or verbal representations of space, they are sensing, codifying, and storing knowledge about the distinction between an inside world and an outside world on a body-felt level (Geller 1978). An early first step is taken when infants use their sensory-motor intelligence to detect, organize, and respond to sensations coming from inside and outside the body. Piaget (1956) has hypothesized that, over the course of development, we gradually learn to coordinate the tactile, visual, auditory, buccal, and postural spaces formed by our bodies. For example, at the beginning of life, sucking objects promotes the coordination of the buccal and tactile-kinesthetic spaces. Spitting food out of the mouth, purposely, perhaps signals the arrival of the discovery of the distinction between the feeling of inside and all of that stuff "out there."

Another developmental landmark in the spatialization of experience is the acquisition of the representational capacities that underlie the sense of being bounded and three dimensional. There are many more directions in which to move or look than merely proceeding outward and inward in three-dimensional space (e.g., here and there; near and far; between, through, and around; right and left; east and west; above and below.)[5] It is well documented that representations that aim at boundedness or defining the limits of self and nonself are subject to wide variation and this is, of course, pertinent to Winnicott's (1971) important notion of transitional space.

The discovery that there are sealed and unsealed enclosures in the physical world lends credence to the preverbal sense that there is a space that extends from the core of the body to the surface. Bachelard (1964) has argued that the forms ultimately taken by our sense of inner space bear the fundamental imprint of the body of images provided by the homes of our childhood and their "spaces of intimacy." Opening and closing drawers and closets, entering and exiting the interior of rooms, houses, cars, and so on, does, at a minimum, reinforce our body-based sense of inside and outside. My catalog of intimate spaces

---

5. Everyday speech reveals that spatial positions tend to acquire connotative meanings, for example, "above" and "below" tend to suggest rank or status.

includes the primal roundness of the cups and plates in our kitchen, our "king-size" bed, the bathroom mirror and toilet bowl. High on my list of intimate spaces is the structural wholeness of the "witness circle" in which I practice Authentic Movement (Whitehouse et al. 1999).

One interviewee described her sense of inner space as an "upside-down vase." She produced the following drawing, Figure 22–2, to clarify what she was saying. She felt as if it ended at her neck.[6] She characterizes the vase as having "fluffy gray borders" that are "arranged harmoniously," and as being "a rich dove gray" in color. She added that the clouds, "not having a discrete edge, signified that things aren't settled." Her first association was to a classical Greek urn. Mine was to the contours of a beech or maple tree in full bloom. For both of us, the shape then brought up images of the folds created by the gray matter of the brain and of the uterus. Life begins in an enclosure.

The human body contains numerous openings and cavities (e.g., the throat, the nostrils, the ears, the anus, the belly). Women additionally possess the containing spaces of the vagina, the womb, and breasts. My granddaughter calls her mother's breasts "nursies," that is, containers of milk. Do these anatomical differences influence how men and women apprehend boundedness and construct representations of inner psychic space?[7]

The developmental trajectory Bert is suggesting is that the forms taken by the body, in stillness and when in motion, representationally prefigure and provide the nonverbal substrate for our psychological experiences of inner space. Like Anzieu (1989), Bert also believes that the sense of boundedness provided by representations of the skin as a sheath or outer envelope that surrounds and contains the bodily self is

6. I am given to thinking of the neck as a transitional space that, in people's imaginations, separates the mind and the body.

7. In 1950, Erikson described the contrasting play configurations of girls and boys. The boys tended to use blocks to build towers; the girls tended to use them to construct enclosures. Many changes have taken place with regard to gender distinctions since this data were collected. Thus, I believe that his data can no longer be cited as evidence of gender differences in the construction of psychic inner space.

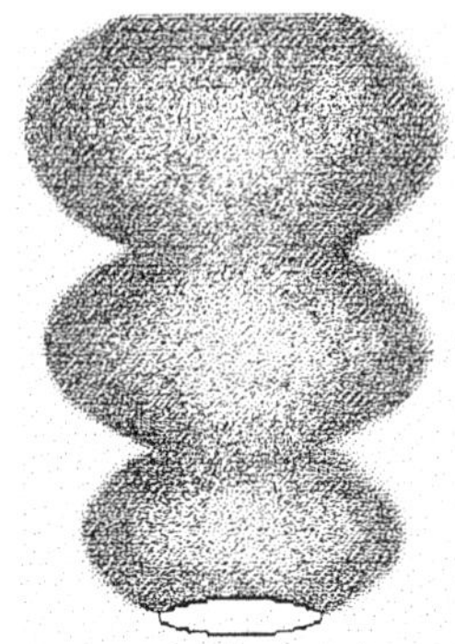

Figure 22–2

another fundamental source of our sense that representational boundaries surround the mind. In other words, conceiving of the self as a three-dimensional bounded entity anticipates and contributes to experiencing the mind as a container that holds our thoughts and feelings.

At the same time, as we begin to experience ourselves as three-dimensional bounded entities, the formation and establishment of representations of the spaces that separate self and others are also occurring. Much anthropological and psychological research indicates that there are cultural and characterological differences in the ways people respond to the felt experience of being close to and far away from the other. Hall's (1959, 1966) studies of proxemics indicate that we usually try to maintain a personal envelope of space around our bodies, and that any violation or infringement upon this sense is acutely experienced. I believe that shifts in the location and permeability of "personal space" (Sommer 1969), like variations in the experience of transitional space, are pertinent to activation of the process of introjection.

INTROJECTION AND THE THERAPEUTIC PROCESS

For the past twenty years my colleagues and I have been studying the therapeutic action of the processes of introjection (Geller et al. 1981).

Since being introduced to Bert's ideas about psychic inner space, I have been rethinking some of the most important findings that our ongoing project has yielded (Geller 1999). Currently, I am intrigued by the idea that the processes of interiorization, of which introjection is a particular instance, make a fundamental contribution to the formation and reshaping of the psychological experience of inner space.

For research purposes we define the concept of introjection as those processes that bring into existence, modify, and reorganize emotionally charged schemas of human interactions. In our model, interpersonal schemas, as such, are not directly knowable or available to consciousness; they are the inferred memory structures whose activation gives rise to emotionally charged representations of the self, others, and interactions between them.

We work with the assumption that within the context of therapy, patients acquire or construct representations that replicate within subjective experience the patterns of listening and talking, seeing and being seen, feeling and being with the therapist that recurrently organize the therapeutic dialogue. Once such schemas are firmly established in long-term memory, patients are no longer dependent on the actual presence of the therapist to continue the therapeutic dialogue, and they do so representationally, in the privacy of consciousness. For example, when we are daydreaming, interpersonal schemas may appear or reappear in awareness in the form of imaginary "felt presences" existing within the confines of the body or mind or both, but which are not experienced as an expression of the subjective self. In other words, the person about whom the fantasy refers may be experienced as if he or she were objectively present; in this sense, they are "inner experiences."

Thus far, our results indicate that patients' representations of the therapeutic process tend to be more imagistic than conceptual (Geller and Farber 1993). Psychotherapy clients drawn from diverse samples typically report that when interacting with the felt presence of their therapists (between sessions, and after termination) they do so in the form of images of being "in" the presence of their therapist sitting *in* his/her chair, *in* his or her office. We have also found that access to vivid, detailed, sensorially rich visual, auditory, and kinesthetic images of a continuing dialogue with one's therapist, in his or her office, increases the probability of a positive therapeutic outcome and its preservation after termination (Orlinsky and Geller 1994).

Psychotherapy sessions typically or solely take place within the intimate confines of an environment created, maintained, and sanctioned by the therapist. Moreover, encounters with the therapist are typically scheduled at regular and predictable intervals. In short, they are rhythmically spaced apart. Do the spatial boundaries and temporal parameters of the work structure of psychotherapy contribute to the creation of a "holding environment" (Winnicott 1971) or "frame" (Langs 1976), which, when introjected, serves as the raw materials for the reshaping of the psychological experience of inner space?

Opinions differ as to which interpersonal conditions set in motion the processes of introjection. The repair of ruptures in the therapeutic alliance, the working through of nontraumatic empathic failures, and the process of mourning all have their share of advocates. My opinion is that in situations of deep intimacy, participating in reciprocal exchanges having the quality of rhythmic synchronization ultimately leads to a blending and sharing of the functions and experiences of the other. This, in turn, makes it possible to "take in" or introject qualities of a caring person, and, in so doing, expand or refine attributes that may not be adequately represented in the patient's own personality.

The novel angle of vision provided to me by Bert's ideas has led me to ponder the following questions. What do patients remember of the places in which their therapists work? Do images of one's therapist inhabiting his or her office replicate the sense of being in a private and protective enclosure? Do aesthetically pleasing images of the therapist's workplace play an influential role in the conscious and preconscious mental activities that occur when patients are attempting to achieve further self-understanding, resolve conflicts, problem solve, or regulate affect? Does the creation of mental models of the spatial configurations encountered in the therapy (e.g., the arrangement of the chairs) promote an internal climate that makes verbal representation of that which must be spoken about in therapy possible? Does the body of images provided by evocative memories of sitting with the therapist in his or her office facilitate or interfere with adaptive utilization of verbalized symbolic thought?

I have many other questions. For example: Is progress in therapy marked by transformations in the forms taken by inner space? What is the route back to the road not taken? What is the shape of a sense of inner emptiness? Does it make a difference whether one's self-representations are higher or lower, larger or smaller, further to the left or right, than one's representations of the therapist? Do patients' representations of the physical identifying properties of the therapists' offices and their contents have iconic properties, similar to those of maps? (In semiotics, an icon is a sign that stands for something else by virtue of being similar to it.)

In an earlier publication (Geller 1984), I argued on behalf of the idea that the processes of introjection can play a vital role in the structuralization of feelings as experienced qualities. I reasoned that by bringing into existence benignly influential representations of relationship episodes with a trusted therapist, the processes of introjection strengthened the capacity to engage in what Bert refers to as "discursive symbolization." Grappling with the questions posed above has led me to hypothesize that a patient's capacity for "dynamic symbolization" will be strengthened when the processes of introjection give rise to representations of benignly influential relationship episodes with the therapist that concern self-reflection. Dynamic symbolization is the name Bert has given to those forms of mentation that underlie subjective awareness of irreconcilable conflicts, the ability to take oneself as an object of consciousness, and to reflect upon consciousness of consciousness.

QUESTIONS FOR PONDERING

If we are to learn whether and how the processes of introjection contribute to the formation and reshaping of inner space within the context of psychotherapy, we will have to develop tools to study questions that are even more fundamental.

1. Do the spatial properties of the representational world take on different qualities when we are retrieving memories, problem solving, theorizing, and so on?
2. What spatial properties of an individual's representational world persist over time and changes in circumstance?
3. What do representations of the places in which memorable events occurred, and their affective valences, contribute to our sense of inner space?
4. Do the representational boundaries that surround the mind regulate what potentially can be brought into the mind?
5. Are the cohesiveness and integrity of the self correlated with the forms taken by inner space?
6. Can spatial representations be characterized in terms of their mimetic complexity?
7. Are there connections between the ways in which we move through spaces outside our bodies and the ways in which our thoughts move through inner space?
8. Like the stars and planets, do thoughts move in regular paths according to discoverable laws?
9. Are there psychologically important linkages between the forms taken by psychic inner space and the ability to perform different mental functions?
10. Do some spatial representations have a referential meaning in their own right, that is, do they themselves signal mental content?
11. Are the forms taken by inner space predictive of the quality of the symbolizing processes taking place within these representational boundaries?
12. Can one infer from the thinness or thickness of the contours of its silhouette the degree to which a particular sense of inner space feels coherent, substantial?
13. Are there resemblances between the visible properties of the

physical world and the forms taken by pictorial representations of inner space?

14. What forms of symbolizing space pave the way for the production and consideration of conflictual ideas from multiple perspectives?

One of the most sophisticated developments in the evolution of the human mind is the capacity for reflexive consciousness. As defined by Humphrey (1984), "reflexive consciousness means not merely observing from outside but from within, not merely looking *at* one's behavior, but looking *in* on it—in on the thoughts and passions which accompany consciousness" (p. 210). Bert Freedman has deepened my understanding of what is required to conduct such introspective inquiries. Tiresias warned Oedipus that "Wisdom is a dreadful thing if it brings no profit to the man who is wise" (Sophocles 1971, p. 23). I have consistently profited, personally and professionally, by knowing a very wise man, whom I have affectionately come to think of as my personal Tiresias.

REFERENCES

Anzieu, D. (1989). *The Skin Ego*, trans. C. Turner. New Haven, CT: Yale University Press.

Bachelard, G. (1964). *The Poetics of Space*, trans. M. Jolas. Boston: Beacon.

Bion, W. R. (1963). *Elements of Psychoanalysis*. London: Tavistock.

Blom, L. A., and Chaplin, L. T. (1982). *The Intimate Act of Choreography*. Pittsburgh: Pitsburgh University Press.

Bloomer, K. C., and Moore, W. M. (1977). *Body, Memory, and Architecture*. New Haven, CT: Yale University Press.

Erikson, E. (1950). *Childhood and Society*. New York: Norton.

Fisher, S., and Cleveland, S. E. (1968). *Body Image and Personality*, 2nd. ed. New York: Dover.

Freedman, N. (1983). On psychoanalytic listening: the construction, paralysis, and reconstruction of meaning. *Psychoanalysis and Contemporary Thought* 6:405–434.

——— (1997a). *On spatialization—personal and theoretical reflections.* Unpublished paper.
——— (1997b). *The spatialization of the representational world.* Unpublished paper.
Freedman, N., and Bucci, W. (1981). On kinetic filtering in associative monologues. *Semiotica* 34:225–249.
Freedman, N., and Lavender, J. (1997). On receiving the patient's transference: the symbolizing and desymbolizing countertransference. *Journal of the American Psychoanalytic Association* 45:79–103.
Geller, J. D. (1978). The body: expressive movement and physical contact in psychotherapy. In *The Power of Human Imagination*, ed. J. L. Singer and K. S. Pope, pp. 347–378. Orlando, FL: Grune & Stratton.
——— (1984) Moods, feelings, and the process of affect formation. In *Emotions in Health and Illness: Foundations of Clinical Practice*, ed. L. Temoshuk, L. S. Zegans, and C. Van Dyke, pp. 171–186. Orlando, FL: Grune & Stratton.
——— (1999). What does it mean to practice psychotherapy scientifically? *Psychoanalysis and Psychotherapy* 15:187–214.
Geller, J. D., Cooley, R. S., and Hartley, D. (1981). Images of the psychotherapist: a theoretical and methodological perspective. *Imagination, Cognition and Personality* 1:123–146.
Geller, J. D., and Farber, B. A. (1993). Factors influencing the process of internalization in psychotherapy. *Psychotherapy Research* 3:166–180.
Grotstein, J. S. (1978). Inner space: its dimensions and its coordinates. *International Journal of Psycho-Analysis* 59:55–61.
Hall, E. T. (1959). *The Silent Language,* Garden City, NY: Doubleday.
——— (1966). *The Hidden Dimension*, 1st ed. Garden City, NY: Doubleday.
Humphrey, N. (1984). *Consciousness Regained.* Oxford, UK: Oxford University Press.
James, W. (1890). *Principles of Psychology*. (2 vols.) Cambridge, MA: Harvard University Press.
Kundera, M. (1984). *The Unbearable Lightness of Being.* New York: Harper & Row.
Langer, S. K. (1948). *Philosophy in a New Key.* New York: New American Library.
Langs, R. (1976). *The Bipersonal Field.* New York: Jason Aronson.
Lewin, B. D. (1946). Sleep, the mouth, and the dream screen. *Psychoanalytic Quarterly* 15:419–434.
Lux, T. (1997). *New and Selected Poems.* Boston: Houghton Mifflin.

Orlinsky, D., and Geller, J. D. (1994). Patients' representations of their therapists and therapy. In *Psychodynamic Treatment: A Handbook for Clinical Practice*, ed. N. E. Miller, L. Luborsky, J. Barbar, and J. Docherty, pp. 423–466. New York: Basic Books.

Piaget, J. (1956). *The Child's Conception of Space*. London: Routledge and Kegan Paul.

Proust, M. (1913). *Swann's Way: Remembrance of Things Past*. New York: Vintage International Books, 1989.

Rafelson, B., director. (1970). *Five Easy Pieces*, co-writers A. Joyce and B. Rafelson.

Rich, A. (1984). Notes toward a politics of location. In *Blood, Bread and Poetry*, pp. 23–75. London: Virago.

Schilder, P. (1950). *The Image and Appearance of the Human Body*. New York: International Universities Press.

Sommer, R. (1969). *Personal Space*. Englewood Cliffs, NJ: Prentice Hall.

Sophocles (1971). Oedipus the king. In *The Complete Greek Tragedies*, 7th ed., ed. D. Greene and R. Lattimore. New York: Washington Square Press.

Styron, W. (1990). *Darkness Visible*. New York: Random House.

Viderman, S. (1970). *La construction de l'espace analytique*. Paris: Denoel.

Wapner, S., and Werner, H., eds. (1965). *The Body Percept*. New York: Random House.

Whitehouse, M. S., Adler, J., and Chodorow, N. (1999). *Authentic Movement—A Collection of Essays*, ed. P. Pallaro. London: Jessica Kingsley.

Whorf, B. L. (1956). *Language, Thought and Reality*. Cambridge, MA: M.I.T. Press.

Winnicott, D. W. (1971). *Playing and Reality*. New York: Basic Books.

Index